HUMAN DEVELOPMENT

HUMAN DEVELOPMENT

FROM CONCEPTION THROUGH ADOLESCENCE

KURT W. FISCHER

University of Denver

ARLYNE LAZERSON

W. H. FREEMAN AND COMPANY

NEW YORK   OXFORD

Cover illustration: *Baby at Play*, by Thomas Eakins (1844–1916), in the John Hay Whitney Collection, National Gallery of Art, Washington, D.C. Reproduced with the permission of the National Gallery of Art.

The letters on pages 627–631 are reproduced from *Fathers to Sons: Advice without Consent*, by A. Valentine. Copyright 1963 by the University of Oklahoma Press.

Library of Congress Cataloging in Publication Data

Fischer, Kurt W.
    Human development.

    Bibliography: p.
    Includes index.
    1. Developmental psychobiology.   I. Lazerson, Arlyne.
II. Title.
RJ131.F47   1984   612'.6   83-25315
ISBN 0-7167-1575-9

Design by Daniel Thaxton

Printed in the United States of America

2 3 4 5 6 7 8 9 0   DO   2 1 0 8 9 8 7 6 5 4

To Josh, Paul, and Seth

BRIEF TABLE OF CONTENTS

CONTENTS

CHAPTER 3
PRENATAL DEVELOPMENT 114

UNIT 2   INFANCY

CHAPTER 4
FROM REFLEX TO ACTION:
THE NEWBORN 160

UNIT 5 ADOLESCENCE

PREFACE

The goal of developmental science is to explain how people become what they are—to provide a coherent portrait of the developments that transform a person from fertilized egg to infant, infant to child, child to adolescent and adult. Because developmental science itself is young, it has been relatively fragmented, characterized by large numbers of disconnected facts. Most textbooks have necessarily reflected this fragmented character, describing long lists of facts without integrating them. Until recently, it seemed that the only other approach to describing development was to pick one of the distinct theories of development, such as social-learning theory or Piagetian theory, and organize a textbook around it, thus producing coherence by only briefly mentioning the data that support other theories.

Recently, the study of development has undergone a major transformation, a movement toward maturity. The distinct approaches are becoming integrated into a unified, coherent portrait of development. The opposing schools of past years—behaviorists, Piagetians, Freudians, ethologists, and so forth—have given way to a host of new bridging approaches, such as cognitive social learning, social cognitive development, developmental psychobiology, neo-Freudian theory, and so forth. The field has moved toward integrating the different perspectives on development so as to understand the whole child, who shows systematic, interrelated changes in cognition, learning, language, social behavior, emotions, personality, and physical development all at the same time.

To date, no textbook in human development has adequately captured this new spirit. Although most books treat several major approaches, their orientation is to present "opposing theories" or to focus primarily on one approach and to discuss other approaches only superficially. In our discussions with instructors of human development around the country, we have repeatedly heard complaints about the absence of a textbook built upon the new integrative spirit in developmental science.

Our textbook is designed to fill this gap by providing a balanced analysis of the whole child. All the major theories play a part in this analysis, not as opposing schools but as frameworks for explaining distinct but related aspects of behavior. The first chapter describes the central themes that are woven throughout the book, including the types of commonalities in development that occur across children and social groups, the kinds of individual differences that children frequently show, and the important methods used in developmental research. The major theories are introduced briefly in the first chapter as complementary perspectives, and later in the book each theory is described in depth in the chapter where its concepts are first used. These special theory sections present the important concepts of each theory and also emphasize how the concepts relate to analysis of the whole child.

The theory sections serve several purposes that are different from the traditional treatment in most textbooks (which present all theories together at the beginning as opposing frameworks). First, these sections represent the new integrative spirit by highlighting how each theory explains certain components of behavior and leaves other components to other theories. Second, by presenting each theory in a chapter that highlights its role in explaining specific behaviors, the special sections help the student to see the theories as concrete tools for understanding real behavior in real children. Third, students are not asked to digest in abstract form all the major concepts of all the theories at the start of the course. We think it is usually a disservice to students to begin with a bulky, difficult chapter including a long discourse on theories. We realize, however, that some instructors will prefer to assign reading on theories in an order different from the one that we have chosen. To assist them, each theory section is prominently marked in the Table of Contents and is typeset differently from the rest of the text.

The Student of Human Development

All people who live or work with children are in a sense students of human development. They observe the week-to-week, month-to-month changes in their children as the years unfold. Most find methods to support and channel the children's growing capacities. Some seek knowledge from popular books on child care, but for many people, learning about children follows in the wake of the children's development: Parents and teachers learn to adapt to the demands of the children's new capacities. Because most people think of parenting as a "natural" human occupation, they believe that no formal education or preparation is required. Yet everyone who plans to be a parent or who plans a career that involves the care or teaching of children should have a foundation of knowledge in human development. They should know what science can tell them about a child's changing capacities and needs and about the environmental conditions that can foster or dull the child's development.

This textbook distills from the vast library of scientific developmental research a coherent and readable account of how children change from infancy to adolescence. It describes what children are like at the various periods of early life—how they think, how they feel, how they interact with others, what their physical abilities are. And it explains, where possible, the processes of development. It does not suggest specific child-care techniques, because it is not the business of developmental scientists to tell people how to handle such matters. People differ in their values concerning toilet training or manners or bedtime schedules, but developmental science can provide knowledge that helps them to realize their values more fully in raising their children.

After the first chapter, each major unit of the book deals with a major period of development, so that the student can see how the several threads of behavior are woven together in each period. The first unit introduces the biology of development, especially prenatal development. The other units typically divide development into two general topics: One chapter deals with cognition, language, and physical change; and the other covers social behavior and personality. Although this division reflects the way most research is done in developmental science, the new integrative spirit in the field leads to many analyses of how developments in one area affect and are affected by developments in other areas—how, for instance, cognitive changes influence social interactions, and how social experiences influence thinking. Also, the vast differences between children in different periods lead naturally to a focus on particular topics in each period, such as language and play in the preschool years, schooling in the elementary-school years, and heterosexual friendships in adolescence.

In preparing to write this book, we sampled students' reactions to the textbooks they had used. Besides the obvious need to learn what development is and how it occurs, one additional desire stood out: Students want a book that communicates concepts to them, not just to their instructors, and that does so in a manner that is intellectually and scientifically respectable. The most common complaints we heard were that "scholarly" textbooks are written for scholars in the field, not for students, and that "student-oriented" books are condescending or simplistic.

Research on reactions to textbooks indicates that most students consider a book to be relatively easy to read if they find it interesting; their reactions are affected very little by the apparent sophistication of the prose or the concepts, so long as the book interests them. By our choice of concepts and examples (many of them tested in the classroom), we have tried to show how interesting the study of development really is. In making those excruciating decisions about what to exclude, as all textbook writers must, we have aimed for clarity and depth of coverage of central developmental concepts. We sought to illustrate important points with good examples that are clear, interesting, and scientifically sound, so that scholarship is combined with good communication. In addition, visual illustrations help to make ideas clear and to bring the results of specific research to life. Photographs, graphs, and drawings have been used generously throughout the text to provide concrete support for the presentations of the central concepts of development.

A Note on Sexism in Pronouns

In recent years, concern has arisen about the problem of sexism in English pronouns. The traditional use of the masculine pronoun "he" to refer to the child in general may lead to an unintentional devaluation of girls and women. However, many of the proposed solutions to this problem create difficulties of their own. The repeated use of "he or she" leads to an unfortunate awkwardness in prose. Use of only the plural "children" is misleading when the topic is the individual child. And the pronoun "it" is depersonalizing. Our solution, which has also been adopted by a number of other authors in recent years, is to use "he" or "she" alternately in large segments of each chapter to refer to a child.

Acknowledgments

We owe gratitude to a number of people who have helped us in producing this book, and we wish to acknowledge that help here. We wish to thank Alastair McLeod for his help in conceptualizing the art, Cathy Caldwell Brown for her editing of the manuscript, and Andrew Kudlacik, Lisa Douglis, and Sarah Segal for their untiring aid in all aspects of producing the final book as well as their good humor throughout a difficult schedule. We want to thank Jacqueline Roberge for typing many drafts of many chapters, Jeff Vanelli for much library work, and David Barkan for exacting and creative photo research. We are grateful to Carol Donner for her fine anatomical drawings. Thanks also go to Daniel Bullock, Joseph Campos, Marshall Haith, Denise Hall, Susan Harter, Sybillyn Jennings, Brian MacWhinney, Marilyn Pelot, Sandra Pipp, Phillip Shaver, Helen Strautman, David Thomas, and Michael Westerman for their contributions to various parts of the project. Some of the conceptual work that laid the foundation for the book was supported by grants for independent research from the Carnegie Corporation of New York and the Spencer Foundation.

Kurt W. Fischer

Arlyne Lazerson

REVIEWERS

The following people helped us with suggestions for revisions of early and late drafts of the manuscript, and we are grateful for their help. However, the statements made and the views expressed in this book are the responsibility solely of the authors.

Curt Acredolo	University of California, Davis
Bennett Bertenthal	University of Virginia
John Bonvillian	University of Virginia
James Brown	San Diego State University
Joseph Campos	University of Denver
Louise Carter	University of Washington
Roberta Corrigan	University of Wisconsin, Milwaukee
Philip Cowan	University of California, Berkeley
Carolyn Edwards	University of Massachusetts, Amherst
Dorothy Eichorn	University of California, Berkeley
Larry Fenson	San Diego State University
Marshall Haith	University of Denver
Lauren Julius Harris	Michigan State University
Susan Harter	University of Denver
Elaine Holder	California Polytechnic State University, San Luis Obispo
John Horn	University of Denver
Dorothy Jackson	Ohio State University
Sharon Karr	Emporia University
William Kessen	Yale University
Charles La Bounty	Hamline State University
Brian MacWhinney	Carnegie Mellon University
Carolyn Mebert	University of New Hampshire
Patricia Miller	University of Florida, Gainesville
Tina Moreau	Queens College
Marion Perlmutter	University of Minnesota, Minneapolis
Clark Presson	University of Missouri, Columbia
Gary H. Ritchey	University of New Mexico, Albuquerque
Lee B. Ross	Frostburg State College
Phillip Shaver	University of Denver
Harold Siegel	Nassau Community College
Frank Sjursen	Shoreline Community College
Harriet S. Waters	State University of New York, Stony Brook
Malcolm Watson	Brandeis University
Marsha Weinraub	Temple University

HUMAN DEVELOPMENT

1

HUMAN
DEVELOPMENT
AND
ITS
STUDY

CHAPTER OUTLINE

1

HUMAN
DEVELOPMENT
AND
ITS
STUDY

Figure 1-1 Mozart at age 7. The precocious development of the boy's musical ability brought him acclaim from the nobility of all the courts of Europe. At age 6, he was a "child star." After his days as an infant prodigy, however, many of these same nobles lost interest in him. They could find no place for Mozart in their establishments, nor money to pay him for his compositions. Dead at age 35, Mozart was buried in a pauper's grave.

When Wolfgang Amadeus Mozart was 7 years old, he was an accomplished performer on several instruments, had already composed his first concerto, and was in the midst of a concert tour of the major cities and royal courts of Europe. The following excerpt from a concert advertisement gives an idea of the spectacle Mozart's audiences were treated to:

> The boy will not only play on the harpsichord or forte-piano, [but will] perform the most difficult pieces by the greatest masters; [he] will also play a concerto on the violin; accompany symphonies on the clavier; completely cover the keyboard of the clavier and play on the cloth as well as though he had the keyboard under his eyes; he will further most accurately name from a distance any notes that may be sounded for him either singly or in chords, on the clavier or on every imaginable instrument including bells, glasses, and clocks. Lastly he will improvise . . . not only on the piano-forte but also on an organ, as long as one wishes to listen and in all keys. (Deutsch 1974)

Such skills in an adult musician would have been remarkable; in a child of 7, they were amazing. People clamored to see this prodigy, this developmental oddity.

In our day, we seem no less interested in child prodigies. Newspapers and magazines unfailingly report the entrance of a 10- or 11-year-old into a university, and television offers us interviews with young computer geniuses and math wizards. The media know that their audiences are interested in people who show accelerated development. People generally recognize retarded development too, but it is not often a matter of such intense interest.

The fact that people recognize developmental oddities reflects their intuitive notions of development. Mozart's parents recognized that their 3-year-old's enchantment with the sounds of the piano, his spending long periods at the keyboard picking out pleasing chords, was way ahead of the developmental "schedule." The parents of Albert Einstein, on the other hand, were greatly distressed because their son was not speaking as fluently as he should at age 3— he was "behind schedule." We all have in mind a developmental schedule of some kind connecting certain physical and psychological changes with certain ages. But how does this intuitive notion of development relate to what scientists mean by development?

THE NATURE OF DEVELOPMENT

The study of development does concern itself with changes in people as they move forward in time. But not all changes are considered to be developmental. In specifying what is meant by development, scientists usually mention three related defining characteristics: Developmental changes are

1. Orderly—they occur in a sequence or series.

2. Directional—they show some kind of accumulation or organization of components; each change in a sequence builds on the results of preceding changes.

3. Stable—their effects do not disappear in a short time.

Even though most children grow their first teeth before they speak their first words, and talk before they start doing math problems, such a sequence of changes is not usually called developmental because the steps are not related to each other. As children acquire language, on the other hand, they pass through an orderly development from speaking one word at a time (at around 1 year of age) to using two- or three-word utterances (at around 2 years of age) to constructing adultlike sentences (at around 3 years of age). Some other developmental sequences are shown in Figure 1-2.

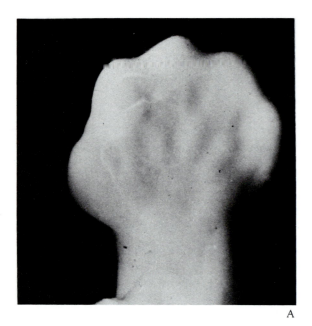

A

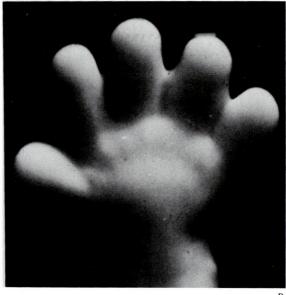

B

A SEQUENCE OF LANGUAGE DEVELOPMENT

Babbling

One-word utterances

Two- and three-word utterances

Multiword adultlike sentences

Sentences with relative clauses

Reading sentences

Writing sentences

Composing a brief essay that describes a sequence of events

Composing an essay that presents an argument

(Based on Bloom and Lahey 1978, Dale 1972, and Hunt 1970)

Figure 1-2　Three sequences of development.

A SEQUENCE OF EMOTIONAL DEVELOPMENT

Smiling at eye-to-eye contact

Distress at separation from mother

Using the caregiver as a secure base from which to explore the immediate environment

Temper tantrums when child is thwarted in attaining a goal

Spontaneous fear of monsters when no monsters are present

Forming a special friendship with a "best friend"

Desiring acceptance by a particular peer group and fearing rejection by the group

(Based on Sroufe 1979 and Hartup 1983)

A SEQUENCE OF PHYSICAL DEVELOPMENT

A　The fifth week of prenatal development: Hands are "molding plates" with finger ridges.

B　Sixth week: Finger buds have formed.

C　Seventh and eighth weeks: Fingers, thumbs, and fingerprints form, with prominent touch pads. By the third month the pads will have regressed and the hands will be well formed.

D　A newborn's hand.

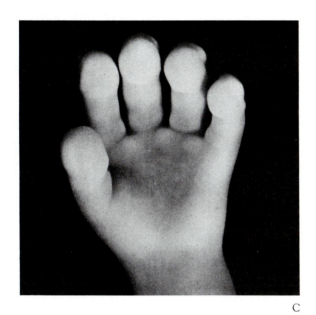
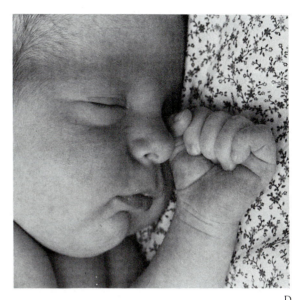

C
D

One major goal of developmentalists is to carefully delineate developmental sequences—to **describe** development in a precise and systematic way. But they also want to **explain** how and why people develop as they do, and to **predict** how they will develop with time. How does a helpless young infant become transformed, in 24 months, into a walking, talking individual with a sense of self? How does a 2-year-old, who is virtually incapable of imagining what other people think or feel, become able, by middle childhood, to easily take on the point of view of those around him? Why do some individuals start the move toward sexual maturity at 11 years, and others not until 16? What enables an 18-year-old to grasp abstract ideas that were impossible for her to understand in childhood? Why do child prodigies like Mozart develop in one domain far faster than they do in other domains (Feldman 1980)?

Developmentalists seek to understand the shared processes by which all infants are gradually transformed into children and then adolescents. Along with these commonalities, they also try to understand the distinct processes that lead each person to develop differently from every other person—that is, the processes that make us individuals.

THREE CHILDREN

Following are short biographical sketches of three 12-year-olds, each growing up in a different culture. (In order to avoid calling up any stereotypes about particular societies or cultures, the children's names are abbreviated and the case studies contain no place names.) These word pictures freeze the developmental action, just for a moment. While reading them, you might look for aspects of development that the three children share: What do they have in common? You might also compare their biographies for the factors that produce differences between them: What differences in their everyday experiences can be traced to differing cultural or social-class values? Note similarities and differences between the children's families—in the organization of the families and in how the adults treat the children. These aspects of development are discussed immediately following the biographies.

N———

N is tall for a 12-year-old girl, 5 feet 6 inches. She has a sturdy build, with broad shoulders and hips, and she is good at athletics. She wears her long blond hair in pigtails and has deep blue eyes. N's schoolmates respect her for her seriousness, her organization, and her ability to enjoy a good joke. Her facial expression does not usually reveal much about her thoughts, but she has a deep capacity for pleasure. When she laughs, her whole body seems to enjoy it.

N lives with her mother, father, and grandmother in a three-room apartment in a large city. Her mother is a doctor, and her father an electronics specialist. An only child, N shares a bedroom with her grandmother, who has cared for her from infancy because both her parents work. Her parents want no more children, partly because of the acute housing shortage in the city.

N was an active baby who was very regular in her sleeping and eating patterns. She sat up and walked earlier than most girls in her country, and seemed to be into everything. Her parents had to rearrange their bookshelves and knick-knacks to protect them from their daughter, and her grandmother had to take her to the park even when it was very cold so that the child could expend some of her boundless energy outside the confines of the small apartment. She cried very little as an infant, but whenever she did, one of the adults in the household immediately came to feed and soothe her. As a toddler, she had tantrums only when she had missed a nap and was extraordinarily tired.

N's parents and grandmother want her to be an obedient child, and they tell N often that she should do as she is told. A best-selling childcare manual that N's parents read says, "If a child does not obey, . . . his independence invariably takes ugly forms. Training in obedience is an essential condition for developing the ability of self-discipline." When N is not properly obedient, her parents and grandmother respond first with a reprimand and then by being cold toward her. If the disobedience is especially serious, they may refuse to talk to her for hours.

N's class at school is divided into groups, named after colors, which are a central focus of activity in the classroom. All the children in one row of desks

Figure 1-3 Like N, these youngsters are at a summer camp, where they swim, sunbathe, and have all kinds of recreational activities. Right now it is time for the group to expose their backs to the warmth of the sun. Soon it will be time to turn over. Then it will be time for the group to swim.

form a group. In the third grade, N was the leader of the blue group. Each morning the teacher asked for her report on her group's behavior the previous day. The kinds of events N reported were that one boy did the wrong problem, one girl forgot to underline certain words in the homework assignment, and another boy had a dirty shirt collar. After all the group leaders had given their reports, the teacher commended some groups and reprimanded others, but she did not praise or scold individual children.

Outside school, N belongs to a group that resembles the Girl Scouts. Most group members go to a camp in the country for three weeks each summer. Last summer, she and some friends from the camp went swimming in a lake that had no lifeguard. Although all the children were good swimmers, swimming without a lifeguard was forbidden, and another child reported their action to the camp director. N was called before the camp council, made up of 14- and 15-year-olds, and asked for the names of the others who had gone swimming with her.

She named her five friends. The council ruled that the children would not be allowed to wear their camp uniforms for two weeks. In addition, the director wrote a note to the parents of each child, describing the disobedient behavior and saying, "I expect that you will give appropriate punishment." N's mother and father did not actually punish her but they suggested that N tell the camp director, if she was asked, that she had been forbidden movies for a month. Her parents warned N, however, that setting herself off from her fellows by breaking the group's rules could be a serious matter.

Except for scout meetings, N goes out very little. She has several hours of homework every night. She wants very much to pass the qualifying tests for the university and become a doctor like her mother.

K———

K is a wiry and energetic boy, with wavy brown hair and green eyes. At 12, he is taller than most of the children in his class, because he started puberty earlier than most boys and so is already in the midst of his adolescent growth spurt. K's high spirits, inventiveness, and daring make him popular with his schoolmates. He expresses his feelings easily, and though they are usually feelings of well-being and enthusiasm, when he is angry or distressed he lets others know it in no uncertain terms.

K lives with his mother, father, and younger sister in a six-room suburban house near a large city. In the 12 years since K was born, his family has moved five times because the company his father works for has transferred him from plant to plant. The company also requires that K's father, a sales representative, spend several months a year traveling. But the family has always lived in a large, comfortable house or apartment, with a bedroom for each child. Despite all the moving, the children have never lived near their grandparents or their aunts, uncles, and cousins. They see their relatives only once a year, when their parents take a vacation.

K gave his parents some trouble when he was an infant. He was colicky and cried a great deal, driving his inexperienced mother almost frantic. He remained very sensitive to stimulation throughout his first year and was easily upset by loud noises and unexpected happenings, so his mother tried hard to keep the house relatively quiet and to guard against surprise visitors. Otherwise, he developed normally, beginning to walk and talk at the average ages for boys in his country.

K's father and mother are eager that he and his sister do well in school. They stress the importance of good marks, and they reward the children with a certain sum of money for each high grade they get. K's sister has always been a good student, but K does not do nearly as well. When he was 11, he had some disciplinary problems at school. His mother was called in to see the principal, who told her that K had been truant the day before, and the previous week had

Figure 1-4 Like K, these youngsters live in a suburban area, where most families are nuclear families—just parents and their children living in their own homes.

rudely refused to take directions from a safety guard about when to cross the street.

When his father asked the boy to explain his truancy and disobedience, K told him that he had skipped school because one of his friends had been given tickets to a professional ball game. But K refused to tell his father the name of the friend he had played hooky with. When asked about his rude behavior to the crossing guard, K told his father that no one at school liked that student, who was a teacher's pet and tattletale, and that K was one of the few kids with the courage to tell him off. K's father, secretly a little proud of the independence shown by these minor transgressions, scolded K but administered no punishment. In fact, he told K about several similar incidents in his own youth, stories K had never heard before. He also mentioned a couple of more recent incidents, in which some fellow workers had made a mistake that he had kept quiet about. Later, K's mother and father quarreled about the boy's behavior and how to handle it. His mother thought K's actions foreshadowed wildness and possible delinquency, but his father said they were a natural part of growing up.

P———

P has straight black hair, and his eyes are such a dark brown that they seem almost black. He is shorter than the average 12-year-old boy in his country and quite thin, like his mother. At home he is usually quiet and reserved, but with his friends he is often boisterous and aggressive and plays a spirited game of soccer.

P lives with his mother, his two older sisters, his grandmother, and her two grown daughters and their children in a four-room house just outside a large city. P's parents are not married and his father lives elsewhere, visiting the family only once or twice a week for a few hours and occasionally bringing money to the household. The woman that P calls grandmother is actually a common-law wife of his grandfather (his mother's father) and is not related to P by blood. P's grandfather built the small house the family lives in, but he no longer lives there himself because he has made a liaison with a younger woman. He built the house outside the city so that the family could have a small yard for raising pigs and chickens to supplement their meager income. P shares a bed with two of his male cousins, and there are two more beds in the room for five other people in the household. Other cousins, aunts, and uncles visit the house quite frequently, and they are always asked to share a meal and sometimes to stay over, sleeping on a mat on the floor.

P's mother was 15 years old when her first child was born; P is the youngest of her three children. Because he is her only son, she makes much of him. Even when he was an infant, she talked of how he would break girls' hearts when he grew up.

P was a quiet baby. He would lie peacefully for long periods and rarely cried from discomfort or wetness. When he did cry, his mother offered him food immediately. She often had one of his older sisters change him or care for him while she went shopping for the day's food or went out in the evening.

P was born and grew up in his mother's one-room tenement in the center of the city. He began to walk and talk a few months later than most boys in his country, and he did not start school until he was 7. He had been ill the year before, and his mother didn't want to send him to school until she was sure he had recovered. After he enrolled, he was sometimes truant for days or weeks at a time, and he never took seriously his mother's sporadic scoldings about it.

When P was 10, the family moved to the house his grandfather had built for them in the suburbs. There were no schools nearby and the family could not afford to transport him to school, so P's formal education ended. Also, after moving to the suburbs, P's family needed extra money, so he helps by carrying water cans to neighbors' houses from the truck that delivers water every day. He can read magazines and newspapers and, with difficulty, do simple arithmetic.

P has a group of neighborhood friends who range in age from about 10 to 15. He calls them his gang. They all work to bring home a little money—shining shoes, selling candies, helping tradesmen. When P moved to this neighborhood, he had to prove himself to the gang in order to be accepted. His credentials came slowly, one by one. P first earned respect by dousing a boy from another neighborhood who was making fun of his water-carrying work.

Figure 1-5   Like P, this 11-year-old boy contributes to his family's income.

Later, P took a slug of strong liquor from a bottle without coughing or blinking. His final test was passed when, after a stone-throwing fight with the leader of the gang, P refused to sign a police complaint against him, even though the leader had knocked P unconscious and opened a big gash in his forehead. The fight had been a man-to-man encounter, P explained to his mother, who had urged him to sign the complaint because she was afraid to say "no" to the policeman.

When P turns 13, his grandfather plans to get him a job washing dishes at the restaurant he works for. The grandfather himself started there as a dishwasher and is now the food buyer. Although the owners have paid him the same low salary for 12 years, he makes money on the side by negotiating payments from the people who supply the restaurant. He has already begun to teach P how to handle such dealings, and P has been so quick to understand this work that his grandfather hopes P might some day make enough money to have a restaurant of his own.

These three short biographies reflect individual lives in three cultures. N is Nadya, who is growing up in the privileged class of Moscow (Bronfenbrenner 1970; Smith 1976). K is Kevin, who lives in a middle-class suburb of Cleveland, Ohio. P is Pedro, a boy growing up in Mexico City in a social class that anthropologist Oscar Lewis (1970) calls the "culture of poverty."

The children differ in many respects. They were born into different cultures and social classes, and are therefore learning some different values and attitudes. Their family situations are not alike. Their sizes, shapes, and coloring are different. Their temperaments at birth differed. Yet Pedro, Nadya, and Kevin also have much in common. Despite the difference in their builds, anyone seeing them would recognize that they are about 12 years old, growing from childhood into adolescence. They all began to walk and talk at about the same age. They all like to play. And despite the differences in the composition of their families, they nevertheless all live in a family, with relatives who care for them physically and teach them the values of their culture.

COMMONALITIES IN DEVELOPMENT

Because we are all members of the same species, *Homo sapiens,* we have a common biological heritage and therefore share a common developmental outline. Like Nadya, Kevin, and Pedro, we all walk upright, and most of us begin to walk within a few months of our first birthday. We all talk, and most of us begin to speak between 1 and 2 years of age. We have a long childhood during which adults care for us and teach us. In healthy environments, we can live to be 70 years old or more. Our environments, too, have some things in common, even though they range from the cold climate of the Soviet Union to the warm, thin air of Mexico City, from rural huts to skyscraper cities. For example, we all live in social groups. The study of human development must begin by tracing these common patterns (McCall 1981; Wohlwill 1973).

Our Biological Heritage

Every species possesses a biological heritage that is passed from parents to offspring by a set of genes. Genes help determine the form and physiology of the species, as well as some of its behaviors. For example, their genes determine that salmon have gills and fins, that robins have lungs and wings, and that human beings have lungs and legs. They also determine that the fish swim, the birds fly, and the human beings walk upright. Not all birds fly exactly the same way, of course (and some don't fly at all). Each species may have its own way of taking off or soaring—or of eating or nest building. Nevertheless, all members of one species do it the same way.

Behaviors in which genes play an important part and that are shared by virtually all members of a species are called ***species-specific behaviors.*** Some behaviors are obviously universal in the human species. Nearly all of us crawl before we walk, and then walk on two legs. We all jump when surprised by a loud noise and blink when an object suddenly approaches our eyes. We all smile and cry, love and hate. We all develop language. And we all learn. The enormous learning ability of human beings, also a part of our common biological heritage, makes our behavior much more varied and flexible than that of other animals.

Human language is a species-specific behavior that is remarkably flexible (Lenneberg 1967). Under normal circumstances, all the birds in a single species develop essentially the same call, but members of our species learn very different languages. Nadya learned Russian; Kevin, English; and Pedro, Spanish. Our genes give us the capacity to learn language, but the specific environment in which a child grows up determines the language that she or he speaks.

Like language, almost all species-specific human capacities depend heavily on environmental circumstances for their final expression. Nadya, Kevin, and Pedro all smile when they are presented with a pleasant surprise, and each cries when seriously upset. But many of the things that constitute pleasant surprises or serious upsets are different for the three children, as a result of the differences between their environments.

The Human Life Cycle   Our biological heritage gives us a common developmental outline—the human *life cycle.* This life cycle is the starting point for the scientific analysis of development. We all pass from infancy to childhood; we undergo the changes of puberty and pass into adulthood and then old age. The changes of the human life cycle are so compelling that people at the same period of life tend to resemble each other more closely than they do others from the same culture or class who are significantly younger or older. In many ways, Nadya, Kevin, and Pedro resemble each other more than they resemble an infant or a 60-year-old from their own culture. Given an array of photographs of infants, children, and adults from a wide range of cultures, almost any adult in the world (provided he or she is accustomed to dealing with pictures) could group them according to periods of the human life cycle— no matter what races or styles of dress were shown. All human beings, then, share a biological heritage that gives us the same basic form, a common range of species-specific behaviors, and a predictable life cycle.

The Environmental Context of Development

People share not only a common genetic inheritance but a **common environment**—the species-specific environment for *Homo sapiens.* We all breathe air containing oxygen and eat foods containing the same basic nutrients. We live in a world where things fall down, never up. We experience a daily cycle of light and dark, as well as an annual cycle of seasonal changes. Because the human species is so versatile, we can live under a wide range of physical conditions, from the arctic to the tropical. But wherever human cultures exist, certain aspects of the **social environment** are similar (Cairns 1979). For exam-

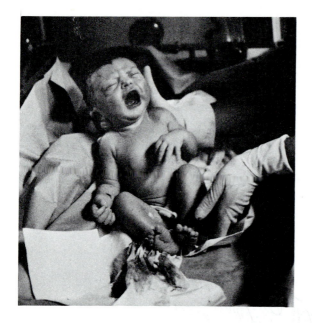

Figure 1-6   Here are the life cycles of organic and inorganic entities. A butterfly goes through such radical developmental changes that its form from one stage to the next is totally different. Shown from left to right are the metamorphoses from egg to larva (caterpillar) to pupa (chrysalis) to adult. A river's characteristic life cycle shows more gradual change. A young river is vigorous and disorganized, with many lakes and swamps, rapids and waterfalls. As it matures, it makes its mark deeper on the earth, carving an enduring channel so that it no longer diffuses itself in lakes and swamps. As it grows older, its channel starts to wander and expand itself into a flood plain. Eventually the plain becomes wide enough for the river to meander back and forth across it without any constraints from the landforms. The people whose photographs appear here illustrate phases of the human life cycle. They represent different races and nationalities, but all are members of the species *Homo sapiens*, so all are going through the same life cycle.

ple, all societies use language to transmit cultural values and teach skills to children and young people.

The long childhood that characterizes our species probably accounts for the existence of the human *family*, another aspect of our shared social environment (Hartup 1979). The human reproductive cycle can result in children being born about one year apart, and children must be cared for, say, through the first ten years of life if they are to survive. Thus, from the early days of human existence, females required assistance in providing food, care, and protection for their young. This need seems to have been the basis for permanent matings and the existence of fairly stable family groups (Linton 1959).

The family is a universal human institution, though its exact nature varies greatly from culture to culture. Pedro lives in what is called an *extended family*, in which a large number of relatives live together and share child-rearing and most other family duties. Kevin lives in a *nuclear family*, now the most common form of family in the United States: It contains only two parents and their children. Nadya's family—her parents, her grandmother, and herself—is called a *stem family*. A number of variations of these basic patterns also exist. For example, some nuclear families consist of only one parent and his or her children, and some extended families are composed of people who are unrelated by blood ties but have chosen to live together in a communal setting.

In all its many variations, the family serves basically the same child-rearing functions. It cares for the helpless infant and immature child so that he or she can survive to adulthood. And it ensures that children are socialized and educated, taught the ways of their culture and the skills they need to get along in life. These kinds of shared experiences and the common biological heritage of all *Homo sapiens* illustrate the unity of human life. The study of individual differences reveals its diversity.

INDIVIDUAL DIFFERENCES

Developmentalists are interested not only in the common pathways that people follow as they live their lives. They are also interested in the qualities and behaviors that distinguish one person from another. They ask questions such as the following: Are there consistent differences between young infants in how they react to stimulation? Are preschool boys more aggressive than preschool girls? How do individual children differ in their approach to solving problems? Why do some adolescents become delinquents? They try to answer such questions by conducting studies of various kinds. These studies have shown that several major factors seem to be important in the development of the wide variety of individual differences that exist: genetic heritage, culture and social class, and interactions between family members.

Individual Genetic Heritage

Besides specifying the characteristics that all people share because they belong to the same species, genes also specify individual differences. In fact, the particular combination of genes that a person inherits from his or her parents is unique—it is unlike the set belonging to anyone else in the world. The only exception is identical twins, who have identical genes.

Many physical characteristics, such as Pedro's black hair and Nadya's blonde hair, are controlled primarily by genes. Most physical characteristics, however, result from the collaboration of genetic and environmental influences. Height, for example, is strongly influenced by genes, but it is also affected by the amount and quality of food that a child eats. Similarly, obesity, physical strength, and many other traits are determined by genes and environmental factors acting together.

For most behaviors, the precise extent of the genes' role is unknown. Some researchers have found that right after birth and for the first months of life, many infants show a consistent individual pattern of responding that seems to depend on inborn physical factors. This pattern of behavior is called temperament (Thomas & Chess 1977). But as children develop and interact with things and people around them, such patterns become very difficult to discern. So if Nadya's father says to her, "You're just like your mother," there simply is no way of knowing how much of Nadya's personality and ways of acting result from the genes that she has inherited from her mother or how much they result from what she has learned in her family.

Culture

Every society has its own values—its own definitions of the good life, the ideal man or woman, good character, valuable work. These shared customs and values constitute a *culture* (Super & Harkness 1980). It is most important for the society's continuance that these values be taught to its young. The process by which they are taught is called **socialization,** and primary agents of socialization in industrial societies are the family, the school, and the peer group. Nadya, Kevin, and Pedro illustrate how values and the methods of socialization differ from one culture to another, producing important individual differences in behavior.

Let us compare Nadya and Kevin. Nadya is growing up in a culture that values the group above the individual (Figure 1-7); in Kevin's society, individual achievement is emphasized. This basic difference leads Nadya and Kevin to develop different ways of thinking and acting. When Nadya and Kevin were disobedient, both children knew that what they had done was against the rules, but the disobedience had very different meanings for the two children.

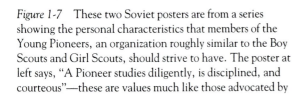

Figure 1-7 These two Soviet posters are from a series showing the personal characteristics that members of the Young Pioneers, an organization roughly similar to the Boy Scouts and Girl Scouts, should strive to have. The poster at left says, "A Pioneer studies diligently, is disciplined, and courteous"—these are values much like those advocated by American scout groups. The one at the right says "A Pioneer tells the truth and treasures the honor of his unit." It shows the Young Pioneer telling the authorities—a troop leader or teacher—about a schoolmate's misdeed (Bronfenbrenner 1970). Most American adults would not see this behavior as wholly desirable.

For Kevin, the emphasis was on his own individual responsibility. When he skipped school to go to a ball game, he knew that he alone had made the decision and that he alone had to take the responsibility for it. When he refused to name the friend he had played hooky with, his father understood his unwillingness and accepted it.

For Nadya, on the other hand, everything about the disobedience was interpreted in terms of the group rather than the individual. Nadya did not hesitate to name the companions she had gone swimming with. She and her friends had jointly made the decision to disobey the camp rule against swimming without a lifeguard, and Nadya had no doubt that it was correct for them to receive joint punishment. The main punishment was delivered not by individual adults but by a group of young people representing the larger group, and it deprived the swimmers of the symbols of their group membership for a time.

Pedro, too, was disobedient to the authorities when he refused to bring a complaint against the companion who had hit him with a stone. For Pedro, the fight had been a necessary step in proving that he possessed the courage and toughness his culture considers a vital part of masculinity.

Because of the differences between their cultures, Kevin, Nadya, and Pedro are learning different social values and behaviors. But people's values and behaviors differ within a culture, too, and one of the most important sources of these differences is social class.

Social Class

Almost every culture has a hierarchy of **social class**—typically an upper class and a lower class, and in many cases, a middle class as well (Robertson 1981). Members of the higher classes have higher status and, usually, greater wealth; they frequently assume positions of leadership or influence in their society. The class that a person belongs to can be either achieved or ascribed. When social class is achieved, the person has done something to attain his or her social position, such as making a large amount of money. When social class is ascribed, its members belong to it by virtue of some inherited characteristic. In old India, for example, children of untouchables (the lowest class) had to remain untouchables forever, and children of Brahmans (the highest class) remained Brahmans, no matter how they spent their lives. In societies in which social mobility is possible, a person may be ascribed a class at birth based on the family's status but can achieve a higher (or lower) class according to his or her attainments.

The values, attitudes, and expectations held by people in one social class may be very different from those held by people in another class (Tulkin 1977). Pedro, for example, comes from a lower-class family. Class distinctions in Mexico are based largely on income, and Pedro's family is poor. Many of the differences between his family and Nadya's and Kevin's families reflect differences in social class rather than differences between the larger cultures. Indeed, Pedro's family is similar in many ways to lower-class families in other Western nations, including the United States. For example, Pedro's family values education less than Kevin's and Nadya's. A child who is going to school cannot at the same time work to bring home income, and Pedro's family needs the income he earns through his water-carrying job. This immediate need outweighs the promise of greater future income through education. Also, lower-class families, sometimes because of racial or ethnic bias in the culture, may be unable to learn about means of making it easier to enter schools or to obtain outside funds such as scholarships.

Kevin's parents, on the other hand, expect that he will go to college after he graduates from high school, even though his academic record through seventh grade has been only mediocre. About 55 percent of American children from families with incomes as high as that of Kevin's do attend college. Only about 30 percent of American children whose family income and occupation place them in the unskilled working class or lower class enroll in college (U.S. Department of Commerce 1981). There are no official Soviet statistics based on class differences (the Soviets do not acknowledge officially that class differences exist in their society), but Americans who have lived in Russia report that most of the top schools are filled with sons and daughters of prominent Russian scientists and bureaucrats (Smith 1976). These youngsters from the privileged class tend to score better than others on the nationwide competitive entrance exams.

In many countries, another difference between classes is that in the lower class, people tend to have extended families, like Pedro's, with a number of relatives living together, while, in the middle class, people tend to have nuclear families, like Kevin's, with just parents and children living together. Pedro's grandfather has a strong sense of obligation to support not only his wives and children but also his grandchildren. Even more distant relatives—aunts, uncles, cousins—know that if they are hungry, they will be offered food at the grandfather's house. Pedro is being taught the same values.

Family Interactions

Variations among families are another important source of individual differences. Parental style has an important effect on a child's personality, especially in the nuclear family typical of the Western middle class (Leiderman et al. 1977). For example, studies in the United States have shown that when parents are firm and authoritative but at the same time warm and supportive, their children tend to become active, individualistic, competent adolescents (Baumrind 1975). When, on the other hand, parents are harsh, arbitrary, inconsistent, and cold, their children may be in danger of becoming delinquents (Maccoby & Martin 1983).

Although parental style is clearly important, the interactions between members of a family are a two-way street (Bell 1979). All children affect their parents, too—the birth of a first child in itself usually changes the parents' style of life dramatically because infants require so much care, no matter what their temperament. Recall how Kevin's parents had to adjust to his irritability as an infant, and how Nadya's family responded to her high level of activity. Pedro's family adapted easily to his birth because of his quiet nature, but his sisters had to devote a good deal of what would have been their play time to caring for him. As the children grew older, all the parents had to respond to their children's disobedient behavior. Nadya's camp director expected her parents to cooperate with the state in punishing her. Allen's parents were drawn into a quarrel with each other about how his behavior should be viewed and whether it should be punished. Pedro's mother had to undergo an anxiety-filled encounter with authorities on his behalf. And these were just single incidents in the lives of these 12-year-olds.

The effects of family interactions, culture, and social class, then, combine with an individual's genetic heritage to make each human being unique.

UNRAVELING DEVELOPMENT: THEORIES

Explaining development is like trying to solve a mystery when you do not know where to find all the clues and are not sure what the nature of the final solution will be. In their search for answers, scientists use tools that fall into two main categories: theories and methods. A developmental *theory* is a system of ideas that can be used to describe, predict, and explain behavior from a certain point of view. Theories tell a researcher where to look for clues. **Methods** are techniques for collecting and analyzing those clues—making careful observations and using those observations to make inferences about development.

Historical Background

Folk wisdom about how children change as they grow up—and about what children need in order to become successful adults—is probably as old as the human species. As a social science, however, the study of development is less than a hundred years old. In the course of this short history, four general theoretical approaches to explaining development have predominated—the biological, behaviorist, cognitive-developmental, and psychoanalytic approaches (Achenbach 1978).

The biological approach originated with Charles Darwin, the biologist who formulated evolutionary theory and applied some of his concepts to descriptions of child development. A great burst of research based on the biological approach took place in the 1920s and 1930s, when a number of large-scale "growth studies" were initiated, charting in minute detail the physical growth and mental functioning of children from infancy to adolescence, often with the aim of establishing standards that would allow the prediction of future abnormalities (for example, Gesell et al. 1938). Since the 1940s, biologically oriented researchers have focused less on pure description and more on explaining development in terms of such biological concepts as genetics and evolution.

The behaviorist approach, also known as learning theory, formulated by the American psychologist John Watson, also had its first major impact on the study of development in the 1920s. Watson emphasized the contribution of learning to development and the way that all behavior is shaped by reward and punishment. This approach dominated American psychology in the 1940s and 1950s, and learning theory—particularly social-learning theory—remains one of the most influential in modern developmental science.

The cognitive-developmental approach grew out of the mental-testing movement, which arose in the early 1900s after the first intelligence test was constructed. Beginning in the 1920s, the Swiss scientist Jean Piaget put items like those on intelligence tests to a new use—the study of how children's thinking, or cognition, develops. He later worked out techniques of his own for studying cognition. Piaget's work, which received little attention from American scientists until the early 1960s, has stimulated much recent research on cognitive development—how children think at different ages.

The psychoanalytic approach originated with the work of the Austrian physician Sigmund Freud. It includes concepts of a number of other theorists, one of the most important being Erik Erikson. This approach began to emerge in the 1930s as a major force in the study of development. Among the most influential of Freud's ideas was the theory that early experiences in the family, such as weaning and toilet training, have a major and lasting impact on the development of emotion and personality.

This chapter presents a brief introduction to each of these four theoretical approaches. Full descriptions of the developmental theories that represent each approach appear as special Theory Insets in later chapters (see Table 1-1). Here, each approach also will be applied to a single situation—Kevin's disciplinary problems in school. Recall that when Kevin was 11 years old, he played hooky and refused to tell the principal where he had been on the day he was absent. He also refused to tell his father or the principal the name of the

TABLE 1-1 INSETS ON THEORIES OF DEVELOPMENT

The biological approach	
Ethology	Chapter 2, page 71
The learning approach	
Conditioning and Learning	Chapter 4, page 172
Social Learning	Chapter 6, page 275
The cognitive-developmental approach	
Cognitive Development	Chapter 5, page 215
A Cognitive-Developmental Approach to Moral Judgment	Chapter 10, page 534
The psychodynamic approach	
The Psychodynamic Approaches of Freud and Erikson	Chapter 8, page 392

boy he had played hooky with. If developmentalists representing each theoretical approach were asked to explain Kevin's actions in this sitution, their analyses might include some of the following points.

The Biological Approach

The **biological approach** emphasizes the organic bases of development (Cairn 1979; Gottlieb 1983). How is a person's development affected by his or her genetic inheritance or by other specific biological influences, such as hormones? And how does a person's development reflect general characteristics that are typical of the human species?

As was mentioned earlier, one species-specific characteristic that is particularly important for developmental analysis is the human life cycle. The general outline of this cycle is controlled by genes, which have their effect through hormones and other biochemical agents. For example, puberty—the development of mature sexual anatomy and physiology—is begun by a sharp increase in the body's production of male or female sexual hormones.

A biological theorist might point out that Kevin's behavior was probably influenced by organic factors related to the onset of puberty. Kevin is on the verge of adolescence. He began puberty early, already showing signs of it when he was 11. The increase in male hormones that comes with puberty tends to produce an increase in assertive and aggressive behavior, and Kevin's playing hooky may have been an instance of such behavior. Some individual biological characteristics that Kevin has inherited might also have affected his behavior. His father had been something of a rebel in childhood, and Allen could possibly have inherited some of his father's temperamental characteristics, such as a tendency to react intensely.

The Learning Approach

The **learning** (or **behavioral**) **approach** focuses on behavior and how it is molded and controlled by events in the person's environment. The direction of an individual's development is determined by the behaviors the person learns, and learning is affected mainly by three mechanisms: (1) reward, or reinforcement, (2) punishment, and (3) observational learning, or imitation (Bandura 1969; Mischel 1970).

When a person's behavior is rewarded, the person is likely to repeat it in the future; when it is punished, the person is likely to refrain from repeating it. Reward and punishment thus shape the learning of specific behaviors. Human beings, in contrast to many other animals, also learn new behaviors through imitation, that is, by watching and listening to other people. They can learn whether a behavior is likely to be rewarded or punished by noting the response that it elicits when performed by other people.

Figure 1-8   Children who grow up in different environments may learn very different things about the world. (Top) The countryside of Iceland. (Bottom) Brooklyn, New York. (Right) Belfast, Northern Ireland.

A learning theorist attempting to explain Kevin's truancy would first specify the exact behavior in question. In this case, there are two behaviors to be explained. Kevin's playing hooky and his refusing to tell who played hooky with him.

Both imitation and reward could account for Kevin's playing hooky. Recall that Kevin's father had confessed to similar youthful escapades, and the stories he had told Kevin clearly implied that he had enjoyed his childhood rebelliousness and was even a little proud of it. In being truant from school, Kevin could have been simply imitating his father's youthful behavior.

Also, Kevin was reinforced, or rewarded, for his truant behavior in more ways than one. First, he got to go to a ball game with a good friend. Second, his father did not punish him, but even subtly communicated approval. These reinforcements apparently outweighed the punishments represented by the disapproval of his mother and the principal. Because behavior that is reinforced tends to be repeated, the learning theorist might point out that Kevin is quite likely to play hooky again.

Kevin's refusal to name his accomplice likewise involved both imitation and reinforcement. Although Kevin's father usually insisted that Kevin tell the truth, he had frequently condemned people who betray their friends, and on several occasions had made a point of refusing to tell higher officials at his company about the misbehavior of his fellow workers. Kevin was imitating his father's faithfulness to friends.

The reinforcements for this second behavior were numerous. His father's subtle approval extended to Kevin's show of loyalty, and it is probable that Kevin's peers overtly admired him for refusing to "rat" on his friend. In addition, Kevin knew that if he named his accomplice, he would be punished with disapproval from both his father and his peers.

The Cognitive-Developmental Approach

The **cognitive-developmental approach** emphasizes thinking processes, or cognition, and how they change as people develop through a series of stages. A stage is a period of development in which a person's abilities are qualitatively different from those of the periods before and after it. In each stage, a person both acquires new abilities and retains those of the stage before, although typically they are reorganized and recombined in some way. By delineating these stages, the cognitive-developmental approach attempts to describe and explain how people gradually build an understanding of their world—how their skills for acting on things and interacting with people change systematically with development (Kohlberg 1969, 1981; Piaget 1952).

An individual's cognitive capacity sets limits on what she or he can learn, understand, and accomplish. According to cognitive-developmental theory, this capacity develops through four stages as the individual matures from newborn to young adult. (The significance of the names given to these stages will become apparent when this approach is discussed in detail in Chapter 5.) In the first stage (the sensorimotor stage), the infant can learn only actions— how to grasp, look, walk. During the second stage (the preoperational stage), the preschool child begins to be able to think about objects and people independently of his or her own actions. But it is not until the third stage (the concrete-operational stage), which occupies the elementary-school years, that the child can organize these thoughts systematically enough to begin to think logically. Adolescence brings with it the beginnings of the fourth stage (the formal-operational stage), which is marked by hypothetical thinking.

A cognitive-developmental theorist might point out that Kevin's thinking abilities had progressed to at least the third stage of development, when children can understand the logic of social rules well enough to apply them both to

Figure 1-9 By age 8 or 9, most children know that they can act and talk with their peers in ways that they cannot with adults.

themselves and to others. He was definitely past the second stage, in which children usually accept the authority of adults without question because they believe that social rules are absolute. By age 8 or 9, however, they know that social rules are made by people and that different rules apply in different situations. They know, for example, that they can talk and act with their peers in ways that they cannot with adults.

When Kevin played hooky, he was following his peer group's social rules, which say that boys are supposed to be independent and to do things that are a little risky, even if their behavior invites disapproval from adults. Playing hooky and going to a ball game fit these rules to a T.

When Kevin was asked by his father to reveal whom he had skipped school with, he had to choose between two sets of social rules—adult rules about obeying those in authority and peer-group rules about not tattling on a friend. After weighing the consequences of telling or not telling, Kevin decided to follow the peer-group social rules, even though he knew that he could expect some disapproval and even punishment from his parents. A few years earlier, Kevin would not have been able to formulate the two sets of rules and keep them both in mind at the same time.

The Psychodynamic Approach

The **psychodynamic approach** focuses on the pervasive influence of emotion on thinking and behavior. According to this view, the three most important determinants of emotional development are a person's ways of dealing with pleasure (especially sexual pleasure) and aggression, the nature of the person's unconscious thoughts and needs, and the relations of the child with his or her parents (A. Freud 1966; Wolman 1972).

According to psychodynamic theory, one of the most important developmental events is the Oedipus conflict, which illustrates how all three determinants interact during emotional development. In this conflict, which takes its name from the legend of the Greek king Oedipus who unwittingly killed his father and married his mother, the 4- or 5-year-old boy wants his mother's affections all to himself and sees his father as a rival. Unconsciously, he wants to be rid of his father, and this desire is expressed in fantasies about his father's disappearing or dying.

At the same time that a boy has these hostile feelings toward his father, he admires and fears him. His father is the person whom his mother loves and is the embodiment of power and authority—someone who might forcefully retaliate against him. He resolves this emotional conflict by identifying with his father. That is, he internalizes his father's values and characteristics and makes them his own, thus developing a conscience and a masculine identity. Problems in resolving the Oedipus conflict are believed to produce lifelong difficulties in interpersonal relations, especially with people whom one loves and with authority figures.

A psychodynamic theorist might explain Kevin's behavior by suggesting that Kevin was hostile to authority figures because of problems he had had in the past with his parents, especially in the resolution of the Oedipus conflict. His father's frequent and prolonged absences from home probably interfered with Kevin's resolution of the conflict. Kevin did not just fantasize about having his mother to himself; while his father was away on his frequent business trips, Kevin in fact had no male rival for his mother's affections. His father's absences also lessened the threat of retaliation for Kevin's hostile fantasies. Thus, a psychoanalytic theorist might conclude that Kevin's identification with his father may have come later than most boys' and was still not complete. Incomplete resolution of the Oedipus conflict may have produced a weak conscience and lingering hostility toward his father and other authority figures. His weak conscience allowed Kevin to break the rules and play hooky. The hostility toward his father may have spilled over into his relationship with school authorities and led him to refuse to tell the principal and his father who had played hooky with him.

The Complementarity of Theoretical Approaches

These four theoretical approaches offer different insights into Kevin's actions because the primary focus of each approach is different. The biological approach stresses organic contributions to Kevin's behavior. The learning-theory approach emphasizes how the environment has molded his specific behaviors. The cognitive-developmental approach focuses on the stage of development of Kevin's thinking. And the psychoanalytic approach seeks to analyze his emotions. Because each theoretical approach deals with a different aspect of Kevin's actions, they are more complementary than contradictory. Each adds something unique to an understanding of Kevin's behavior.

Although Kevin's sudden rebelliousness might have been stimulated by the hormonal changes of puberty, the biological analysis does not explain why Kevin chose to rebel through the particular behavior of truancy instead of, say, smoking or shoplifting. Learning theory helps to understand that choice: Kevin was imitating his father's youthful behavior, and he received approval for this not only from his father but from his buddies. However, Kevin's actions violated the social rules adhered to by the school principal and the adult "establishment." The cognitive-developmental approach helps us see how a child whose thinking abilities have reached a specific stage of development could come to understand two sets of social rules—the peer group's and the school's—and choose between them. Kevin understood both sets of rules but chose to abide by the set that called for disobedience to authority. The psychoanalytic approach suggests that his choice may have been motivated by some hostile feelings toward authority figures, perhaps including his father.

Kevin's behavior probably was determined by a combination of all these factors—even seemingly contradictory ones. For example, Kevin could act in ways that would win approval from his father, and yet, at the same time, he could harbor hostile feelings toward his father. Applying all four theoretical approaches, rather than any one, gives a fuller and probably more realistic account of Kevin's behavior. That is why in the last decade, many developmentalists have stopped treating these theories as contradictory and, instead, have begun to move toward an integrated, more comprehensive approach to development (Achenbach 1978). In practice, however, not all four theoretical approaches are generally used to interpret every developmental phenomenon. This is because each approach concerns itself with somewhat different kinds of data. The biological approach, for example, is not likely to yield much information about why identical twins grow up to have some different personality traits. The psychoanalytic approach probably would not be useful in explaining why older children can perceive optical illusions that younger ones cannot.

Likewise, there are behaviors that would not be usefully explained from the cognitive-developmental or learning-theory perspective. This book presents the rich array of theoretical approaches in detail in the Theory Insets, and selectively applies them throughout the book to the developmental phenomena they can best explain.

UNRAVELING DEVELOPMENT: METHODOLOGY

Theories can tell researchers where to look for clues in their quest to unravel the mysteries of development, but theories by themselves cannot provide solutions. After researchers have examined the clues that theories point to, they must devise a hypothesis about how or why a certain developmental event takes place and then test that hypothesis, using the accepted methods of science.

To test hypotheses, researchers use a number of standard methodologies— techniques for (1) observing and recording behavior, and (2) analyzing the data from observations in order to explain what has been observed.

Observational Techniques

The solution of real-life mysteries often requires that witnesses to an event describe what they saw. The problem is that witnesses' descriptions rarely agree on all points. Even more difficult than getting an accurate account of a certain sequence of behaviors is knowing what the behaviors mean. Was the man observed running away from the scene of a crime an associate of the criminal? A frightened onlooker? A good Samaritan going for help? Or merely an oblivious passer-by, late for an appointment?

The specialized methods of observation developed by researchers are designed to deal with such difficulties. Their function is to make observation as objective as possible, in order to obtain accurate measures of behavior. Three **observational techniques** often used by developmentalists are ethological observation, the clinical method of observation, and controlled observation. Each has its special strengths and shortcomings.

Ethological Observation   Ethology is the study of animal behavior. In particular, the behavior of an animal species in its natural environment is studied in order to discover the meaning of a behavior for the species. Ethological observation of human behavior likewise focuses on understanding the meaning of that behavior in its natural context (Hess 1970).

Ethologists always begin their study of a species by using observational techniques designed to keep the observer from affecting the animals' ongoing behavior. Such **naturalistic observation** techniques are also used by developmental researchers. (In fact, some of the earliest developmental studies—baby biographies—made use of naturalistic observation. Charles Darwin made close observations of his infants' behaviors and described them in detail.) Researchers wishing to study the behavior of preschool children, for example, might watch the children from behind a one-way mirror in a nursery school. If that technique was not available, or seemed too confining, the researchers might attend the preschool session for several weeks before beginning formal observations so that the children would become accustomed to their presence.

An essential aspect of naturalistic observation is the attempt to prevent the observer from projecting his own viewpoint and assumptions onto the organism under study. Even when the organism is fairly uncomplicated, say, a fish or a bird, it is not always easy to discover what a particular behavior means for it. For example, why do female mallard ducks tending their eggs make certain clucking sounds? To ward off strangers? To communicate with other adult ducks? One ethologist observing these ducks concluded that ducklings in the egg can hear sounds before they hatch and that the mother mallard is therefore clucking to give the ducklings experience in hearing her call so that when they hatch, they will follow her. The ethologist went on to test his interpretation with experiments. He played a recording of a human voice saying "Come, come, come" to a group of unhatched ducklings instead of allowing them to hear the mother's clucks. When these ducklings hatched, they readily followed a decoy duck that was rigged to play the "Come, come, come" recording (Hess 1973).

Ethological observation is also useful for understanding human behavior. Scientists can easily misread the significance of a person's behavior if they do not carefully note the conditions under which it normally takes place. Only in this way can the meaning of the behavior for the person being observed be taken into account. Misinterpretations are especially likely to happen when scientists are observing the behavior of people whose lives are very different from their own, such as those of a different culture, social class, race, sex, or age group.

Ruth Weir, a psycholinguist, used the technique of ethological observation in studying her son Anthony. She had noted that after the 2-year-old was tucked in at bedtime he continued to talk, even though he was alone. She wondered what function such extended monologues might play in the child's development, so she set up a tape recorder in his bedroom. She was thus able to assemble an accurate account of her son's bedtime verbal behavior without affecting that behavior by her presence (Weir 1962). If she had remained in the room with the boy, he probably would have directed his talk to her, and she would not have heard a monologue. Here is one of the bedtime soliloquies that she recorded:

Figure 1-10 A psychologist observing human behavior in a natural setting, a schoolroom.

1. Step on the blanket
2. Where is Anthony's blanket (2 times, falsetto)
3. Where's hiding (falsetto)
4. Books
5. Down (2 times)
6. Have the books today
7. I take the white blanket off
8. On the blanket
9. Under the blanket
10. Sleep go
11. What a blue blanket
12. What the take the blanket

Dr. Weir found, in excerpts like this, that the child was not only recalling events of the day but was practicing newly acquired language skills. In phrases 7, 8, and 9, for example, he appears to be testing his mastery of the prepositions "off," "on," and "under."

Because the goal of ethological observers is noninterference in the activities they observe, one drawback of this method is that there can be no direction or control of situations. The method, therefore, can yield detailed descriptions of behavior but it often cannot provide an explanation for why or how development takes place. Generally, this method can suggest answers to questions about what causes certain behaviors but cannot verify them with very much certainty. Another drawback is that the data obtained usually characterize an entire group of organisms—all nesting mallards or all 2-year-olds—and so offer little insight into individual differences.

The Clinical Method   The *clinical method* of observation is designed to obtain an accurate measure of a person's motives, thoughts, or abilities. In the clinical method, unlike most ethological observation, the emphasis is on careful analysis of an individual's behavior. To avoid misinterpretation, the observer takes an active part in the situation, probing as sensitively as possible to determine what the person's behavior means. The observer thus is able to structure the event in order to elicit the behavior he or she is interested in; the naturalistic observer, in contrast, can only try to choose a situation in which the behavior of interest is likely to occur.

Jean Piaget used the clinical method of observation to assess individual children's cognitive abilities. He named this technique the clinical method to indicate that although the observer participates actively, he assumes a "clinical detachment" similar to that of a physician examining a patient (Vinh Bang 1966). The following excerpt from a study by Piaget (1932) shows how he used the clinical method to find out how a 6-year-old boy (Clai) reasons about lies.

Piaget: Do you know what a lie is?

Clai: It's when you say what isn't true.

Piaget: 2 + 2 = 5. Is that a lie?

Clai: Yes, it's a lie.

Piaget: Why?

Clai: Because it's not right.

Piaget: The boy who said 2 + 2 = 5, did he know it was wrong, or did he just make a mistake?

Clai: He made a mistake.

Piaget: Then, if he made a mistake, did he tell a lie or not?

Clai: Yes, he told a lie.

Piaget: A bad one or not?

Figure 1-11 Jean Piaget among some of the children that he studied in Switzerland.

Clai: Not very bad.

Piaget: You see this gentleman? (Piaget points to a graduate-student assistant.)

Clai: Yes.

Piaget: How old do you think he is?

Clai: 30 years old.

Piaget: I would say 28.

(The student says he is 36.)

Piaget: Have we both told a lie?

Clai: Yes, that's a lie.

Piaget: A bad one?

Clai: Not too bad.

Piaget: Which is the worst, yours or mine, or are they both the same?

Clai: Yours is the worst, because the difference is biggest.

Piaget: Is it a lie, or did we just make a mistake?

Clai: We made a mistake.

Piaget: Is it still a lie, or not?

Clai: Yes, it's a lie.

The major limitation of the clinical method is that because the observer takes such an active role, he or she may influence or misinterpret the child's behavior in some way, creating the very problem the method is intended to prevent. Although Piaget's own observations have proved to be exceptionally accurate (that is, his findings have been replicated, or duplicated, by other researchers), many investigators have been less successful at maintaining objectivity while using the clinical method.

Controlled Observation   What a scientist "observes" can be affected by what he or she expects to observe. That is, the observer's expectations can affect what is noticed or even what is actually seen. This phenomenon, known as *observer bias*, can affect observations of any kind. Suppose, for example, that you are a researcher who suspects that watching aggression on television stimulates aggressive actions in young children. You are observing a group of young children who have just watched several TV cartoons filled with episodes of aggression. Even with the strongest will to be an objective observer, you may inadvertently classify some neutral acts as aggression: A child knocks over a chair out of clumsiness, but because you are looking for aggression, that is what you perceive as the chair crashes to the floor.

To guard against observer bias, researchers employ methods of *controlled observation.* First, they often use a "blind" scoring procedure, in which the observer is someone other than the researcher who designed the study. This observer is kept from knowing the experimental conditions of the study and the hypothesis being tested. In a study of the effects of TV on aggression, for instance, the observer would be asked to record the number of aggressive acts the children perform but would not be told the experimenter's hypothesis— that watching aggression on TV stimulates aggressive behavior. In addition, the observer would score behavior not only for children who had just been watching television but also for a *control group,* who had just been doing something else. In a blind scoring procedure, the observer would not know which group was which, or even what they had just been doing.

Second, the researcher carefully defines the categories of behavior that she or he wants recorded and trains the observers to catalog the children's behaviors in terms of these particular definitions. For example, in a study of mother-child interactions in the first year of life, the researchers gave their observers the list shown in Figure 1-12. Each behavior on the list was represented by an abbreviated code, so that recording it took only a moment.

In most studies, two or more observers independently record the behaviors of interest, and their records are compared to see how well they agree. If the behaviors have been clearly defined and the observers well trained, there is usually good agreement. If the agreement is poor, further efforts must be made to clarify the behavioral categories or to train the observers more carefully.

1. Location: distance of mother from infant, scored each time it changes.
   a. Face to face.
   b. Within 2 feet (within arm's distance).
   c. More than 2 feet away.
2. Physical contact.
   a. Kiss: Mother's lips touch child.
   b. Hold: Mother supports child's weight—mother carries child, child sits on mother's lap, etc.
   c. Active physical contact: Mother tickles child, bounces child on lap, throws child in air, etc.
3. Prohibitions: Mother interferes with or stops an act of the child's that has begun.
   a. Verbal: negative command (e.g., "stop that" or "don't do that").
   b. Physical: Mother stops child's motor activity or takes object from child.
   c. Prohibition ratios: (*i*) To control for possible differences in infants' activity levels, which could result in some infants receiving more prohibitions than others, a ratio was computed in which the total number of maternal prohibitions was divided by the number of 5-second intervals in which the infant was either walking or crawling. (*ii*) Another possible bias was that infants moving around on the floor would have more opportunities to engage in behaviors that might be prohibited; thus, a second ratio was computed in which the total number of maternal prohibitions was divided by the amount of time that the infant was free to crawl or walk on the floor.
4. Maternal vocalization: Mother says words to child. This category was analyzed separately for each location in category 1.
5. Keeping infant busy: Mother provides activity for child.
   a. Entertain: Mother holds attention of child by nonverbal sounds, body movements such as peek-a-boo, or the use of a toy—such as shaking a rattle. If words were used with an entertainment behavior, category 4 was also scored.
   b. Give object: Mother gives child an object and makes no effort to hold child's attention.

Figure 1-12 A description of the detailed instructions for scoring given to observers in a study of mother-child interactions (Tulkin and Kagan 1972).

The clinical and ethological methods of observation can provide rich descriptions of the behavior of an individual or a group, and the method of controlled observation, although it provides more limited descriptions, can eliminate problems of observer bias. Together, these techniques of observation can provide a detailed and accurate description of behavior. But developmentalists want to do more than describe behavior: They want to explain it, and to test their explanations rigorously. Such testing requires special techniques for interpreting what has been observed.

Techniques for Making Inferences

To test an explanation, an experimenter must try to infer a relation between two or more factors—for example, that the ability to understand the rules of games is related to age, or that seeing a person rewarded for a given behavior is related to one's later performance of that behavior. But for researchers (just as for detectives), it is often no easy matter to determine what relates to what. The two most basic techniques for inferring relations are the experiment and the correlation.

The Experiment *Experiments* allow the testing of causal hypotheses—explanations of how one factor affects another. In an experiment, researchers manipulate one factor and then measure how another factor changes (Achenbach 1978). The factor that they manipulate is called the **independent variable.** The factor that, according to the experimenter's hypothesis, should be affected is called the **dependent variable,** so named because changes in it are hypothesized to *depend* on changes in the independent variable.

To be certain that changes in the dependent variable are due to changes in the independent variable, and not to other factors, the experimenter must establish a **control condition.** Subjects in the control condition are exposed to the same experimental circumstances as the other subjects (those in the **experimental condition**) and are tested and measured in the same manner—with one crucial exception: They do not undergo the experimental manipulation, the change in the independent variable. Identical results in both conditions would thus rule out the independent variable as the cause of the results. A control condition, then, controls for bias or error arising from irrelevant variables, just as controlled observation controls for sources of observer bias.

An experiment by Yvonne Brackbill (1971) illustrates how the experimental method is used. One hypothesis that she tested was that swaddling—wrapping babies tightly with strips of cloth so that their movement is restricted—would calm 1-month-old infants. Swaddling was therefore the independent variable. Activity level, the dependent variable, was assessed by means of four measurements: the infant's heart rate, respiration, amount of movement (general restlessness, measured by wires in the crib-mattress), and state of arousal (the amount of time spent asleep, awake and quiet, or awake and crying).

Babies in the control condition were treated exactly the same as those in the experimental condition, except that they were not swaddled. Because of this control condition, Brackbill could be certain that any difference in activity level between the experimental and control groups resulted from swaddling and not from another factor. For example, attaching electrodes to the infants to measure heart rate and respiration might affect their activity level. By attaching electrodes to *all* the infants, including those in the control condition, Brackbill equalized the effect of this manipulation in both groups and thus kept it from distorting the experimental results. Also, to avoid results that might have been distorted by individual differences between the babies, each infant served as its own control. That is, each baby spent some time swaddled and some time in the control condition.

Figure 1-13 A swaddled Navaho infant. Parents in many cultures around the world swaddle their babies, but American child-care practice has looked at swaddling with disfavor. Many American parents, if asked, would say that babies should be free to move their limbs about. Brackbill's experimental results prove that swaddling has a calming effect on one-month-old infants.

Brackbill found that the swaddled, experimental group was substantially calmer than the unswaddled, control group. In particular, the swaddled babies cried much less and slept much more than the unswaddled ones. Brackbill therefore concluded that swaddling—an ancient practice that goes back thousands of years in human history—produces a quieting effect in infants.

An experiment can include more than one independent variable. In fact, Brackbill's study included four types of constant stimulation: (1) the sound of a heartbeat, (2) a constant low level of illumination, (3) a constant room temperature (88°F), and (4) swaddling (constant skin pressure). Her full hypothesis was that the effects of more than one kind of constant stimulation would be cumulative. For example, she expected swaddled babies exposed to a constant sound to be quieter than those only swaddled or those only exposed to the sound.

To test this hypothesis, Brackbill observed the reactions of twenty-four 1-month-old babies, each of whom was exposed for 24 hours to one of the five different conditions shown in Figure 1-14A. Her results showed that when the babies were exposed to only one type of continuous stimulation at a time, swaddling was the most effective in reducing crying and promoting sleep. Figure 1-14B shows further that babies exposed to all four types of stimulation slept the most and spent the least time awake and crying.

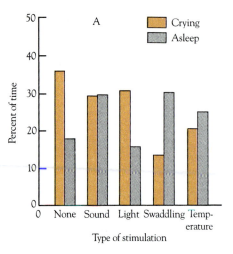

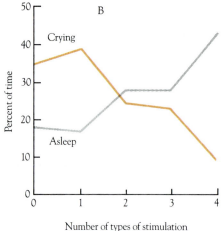

Figure 1-14　In Brackbill's experiment, the subjects were 24 normal 1-month-old infants. Her independent variables—the variables she manipulated—were the four types of stimulation: sound, light, temperature, and swaddling. Her dependent variable—the variable she measured—was activity level, which was assessed in the four ways described in the text. The experiment included a *control condition:* All the babies who were exposed to stimulation also were observed during a period of time during which they received no special stimulation, though in all other ways they were handled just as they were in the experimental condition. (A) This graph shows the effects of each type of stimulation (and of no stimulation) on the amount of time the infants spent crying or asleep. Swaddled babies cried less and slept more than babies receiving the other types of stimulation. (B) This graph shows the cumulative effect of the four types of stimulation on crying and sleeping times. Infants exposed to all four spent more time asleep and less time crying than those exposed to three or less (Brackbill 1971).

From these results, Brackbill drew certain cause-and-effect conclusions. First, under her experimental conditions, several different types of continuous stimulation caused infants to become quieter, especially when two or more types were used in combination. Second, swaddling was the most effective single quieter of babies.

Correlations　　In her experiment, Brackbill could manipulate the independent variables—she could test her hypothesis by swaddling some babies and not swaddling others. In much developmental research, by contrast, direct experimental manipulation either would be ethically undesirable or is simply impossible. For example, an investigator who believes that malnutrition in infancy results in lowered intelligence may not starve children to test that hypothesis. Some research investigates characteristics that cannot be manipulated at all, such as sex, age, or social class.

In much developmental research, changes with age are the point of interest. But researchers cannot magically turn some 2-year-olds into 4-year-olds in order to test directly for the effects of age. Certainly, 2-year-olds and 4-year-olds can be given the same tests or observed under similar circumstances, and their scores can be compared. But there are bound to be many differences between the two groups, besides age, that are not subject to a researcher's control—attention span, for example, or control of body movements. In cases like these,

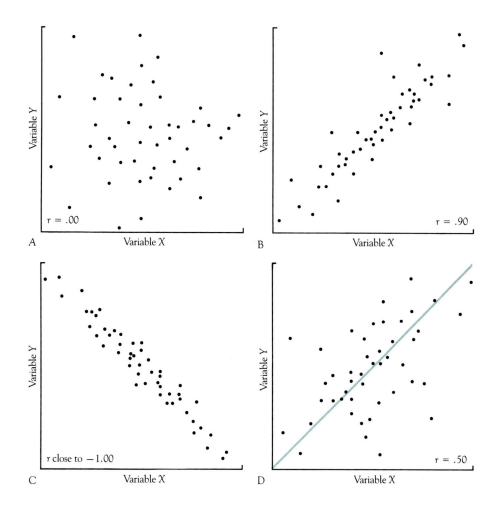

Figure 1-15 Scatterplots representing four correlations. The place of each point on a plot is determined by a pair of measurements, one of variable X and the other of variable Y. X might be a person's IQ at age 5 and Y the same person's IQ at age 30, or X might be the height of a person and Y the weight. In A, there is no relation between X and Y; the correlation coefficient (r) is zero. In B, high scores on X are associated with high scores on Y, and low scores on X are associated with low scores on Y; this pattern indicates a high positive correlation, with r = .90. In C, high scores on X are strongly associated with low scores on Y, and vice versa; this pattern indicates an exremely strong negative correlation, with r very close to − 1.00. D shows a positive correlation of moderate strength; developmental research has identified many correlations of about this strength. The colored line is where all the dots would fall if the correlation were positive and complete, that is, if r were 1.00.

in which experiments are not possible, developmental researchers often do observational studies that yield correlations between age (or sex or social class) and other factors (Wohlwill 1973).

A ***correlation*** is a measure of how well the rankings of individuals on one factor can be used to predict the rankings of the same individuals, or a matched group of individuals, on another factor. For example, students might be ranked according to their grades on a test: Those who get an A are ranked first; B +, second; B, third, and so forth. The same students could be ranked separately according to their IQ scores. These rankings would then be compared, or correlated. Correlations indicate only whether there is a systematic relation between two factors; they do not show whether one factor causes the other.

Correlations may be either positive or negative. In a **positive correlation,** a high rank on one factor predicts a high rank on the other. In fact, IQ scores and school grades show a moderate positive correlation: People who score high on IQ tests tend to achieve high grades in school, and people whose grades are high tend to have high IQ scores. When a low rank on one factor predicts a low rank on the other, and a middle rank on one predicts a middle rank on the other, there is also a positive correlation between the factors.

A negative correlation reflects a regular relationship, just as a positive correlation does. The only difference is the direction of prediction: In a **negative correlation,** a high rank on one factor predicts a *low* rank on the other. High levels of test anxiety, for example, have been shown to predict low scores on achievement tests, whereas low levels of test anxiety may predict higher scores (Culler & Holahan 1980).

The strength of a correlation is measured by a number called a **correlation coefficient.** The strongest positive correlation is assigned a coefficient of +1.00; the strongest negative correlation is assigned a coefficient of −1.00. A correlation coefficient of 0.00 means that there is no relation between the two factors. A positive or negative correlation coefficient of 0.80 or 0.90 indicates a very strong relation between two factors. A correlation coefficient of 0.50 or 0.60, which is common in psychological research, indicates a moderate relation (Figure 1-15).

Although even strong correlations do not allow inferences about what causes what, they do allow prediction. If two factors are well correlated, scholars can use either factor to make predictions about the other. It can be predicted that a person who has a high IQ score will probably do well in school, and vice versa. Because the correlation between IQ scores and school performance is not perfect, these predictions will not always be right, but they will be right more often than wrong.

Techniques for Analyzing Developmental Change

The most common correlations in the study of development are between age and some other variable. During infancy and childhood, for example, there are strong positive correlations between age and size of vocabulary, age and height, age and ability to act independently. But does age itself produce the observed changes in vocabulary size and so on, or are they produced by other factors that happen to be related to age? To determine the meaning of correlations in which age is a variable, developmentalists use two basic designs for their studies—cross-sectional and longitudinal (Achenbach 1978; Wohlwill 1973).

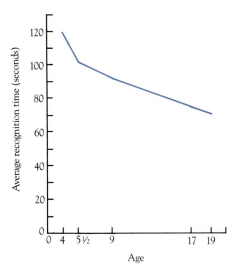

Figure 1-16 Here are some photographs from the sequence that Mary Potter showed to subjects in her cross-sectional study of hypothesis formation. The subjects saw 10 or 12 slides of the same scene, in increasingly better focus, and they were asked at each step to offer a hypothesis about what was pictured. The stages of focus were presented at a fixed rate to all the subjects; as the graph shows, the time that it took to recognize the red-haired woman and the cow declined steadily with age. Listed on the next page are some hypotheses about the sequence of photographs, by a 4-year-old, a 9-year-old, and a 19-year-old (E indicates a statement by the interviewer). The 4-year-old's hypotheses were based more on her own thought chains than on the perceptual evidence, and she had trouble focusing her attention. The 9-year-old had trouble modifying his initial hypothesis, and it tended to shape his perceptions. The college student's hypotheses were elaborated but not rigid. He accounted for the many details he perceived, yet abandoned a hypothesis when it no longer accounted for what he was seeing (Potter 1966).

Cross-sectional Designs In a *cross-sectional design,* groups of people of different ages are studied. All groups are observed at the same time and measured in the same way; if the groups are similar in all important respects but age, behavioral differences between them can be assumed to be due to developmental changes related to aging.

In one cross-sectional study, groups of people of different ages were shown the sequence of photographs reproduced in Figure 1-16. The groups were 4, 5½, 9, 17, and 19 years of age. People in all groups stated what they thought was depicted as the photographs gradually changed from fuzzy to clear. Not surprisingly, the time required to identify the object decreased with age, as the graph shows. More important, there were changes with age in the way people

Figure 1-16 (continued)

A 4-YEAR-OLD GIRL

1. (*E: What do you think it could be?*) All different colors. It's a picture. (*E: It's a picture, yes.*) Maybe it could be a little girl before it has long hair.
2. . . . That picture could be a little, a little, a big round orange ball.
3. (*E: What do you think it could be?*) A bunny rabbop. (*E: Keep watching.*) Oooh, you know my sister calls rocks and a rabbit a bunny rabbop. (*E: Really? Keep watching.*)
4. (*E: What do you see now?*) That has a little eye. I think it's a skunky. (*E: Maybe.*)
5. It could be. . . . That could be a Indian. . . . I know all the animals.
6. That could be Queeny. Do you know what's Queeny? (*E: No.*) That's Molly's horse. See, it's a girl horse and she's, she's pretty tall.
7. (*E: Well, let's see what's in the picture. Keep watching all the time.*) Ooooh, there's a little round nose and mouth. . . . I think it's a face and it's an Indian.
8. Another Indian. . . . Indian. What's in that black books? (*E: We'll look at those later.*)
9. It's, isn't he a cow. . . .
10. Another cow. (*E: And what else?*) I don't know. My sister doesn't know all the animals like I do.

A 9-YEAR-OLD BOY

1. Oh, that looks like the shadow of a person—like in New York . . . the colored lights, not in focus.
2. But that looks like car lights, and the very lighter shadow, the people.
3. That looks like other lights, around here, or a car behind that car, over here with its car lights in different colors.
4. Those look like people, and these look like decorations, and the cars, and the cars in back of them and you can see the . . .
5. I see different colors. . . . in the stream of lights here.
6. I see a diff . . . like a little mouth, and very lightly, very very lightly . . . two eyes.
7. In the what I call a person . . . I see darker colors on decorations over here and darker lighting, like the lights of the car.

A 19-YEAR-OLD MALE COLLEGE STUDENT

1. It's in color too. It looks like two people in fencing outfits, with the white jacket-like things that they wear.
2. And it still looks, er, like that, though the floor has an awful lot on it for two people to be fencing. There's too much going on . . .
3. Ah . . . still don't er . . .
4. Know . . . these, er, look sort of like they might be round chestnuts or something, with these black spherical-looking things.
5. Uh . . . possibly a bowlful of something or other . . .
6. It's starting to look like a dissection in a biology lab.
7. Oh . . . oh . . . here, well this looks kind of ridiculous, but it looks like a fellow in a white shirt, with red hair kissing a cow wearing a white nightcap.
8. And, er, I suppose he's looking at a cow in a stall.
9. I'm pretty sure it's a cow. And I think it's a woman not a man, that's looking this cow in the eye.

expressed their hypotheses about the photographs, as illustrated above. The youngest group, the 4-year-olds, could not even formulate effective hypotheses. The older the group, the more effectively its members formulated and revised hypotheses.

Does the positive correlation implied here between age and the ability to make and revise hypotheses allow the conclusion that this ability improves with age? Strictly speaking, it does not. Often, a correlation of this sort does reflect developmental change with age, but sometimes it reflects the influence of some other factor. The difficulty of ruling out such influences is one drawback of the cross-sectional method.

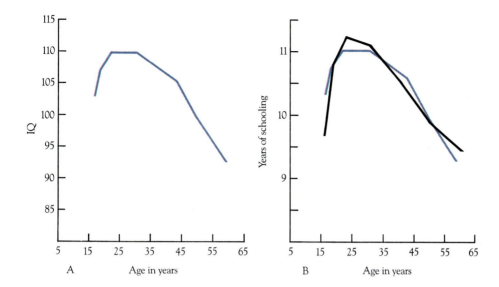

Figure 1-17 (A) Cross-sectional data relating age and IQ. People in different age groups from 15 to 60 years old were given IQ tests at about the same time. (The data were collected by the developers of the widely used Wechsler Adult Intelligence Scale.) The curve connecting the data points seems to show that IQ declines after age 30—that people become less intelligent beginning at about their thirtieth birthday. (B) However, things change when the education level of each of the tested age groups is plotted and the curve in (A) is superimposed on the plot. Now it seems clear that the curve represents not a decline in IQ with age but an increase in amount of education received by different age groups over the years. (Adapted from Kimmel 1974)

For an illustration, look first at the data in Figure 1-17A, which are from a cross-sectional study of the relation between age and intelligence (as measured by an IQ test). The graph seems to show that IQ decreases with age throughout most of adulthood. However, because the study was cross-sectional, the 60-year-olds tested were not the same individuals as the 20-year-olds, and there were many differences between the 20-year-olds and the 60-year-olds besides their age. In fact, the members of each age group, or **cohort,** share experiences and a background that are significantly different from those of the other cohorts. The cohort of 60-year-olds, for example, experienced the Great Depression of the 1930s and were young adults during World War II.

An important difference between these cohorts—the one that probably accounts for the apparent decline in IQ—is shown in Figure 1-17B, where the amount of education is plotted for each cohort. When the IQ-score curve from Figure 1-17A is superimposed on this plot, the cross-sectional results seem to reflect not a decline in IQ with age but rather an increase in the amount of education received by the younger cohorts (Rosow 1978; Schaie 1973). Such differences between cohorts mean that a cross-sectional study alone cannot be used to determine changes in IQ with age.

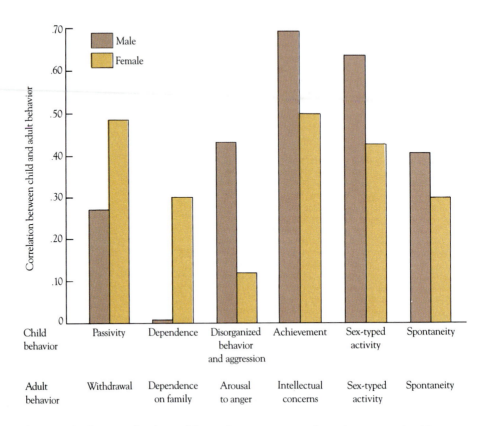

Figure 1-18   Some results obtained during the classic Fels longitudinal study. The study took 30 years to complete. The subjects were observed, tested, and interviewed repeatedly, and earlier measures were compared with later ones to look for continuity in behavior and personality. Measurements of dependence, passivity, and disorganized behavior and aggression when subjects were 6 to 10 years old were compared with measurements of similar behavior when the subjects were adults. Sex-typed activity, spontaneity, and achievement were rated when subjects were 10 to 14 years old and compared with their adult behavior. (Adapted from Kagan and Moss 1962)

Longitudinal Designs   One way of dealing with the cohort problem is to use the ***longitudinal design***, in which the same people are repeatedly tested or studied as they grow older. Some of the most extensive longitudinal studies have followed the same group of people for 30 years or more. In longitudinal studies of intelligence, IQ scores tend to remain steady or increase slightly during adulthood—a very different pattern from the cross-sectional results shown in Figure 1-17A (Botwinick 1977; Horn & Donaldson 1976).

Longitudinal studies also provide valuable kinds of information that cannot be extracted from cross-sectional studies—information about patterns of development in individuals. Figure 1-18 presents such results from a classic longitu-

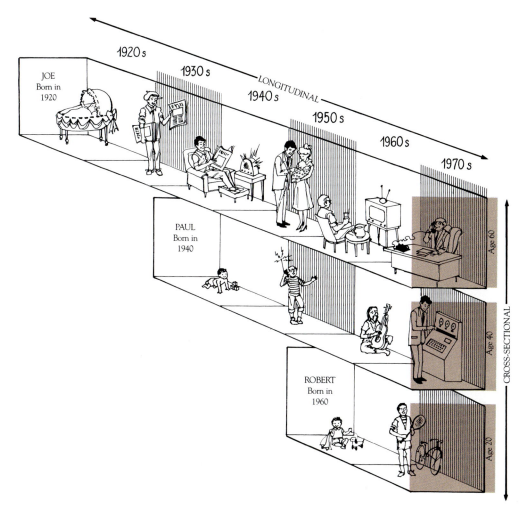

Figure 1-19   The two major types of study design used by developmentalists, the cross-sectional and longitudinal, are illustrated here. In a longitudinal study Joe and other subjects would be observed or tested a number of times over the years. Earlier measurements would be compared with later ones to discover and describe developmental changes. A cross-sectional study might have as subjects Robert at age 20, Paul at age 40, and Joe at age 60. Suppose the study gave the same personality test to these men and others in the same three age groups, and scoring showed that the 60-year-olds were, on the average, more cautious than the 20- and 40-year-olds. The researcher might conclude that males become more cautious as they age. However, a longitudinal study would show that all the individuals born in the 1920s were school-age children during the Great Depression of the 1930s, when joblessness was widespread and many families were concerned about being able to buy enough food: This historical experience, rather than age itself, might account for the greater cautiousness of the 60-year-olds in such a cross-sectional study. A longitudinal study that followed Paul and other 20-year-olds and Robert and other 40-year-olds to age 60 might not find any increase of cautiousness as these cohorts age.

dinal study, carried out at the Fels Research Institute in Ohio. Jerome Kagan and Howard Moss (1962) analyzed the Fels data in an effort to identify consistencies and inconsistencies in personality as children became adolescents and young adults. They calculated the correlations between the behavioral patterns of these individuals when they were children and the same types of patterns after they had become adults.

Although longitudinal studies have some virtues lacking in cross-sectional studies (Figure 1-19), they, too, have their drawbacks (Horn & Donaldson 1976). Longitudinal studies are expensive, time-consuming, and difficult to carry out. Equally important, some subjects eventually drop out of the study, and these people tend to be different from those who stay—they are slightly less intelligent and less healthy, for example—so that the study group gradually changes in ways that are not due to development. Finally, repeated testing often produces *practice effects:* The experience of testing itself affects the results. For example, repeatedly taking intelligence tests tends to lead to higher IQ scores.

Because both cross-sectional and longitudinal studies can produce misleading results, many researchers who take age as one variable have begun to use a combination of cross-sectional and short-term longitudinal designs (Baltes 1979; Schaie 1973). Several different cohorts are studied longitudinally for a few years, while similar groups are tested cross-sectionally. This combination substantially reduces the problems of using either method alone.

The methods used to unravel development include, in brief: (1) careful observation, (2) the use of experiments when possible, (3) the analysis of correlations when experiments are not possible, and (4) the investigation of age-related changes by means of both cross-sectional and longitudinal studies. Often guided by the major theories of human development, scientists use all these methods, singly and in combination, to analyze development—to describe and explain the developmental changes that take place during the human life cycle.

SCIENTIFIC ANALYSIS AND THE WHOLE PERSON

Scientific analysis requires that human behavior be broken down into parts, even though all the parts operate simultaneously. In developmental studies, researchers usually investigate one aspect of human behavior during one phase of the life cycle: say, physical development in infancy, social development in childhood, or cognitive development in adolescence. Similarly, each unit in this book considers one phase of the life cycle, and the chapters in the unit focus on different aspects of development. Unit 3, for example, consists of two chapters about preschool children. One chapter discusses their cognitive, linguistic, perceptual, and physical development. The other describes the development of social interaction and personality during the preschool years. In reading these chapters, and any other, you should keep in mind that the well-defined categories of behavior they describe are not separate in real life. An example may help illustrate this point.

When a child begins to crawl and then walk, she has taken an important step in physical development. Her crawling shows that her bones, muscles, nerves, and brain have matured enough for her to carry her weight and control the movements of her arms and legs; walking shows even greater maturity. But crawling and walking are not isolated physical events. They introduce important new elements into the child's social and thinking life. For one thing, they change the social relationship between the child and her parents. Parents rarely need to say "no" to an infant. If there are objects the parents want to keep away from the baby (or keep the baby away from), they can just deposit her where she cannot reach those precious or dangerous objects. As soon as the child becomes mobile, however, the parents must increase their efforts to teach the child to control her own behavior. They usually begin saying "no" a lot: "No, don't touch the vase." "No, you can't go into the bathroom when Mrs. Gold is in there." "No, you can't play in the street." Crawling and walking are thus important milestones in social development as well as physical development.

This change in social relations also requires a lot of thinking on the child's part. Cognitive development and social development go hand in hand. The baby who suddenly begins to hear "no" a lot has to figure out many new things. It is all right to bang with a spoon on a shiny pot, but not on a shiny vase. It is all right to go into the bathroom when Mother is in there, but not when Mrs. Gold is in there. It is all right to play on the blacktop called the driveway, but not on the one called the street. Practically speaking, every new "no" means something else to learn.

Personality also plays an important part in the social changes that accompany the development of crawling and walking. Some babies are extremely active. When they begin to crawl, it is as if they cannot stay still for a moment. They keep on going until they drop from exhaustion, napping wherever they happen to stop. Others are content with only a little activity and will stay happily playing in one place for an hour or more. Naturally, the amount and intensity of the new social interactions—in particular, the teaching of control—will differ greatly for these two kinds of babies.

Each baby has a mother with *her* own style, too, and compromises are often necessary. Suppose a mother who likes well-structured days—meals and naps on a regular schedule—has a very active baby, who hates being penned up in a crib before he is ready to sleep. The baby can scream and throw himself around in the crib for more than an hour if he is not tired. To avert this, the mother may have to compromise by watching for sure signs of weariness before putting the baby down. If she then consistently waits out the first few minutes of complaint, the baby will probably learn to compromise by complaining less before giving in to his obvious fatigue.

Almost everything a person does has roots in, and repercussions for, every aspect of his or her development, but the field of development cannot be presented that way. Each piece of the puzzle of human behavior must be analyzed before the pieces can be put together. Periodically throughout this book, the authors will point out how several developmental strands intertwine, and you should regularly remind yourself that the person develops as a whole, not as a collection of separate parts.

SUMMARY

1.   The changes that constitute development have three defining characteristics: They must be (a) orderly, occurring in a sequence, (b) directional, or cumulative, and (c) stable.

2.   The basic goals of the study of development are to *describe* systematically the ways in which people develop, to *explain* how and why they develop as they do, and to *predict* the ways in which they will develop.

3.   All human beings share a number of *commonalities* in development.
    a.   We share a biological heritage and therefore share certain *species-specific behaviors*—language, for example.
    b.   We develop at much the same rate through the same *life cycle.*
    c.   We share a *common physical and social environment.* For example, most of us grow up within a *family.*

4.   Besides studying commonalities in human development, researchers try to identify *individual differences* and to explain how they come about.
    a.   Some individual differences—eye color, for example—can be traced mostly to genetic differences.
    b.   Among the environmental determinants of individual differences are the *culture* in which a person grows up, his or her *social class* within that culture, and *interactions* between members of his or her *family.*

5.   To unravel development, scientists have devised two basic categories of research tools—theories and methods. A *theory* is a system of ideas that is used to describe, explain, and predict some aspect of behavior. Four general theoretical approaches currently predominate.
    a.   The *biological approach* focuses on organic bases of behavior, explaining development in terms of genetic inheritance, species-specific characteristics, and other biological influences, such as hormones.
    b.   The *learning* (or behavioral) *approach* focuses on behavior and explains its development in terms of shaping and control by events in the environment.

    c.   The *cognitive-developmental approach* focuses on thinking processes, or cognition, and how they change systematically at different stages of development.

    d.   The *psychodynamic approach* focuses on emotion and how it affects thinking and behavior.

6.   Scientists studying human development use particular *methods*—standard techniques for observing and recording behavior and for making explanatory inferences from the resulting data.

7.   Variations of three *observational techniques* are commonly used in developmental research.

    a.   In *ethological* or *naturalistic observation,* the behavior of animals or people is observed in its own environmental context.

    b.   In the *clinical method,* the observer sensitively interacts with the person being observed in order to assess the individual's behavior more fully and accurately.

    c.   To guard against *observer bias,* researchers may use techniques of *controlled observation.* One example is the "blind" scoring procedure, in which observers who record the behavior are not aware of certain features of the study, such as the hypothesis being tested.

Observation permits precise description of behavior, but it can seldom explain what factors produce the behavior. Experiments and correlations are the most important techniques for making inferences about the causes of behavior.

8.   *Experiments* allow researchers to test causal hypotheses—explanations of how one factor affects another.

    a.   In an experiment, researchers manipulate one factor, the *independent variable,* to see how the manipulations affect a second factor, the *dependent variable.*

    b.   To ensure that observed changes in the dependent variable are due to changes in the independent variable and not to other factors, experimenters must include a control condition. Subjects in the *control condition* are treated and tested exactly like the experimental subjects (those in the *experimental condition*) except that they do not undergo the experimental manipulations.

9.   Because most developmental changes cannot be experimentally manipulated, much developmental research produces results in the form of correlations. A *correlation* is a measure of how well the rankings of individuals on one factor predict the rankings of the same individuals, or a matched group of individuals, on a second factor. Correlations indicate whether there is a systematic relationship between two factors, but they do not allow researchers to make causal inferences. The strength of a correlation is measured by a *correlation coefficient,* which is a number between -1.00 and $+1.00$.

10. To describe and explain how behavior changes with development, researchers use cross-sectional and longitudinal designs in their studies.

    a. In a **cross-sectional design,** groups of people of different ages are observed at the same time and measured in the same way. If the groups are similar in all respects except age, behavioral differences between the groups are assumed to be due to developmental change.

    b. In a **longitudinal design,** the same group of people is repeatedly studied as they grow older. Behavioral changes with age are assumed to result from development, but the group may change in other, uncontrolled ways that can make interpretation difficult.

    c. To overcome the respective weaknesses of the longitudinal and cross-sectional designs, researchers frequently need to design studies that combine the two methods.

SUGGESTED READINGS

ACHENBACH, THOMAS M. *Research in Developmental Psychology: Concepts, Strategies, and Methods.* New York: Free Press, 1978.

Although written for advanced undergraduates, this well-organized book might be of particular interest to students thinking of majoring in developmental psychology or human development.

ARIES, PHILIPPE. *Centuries of Childhood: A Social History of Family Life.* New York: Random House, 1965.

A historian looks at how people in the past felt about and dealt with the young.

BOSTON WOMEN'S HEALTH BOOK COLLECTIVE. *Ourselves and Our Children: A Book by and for Parents.* New York: Random House, 1978.

Real parents talking about real children. This is a collection of vivid, heartfelt essays about what it is like to raise children—the joys and triumphs, the pains and troubles of being a parent.

KESSEN, WILLIAM. *The Child.* New York: Wiley, 1965.

This short book about the history of child study presents and comments on excerpts from the writings of child experts, beginning with the reformers of the eighteenth century and ending with Sigmund Freud and Jean Piaget, two giants of the twentieth century.

KESSEN, WILLIAM, ed. *History, Theory, and Methods,* Vol. I of P.H. Mussen, ed., *Handbook of Child Psychology.* New York: Wiley, 1983.

In this definitive, up-to-date sourcebook, well-known researchers present scholarly analyses of the major theories and methods in child development. A history of the study of child development is also included.

MILGRAM, JOEL I., and DOROTHY J. SCIARRA, eds. *Childhood Revisited.* New York: Macmillan, 1974.

Excerpts from the autobiographies of well-known men and women recounting their childhood experiences. The editors comment on the relation of these experiences to concepts in the study of development.

All human beings are born with a long history, which lies partly encoded in their genes. For a short period at the beginning of prenatal development, the human embryo has a tail. It disappears before birth, but its brief appearance reminds us that we are a species of animal, that—in the course of millions of years—we have descended from other species, and that all members of our species share the same biological history and therefore the same basic behaviors. At the same time, the mechanisms of inheritance—and, of course, the extraordinary range of human environments—ensure that each member of the species is unique. Chapter 2 discusses human behavior in terms of our species membership and presents the basic mechanisms of genetic inheritance. Chapter 3 describes prenatal development and birth.

UNIT

1

BEGINNINGS

2

THE
HUMAN
SPECIES:
EVOLUTION,
HEREDITY,
AND
ENVIRONMENT

CHAPTER OUTLINE

2

THE HUMAN SPECIES

In 1859, Charles Darwin published *The Origin of Species*, persuasively setting forth his theory of evolution and thus radically altering mankind's view of itself. Darwin proposed that all living things have evolved by the process of natural selection—all living things, including people. In fact, all species of animals, including the human species, seem to have evolved from a common ancestor and so are related to each other. Darwin thus firmly placed human beings within the animal world and helped lay the foundation for the scientific study of the human animal. What kind of an animal are we, then? How did we evolve? In what ways are we like other animals, and in what ways are we different? How does our behavior reflect the type of animal we are? And how does this behavior develop as we grow from infants to adults?

All human beings belong to the species *Homo sapiens*. As members of this species, we have a common biological heritage; we share a number of physical and psychological characteristics that have evolved through time and that provide a basis for our behavior. The first part of this chapter examines some of the behavioral and physical characteristics that we share as a species and how they may have evolved. The second part of the chapter explains the genetic process by which inherited characteristics are transmitted from generation to generation. The final section discusses how genetic inheritance and environmental factors interact to produce differences and similarities between human beings.

SPECIES AND EVOLUTION

A *species* is a group of organisms—animals or plants—that are capable of interbreeding. The members of a species are alike in many ways, and a similar appearance is often a clue that two living things belong to the same species. But in many species, individuals show extreme variations. Dachshunds, great Danes, and chihuahuas, for example, look strikingly different from each other, yet they are all dogs—members of the species *Canis familiaris*.

The key defining characteristic of a species is that it is a **breeding population.** Chihuahuas can mate with dachshunds, and poodles with great Danes, and such matings can produce healthy offspring, which will in turn grow up to have offspring of their own. Dogs cannot successfully interbreed with cats, monkeys, or ponies, because these animals belong to different species. Because all types of human beings, no matter what their size or shape or color, can mate and produce offspring, we constitute a species—*Homo sapiens*.

Adaptation by Natural Selection

The concept of evolution existed before Darwin put forth his theory. For a long time, scientists had known that fossils, the remains of ancient animals and plants embedded in rocks or soil, included many species different from those currently alive. From time to time, someone would point out that these fossils suggested that species had changed with time, or evolved, but none of these proposals gained wide acceptance. Darwin established evolution as a scientific concept both by gathering an overwhelming array of evidence and by putting together a framework for explaining how evolutionary changes could take place (Gruber 1981).

The theory of evolution rests on three key ideas: ***variation, heredity,*** and ***adaptation by natural selection.*** Within a species, individuals typically vary in many characteristics, such as size, coloring, and keenness of vision. In competing with other creatures for food and the necessities of life, organisms with characteristics favorable to success in their environment are more likely than others are to reach maturity and bear offspring. If these characteristics can be inherited, then the successful organisms will pass them on to their offspring, who in turn will also have a competitive advantage. In this way, from generation to generation, favorable characteristics are naturally selected.

As a result of this process of natural selection, a species becomes ***adapted*** to the special features of its environment (Lewontin 1978). That is, each species tends to evolve a special "fit" between its physical and behavioral characteristics and the environment in which it lives. One of the famous examples Darwin used to illustrate this adaptation was the beaks of the various species of finches in the Galapagos Islands. Although he found that the species of finches were similar in many ways, the shapes of their beaks differed widely, as shown in Figure 2-1. The various shapes of their beaks matched perfectly the types of food that they ate. Similarly, species of fish have types of fins adapted to the type of swimming they must do to survive in their habitats.

When environmental conditions change, natural selection can lead to major evolutionary changes in a species (Stanley 1981). About 375 million years ago, for example, repeated droughts apparently led certain species of freshwater fish, by natural selection, to develop primitive lungs and fins strong enough for them to waddle, dragging their bellies, along the muddy bottom of a drying stream bed to seek deeper water (Curtis 1983). As generations passed, some of these fish came to spend more of their lives on land, where they could take advantage of their unusual abilities to breathe air and "walk." Eventually, the process of natural selection improved both of these abilities, adapting them better to life on land: The lungs became more effective and the fins changed into legs. The new species of land animals moved into many different environments, where the legs were adapted to diverse uses—the legs of antelopes for running fast, the wings of birds for flying, the hands of human beings for manipulating tools. This diversity of adaptations is one of the most remarkable results of evolution.

Because the human species originated so long ago, we can describe its evolution only by re-creation from the evidence of fossils. Although there are still many gaps in the fossil record of human evolution, it is currently estimated that the first creatures in the hominid, or humanlike, line of descent lived about

Figure 2-1   Some of the types of finches that Darwin saw in the Galapagos Islands. From top left to top right: warbler finch, small insect-eating tree finch, large ground finch, cactus ground finch, woodpecker tool-using finch, vegetarian tree finch. It was postulated that the finches all descended from a common ancestor and that each became adapted, by natural selection, to its particular environment.

Figure 2-2 (at right)   The evolution of *Homo sapiens*.

4 million years ago (Stanley 1981; Washburn 1978). Before that, the creatures ancestral to us were not recognizably human.

Figure 2-2 outlines the path by which we probably evolved. We are members of the class of mammals, warm-blooded animals with hair who suckle their young. Among the many types of mammals, we belong to the order of primates, which includes our cousins the apes, as well as monkeys, lemurs, and tree shrews. Among primates, we belong to the family of hominid species. After hominid creatures first appeared, about 4 million years ago, several different species seem to have evolved, including *Australopithecus africanus* and our ancestor, *Homo habilis*. Somehow all of them became extinct except *Homo sapiens*, the earliest fossils of whom are about 250,000 years old.

MODERN MAN. People physically indistinguishable from us appeared about 40,000 years ago, just as the Neanderthal people disappeared. The Neanderthals, a large-brained but anatomically distinct form of *Homo sapiens,* had first appeared about 250,000 years ago.

TRUE MAN. Creatures whose brains were close to modern human size and whom we would recognize as human in form and behavior appeared about 1.5 million years ago.

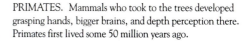

APE-MAN. The early hominid *Australopithecus,* who walked erect on two legs and made primitive tools, appeared some 4 million years ago.

APES. Some primates returned to the ground and competed with other ground-dwelling foragers and predators. Apes appeared about 25 million years ago.

PRIMATES. Mammals who took to the trees developed grasping hands, bigger brains, and depth perception there. Primates first lived some 50 million years ago.

MAMMALS. These animals have internal control over their body temperature and they suckle their young, which are born live rather than from an egg. Like the dinosaurs, mammals evolved from reptile stock about 200 million years ago, but they were versatile and agile enough to outlast the dinosaurs.

REPTILES. These creatures could live and reproduce wholly out of the water, unlike their predecessors, amphibians and fish. Reptiles first appeared about 300 million years ago.

Figure 2-3 One characteristic we don't usually think of ourselves as sharing with other primates is the ability to make and use tools. For a long time, the use of any kind of tool was thought to be a uniquely human ability. Yet here is a chimpanzee using a long blade of grass to scoop delicious ants out of an anthill. Although it is unsophisticated, the piece of grass is definitely a tool.

Homo sapiens

Homo sapiens is a successful species. We have spread throughout most of the land masses of the world and have dominated most other forms of life. By most criteria, we have been more successful than any of our primate relatives, yet many of the characteristics that we consider distinctly human are also typical of other primates. We have excellent color vision, but our sense of smell is not as good as that of some other mammals. We stand and walk on our hind limbs, and we use our forelimbs for skilled manipulation of objects (Figure 2-3). We have flat faces that we use to communicate emotions and other social cues. We live in social groups, which are organized by status. We have a relatively long childhood, during which we are dependent on our parents and learn how to get along in our social group. We have a large brain. We are intelligent and use our resulting behavioral flexibility to adapt quickly to changes in our environment. All these characteristics, and many more, would describe chimpanzees, gorillas, rhesus monkeys, or baboons as well as people (Napier 1970).

In the human species, some of the traits of primates have been carried to an extreme. For example, primate adults generally retain many of the physical characteristics of infants, such as flattened faces and large heads. This tendency has been carried much farther in *Homo sapiens* than in other primates (Gould 1977b). Similarly, the prolonged childhood typical of all primates, during which they are dependent on parental care, is longest of all in our species. We do not reach sexual maturity for 12 or more years, and we usually remain somewhat dependent on parental care even after that age, although cultural norms affect the total length of the period of dependency.

Human childhood seems to be longer at both ends. At the start, we are carried in the womb for a shorter proportion of our total lifespan than other

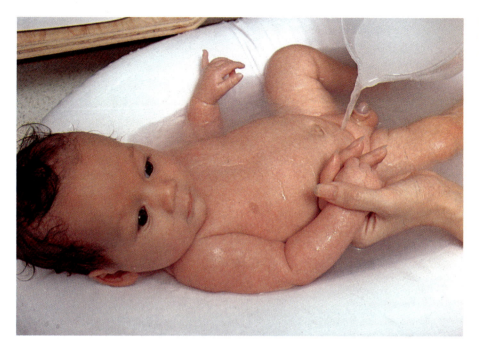

Figure 2-4 Species: *Homo sapiens.* Life stage: infancy.

primates are (see Table 3-1). That is, we are born "early" and, perhaps for this reason, have an unusually long infancy. If we followed the pattern of other primates, we would be born from 3 to 9 months later than we are (Montagu 1961; Passingham 1975): Our mothers would carry us for as long as 18 months instead of merely 9. The fact that human babies are born in a somewhat underdeveloped state is probably due to the large size of the human brain. At birth the human brain is only one-fourth its final size, but it is growing fast. If it were to develop much further before birth the infant's head would not be able to pass through the birth canal.

Human beings also live much longer than they "should." In most of the animal kingdom there is a systematic relation between body size and life expectancy: The larger the normal size of the species, the longer the life expectancy (Gould 1977b). According to this relation, an animal our size should survive only about 25 to 35 years, but we live into our 70s and beyond.

THE HUMAN BRAIN

As a rule, larger animals have larger brains. Apparently, more neural tissue is required to operate a large body than a small one. But some animals seem to have more brain than their bodies "require." Chimpanzees, for example, are notably smaller than gorillas, but their brains are nearly the same size. Human beings are larger than 99 percent of all animals on earth; among primates, only

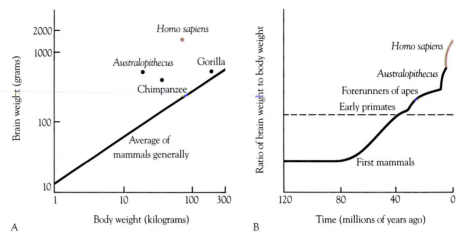

Figure 2-5   (A) The human brain is much larger than it "should" be according to our body size. A sheep, for example, is about as large as an adult human being, but its brain is only one-sixth the size of ours. The diagonal line on this graph indicates the usual relation between brain weight and body weight in modern mammals. Primates lie above this line because their brains are larger than those of typical mammals of the same size. (B) The large brain of *Homo sapiens* is the result of an evolutionary spurt that began about 4 million years ago. Notice the almost vertical curve that traces the growth of the brain from *Australopithecus* to modern human beings. (The broken horizontal line represents the average ratio of brain weight to body weight in modern mammals.)

gorillas are larger (Gould 1977a). Given our body size, our brains should indeed be heavy—at least 200 grams and as high as 400 to 550 grams (Lewontin 1978; Pilbeam & Gould 1974), or roughly 100 grams less than the gorilla's (Figure 2-5). Instead, they weigh about 1300 grams, three times what they "should." This seems to be the most important unique physical characteristic of the human species: The brain is much larger than it should be.

The significance of this large brain can hardly be overemphasized, for the brain gives us the great intelligence that is the basis for our success as a species. It has enabled us to invent tools, such as the hammer, the wheel, the internal combustion engine, and the computer, and to use them to modify and manipulate our environment. It enables us to communicate by means of a complex language, which not only binds together our social groups but allows us to give detailed information to our companions and descendants—from where to find food and how to build fires to philosophical treatises on moral action and poetry about heroism and love. With language, we can build sciences and cultures and pass them on to future generations.

Because the brain seems to be our most important evolutionary specialization and clearly plays a central role in the development of our behavior, scientists have given much effort to investigating the biology of the brain and relating that biology to human behavior. In recent years, our understanding of the brain and the nervous system has advanced enormously.

S. Harris

"Although humans make sounds with their mouths and occasionally
look at each other, there is no solid evidence that they
actually communicate among themselves."

The Evolution of the Brain

In the evolution of our species, brain size has increased exceptionally fast
compared with similar changes in other species (see Figure 2-5B). Bottle-nosed
dolphins, for example, which may be the most intelligent nonhuman animals
on earth, have approximately the same brain–body ratio as human beings, but
the increase in brain size that took 15 to 20 million years in the dolphin took
only 3 to 4 million years in hominids (Jerison 1976).

The structure of the human brain reflects the evolutionary history of the
animal kingdom (Rose 1975). Reptiles, fish, and amphibians have fairly simple
brains, which control most of their basic bodily processes, such as heart rate
and breathing, and allow simple behaviors and simple learning. Remnants of
this simple brain are retained in all mammalian species. The central core of the
human brain, including the brain stem, is our inheritance from classes of
animals more ancient than our own (Figure 2-6).

Mammals also evolved several brain structures that are not found (except in
very rudimentary form) in older classes. One is the limbic system, a group of
structures that regulate body temperature and also have other important functions. The limbic system is the chief basis of the emotional reactions of
mammals, which are extreme and complex relative to the emotions displayed
by insects or lizards or birds. Another structure that is much larger and more
complex in mammals is the cerebellum. It provides for very fine control of
movements: the quiet grace of cats, the tree-climbing abilities of monkeys, and
the manual dexterity of human beings.

Perhaps the most distinguishing feature of the mammalian brain is its large
cerebrum—the structure at the top of the brain that enables flexible, intelligent
behavior. The cerebrum has become especially large, and its surface has become
intricately folded in primates, whales, and dolphins. Its most extreme development is in human beings and bottle-nosed dolphins.

Figure 2-6 (A) This extremely simplified diagram shows the evolutionary age of various parts of the brain. The "oldest" part of the brain, which corresponds in some ways to the brains of more primitive creatures, seems to regulate stereotyped patterns of behavior. A "newer" set of structures, present in primitive mammals, encircles the inner core and seems to regulate emotional experience. The "newest" part, which is highly developed in our species, is the large cerebrum, which seems to be responsible for rational thought. (B) The brains of four different animals (not drawn to scale). The human brain is shown in front-to-back cross section, so that parts normally covered by the cerebrum can be seen.

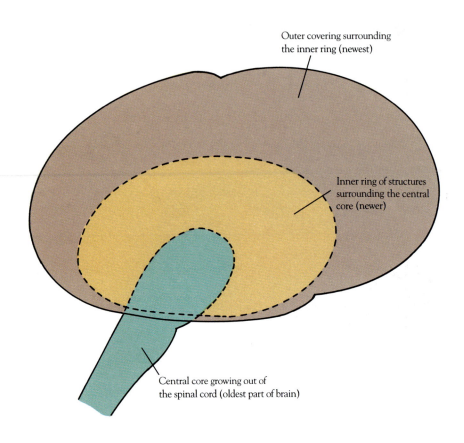

Outer covering surrounding the inner ring (newest)

Inner ring of structures surrounding the central core (newer)

Central core growing out of the spinal cord (oldest part of brain)

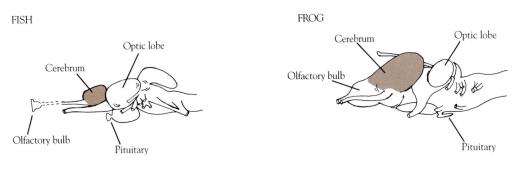

FISH

Cerebrum

Optic lobe

Olfactory bulb

Pituitary

FROG

Cerebrum

Optic lobe

Olfactory bulb

Pituitary

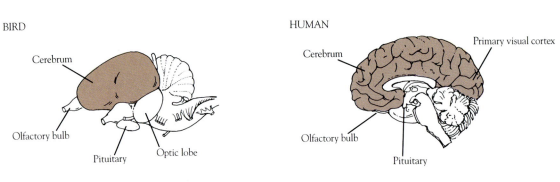

BIRD

Cerebrum

Olfactory bulb

Pituitary

Optic lobe

HUMAN

Cerebrum

Primary visual cortex

Olfactory bulb

Pituitary

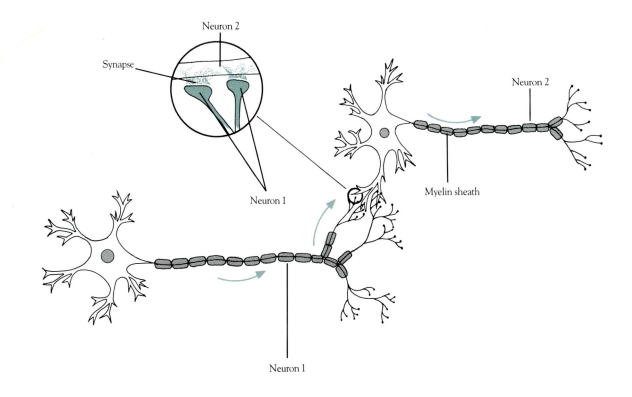

Figure 2-7 A simplified drawing of two neurons. Neurons differ considerably in size and shape and may have many more branchings than are shown here. One neuron may have thousands of contact points with surrounding ones. Impulses always travel in the same direction (arrows) down the long extension of a neuron. When an impulse reaches the knobs at the end of the extension, small amounts of certain chemicals are released from inside the knob (magnified inset). The chemicals cross the short space between the neurons—the synapse—and cause the receiving neuron to fire. This is the basic process by which information is transmitted through the nervous system; it is the basis of all psychological processes.

An electrically insulating sheath of myelin (shown surrounding the long thin part of each neuron) forms on many neurons as the nervous system develops after birth.

The Nervous System

The human brain is the command center of a vast communications network, the **nervous system,** which in large part controls the action of every bone, muscle, organ, gland, and blood vessel in the body (Kimble 1978). Messages between the brain and the various parts of the body are carried by nerves, which are composed of bundles of long, thin cells called **neurons.** Much of the brain itself consists of neurons, at least 10 billion of them. Messages within the brain and in the rest of the nervous system are electro-chemical impulses that move along a neuron much as a flame travels along a fuse, but faster.

As Figure 2-7 shows, adjacent neurons are not directly connected to each other. There is a tiny gap between them, called a **synapse.** One neuron

Figure 2-8   A network of nerve cells in a human brain.

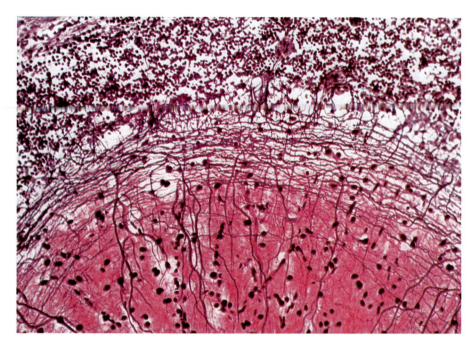

transmits a message to the next by releasing certain chemicals into the gap. These chemicals act like a spark, "igniting" an impulse in the second neuron and sending the impulse rushing along to the next synapse. A single neuron may have synapses with many other neurons, so that it can receive and combine messages from all of them. One message between brain and body can involve large numbers of neurons and synapses.

Even for seemingly simple actions, the brain coordinates many messages. Consider all that is involved just in eating an apple. Messages travel from your eyes to your brain about the shape, color, and condition of the object, allowing you to retrieve from memory such things as the word "apple" and the fact that it appears to be ripe and edible. Messages travel to and from your hand and arm about bringing the apple to your mouth; to and from your jaw about coordinating its movements with those of your hand and arm; to and from your nose, tongue, and throat telling you what is happening in your mouth—the smell of the apple, its taste, and the actions of chewing and swallowing. And the taste and smell messages may evoke a certain memory about the last time you ate this kind of apple. All these messages involving your first bite of apple normally occur in a fraction of a second, so they seem instantaneous.

The **central nervous system** (the brain and spinal cord) contains not only neurons but also other types of cells, called **glial cells.** There are actually more glial cells than neurons in the brain, but less is known about their function. They provide the neurons with nourishment and help remove waste products. Some scientists have proposed that they also play a more direct role in transmitting impulses or in storing memories.

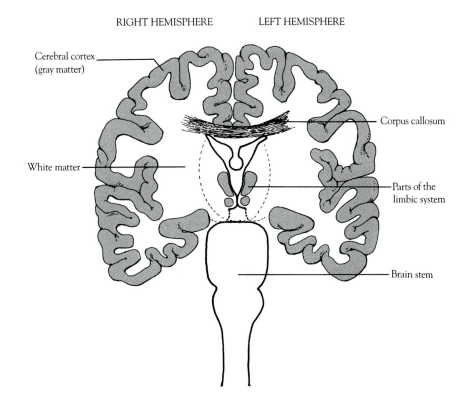

RIGHT HEMISPHERE   LEFT HEMISPHERE

Cerebral cortex
(gray matter)

Corpus callosum

White matter

Parts of the
limbic system

Brain stem

Figure 2-9 The human brain in cross section (from side to side). You can see the two hemispheres connected by the corpus callosum. The many-folded cerebral cortex, or "gray matter," is the information-processing part of the brain. It enables higher intellectual functioning in human beings. The two hemispheres tend to specialize in somewhat different mental functions. The inner area, or "white matter," carries information between the surface and the "older" structures, such as the brain stem and the limbic system.

Throughout the nervous system, neurons, synapses, and glial cells are linked into miniature systems with specific functions. For one example, the reticular activating system monitors sensory messages from the whole body; with this information, it controls the body's general level of arousal and helps determine whether one is in a state of wakefulness or asleep. For another, a small system of structures most commonly found on the left side of the cerebrum controls the production of sentences in normal speech (Geschwind 1972).

The Cerebral Cortex

Because it is responsible for much of our learning ability, the brain structure of greatest interest to developmental scientists is the *cerebral cortex,* the surface layer of the cerebrum, which has become so large and complicated in human beings. Some parts of the cortex perform well-defined functions in the use of a particular sense, such as vision, or a particular motor activity, such as movement of an arm or a hand. Other areas, called association cortex, are thought to play a role in higher mental processes, such as solving problems, imagining, and planning for the future.

Two Brains in One   The many different parts of the cortex are organized into two separate hemispheres, roughly mirror images of each other, which are connected by a thick band of nerve fibers called the *corpus callosum* (Figure 2-9). The differences between the two hemispheres have been the subject of much research in recent years. In 1981, Roger Sperry was awarded the Nobel Prize for his contributions to this research.

For the most part, the two hemispheres control different sides of the body. The *left hemisphere* controls the movements and sensations of the right side, and the *right hemisphere* controls those of the left side. When you move your right hand, the movement is controlled by the left hemisphere; when you move your left hand, it is controlled by the right hemisphere. This right-left connection does not apply to all parts of the body, and it is not evident in all people, but it is the general rule, applying to approximately 90 percent of all human beings. In addition, the left hemisphere seems to be specialized to work in a logical, sequential way, so it tends to control more of our speech and language. The right hemisphere seems to be specialized for the integration or synthesis of information into a whole or a unit, so it tends to deal more with spatial information (Kinsbourne 1978).

When the corpus callosum has been cut, the two hemispheres lose most of their ability to communicate with each other, and their separate roles are clearly revealed (Gazzaniga 1967; Sperry 1964). This separation was first observed in human beings when certain medical problems were treated surgically by cutting through the corpus callosum. One patient, W. J., had suffered from severe epilepsy resulting from a wartime injury to one side of his brain. Surgeons cut his corpus callosum, hoping to prevent the epileptic seizures from spreading from the injured hemisphere to the other. After the operation, W. J. displayed a number of odd behaviors. For example, when given a verbal command such as "bend your knees," he would bend only his right knee. This happened because the left hemisphere, which controlled most language and movement in the right side of his body, responded to the verbal command, but it could no longer pass on this information to the right hemisphere, which controlled movement in the left side of his body.

At first, it seemed that the right hemisphere was useless, or at best unintelligent. But when the researchers asked W. J. to draw a copy of a figure such as a cross with his left hand, he proceeded to make a perfect drawing, using one continuous line. When he tried to draw the same figure with his right hand, he could not make a decent copy, even though he was right-handed. This experiment and many subsequent ones like it have shown the superiority of the right hemisphere in dealing with spatial concepts.

Further research has shown that although hemispheric specialization is common in human beings, it applies much more strongly to right-handed people than to left-handed ones. Whereas 99 percent of right-handers show a specialization of the left hemisphere for language, for example, only about 60 percent of left-handers show it (Hecaen & Albert 1978). But left-handers constitute no more than 10 percent of the population, so about 95 percent of the general population demonstrates this specialization. Why the brains of left-handers are different from those of right-handers is not well understood.

For some time after the initial discovery of hemispheric specialization, scientists tended to focus exclusively on the differences between the hemispheres. Recent research, however, has demonstrated that both sides of the brain take part in most behavior (Corballis 1980). For example, although language tasks tend to depend more on the left hemisphere and spatial tasks more on the right, both sides take part in both types of tasks. When the flow of blood to various parts of the brain was measured, spatial tasks, such as determining the size of an angle in a drawing, increased the flow of blood to both hemispheres, although more flowed to the right. Language tasks, such as vocabulary tests, also increased the flow to both hemispheres, although more flowed to the left (Lassen et al. 1978; D. Weinberger 1983).

Cortical Development   During the prenatal period, the "old" parts of the brain, the parts that we share with reptiles and other mammals, begin to develop first. The cerebral cortex develops last, and at birth it is still very immature. It continues its development not only throughout childhood but into adolescence and adulthood (Tanner 1978).

After birth, the neurons in the cortex increase in size and complexity rather than in number, adding more and more connections with other neurons (Goldman-Rakic et al. 1983). Many neurons both in the brain and in the nerves develop a sheathlike coating, called *myelin,* around their longer fibers (see Figure 2-7). The myelin coating acts much like insulation on an electric wire, reducing interference and speeding up the transmission of impulses along the neuron (Morell & Norton 1980).

Recent research suggests that the general growth of the brain, and especially the cortex, may alternate between periods of rapid and slow increase (Lampl & Emde 1983). The times of fast growth, called spurts, seem to coincide with major cognitive-developmental changes (Epstein 1979; Kagan 1982). The ages at which these spurts occur and the corresponding cognitive developments will be described in more detail in later chapters.

The timetable of development for the specialized functions of the two hemispheres is not yet clear. Studies of electrical patterns in the brain indicate that the hemispheres are already somewhat specialized within a few months after birth (Molfese et al. 1975; Shucard et al. 1979). The effects of brain damage on children, however, show that this specialization is not complete for at least 12 to 15 years. Many children less than 2 years old who have suffered damage to the language areas of the left hemisphere nevertheless develop language ability without difficulty. Apparently, the right hemisphere of these children was still unspecialized enough to take over major language functions quickly. In some children from 4 to about 11 years of age, damage to the left hemisphere produces only a temporary loss of language. Within months, these children recover normal language use, apparently developing the necessary language skills in the right hemisphere. By the midteens, however, the pattern is exactly like that of adults. After major damage to the left hemisphere, most people never recover full use of language. Presumably, the right hemisphere has become too specialized to change its course and take over language functions. Many of those adult patients who do recover are found to have been left-handed or ambidextrous (Kinsbourne & Hiscock 1983; Lenneberg 1967).

The brain shows a similar flexibility in recovering from many kinds of major trauma during childhood, although recovery is by no means guaranteed. Apparently, a variety of brain functions, especially those found in the cerebral cortex, can be assumed by other parts of a child's brain (Hecaen & Albert 1978). The extraordinary flexibility of function shown by the developing brain seems to reflect the adaptability that children generally show in their learning and behavior. Recent research with monkeys shows specifically how one part of the cortex can take over functions normally reserved for other parts (Goldman-Rakic et al. 1983). It also shows that some types of early damage cannot be compensated and have devastating long-term consequences for behavioral development.

ETHOLOGY AND HUMAN DEVELOPMENT

Every species has not only its own physical characteristics (most notably, in our case, the large human brain) but also its typical psychological characteristics. With regard to the human species, scientists commonly cite three such psychological characteristics as most important (Pilbeam 1979):

> *People are intelligent.* We can adapt our behaviors to many environments and solve a wide range of problems.
>
> *People use language.* We communicate large amounts of information to our fellow human beings, by both speech and writing.
>
> *People have cultures.* Each human society has a set of traditions, customs, and values for dealing with such matters as how to obtain food, how to build dwellings, how to select a mate, how to raise children, how to be a productive adult.

Understanding these shared characteristics and their development, like understanding the behaviors that typify any species, requires the viewpoint of ethological theory.

THEORY: ETHOLOGY

One of the remarkable facts of evolution is that each species is anatomically well adapted to its own particular environment. Among other things, its mouth and digestive system are appropriate for what it eats; its limbs provide the kind of locomotion it needs; its eyes are suited for the type of light stimulation it must process in its environment. But when Darwin set forth his theory of evolution, he recognized that a species is characterized by distinctive behaviors as well as by a distinctive anatomy. The courtship rituals of pigeons, the hibernation patterns of bears and woodchucks, the hunting strategies of hyenas, the communication techniques of honey bees, and the emotional expressiveness of human beings—such behaviors are characteristic of each species. Indeed, these behavioral characteristics are just as well adapted to the environment and just as important to survival as the body structure of each species is.

Following Darwin's lead, other biologists set out to study the behaviors that characterize a species—that is, its species-specific behaviors—thus founding the science of ethology. The most important figures in ethology include Konrad Lorenz, Niko Tinbergen, and Karl von Frisch, who in 1973 shared a Nobel prize for their work on the behavior of birds, fish, and honeybees. Most ethological research is done by biologists who study variations in the natural behavior of animals. In the past two decades, however, many psychologists and other behavioral scientists have also taken an ethological approach to the study of human development.

OBSERVATION

According to ethologists, the close fit between the behavior of a species and its environment dictates that the study of a species must begin with careful observation of the organism in its natural surroundings and with a thorough description of its behavior there (Eibl-Eibesfeldt 1970). What are the species' feeding behaviors? What are its mating behaviors? What are all the common behaviors that the species shows, and when and how does each of them occur?

The goal of such a description, called an ethogram, is to identify the meaning of the behaviors for the species—in other words, to understand the behaviors from the viewpoint of the species. Only after this careful observation and description do ethologists attempt to explain the species' behaviors in a systematic way, sometimes by conducting experiments in the somewhat unnatural but controlled environment of the laboratory. Without an extensive description of the natural behaviors of a species and their contexts, a scientist may fail to get beyond his own viewpoint and thus may misunderstand the behaviors.

This effort to observe behavior objectively can also be useful with members of our own species who are very different from ourselves, such as infants. Newborn babies show many reactions that are superficially similar to the behaviors of adults, but they do not have the same meaning. For example, in the first few days of life, an infant's smile seems to have nothing to do with pleasure or social interaction but is merely a reflex of the facial muscles. Likewise, newborn boys have frequent erections that have nothing to do with sexuality but simply reflect the child's state of wakefulness; most occur when the babies are in one particular state of sleep (Emde et al. 1976). (Adult males in a similar state of sleep also experience erections that are unrelated to sexuality.)

Figure 2-10 Some emotional expressions in human beings are species-specific behaviors. Laughter from delight is one such expression. Crying in distress is another. Ethologists have systematically described such expressions in terms of their components, such as mouth shape and eyebrow shape (Ekman & Friesen 1975; Izard 1977).

SPECIES-SPECIFIC BEHAVIORS

The central focus of ethologists is *species-specific behaviors*—the behaviors that characterize a species. In some cases, these behaviors are unique to a species. Human beings, for example, have a mode of locomotion that no other living species has. In other cases, a species-specific behavior may be exhibited by a number of species; it is nonetheless species-specific for all the species that show the behavior. Both chimpanzees and people laugh, for example, and many primate species let out a scream when they are injured. The laugh and the scream are species-specific behaviors of both human beings and these other primate species (Figure 2-10).

Fixed Action Patterns and Sign Stimuli

When analyzing species-specific behaviors, ethologists often focus on two phenomena—fixed action patterns and sign stimuli (Hinde 1983; Lorenz 1971). A *fixed action pattern* is a frequently repeated pattern of movements that varies little from animal to animal within a species. All pelicans dive for fish in the same way. All horses use the same pattern of movements in galloping.

Sign stimuli are patterns of sensory stimulation—colors, shapes, sounds, touches, facial expressions—that reliably elicit fixed action patterns. The bellies of male stickleback fish turn red during mating season, and the red color serves as a sign stimulus for attack by other males (Tinbergen 1951). Many of the young human baby's responses are elicited by sign stimuli, according to classic ethological analyses (Eibl-Eibesfeldt 1970). A light touch on a baby's lips elicits sucking; a similar touch on the palm elicits grasping. When a baby is a few months old, a human face (real or drawn) that is moved up and down in a nodding motion elicits smiling (Spitz & Wolf 1946). Many sign stimuli function later in development, too. Tickling elicits laughing in most preschool children, for instance.

The original work of ethologists on fixed action patterns and sign stimuli dealt with species of insects, birds, fish, and reptiles, whose behavior is highly inflexible. Consequently, these two concepts at first referred to rigidly fixed behaviors and reactions that do not vary among individuals and that are completely innate, appearing automatically according to an inborn developmental "timetable" (Marler &

Hamilton 1966). But as ethological research was extended to more intelligent species, it had to deal with species-specific behaviors that were more flexible and variable. Many primates, including people, use a small number of vocalizations and facial expressions, such as the cry, the frown, and the stare, to communicate how an individual feels or what he wants. But a chimpanzee can use its warning scream to tease other chimps, and a human being can hold back or intensify a smile to suit the social purpose. Also, the development of such behaviors is not completely innate but can depend on environmental influences as well as heredity.

Consequently, ethologists have changed their concepts of fixed action pattern and sign stimulus. A fixed action pattern has been redefined as a recurring species-specific behavior that, once begun, seems to run off by itself, without any need for further stimulation to elicit each part of the behavior (Barlow 1968; Hinde 1970). The new definition still includes the rigid patterns of behavior that had first caught the attention of ethologists, but it also can include behaviors that are neither rigid nor innate. There can be considerable flexibility in how the animal uses the behavior and how it developed. Because of these changes, even some adult human behavior can be described in terms of fixed action patterns and sign stimuli. For example, many human facial expressions for emotions, such as the smile, the frown, and the expression for disgust, can be classified as fixed action patterns.

Nevertheless, one of the most important characteristics of human behavior is its flexibility and variability, and so behavioral scientists have had to build concepts that emphasize these characteristics. In most research on human development, the ethological approach focuses not on fixed action patterns and sign stimuli but on broad categories of activity known as behavioral systems.

Behavioral Systems

A **behavioral system** consists of a group of related species-specific behaviors that can be expressed in flexible ways by members of the species. Honeybees use a set of "dances" to communicate the location of honey to other bees in the hive (von Frisch 1967). All mother rhesus monkeys hold, nurse, and groom their babies, but they perform these actions in many different patterns (Hinde 1970; 1983).

Human language is a clear example of a behavioral system. It is obviously species-specific to *Homo sapiens,* yet we speak hundreds of different languages in different places around the globe. Tool use is another human behavioral system that is highly flexible and variable. We can adapt our behavior to hammer, screwdriver, automobile, or spaceship. We can use either a modern carpenter's hammer or a crude stone hammer to drive a nail effectively.

Human social interaction is a third behavioral system (Savin-Williams & Freedman 1977; Hinde 1981). For example, all human societies have status hierarchies, but every society defines its hierarchies in different ways. Even within one society, status can vary according to context. A person who has high standing with some people because of personal wealth may have low standing with others because of the way that wealth was obtained. Someone who is a leader on the job or in the classroom may be strictly a follower with friends and at the low end of the totem pole at home.

In studying behavioral systems, ethologists follow the same approach that they use to study fixed action patterns and sign stimuli. They observe a species in its natural environment and then describe the characteristic patterns of behavior displayed there. Only after this careful observation and description do they attempt to analyze and explain the behaviors.

PROCESSES OF LEARNING AND DEVELOPMENT

Even though as humans we have a hereditary disposition toward language, tool use, and social interaction, the development of these behavioral systems clearly depends on learning (Hess 1970; Hinde 1970). Every person must learn to speak, to use tools, to use facial expressions properly in social situations, even to walk. In fact, our learning ability is itself a species-specific characteristic. Each species has certain **learning capacities** that typify it and are essential to its normal behavior. In some species, these learning capacities are very narrow and specialized. Those of human beings, however, are extremely general. We can learn almost anything.

Figure 2-11 This little troupe of goslings is following the famous ethologist Konrad Lorenz. They are behaving toward him as if he were their mother, because within a few hours of hatching they were exposed not to the goose that laid the eggs but to him.

Imprinting

The phenomenon known as imprinting illustrates a species-specific learning capacity that is highly specialized and time limited. **Imprinting** is a learning mechanism that works during a restricted period early in the life of certain species of birds; it enables these birds to learn to recognize kindred members of the species. The concept of imprinting first became widely known through the work of Konrad Lorenz, who found that a recently hatched duckling, chick, or gosling will follow, and develop an attachment to, the first moving object it encounters, whether the object is its mother, a person, a ball, or a mechanical toy—almost anything that moves (Lorenz 1971; Figure 2-11). A bird that is a day or two older when exposed

to the moving object will not follow it and is much less likely to form such an attachment.

In its natural environment, the first moving object that a hatchling encounters is its mother, so that under normal circumstances, imprinting helps to form a social bond between mother and offspring. Lorenz has shown that this first bond is essential to the formation of general social bonds within the bird's species. If a gosling's initial bond is with a toy or a person instead of with a member of its own species, the animal's later social and sexual behavior is often directed toward toys or people instead of geese.

The limited time during which imprinting can occur is called a critical period, or **sensitive period.** In nonhuman animals, many developmental events require some particular response to definite stimuli during a brief, restricted sensitive period. Many birds learn the song of their species during a sensitive period of their lives; if they are not exposed to the song during this period, but only before or after it, they will learn the song poorly or not at all (Hinde 1970; Marler et al. 1981). Puppies most easily form social bonds—with people as well as dogs—during a sensitive period encompassing the first few months of life (Scott 1970).

Human Sensitive Periods

Human beings do not appear to experience the short, rigid sensitive periods for learning seen in animals. But we do seem to have some long, fairly flexible sensitive periods, during which we are especially skilled at learning certain types of behavior. Several theorists have speculated, for example, that the first year or two after birth may be a sensitive period for the formation of normal human social attachments (Ainsworth et al. 1978; Bowlby 1969).

Probably the best-documented human sensitive period occurs in the acquisition of language. Eric Lenneberg (1967, 1969) has suggested that between about 2 years of age and 12 to 15 years of age, children go through such a sensitive period. His evidence comes mostly from studies of language learning by deaf children and by children with brain damage. If children become deaf before 2 years of age, they seem to have great difficulty learning to speak later. Children who become deaf at 3 to 4 years of age also may stop speaking temporarily, but with training they can learn to speak again much more quickly than those who become deaf at an earlier age. Between 12 and 15 years of age, deaf children stop showing major improvements in their language; mentally retarded children also stop showing improvement at this age.

Studies of people whose brains have been damaged in the language areas also offer evidence for the sensitive period. Brain-damaged preschoolers quickly regain their language ability after a temporary loss, but older children recover a bit more slowly; many brain-damaged adolescents and adults lose their language ability permanently (Hecaen 1976; Lenneberg 1967, 1969). The age span between 1 or 2 years and 4 or 5 years is generally recognized as the peak of the sensitive period for language, a time when, as both research and casual observation confirm, the child is especially primed to learn to speak (DeVilliers & DeVilliers 1978).

The human sensitive period for acquiring language is very different from a bird's sensitive period for learning its song or from other rigid learning periods in nonhuman animals. Not only is it vastly longer, but it lacks definite boundaries—people can learn much language before 2 years of age and after 15 (Snow & Hoefnagel-Hohle 1978). Such major differences are sometimes ignored in books and magazine articles that might be called "popular ethology." The discovery of imprinting in geese, for example, led some people to conclude that such imprinting must occur in people too. What must be remembered is that scientific ethology emphasizes species specificity, which means that behaviors and learning processes in two diverse species must be assumed to be different unless there is very convincing data showing that they are alike. In species as different as humans and geese, a biologist would not expect imprinting or other learning processes to be closely similar.

An Emphasis on Acquisition

Early in the twentieth century, when most ethological research dealt with birds and other animals much less intelligent than human beings, almost all the data indicated rigid hereditary limits on learning and behavior in the species under study. On the basis of this evidence, scientists were often content to say that the species-specific behaviors of *all* species were inherited and to go no further in analyzing the way behaviors are acquired.

Subsequent ethological and psychological studies of more intelligent species, such as cats, chimpanzees, and people, have revealed the importance of learning in the acquisition of species-specific behaviors. In the light of these findings, ethologists have begun to reconsider some of their earlier assumptions. The result has been a revision of ethological theory, with the main emphasis shifting away from heredity alone to the interaction of heredity and environment in the acquisition of behavior.

This **interactional approach** now seems to dominate American ethology and psychology. It stresses the need to describe in full the sequence of events that leads to the normal appearance of a behavior (Hebb 1953; Hinde 1983). Interactional analysis shows that even relatively rigid processes such as imprinting do not simply follow automatic timetables. As Eckhard Hess (1973) demonstrated, the sensitive period for imprinting depends on at least two developing behaviors. First, the sensitive period does not begin until the newly hatched bird can walk well enough to follow a moving object—for chicks, usually at about 16 hours after hatching. Second, the sensitive period ends when the bird develops a fear of novel objects. In chicks, this fear appears some 24 hours after hatching, when the bird has presumably had enough time to become familiar with its environment. Figure 2-12 shows how these two factors interact to define the sensitive period for imprinting in chicks.

A third factor that seems to affect imprinting, under normal circumstances, is familiarity with the mother bird's call (Gottlieb 1983; Shaw 1976). Baby ducks imprint better on objects that make sounds, and they appear to imprint best when the sound is the call of their own species. This preference seems to be learned before hatching. As she tends her nest, the mother duck makes clucking sounds that the duckling hears inside the egg. The duckling also begins to make calls before hatching (Gottlieb 1963), and apparently becomes acquainted with the call of its species by hearing its mother and itself calling. As a result, during imprinting the duckling is attracted to the call its mother makes (Hess 1973).

If imprinting in birds is shaped by the interplay of at least three factors—walking ability, fear of novel objects, and familiarity with the normal call of the species—consider how complex the development of behavioral systems in the human species must be. Scientists are only now beginning to understand how language and other complex human species-specific behaviors develop.

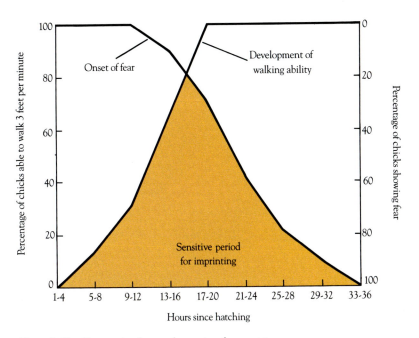

Figure 2-12   Two major factors determine the sensitive period for imprinting in chicks: ability to walk and fearfulness. A chick too young to walk well cannot follow a moving object; most are able to walk skillfully by about 16 hours after hatching. And a chick fearful of strange objects will not follow one; by about 24 hours after hatching, most chicks have developed fear. The combination of these two factors delimits the sensitive period that is graphed here. Notice that the graph of the percentage of chicks showing fear is "upside down," so that it actually represents "not fear." It is this plus the ability to walk that makes imprinting possible.

Human Emotion, a Species-specific Psychological Characteristic

The human characteristic that has been of most interest to ethologically oriented developmentalists is emotion. A high degree of emotional behavior is characteristic of all mammals, but, in general, the more intelligent a mammalian species is, the more emotionality it shows (Hebb & Thompson 1968). Dogs seem more emotional than mice; monkeys more emotional than dogs; chimpanzees and other apes more emotional than monkeys. Human beings are the most emotional of all.

Because we understand so much more than other animals do, we react emotionally to all sorts of things that simply pass them by. We can be afraid of ideas, such as Marxism or evolution. We can be angry about social slights, such

 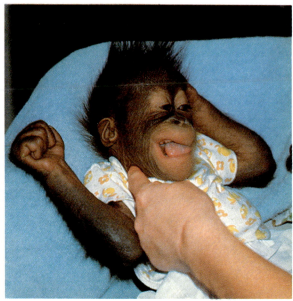

Figure 2-13   Specimens of the young of *Homo sapiens* (human) and *Pongo pygamaeus* (orangutan), two fairly closely related species, exhibiting a stereotyped species-specific response (laughing) to tactile stimulation (tickling).

as back-handed compliments. We can be awed by great art or music. We can be amused by a pun or by satire. And when something upsets us, we can have an emotional reaction than continues for a long time, as when we feel recurring guilt over some past act or when we sulk over some slight. Mice never sulk. Also, our intelligence leads us to distinguish between similar emotions, such as embarrassment, shame, and mortification. Virtually all human experience is infused with some kind of emotional tone (Osgood et al. 1957; Zajonc 1980).

Humor illustrates clearly the greater range of emotional behavior that comes with our greater intelligence. All normal human beings find some things humorous, but almost no other animal is capable of humor. The one established exception is the sense of humor of apes, who are the most intelligent primates after human beings. Baby orangutans laugh when tickled, for example (Figure 2-13), and adult chimps often play crude jokes on each other and on their human keepers. In one common scenario, a chimp takes a mouthful of water as someone approaches, waits quietly, and then suddenly spits the water at the person. The victim's surprised reaction usually provokes the chimp to riotous laughter. Human beings also enjoy slapstick of this sort, but most of us can also appreciate more cerebral humor that would fail to amuse a chimp.

Another emotionally charged behavior that is associated with intelligence is sex. Most animals seek sex only when offspring can be conceived, that is, when the female is in estrus (in "heat"). But among mammals in general, the smarter the species, the more likely it is that some sexual behavior will occur outside the female's fertile period (Beach 1965). Human sexual behavior occurs throughout the female's menstrual cycle, regardless of the time of ovulation. This constant sexuality is extremely unusual in the animal kingdom. Apparently only dolphins, who are also exceptionally intelligent, show such a high degree of sexual behavior (Wursig & Wursig 1979).

Strong negative emotions, such as fear and rage, are also part of the human behavioral repertoire. However, the social rules created by human intelligence produce a fairly predictable environment, which minimizes the occurrence of such emotions. In fact, when they do occur, it is likely to be in response to a seemingly minor violation of some social rule. Most people are outraged when someone slips into a parking space they have obviously been waiting for or tries to cut in front of them in a line to buy movie tickets.

Certain other primates will display similar reactions to violations of their social rules. If a young male chimp ignores his low status in the established hierarchy and approaches an older female, the males at the top of the hierarchy become enraged and behave ferociously toward him.

Although adult human beings and other primates react emotionally to violations of rules and expectations, their infants do not. In one study, chimps were shown a clay model of a chimpanzee head—that is, a "detached" head. Young chimps virtually ignored the object, whereas adult chimps reacted in ways that indicated strong fear (Hebb & Thompson 1968). Adult chimps had learned the standard for chimpanzee anatomy, and deviations from that expectation were frightening. Human adults react intensely to snakes, but young children do not. Adults not only have learned that snakes may bite and may even be poisonous, but also accept their culture's view of snakes as loathesome creatures.

Unfortunately, emotional development has not received much attention in psychological research. Sigmund Freud, the founder of psychoanalysis, pointed out the pervasiveness of emotion and sexuality in human behavior (thereby evoking an emotional reaction of extreme disgust in his Victorian scientific colleagues.) But when research findings failed to support many of his hypotheses about emotional development (Caldwell 1964), psychologists turned to other avenues of exploration.

In recent years, the attention of ethologists to human emotional development has renewed the interest of other developmental researchers as well. Ethological research has focused especially on the emergence of smiling and fears in infancy. The approach has been mostly descriptive, as early research on any topic must be, according to the methodology of ethology.

Newborn infants frequently turn up the sides of their mouths as if smiling. Parents say that these smiles are not "real," however, because they do not seem to be evoked by any clearcut external event, such as the sight of another person. At about 2½ months, most infants develop a *social smile,* which they use when

ESSAY
THE INCEST TABOO

The incest taboo, which forbids matings between parents and their children and between brothers and sisters, is universal in human cultures. In some societies, such as the Cheyenne, the prohibition extends to in-laws and even to the in-laws of in-laws.

What is the origin of the incest taboo? Is it a cultural creation? Or is it biologically based? These questions reflect the long-standing controversy between biologists and social scientists about the question of incest. Anthropologists and sociologists assert that the taboo was created to serve the needs of people living in groups; biologists contend that the prohibition of matings between close relatives serves an evolutionary purpose.

Certain anthropologists argue that the taboo arose among early groups of hunters and gatherers in order to force marriage outside the group and thereby create alliances among these small groups. These new social links afforded better protection against enemies and enlarged existing trade networks (Cohen 1978; Lévi-Strauss 1956).

Sociologists believe the taboo arose because the proper functioning of the family required it, in order to maintain both a clear system of status and emotional stability. If incest were permitted, the confusion in the family would be intolerable. A boy born of an incestuous father-daughter union, for example, would be a brother of his mother, a son of his sister, a grandson of his father (Davis 1948). Also, the emotional confusion arising from sexual rivalry and status would seriously disrupt the normal family roles—a father mating with his daughter, for example, would experience conflict between the roles of disciplinarian and lover. Such continuous conflict and tension could even lead to disintegration of the family unit (Robertson 1981).

Anthropologist Claude Lévi-Strauss, who believes that the incest taboo was created by groups to forge new alliances, views it as marking the passage from animal to human life, because the taboo "remodels" the biological conditions of mating and procreation. This contention rests on the assumption that animals have no prohibitions with regard to matings. But is this assumption correct? Recent ethological findings suggest that it is not.

Ethologists have found evidence that some nonhuman primates avoid incest. In two long-term ethological studies, one of rhesus monkeys on an island off Puerto Rico (Sade 1968) and one of Japanese macaques (Imanishi 1960, 1963), researchers were able to identify individual monkeys and construct genealogies so that incestuous matings could be noted. In the Puerto Rican study, only 4 of the 363 copulations observed were between mother and son; in the Japanese study, no matings between mother and son were observed. Jane van Lawick-Goodall (1971), who observed a colony of chimpanzees over a long period of time, never saw a mother-son mating and reported that brother-sister matings were rare.

One way that the likelihood of incestuous matings by primates is decreased is the voluntary or forced emigration of young animals away from the group in which they were born. Among baboons and macaques, nearly all young males emigrate to other groups. Female chimpanzees leave their group to join another when they attain sexual maturity (Nishida & Kawanaka 1972). In gibbons, which are monogamous apes, the parents drive their offspring out of the home range (Ellefson 1968). After reviewing a number of such studies, William J. Demarest (1977) concluded that "incest avoidance appears to be universal among higher primates."

The observations of psychologist Maurice Temerlin (1975), who raised a female chimpanzee named Lucy from infancy as a member of his family, highlights this conclusion. After Lucy reached sexual maturity, at about age 8, her relationship with her "father" underwent a profound change. Lucy stopped the hugging, kissing, and skin contact that had always been part of their play. Especially during her periods of estrus (times of sexual responsiveness and fertility), Lucy would make blatant sexual overtures to other men—friends and strangers alike—but would abruptly walk away from her "father" if he even walked in her direction.

If we and our primate relatives alike actively seek to avoid incest, it seems likely that there is a biological basis for that avoidance. Psychologist Gardner Lindzey (1967) has provided a succinct statement of the reason: "The biological consequence of inbreeding is a decrease in fitness. . . . A human group practicing incest operates at a selective disadvantage in competition with outbreeding human groups and ultimately would be unlikely to survive."

Evidence for the lowered fitness of inbreeding groups in animals has been abundant for a long time (Gates 1926; Law 1938). Inbred strains of mice, chickens, and laboratory animals have proved to be smaller, shorter-lived, and less resistant to disease than cross-bred animals. Also, people who raise cattle and sheep have found that inbreeding eventually produces offspring that are infertile.

Direct evidence about the effects of inbreeding on human beings is more difficult to obtain, both because breeding experiments with humans are not possible and because people who violate the incest taboo are unlikely to acknowledge the fact publicly. However, in several studies researchers have been able to examine the offspring of incestuous matings.

In one study of babies given up for adoption, 18 children born of parent-child or brother-sister matings were compared with a control group, 18 adoptive children matched with the first group in age, intelligence, social class, and body build. By 6 months of age, 5 of the incestuous offspring had died; 2 were severely mentally retarded and subject to seizures; 1 had a cleft palate; and 3 showed evidence of mental retardation. Only 7 of the 18 children were considered healthy and ready for adoption. Of the control group of babies, 15 were considered healthy (Adams & Neel 1967).

In another study, an English physician examined 13 incestuous matings (Carter 1967). His observations began before the pregnancies came to term and ended when all the living children were between 4 and 6 years old. Six children were the offspring of father-daughter matings, and 7 were from brother-sister matings. Only 5 of the 13 children were normal; 3 died of disease in early childhood; 1 was severely retarded, able to speak only a few words at 5 years of age; and 4 had IQs between 50 and 75.

Similarly unfortunate results were found in a study conducted in Czechoslovakia (Seemanova 1971). Of 161 children born of incest, 2 were stillborn, 21 died soon after birth, and 60 were judged to be significantly abnormal. Forty-six of the mothers in this study also had had children with a man who was not related to them. Out of a total of 92 outbred children borne by these mothers, only 5 had died and only 3 suffered abnormalities (9 percent), but of the 50 children fathered by the women's brothers or fathers, 6 had died and another 20 were significantly abnormal (52 percent).

The human evidence that exists, then, indicates that incestuous matings have harmful effects. Genetics and evolutionary theory help explain these data and suggest why incest avoidance might be biologically determined. Inbreeding decreases genetic variability, and a species requires such diversity to avoid major problems of health and fitness.

All of this indicates that there are very good genetic reasons for us to shun incest. And likewise there are very good social reasons—the disruption of status within the family, sexual conflict, and the need for new alliances. Thus, both points of view, the biological and the social, give insight into this fascinating bit of human nature.

Figure 2-14   At about 8 months of age, the attachment of an infant to his parents grows very strong, almost as if the baby could not differentiate between himself and his parents. The infant focuses all his needs and demands on the parents. A parent's departure, then, can arouse distress, even if the mother or father is only going out to the backyard or down to the basement.

another person is looking at them (Emde et al. 1976). Laughing seems to first appear about a month or two after the social smile.

At about 8 months of age, infants show a major increase in fears—fear of being separated from their mother, fear at being held by a stranger, fear of heights (Campos et al. 1983). Some of these fears seem to arise from infants' developing attachment to their mothers. Babies fear separation from their mother and fear adults who look different from her (Figure 2-14; and see Chapter 6). There is also some evidence that these new fears reflect developments in the infants' intelligence. Several studies indicate a major spurt in intellectual ability at the same age that infants begin to show this increase in fear (McCall 1983).

Although little work has been done on emotional development beyond infancy, there is ample material for study. Temper tantrums are very common among 2-year-olds. Adolescents often seem to undergo a period of emotional turmoil stimulated by their new sexuality and new need for independence. Much remains to be done to define the scope of our species-specific emotionality and to describe and explain how various emotions develop.

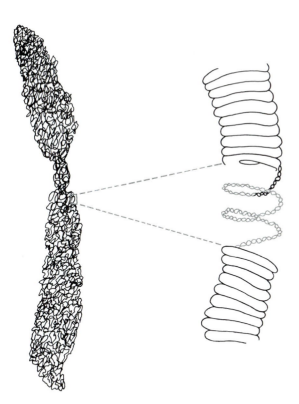

Figure 2-15 The relation of DNA, genes, and chromosomes. A chromosome seen with a light microscope looks like two tangled masses joined at one point. The masses are formed by the coiling of a single threadlike DNA molecule (see Figure 2-17). A single gene is a segment of this long thread, such as the one shown in gray here. Each chromosome includes thousands of genes. Chromosomes are usually visible like this only at certain stages of cell division, when the DNA is tightly coiled.

MECHANISMS OF GENETIC INHERITANCE

When we try to understand ourselves as a species, we describe and analyze traits and behaviors characteristic of the species. But how is it that all people have these common characteristics? Answering this question requires, among other things, an understanding of the mechanisms of genetic inheritance.

Gregor Mendel, an Austrian monk who studied heredity in plants, proposed in 1865 that each parent passes on to its offspring a set of "hereditary factors"— later named *genes*—containing the information that accounts for heredity. Mendel's hypothesis went unnoticed until about 1900, when the science of modern genetics began to take shape. Since the turn of the century, scientists have made huge advances in understanding how genes operate.

Genes, Chromosomes, and DNA

Genes are segments of chromosomes, rod-shaped structures that are found in every cell of the human body (Figure 2-15). With one important exception, every cell in a person's body contains a set of 46 chromosomes. The exceptions are the egg cells produced by a woman's body and the sperm cells produced by a man's—each of these contains only 23 chromosomes. When a sperm and an egg unite as a result of sexual intercourse, they form a single cell having 46 chromosomes. In the normal course of prenatal development (see Chapter 3), this cell grows and divides in half repeatedly, until after nine months a child is

Figure 2-16 Mitosis is the process of cell division through which all growth and maintenance of body tissues takes place. Its genetic function is to preserve information. It does so by copying each chromosome and then distributing one of the duplicates to each half of a dividing cell. For simplicity, this diagram shows only four chromosomes—two from the mother (color) and two from the father.

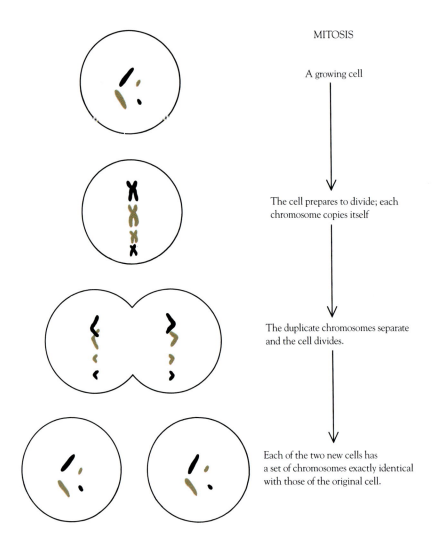

MITOSIS

A growing cell

The cell prepares to divide; each chromosome copies itself

The duplicate chromosomes separate and the cell divides.

Each of the two new cells has a set of chromosomes exactly identical with those of the original cell.

born whose body contains about a trillion cells. All of these cell divisions take place by *mitosis,* a process that duplicates each chromosome and then distributes an identical set of chromosomes to each half of the dividing cell (Figure 2-16). Thus, every cell in the child's body contains an identical set of chromosomes—half of them descended from the mother's egg and the other half from the father's sperm. Because each chromosome includes roughly 20,000 genes, each of us has just under a million genes in almost every cell of our bodies.

Genes are composed of DNA (deoxyribonucleic acid), a long threadlike molecule that runs along the length of each chromosome. Each gene is a segment of one of these long molecules. The DNA molecule is particularly well suited for passing on hereditary information. Each molecule consists of two long strands wound about each other as if someone had twisted a rope ladder (Figure 2-17). Just before a cell divides, the two strands "unzip" down the middle and

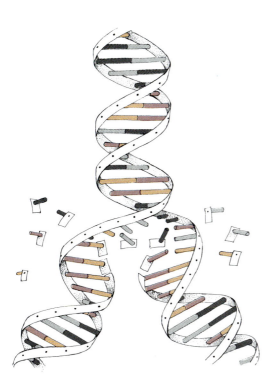

Figure 2-17 A close-up of a portion of DNA that is making a duplicate of itself. The double helix unwinds and the strands separate. Each separate strand builds a new double helix identical to the old one. The identity of the double helixes is assured because each base can join across the "ladder" only with a certain other base. In this diagram, for example, brown can connect only with gold, and black can connect only with gray. This rule holds both in the old double helix and in the new ones.

then a new second strand forms alongside each original one. The two new DNA molecules are identical with the old. In this way, chromosomes—and the genes that they include—are copied precisely. The DNA strands are made up of only four different linked chemical units, called bases: adenine (A), guanine (G), thymine (T), and cytosine (C). These bases can occur along a strand in any sequence and in segments of various lengths. Most genes are a few hundred bases long.

The genes control the production of important chemical substances in all of our cells, as well as the timing of their manufacture. It appears that each gene specifies and controls the production of one chemical substance. By this means, in the developing fetus, the genes specify that some cells become nerve cells, some muscle cells, and others bone cells, even though all these cells are descended from the original single cell through mitosis. (No one can yet describe the process that produces this specialization.) Thus, genes determine both the general outlines of our species-specific characteristics and the general course of our development. They specify, for example, that we have two eyes, a four-chambered heart, lungs rather than gills, and the apparatus that permits us to use speech. They specify that we have a brain with a large cerebral cortex, and certain kinds of connections between that brain and other parts of our body. They also specify how each of the other organs develops. Finally, because our psychological traits are determined largely by our physical capacities, the

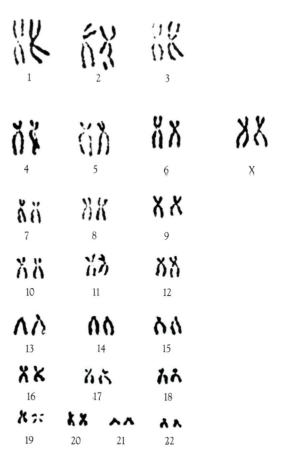

Figure 2-18 A set of human chromosomes arranged in matching pairs. This sort of arrangement is called a karyotype. It is produced by photographing a cell in the process of division, when its chromosomes are easiest to see and tell apart—this is when the chromosomes have just duplicated themselves but the duplicates have not yet separated. The photograph is cut up and the pictures of the chromosomes are arranged in order of size. The chromosome pairs are then numbered from the largest to the smallest. The only chromosomes not numbered in this way are the ones marked X. These are the chromosomes that determine a person's sex, in this case, female.

genes *indirectly* specify, among other things, our intelligence, our language ability, our social behavior, and our emotionality.

Besides determining our overall structure and functions as members of the species *Homo sapiens,* our genes provide us with an individual inheritance from our parents.

Pairs of Genes

Dominant and recessive genes   The chromosomes that we each inherit from our mother and father are well-matched sets, so that each of our cells actually has 23 *pairs* of chromosomes (Figure 2-18). In each pair, one chromosome is descended from the mother and one from the father. As a rule, the two chromosomes in a pair have matching genes all along their lengths. In most cases, the matching genes are identical and so contain the same instructions: Both genes of a pair that specify eye color, for example, may specify brown. Such gene pairs are said to be **homozygous.** In other cases, the genes of a pair may differ slightly and so contain different instructions: In an eye-color pair, one gene may specify brown, the other blue. Such gene pairs are said to be **heterozygous.** When a gene pair is heterozygous, one of the genes may dominate

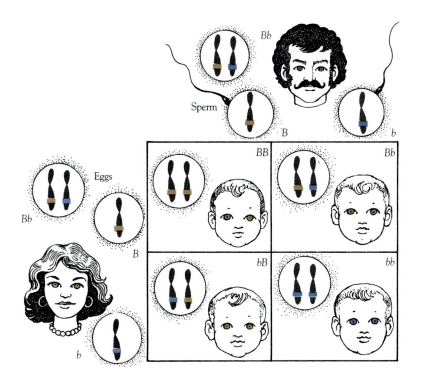

Figure 2-19   Eye color is determined by a pair of genes that specify the presence of pigment-bearing cells near the iris of the eye. A person with brown eyes has these cells, which contain brown pigment (just which shade of brown depends on other genes). A person with blue eyes does not have these cells. This diagram shows how parents who both have brown eyes may produce a blue-eyed child. The brown-eye gene (B) is dominant over the blue-eye one (b), because even one brown-eye gene is enough to produce pigment cells in the iris. Therefore, a person with brown eyes may have the gene pair *Bb*. Both parents here have the gene pair *Bb*, and so together can produce the four combinations shown. One out of four offspring, on the average, should have blue eyes.

the other. The substance produced by this **dominant** gene may completely mask the effect of the substance produced by the other, **recessive** gene. For example, when a pair of genes that specifies eye color is heterozygous, the brown-eye gene is always dominant over the blue-eye gene. Only when both genes of the pair specify blue eyes will the person's eyes be blue.

You may have heard someone say to parents of a young child, "But how is it that your daughter has blue eyes when both of you have brown ones?" The dominance of the brown-eye gene explains this phenomenon. In every gene pair, one of the genes comes from the mother and one from the father. When the mother and the father each have one brown-eye gene and one blue-eye gene, their eyes are brown because the brown-eye gene is dominant. But if any of their children inherits the blue-eye gene from both of them, the child will have blue eyes. On the average, one of every four children born to couples like this one will have blue eyes. Figure 2-19 shows how the process works.

Many gene pairs show this pattern of dominant and recessive inheritance of particular traits. For example, in human beings, curly hair is dominant over straight hair, dark hair is dominant over light hair, and the ability to roll up the sides of the tongue is dominant over the lack of this ability. In many other gene pairs, however, both genes are expressed at the same time. One example of this blending pattern is the gene pair for sickle-cell anemia, described in the essay "The Sickle Cell: Adaptive and Destructive."

Genotype and Phenotype   The genes carried by a person for any given trait are his or her *genotype* for that characteristic. The trait the person actually displays is his or her *phenotype.* Different genotypes (either *BB* or *Bb* in Figure 2-19) can produce the same phenotype (brown eyes). The terms are also used in a broader sense, "genotype" referring to a person's total set of genes and "phenotype" to a person's total appearance and behavior.

The same genotype also can result in different phenotypes because of environmental circumstances. People with a genotype for a certain height may not reach that height because of poor nutrition. When the diet of most Japanese changed after World War II to include more protein and other nutrients, many Japanese children grew to be markedly taller than their parents. There are, however, limits to the height that can be produced by variations in nutrition. Even the best nutrition would probably not produce Japanese who average more than six feet in height, and even with very poor nutrition some Japanese would be relatively tall and others relatively short. For height and for other characteristics, the range of phenotypes that a specific genotype will produce in different environments is called its *reaction range.*

Polygenic Inheritance   Although eye color and a few other traits are strongly affected by a single pair of genes, few traits seem to be specified entirely by a single pair. Most traits appear to be *polygenic;* that is, they depend on the combined effects of several genes. A person's height, for example, is affected by genes that specify such factors as hormone production, bone formation, and growth rate, all working together. Skin color depends on at least five gene pairs, and eye color on at least two, which also help to determine skin color (Nicholls 1973). Brain development and intelligence depend on at least 150 genes, because mental retardation has been traced to at least that many; several hundred other genes probably also contribute to brain development.

Genetics and Evolution

The variations that exist in living things, both within species and from one species to another, arise in part from mutations, changes in genes that either

ESSAY
THE SICKLE CELL:
ADAPTIVE AND DESTRUCTIVE

Under high magnification, normal red blood cells look round and plump, something like jelly donuts. In about 8 percent of American blacks, however, and in close to 30 percent of certain African populations, some red blood cells are much smaller than normal and have a sickle, or crescent, shape.

Sickling of the red blood cells is an inherited trait, which has been traced to a mutation in a single gene (Wallace 1978). This gene specifies the structure of hemoglobin, the protein that carries oxygen in red blood cells. People who are heterozygous for sickling—with one gene for normal hemoglobin and one for abnormal hemoglobin—ordinarily suffer few adverse effects. Both genes are active, so that each gene specifies the formation of some hemoglobin and there is a blending of normal and abnormal hemoglobin in the red blood cells. Under most circumstances, this mixture carries enough oxygen, and there are no obvious symptoms of the sickle-cell trait. However, when the concentration of oxygen in the blood falls below a certain level, the abnormal hemoglobin causes many of the cells to collapse into a sickle shape. For example, at high altitudes, where the air is thin, strenuous exercise can cause as many as 40 percent of the red blood cells to collapse into sickles.

A person who is homozygous for sickling—that is, one who inherited two sickling genes—is said to have sickle-cell anemia, a severe and chronic condition that is often fatal. Sickle cells carry much less oxygen than normal cells, and because these people have only sickle cells, their body frequently suffers from insufficient oxygen. In addition, because of the cells' shape, they often clog blood vessels, causing severe pain, tissue damage, and even death if vessels supplying the brain or lungs are blocked.

People with sickle-cell anemia frequently die at an early age and are therefore unable to reproduce. Yet there is a high incidence of the sickling gene in certain African populations. Why? Researchers uncovered the answer to this question when they noticed that the populations with a high percentage of sickling lived in

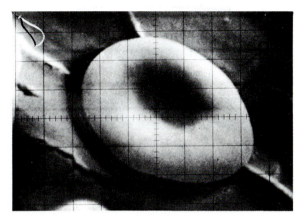

A normal red blood cell

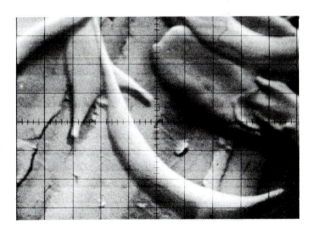

A sickled red blood cell

areas with a high incidence of malaria, a parasitic disease transmitted by mosquitoes in which the parasites attack the red blood cells and produce fever, chills, sweating, weakness, and often death. The investigators noted that people with the sickle-cell trait (one sickling gene and one normal gene) had a substantially lower incidence of malaria than the rest of the population (Allison 1954; Livingstone 1971). Apparently, having one sickle-cell gene improves a person's chances of surviving malaria.

If possessing a single sickle-cell gene does have survival value, then the sickle-cell trait should be more common in adults than in infants because children with the gene will be more likely than those without it to survive malaria and live to be adults. A study

sponsored by the World Health Organization and the government of Nigeria supported this prediction (Fleming et al. 1979). Researchers studied the population living in Nigeria's Sudan savanna region, which has a severe malaria problem. The prevalence of the sickle-cell trait was 24 percent among newborns and 29 percent among adults. Also, the blood of children 4 years old and younger with the sickle-cell trait carried fewer malaria parasites than the blood of those without the trait. Because of the strong advantage of having a single sickling gene in areas with malaria, the

gene remains in the population, despite the severe handicap of having two sickling genes.

For American blacks, the sickling gene has no adaptive function, because malaria is no longer a medical problem in this country. However, in one small population that lives on James Island, off the shore of South Carolina, researchers found a frequency of 20 percent for the sickle-cell trait (Livingstone 1967). According to historical record, this island had a very high incidence of malaria during the time the colonies were being settled (Childs 1940). There, the gene persisted in large numbers because it had an adaptive value. Also, because the same people continued to live on the island after the danger of malaria had been eliminated, and because there was little admixture of genes from outside populations, the high percentage of sickling genes has been maintained into the twentieth century.

The sickling trait, then, is destructive in people with two sickling genes but survives in many people with only one because it makes them fitter in areas where malarial infection is a hazard. Malaria kills a significant number of individuals in these areas, so those with the sickle cell are more likely to survive and reproduce. If malaria is ever eliminated in Africa, as it has been in North America, the sickle-cell trait is likely to decrease over the generations because it will no longer have an adaptive value.

occur spontaneously or are caused by chemical or physical agents, such as radiation (see Chapter 3). Variations caused by mutation are a chief source of the new genetic characteristics upon which evolution depends. Many of the mutations that occur are harmful, but a very few are advantageous and so can lead to evolutionary change through the process of natural selection. When a species evolves into distinct races, for example, the variations between races result from differential selection acting on a relatively small number of genes. The variations in the finches shown in Figure 2-1, who most likely evolved from a common ancestor, were selected for the particular environments that flocks of finches found themselves isolated in. A mutation may have produced the first individual with the changed beak shape, and that shape happened to be advantageous for, say, capturing tree insects. If this individual lived in a place that had plenty of trees, the bird therefore ate well and reproduced, passing on the new gene to offspring, who also had a better diet than their "normal" peers—and so a new race of finches evolved. In human races, the genes selected specify such traits as skin color, nose size and shape, and hair color and texture.

In the formation of new species, however, the variations frequently seem to involve the way genes are arranged into chromosomes (Stanley 1981). For example, chimpanzees neither look nor act like people. They are much less intelligent, cannot talk, and cannot walk upright for long. They also have many characteristics and abilities that we do not. They can use their feet as hands, for instance, and they are much stronger than we are. Yet they have almost all the same genes that we do (King & Wilson 1975). However, their genes are organized into 48 chromosomes, whereas ours are organized into 46. How such differences can produce radical differences between organisms is not yet understood, but some fairly drastic human abnormalities seem to be due to an abnormal organization of chromosomes that arises when eggs and sperms are formed.

The Production of Eggs and Sperms

Our genes dictate that one kind of cell undergoes a special kind of division called *meiosis.* This is the process that produces egg cells (ova) in women and sperm cells in men, cells with only 23 chromosomes, half the normal complement. This process is illustrated in Figure 2-20. When egg and sperm unite, they form a cell that contains, once again, 46 chromosomes. The exact copying and sorting of chromosomes and genes in meiosis is essential to normal development. If the correct components are not reproduced in their proper organization in an egg or in the sperm that fertilizes it, the consequences can range from spontaneous abortion to serious abnormality or disease, including cancer.

MEIOSIS IN THE MALE

Father's cell with a full number
of chromosomes, two of each type.

The cell prepares to divide;
each chromosome copies itself
and lines up with its partner.

FIRST DIVISION: The members of
the chromosome pairs separate.

Each of the two intermediate cells
receives one member of each original pair
of chromosomes.

SECOND DIVISION: The duplicate
copies of each chromosome separate.

Four sperm cells are the final result;
each of them has half the original number
of chromosomes — one from each original
pair (or an exact copy of it).

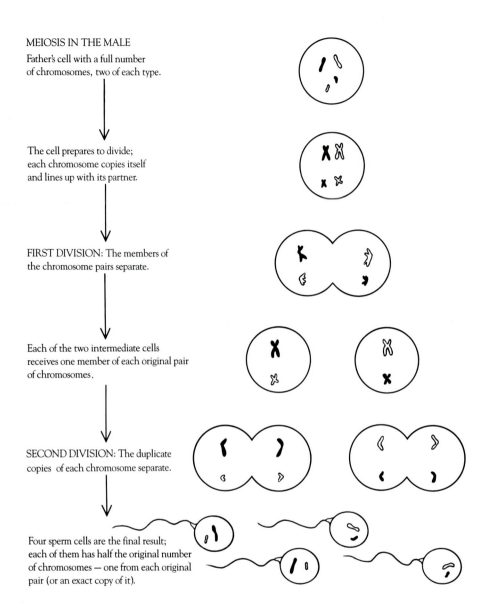

Figure 2-20 Meiosis is the special process of cell division that makes the sexual cycle of
reproduction possible. The biological function of sex is to mix the genes of individuals within a
species so that offspring are variations on a theme, rather than rigid copies of their parents. In
fertilization, genetic material from two individuals is combined; to prevent a doubling of the
quantity of genetic material in each generation, a way of reducing it is needed. Meiosis
accomplishes this by copying the chromosomes once but then causing the cell to divide twice.
For simplicity here, only two pairs of chromosomes are shown in each parent cell that undergoes
meiosis.

   In the production of sperm, one body cell gives rise to four sperm cells, each containing half
the original number of chromosomes. Meiosis in females is identical in principle, but only one
of the cells produced survives. Also, the process is not completed until after the ovum has been
penetrated by a sperm. When a sperm fertilizes the ovum, the new cell has the full count of
chromosomes that the parent cells had.

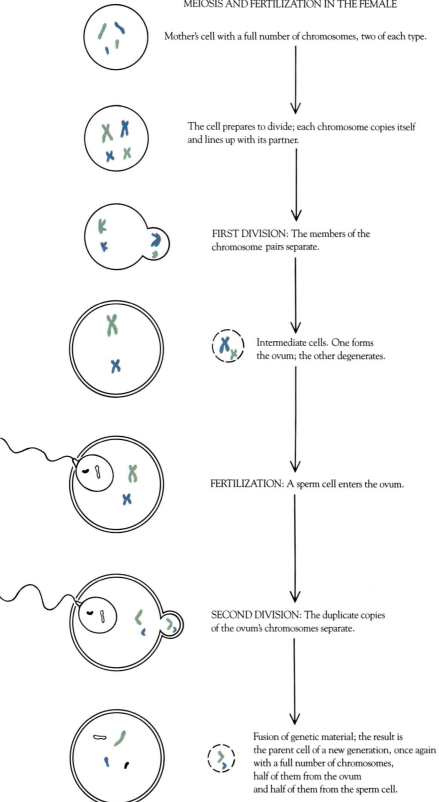

Mother's cell with a full number of chromosomes, two of each type.

The cell prepares to divide; each chromosome copies itself and lines up with its partner.

FIRST DIVISION: The members of the chromosome pairs separate.

Intermediate cells. One forms the ovum; the other degenerates.

FERTILIZATION: A sperm cell enters the ovum.

SECOND DIVISION: The duplicate copies of the ovum's chromosomes separate.

Fusion of genetic material; the result is the parent cell of a new generation, once again with a full number of chromosomes, half of them from the ovum and half of them from the sperm cell.

Figure 2-21 Many children with Down's syndrome can function as cherished family members, despite their retardation.

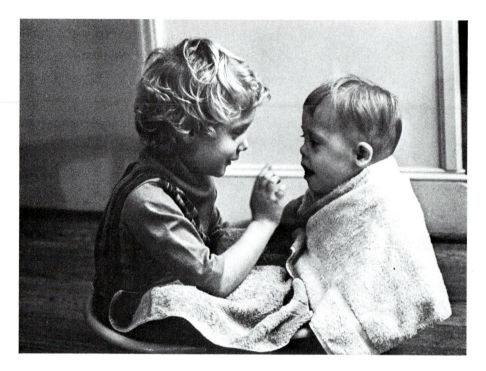

The best-known outcome of a chromosomal error is **Down's syndrome.** People with Down's syndrome are unusually short, with stubby hands and feet. Most of them are severely mentally retarded. They usually suffer from serious congenital malformations, especially of the heart, and therefore many die before reaching adulthood. The syndrome was originally called mongolism because the eyelid fold that is another of its symptoms superficially resembles that of Orientals.

Down's syndrome is caused by a chromosomal error in which the person has three chromosomes in the 21st position (see Figure 2-18) instead of the normal two. Several different processes can produce this extra chromosome. The most common is called **nondisjunction.** During meiosis in either the male or the female parent, the chromosomes in the 21st pair do not separate, so that one egg or sperm ends up with two of these chromosomes and the other with none at all. If either of these defective germ cells joins with a normal egg or sperm, the resulting fertilized egg is seriously defective. When the 21st chromosome is missing, the embryo dies quickly. When there is an extra 21st chromosome, the child shows Down's syndrome (Lejeune et al. 1959). Nondisjunction apparently can occur for every one of the 23 pairs of human chromosomes, but in most cases it is lethal to the embryo at a very early stage of pregnancy.

Children with Down's syndrome are much more likely to be born to women over 35 years of age (Goad et al. 1976). The reason for this is not known but seems to be related to the age of the mother's eggs. At birth, a female's ovaries contain all the egg cells she will release during her mature years. The eggs released by a 40-year-old woman, then, are twice as old as the eggs she released at age 20. Although Down's syndrome can also be produced by sperm cells, this and the many other types of nondisjunction seem to be more common in eggs.

Many women who are over 35 when they become pregnant, or who have some other reason for concern about genetic defects, are now electing to undergo a procedure called *amniocentesis* (Fuchs 1980). The physician inserts a hypodermic needle through the woman's abdomen into the uterus and takes a sample of the amniotic fluid that surrounds the fetus. This fluid contains cells sloughed off the skin of the fetus. Examining these cells by karyotyping (see Figure 2-18) and other methods can reveal nearly a hundred types of hereditary problems, including the extra chromosome of Down's syndrome and some problems due to single-gene defects, such as sickle-cell anemia and Tay-Sachs disease. If a serious condition is found for which there is no treatment, the parents then have the option of electing a therapeutic abortion.

THE TAPESTRY OF HEREDITY AND ENVIRONMENT

Genetic mechanisms are, of course, essential to human development, but it has long been recognized that environmental determinants are at least equally or even more important. The rules that govern social behavior, for example, vary widely between cultures and are determined primarily by environmental factors. The teaching of these rules to children, a process called socialization, has a powerful influence on development.

Research on the hereditary basis of behavior, called behavior genetics (Henderson 1982), has tended to show just as much about environment as about heredity (Plomin & DeFries 1980). Even behavior formerly thought to be controlled almost entirely by hereditary factors, such as the development of motor abilities during infancy, is turning out to have important environmental determinants as well. Sex differences, too, clearly have an environmental as well as a genetic basis. Sexual anatomy is strongly controlled by genes, yet most psychological differences between the sexes seem to be controlled more by social learning than by heredity.

It is extremely difficult to separate the influence of heredity and environmental factors in the study of human development. Obviously, controlled breeding experiments or those requiring subjects to be raised under possibly harmful conditions cannot be carried out with people. With plants, however, experiments can be conducted that allow genetic and environmental factors to be sorted out. Figure 2-22 shows how differently several specimens of the same

Figure 2-22 Heredity and environment interact in plants as well as in animals, but in plants their separate effects are easier to demonstrate. (A) These three plants, of the same species and subspecies, were found growing together on a northern California hillside and were transplanted to an experimental garden, where they were grown under identical environmental conditions. The differences between these plants—which are considerable—are due entirely to individual genetic variation. (B) These four plants were obtained by taking cuttings from a single original plant and growing them under different conditions of moisture and light. The striking differences between them are entirely the result of variations in their environment.

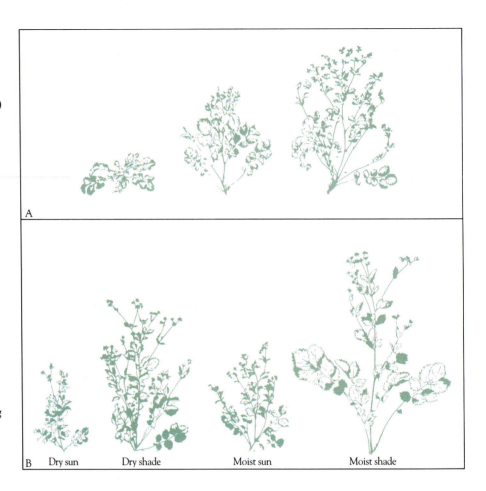

A

B   Dry sun   Dry shade   Moist sun   Moist shade

kind of plant can develop when either their heredity or their growing conditions are varied.

In human development, heredity and environment collaborate so closely that their relationship resembles that of the warp and woof threads in a tapestry. Although the one set of threads runs vertically, while the other runs horizontally, they are hardly distinguishable in the final product. As a tapestry is woven, it changes constantly. The interaction of warp and woof threads, the addition of new colors, the finishing of some parts of the pattern and the start of new parts all make the weaving itself a dynamic process.

In the development of a human being, the warp and woof of environment and heredity begin to interweave at the moment of conception, as uterine environment and genetic program start to interact. It is the beginning of a dynamic meshing of hereditary and environmental influences that will continue throughout life.

PKU, A Single-Gene Defect

The collaboration of heredity and environment in development is strikingly demonstrated by the disease called PKU. Recall that every gene specifies the production of a substance important to the body's functioning. Some of these substances are structural proteins that make up such body parts as muscle and

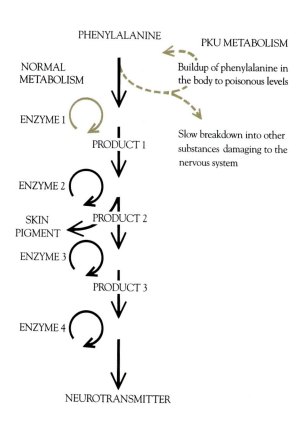

NORMAL
METABOLISM

PHENYLALANINE

ENZYME 1

PRODUCT 1

ENZYME 2

SKIN
PIGMENT

PRODUCT 2

ENZYME 3

PRODUCT 3

ENZYME 4

NEUROTRANSMITTER

PKU METABOLISM

Buildup of phenylalanine in
the body to poisonous levels

Slow breakdown into other
substances damaging to the
nervous system

Figure 2-23 A simplified
diagram comparing the
body's normal use of
phenylalanine with its use
in children who have
PKU. Such children lack
the gene for an enzyme
(color) that begins the
conversion of
phenylalanine into
substances useful to the
body. Consequently,
phenylalanine and its
breakdown products can
build up to concentrations
that poison the child's
brain.

connective tissue; others are enzymes that control chemical changes or some
other bodily processes. In phenylketonuria, or **PKU,** a particular gene pair is
defective in that both genes fail to produce an enzyme needed to convert the
chemical phenylalanine into other useful substances. Phenylalanine is present
in many common foods. As Figure 2-23 shows, when the required enzyme is
present, phenylalanine is converted, through a sequence of chemical changes,
into various substances—a pigment, various hormones, and chemicals that
transmit impulses from nerve cell to nerve cell (neurotransmitters). Lack of
that one enzyme, then, results in pale-colored skin, hair, and eyes, and also
prevents normal production of certain hormones and neurotransmitters. The
danger to health arises because the high concentration of phenylalanine that
builds up when there is no conversion acts as a poison to the brain. Consequently, a child who has untreated PKU suffers epileptic-like seizures and
mental retardation.

Although PKU clearly is caused by a defective gene, it is also caused by an
environmental factor—diet. People normally eat many foods that are high in
phenylalanine; the body does not manufacture it. The chemical can build up
in children who have the defective gene only if it is ingested. For this reason, a
PKU child's diet should be chosen to include only foods low in phenylalanine.
(Some phenylalanine is needed for normal functioning even by children who

have PKU.) With such a diet, the chemical does not accumulate and the brain damage is prevented. Infants who have PKU cannot drink milk or eat ordinary foods, but are given a special formula containing all other essential nutrients plus a small amount of phenylalanine. Toddlers with PKU may eat sugars, starches, and fats, but their intake of protein-rich foods must be closely monitored. Children on this diet still have light skin, hair, and eyes, but the other functions of the missing enzyme (production of certain hormones and neurotransmitters) apparently are taken over by other bodily processes.

In one study, babies who had PKU were put on a low-phenylalanine diet at 3 months of age. These infants showed later IQs of 102 to 118, while their older brothers and sisters with PKU, whose treatment had not started until after age 1 (because the diagnosis had not been made earlier), showed IQs of 55 to 83 (Berry 1969). The disorder is easy to detect, and most hospitals now routinely check newborns for it.

Not long ago, it was thought that an excess of phenylalanine affected the brain only during a sensitive period between birth and about 7 years of age, so dietary restrictions could be eliminated during later childhood. But a 1976 study (Brown & Warner) found that children with PKU who were taken off the diet after age 6 lost 9 to 10 IQ points by age 16, while the IQs of those on the low-phenylalanine diet remained about the same. Therefore, even though the risk of *severe* mental retardation is gone by age 6 or 7, it seems best for these children to remain on the diet until adolescence.

Motor Development

Until recently, scholars firmly asserted that hereditary factors were almost solely responsible for **motor development** (also called sensorimotor development), that is, the development of skills involving body movements. During infancy, it was thought, the environment had little or no effect on motor development, except when infants received virtually no stimulation. Several classic studies seemed to show that the speed with which infants develop the ability to sit up, to manipulate objects, and to crawl is unaffected by practice or other environmental factors (Gesell & Thompson 1929; Dennis & Dennis 1940). Most developmental scientists accepted these findings as conclusive and assumed that motor development was controlled by an inherited timetable of maturation.

As a result of this apparent evidence, certain findings on motor development were misinterpreted. A number of studies had demonstrated that African infants showed faster motor development than European or American infants (Geber & Dean 1957; Warren 1972). Because they assumed that the environment played no part in this outcome, many scientists concluded that these developmental differences must be the result of hereditary differences between the Negro and Caucasian races.

Recent studies have shown that this conclusion was incorrect. One of these, an experiment with American infants, demonstrated the effect of practice on walking (Zelazo et al. 1972; this experiment is described at greater length in Chapter 4, Figure 4-3). For 8 weeks, some infants less than 3 months old were given practice with the stepping reflex. These infants were able to walk alone 6 to 8 weeks earlier than the infants in a control group, who did not practice the stepping reflex. This effect is especially interesting because children do not walk alone until about the end of the first year; thus, there was a delay of many months between the practice and the onset of walking. Other recent studies show that practice can hasten the development of a wide range of motor abilities (Thelen 1981; Yarrow et al. 1977).

Further research has also revealed the role of practice in the development of the motor skills of African infants. Mothers in a variety of African cultures deliberately teach many motor skills to their infants, including sitting, standing, and walking (Konner 1977). Some of the mothers insist that if they did not teach these skills, their infants would never learn them. In one study, African infants were indeed precocious, but only in the skills that they had practiced, not in other motor skills (Super 1976). Thus, even for basic species-specific behaviors such as walking, environment interacts with heredity to determine the developmental timetable of a child's behavior.

Sex Likenesses and Differences

Much of the research on the interplay of heredity and environment has focused not on specific behaviors, such as walking, but on large, complex clusters of behaviors—especially on the characteristics called "intelligence" and "sex differences." Intelligence is discussed in Chapter 9. For sex differences, scientists have succeeded in discovering some of the hereditary mechanisms and how they collaborate with environmental influences to produce the different behaviors that we see in girls and boys, women and men.

In exploring the hereditary and environmental sources of sex-related behavioral differences, however, one should keep firmly in mind that for almost all traits, males and females are very similar. We are, after all, members of the same species, sharing almost all the same genes and chromosomes and inhabiting the same species-specific human environment. Most psychological research about the sexes is aimed at identifying differences. Therefore, differences are emphasized while likenesses are only implied.

When psychologists talk about a difference between the sexes on some trait, they mean only that there is an *average* difference. On most psychological tests, the scores of the two sexes on a trait largely overlap, although the average score on the trait for one sex may be slightly higher than the average for the other sex (Plomin & Foch 1981). On intelligence tests, for example, women as a group

Figure 2-24   (A) The sex-determining pair of chromosomes as they would appear in a karyotype (see Figure 2-18). (B) The sex of a child depends on whether he or she receives a Y or an X chromosome from the father.

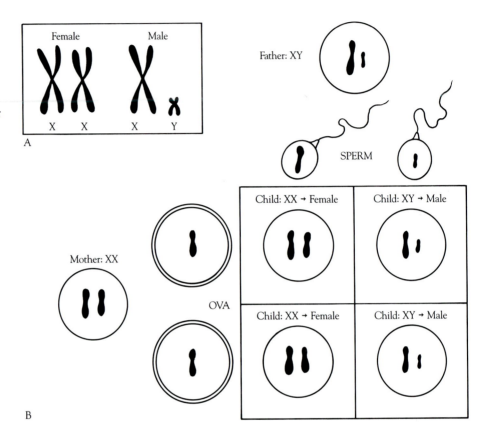

show higher average verbal abilities than men as a group. Women tend to have larger vocabularies, better writing skills, and so forth. But most men and women fall in the large middle range of the distribution, having about the same scores, and some men have better verbal abilities than most women. Similarly, men tend to score higher on arithmetic and spatial problems than women, but only on the average. In everything except perhaps sexual anatomy and physiology, males and females are more alike than they are different.

Sex Determination   As described earlier (see Figure 2-18), the chromosomes in body cells are in pairs, with the members of each pair well matched in size and in the genes that they contain. In human beings and many other animals, there is one exception to this rule: In a male, one of the pairs consists of one large chromosome, designated X, and one much smaller one, designated Y. A female's cells always contain two X chromosomes, and no Y (Figure 2-24). As a result of meiosis, half the sperm cells that a male produces have an X chromosome and the other half a Y. All the eggs that a woman produces have one X chromosome.

When an X-carrying sperm unites with an egg, the child will be a girl; when a Y-carrying sperm unites with an egg, the child will be a boy. The father's sperm, then, always determines the sex of the child. Soon after the egg has been fertilized, the process of sexual development specified by the chromosomes begins. At first, the sex glands, or gonads, are the same in male and female embryos. But in the ninth week, when the embryo is not much more than an inch long, the gonads begin to differentiate into testes or ovaries. In a male, the testes then begin to secrete a hormone that triggers the formation of male genitals. In a female, this hormone is not secreted, and female genitals develop.

Even at this very early point in development, the environment must collaborate with heredity to produce a normal infant. If the hormone secreted by the testes of a male embryo is destroyed by an abnormality of chemistry within the mother's uterus (or if the testes fail to secrete the hormone), female genitals develop even though the embryo's chromosomes are male. Likewise, a female embryo develops male genitals if the uterine environment exposes it to male hormone—for example, if the mother's body produces more than the normal low level of male hormone that is present in all women (Money & Earhardt 1972). In most such cases, the individual does not simply become a member of the "wrong" sex but instead has ambiguous sexual characteristics. For example, most genetic males who develop external female genitals because of an absence of male hormone do not develop a uterus. Fortunately, such sexual anomalies are extremely rare.

Physical Differences   In all known human populations, there are physical differences between men and women besides the obvious differences in sexual anatomy. Genes play an important role in specifying these differences. Men are taller than women; they have a higher ratio of muscle to fat and broader chests. Women are wider in the pelvis; their hip joints are formed a little differently; their bodies use energy more efficiently.

In many cases, environmental factors exaggerate the degree of these genetic differences between the sexes. For example, genetic differences do produce stronger muscles in men than in women, but most modern cultures provide a social environment that magnifies this genetic difference. Men do more heavy physical work than women, so their muscles become even stronger. Women are discouraged from heavy physical work, so they become soft and "feminine." In the same way for many other physical traits, cultures tend to build upon and accentuate genetic physical differences between the sexes.

Despite the stereotype of females as the weaker sex, in several important ways women are stronger than men. In tasks that require long-term endurance rather than brute strength, such as work on an assembly line or day-long spadework in a garden, women, on the average, perform better than men (Tavris & Offir 1983).

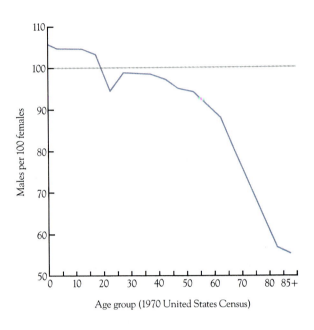

Figure 2-25 The ratio of males to females from birth through old age. More males than females are born, and there are more males throughout childhood, even though more boys than girls die as infants. At about 60 years of age, the surviving women begin to outnumber surviving men, and by 85 years of age, there are twice as many women as men. Because this curve is based on 1970 Census data, the sharp dip at around age 20 may represent the loss of male lives in the Vietnam War.

The superior endurance of females is also reflected in their consistently lower death rate. To begin with, there are many more miscarriages of males than females. It is estimated that about 140 males are conceived for every 100 females (Lowry 1979), but only about 106 boys are born for every 100 girls. Figure 2-25 shows how the ratio of males to females changes over the life cycle. Males are more susceptible to most serious diseases than females are, and more boys than girls die in infancy (Beatty & Gluecksohn-Waelsh 1972). The difference in susceptibility to disease continues throughout childhood and even into adulthood. By the time people are in their 80s, there are several surviving women for every man (Parkes 1978).

Females have superior endurance for several reasons. First, weaker females are less likely to reproduce than weaker males. It requires less strength and health for a man to impregnate a woman than it does for a woman to carry and nourish a developing fetus through 9 months of pregnancy (Trivers 1972). Thus, evolutionary selection for good health is much stronger in females than in males.

A second reason for males' poorer health lies in the structural differences between the X and Y chromosomes. Because the Y chromosome is smaller than the X, it carries fewer genes, and some genes on a male's X chromosome thus have no partners on the Y. When an unpaired gene on a male's X chromosome determines a harmful trait, it will necessarily be expressed because there is no second gene to counteract or moderate its effects. Females who have the harmful gene are much less likely to show the trait because the harmful gene on one X chromosome is likely to be paired with a gene masking the trait on the other X chromosome. (Of course, a female who inherits the harmful gene from both parents will express the trait.) A male who has such a trait always inherits it from his mother, even if she did not express it, because he received his X chromosome from his mother. Thus, women are carriers of the trait, but for the most part only their sons are afflicted, although their daughters, too, may be carriers.

Minor problems such as color blindness and pattern baldness are examples of such **X-linked traits.** A more serious example is hemophilia, a disorder that prevents the production of a protein the body needs to make the blood clot properly. As a result, hemophiliacs bruise very easily and may lose large amounts of blood from minor cuts. Also, during their growing years, they bleed into their knees, elbows, and other joints, for reasons not entirely understood. This bleeding causes great pain and is sometimes crippling (Massi 1975). The most famous example of this disorder is the hemophilia that has afflicted certain of the royal families of Europe since the nineteenth century. In this instance, the origin of the disorder has been traced to Queen Victoria of Great Britain. Because there is no history of hemophilia in her ancestors, it is likely that there was a spontaneous mutation in a gene she received from one of her parents. Figure 2-26 shows the incidence of the disease in some of her descendants.

In addition to these genetic reasons for greater male mortality, there are environmental ones associated with traditional sex roles. The most obvious is that men typically fight in wars, and so die in them. The dip in the curve in Figure 2-25 at about age 20 results mostly from the large number of men who died in the Vietnam war. Likewise, many traditionally male jobs and hobbies, such as mining and car-racing, are more likely to lead to early death than the traditionally female role of housewife.

Differences in Behavior   Genetic factors seem to be less important in behavioral differences between the sexes than in physical differences. In fact, most of the behavioral differences that people think they see between men and women have not been confirmed by research. Eleanor Maccoby and Carol Jacklin (1974), in their comprehensive review of research on sex stereotypes, concluded that only four of the many characteristics studied actually show sex differences. These differences seem to appear in almost every culture and so may have a genetic component:

1.   Boys and men tend to be more aggressive, both physically and verbally, than girls and women. Studies in many different cultures affirm the greater aggression of males, particularly toward other males.

2.   Girls tend to have greater verbal ability than boys. They learn to speak and read earlier, and fewer girls have difficulty learning to read. Beginning at about age 11, girls are also better than boys on both abstract verbal tasks (analogies, comprehension of difficult written material) and concrete tests of verbal fluency (grammar, spelling).

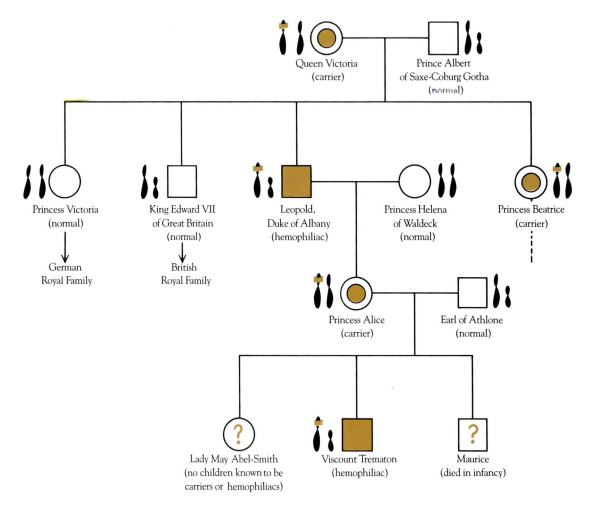

Figure 2-26   The transmission and expression of the genetic defect causing hemophilia in some of the descendants of Queen Victoria. (Victoria actually had nine children, three of whom carried the defect, but only four of her children are represented. Through marriage, the illness was brought into the royal families of Prussia, Russia, and Spain.) Victoria carried the defective gene—represented by the band on one chromosome—but did not herself suffer from the disease because the corresponding gene on her other X chromosome was normal and dominated the defective gene. Her husband did not carry the gene. The four offspring of this marriage represented here show the four possible outcomes. Princess Victoria has the normal X chromosome from her mother and an X from Albert, so the German royal family was spared the disease. King Edward has the normal X from his mother and his father's Y, so the British royal line was also spared. Leopold inherited the chromosome with the defective gene from his mother and so suffered from the disease, because the Y chromosome from his father had no matching gene to counter the ill effects. Princess Beatrice also inherited the defective gene, and although the X she inherited from her father masked its effects for her, she did pass on the disease to several of her male descendants.

3. In visual-spatial ability, men and adolescent boys tend to perform better than women and adolescent girls, but this difference may or may not exist before adolescence (Wittig & Petersen, 1979). Also, women who have only one X chromosome, an anomaly called Turner's syndrome, show a specific deficiency in visual-spatial ability (McClearn & DeFries 1973). This fact suggests that visual-spatial ability is determined in part by genes on the sex chromosomes. Some verbal and visual-spatial problems on which the sexes typically obtain slightly different average scores are shown in Figure 2-27.

4. Men and adolescent boys also tend to show greater mathematical ability, although there seems to be no such difference among children. This difference in mathematical ability, however, varies widely among social groups and in general is not as great as the other differences.

Some other behaviors may show consistent sex differences across cultures, but there are not yet enough data to be certain (Block 1976; Huston 1983). For example, some findings suggest that girls and women may be more nurturant than boys and men (Edwards & Whiting 1980) and that this difference may increase in adolescence (Chandler 1977). That is, women may be generally more attracted to infants and children and more likely to want to care for them.

Although the near universality across cultures of the differences described by Maccoby and Jacklin suggests that there is probably *some* genetic contribution to them, environmental influences are certainly important, too. For example, in most cultures little boys are often given toys and games that encourage competition and aggression; little girls are given dolls and are encouraged to play house.

Environmental Determinants: Sex Roles   All cultures define the sex roles of men and women somewhat differently and teach children from an early age to fit those roles. The roles are based to some degree on the biological differences between the sexes, especially the fact that only women bear children. But they also stem from relatively arbitrary cultural rules about what activities are appropriate for women and for men. In most cultures, care of children and the home are defined to be the concern of women, whereas matters of public life, politics, and war are defined to be the concern of men (Maccoby & Jacklin 1974; Mead 1963). Beyond these few commonalities, cultures differ widely in their definitions of sex roles.

Indeed, the variety of sex role definitions in different cultures is astounding (d'Andrade 1966). It is evidence of the striking degree to which human behavior can be shaped. For instance, among the Tchambuli, one of several New Guinea tribes studied by Margaret Mead (1963), the sex roles were completely different from those familiar to us in Western culture: The women were the actual holders of power, and they also appeared generally more "masculine," in Western terms, than the Tchambuli men. The women did the tribe's fishing and practiced its chief commerce, manufacturing the mosquito

A In the next three minutes, write down as many original five-word sentences as you can think of, beginning the words with the following initial letters:
F_____ D_____ O_____ R_____ L_____.
(For example, Flying Dogs Often Require Labor.)

B Show where this figure

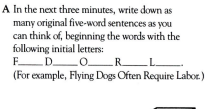

is contained in these:

C Do the following problem in your head: Fold a piece of paper, ABCD, into a triangle, and then fold it again into a smaller triangle, as shown at right. Punch a hole in corner BD. Where will the holes be when you unfold the piece of paper–as shown in 1, 2, 3, or 4?

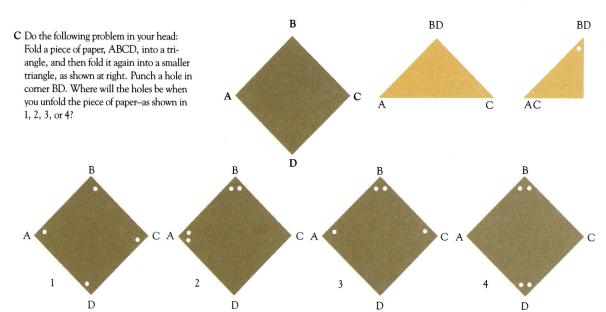

D Color is to spectrum as:
(a) tone is to scale.
(b) sound is to waves.
(c) verse is to poem.
(d) dimension is to space.
(e) cell is to organism.

Figure 2-27 A and D are problems of the sort that females do better than males, on the average. B and C are problems that males do better than females, on the average.

netting that was their people's main source of income. They shaved their heads and did not adorn themselves at all. And when it came to the selection of marriage partners, the women did the choosing, even though formal ritual made it seem that it was the men who chose.

The men, on the other hand, were mainly artists—musicians, dancers, wood carvers. They wore elaborate hairdos and were very particular about the way they dressed. In general, they showed much more concern with social relations and the details of everyday life than with power and wealth.

In Tchambuli child rearing, boys and girls were treated quite similarly until they were 7. Then the women began to teach the girls to fish and weave. The boys, meanwhile, were pretty much ignored until they were initiated into manhood at puberty. At that time, they moved into the men's houses and began their training in the arts. Mead stated that the Tchambuli had the only society she had seen as an anthropologist in which girls of 10 and 11 were brighter and more enterprising than boys of the same age. The fact that some cultures exist where sex roles, as defined in contemporary Western societies, are reversed indicates the power of the social environment to shape sex-role behaviors.

Western sex roles and their opposites are only part of a wide range of male and female roles and personalities that different cultures consider appropriate, as illustrated by other tribes that Mead (1963) studied in New Guinea. In some societies, such as the Arapesh, both men and women were "feminine" by Western standards. Aggression was rejected by both sexes, and everyone strove to be sensitive, compassionate, and liked by his or her peers. In other societies, like the Mundugumor, both men and women were "masculine" by Western standards: independent and aggressive.

Within any one culture, too, most of the psychological differences between the sexes are probably environmentally controlled. Various socializing agents— parents and other family members, peers, and in modern cultures, schools and television—teach children how boys and girls, and men and women, are supposed to feel and act. In most Western nations, it is a pervasive process that begins almost from birth. Newborn girls are wrapped in a pink blanket and their nursery is decorated with flowered wallpaper; boys are wrapped in blue and their wallpaper may bear a sports or airplane motif. Less obviously, it is reflected even in the way parents talk to and play with an infant daughter or son (Maccoby & Jacklin 1974). By the time they are 3 years old, if not sooner, children know what sex they are. From 4 to 7 years they also tend to demonstrate extremely stereotyped ideas of what girls and women do versus what boys and men do (Maccoby 1980). Once children have learned how males and females should act, violations of the normal sex roles tend to be seen as moral transgressions. Given the power of socializing agents, it is hardly surprising that in each culture men and women should behave so differently. (The contributions of socializing agents to development are discussed more fully in later chapters.)

Sex differences, then, demonstrate the collaboration of heredity and environment. Genes and chromosomes determine whether a person is a male or a female. They may also specify some sex differences in certain psychological characteristics, though it should be emphasized again that the few scientifically established sex differences in behavior are modest in degree. But sex-typed behavior, like human behavior generally, varies greatly, both between and within cultures. Every culture teaches its boys to act "masculine" and its girls to act "feminine," but one culture's definition of "masculine" or "feminine" may bear little resemblance to that of another. Within a culture, too, especially one as diverse as that of the United States, a wide range of behaviors is accepted as appropriate to either sex. Although sex roles still exist in modern societies, they seem to be becoming more and more flexible (Tavris & Offir 1983).

In most other species of animals there is considerably less variability among individuals, and the differences between male and female behavior are very clearcut and consistent. For example, most adult male baboons strive to dominate the other members of their troop, protect the troop from intruders, and mate with as many females as possible. Most female baboons take care of their babies, try to maintain themselves in a stable social position within their troop, and mate with one or a few males each time that they are in estrus. These patterns of male and female behavior are similar in all troops within a baboon species.

This difference between us and other species demonstrates again one of the prime species-specific characteristics of human beings: the malleability of our behavior. The capacity for an enormous range of behaviors is part of our genetic heritage. Although developmental studies have focused more on the effects of environmental events than on "inborn tendencies," as the chapters that follow demonstrate, our very responsiveness to environmental events is itself inborn. In this extremely broad way, as in innumerable more specific ones, heredity and environment interact to create the tapestry of human life.

SUMMARY

SPECIES AND EVOLUTION

1. A *species* is a breeding population of organisms that share a group of common characteristics. All human beings, despite superficial differences in physical or behavioral characteristics, are members of the species *Homo sapiens*.

2. Over many millions of years, species have evolved and have **adapted,** both physically and behaviorally, to their particular environment. Charles Darwin's **theory of evolution** uses three main ideas to explain how species change and adapt: variation, heredity, and natural selection. Within every species, the characteristics of individuals vary, and many of these variations are passed on to their offspring. Species members compete with each other and with members of other species for the resources of life. Individuals whose inherited characteristics allow them success in such competition tend to survive and pass on these advantageous characteristics to their offspring. Favorable characteristics are thus **selected** over less favorable ones.

3.   The species *Homo sapiens* belongs to the class of mammals and the order of primates, which also includes monkeys and apes. Some of the traits we share with our fellow primates have become exaggerated in humans. We have an unusually long childhood and, given our body size, a longer life expectancy than we "should." Our brain is also much larger relative to body size than that of other primates.

THE HUMAN BRAIN

4.   The brain and nerves together are called the **nervous system.**
   a.   The nervous system is composed of a network of long, thin cells called **neurons,** which carry messages—electrochemical impulses—between the brain and the rest of the body.
   b.   Neurons are separated from each other by small gaps, called **synapses,** which are bridged by chemical messengers.
   c.   The central nervous system (the brain and spinal cord) also contains **glial cells,** which nourish the neurons and remove their waste products.

5.   The brain's **cerebral cortex** is made up of two hemispheres, connected by a band of nerve fibers (the corpus callosum). In general, the **right hemisphere** controls the left side of the body, and the **left hemisphere** controls the right side. The two hemispheres appear to be partly specialized for particular kinds of thinking: the left hemisphere for logical, sequential thought, as with speech and language, and the right hemisphere for integrating information into a whole, as with spatial information. Hemispheric specialization develops gradually throughout childhood.

6.   Although no new neurons are produced after birth, neurons do grow larger and form more complex connections with each other. Also, the long thin extensions of many neurons become covered by **myelin,** a coating that increases their efficiency.

ETHOLOGY AND HUMAN DEVELOPMENT

7.   Every species displays species-specific psychological characteristics. In human beings, the complexity of the brain and nervous system is the basis of highly complex characteristics, most notably, **intelligence, language,** and **culture.**

THEORY: *ETHOLOGY*

8. Ethological theory offers an important perspective on human development. Ethologists study a species to describe its typical, naturally occurring behaviors, called *species-specific behaviors,* many of which can be analyzed into two related phenomena: fixed action patterns and sign stimuli.

  a. *Fixed action patterns* are frequently repeated patterns of movement that virtually all members of a species perform in a similar way.

  b. *Sign stimuli* are sensory inputs that reliably elicit fixed action patterns.

9. Because human behavior is so flexible and varied, ethologists studying people go beyond fixed action patterns and sign stimuli to focus on species-specific *behavioral systems,* which combine many separate but related behaviors, as in language and the use of tools.

10. Most animal species show species-specific *learning capacities.* In some species, learning abilities are highly specialized and limited, but in human beings, they are extremely general.

  a. A *sensitive period* is a limited time during which a particular influence can affect development. In *imprinting,* for example, birds of certain species learn to follow their mother and thus form a social attachment to her, but this learning normally occurs only during a few hours shortly after hatching.

  b. In human beings, there seems to be a long sensitive period (from 2 years to 12 or 15 years of age) for acquiring language.

11. Many ethological researchers now take an *interactional approach* to the behavior of more intelligent species. This approach attempts to describe all the factors leading to the acquisition of a behavior, including the way environmental factors interact with heredity.

12. The methods and findings of ethologists have rekindled the interest of developmental psychologists in human *emotions.* Human beings show more varied emotional reactions to a wider range of events than less intelligent animals do. So far, most research on emotional development has focused on infancy.

MECHANISMS OF GENETIC INHERITANCE

13. Species-specific characteristics are passed on from parents to offspring by means of hereditary factors called *genes.*

14. Genes are segments of *chromosomes,* which are composed of a chemical called **DNA.**

  a. Almost all human cells contain 46 chromosomes. The only exceptions are sperm cells and egg cells, which contain only 23 chromosomes.

  b. When a sperm and an egg fuse as a result of sexual intercourse, the chromosomes from the father and mother are combined into one cell. This cell grows and divides repeatedly by **mitosis** to produce all the cells in a human body.

    c.   Each gene specifies and controls the production of one chemical substance in the body. Together, the genes establish both the general outline of the characteristics of a species and the timetable for their development.

15.   In all human cells (except sperm and egg cells), the chromosomes exist in pairs. Human cells contain 23 pairs. As a rule, the two chromosomes in a pair have matching genes all along their length.

    a.   The genes in a pair may be identical **(homozygous)**. When the genes are different **(heterozygous),** one may be **dominant,** which means that its instructions override the instructions of the other, **recessive** gene.

    b.   The genes a person carries are called his or her **genotype.** The **phenotype** is the trait the person actually displays. The range of possible phenotypes that one genotype can produce is called its **reaction range.**

    c.   Almost all human traits are **polygenic:** They depend on the combined effects of two or more genes.

16.   Changes in genes, or mutations, may occur spontaneously or may be produced by chemical or physical agents. Many mutations are harmful, but a few produce the potentially useful variations in characteristics upon which evolution depends.

17.   The cell-division process called **meiosis** produces egg cells and sperm cells, each containing 23 chromosomes, one-half the usual number. When a sperm fertilizes an egg, the result is a single cell with the full complement of 46 chromosomes, 23 from each parent. When chromosome pairs do not separate correctly during meiosis, the error is called **nondisjunction,** which can result in serious genetic defects such as **Down's syndrome.**

THE TAPESTRY OF HEREDITY AND ENVIRONMENT

18.   Heredity and environment always collaborate in the course of development. In **PKU,** a defective gene can lead to brain damage, but a change in diet soon after birth can prevent the damage. Even early **motor development** depends more on environmental factors than was previously thought.

19.   Human sex differences illustrate the collaboration of heredity and environment.

    a.   The anatomical differences between males and females are specified by the sex chromosomes: Females have two X chromosomes, and males have an X and a Y.

    b.   Males are subject to many more diseases than females are. These diseases include genetic disorders known as **X-linked traits.** Because the Y chromosome is smaller than the X, harmful recessive genes on a male's X chromosome typically do not have a corresponding dominant gene on the Y.

   c. Environmental factors ranging from prenatal hormones to cultural expectations can produce behavioral differences between the sexes.

20. Behavioral differences between the sexes are much less prevalent than is commonly assumed. The sexes are generally more alike than they are different.

   a. Research has so far confirmed only four consistent behavioral differences between males and females: On the average, males are more aggressive, females have greater verbal ability, and males have greater visual-spatial and mathematical abilities.

   b. *Sex roles,* behaviors deemed characteristically masculine and feminine, vary enormously from culture to culture, so that a behavior seen as characteristically masculine in one culture may be viewed as feminine in another.

SUGGESTED READINGS

GOULD, STEPHEN. *Hen's Teeth and Horse's Toes: Reflections on Natural History.* New York: W. W. Norton, 1983.

A series of articulate, informative essays by an evolutionary biologist on evolution, science, and humanity. The essays originally appeared in the popular magazine *Natural History.*

GOLDMAN-RAKIC, PATRICIA, AMI ISEROFF, MICHAEL SCHWARTZ, and NELLIE BUGBEE. "The neurobiology of cognitive development." In M. M. Haith and J. J. Campos (eds.), *Infancy and Developmental Psychobiology,* Volume 2 of P. H. Mussen (ed.), *Carmichael's Handbook of Child Psychology.* New York: Wiley, 1983.

A definitive analysis of the latest research on the nature of brain development in monkeys and people.

LEWONTIN, RICHARD. *Human Diversity.* New York: W. H. Freeman and Company, 1982.

A scholarly treatment of human variety and its basis in evolution, heredity, and environment, including an up-to-date overview of the nature of genetic mechanisms.

LORENZ, KONRAD. *King Solomon's Ring: New Light on Animal Ways.* New York: T. Y. Crowell, 1952.

A collection of stories about animals by one of the founders of ethology. The book is a particularly entertaining introduction to ethological thinking.

MILLER, JONATHAN. *The Body in Question.* New York: Random House, 1979.

A well-written, nicely illustrated book on the physiology of the body. The book relates physiology to behavior and to medicine and traces the historical roots of modern physiology. The chapter on genetics is especially relevant here.

ROSE, STEPHEN. *The Conscious Brain.* New York: Random House, 1976.

A comprehensive presentation of brain physiology and how it relates to human consciousness and personality.

TAVRIS, CAROL, and CAROLE OFFIR. *The Longest War: Sex Differences in Perspective.* New York: Harcourt Brace Jovanovich, 1983.

A lively and authoritative inquiry into sex differences that attempts to separate the real from the imagined.

3

PRENATAL

DEVELOPMENT

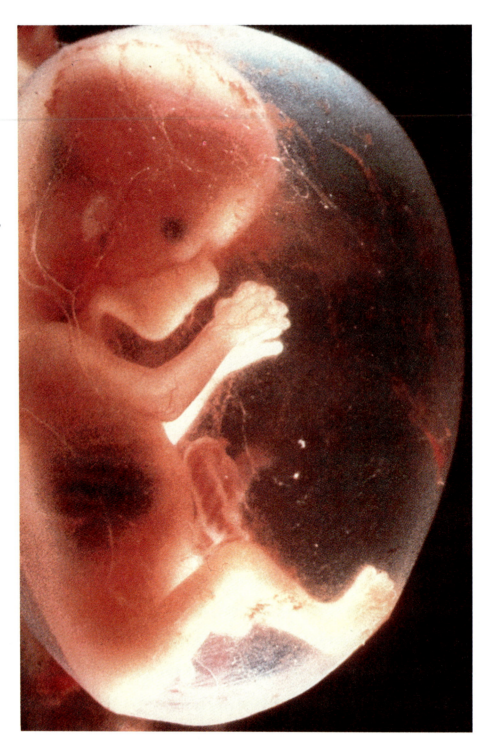

CHAPTER OUTLINE

3

PRENATAL
DEVELOPMENT

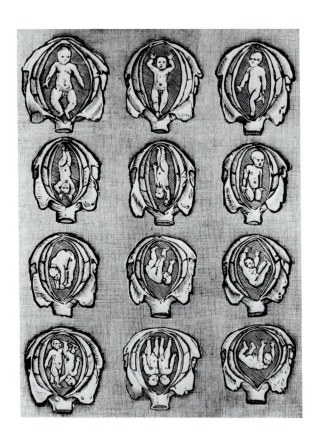

Figure 3-1 (Right) These woodcuts were made about a hundred years before the invention of the microscope. They were published to show midwives the various positions in which babies may present themselves at birth. Such drawings were based on midwives' experience rather than on scientific observation. No one connected with these woodcuts had ever examined fetuses *in utero.* (Left) Fanciful drawings like this one may have influenced the perception of seventeenth-century spermists, who claimed that with the help of the microscope they saw in each sperm a homunculus ("little man").

In the middle of the seventeenth century the Dutch naturalist Anton van Leeuwenhoek, inventor of one of the earliest microscopes, looked at magnified human sperm for the first time. Soon others followed his example, and saw what they believed to be a minuscule but perfectly formed human creature in each sperm cell. They believed that this miniature baby, which they called a *homunculus* (meaning "little man"), was simply carried by the sperm into the mother's womb, where it grew until it was large enough to be born. At about the same time a Dutch physician, Regnier de Graaf, described for the first time the structure of the human ovary. Although he never actually saw a human ovum, he conjectured that women form eggs, just as birds do. De Graaf thought that the egg, not the sperm, contained a miniature human being and that the sperm's role was merely to stimulate its growth. Controversy between scientists who favored the first theory, called spermists, and those who favored de Graaf's, called ovists, continued for a century.

When challenged to explain the origins of homunculi, both ovists and spermists theorized that each homunculus carried within it another, tinier being—which, in turn, contained another even tinier one, and so on. Some ovists, carrying the argument to its ultimate conclusion, said that Eve had

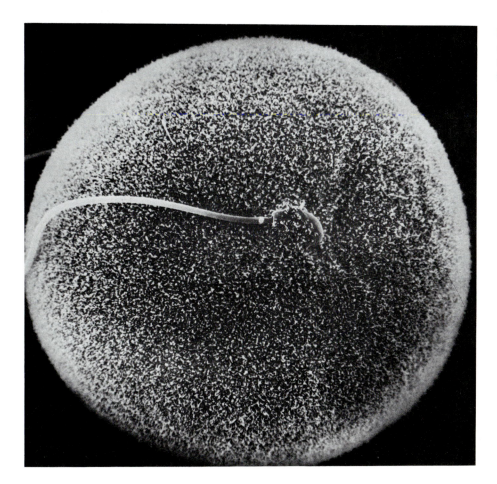

Figure 3-2 A human sperm penetrating an egg at the moment of fertilization.

contained within her body all the generations to come. They calculated that she had carried enough eggs within eggs to give the world 200 million generations. After that, they believed, human life would come to an end (Guttmacher 1973).

Some scientists did not find these explanations of prenatal development satisfactory. In 1759 the German anatomist Caspar Wolff made a dramatic claim: The human infant does not exist preformed inside one parent or the other, he said, but develops after sperm and egg join. Development begins with two equally important cells, one from the father and one from the mother (Needham 1959). This explanation is correct.

Human development begins with fertilization: A sperm and an egg fuse inside a woman's body to become, briefly, one cell (Figure 3-2). Combination of the mother's and father's chromosomes at the time of conception gives the new organism its genetic inheritance. Part of this inheritance is the genes that direct

118

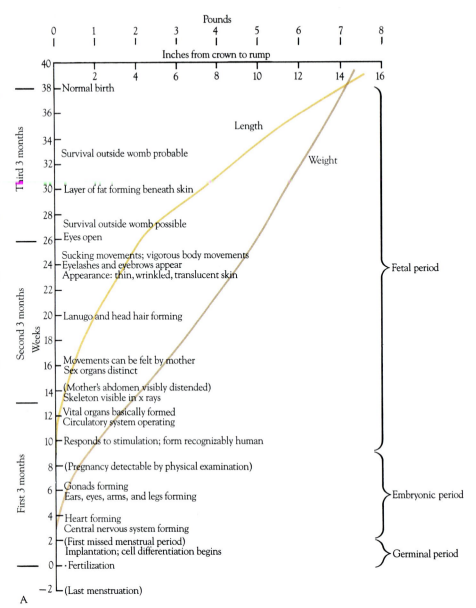

Figure 3-3 A summary of prenatal development. The curves reflect growth in weight (brown line) and length (gold line) during the 9 months. Important physical and behavioral developments are shown at the time they occur. You can see that most of the fetus's anatomy is well established within the first 3 months of development, even though at 3 months it is the size of a mouse and weighs only a few ounces. The drawings at the right show the relative size of the human embryo at various stages in its development.

development throughout the human life cycle, including the 9 months of prenatal development. Embryologists have closely described the day-to-day developmental changes that occur, so the 9-month process that transforms the single microscopic cell inside a woman's body into a complex living being is now well charted (Curtis 1983; Nilsson et al. 1977).

The course of prenatal development is summarized in Figure 3-3. The first 2 weeks of the new organism's life are called the **germinal period.** The main developmental process during this period is cell division. The next 6 weeks, called the **embryonic period,** are characterized by cell differentiation and

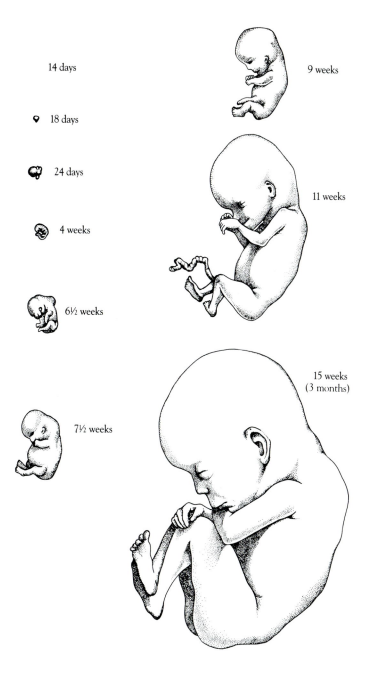

14 days

18 days

24 days

4 weeks

6½ weeks

7½ weeks

9 weeks

11 weeks

15 weeks
(3 months)

specialization. Cells destined to become nerve tissue, for example, become differentiated from those that will make up muscle or bone, and different cell types in turn become specialized for particular functions. For instance, nerve cells destined to function as part of the visual system take on characteristics quite different from nerve cells in the skin. By the end of the embryonic period, the developing organism has a beating heart and a functioning brain (both still very simple) and the rudiments of most other organ systems. The final 7 months of prenatal life are called the *fetal period.* For the most part, this is a time of maturation and growth rather than the creation of new structures.

Prenatal development, like all development, involves the collaboration of heredity and environment. Although many people do not think of the womb as an environment, it is every human being's first—and in some ways most important—home. Each developing person lives in a uterine environment that has its own distinctive characteristics. Even identical twins, who have identical genes, may have different enough uterine environments to cause them to differ somewhat at birth. The positions of the twins in the uterus are different, for example, so that one fetus's movements may be more restricted than the other's. Also, even identical twins may have separate placentas, and one may function better than the other, providing more nutrients.

Besides such slight differences in normal uterine environments, there are environmental agents and events that can seriously disrupt development. Curiously, the unborn human organism is well protected against many severe shocks but is exquisitely sensitive to a small number of seemingly minor events. A pregnant women can break a leg, undergo many types of major surgery, or suffer a schizophrenic breakdown, and her chances of bearing a healthy, full-term infant are still good. But if she contracts a mild case of German measles early in pregnancy, the result can be disastrous. This chapter discusses some of these potentially harmful agents, after describing the developments that take place during each of the three periods of prenatal life.

THE FIRST 3 MONTHS

The Germinal Period: Fertilization to 2 Weeks

During sexual intercourse, the male's ejaculation of semen typically deposits 300 or 400 million sperm cells in the vagina. However, only a few thousand of these sperm survive the trip through the vagina, cervix, and uterus into the Fallopian tubes, which is where fertilization usually takes place. Sperm that succeed in making the journey have, at most, 48 hours in which to fertilize an egg before they degenerate.

Normally, a woman's ovaries release one egg each month about two weeks after the start of each menstrual period—that is, ovulation takes place. The egg travels from the ovary through the Fallopian tube that leads to the uterus. If the egg is not penetrated by a sperm within 12 to 24 hours after ovulation, it begins to degenerate and is soon expelled from the body.

When a sperm does reach an egg, the sequence of events diagrammed in Figure 3-4 is set in motion. The membranes of the two cells fuse, and the sperm nucleus (located in the head of the sperm) enters the egg. The outer membrane of the egg immediately undergoes chemical changes that prevent penetration by any other sperm. The egg and sperm become a single cell, called the zygote.

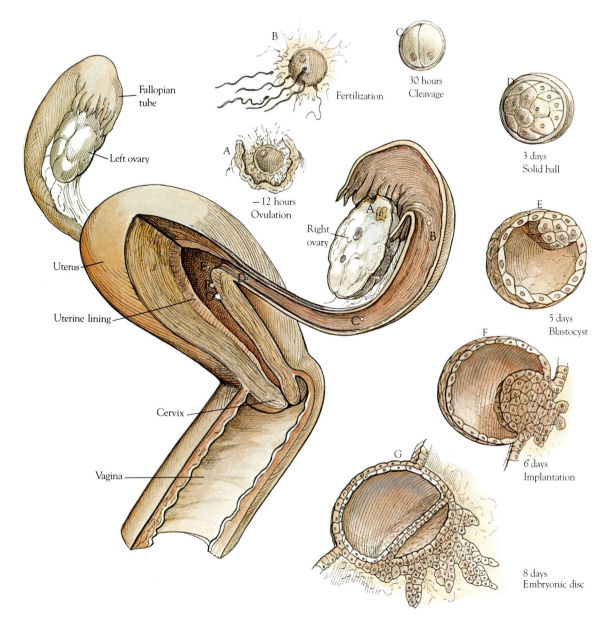

Figure 3-4 The first week of prenatal development. As the large drawing shows, most of the first week's development takes place in the Fallopian tube, as the organism makes its way to the uterus. (A) The egg is released from the ovary and begins its journey through the Fallopian tube toward the uterus. (B) If sperm have been deposited in the vagina during sexual intercourse, a few make their way to the far end of the Fallopian tube. As soon as one sperm penetrates the egg, chemical changes make it impossible for other sperm to enter. The sperm's genetic material combines with the egg's to form the zygote, a new cell with the full human complement of 46 chromosomes. (C) Cleavage, or cell division, first takes place about 30 hours after fertilization, as the zygote continues its passage through the Fallopian tube toward the uterus. Cell division continues until (D) a solid ball of cells has formed. This ball is no larger than the original egg. (E) As cell division continues, the spaces between the inner cells of the ball become larger until the ball becomes the blastocyst, a hollow sphere of cells with a small mass of cells adhering to one point in its inner surface. (F) Now within the uterus, the blastocyst makes contact with the uterine lining, where it implants itself. (G) By the eighth day, the thickened cell mass that was evident inside the blastocyst at five days has become the embryonic disc, from which the baby will develop.

Cell Division   Soon after sperm and egg have joined, the cell-division process known as mitosis begins. (Mitosis is described in Chapter 2.) It is through mitosis that a single cell becomes a 7-pound newborn (Guttmacher 1973; Nilsson et al. 1977).

The first mitotic cell division takes place about 30 hours after fertilization and produces two cells. At 60 hours, the two cells divide to form four cells. At 3 days, the four divide to form eight. All this time the dividing zygote is traveling down the Fallopian tube toward the uterus. By about the fifth day, the original cell has become a hollow ball composed of some 100 cells and is called the *blastocyst.* Certain cells on the outside of the ball are not destined to become part of the developing organism. Instead, they will form the placenta, the umbilical cord, and the lining of the sac in which the fetus will grow. These cells are called the *trophoblast,* from the Greek word *trophos,* meaning "feeder." A small mass of cells attached to the inside of the ball will become the fetus.

Soon the blastocyst enters the uterus and begins to burrow into its lining. If *implantation* proceeds successfully, the blastocyst will be fully buried there by about the ninth day after conception.

At first, the mother's body reacts to implantation as if it were being invaded by foreign tissue—as in a sense it is, because half of the new organism's genes come from the father. Cells in the mother's body that serve as protectors against infection rush to the site of implantation, and the blood supply to the area increases. The trophoblast then begins to function as a primitive placenta, absorbing nourishment for the new organism from this increased blood supply. Soon it secretes hormones into the mother's bloodstream that quiet the alarm reaction and further prepare the uterus for its new tenant. (These hormones are the basis for pregnancy tests; they can usually be found in the urine of a pregnant woman by 5 or 6 weeks after her last menstrual period.)

As the organism becomes implanted, its membranes begin to develop. The inner cell mass detaches itself from the outer ball (except in one place, which will become the umbilical cord) and forms a flat disc, called the *embryonic disc* (see Figure 3-4G). Cell differentiation begins within a week, and the disc is soon made up of two distinct layers of cells. One layer, called the ectoderm, will become the nervous system, skin, hair, and nails. The other layer is the endoderm, from which the digestive tract, respiratory system, and related glands develop. Soon a third layer, the mesoderm, forms between these two; it becomes the muscles, skeleton, and circulatory system. In all animal species, from the simplest to the most complex, the formation of these three layers of cells is the first step in the development of a new individual, and each layer forms the same types of organs in every species. The formation of these three layers is just the beginning of cell differentiation. Although scientists know the form and function of the various kinds of cells that develop during this process, the mechanisms that trigger and control differentiation remain largely a mystery.

The Placenta   The *placenta* is an organ formed partly from the trophoblast and partly from cells in the lining of the uterus. It is a disc-shaped mass of spongy tissue that adheres to the wall of the uterus, with the center of the disc at the site of implantation, and it is connected to the fetus by the **umbilical cord** (Figure 3-5). The placenta has two separate sets of blood vessels, one set going to and from the fetus through the umbilical cord, the other going to and from the mother through arteries and veins supplying the placenta. These two blood systems are entirely separate, but because they are intermeshed in the placenta, the mother's system can supply oxygen and nutrients to the fetus and carry off its wastes and carbon dioxide, which are expelled from the mother's body by her kidneys and lungs. In addition, antibodies that have been manufactured by the mother's immune system in response to disease in her own body can pass through the placenta into the fetus's bloodstream. The fetus can thus receive temporary immunity to some diseases. By 1 or 2 months after birth, these antibodies cease to function and are replaced by antibodies manufactured by the baby's own immune system.

Another important function of the placenta is the screening out of substances potentially harmful to the fetus, as well as most bacteria. Some years ago it was thought that the placenta acted as a barrier to *all* such substances and organisms, but this is now known to be incorrect. As explained later in this chapter, among the harmful substances that can cross the placental barrier and impair the fetus's development are certain viruses and some drugs.

It is also the function of the placenta to produce the hormones that adapt the mother's body to pregnancy and approaching childbirth. These hormones cause her blood supply to increase, prepare her breasts to produce milk, and bring about other significant changes in almost every organ system of her body. After the baby is born, the placenta is expelled from the uterus as the afterbirth, and the production of these hormones ceases (Eichorn 1970).

The Embryonic Period: 2 Weeks to 2 Months

In general, prenatal development begins with the most indispensable body parts and adds the details later (Nilsson et al. 1977). For example, the brain and heart begin to develop very early, during the third week after fertilization, followed quickly by the digestive tract, skeleton, and muscles. Arms and legs appear in the fourth week, and fingers and toes about 2 weeks later. Hair does not appear until the fifth month, and eyelashes and eyebrows not until the sixth month (Guttmacher 1973; Tanner 1970).

The Formation of Body and Organs   The central nervous system (the brain and spinal cord) begins when parallel ridges emerge across the top "plate" (the ectoderm) of the embryonic disc, forming a groove. The edges of the groove join and seal, creating a hollow tube. The front part of the tube thickens and

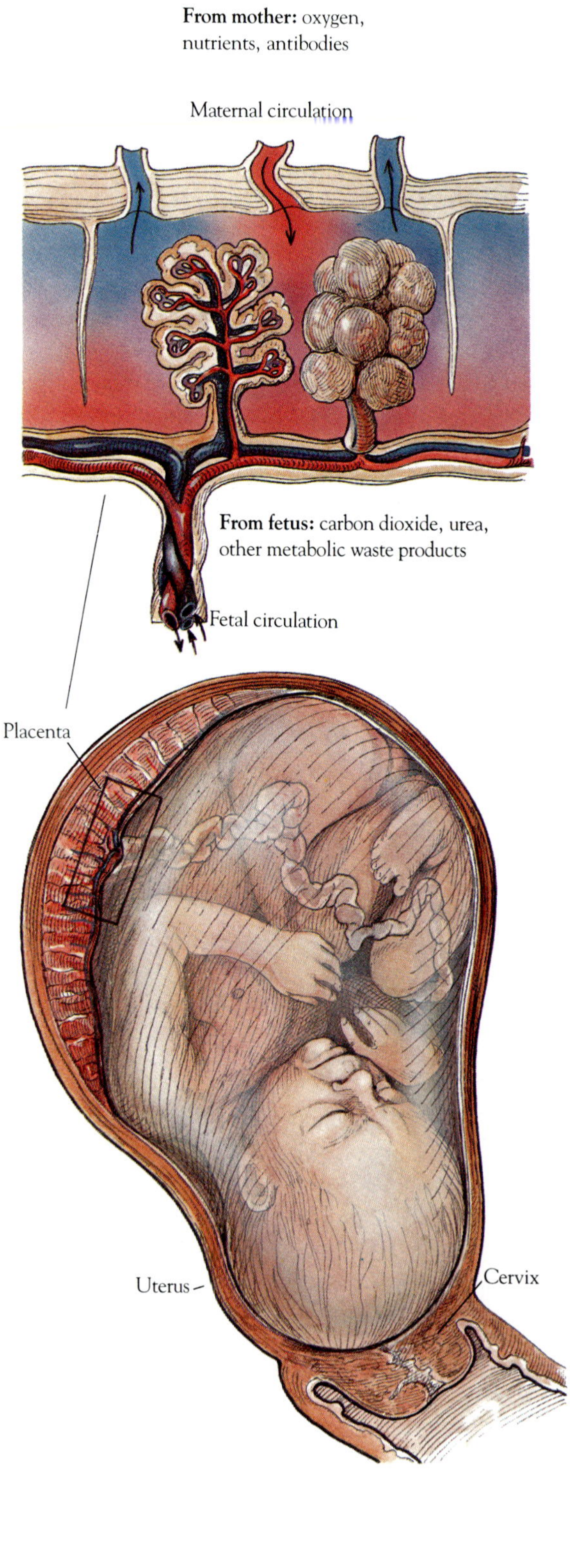

Figure 3-5   The placenta and fetus drawn here are well developed—about 22 weeks prenatal age—in order to show clearly how the placenta functions. The placenta forms a number of compartments, or basins, into which the mother's circulatory system pumps blood, something like a series of upside-down fountains. Her system also drains blood from these basins. Into the basins grow frondlike tissues containing small blood vessels connected to the fetal circulatory system through the umbilical cord. These fronds are bathed in maternal blood but normally the two bloodstreams never mix. Instead, substances diffuse across the frond membranes that divide fetal and maternal blood. Blood containing oxygen and nutrients (red) comes from the maternal circulation, and the fetal circulation picks up these substances. Blood containing wastes (blue) comes from the fetal circulation, and the wastes are passed on to the maternal circulation to discharge.

From mother: oxygen, nutrients, antibodies

Maternal circulation

From fetus: carbon dioxide, urea, other metabolic waste products

Fetal circulation

Placenta

Uterus

Cervix

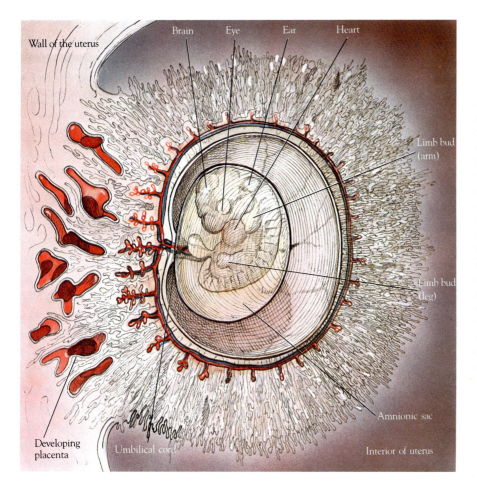

Wall of the uterus

Brain Eye Ear Heart

Limb bud
(arm)

Limb bud
(leg)

Amnionic sac

Developing
placenta

Umbilical cord

Interior of uterus

Figure 3-6 The embryo at four weeks. All the major organs of the body can be seen in a simple form at this time, even though the embryo is only a fifth of an inch long. At this developmental phase, it is difficult to distinguish the embryos of fish, chickens, rabbits, and human beings. Notice that the embryo is surrounded by a thin membrane (the amnion), which contains the amniotic fluid the fetus floats in weightlessly during its prenatal life.

expands to become the brain, while the back part becomes the spinal cord. By the end of the second month, when the embryo has assumed a roughly human shape, it seems to be bent forward by the weight of its head, which accounts for almost half its total length.

The heart likewise starts out as a tube, and begins pulsating immediately. By the end of the first month, though much development is still to come, the heart is a four-chambered vessel that pumps blood through the embryo and primitive placenta. Another organ that begins as a tube is the digestive tract. Near the top of the tube is a pouch, which pushes forward and breaks through to form the mouth. At the end of the first month, rudimentary eyes, ears, nose, jaws, and cheeks begin to appear, giving the face a human look. During the second month, the embryo acquires a liver, gall bladder, and pancreas.

Late in the first month, little flippers called limb buds appear (Figure 3-6). During the next few weeks, these become arms and legs complete with elbows and knees, hands and feet, fingers and toes. By the end of the second month, the embryo has developed a skeleton composed mainly of cartilage, a more flexible material than bone. Before birth, much of the cartilage will be replaced by bone, although bone formation will not be complete until after puberty. The large muscles have also appeared by the end of the second month, and they are attached to the skeleton of cartilage.

At this time the embryo has a tail—a reminder of our animal ancestry—that reaches its greatest length during the second month and disappears before the baby is born. In the neck region can be seen what look like the gill slits of a fish, but these turn out to be rudimentary versions of structures in the neck and face.

The development of the kidneys is an unusual three-stage process that seems to mimic evolutionary trial-and-error. Near the end of the first month, the embryo forms a type of kidney found only in a few very primitive fishes and eels. Within a few days, this kidney disappears and a second, more complicated one develops. This kidney, too, soon vanishes. In the third month a final, even more complex kidney forms and begins to function.

During the second month of life, the embryo has increased approximately four times in length and about fifty times in weight. At the end of this growth spurt, it is about 1 inch long and weighs a little less than an aspirin tablet. The new organism, though by no means finished, is a recognizably human creature complete with all vital organs and most other body parts. Some parts, such as the sex organs, are still in very primitive form; others, such as the heart, are remarkably well developed. The nervous system is well enough developed to show the beginnings of reflex responses, such as an overall startle reaction to touch.

Birth Defects   It is during the embryonic period, when the organism's body parts and vital organs are being formed, that most serious birth defects originate (Kopp & Parmalee 1979). Some developmental abnormalities are the result of genetic or chromosomal errors. For instance, nondisjunction of chromosomes (discussed in Chapter 2) may result in an embryo that lacks a chromosome and therefore also lacks the genes specifying the development of some part of the body. Because of abnormalities in the embryo (or in the placenta), an estimated 30 percent of embryos are spontaneously aborted, usually without the mother's knowledge (Tanner 1970).

It is also during these early weeks that many organs or parts are most vulnerable to harmful environmental agents. The risk of harm is increased by the fact that during most of the embryonic period a woman may not even be aware that she is pregnant. Each organ or part appears to have a *sensitive period,* during which specific substances or events are likely to affect its formation. Both before the sensitive period and after it, these substances or events will not usually alter the normal developmental process.

For example, arms and legs begin to develop late in the first month after conception and are well formed by the end of the second month. The drug thalidomide, a tranquilizer, interferes with the formation of these limbs if taken during the sensitive period of 27 to 40 days after conception. Before this effect was discovered and the drug was removed from the market, many children with ill-formed limbs were born to mothers who had taken the drug during the sensitive period (Taussig 1962). Women who took the drug after the fortieth day of pregnancy bore infants who had normal limbs. The publicity about the thalidomide tragedy helped to focus public awareness on the potential dangers of drugs and other agents during the early months of pregnancy.

The Third Month: The Beginning of the Fetal Period

Most of the fetus's organs are basically formed by the end of the embryonic period and need only to grow and mature. The sex organs, however, form during the third month (Tanner 1978). In the sixth week after fertilization, the embryo develops sex glands (gonads), which initially are the same for both males and females. Early in the third month, one or more genes on the male's Y chromosome triggers the differentiation of his gonads into testes, which secrete the male hormone androgen. The androgen then stimulates the growth of the male external sex organs. The female gonads do not need to produce a hormone, because there is plenty of the female hormone estrogen circulating in the mother's bloodstream. In the absence of androgen, the embryo develops as a female. By the end of the third month, both male and female fetuses are developed well enough that their sex can be identified from their external organs.

During the third month the final kidneys begin to function, although the fetus's waste products are still disposed of through the placenta. The baby teeth originate at this time, as twenty inverted cups. The 3-month fetus can suck and swallow, and its face has become expressive—it can squint, frown, or look surprised. A live fetus born at this time will curl its fingers into a fist when its palm is touched. At the end of the third month, the fetus is between 3 and 4 inches long and weighs a few ounces.

THE SECOND 3 MONTHS

The most dramatic development between the fourth and the fifth month is that the mother feels her baby move for the first time (Guttmacher 1973). This movement, which is sometimes called quickening, occurs fairly consistently at 4½ months and so is sometimes used to check the baby's estimated date of birth. At first the mother experiences only a faint fluttering sensation, but soon the kicks and jabs are strong enough to feel, and later they can be seen on the outside of her abdomen. The fetus not only exercises its limbs but, from time to time, turns from front to back or executes a somersault. These larger movements tend to fade out near the end of pregnancy, when the fetus no longer has much room for them, but fetuses have been known to turn from a breech position (buttocks or feet down) to the usual head-down birth position just a few days before delivery, and sometimes even after labor has begun.

At 2 months, the embryo's body was curled forward in a C shape: it was mostly back, with very little front. In the fourth and fifth months, the neck, abdomen, and pelvic walls build up and the body straightens out. As the abdominal cavity enlarges, the liver, stomach, and other abdominal organs begin to move downward from the chest, where they formed earlier. Some organs, such as the bladder and uterus, do not complete their descent into the pelvic area until after birth. One of the most interesting features of human anatomy is a result of this descent of organs during development. The nerves connecting these organs to the spinal cord also develop high up in the chest. Later, as the body cavities develop and the organs descend into them, the nerves are dragged along with them. Thus, in adults, the nerves to the heart and diaphragm still join the spinal cord in the neck area and wind their way downward to the chest. Likewise, the nerves that connect the intestinal and pelvic organs to the spinal cord join the cord high in the chest cavity.

The eyelids, which remained closed while the eyes were developing, open toward the end of the sixth month. Infants born prematurely at this time react to strong light: Their pupils contract.

Although the fetus gains an impressive amount of weight during the fourth and fifth months, at the end of the sixth month it is still a skinny creature. Its height from crown to rump is about 11 inches, roughly two-thirds of what it will be at birth, but its weight is only about 2 pounds, or less than one-third of the average birth weight. The fetus has only begun to develop a layer of fat. Its skin is wrinkled and so translucent that a cross-hatching of blood vessels can be clearly seen. Its head, back, and shoulders are covered with a blanket of soft, fine hair called lanugo (from the Latin word for "down"), most of which will be lost before birth. It is covered with a greasy, cheeselike substance manufactured by glands in the skin. This covering probably protects the skin from irritation caused by constant contact with the fluid in the amniotic sac.

At 6 months (180 days after fertilization) a fetus usually has *viability:* If born at this time, the infant has at least a small chance of surviving. Although most babies born three months early live for only a few hours, some are sufficiently mature to sustain themselves if supported by the artificial breathing equipment and other facilities of a modern hospital nursery. The critical question seems to be whether the baby's respiratory system and central nervous system (which regulates breathing) are developed well enough to function adequately.

THE FINAL 3 MONTHS

During the seventh and eighth months, the fetus's chances of survival if born early go from near zero to almost 100 percent. The lungs continue to mature, and the capacity of the central nervous system to regulate breathing, swallow-

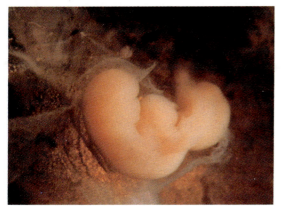

4 Weeks

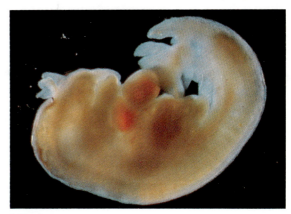

5 Weeks

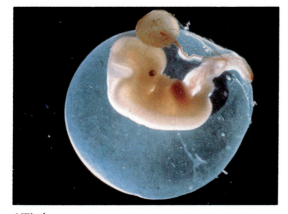

6 Weeks

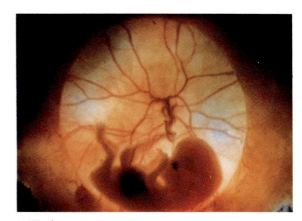

11 Weeks

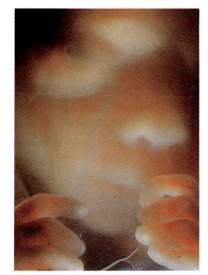

5½ Months

5½ Months

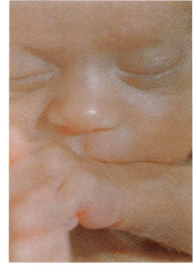

7 Months

TABLE 3-1 GESTATION PERIODS OF VARIOUS SPECIES OF MAMMALS

SPECIES	GESTATION PERIOD (DAYS)	AVERAGE LIFE SPAN (YEARS)
Rat	21	1–3
Wolf	62	10–12
Lion	108	10–15
Macaque	160	25
Gibbon	210	33
Chimpanzee	231	20
Hippopotamus	240	25–30
Gorilla	257	20
Homo sapiens	266	70
Orangutan	270	30
Cow	280	10–15
Horse	336	20–25
Rhinoceros	450	15–20
Elephant	624	30–40

SOURCE: Gould 1977b. Animals in zoos commonly live longer than animals in the wild, and people in modern industrial societies commonly live longer than people in societies with less effective systems of medical care.

ing, and body temperature increases. A layer of fat grows between the skin and muscles, smoothing the skin somewhat, though the baby will still be red and wrinkled at birth.

The fetus gains almost 2 pounds a month, or an ounce a day, during the final three months. Although good nutrition is very important throughout pregnancy, it may be most important in the final months, when some 85 percent of the calcium and iron in the mother's diet is being used to manufacture fetal bones and blood cells (Wallace 1978).

A week or two before labor begins (but sometimes not until it has started), the fetus drops slightly, wedging its head between the bones of the mother's pelvis. At this point the fetus has achieved its final position within the womb. Further twists and turns are very unlikely, though the kicks and pokes continue. The bones of the fetus's skull are not yet fused, and there are six "soft spots" on the head, allowing some compression of the skull during birth.

Because a fetus obtains its oxygen through the placenta, its blood bypasses the lungs and flows directly from the right half of the heart to the left half, through a hole in the partition that bisects the heart. As soon as the baby is born and takes a breath, a flaplike valve closes this hole, forcing the blood to flow through the lungs. During the next 6 to 8 weeks, fibers grow across the hole and seal it permanently.

The length of prenatal development differs greatly among different species (Table 3-1). Most human infants are born about 280 days from the beginning of the mother's last menstrual period, or 266 days from the time of conception. The birth may occur much earlier, or it may be delayed well beyond the due date, although physicians are likely to induce labor if the due date is passed by several weeks. Premature birth is discussed in the section starting on page 139.

BIRTH

The process of birth, called **labor,** is divided into three stages (Figure 3-7) of which the first is the longest and hardest (Guttmacher 1973). Stage 1 begins with mild contractions of the uterus, usually about 15 or 20 minutes apart. No one knows why the contractions start at the moment they do, though some investigators believe that a change in placental hormone production is responsible. The question is important, because identifying the "alarm clock" that makes labor begin might suggest ways of preventing premature births.

As the first stage continues, the contractions get stronger and closer together. Strong muscles near the top of the uterus press the fetus downward against the cervix. Gradually, the cervix dilates until it is 4 inches in diameter, wide enough for the fetus to pass through into the vagina, or birth canal. This stage usually takes some 8 to 16 hours for a first baby and about half that long for later-borns. By the end of Stage 1, the contractions are strong and only a minute or two apart.

The second stage of labor begins when the cervix is fully dilated, allowing the fetus's head to enter the birth canal. During this stage the woman can help by pushing vigorously during contractions, so that her abdominal muscles and diaphragm aid the uterus in propelling the fetus toward the outside world. The second stage may be very fast, only a few minutes, or it may take more than an hour. Sooner or later, the crown of the head becomes visible through the expanding vaginal opening, and with a few more contractions the baby is born.

During the third (and easiest) stage, the contractions continue until the placenta, or afterbirth, is expelled. As soon as the baby is born, the normal hospital routine is to clear the baby's mouth and throat of fluid, cut and tie the umbilical cord, and observe the infant closely to see that regular breathing has begun and that the skin is a good color. A blue or yellow tinge indicates that some system is not functioning correctly. In the United States, the baby's overall condition is measured on the **Apgar scale:** The infant is rated 0, 1, or 2 on color, heart rate, reflex irritability, muscle tone, and breathing (Table 3-2). The maximum score is 10; a score of 4 or less is reason for immediate examination and treatment (Apgar et al. 1953; Self & Horowitz 1979).

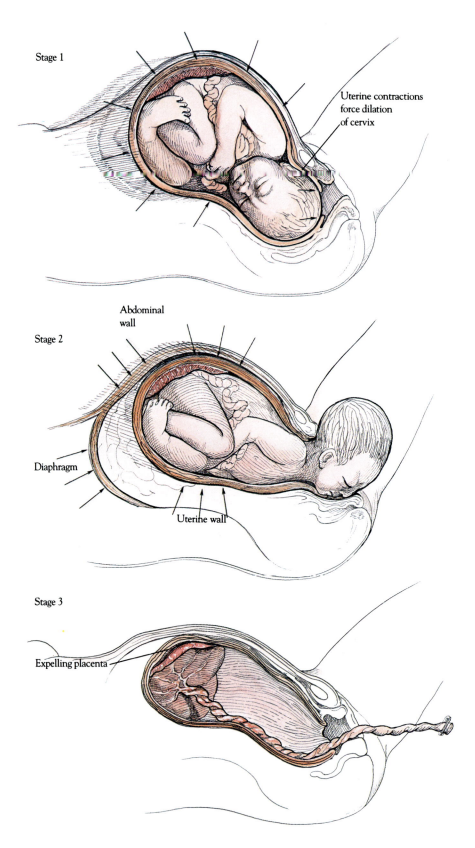

Figure 3-7 The three stages of labor. Stage 1: When labor begins, the uterus begins to contract and exert pressure on the baby, pushing its head against the cervix. This pressure causes the cervix to dilate. During Stage 2 the baby passes through the birth canal. Stage 3 is the expulsion of the placenta, or afterbirth.

Stage 1

Uterine contractions force dilation of cervix

Abdominal wall

Stage 2

Diaphragm

Uterine wall

Stage 3

Expelling placenta

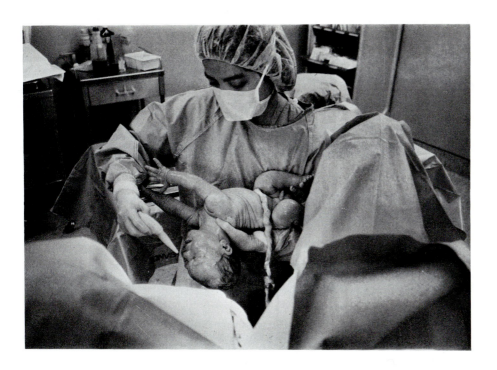

TABLE 3-2 THE APGAR SCALE

SIGN	CRITERION*	SCORE
Heart rate (beats/minute)	100 or more	2
	Less than 100	1
	Not detectable	0
Respiratory effort	Lusty crying and breathing	2
	Any shallowness, irregularity	1
	Not breathing	0
Reflex irritability	Vigorous response to stimulation (e.g., sneezing or coughing to stimulation of nostrils), urination, defecation	2
	Weak response	1
	No response	0
Muscle tone	Resilient, limbs spontaneously flexed and resistant to applied force	2
	Limpness, lack of resistance	1
	Complete flaccidity	0
Skin color	Pink all over	2
	Partially pink	1
	Bluish or yellowish	0

*Observations made at 60 seconds after birth.
SOURCE: Apgar et al. 1953.

Shortly after birth, silver nitrate drops are placed in the baby's eyes to prevent a type of blindness that can result from gonococcus bacteria the mother may be harboring. The baby's footprint is also taken right after birth, to ensure that there are no mix-ups later. Like fingerprints, no two footprints are exactly the same.

Medication during Childbirth

How a woman experiences childbirth depends very much on the culture in which she lives. Some cultures equate childbirth with illness; others look on the process as a healthy one. According to the eminent anthropologist Margaret Mead, having a baby may be "an experience that is dangerous and painful, interesting and engrossing, matter of fact and mildly hazardous, or accompanied by enormous supernatural hazards," depending on what a woman has learned to expect (Mead & Newton 1967). In American society, where most babies are born in hospitals—places people go when they are sick—the equation between illness and childbirth seems to hold.

In most hospital births, the mother is given some kind of medication for relief of pain (Brackbill 1979). Often, a local anesthetic is injected at the base of the spinal cord; this blocks transmission only along the nerves carrying sensation from the legs and abdomen. Other drugs may be given orally—sedatives to reduce anxiety and relax muscles, analgesics to reduce pain, drugs to alter consciousness so that pain is forgotten. Some drugs, such as nitrous oxide, are inhaled. Some inhaled or injected drugs may be used late in labor to induce general anesthesia (complete unconsciousness).

What all these drugs—except local anesthetics—have in common is that they can cross the placental barrier and affect the fetus. Although the amount of medication is closely monitored by physicians and anesthesiologists, most newborns show some effects if their mothers have received heavy medication. There is a significant correlation between the amount of medication the mother receives and the newborn's alertness, muscle tension, and vision. In a number of studies, babies of mothers who had received highly potent drugs, especially anesthetics, functioned less well than other babies in the days immediately after birth. They were not as good at suckling, for example. A few studies suggest that heavy medication of the mother may lower her baby's intelligence slightly throughout the baby's first year and perhaps even into childhood (Brackbill 1979).

The committee on drugs of the American Academy of Pediatrics has recommended that medication during childbirth be kept to a minimum. In some other industrialized countries, medication is given in very few births. In the Netherlands, for example, drugs are given for pain in only 5 percent of deliveries, and in Sweden, in only 12 percent (Macfarlane 1977).

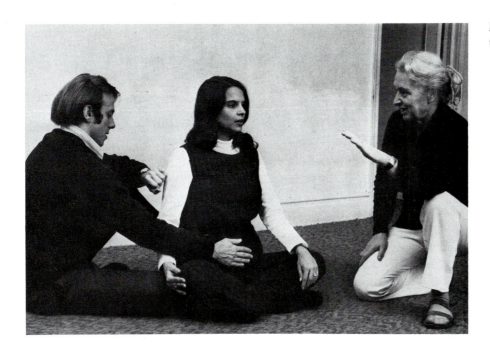

Figure 3-8 A Lamaze
training class.

Natural Childbirth

Growing numbers of people in the United States wish to make childbirth a less
frightening and painful process. Some believe that properly prepared mothers
who have experienced no complications during pregnancy can often do without
medication and deliver their children with minimal discomfort. Preparation for
such **natural childbirth** includes both psychological and physical training. The
term "natural childbirth" was brought into use in the 1930s by Grantly Dick-
Read, a British physician. He said that difficulty in labor arises, in most cases,
because of a woman's fear and tension, which cause resistance to the work being
done by the muscles of the uterus. He advocated preparing for childbirth by
training in breathing and relaxation.

   A similar technique is employed in the widely used Lamaze method of natural
childbirth, which is based on principles of classical conditioning (see the theory
inset "Conditioning and Learning," in Chapter 4). According to its originator,
Dr. Fernand Lamaze (1970), "The anticipation of pain is a conditioned emotion
that education has turned into fear." The Lamaze method is aimed at replacing
these conditioned fears with new conditioned reflexes that facilitate the birth
process. Because the mother has learned techniques for participating actively
in childbirth, she focuses on using those techniques instead of on her fears.

Training before labor and control during it, say the advocates of natural childbirth, take much of the pain out of giving birth. Expectant mothers who receive Lamaze training learn all about the physical process of birth. They do exercises to firm the pelvic floor muscles and to give the hip and knee joints greater flexibility. They learn to relax deeply, to coordinate their breathing with the intensity of their contractions, and to push effectively after the cervix has dilated. Fathers participate in the training and are expected to be present during labor and delivery to help the mother with her breathing and relaxation techniques and to give support and affection. This makes the father an active partner in his child's birth.

Lamaze and Dick-Read agree that childbirth should take place under medical supervision and that pain-relieving medication should be given for difficult births. Advocates of natural childbirth say that when prepared women request medication at all, they usually do so late in labor, so the total amount administered is small. They also claim that an unmedicated labor tends to be shorter and that the combination of less medication and shorter labor produces healthier newborns.

Although natural childbirth has received many testimonials from those who have used it (Elkins 1976; Tanzer & Block 1972), there have been virtually no controlled studies of its effects. One of its advocates in the United States, Colorado physician Robert Bradley (1965), recommends that women enlist the assistance of the force of gravity by delivering their babies in a squatting position, with their husbands supporting their backs. Dr. Bradley has claimed that of the tens of thousands of American women who have had their babies by his method, more than 95 percent required no drugs (*Newsweek* 1976).

Many hospitals now give training in natural childbirth, and some are trying to do away with the traditional hospital atmosphere in their maternity wards to make them more comfortable and homelike. Many now accept the father's presence in the delivery room as well as the labor room.

In the Netherlands, a substantial number of deliveries occur in the home. Obstetric practice in that country divides expectant mothers into two groups: those who appear likely to have a trouble-free delivery and those who show any signs that they will have difficulty during childbirth. Women in the first group routinely have their children at home, in the care of a midwife or a general practitioner with training in obstetrics. Women in the second group give birth in hospitals, attended by medical specialists (Macfarlane 1977).

Some people, both parents and professionals, wish to see home delivery become an accepted practice in the United States. However, most American obstetricians strongly discourage home births. Unexpected complications can occur at any time, they say, and the sophisticated equipment of a delivery room ensures that these emergencies can be dealt with promptly and efficiently. A number of recently developed instruments and techniques have helped lower the newborn mortality rate in this country from 20.7 deaths per 1000 births in

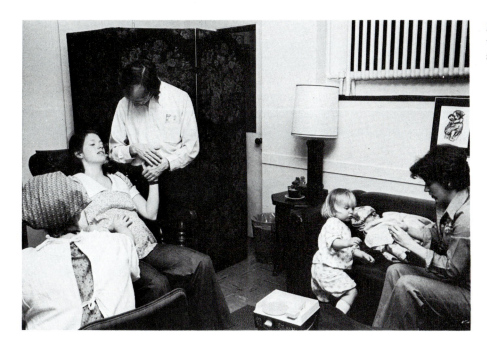

Figure 3-9   A maternity ward with a homelike atmosphere.

1969 to 13.0 in 1979 (United States Bureau of the Census 1980). A device that uses sound waves can show the exact position of the fetus, umbilical cord, and placenta before and during labor, and it does not entail the substantial health risks of other methods, such as x ray. Electronic monitors attached to the mother's abdomen during labor can continuously report fetal heart rate and activity level.

If there are signs of serious fetal distress, if labor is not progressing satisfactorily, or if the fetus seems unable to pass easily through the birth canal, the infant can be delivered immediately by cesarean section. In cesarean births, the baby is removed through an incision in the wall of the abdomen and uterus. (The procedure is named after the Roman emperor Julius Caesar, who was born in this way.) Partly as a result of the use of fetal monitors, the number of cesarean sections performed in the United States rose nearly three-fold in the 1970s, from 5.5 percent in 1970 to 15.2 percent in 1978, and in some large teaching hospitals the rate is now 25 percent (National Institute of Health Consensus Development Summary 1981). Part of the reason for the increase is that more than 98 percent of women who have had one baby by this method have subsequent cesarean deliveries.

Some studies indicate that the increase in cesarean sections has led to a decrease in certain types of birth defects, such as severe cerebral palsy, which is typically caused by brain damage during the birth process. Some physicians argue, however, that the large increase in the use of this surgical procedure is not justified (Guillemin 1981). More data are needed for resolution of this medical controversy.

Whether to undergo natural childbirth and where delivery should take place must be decided by individual couples, with advice from the doctor who has provided prenatal care. Many publications are available that give details and goals of training for natural childbirth, and some present arguments for and against home delivery. Prospective parents should feel free to inquire about the facilities and routines of the hospital maternity ward they are considering. They might also ask whether medication is administered routinely or only upon request, whether natural childbirth classes are available, whether fathers are welcome in labor and delivery rooms, and what procedures are followed after the baby is born.

The First Hours and Days

It used to be standard delivery-room procedure to give the mother a quick look at the newborn and then whisk the baby away to a nursery. Thereafter, the baby was brought to the mother only for feeding every four hours during the day. Although this procedure is still common, many hospitals now offer the option of rooming-in: If the mother wishes, her baby stays in her room or the next one so that she can see and care for the child whenever she likes. Still, even in hospitals that allow rooming-in, mother and newborn are usually separated for a time just after birth. Hospital procedures that call for such a separation have been criticized by some physicians and psychologists.

One French physician, Frederick Leboyer, believes that immediately after birth, even before the umbilical cord is cut, the baby should be placed on the mother's abdomen, where she can massage and comfort it. Leboyer (1975) advocates and practices what he calls "birth without violence." He believes that the passage from the uterus into the world, harsh in itself, is made traumatic by the bright lights, noise, and rough handling in the delivery room. Babies that he delivers are given contact with the mother immediately, until the umbilical cord stops pulsating. After the cord is cut, the baby is gently bathed in warm water for a few minutes, so that the transition from prenatal to postnatal environment is not so abrupt. The lights in the delivery room are dim, and noise is kept to a minimum.

Leboyer's methods have received acclaim from some quarters. Many parents whose babies were delivered according to his recommendations reported that their children showed fewer difficulties with eating and sleeping and were more socially responsive than other babies (Englund 1974). As with natural child-birth techniques, there are no controlled studies that can support or disprove such claims. Many physicians say that Leboyer's methods are unnecessary, even dangerous. They insist, for example, that bright lights are required in the delivery room in order to assess the newborn's skin color. Leboyer's critics also point out that taking the newborn from a warm bath into the air of the delivery room right after birth doubly upsets the baby's temperature-control mechanisms. There are also claims that some newborns stop breathing when they are bathed in warm water, responding as if they have returned to the womb.

Another change in hospital procedures has been effected by the report of a phenomenon called bonding. Several American pediatricians have argued that mother-infant contact soon after birth and during the first few days is important for establishing a bond of affection between the mother and her child (Klaus & Kennell 1976). In one study, some mothers were given their naked babies to hold and caress immediately after they had left the delivery room, while other mothers were separated from their newborns. The babies in both groups were then sent to the newborn nursery for 12 hours. When the babies were brought to their mothers for their first feeding, observers noted that the mothers who had had the early contact spent more time fondling and kissing their babies and gazing into their faces (Klaus & Kennell 1978). In other studies, mothers who had had early and extended contact during the first days after birth showed more positive maternal behavior when the children were a year old than did mothers who had not had such contact (Kennell et al. 1974).

There have been serious doubts about these findings, however. Some researchers have questioned the adequacy of the original studies of bonding, and attempts to replicate the results have generally not been successful (Carlsson et al. 1979; Svejda et al. 1980, 1982). If separation immediately after birth does have a substantial effect on the mother's relation to her infant, it is probably limited to high-risk mothers, that is, those who have gone through an unwanted pregnancy or who, for some other reason, are ambivalent or anxious about their new role as a mother.

Even though the studies on bonding may have been inadequate, they have had a humanizing effect on the policies of many hospitals throughout the United States. Procedures have been changed so that mothers can hold their babies immediately after birth and spend a considerable amount of time with them in the hospital. When infants must be kept in the hospital for weeks or months because they require special medical care, efforts are mde to help the mothers (and the fathers) see their babies often and develop a relationship despite this forced separation. Babies who are born considerably before term or who weigh very little at birth often require such prolonged hospital care.

PREMATURITY

The designation "premature" has recently been dropped from scientific use because it does not distinguish between early birth and retarded prenatal growth

(Kopp & Parmalee 1979). Instead, babies who are born after a shorter-than-usual period in the uterus are now called **short-gestation** infants, whereas those who weigh less than 5½ pounds after a normal gestation period are called **low-birth-weight** babies. The distinction between the two types is important because they may require different treatment after birth and also because the prognosis for their later development is different. It is clear now that a somewhat shorter-than-normal period of gestation is not necessarily harmful, whereas retarded prenatal growth implies that something has been wrong with the fetus, the placenta, or the mother's health (Kopp 1983).

The nervous system of short-gestation infants continues to mature after birth at about the same rate as if they were still developing in the womb. An infant born at 28 weeks will show, some 6 weeks later, the same general neurological maturity that an infant born at 34 weeks demonstrates at birth (Dreyfus-Brisac 1966; Minkowski 1966).

Low-birth-weight babies may simply be small babies born to genetically small parents. Also, twins and triplets are often much smaller than average at birth. These babies typically grow faster than other babies during the first 2 years, so they catch up somewhat. However, most will be smaller-than-average 5-year-olds—and probably smaller adults as well. Furthermore, for low-birth-weight babies, the lighter the baby, the less are its chances for survival. The survival rate of infants between 2½ and 3½ pounds has improved greatly in the past decade. In the late 1960s, mortality in this group was about 35 percent; in the late 1970s, it was about 15 percent. Babies born weighing less than 2½ pounds have only about a 50 percent chance of survival (Fanaroff & Martin 1983). For low-birth-weight babies who survive, there is a strong relation between birth weight and the likelihood of impairment later in life (Tanner 1970). Babies who weigh at least 4½ pounds at birth show only a slight size deficit later in life and almost no other kind of impairment that can be related to their birth weight. Babies weighing less than 3 pounds, however, often suffer some later developmental difficulty. A study conducted at a university hospital in Cleveland followed a group of low-birth-weight babies until their second birthday, when they were tested for developmental status. Of 90 babies born weighing less than 3 pounds, 54 had died. Of the 32 survivors tested (4 could not be tested), 7 (22 percent) showed some motor or sensory abnormality (Hack et al. 1979).

Anoxia—the lack of oxygen during and shortly after birth—occurs most often in short-gestation and low-birth-weight infants and has been implicated as a cause of later retardation. Anoxia can also occur in normal-weight and normal-term babies. For example, if the umbilical cord becomes compressed during the infant's passage through the birth canal, the supply of oxygen-rich blood from the mother may be either cut off or severely reduced. With short-gestation and low-birth-weight infants, the anoxia more often occurs after birth because the infant's respiratory system is not well enough developed to initiate and regulate breathing.

Birth-related anoxia has long been thought to cause brain damage, ranging from minor to severe. Early studies, which identified retarded children and adults and then tried to trace their birth histories, seemed to show that the retardation was often caused by anoxia at birth (Schreiber 1939). Later studies of children who were known to have suffered anoxia during birth also showed intellectual deficits (Benaron et al. 1960). One longitudinal study, for example, followed hundreds of newborns and found that anoxic newborns were impaired for several years after birth (Corah et al. 1965). At age 3, they scored lower than a control group of normal-birth children on all tests of cognitive functioning. By age 7, however, almost all the differences between the anoxic and normal-birth groups had disappeared. The 7-year-olds were tested with 21 measures of intellectual and perceptual functioning, and the anoxic group scored lower on only one vocabulary and one perceptual task.

Physicians and psychologists are moving toward the view that in many cases anoxia is a symptom rather than a cause of brain damage (Amiel-Tison 1982). That is, the brain damage may exist prenatally, with anoxia merely being the first postnatal expression of it. The brain may simply be unable to control breathing properly. Such a malfunction might have a genetic cause, or it might result from a complication of pregnancy that deprived the fetus of sufficient oxygen over a long period of time—a malfunction in the placenta, perhaps.

In the case of short-gestation and low-birth-weight infants, however, it is usually immaturity that causes postnatal breathing difficulties. In well-equipped hospitals, oxygen is quickly supplied to babies in trouble, and it appears that a few minutes of oxygen deprivation at birth (before extra oxygen is supplied) does not necessarily cause serious or lifelong developmental difficulties (Sameroff 1975).

Middle-class children who had low birth weights seem to make up early deficits more fully than children from less privileged homes. In one study, few low-birth-weight children from middle-class homes were retarded at 5 to 7 years of age, although some whose birth weight had been less than 3½ pounds were retarded. Among children of similarly low birth weights from lower-class homes, however, there was a "marked excess of retarded and very dull children" (Drillien 1964). Other studies have also found that the environment plays a large part in minimizing difficulties stemming from early birth or low birth weight (Kopp & Parmalee 1979). Indeed, middle-class children seem to have a major advantage in recovery from a wide range of potentially harmful circumstances (Kagan 1982; Sameroff et al. 1982).

Early developmental difficulties, such as anoxia, short gestation, or low birth weight, then, are not necessarily predictive of later physical or psychological problems. One large study reported on all children born on the Hawaiian island of Kauai in 1955. All kinds of birth complications, including short gestation

Figure 3-10   Newborns in trouble because of low birth weight, short gestation period, or some other problem can be kept alive and treated in modern hospital newborn centers equipped like this. Temperature and oxygen flow are controlled and the babies' vital signs are monitored. Signals alert nurses and doctors to any problems. Some babies need to spend only a few days under such close scrutiny, others may need such attention for months.

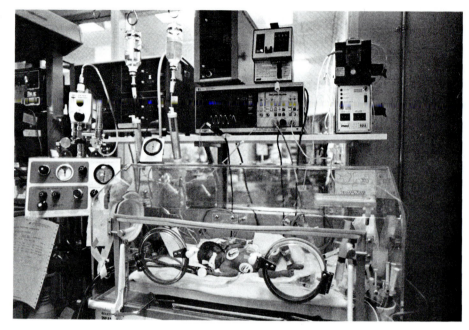

and low birth weight, were noted, and the children were followed through age 10 (Werner et al. 1971). The investigators found that although 34 percent of the children born that year were having problems at age 10, only a small proportion of the problems could be attributed to birth complications. They concluded that "ten times more children had problems related to the effects of poor environment than to the effects of perinatal [birth-related] stress."

The first external environment of many short-gestation and low-birth-weight infants is an incubator, a criblike apparatus in which the baby is protected from infection, kept warm, and monitored in various ways. The use of incubators has raised the survival rate of these infants considerably in recent decades (Stewart & Reynolds 1974).

A problem with incubators, however, is that they separate infants from their parents, often for many weeks, and the separation may make the formation of early affective bonds difficult. Fortunately, studies of babies who were separated from their mothers for several weeks suggest that attachment difficulties caused by the separation are usually temporary. These studies found some differences between separated and nonseparated mother-infant pairs for the first few months that the baby was at home. The separated mothers and babies spent less time gazing and smiling at each other, the babies cried more, and the mothers caressed and cuddled the babies less (Seashore et al. 1973; Whiten 1975). But by the time the babies were 1 year old, the effects of the early separation were no longer evident. It may have been that the effects detected earlier resulted partly from the mother's fear of handling this seemingly frail and vulnerable child.

THE MOTHER'S CHARACTERISTICS AND EXPERIENCES

In 1978, about 7.1 percent of all live births in the United States were of children weighing less than 5½ pounds. The percentage is about twice as high among nonwhites as it is among whites (United States Bureau of the Census 1980), and it is higher for younger teenagers and for poor people than for the middle and upper classes (Ricciuti 1976). The chief reason for such statistics is that many of these women do not have the same kind of care and diet during pregnancy that women of the middle and upper classes have. The effects of poor nutrition and lack of prenatal care are most evident in impoverished countries, where as many as 40 percent of all newborns are undersize (Chavez et al. 1974).

Besides diet and prenatal care, there are a number of maternal experiences and characteristics, unrelated to poverty or social class. that can affect prenatal development (Kopp 1983; Kopp & Parmalee 1979). Smoking, maternal stress, certain drugs, radiation above a certain level, and some diseases all appear to have the potential for interfering with normal development.

Nutrition and Malnutrition

The developing fetus gets all its nourishment from its mother. If the mother's diet is deficient in certain important nutrients, the fetus may be able to obtain them from some substances that are stored in the mother's body tissues. For example, the needs of the developing fetus can "demand" the release of calories stored as body fat or calcium from her bones. (In fact, changes in the mother's body during pregnancy allow her to absorb calcium from foods much more easily than when she is not pregnant.) Certain nutrients, therefore, are required in particularly large amounts to meet the demands of both fetus and mother. These are the minerals calcium and iron and certain vitamins, such as folic acid and vitamin B_6. The mother should also increase her intake of protein (by about 30 grams) because otherwise the fetus will break down the mother's muscle tissue to supply itself (Winick 1981).

Severe **malnutrition** is damaging to mother and fetus alike. Studies of babies conceived and born during World War II show that, under famine conditions, there is an increase in the number of stillbirths and short-gestation and low-birth-weight babies. A study of Dutch babies born during famine conditions found that they were much smaller than babies born before or after the famine. Infants whose mothers were severely undernourished during the last three months of pregnancy were the smallest (Stein et al. 1975). Another study showed that many Russian women who withstood the German siege of Lenin-grad in 1942 were so malnourished that they stopped ovulating. Of those who

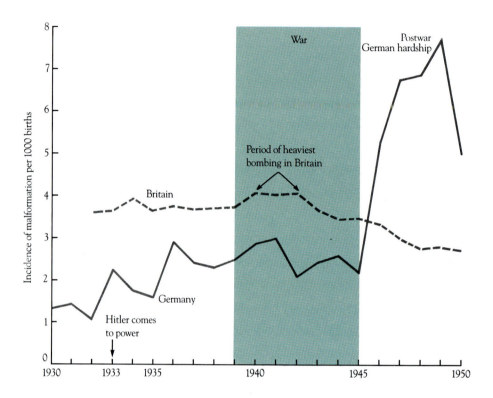

Figure 3-11   Can stress during pregnancy increase the likelihood that a child will be malformed? The data presented here comparing malformation rates in Britain and Germany during the World War II period suggest that stress may be implicated. (The German data arc for malformations per 1000 births; the British data report neonatal deaths from malformation per 1000 live births.) But the many interpretations possible for these data show why it is so difficult to gain reliable knowledge about this subject. Did the number of malformed babies in German hospitals show a sharp rise after the war because of the psychological shock of defeat and ruin or because of malnutrition and poor medical care in the aftermath of defeat? The fact that malformations began to rise as soon as Hitler came to power suggests that psychological factors may have played an important role. Did the increased rate of malformations in Britain during the heavy bombing reflect psychological stress or only physical factors, such as overwork, lack of heat, and irregular sleeping patterns? No one knows for certain (Stott 1969).

did get pregnant, 41 percent gave birth well before term, and 31 percent of these short-gestation infants died soon after birth (Antonov 1947).

In contrast, women who became pregnant in England during World War II were given special, highly nutritional rations. For many of these women, this diet was better than their prewar diet. Consequently, the stillbirth rate fell about 25 percent from prewar levels (Stott 1969). Figure 3-11 compares these English women with German women during the same war years.

Malnutrition probably also has some negative effects on the development of the fetal brain, although these may be reversible after birth. In studies of rats, severe maternal malnutrition produced offspring with a reduced number of brain cells at birth and poor problem-solving abilities later in life (Winick 1974). A number of psychologists believe that maternal malnutrition has similar effects on human children (Vore 1970; Winick 1976), but unequivocal scientific findings about human beings are difficult to obtain because most malnourished children are also deprived in other ways. A study of the young men born in Holland during the World War II famine showed no detectable physical or intellectual differences between them and other young Dutch men (who had not been malnourished) when tested for army entrance at age 19 (Stein et al. 1972).

Even though a supportive environment after birth sometimes can erase the behavioral traces of developmental damage caused by prenatal malnutrition, it seems that both mother and fetus will benefit from a good, well-balanced diet during pregnancy. According to the U.S. Department of Health, Education, and Welfare (1981), the daily diet should include:

four servings of milk and dairy products

two or more servings of meat, poultry, fish, or eggs

four or more servings of vegetables and fruit, including at least one fruit high in vitamin C, one green leafy vegetable, and one yellow vegetable

four or more servings of bread or cereal products

A pregnant woman should consume about 2200 calories every day. For most women, this should be between 300 and 500 calories more than they took in before, and they should gain about 25 pounds during the course of pregnancy (National Research Council 1981; Winick 1981). Doctors used to restrict women to a weight gain of only 10 to 15 pounds, until research showed that taking this advice tended to result in low-birth-weight babies.

Maternal Stress

Folklore and popular literature are full of anecdotes that relate maternal emotion to the state of the fetus or its development. In the Bible, Elisabeth says, "For, lo, as soon as the voice of thy salutation sounded in mine ears, the babe leaped in my womb for joy" (Luke 1:44). Although a mother's passing emotional states probably do not affect fetal development, prolonged **maternal stress** or continuing anxiety may have some ill effects.

Research into the effects of maternal stress is difficult to carry out. Obviously, pregnant women cannot be subjected to prolonged anxiety in order to examine its effects on the developing fetus. Stress-inducing circumstances such as war offer natural opportunities for research, but the results must be qualified by the fact that the emotional stress of war-time conditions is almost always accompanied by physical stress of some kind—malnutrition, extreme cold, enforced labor, even physical punishment. One study found that among children born to Jewish women who had become pregnant while in concentration camps, the incidence of malformation was far above the norm. For example, the incidence of Down's syndrome was reported to be 1 in 35 in those women who were under 30 compared to the norm of 1 in 650 found in other European populations (Klebanov 1948). But these women had been subjected to extreme physical abuse as well as unrelenting psychological stress, and there is no way to know whether their infants' abnormalities resulted from psychological or physical stress.

The mechanism by which maternal stress is presumed to affect the fetus is a chemical one. Strong emotion is accompanied by changes in the mother's endocrine system, including the release of powerful hormones from the adrenal glands. These hormones can cross over the placental barrier and enter the fetus's bloodstream (Thompson & Grusec 1970).

One longitudinal investigation that studied women closely during pregnancy found that when the women were undergoing emotional disturbances, the fetus markedly increased its body movements (Sontag 1941, 1944). The researchers conjectured that babies of women who experience long periods of stress may be much more active before birth and thus use up more energy and gain less weight. This hypothesis would help to explain the researcher's findings that babies of mothers who reported prolonged psychological stress weighed less at birth than other babies. These babies also seemed to be more irritable and they had more feeding difficulties. Their crankiness could also have had other causes, however, including the mother's emotional state after giving birth (Sameroff et al. 1983).

Smoking

Researchers suspect that a pregnant woman's smoking may be harmful to the developing fetus in a number of ways, and so far they have documented one major effect: Babies born to women who smoke during pregnancy are, on the average, almost half a pound lighter than babies born to women who do not smoke. The more the mother smokes, the less the baby's birth weight. More than fifty different studies in the past 20 years have confirmed this correlation (National Research Council 1982; United States Department of Health, Education, and Welfare 1979).

Some researchers have suggested that the psychological makeup of smokers may itself be a cause of both the smoking and the low birth weight of the babies. One study found that women who did not smoke while pregnant but who began to smoke afterward had babies as underweight as the babies of those who had smoked throughout pregnancy (Yerushalmy 1972). It is not yet possible to determine whether it is smoking itself or some characteristic of the smoker that leads to the reduction in birth weight (Silverman 1977).

A number of investigators have searched for differences between the offspring of smoking mothers and those of nonsmokers in fetal and infant mortality rate. These studies have produced inconsistent results, largely because it is difficult to separate the effects of smoking from the effects of other crucial factors, such as the mother's age, social class, and history of previous pregnancies and births.

Some studies have used sophisticated statistical methods to analyze relations between smoking and other variables. In one, women who were light smokers (less than a pack a day) and who were also young and healthy, with no history of previous pregnancy problems, showed a fairly small increase in the risk of their infants' dying—10 percent more than that for comparable nonsmokers (Meyer et al. 1975). At the other extreme, women who had already had problem pregnancies and births, who were anemic, who were poor, and who were also heavy smokers had an increase in risk of 70 to 100 percent. When further statistical analysis was used to separate the effects of smoking from those of the other factors, the researchers concluded that light smoking increased the risk of fetal and newborn mortality by 20 percent, and heavy smoking by 35 percent (Meyer et al. 1976). If a baby survives the newborn period, however, the effects of the mother's smoking during pregnancy do not seem to last. In one recent study, for instance, 10-year-old children of smoking and nonsmoking mothers showed no differences in physical development, intelligence, school performance, self-esteem, and a host of other psychological characteristics (Lefkowitz 1981). For the mother herself, smoking poses enormous health risks. Heavy smokers can expect to live, on average, 10 or 15 years less than nonsmokers.

Drugs and Environmental Chemicals

Almost all drugs can cross the placenta and enter the circulatory system of the fetus. Fortunately, most appear to produce no gross abnormalities in fetal development. One investigation of more than 3000 women first separated the subjects into two groups—those who had borne children with some developmental defect (8.4 percent) and those whose newborns had been normal. Then the number and types of drugs taken by the two groups during the first 3 months of pregnancy were compared. It was found that the groups did not differ in any significant way with regard to the drugs they had consumed, so the cause of any developmental defects was apparently something other than drugs (Mellin 1964).

In fact, only 2 or 3 percent of developmental defects are estimated to be caused by drugs and environmental chemicals. Most of the drugs currently *known* to be harmful to the developing fetus are those used to treat serious or chronic illnesses, such as cancer. Other, more common drugs *suspected* of causing damage include certain amphetamine compounds used as appetite suppressants or as stimulants (Wilson 1973).

It is usually not easy for drug researchers to connect cause and effect with any certainty. A pregnant woman may come into contact with many potentially hazardous substances, including viruses, environmental pollutants, and food additives as well as various drugs, thus making it hard to identify the exact source of a given problem (Bowes 1970). Although controlled experiments on drug effects can be conducted with animals, their results are not conclusive for human beings. Some drugs affect the prenatal development of test animals but have no ill effects on humans, whereas other drugs have no effect on animals but are damaging to humans. Thalidomide, a drug now known to be extremely damaging to human embryos, had no ill effects on the test animals who were exposed to it.

Thalidomide was a popular tranquilizer that was used during the 1950s and 1960s in many European countries to prevent nausea in pregnant women. It was sold without prescription. Taken between the fourth and sixth weeks of pregnancy, however, the drug not only arrested the development of arms and legs but, in some children, damaged heart and blood vessels, ears, and the digestive tract. Some mothers of affected children reported having taken the drug for only a few days, or even on just one day (Taussig 1962).

Before the effects of thalidomide became evident, its use had spread throughout Europe and then to Canada, South America, the Near East, and Japan. In the United States, Frances Kelsey, a physician employed by the Food and Drug Administration, repeatedly refused applications to allow the manufacture and distribution of the drug until she had convincing evidence of its safety. The drug was never sold in the United States.

Another drug appeared to be perfectly safe for human beings until 15 years after it began to be used. In the 1950s and 1960s, DES (diethylstilbestrol), a synthetic hormone related to the natural female hormone estrogen, was used extensively to treat problems of pregnancy—cramps, bleeding, threatened miscarriage. But in the 1970s and 1980s some adolescent girls and young women whose mothers had been treated with DES developed vaginal cancer. Because of such experiences, physicians are generally very cautious about prescribing or recommending drugs during pregnancy, and no pregnant women should take any drug—even ordinary cold remedies—without checking first with her physician.

Some nonmedical drugs—heroin and other narcotics—do not cause physical malformations but have other serious effects. The baby of a heroin addict is born addicted to the drug its mother takes. Right after birth, the baby begins to undergo withdrawal symptoms. It suffers breathing difficulties and intestinal troubles, sometimes accompanied by fever and convulsions. The severity of the withdrawal symptoms depends on how long the mother has been using heroin, how much of it she usually takes, and how soon before the baby's birth she had her last "fix." If a severely addicted baby is not treated right away, it may die. Doctors are usually able to recognize the problem in time to treat the baby's symptoms successfully.

Alcohol in small amounts does not appear to produce developmental abnormalities in a fetus, but it does increase the risk of spontaneous abortion, especially during the fourth, fifth, and sixth months of pregnancy. Even one drink a day, taken regularly, appears to increase the risk of miscarriage (Harlap & Shiono 1980; Kline et al. 1980). A mother's heavy consumption of alcohol definitely puts the fetus at risk. One large study of fetal effects arising from alcohol consumption defined heavy drinking as consumption of five or more drinks on some occasions, amounting to at least 45 drinks a month. Moderate drinking was fewer than 45 drinks a month, but drinking more than once a month. Light drinking was consuming alcohol less than once a month and never having five drinks on one occasion. A drink refers to the usual serving of beer, wine, or liquor, because all contain approximately the same amount of alcohol (Oullette et al. 1977). Babies born to women who drink heavily may undergo delirium tremens after birth—shaking, vomiting, and extreme irritability—caused by the babies' withdrawal from alcohol addiction. Also, several studies have found a number of abnormalities in children of chronic heavy drinkers, ranging from low birth weight to fetal alcohol syndrome, a rare clinical entity that includes retarded growth, central nervous system problems, and facial abnormalities (flattened jaw, thin upper lip, small eyes) (Ashley 1981; Sokol 1981).

Some chemicals present in the environment can also be harmful to the developing fetus. Lead circulating in a pregnant woman's blood can cross the placenta and cause her unborn child to be mentally retarded (Needleman 1973; Scanlon & Chisolm 1972). Some industrial chemicals that pregnant women may be exposed to in their work environment are also suspected of being hazardous to the fetus. Some that have been implicated are vinyl chloride, formaldehyde, asbestos, naphtha, and benzene (American College of Obstetrics and Gynecology 1977).

Radiation

After the atomic bombing of Hiroshima and Nagasaki that ended World War II, many pregnant women who had been within 1½ miles of the blast sites suffered miscarriages and stillbirths. Many others bore infants who had deformities or leukemia (Murphy 1947). Subsequent studies have shown that the organ most likely to be affected by radiation is the central nervous system.

An embryo or fetus can be damaged by a much lower level of radiation than an adult. In addition, the effects of radiation are cumulative; that is, they build up in the body over the years. Dental examinations and other diagnostic x rays, however, deliver only a small amount of radiation, so a woman whose doctor orders an x ray of an aching tooth or a broken bone need not worry that her child will be hurt (though she should be sure that the physician or dentist knows she is or may be pregnant). Radium or x-ray treatments, such as those given for some cancers, are another matter because the doses are much larger and so may have a high probability of producing physical abnormalities.

Disease

As stated earlier, the placenta acts as a barrier that prevents many disease-causing organisms from reaching the developing child. Most bacteria that cause disease in the mother cannot pass through the placenta, but a number of viruses, which are much smaller than bacteria, can.

By far the most dangerous viral disease for a woman to contract during the early months of pregnancy is rubella, or German measles. Depending on exactly *when* the mother has the disease (which is mild for her, entailing only a few days of minor discomfort), it can cause blindness, deafness, mental retardation, heart malformations, and other serious problems in the unborn child. The danger seems to be greatest very early in the pregnancy. One study showed that 47 percent of babies born to mothers who had rubella in the first month of pregnancy suffered one or more such defects; in the second month, 22 percent were affected; in the third month, 7 percent (Michaels & Mellin 1960).

A vaccine for rubella exists, but it cannot be administered to women who are already pregnant because it is made from live virus. A simple blood test will show whether rubella antibodies are present in a person's blood, indicating that she has had rubella and is therefore already immune. It would be best for all children to be given the vaccine, but, because they are not, any female old enough to become pregnant should have this blood test, and if she does not already have antibodies, she should request the vaccine as long as she is certain that she is not pregnant.

One bacterial disease that *can* cross the placenta is syphilis. If the disease in the mother is untreated, there is an 80 percent chance that the fetus will be infected, and the infection can cause stillbirth or premature birth, infant death, or deformities (Dwyer 1976). Syphilis detected in a pregnant woman can be cured with large doses of penicillin, an antibiotic that crosses the placenta and also eliminates the disease in the fetus.

Recently, there has been a great deal of interest in another widespread venereal disease, genital herpes. Herpes is a virus infection and has therefore been more difficult to treat than the bacterial infections (viruses are not affected by antibiotics). Very little has been published about the effect of a mother's herpes infection on the fetus. In most cases, the mother's herpes infection is localized in the genital area and, in fact, may be "silent," with no outward evidence of infection. However, in some cases it may spread to other parts of the body, especially the liver. Early studies showed that newborn infants who contracted the herpes infection, presumably from their mothers during birth, were in danger of death or neurological damage (Nahmias et al. 1975). Babies born to mothers whose infection had spread—and the mothers themselves—appear to have an especially high risk of dying. A review of seven such cases reported that three of the mothers and three of the babies died (Peacock & Sarubbi 1983). One large study of women with localized infection, however, reported no deaths as a result of infection. Because the physicians conducting the study followed the women throughout their pregnancies, monitoring them weekly to see whether the infection was active, a number of babies were delivered by cesarean section. Two babies, however, were delivered vaginally to mothers who had active local infection. None of the infants seemed to be infected at birth or was otherwise abnormal. The physicians who conducted this study suggest that maternal antibody to herpes may pass across the placenta and protect the infant from infection (Grossman et al. 1981).

Although a few disease-producing agents can cross the placenta and affect the fetus, in general, the exchange of disease-related substances through the placenta is in the baby's favor. During the last months of pregnancy, the mother's antibodies against disease normally pass through the placenta to the fetus. Such antibodies are also transmitted to nursing babies in their mother's milk. These antibodies protect the newborn against many common diseases for the first few months of life, until the baby's own immune system starts to work.

Rh-Factor Incompatibility

The blood is made up of many complex substances, some of which can cause a developing fetus serious harm. The most common of these is the Rh factor, a substance on the surface of red blood cells. The blood cells of the great majority of human beings bear the Rh factor because it is determined by a dominant gene. Such people are called Rh positive. A small number (15 percent of whites; 7 percent of blacks) show the recessive Rh-negative trait. When an Rh-negative woman conceives a child with an Rh-positive man, some of their children are likely to be Rh-positive.

In such a case, as in all pregnancies, blood cells from the fetus enter the mother's bloodstream; a few pass through the aging placenta in the last weeks of pregnancy, but large numbers of the cells enter her bloodstream during the baby's birth, when the placenta separates from the wall of the uterus. The Rh-negative mother's immune system reacts to this invasion of "foreign" (Rh-positive) matter by creating antibodies to the Rh factor. The first Rh-positive baby is not affected. But in a subsequent pregnancy with an Rh-positive fetus, antibodies created at the time of the first birth cross the placenta and begin to destroy the blood cells of the fetus, causing anemia (Figure 3-12). A severe case may cause miscarriage or stillbirth (Guttmacher 1973).

FIRST PREGNANCY

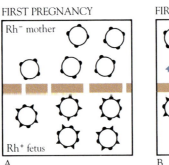

A

FIRST PREGNANCY

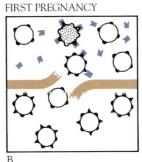

B

SECOND PREGNANCY

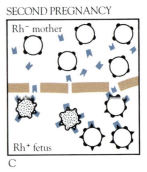

C

Figure 3-12 The danger to a fetus whose blood cells have the Rh factor while its mother's do not arises in the following way. (A) The fetus of a mother's first pregnancy is in no danger, because blood cells normally cannot be exchanged through the placenta (heavy broken line). (B) At the first child's birth, however, breaks in the placenta inevitably occur, and the bloodstreams of mother and child mix. The mother's immune system reacts to the child's Rh-positive cells just as if they were foreign invaders, and it manufactures antibodies (colored particles) against them. (C) During her second pregnancy, although the mother's blood cells cannot cross the placenta, her antibodies can, including antibodies to Rh factor. Therefore, if the second fetus is Rh-positive, these antibodies attack the fetus's red blood cells and kill them (speckled cells). Giving the mother an injection shortly after the first birth and each subsequent one can now prevent the problem.

A simple method of preventing the problem now exists. Within 72 hours after birth (or after an induced abortion or miscarriage), the woman can be given an injection that prevents the production of Rh antibodies by eliminating fetal cells in her bloodstream before her immune system can react to them. Used properly, this method is 99 percent effective in preventing the problem of Rh incompatibility (Clarke 1968).

BEHAVIOR BEFORE BIRTH

The mother is not the only one whose experiences during the months of pregnancy are important to prenatal development. Long before it is born, the fetus can sense many things and behave in ways that may affect its development (Carmichael 1970).

The fetus's behavior—its movement within the womb—is particularly important. A fetus makes spontaneous movements by 8 weeks after conception. By 12 weeks, it can kick its legs, close its fingers, bend its wrists, and turn its head. It makes facial movements and swallows amniotic fluid from time to time. By 24 weeks, it performs many spontaneous movements, some of them resembling crawling or walking motions. It can also open and close its eyes, and move them as if looking up, down, or sideways (Macfarlane 1977).

Studies of fetuses aborted for medical reasons show that they display a number of reflexes and reactions. The skin is sensitive to touch and temperature well before birth. As early as 8 weeks, the fetus will bend its head away from a touch around its mouth. (Later, the fetus will turn its mouth toward the touch. In newborns, this reaction is called the rooting reflex.) At 14 weeks, a touch to the hand will cause the fingers to close slightly. By 18 weeks, the touch elicits a rudimentary grasping reflex. By 24 weeks, the grasping reflex is strong enough to pull the fetus's upper body up (Hooker 1952). By 25 weeks, the fetus makes strong sucking movements, and it may suck its thumb. By the final weeks of gestation, the fetus performs most of the reflex movements that a newborn

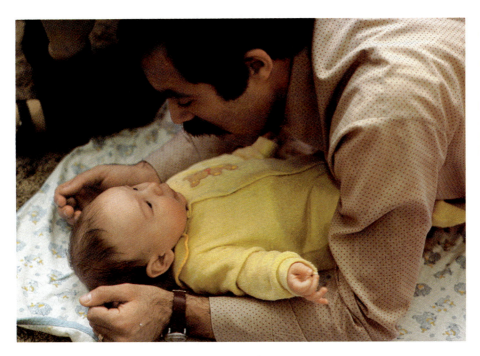

Figure 3-13 Many developmental difficulties that exist at birth can be overcome when a child's environment is peopled by loving adults who feed and care for his mind and feelings as well as his body.

shows. In fact, toward the end of their uterine stay, fetuses make breathinglike chest movements, which can sometimes be detected by the mother.

When scientists discovered the degree and complexity of the activities of the fetus, they asked themselves what function these activities might serve. For example, would a fetus that has remained immobile be the same at birth as one that has kicked and jabbed and swallowed and sucked?

Prenatal activity seems to be necessary for normal prenatal development (Gottlieb 1976). The use of incompletely formed structures apparently contributes to their final form and function. Animal studies suggest that when it is impossible for fetuses to put newly developed structures into action, the lack of experience shows itself after birth. In one experimental study, a chick embryo inside an egg was prevented from moving one of its legs for several days by injecting the leg with a chemical that temporarily paralyzed it. When the chick hatched, the joints in that leg were fixed and virtually immovable. The leg resembled what is called "clubfoot" in human beings (Drachman & Coulombre 1962). Inactivity or immobility in human fetuses may be a cause of clubfoot and also of cleft palate, two fairly common birth defects (Humphrey 1970).

Even before birth, then, experience in an environment seems to interact with genetic inheritance. In the uterine environment, the genes have programmed both the development of structures and their activation. The active use of those structures may contribute to their final development. If the environment is not a normal one—if it is toxic or so restrictive that the activity cannot take place—the lack of experience may slow or even distort the development of a particular structure. Fortunately, however, this first environment is usually a wholesome one. Even when it is not, its deficiencies are usually minor, not causing serious or long-lasting damage in the vast majority of infants. Most of the minor developmental difficulties that originate before birth disappear in later life, particularly if the child's environment after birth is a healthy one.

SUMMARY

1. The 9-month course of prenatal development begins with fertilization—the fusion of a sperm and an egg to become one cell.

THE FIRST 3 MONTHS

2. The first 2 weeks of prenatal development are called the **germinal period.** The main developmental process during this period is **cell division,** which begins about 30 hours after fertilization. By the fifth day, there are about 100 cells, which are in the form of a hollow ball called the **blastocyst.** The cells on the outside of the blastocyst are called the **trophoblast,** from which develop the placenta, the umbilical cord, and the sac surrounding the fetus. A small mass of cells on the inside of the ball will become the fetus.

3. **Implantation** takes place when the blastocyst burrows into the lining of the uterus. At the time of implantation, cells inside the blastocyst arrange themselves into a flat disc, called the **embryonic disc,** which develops three layers of cells: the ectoderm, which will become the nervous system, skin, hair, and nails; the mesoderm, which will become the muscles, skeleton, and circulatory system; and the endoderm, from which the digestive tract, respiratory system, and related glands develop.

4. The **placenta,** a disc-shaped organ that adheres to the wall of the uterus and is connected to the fetus by the **umbilical cord,** supplies oxygen and nutrients, carries off wastes, and acts as a barrier against many harmful substances.

5. The period from 2 weeks to 2 months after fertilization is called the **embryonic period,** during which cell differentiation and specialization produce rudimentary forms of the brain, heart, digestive tract, skeleton, muscles, and limbs.

6. During the embryonic period, when so many vital organs and body parts are forming, there are a number of sensitive periods during which specific substances—such as drugs or viruses—can affect development to produce birth defects.

7. The third month after fertilization marks the beginning of the **fetal period,** during which most of the remaining organs form, including the sex organs.

THE SECOND 3 MONTHS

8. During the second 3-month period, the fetus's body straightens out from its curled-up position, and the fetus is now able to respond to external stimuli and move parts of its body. At 6 months, most fetuses have achieved **viability;** that is, if born now they have a small chance of surviving.

THE FINAL 3 MONTHS

9. During the final 3 months of prenatal life, the fetus gains a great deal of weight, and its lungs and central nervous system mature rapidly.

BIRTH

10. The birth process, called **labor,** is divided into three stages. During the first stage, the uterus contracts and the cervix dilates. During the second stage, contractions of the uterus and vigorous pushing by the mother propel the fetus through the birth canal, and the baby is born. In the third stage, the contractions continue until the placenta is expelled.

11. As soon as the baby is born, its overall condition is measured by the **Apgar scale.**

12. In hospital childbirths, most American women are given some form of medication to relieve pain. Except for local anesthetics, all such drugs cross the placental barrier. Especially for the stronger drugs, such as anesthetics, there is a significant correlation between the amount of medication given the mother and the newborn's alertness, muscle tension, and vision. The drugs may also have more long-lasting effects.

13. Many mothers trained in **natural childbirth** require little or no medication. The training classes include breathing and relaxation exercises and teach a thorough understanding of the entire birth process.

PREMATURITY

14. The term "premature" has been replaced by two categories that are more precise.
   a. Babies born after a shorter-than-normal period in the uterus are called **short-gestation** infants.

b.   Babies who weigh less than 5½ pounds after a normal gestation period are called **low-birth-weight** babies.

A common problem in both types is **anoxia,** the lack of sufficient oxygen during and after birth, usually because of immaturity of the baby's respiratory and central nervous systems. Recent studies seem to show that most cognitive defects that might be traced to short gestation or low birth weight disappear by age 7 in children who grow up in good environments.

THE MOTHER'S CHARACTERISTICS AND EXPERIENCES

15.   A number of the pregnant mother's characteristics and experiences can affect the course of prenatal development.

a.   Severe **malnutrition** or extreme deficiencies of certain nutrients in the mother's diet can produce short-gestation or low-birth-weight babies or even stillbirths.

b.   Prolonged **maternal stress** may induce spontaneous abortion and seems to cause greater fetal activity and lower birth weight.

c.   Mothers who smoke tend to have low-birth-weight babies.

d.   Some drugs (for example, thalidomide, alcohol, heroin) and environmental chemicals (for example, lead) are known to be harmful to the fetus.

e.   Massive doses of radiation, such as are sometimes required to treat cancer, have a high probability of producing defects in a fetus.

f.   A few disease-producing agents—mostly viruses—can cross the placenta and affect the developing organism.

g.   Rh-negative mothers, whose red blood cells lack the Rh factor, once had serious problems in bearing more than one Rh-positive child because maternal antibodies created at the birth of the first child can attack the blood cells of later Rh-positive fetuses. Injections can now be given to Rh-negative mothers to prevent them from producing such antibodies.

BEHAVIOR BEFORE BIRTH

16.   A fetus is normally very active—moving its arms, legs, fingers, and head, swallowing, opening and closing its eyelids. This prenatal activity seems to be necessary for normal physical development.

SUGGESTED READINGS

BORG, SUSAN, and JUDITH LASKER. *When Pregnancy Fails: Families Coping with Miscarriage, Stillbirth, and Infant Death.* Boston: Beacon Press, 1981.

Two authors who themselves each lost an infant discuss what happens when a family loses an infant and how to deal with the loss.

GOLDBERG, SUSAN, and BARBARA DeVITTO. *Born Too Soon: Preterm Birth and Early Development.* San Francisco: W. H. Freeman and Company, 1983.

Two developmental scientists summarize findings from the extensive research on the development of short-gestation and low-birth-weight infants and relate those findings to the concerns of parents.

GUTTMACHER, ALAN F. *Pregnancy, Birth, and Family Planning.* New York: New American Library, 1973.

A comprehensive, practical guide to pregnancy and childbirth, written for expectant parents.

MACFARLANE, AIDAN. *The Psychology of Childbirth.* Cambridge, Mass.: Harvard University Press, 1977.

A pediatrician takes a careful look at some important psychological aspects of childbirth: emotional attitude and morning sickness, bonding of mother and infant, hospital or home delivery, the trauma of birth, and more.

NILSSON, LENNART. *A Child Is Born,* rev. ed. New York: Delacorte Press, 1977.

A step-by-step description of prenatal development, filled with remarkable photographs of every step from fertilization through birth.

The birth of a baby is almost always a cause for rejoicing. The newborn is welcomed and tenderly cared for. But many parents report that at first, and for a few months after the baby's birth, they feel a little disappointment because the newborn seems "unfinished," unable to respond or even to communicate by meeting a parent's glance. There may be a good reason for the newborn's rawness. We human beings seem to be born too early, compared to other animals that share our characteristics—long life spans, big brains, and complex social behavior. The brain, which is only one-quarter of its adult size when we are born, seems to be the culprit in our too early birth. If the duration of human pregnancy were comparable to that of monkeys and apes, our brains would become so large that our heads could not pass through the birth canal. The first three months of life, then—the "finishing" period—is discussed separately in Chapter 4. After 3 months, babies are much more responsive, and Chapter 5 looks at the growth of intelligence from 3 months to 2 years. This is the period when babies master the basic uses of the human body and build the foundations for thought and language. Chapter 6 examines the origins of personality in temperament and the parent-child relationship.

UNIT

2

INFANCY

4

FROM REFLEX TO ACTION: THE NEWBORN

CHAPTER OUTLINE

4

FROM
REFLEX
TO
ACTION:
THE
NEWBORN

Although human infants develop rapidly during the 9 months after conception, at birth they are less mature and much more helpless than the offspring of many other animals. Baby chicks, you will recall from Chapter 2, follow their mothers around within 1 day of being hatched. A newborn calf stands up, finds it mother's udder, and begins to nurse within minutes after birth. Rhesus monkeys can walk clumsily and cling to their mother's fur shortly after they are born.

In contrast, a newborn child cannot raise her head or turn over, much less crawl or walk. She cannot provide herself with food, keep herself clean, or even remove the corner of a sheet that happens to cover her face.

Yet the newborn's helplessness is by no means total. Human beings are born with a wide range of capacities that promote their survival. They have reflexes for the basic biological functions—breathing, eating, defecating, urinating. They also have reflexes that lay the foundation for more controlled behaviors, such as grasping, crawling, walking, and talking, that appear later. Their basic sensory capacities for seeing, hearing, touching, smelling, and tasting are already functioning, and many newborns are surprisingly competent in these capacities.

In addition, the newborn's helpless appearance promotes survival by striking a responsive chord in parents and other adults entrusted with the baby's care. People who, before parenthood, slept like stones—who could curl up and take a nap in an automobile factory—suddenly find themselves awake and alert at their baby's smallest whimper, no matter what hour of the day or night. Diapering their newborn child, they wonder at the baby's seeming fragility, the incredibly tiny hands and feet, and feel the need to protect and care for the baby.

The adults' attraction to the newborn is in a sense remarkable, because babies right after birth are not beautiful. The trip through the birth canal compresses the unfused bones of the skull, and many babies' heads are temporarily cone-shaped. The pressure also pastes back their ears. Newborns are covered with vernix, a white protective skin coating that looks like cheese, and are splotched with their mother's blood. Some have virtually no hair on their heads, and some are born with a coat of fine hair (lanugo) all over their bodies. Even after they're cleaned up, most have mottled red skin from their arduous passage to birth. The struggle to be born is so exhausting that most newborn babies fall asleep within a couple of hours and stay fast asleep for many hours afterward.

In the past two decades, developmental researchers have shown a great surge in attention to the newborn and very young infant. Newborns are of particular scientific interest partly because they are the baseline for the study of development. Any abilities that newborns do not have but that appear in later life are ones that must have developed. A first task of developmentalists, therefore, is to carefully observe and describe newborn characteristics and behaviors.

Important developments begin to take place very soon after birth. Recent research has shown that in the first 2 or 3 months of life, for example, many

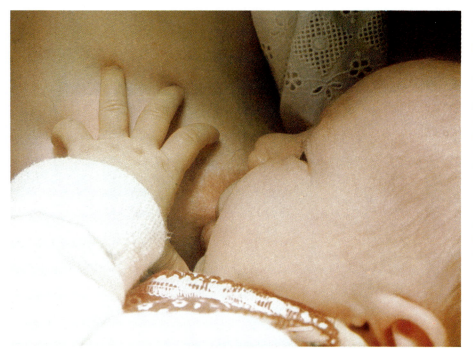

Figure 4-1 This contented newborn was born with an ability to suck, which she fine-tuned during the first weeks of her life. She has been able to adapt her sucking patterns to the flow of her mother's milk and also to the flow from the bottle when her father does the feeding, so she gets plenty to eat in a comfortable way. When the baby nurses, she gets not only physical nourishment but also stimulation of her muscles and senses as she is picked up and moved around. She also experiences the physical contact and closeness that are the beginning of human communication.

reflexes disappear, and babies begin to look into their parents' eyes, to smile, and to learn things more easily. By 3 months of age, they are generally much easier to live with than they were as newborns—their schedules of sleeping and eating become more regular, they seem to cry less, and they begin to respond socially (Haith & Campos 1977).

The major psychological development that seems to underlie all these changes is the transformation of the newborn's rigid reflexes and sensory capacities into the 3-month-old's skilled voluntary actions. A 3-month-old can feel around for her rattle until she can grasp it, and she can look at her mother's face, examining systematically the eyes and mouth and hairline. A newborn has neither of these abilities—she can merely grasp things reflexively and look at whatever happens to catch her eye. How do these skilled actions develop from the narrow, virtually automatic capacities of the newborn?

REFLEXES

The newborn can, among other things, suck, cry, see, hear, and grasp. At birth, each of these behaviors is a ***reflex,*** that is, an automatic or stereotyped reaction, usually to a specific stimulus. A touch on the newborn's lip causes the baby to start sucking. A touch on the palm elicits grasping. Bright light makes

TABLE 4-1 SOME NEWBORN REFLEXES

REFLEX	DESCRIPTION	DISAPPEARANCE
Babkin	When the baby is lying on her back and pressure is applied to the palms of both hands, the baby opens her mouth, closes her eyes, and brings her head to face front at the midline of the body.	Weakens after 1 month; disappears by 3 months.
Crawling	When an infant is placed on her stomach and pressure is applied to the soles of her feet, she makes rhythmic movements of her arms and legs, as if crawling.	Disappears by 3 to 4 months.
Grasping	When something is pressed against the infant's palm—a finger, for example—the infant will tightly grasp the object.	Weakens after 3 months; disappears by 11 months.
Moro	When someone holding the baby lets her head drop a few inches or when there is a sudden loud noise, the baby first throws her arms out, then brings them back toward her body, with her hands curling, as if to grasp something.	Easily elicited before 3 months; disappears by 7 months.

SOURCE: Peiper 1963; Touwen 1976; Zelazo et al. 1972.

the pupils of the eyes contract, and darkness makes them dilate. Reflexes sometimes occur without any apparent stimulus, as when a baby sucks for a few seconds even though nothing is touching the mouth.

Some reflexes, such as sucking, blinking, and crying in response to pain, have obvious value for the baby. The usefulness of other reflexes is not always clear, but their absence at birth usually signals some problem in the baby's nervous system. Absence of the Moro reflex, for example (see Table 4-1), indicates a serious disturbance, perhaps even brain damage. It is now standard practice to test a newborn's reflexes to ensure that the nervous system is responding normally (Self & Horowitz 1979).

Many reflexes, such as coughing, gagging, sneezing, yawning, and blinking, persist throughout life. These reflexes are important for the health and survival of adults as well as infants. The reflexes that are of special interest to developmentalists, however, are those that disappear within a few months, as the cerebral cortex matures and the infant establishes voluntary control over some actions (Table 4-1). For example, a newborn startled by a sudden loss of support, especially of her head, will display the Moro reflex. With a cry, she stretches her arms wide and then brings them back toward her body, curling

REFLEX	DESCRIPTION	DISAPPEARANCE
Rooting	When the infant's cheek is lightly touched, she will turn her head in the direction of the touch and open her mouth, as if seeking something to suck on or to eat. Rooting is hard to elicit when the infant is satiated.	Disappears by 3 to 6 months.
Stepping	When someone holds the baby upright with her feet touching a surface and moves her forward, the baby will make rhythmic stepping movements, as if walking.	Disappears by 1 to 4 months.
Sucking	When the baby feels something in her mouth, she sucks on it. This reflex is sometimes hard to elicit when the infant is satiated.	Becomes a sucking skill by 2 to 3 months.
Tonic Neck	When an infant is placed on her back, she will turn her head to one side and extend the arm and leg on that side while flexing the other arm and leg.	Gradually disappears between 2 and 10 months.

her fingers as if to grab hold of something (see Figure 4-2). At 3 months, this reflex begins to disappear gradually, and it is completely gone by 7 months (Touwen 1976).

Several reflexes, such as grasping, sucking, and crying, provide a behavioral foundation upon which the infant's later actions are built (Zelazo 1976). In contrast to these reflexes, over which the baby has only slight control, an **action** is the use of an organized ability that is under voluntary control, that allows flexible behavior, and that can be affected by rewards and punishments (Bruner 1973). Jean Piaget, whose theory is presented in Chapter 5, called such abilities "schemes" (Piaget 1952).

The newborn's grasping reflex, for example, will develop into the grasping action of the 3-month-old. If you put your finger in a newborn's hand, she will reflexively curl her fingers around it. Some newborns hold on so strongly that, with both hands grasping an adult's fingers, they can support their own weight as they are lifted into the air. But a newborn cannot grasp something unless it happens to stimulate the grasping reflex. A few months later, after the grasping scheme has developed, the infant will be able to search out something to grasp—to feel for a blanket or a rattle or a parent's hair and deliberately take hold of it.

Sucking

One of the infant's most important inborn capacities is the ability to suck competently enough to take in nourishment. Newborns even have special muscles in their mouths so that they can suck efficiently—muscles that adults no longer have.

The sucking ability begins as several closely related reflexes, including rooting and sucking. The rooting reflex occurs when a newborn's cheek is touched: She moves her head toward the touch and opens her mouth, a response that is obviously useful in feeding. A mother who wants to lead her baby to take the nipple need only lightly touch the cheek nearest the nipple. Gently pushing the other cheek does not work well at all, because the rooting reflex causes the baby to turn toward the touch.

When the rooting reflex brings the newborn's mouth into contact with an object, the sucking reflex is elicited. If the object fits comfortably into the mouth, the baby will suck on it, whatever it is. Usually, of course, the object is the nipple of a breast, a bottle, or a pacifier. Gradually, as the baby becomes accustomed to sucking on these familiar nipples, she will begin to reject most other objects that touch her mouth when she is hungry. When she is full and satisfied and sleepy, she may not even respond to a touch on the lips.

There are great individual variations in the pattern and strength of sucking (Crook, 1979). Some infants suck forcefully from birth. Others suck less effectively; they have to put in much more effort to get the milk they need and may tire before they are full. It takes most babies a week or two to get the sucking response running smoothly. A baby must coordinate her sucking pat-

 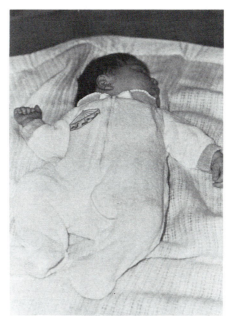

Figure 4-2 The three reflexes shown here (and described in Table 4-1) all disappear during early infancy, but all seem to be related to later childhood and adult behaviors. (Far left) The Moro reflex. This response may be related to the "startle" response shown throughout life, and it may reflect some early evolutionary step in human history: The baby looks as if she is trying to grab a branch or her mother's fur to keep from falling. (Middle) The stepping reflex. (Right) The tonic neck reflex.

tern with her mother's way of holding her, with the flow of milk from breast or bottle, and with her own preferred tempo. But within a few weeks the baby's ability to suck becomes smooth and efficient (as long as she is given the nipple she is accustomed to).

Sucking is not only a means of obtaining nutrition; it also seems to be a pleasurable, calming activity for infants (Kessen 1967). In one classic study, 70 infants were examined for more than a year to see how much sucking they did when they were not nursing and how their sucking changed with age. Sixty-one of the infants did quite a bit of sucking that had nothing to do with nutrition—on fists, fingers, pacifiers. Most of them were doing it by the time they were 6 weeks old, yet by the time they were a year old, all but four of the babies had stopped (Brazelton 1956).

Some babies who have a strong sucking need or who cry a lot can be calmed by giving them pacifiers. One of the authors, a mother of twins, still recalls the day she personally discovered just how aptly these devices are named. Both 5-pound boys were crying irritably, even though they had been fed and burped and changed. She popped a pacifier in each mouth—and then luxuriated in the sudden hush that was broken only by the sounds of contented sucking.

T. Berry Brazelton, the pediatrician who conducted the study described above, concludes that most babies enjoy sucking and should not be discouraged from doing so. Contrary to popular belief, sucking can deform dental arches only if the habit continues until the child is 5 or 6 years old, and as Brazelton's study showed, virtually all babies stop most of their sucking by 12 months, when there are a lot more interesting things to do.

ESSAY:
THE BATTLE OF THE BREAST

Since at least as long ago as the Roman Empire there has been a running battle between child-care experts—the philosophers, physicians, psychologists—and mothers. The experts exhort the mothers to breastfeed their children, and mothers quietly refuse, using wet nurses or bottles. In the second century, the writer Plutarch told Roman matrons that

> the affection of wet nurses and governesses is spurious and constrained, for they love for hire. Nature itself makes it plain that mothers should themselves nurture and sustain what they have brought forth. (Plutarch 1969)

What William Kessen (1965) calls "the war of the breast" continued through the early centuries of Christian Europe, and the battle cry of the experts found mass distribution with the first printing of books in European languages:

> Therefore the child should delight in taking its mother's breast. On that it subsists better and without harm than on that of any other woman, because it became accustomed to it in the mother's womb. (H. V. Louffenburg 1491, quoted in Ruhrah 1925)

John Comenius, a famous Czech educator and philosopher, continued that harangue in 1633, when he held up to errant human mothers the example of wolf mothers, who always tenderly suckled their own young. He also warned the mothers who hired wet nurses from among the peasants or urban poor that

> babies imbibe, along with the alien milk of the foster mother, morals different from those of their parents. (Comenius 1956, p. 79)

In the eighteenth century, Jean-Jacques Rousseau kept up the fight and promised that if mothers would only nurse their own babies, "natural feeling will revive in every heart." (Rousseau 1911, p. 13) When physicians began to add the weight of scientific authority to the

argument, its tone sometimes became positively menacing. J. B. Davis, a physician, threatened English mothers in 1817:

> The mother's breast is an infant's birthright and suckling a sacred duty, to neglect which is prejudicial to the mother and fatal to the child. (McCleary 1933, p. 19)

Mothers had a brief rest from all the sermonizing in the 1920s and 1930s, when scientists decided that the war on germs was more important than the battle of the breast. Physicians actually recommended that babies be fed by means of sterilized glass bottles. However, Freud's ideas about the importance of early experiences began to have a strong influence in the 1950s. The necessity of breastfeeding again became policy—this time, of the psychological establishment—and the truce ended. Psychiatrists and experts on child care again admonished mothers to breastfeed their babies—this time, for the children's psychological health.

In the 1970s and 1980s the argument has returned to the health benefits of breastfeeding, although psychological benefits are also invoked. The terms are somewhat different, of course, because earlier it was the mother's own milk versus the mother's milk of a wet nurse, whereas now it is mother's milk versus sterilized formula made of cow's milk, goat's milk, soy beans, or synthetic substances.

The American Academy of Pediatrics issued an extensive report in 1978 urging mothers to breastfeed their babies. The physicians cite many recent medical findings to support their strong advice. They cite evidence showing that mother's milk protects babies from infections because it contains antibodies to various germs. Babies who nurse are less likely to develop severe and potentially fatal diarrhea, respiratory disease, and meningitis. These babies also seem to be less prone to allergies.

The report contains a number of theories about the advantages of mother's milk. For example, because it contains more cholesterol than many synthetic formulas do, doctors theorize that the additional cholesterol may trigger a biochemical change that will lower the level of cholesterol in later life and help prevent heart disease. The report cites one study in which 30-year-olds who had been breastfed had lower levels of blood cholesterol than those who had not been breastfed, on the average. Also, some doctors suspect that breastfeeding may reduce a baby's risk of adult obesity because the baby is rarely urged to continue feeding when he leaves the breast, whereas babies fed with bottles are often urged to finish the contents of every bottle.

For the moment, such arguments are only medical speculations. However, they are clearly directed toward urging mothers to breastfeed their babies. It is likely that breastfeeding is better for babies in some respects, but many mothers either cannot breastfeed—because they work, perhaps—or will not, for any number of reasons. And so the battle of the breast continues.

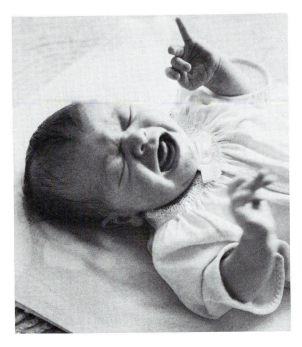

Figure 4-3   People tend to respond with feeling even to photos of infants crying or smiling. The power of those behaviors in person—face-to-face with mother or father—is incalculable. Here a newborn cries all out, and a 3-month-old offers a melting social smile.

Crying and Smiling

Like the newborn's helpless appearance, some infant reflexes, such as crying, seem to serve the function of stimulating adults to take care of the child. Crying is elicited by pain or discomfort but may also occur spontaneously. Newborn babies usually cry the moment they are born (unless their mothers were given heavy sedation during labor). For the first several months of life, this cry is the infant's primary means of communicating distress to her adult caretakers.

Young babies differ greatly in how much they cry and fuss; some cry only a few times a day and others cry frequently throughout the day and night. In the early weeks of life, much of this crying has no obvious cause and is commonly labeled "unexplained fussiness" (Emde et al. 1976). With many infants, there is a sharp decline in such fussiness by 3 months—to the parents' great relief. With other infants, however, fussiness does not decline for several more months. Newborns also make some other sounds, mostly gurglings and grunts. At 1½ to 2 months they start to make a few speechlike sounds, mostly vowel sounds such as "ooo." However, these early sounds are usually overshadowed by crying.

It is extremely difficult to ignore a baby's crying. It is also hard to know how to respond appropriately. The quality of babies' cries seems to vary, depending on whether the baby is hungry, in pain, or irritable for some reason parents cannot discern, but it is not certain that parents can distinguish among the cries (Muller et al. 1974; Wolff 1969). Often, they must resort to a long series of attempts to relieve the baby's distress. They will change her diaper and offer milk. They will burp her to relieve gas pains, reassure her with calming voices and caresses, and rock or walk her. And all the baby has to do to provoke this flurry of activity is to cry.

About 1 month after birth, a smilelike expression is added to a baby's repertoire of response-getting activities, but the smiling seems to be reflexive and unrelated to specific events in the external world. Parents nevertheless react to the expression as if it were an attempt to communicate. At 2½ months or so, this unexplained smile turns into a *social smile,* which appears regularly at the sight of a face (Emde et al. 1976). Parents usually respond wholeheartedly, eagerly repeating whatever they did that might have caused the smile, just to see it again. How smiling facilitates interaction between parents and child is discussed at greater length in Chapter 6.

LEARNING IN EARLY INFANCY

Although a baby's social smile is different from the earlier smilelike expression, there is continuity between the two. Both smiles use the same facial muscles; in fact, the earlier reflex smile seems to be the foundation upon which the later smile is built. As the child develops, the relatively automatic early smile seems to be gradually transformed into the social, communicative smile. Similarly, the early grasp reflex develops into the voluntary grasp; the early sucking reflex changes into controlled, adaptable sucking; and the early rooting reflex is transformed into the ability to turn the head to seek an object to suck (Kaye 1982; Thelen 1981).

For many reflexes, the continuity between early reflexes and later behaviors is less obvious, mostly because the voluntary action does not fully develop until well after the reflex has disappeared (Connolly 1981). In these cases, too, the behavior develops gradually from a reflex to an action. The process of development merely takes longer.

Walking is a good example of this kind of continuity. The stepping reflex (see Figure 4-2B) occurs when a baby is held upright so that the soles of her feet just touch a horizontal surface. This touch causes the baby to move her legs as though walking, which suggests that some of the neurological connections for walking already exist. Ordinarily, the reflex disappears by the third month, and babies do not start walking until about 1 year of age. In the interim, they work with many of the components of walking, including standing and moving their legs one at a time (Thelen & Fisher 1982).

The research of Philip Zelazo, which was discussed briefly in Chapter 2, concerned infants who had had their stepping reflex exercised in the early months. When they were tested, these infants showed the stepping reflex more

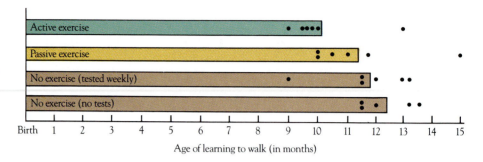

Figure 4-4 The active exercise of the stepping reflex in the Zelazo experiment was carried out daily until the infants were 2 months old. The mothers held the babies upright, as shown in Figure 4-2, to stimulate the reflex while the fathers supported the babies' knees, trying to teach them to use their knees to bear their weight. The infants in the passive exercise group had their legs exercised while they were lying down. Among the subjects in the experiment, there were marked individual differences in the time of learning to walk (indicated by the dots). On the average (indicated by the bars) babies in the group that was exercised actively began walking at least a month earlier than babies in the other groups.

frequently than the infants did who had not been exercised. Later, toward the end of the first year, they learned to walk, on the average, 6 to 8 weeks earlier than infants who had received no such exercise, as shown in Figure 4-4 (Zelazo 1976; Zelazo et al. 1972).

These findings do *not* mean that parents need to make a special effort to exercise their babies' stepping reflexes. Rich and varied experience is important for an infant, but the stimulation of any specific ability is not advantageous. Early walkers do not appear to be better athletes or better scholars later in life (Horn 1976). What the findings *do* show is that the walking reflex lays the foundation for the skill of walking, even though the ability to walk develops many months later. Many of the newborn's reflexes seem to have a similar connection with later skills.

Just as practice with the stepping reflex causes an increase in the use of that reflex and affects later development of the walking skill, most of an infant's other reflexes are also subject to such effects. Although newborn reflexes are relatively rigid and automatic, they still can be molded by learning, as a number of studies have shown (Rovee-Collier & Lipsitt 1982; Sameroff & Cavanaugh 1979). This early learning that makes use of reflexes seems to contribute to the later development of specific actions.

The theoretical approach that focuses on the role of learning in development is called learning theory. Most theories of development deal with learning in some way, but the approach called "learning theory" emphasizes the basic importance of conditioning—not only in newborns but in all human beings.

THEORY: CONDITIONING AND LEARNING

In the 1910s and 1920s, there was a revolution in American psychology—the behaviorist revolution. Led by John B. Watson, the revolt was against the psychological assumption that the mind was entirely separate from the body. Perhaps an even more important target of Watson's criticism was the introspective methodology of the day. In the introspective method, psychologists were carefully trained to report on the workings of their own minds, and they based general psychological principles on these subjective observations. Watson argued that such an approach was entirely unscientific: The findings it yielded could never be verified because no one has access to another person's consciousness. In fact, said Watson, because mental phenomena such as thoughts and feelings cannot be measured, scientists should not try to study these things. Instead, they should confine themselves to the study of observable behavior—what people and animals actually do. The approach based on these ideas is therefore known as **behaviorism**—the study of organisms with the aim of explaining their overt activities (behaviors) as the result of environmental influences.

Watson believed that all infants are "blank slates" at birth and that how they behave as they grow up depends mostly on what they have learned. This belief implies that people can be molded by their environments to become almost anything. The focus on learning has been maintained by behaviorists ever since Watson.

Watson emphasized the need to tie all psychological concepts to direct observation—more specifically, to the observation of changes in **performance.** In other words, he made a distinction between learning and performance. When a psychologist studies learning, what he or she actually observes is a change in performance: A 1-year-old may eat more skillfully today than she did yesterday, getting more food in her mouth and less all around her. But does this change in performance necessarily mean that she has learned something? Perhaps she had an upset stomach yesterday or is simply hungrier today. Performance can improve for many reasons, and not necessarily as a result of learning.

In order to establish that a behavioral change was due to learning and not to some extraneous factor, researchers needed good experimental techniques. The development of classical conditioning techniques in the early 1900s by the Russian physiologist Ivan Pavlov gave Watson and other behaviorists an important tool for studying learning. Later, the description of operant conditioning by E. L. Thorndike and B. F. Skinner gave them a second tool (Schwartz 1983).

CLASSICAL CONDITIONING

Pavlov discovered the process of **classical conditioning** in the course of his research on the digestive system in dogs. While monitoring the dogs' output of saliva, he and his assistants noticed that some dogs began to salivate before they ate: The sight of the laboratory attendant who regularly brought them food was enough to make the dogs' mouths water.

Pavlov determined that the dogs had learned to associate the arrival of the attendant with the arrival of food. Recognizing the importance of this process, he turned his attention to studying how such associations were established. He tried pairing the presentation of food with various stimuli—the sound of a bell or buzzer, the flashing of a light, and so on. If one of these neutral stimuli was repeatedly presented just before the food, the dogs would eventually salivate as soon as they heard or saw the stimulus alone.

Classical conditioning, which is also called Pavlovian conditioning, establishes an association between a neutral stimulus and a response, so that the neutral stimulus begins to elicit the response. A neutral stimulus (such as the buzzer used by Pavlov) is paired with a stimulus that normally elicits a response (food elicits salivation). In this example, the food is the **unconditioned stimulus,** because a dog

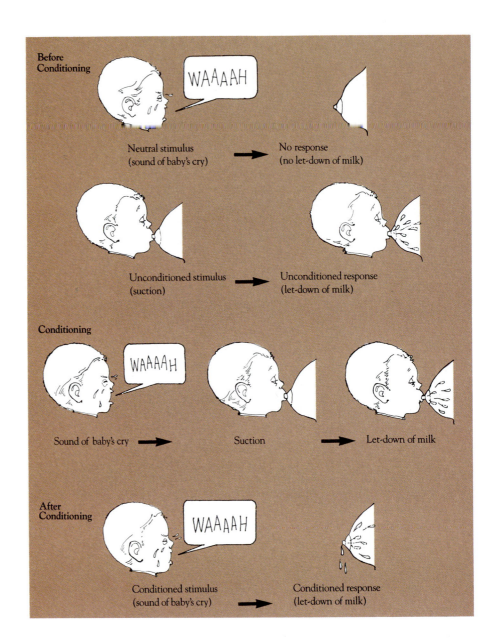

Figure 4-5 Classical conditioning is learning in which a neutral stimulus elicits a response just by being associated with the response. One common example of classical conditioning starts with the "let-down reflex" of lactating mothers; this reflex releases the milk from glands within the breast into ducts from which the infant sucks it. At first, let-down happens automatically only when the infant takes the nipple in his mouth. The touch of the infant's mouth on the nipple is the unconditioned stimulus, and the letting down of milk is the unconditioned response. Because the sound of the baby's cry often precedes feeding, this initially neutral stimulus turns into a conditioned stimulus for the letdown reflex—a mother's milk will flow just because she hears the baby cry.

naturally salivates when presented with it, and the buzzer is the **conditioned stimulus,** because the experimental procedure conditions the dog to respond to the buzzer by salivating. The dog's salivation in response to the unconditioned stimulus (food) is the **unconditioned response,** and its salivation in response to the conditioned stimulus (buzzer) is the **conditioned response.**

Figure 4-5 presents an instance of classical conditioning in human beings. The let-down reflex of a nursing mother becomes conditioned to the cry of her baby at feeding time. The cry is a neutral stimulus in the sense that it does not initially elicit the let-down reflex. At first, the mother's breasts let down milk only at the touch of the infant's mouth. After a few breast-feedings, however, her breasts let down milk at the sound of her infant's cry.

Besides such physiological responses, human emotions also can be conditioned. Some fears, in particular, can be learned through association. A girl who is easily disturbed by loud noises, for example, may learn to fear trains because of the noise that they make as they go by. Although the noise is initially what upsets the child, she comes to fear even trains that aren't moving. The train becomes a conditioned stimulus for fear.

Classical conditioning applies primarily to responses—many of them reflexes—that are elicited by a specific stimulus. In the other main technique for studying learning, operant conditioning, the focus is on behavior that an organism naturally and spontaneously performs, or, in the words of B. F. Skinner, behavior that the organism *emits.*

OPERANT CONDITIONING

Operant behavior is any behavior spontaneously performed by a person or animal. In everyday terms, it is often called voluntary action, although it, too, may first appear as an automatic reflex, especially in babies. Because voluntary behavior goes through major developmental changes, the theory of **operant conditioning** has proved to be somewhat more important to developmental psychology than the theory of classical conditioning is.

Much of learning theory and most of the theory of operant conditioning is the creation of the American psychologist B. F. Skinner, who published his first major work, *The Behavior of Organisms,* in 1938. Skinner was strongly influenced by Watson's approach to psychology, especially his insistence on the study of observable behavior. He was also influenced by the work of E. L. Thorndike, who at the turn of the century formulated what he called the law of effect: Behavior is affected by its consequences. A favorable consequence leads to repetition of the behavior, and an unfavorable consequence leads to extinction, or disappearance, of the behavior.

Reinforcement and Punishment

The basic principles of operant conditioning, which is also called instrumental conditioning, are extensions of the law of effect. One principle states that whether the frequency of a behavior increases or decreases depends on whether that behavior is followed by reinforcement or punishment. As Figure 4-6 shows, a **reinforcer** is an event that *increases* the frequency of the behavior that it follows. Reinforcers may be positive or negative. In **positive reinforcement,** also called reward, the increase in frequency results from the occurrence of a favorable event. In **negative reinforcement,** the increase in frequency results from the removal of an aversive event. Thus, a child may pick up her room either because she is praised

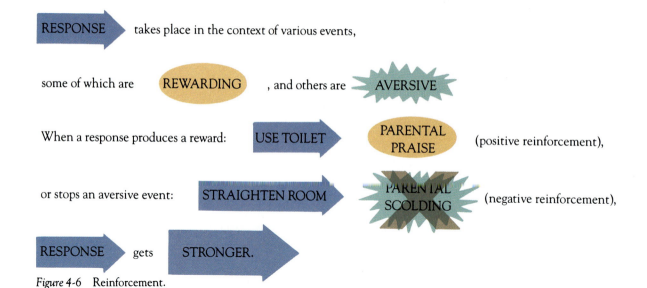

Figure 4-6   Reinforcement.

PUNISHMENT

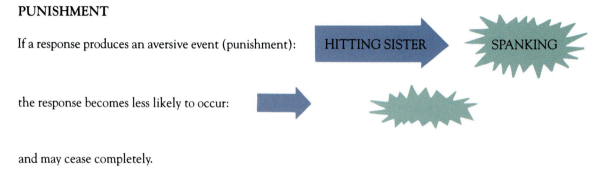

EXTINCTION

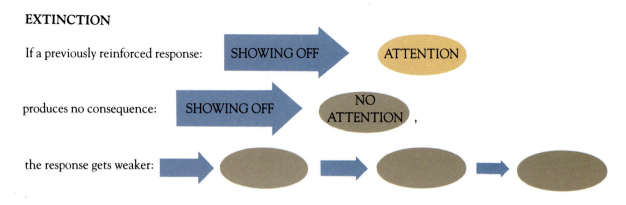

Figure 4-7   Punishment and extinction.

for it (positive reinforcement) or because doing so makes her parents stop scolding her (negative reinforcement). Similarly, a laboratory rat may press a bar in a cage either to obtain food or to stop the sound of a loud buzzer. For a reinforcer to be effective, it must immediately follow the behavior being reinforced.

A *punishment* (Figure 4-7) is an event that *decreases* the frequency of the behavior that it follows. Scolding a child for a particular behavior, for example, usually leads to a decrease in the frequency of the behavior, at least while the scolder is present. Another way of reducing the frequency of a behavior is by **extinction.** After a behavior that has been reinforced (either positively or negatively) stops being reinforced, its frequency gradually drops (often to near zero). The behavior is said to have been extinguished.

These definitions of reinforcement and punishment avoid the need for subjective judgments about what is reinforcing or aversive for a particular individual. Some people assume, for example, that children always dislike being scolded. Yet under some circumstances for some children, scolding can serve as a reinforcement; that is, it seems to cause an increase in the frequency of the problem behavior. The scolding presumably provides the children with something that they value, such as attention from a parent or teacher.

Reinforcement does more than increase the frequency of a behavior. It also tends to bring the reinforced behavior under **stimulus control.** That is, the behavior is repeated when stimuli associated with reinforcement are presented. For example, suppose that a baby is always served her favorite pudding in a particular blue bowl. Whenever she happens to see the bowl, she will "emit behaviors" that go along with eating pudding. She may smack her lips and point at the bowl with anticipation, even if the bowl is empty or she is not hungry. The delicious taste of the pudding has reinforced this behavior and has brought it under the stimulus control of the blue bowl.

Stimulus control in this instance has resulted in the baby's learning a **discrimination.** She can tell the difference between the blue bowl and other bowls: If her father holds up a red bowl, she will not give a "pudding response." On the other hand, stimulus control by the blue bowl is not rigid. If she sees a similar blue bowl, or even a blue-green bowl that is the same shape, she may respond. Such extension of a response to stimuli that are similar to the original stimulus is called **generalization.** This is a vital learning process, for it allows children to use their learning in new situations.

Conditioned Reinforcers

A stimulus associated with a reinforced operant response tends to become a **conditioned reinforcer,** gaining its own power to increase the frequency of a behavior. The sound of a food pellet dropping into the food cup becomes a conditioned reinforcer for a rat in a laboratory cage, because the sound signals the arrival of the **primary reinforcer** (food). Once a rat has learned the sound as a conditioned reinforcer, an experimenter can use the sound to direct the rat's behavior. Likewise, the sound of pudding plopping into a dish becomes a conditioned reinforcer for the baby who likes pudding. Even the blue bowl itself can become a conditioned reinforcer, as long as the child sees it only when she is about to receive her pudding.

One of the most potent conditioned reinforcers in human society is money. Coins and bills, of course, have no function as primary reinforcers—they cannot be eaten or protect one from pain. By 2

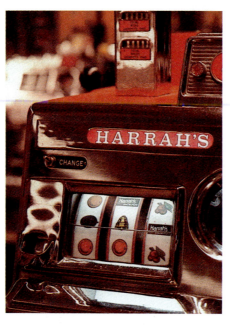

or 3 years of age, children begin to enjoy receiving money and playing with it. Even chimpanzees, which seem to be roughly as intelligent as human 2-year-olds, can be trained to use "money." In a classic study, one researcher first taught some chimps that when they put a poker chip into a vending machine, they would receive a banana. Then the chimps learned to perform certain tasks for a reward of poker chips—conditioned reinforcers that could only later be used to "buy" the primary reinforcer, bananas. Some chimps saved up the chips they earned until they had enough for a banana binge, and some tried to steal chips from other chimps (Wolfe 1936). Some common conditioned reinforcers in human society are compliments for looking good or doing a good job, and applause or cheers for a good theatrical or athletic performance.

Schedules of Reinforcement

The strength of the tie between a behavior and a reinforcer is affected by the *schedule of reinforcement,* that is, the pattern in which reinforcements are awarded (Ferster & Skinner 1957). Early in operant conditioning, the best way to strengthen a behavior is to use a schedule of *continuous reinforcement,* reinforcing the behavior every time it occurs. But once the behavior has been learned, only occasional reinforcement—called *partial reinforcement*—is needed to ensure its repetition. How effective the partial reinforcement can be is shown by that mainstay of gambling houses, the slot machine—which keeps its devotees pulling that handle through carefully scheduled partial reinforcement.

LEARNING THEORY AND CHILD REARING

Principles of operant conditioning can be of great value to parents in helping them shape desired behaviors, particularly in their young children. Most parents have fairly clear ideas of how they would like their children to behave and what they would like them to learn, but very few have any coherent techniques for teaching these things. To use learning principles in raising their children, parents must monitor very closely what they are rewarding and punishing to ensure that they are reinforcing the behaviors that they want and not reinforcing those that they don't want.

For example, one behavior that most parents dislike in their children is whining. Almost everyone has seen a mother in a market with her 2- or 3-year-old. The child tugs at the mother's skirt and whines, "I want gum. Mommeeee, buy me gum." The mother holds off for a while, saying, "No, you can't have any gum. Stop whining."

If this mother is familiar with learning principles, she will not reward the whining by giving in and buying the gum. Instead, she will ignore it, allowing it to extinguish. Although ignoring the behavior may mean a few exasperating shopping trips, the whining will eventually stop if it is not reinforced. But if the mother instead does buy the gum, even once in a while, she has rewarded the child's whining with partial reinforcement. The next time they are in a supermarket, the same scene will probably take place.

In order to eliminate the whining, the mother should not only avoid reinforcing it but should look for situations in which to reinforce *not* whining. If one day the child asks for gum, is refused, and quietly accepts the refusal, the mother should offer approval: "You acted like such a good and grown-up girl by not whining. I'm very pleased with you. Would you like to help me push the cart?" Similarly, a parent's efforts to teach a toddler not to go into the street will be more successful if the parent not only punishes the child for doing so (for instance, by making her come inside) but also praises her on those occasions when she is near the curb and does *not* go into the street.

Reinforcement and punishment should closely follow the targeted behavior. The young child who whined at the supermarket should not be punished when she gets home an hour later because she probably will not be able to connect the punishment with her whining. The ability of children to relate reinforcement or punishment to their behavior increases as they develop. By the time children are 8 or 10 years old, they can usually understand a slightly delayed punishment. In infancy, on the other hand, children can learn only the most concrete relations between behavior and reinforcer or punisher. Newborns seem to be able to learn only when the reinforcer or punisher is an integral part of the behavior, as when they receive milk for sucking.

Conditioning and Habituation in the Newborn

Studies of newborns have shown that they are capable of simple learning. They can learn the association between a neutral stimulus and a response through classical conditioning. And through operant conditioning, they can learn to increase a naturally occurring behavior when it is reinforced. A baby can learn to change the frequency of her sucking, for example, as long as the behavior is promptly and directly reinforced. If sucking produces a sweet liquid in the mouth, babies who are just a few days old quickly start to suck at a high rate. In newborns, operant conditioning seems to be easier to demonstrate than classical conditioning (Sameroff & Cavanaugh 1979).

Newborns can even be conditioned to suck in a specific way. Usually they suck by combining two techniques: They create suction in their mouth, and they also force milk from the nipple by squeezing it against the roof of their mouth with their tongue. When a baby is reinforced for squeezing the nipple but not reinforced for creating suction (by means of an artificial nipple that releases milk only when it is squeezed), she decreases her suction and concentrates on squeezing (Sameroff 1968). She can thus learn to adapt her sucking to the particular nipple from which she is feeding, an ability that is obviously important for the infant's health and survival. A breast and a bottle have

RESEARCH:

HOW MOTHER AND NEWBORN TAKE TURNS

One of the most basic facts about social interaction is that people take turns. When two people have a conversation, for example, one person talks, then the other person talks, then the first one talks again, and so forth.

In at least one situation, even newborn babies seem to take turns with their mothers. When nursing, a newborn sucks several times at the breast or bottle and then pauses; the mother jiggles the baby for a few seconds—rocking or bouncing him gently—and pauses; the baby sucks again, the mother jiggles again, and so forth. Asked why they jiggle the infant, mothers often reply that "it wakes the baby up" or stimulates him to resume feeding. Mothers do not jiggle their infants every time the infants pause, but they do it frequently. This pattern of taking turns commonly appears even the first time the mother nurses the baby, and for almost all infants it is established within a few days after birth. To all appearances, the newborn is already taking part in social interaction, taking his turn and then pausing so that his mother can take hers.

Is the newborn actually taking turns, or is something much simpler going on that merely looks like it? In general, newborns have such limited abilities that it would be surprising if they were truly able to suck and then systematically wait for their mother to take her turn.

Kenneth Kaye and his colleagues have carefully studied this first turn-taking and shown how it comes about (Kaye 1982; Kaye & Wells 1980). They start with a description of a newborn's pattern of sucking. Hu-

man babies have a characteristic way of sucking when they nurse: They suck a few times and than pause for several seconds, suck again a few times, and then pause again (Wolff 1966). The bursts of sucking and the pauses are highly regular, with three to ten sucks in each burst and four to fifteen seconds of no sucking in each pause. Babies follow this pattern even when they are lying by themselves nursing on a bottle, so the pattern does not seem to include waiting for mother to take her turn. Pausing is just a natural part of the infant's way of sucking. It is the mother who takes advantage of the pattern. By turning it into a system of taking turns, she starts the infant on the path toward learning about social interaction.

Does the newborn contribute to the system at all, or does the mother merely fit in her jiggling during the infant's pauses? To answer this question, Kay looked for the kinds of simple adaptations that newborns can make. He found evidence that babies adapted their sucking in two different ways. First, while a mother was jiggling, her newborn less often started a burst of sucking (although occasionally a baby would start sucking during jiggling). Therefore, the infant usually paused as long as his mother was jiggling him. Second, the baby was more likely to start sucking soon after his mother stopped jiggling him.

These changes in an infant's behavior reflect only the likelihood, or probability, of pausing or of starting to suck—minor changes in the basic burst-pause pattern. Nevertheless, a newborn can adapt in a small way to his mother's jiggling and thus, from the first few days of life, take turns with his mother.

Although newborns do not "know" what they are doing, they do take part in social interactions that lay the foundations for turn-taking later in infancy and childhood.

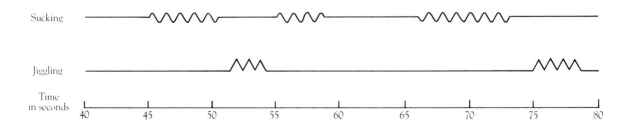

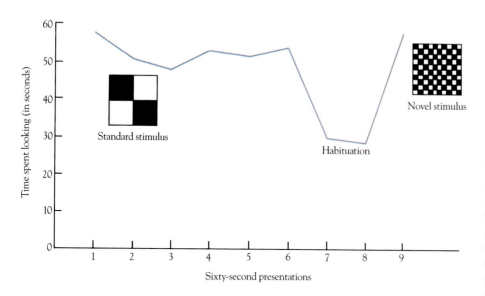

Figure 4-8 Habituation and dishabituation. This is one newborn's response to 60-second presentations of the visual stimuli shown. The baby paid attention to the large checkerboard when it was first shown and for five more presentations. Then the baby became habituated to this stimulus. When the unfamiliar small checkerboard was presented, the baby's attention increased to the earlier level, demonstrating dishabituation (Friedman 1972).

different nipples, and a baby must be able to adapt to such differences in order to obtain enough milk.

Besides conditioning, newborns show a type of learning called **habituation,** which is a decrease in response to a stimulus that originally excited interest. Habituation indicates that the stimulus has become familiar (has been learned). For example, when a newborn is shown the same object repeatedly, she gradually becomes "bored" with the object and stops looking at it. A new object is presented at that point, one that is different but has some similarity to the first one. If the infant notices the difference, she quickly resumes looking. This response to the new stimulus, which is called **dishabituation,** shows that the baby both remembers the initial stimulus and can discriminate between it and a new one.

In one study, newborns were propped in front of a TV screen on which patterns like those shown in Figure 4-8 were displayed. The graph shows habituation to the first pattern and then dishabituation as the second one appears (Friedman 1972). A number of researchers who study newborns use this learning technique, and they have been able to show that newborns can remember and distinguish between many sights, sounds, and smells (Horowitz 1975; Rovee-Collier & Lipsitt 1982).

Although there is no doubt that newborns are capable of both conditioning and habituation, experimenters sometimes find it difficult to demonstrate these simple learning abilities. Whether this simple learning will take place depends a great deal on the infant's state of arousal.

TABLE 4-2 STATES OF THE NEWBORN

STATE	BREATHING PATTERN	SELECTED CHARACTERISTICS
Deep sleep		Infant is sound asleep, with low muscle tone and no motor activity; *breathing is regular*; no facial expressions or mouthing.
Periodic sleep		Infant is asleep, but with some muscle tone and occasional general body movements; *breathing alternates between regular and irregular*; infant shows occasional facial expressions and mouth movements.
Irregular sleep		Infant is asleep but shows some muscle tone and periodic general body movements; *breathing is irregular*; infant shows frequent facial expressions, including smiling, frowning, and pouting, and intermittent mouth movements, including chewing, tonguing, and licking.
Drowsiness		Infant's eyes open and close intermittently but have a dull, heavy appearance when open; infant occasionally shows some gross motor activity but less often than in periodic or irregular sleep; *breathing is usually regular but faster than during deep sleep*; facial expressions, including smiling, are fairly frequent.
Alert inactivity		Infant is awake, with open eyes and a relaxed face; motor activity is minimal; *breathing is regular*; facial expressions are seldom seen; infant seems alert and actively looks at objects around her. (This is the state in which learning and complex behaviors are most likely to occur—the ideal state for most psychological testing, as well as for interacting with her parents.)
Waking activity		Infant is awake and shows frequent bursts of motor activity; *breathing is irregular*; facial expressions related to fretting are frequent, as are grunting, whimpering, and fretting.
Active crying		Infant is awake, shows much motor activity, and often cries; *breathing is irregular*; face shows a cry grimace.

SOURCE: Emde et al. 1976; Prechtl & O'Brien 1982; Wolff 1966.

Figure 4-9 Newborns spend about three-quarters of their day sleeping.

State of Arousal

The newborn's **state** is her level of arousal, which ranges along a continuum from "deep sleep" to "active crying," as outlined in Table 4-2. Each state is characterized by a specific, limited repertoire of behaviors that tend to be performed together rather than independently and that appear to be strongly associated with changes that are biological (physiological) rather than behavioral (Prechtl & O'Brien 1982; Wolff 1966). In fact, the pattern of breathing is a good index of where an infant is on this arousal continuum.

The baby's state is important to both scientists and parents. Newborns sleep about three-quarters of every day—sleeping a few hours, waking up and eating, drowsing a little, and then going back to sleep for a few hours. When they awake they are usually hungry and sopping wet. (Newborns urinate as often as twenty times a day—and may have a half-dozen bowel movements.)

Usually, the best state for getting a newborn to learn is "alert inactivity," which occurs only a few times a day and usually lasts no longer than 15 minutes at a time (although there are large individual differences). Thus, the infant learns easily during only a tiny fraction of her day. Unfortunately for researchers, it is difficult to predict the time of day that a newborn will be awake, alert, and inactive. But parents are usually aware of these brief periods, whenever they do occur, as pleasant times to interact with the baby.

BASIC SENSORY CAPACITIES

An infant is born with all the basic human *sensory capacities*—abilities to receive and respond to information from the senses, including vision, hearing, touch, taste, and smell. These sensory capacities seem to be relatively automatic compared to the corresponding skills of an older child, but they seem to lay the foundation for the later skills, just as the newborn's motor reflexes do. Because of this resemblance, Jean Piaget and many other developmental psychologists use the term "reflex" to refer to any inborn, relatively rigid behaviors, including those involving the senses.

Vision

The newborn visual system has been investigated and described more fully than any other newborn behavioral system, either sensory or motor (Cohen et al. 1979). From this research, a picture emerges of a behavioral system that is highly complex in spite of the automatic way it works in the weeks just after birth.

The Visual World of the Newborn   It is difficult to imagine the visual world of newborns. They certainly do not see the world as we do. They seem to sense things but not to perceive them (Cohen & Salapatek 1975). In *sensation,* the sense organs and the nervous system receive some type of energy, such as light, and transform that energy into a sensory experience, such as an edge or a color. In *perception,* sensory information is interpreted and given meaning.

To demonstrate the difference to yourself, look at Figure 4-10. If you see just a random pattern of black, white, and gray, your experience is roughly analogous to the sensation that a newborn probably has. But when you see a pattern that represents something, you are exercising perception—that is, you are organizing the sensory information in some meaningful way. In part, perception is based on past experience. Because a newborn child has had no visual experience, no pattern or object is familiar, so only visual sensations seem to be possible.

Although newborns do not seem to be able to perceive visually, they can look at things, and much research has been done on the ways in which they look. Exercising this inborn ability during the first few weeks of life seems to give the infant experience with particular visual sensations. This experience, in turn, probably helps to develop the ability to perceive.

Most functions of the visual system are present at birth in at least rudimentary form. Newborns can see objects directly in front of them, as well as objects on the periphery (Lewis et al. 1978). They can distinguish some basic colors, although which ones they are is a matter of some controversy (Werner & Wooten 1979; White et al. 1977). The pupil, the opening that regulates the

Figure 4-10 Most adults would not be satisfied to view this picture as a random arrangement of black blobs on a white background—to experience the sensation of clusters of black on white. Adults begin immediately trying to interpret the pattern, trying to see the whole thing or some part of it as similar to a pattern experienced in the past. For most adults, the pattern will suddenly simplify itself, and they will perceive a spotted dog sniffing the ground, its head at the center of the picture, its hindquarters to the right. An adult who had never seen a Dalmatian dog—a dog spotted black on white—would have difficulty perceiving the dog in this picture.

amount of light entering the eye, functions well at birth, contracting in bright light and dilating in darkness. However, some parts of the newborn's visual system are only partly developed. For example, an infant sometimes fails to adjust the lens of the eye to differences in distance. A young infant focuses best on objects 8 to 20 inches away, just about the distance of the face of a person feeding or caring for him. Objects closer or farther away can be seen, but not as sharply (Atkinson & Braddick 1982).

Visual Scanning Behavior A piece of equipment designed by Marshall Haith (1980) has allowed him to trace the eye movements of newborns in light and darkness. On the basis of his findings and those of others, Haith proposed a set

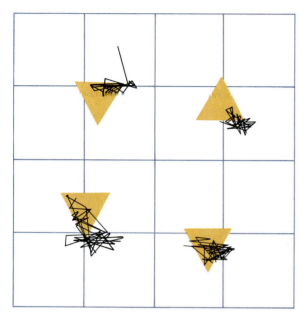

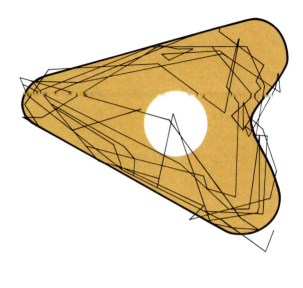

Figure 4-11 (A) In a study by Salapatek and Kessen of visual scanning in newborn infants, babies were shown large equilateral triangles in various orientations. Infrared lights (invisible to the child but not to the infrared camera) were used to track the babies' eye movements. Here are sample records from four of the babies. Notice that the babies do direct their scanning to the triangle, particularly to its edges and the corners, where two edges meet, but they do not scan the entire shape. (B) In a study reported by Zaporozhets (1965), the scanning eye movements of older children were recorded after they were told to examine various shapes. Shown here are the eye movements of a 7-year-old scanning a roughly triangular shape. The circle in the center represents the lens of the camera that photographed the eye movements. Unlike newborns, this child scanned all around the shape.

of **visual scanning rules** that describe the way newborns survey their visual field:

RULE 1   If you are awake and alert and the light is not too bright, open your eyes.

RULE 2   If you find darkness, initiate an intensive controlled scan. (Strangely, newborns in the dark not only open their eyes wide and actively scan their surroundings but also seem to move their eyes more smoothly than in the light.)

RULE 3   If you find light but no edges, engage in a broad, sometimes jerky, uncontrolled "searching" scan.

RULE 4   If you find an edge, stay near it and attempt to cross it.

RULE 5   Stay near areas with the most edges; scan broadly in areas with few edges and narrowly in areas with more edges.

Haith's theoretical rules can explain much of the data on newborn visual scanning. For example, Figure 4-11A, from a study by Phillip Salapatek and William Kessen (1973), shows the eye movements of four newborns scanning a triangle. As you can see, these newborns seemed to follow Haith's rules, particularly the one about crossing edges. You can also see that what seemed to receive the infant's attention was not the triangle as a shape—none of the newborns scanned all three of its angles or sides. What determined where they looked was the visual characteristic of high contrast at one or two edges of the figure. Compare the scanning patterns of these newborns with those of an older child (Figure 4-11B), who clearly scanned the entire shape.

Thus, newborns do not look for meaning in what they see. They simply follow an inborn pattern in their visual scanning. They scan a blank white field even though there is nothing to see. They scan the edges of a shape because they are edges, not because they form a recognizable shape. However, because the shape of an object is defined by its edges, one result of a newborn's scanning behavior is that the baby gains repeated visual experience with the shapes of common objects in his environment. This experience shows up in the greater sophistication of visual scanning by infants 2 to 3 months old.

Development to 3 Months of Age   Gradually, during the first few months of life, the newborn's complex but relatively automatic visual responses develop into a flexible looking skill. Even at one month of age, a baby's way of looking at things differs from what it was at birth. For example, although a newborn will continue to scan a blank white field for several minutes, a 4-week-old is likely just to glance at it and look away (Pipp & Haith 1977). By 3 months, babies begin to prefer looking at certain simple but meaningful shapes, such as faces. When newborns being tested in the set-up shown in Figure 4-12 are shown a normal face and a scrambled pattern of a face, for example, they demonstrate no preference for one or the other. But by 3 months of age, infants show a preference for the normal face (Fantz 1966).

In another study, infants' scanning patterns were recorded as each looked at its mother's face or at the face of a stranger. At 1 month of age, infants were still following Haith's rules, looking mostly at high-contrast areas such as the hairline. But by 2 months, infants spent most of their time looking at significant features, especially the eyes, rather than at the hairline. This was true for the stranger's face as well as the mother's (Haith et al. 1977). This preference indicates that the face had become a meaningful object.

Many parents have observed that around 2 months of age their babies begin to look at them instead of "through" them. Other parents have reported that when their baby began to look into their eyes, they felt that the child was "becoming a person" (Robson 1967). Eye contact may make it easier for an infant to attract the attention and care of its parents, and may also strengthen

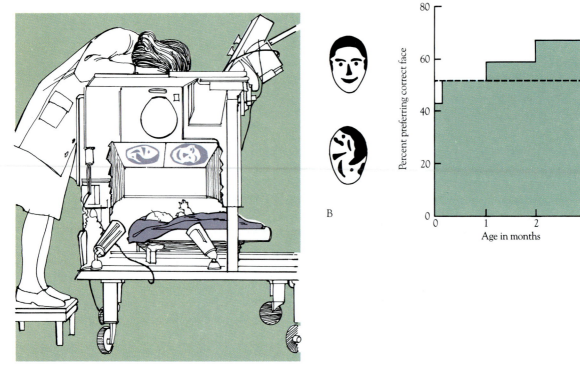

Figure 4-12 (A) Robert Fantz used this apparatus in one of the first systematic studies of what babies like to look at. Subjects were laid in a crib, which was slid under a stand. The baby could look up at the stand, which held a pair of patterned cards. The experimenter recorded the amount of time the infant's eyes were directed to each pattern. The pattern most looked at was said to be "preferred." (B) When infants of various ages were tested, equal numbers of newborns liked the scrambled features and the face. More of the older infants preferred the correct face.

the attachment between parent and child. Mothers of children born blind often report feeling estranged from their baby because of its inability to gaze into their eyes or respond to their facial expressions (Fraiberg 1974).

The ability of 3-month-olds to look into their parent's eyes does not mean that they can recognize their parents. At this age, babies cannot even tell the difference between their mother's face and the face of another woman of the same race (Haith et al. 1977). The ability to analyze the relations among parts of the face and to discriminate parent from stranger requires a few more months to develop (Caron et al. 1973; Emde et al. 1976).

Hearing

Like vision, hearing is a complicated inborn ability. The fetus appears to respond to loud noises even before it is born, and at birth all normal babies can hear. Hearing in infants has not been studied as much as vision simply because it is harder to study. Eye movements can be observed directly, but no similarly observable behavior accompanies hearing. Nevertheless, the results that have been obtained show remarkable hearing capacities in the newborn.

To find out what babies hear, researchers often rely on the learning processes of habituation and dishabituation. By monitoring a baby's heart rate, respiration, or rate of sucking, they can determine when the infant has become

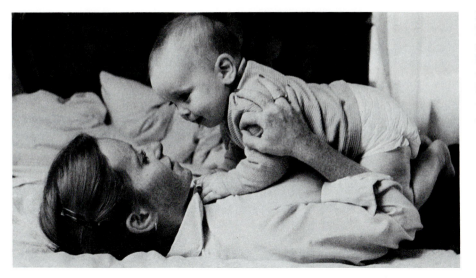

accustomed to a stimulus and when it responds to (hears) a different stimulus.

In one such study, newborns' sucking was monitored while different tones were played. As you can see in Figure 4-14, when the same tone was sounded repeatedly, a baby would stop sucking and listen to it only a certain number of times. Eventually, he would ignore the sound and continue sucking—as if to say, "Oh, that old thing again." That is, the baby habituated to the tone. But

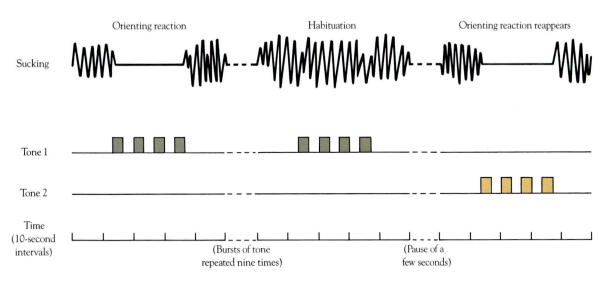

Figure 4-14 These records were made by a baby only 4 hours old sucking on a pacifier that contained a sensor. The sensing device activated a pen, whose tracings show the pressure in the baby's mouth rising and falling roughly once a second when he is sucking. The record at the left here was made as Tone 1 was first played; you can see how the baby's sucking stops while he is listening to the sound. The middle record shows the baby's sucking when Tone 1 is played for the tenth time; the baby does not even pause in his sucking. He has habituated to Tone 1. The record at the right shows what happened when Tone 2 was first played. (Tone 2 is about as different from Tone 1 as two adjacent notes in a musical scale.) The baby again stopped sucking in order to listen. This reaction demonstrates to experimenters that the baby can hear the difference between the two tones.

when a new tone was played, the baby again stopped sucking and attended to the sound—he dishabituated. Some newborns in this study could discriminate between tones only one note apart on the musical scale (Bronshtein & Petrova 1967).

Newborns can also distinguish between the human voice and other sounds. In one study, researchers monitored changes in heart rate, respiration, and muscle activity of 3- to 8-day-olds while playing them different sounds. The sound that had the most effect was a human voice (Hutt et al. 1968).

Young infants can detect very slight differences between speech sounds. Indeed, this may be the most impressive of all their abilities. By 1 or 2 months of age (and perhaps earlier—no way has yet been found to test newborns), babies can hear differences as subtle as the ones between "pa" and "ba," "ma" and "na," and "bad" and "bag" (Eimas & Tartter 1979).

Infants also seem to have an inborn disposition to relate what they hear to what they look at. This capacity has been tested by recording their eye movements while a short tape of a human voice was played. What the babies heard affected what they did with their eyes. For instance, when the voice came from one side, a baby's visual scanning movements would shift in that direction for a moment (Mendelson & Haith 1976). Apparently, newborns have a reflex that causes them to turn toward the source of a sound, as long as the sound is not loud enough to be startling (Turkewitz et al. 1966). This reflexive association between sight and sound in the newborn becomes a skilled action a few months later, when the infant can begin actively to use sound in deciding where to look (Haith et al. 1977; Lyons-Ruth 1974).

Touch, Taste, and Smell

Research on the other senses, though sparse, does indicate that the newborn has complex inborn capacities for them, too (Kessen et al. 1970). Babies show good sensitivity to touch soon after birth, when they are examined for common reflexes (rooting, sucking, stepping). They also have functioning taste buds, and prefer sweet things to those that are salty, sour, or bitter (Crook 1978; Engen et al. 1974). (Even fetuses show a sweet tooth; they swallow amniotic fluid more if a sweetener is added to it.) This preference is an adaptive one, because human milk has a sweet taste.

Smell is less important for people than for many other animals. But newborns do react to smells, and they show an ability to distinguish between odors, as shown by studies of habituation (Alberts 1981; Rovee 1972).

Because there has been so little research on touch, taste, and smell in the newborn, the development of these senses cannot be described with certainty. It is reasonable to assume, however, that developmental changes like those observed in seeing and the motor reflexes also take place in hearing and the other senses.

THE DEVELOPMENT OF ACTIONS

As the rigid inborn behaviors of the newborn develop into the flexible actions of the 3-month-old, the infant becomes able to perform many behaviors voluntarily. At this age, as was pointed out earlier, the infant is much more recognizably human in his behavior. He looks people in the eye. He smiles when he is interacting with them. His hand searches for the rattle in his crib until he can grasp it. He keeps his gaze on his favorite mobile while being carried across the room.

By 3 months, infants learn much more easily, too. Newborns often take a very long time to learn a simple response through operant conditioning—if they can learn it at all—but 3-month-olds can learn the same response quickly. In one experiment, newborns and 3-month-olds were conditioned to turn their heads to the left when they heard a bell and to the right when they heard a buzzer. When the bell sounded, the infant's left cheek was stroked, and if he turned his head to the left, he was fed milk. When the buzzer sounded, his right cheek was stroked, and he was similarly rewarded from the right if he turned that way. Most of the infants at all three ages learned to turn their heads in the appropriate direction, but the newborns required an average of 177 trials spread over 3 weeks, whereas the 3-month-olds learned in an average of only 42 trials over a few days (Papoušek 1967).

Besides growing in skills, beginning to show social behavior, and learning more quickly, infants undergo striking physical changes. By 2 to 4 months, they begin to show mature brain-wave patterns when they are sleeping, and the average amount of time they spend awake each day stabilizes at 8 to 9 hours. Much to their parents' relief, they start to stay awake mostly during the day and sleep mostly at night, and they become much less fussy (Emde et al. 1976). These changes seem to depend on developments in the brain's cortex, which are described below.

Most of the behavioral changes during the first 3 months represent the development of reflexes into voluntary actions (which also depend on the cerebral cortex). Grasping illustrates the nature of this developmental change (Touwen 1976). At birth, an infant exhibits the grasping reflex when his palm is touched. If a rattle is put in his hand, he will curl his fingers around it automatically and perhaps hold the rattle for a while. But by 3 months, the infant appears to grasp with a purpose. If a rattle is put in his hand, he seems to *want* to grasp it. After a few seconds, he may drop it, seemingly accidentally, and then feel around for it with his hand and grasp it again if he finds it. The search is performed without any guidance from looking, because an infant this age is not yet *able* to use looking to guide his grasping. But the grasping activity itself is more skilled, flexible, and persistent than the reflexive grasping of a newborn.

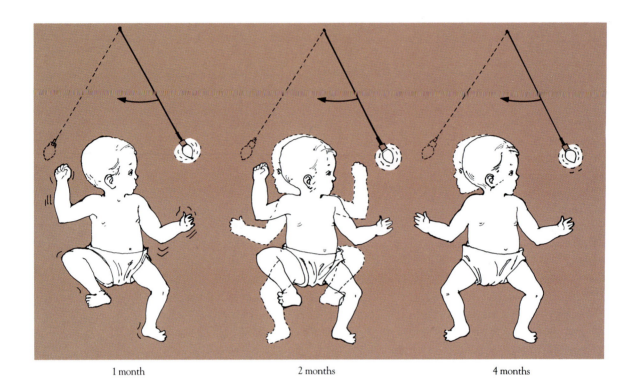

1 month   2 months   4 months

Figure 4-15   From reflex to action. The tonic neck reflex keeps the 1-month-old from visually following the interesting toy with its flashing light as it swings across his line of vision from left to right. The baby's head is turned to the left, and his left arm and leg are extended. This position seems to be wired together by the reflex. While the left arm and leg are extended, the 1-month-old cannot turn his head to the right. At 2 months, the child is able to keep his eyes on the moving toy by moving his head from left to right, but this head movement can be accomplished only when the arm and leg positions change as shown. The infant switches from the left-looking posture to the right-looking one so that he can follow the object with his eyes all the way from left to right. At 3 to 6 months, the infant's tracking action becomes entirely independent of any reflex postures. Consequently, the baby can now use his arms for other, independent movements—he can reach out for the pretty toy.

Combining Reflexes to Produce an Action

Looking shows the same kind of developmental change that grasping does, proceeding from reflexes—automatic, rigid behaviors—to actions, or voluntary, skilled behaviors.

An experiment by André Bullinger (1977, 1981) illustrates how this development seems to take place. As Figure 4-15 shows, two reflexive behaviors—looking and the tonic neck reflex—gradually combine, or become coordinated, allowing the infant of about 3 months to control the action of looking in any posture. In the tonic neck reflex, when an infant's head is turned to one side, his arm and leg on that side extend out straight while his other arm and leg bend, as in a fencer's posture. If his head is turned so that it faces to the other side, the posture also reverses.

During the first month of life, the infant is not able to switch postures on his own, so the tonic neck reflex controls where he can look. When he is in the right-looking posture, he can look only to the right. If an object he is looking at moves from right to left, he cannot turn his head to the left side. For the same reason, when he is in the left-looking posture, he cannot turn his head to the right.

In the second and third months, the infant begins to be able to change his posture so that he can look to either side. Although he has begun to form a looking skill that allows him to track objects visually, he must manipulate his postural reflex in order to track visually from side to side.

By 3 to 6 months, the infant has a looking action that is independent of the tonic neck reflex. He can turn his head from one side to the other and visually follow a moving object with only minor adjustments in his posture (Touwen 1976). Thus, as his mother moves around the crib, he has no trouble moving his head and eyes in order to continue looking at her face.

The development from reflex to voluntary action presumably progresses in a similar way for other behaviors as well. At first, the infant is completely at the mercy of his reflexes and other inborn capacities. During the first 2 months, he develops the ability to control his reflexes to some degree in order to reach particular goals. By about 3 months of age, he has developed abilities that allow him to carry out certain actions that are quite independent of earlier reflexes. Many reflexes, such as grasping, disappear at about the time the action develops.

The Development of the Cortex

Major physical developments make possible the changes in behavior from birth to 3 months of age. The most important of these seems to be that parts of the cerebral cortex begin to function efficiently (Emde et al. 1976; Peiper 1963). The cerebral cortex, you will recall from Chapter 2, is the part of the brain primarily responsible for voluntary behavior and the high level of human intelligence.

At birth, the brain averages 25 percent of its adult weight; only 3 months later, it is approaching 40 percent of adult weight. The cortex at birth is still quite immature in appearance; apparently it functions very little. During the first 3 months, however, it develops rapidly. Neurons grow in size and develop more connections with other cells. By 1 month the primary motor area controlling the upper body and arms appears to be functioning, and at 3 months most of the rest of the primary motor areas seem to be functioning. By 3 months, too, all the primary sensory areas of the cortex are mature enough to suggest that simple vision and hearing have begun to operate. The changes in the motor and sensory cortexes are undoubtedly related to the shift from reflex to action at this age—from a grasping reflex to a grasping action, from rigid visual scanning rules to flexible scanning actions, from the tonic neck reflex to flexible movement of the head (Cohen & Salapatek 1976).

Cortical development during the first months after birth results, in part, from genetically programmed changes. But this development also is molded by sensory experiences. After birth, babies are flooded by stimulation—sights, sounds, warmth and cold, textures of cloth and skin—all of which serves to mold cortical development. Most research on this molding effect has centered on the visual system, and it has vividly shown the essential contribution of experience to normal visual development. Most scientists assume that experience has the same sort of effect on the development of other parts of the cortex (Eimas & Tartter 1979).

Studies of both animals and people have shown that the developmental course of the brain's visual cortex depends on the kind of visual experience an animal or person has (Movshon 1981). That is, experience affects the anatomical structures themselves. The general outlines of visual cortical development are programmed by genes, but the specific details are shaped largely by experience. In people, for example, visual experience is known to speed up the myelination of nerves in the visual cortex. Myelin is the insulation-like coating around nerve fibers that enables the nerves to operate more efficiently (see Figure 2-6). Electrical impulses travel more than ten times faster through a myelinated nerve fiber than through one that is not myelinated. Myelin probably also reduces random interference, or "noise," between adjacent nerve fibers, which lessens the chance of an error (Morrell & Norton 1980).

Figure 4-16 illustrates the degree of myelination in the visual cortexes of four different infants. A is a cross-section of the brain of a premature baby who died at birth. B is that of a baby who was born at term (9 months) but died immediately. C is that of a baby who was born about 1 month prematurely and survived for more than a month. D is that of a baby born at term who lived for several months. The nerve fibers in A and B are not myelinated and are virtually indistinguishable from each other. Even though baby B was older than Baby A, neither had had any visual experience. The nerve fibers in C and D do show myelination and look very much alike, even though baby D was several months older than baby C. Both babies had had more than a month of visual experience. Clearly, then, the key factor in myelination is not maturation but visual experience. In particular, visual experience immediately after birth seems to promote rapid myelination.

In experiments with animals, an absence of visual stimulation has had serious effects on neural development. When one of an animal's eyes is sealed shut at birth, the optic nerve (which connects the eye to the brain) shows much less myelination than the optic nerve of the open eye.

Additional animal research suggests that what shapes the specific neural

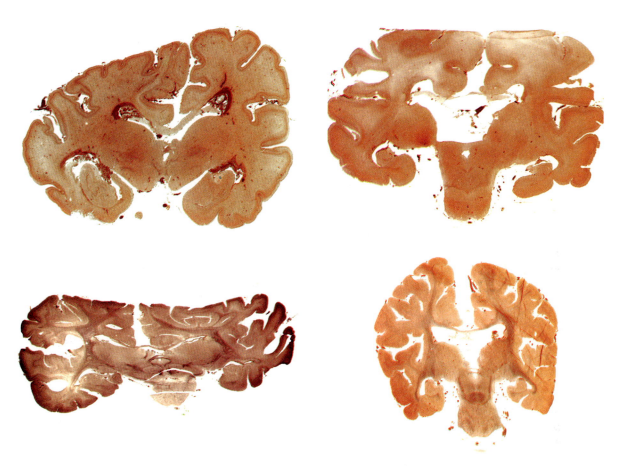

Figure 4-16   These are cross-sections of the brains of babies who died of natural causes early in life. Do not pay attention to the different overall shapes of these brains; some were distorted in the process of being sectioned and photographed. The things to look for are the grayish tracks running through the inner parts of the brain; gray is how myelinated nerve fibers show up in this kind of tissue preparation. These brain sections cut through the part of the brain where fibers carrying information from the eyes radiate outward toward the cortex from a central receiving area. The two brains at the top, A and B, are from babies who died on being delivered from the womb; baby A was born prematurely, at about 7½ months, and baby B was born at the end of a normal 9-month term. Brains C and D are from babies who lived for at least a month after birth; baby C was born prematurely, at about 7½ months, and died 1½ months later. Baby D was born at the end of a normal 9-month term and lived for about 3 months. It is easy to see here that it is not maturity in terms of age but visual experience that produces myelination of the visual nerve pathways. Only the brains of babies who lived in a lighted environment with their eyes open for some period of their short lives have any myelination. The brain of the premature baby in C has myelination, even though it lived no longer after conception than the baby in B, whose brain has no myelination.

connection between the eyes and the cortex is the nature of the visual experience rather than just the amount of it. Pioneering studies of the visual cortex of cats and monkeys have shown that particular nerve cells are specialized for detecting various features of the visual environment (Grobstein & Chow 1975; Singer 1979b). Certain cells in cats' brains, for example, normally respond best to horizontal lines, whereas other cells respond best to vertical lines. Large numbers of both types of cells are present in kittens before they first open their eyes (Hubel & Wiesel 1979). When kittens are raised for several months after birth in an environment in which they see only horizontal lines, their ability to detect vertical lines does not develop normally (Hirsch & Spinelli 1970). Because of their experience with only horizontal lines, very few of the kittens' nerve cells respond to vertical lines, certainly far fewer than in normally reared kittens. Lack of visual experience thus blocks the development of important connections between eye and brain, even though the genetic potential for forming those connections is there.

Visual experience also determines the effectiveness of binocular vision. In normal kittens, monkeys, or children, a large number of cells in the visual area of the cortex respond best when both eyes see the same thing. The visual cortex has this property when the eyes first open, but visual experience can mold it in at least two ways (Grobstein & Chow 1975). First, visual experience fine-tunes the binocular response. At birth and soon after, the nerve cells in the visual cortex respond to objects anywhere within a fairly wide region of the field of vision of either eye. But with experience, these nerve cells become more selective; each responds only to stimuli from a much narrower region of the field of vision in both eyes. Second, experience can change the inherited binocular organization of the visual cortex. If one of an animal's eyes is covered at birth so that it can see with only one eye, most nerve cells in the visual cortex lose their binocular sensitivity. If vision is later permitted to both eyes, the cells continue to respond to stimulation only from the eye that was previously used (Buisseret et al. 1978; Singer 1979a).

For visual experiences to have their shaping effect on the development of the visual cortex, the animal must undergo them while awake and in control of its eyes. If the animal is given an anesthetic that keeps it from moving but allows it to keep its eyes open, or if it is given a drug that allows vision and the movement of all body parts except its eyes, visual experience seems to have no effect. Thus, it seems that the effectiveness of experience in guiding neural development requires active participation by the organism; that is, the organism's own actions must be part of the experience.

Human neural development probably has the same requirement, as is shown by a study of adults with uncorrected astigmatism (Freeman & Thebos 1973). Astigmatism usually results from a sort of wrinkle, either vertical or horizontal, in the cornea: It causes the visual input to the eye and brain to be blurred in one dimension or the other. Using a viewing apparatus that corrected for astigmatism, the experimenters measured the neural activity of the subjects' visual cortex in response to various patterns. Even though each of the subjects reported being able to see all the patterns through the apparatus, there was less cortical response in the dimension that had always been blurred by the astigmatism. As with the visually deprived kittens, apparently, the experience of

Figure 4-17 Faces are fascinating, especially the face of someone who loves you, cares for you, and even entertains you.

poor visual input along a certain dimension had caused the brain cells that responded to that dimension to be underdeveloped.

In light of such findings, the newborn scanning rules described by Haith (1980) make very good sense. The strategy that causes newborns to seek out edges and areas of high contrast gives the greatest possible experience to the visual cortex and thereby promotes cortical development.

Presumably, the development of other parts of the cortex during the first months of life follows the same general principles as the development of the visual cortex. The genes lay down some general patterns for development of the cortex. However, the stimulation of nerve cells through the senses and through motor movement determines exactly how individual cells will develop and what they will respond to later.

Virtually all ordinary environments provide the kind of stimulation needed for normal development. Only kittens in special laboratory settings see a world of edges running only in one direction. Kittens growing up in households or barns see plenty of horizontal and vertical patterns—enough to stimulate growth of all the cells in their visual cortex. For human infants, too, the range of ordinary environments is enough to promote normal development, even though the differences across cultures may seem extremely wide. Infants in some parts of the world, for example, are swaddled most of the time, whereas other infants may never have their limbs wrapped. Yet both kinds of stimulation produce normal sensorimotor development.

Thus, through this interaction of heredity and active experience with the environment, parts of the cortex begin to function effectively by 3 months of age. The baby is now at the point where he can do some things purposefully. Unlike the newborn, who is limited to reflexive responses, the 3-month-old can, for example, purposefully clutch the corner of his blanket or his rattle. He can search out eyes and look into them. He can discriminate common speech sounds. He can easily learn to adapt these simple actions and perceptions to new situations. These actions, which are controlled by the child and become more and more flexible, are the roots of intelligence, which grow deep and strong during the first 2 years of life.

SUMMARY

1. Despite the apparent helplessness of human newborns, they come into the world with a wide range of capacities for doing what is necessary to survive and develop into healthy children.

REFLEXES

2. Infants are born with **reflexes,** automatic reactions that usually occur in response to particular stimuli. The reflexes of particular interest to developmental scientists are those that disappear within a few months after birth, as the cortex of the brain matures and infants establish voluntary control over their actions. During the early months, these reflexes develop into **actions,** which reflect organized abilities that are under voluntary control, allow flexible behavior, and can be affected by rewards and punishments.

3. The newborn's sucking ability is composed of several related reflexes, including rooting and sucking. The rooting reflex causes a baby to turn his head in the direction of a touch upon his cheek and to open his mouth. When rooting brings the baby's mouth into contact with an object, the sucking reflex is elicited.

4. Crying, which is elicited by hunger, pain, or discomfort, serves as a signal to adults that the baby needs care and attention. Between 2 and 3 months of age, the baby begins to smile at caretakers. This **social smile** helps infants obtain the care and attention they need.

5. Continuity between certain early reflexes and later skills exists even though the particular reflex may disappear long before the full-fledged action emerges. The *stepping reflex,* for example, lays the foundation for development of the action of walking, although this reflex disappears by 4 months and infants do not walk until about 1 year.

THEORY: *CONDITIONING AND LEARNING*

6. *Behaviorism* focuses on the analysis of the observable activities of people and animals, especially how they are affected by events in their environment. The main tools of behaviorism and learning theory in general are classical conditioning and operant conditioning.

7. *Classical conditioning* begins with a stimulus (the *unconditioned stimulus*) that naturally elicits a given response (the *unconditioned response*). The unconditioned stimulus is repeatedly paired with a neutral stimulus until the previously neutral stimulus (the *conditioned stimulus*), when presented by itself, comes to elicit the response (now the *conditioned response*).

8. *Operant conditioning* results from the effect of reinforcement or punishment on the frequency with which a spontaneously performed behavior occurs.
   a. A *reinforcer* is an event that increases the frequency of the behavior it follows. In *positive reinforcement,* the person or animal receives a reward after performing the behavior; in *negative reinforcement,* an aversive event stops happening after the behavior is performed.
   b. A *punishment* is an event that decreases the frequency of the behavior it follows.
   c. In *extinction,* the frequency of the behavior decreases to near zero because the reinforcement for the behavior is no longer presented.

9. Besides increasing the frequency of a behavior, reinforcement also tends to bring the behavior under *stimulus control.* That is, a stimulus that signals the arrival of reinforcement begins itself to elicit the previously reinforced behavior.
   a. Stimulus control allows people and other animals to learn a *discrimination:* They begin to respond to a stimulus that has been associated with reinforcement, but not to other, somewhat similar stimuli.
   b. People and animals also show *generalization:* They respond to stimuli that are similar to one that was associated with a reinforcer.

10. *Primary reinforcers* are objects or events that increase the frequency of a behavior without specific training. Food, for example, is a common primary reinforcer. Stimuli associated with primary reinforcers become *conditioned reinforcers,* which can themselves increase the frequency of the behavior they follow.

LEARNING IN EARLY INFANCY

11. The *schedule of reinforcement*—the pattern in which reinforcers are given—affects learning. Early in the conditioning of a behavior, a schedule of *continuous reinforcement* is often required to establish learning. But once the behavior has been conditioned, it can be maintained by *partial reinforcement,* in which the behavior is only sometimes reinforced.

12. Newborns can learn by both classical and operant conditioning, although operant conditioning seems to be easier to demonstrate.

13. Besides conditioning, a second type of learning shown by newborns is *habituation,* a decrease in response to a stimulus that originally excited interest. After babies have become habituated to a particular stimulus, they may again respond at a high level if they are presented with a slightly different stimulus. This renewed responding, called *dishabituation,* indicates that the baby remembers the initial stimulus and can distinguish it from the new one.

14. An infant's *state* is his or her level of arousal, on a continuum from deep sleep to active crying. The best state for getting a newborn to learn something is "alert inactivity," in which the infant is awake, attentive, and inactive.

BASIC SENSORY CAPACITIES

15. Infants possess basic *sensory capacities* at birth; they can receive and respond to information from each of the senses, including vision, hearing, touch, taste, and smell.

16. The most thoroughly researched newborn sensory system is vision.
   a. Newborns seem capable of *sensation,* in which the sense organs and the nervous system transform a stimulus into a sensory experience. They do not seem to be capable of *perception,* the interpretation of sensations in meaningful ways.
   b. Studies of the eye movements of young infants show that newborns seem to follow an inborn set of *visual scanning rules.* One rule is to look for edges; this gives newborns active visual experience with the shapes of objects in their environment.

17. With regard to hearing, newborns can distinguish between musical tones, and by 2 months they can distinguish between such speech sounds as "pa" and "ba." Newborns also seem to have an inborn disposition to coordinate hearing and vision by turning their eyes toward the source of a sound.

18. Newborns also appear to have complex inborn capacities for touch, taste, and smell.

THE DEVELOPMENT OF ACTIONS

19.   During the first 3 months of life, many of the reflex behaviors and rigid inborn sensory capacities of newborns develop into flexible voluntary actions.
   a.   Infants seem to construct each action by combining simple reflexes to produce complex, flexible abilities.
   b.   There is rapid development of the cerebral cortex of the brain during the first 3 months of life, especially in the motor and sensory areas. These developments result from both genetically programmed changes and the effects of experience.

SUGGESTED READINGS

KAYE, KENNETH. *The Mental and Social Life of Babies: How Parents Create Persons.* Chicago: University of Chicago Press, 1982.

Written by a well-known researcher on infant development, this book includes an insightful discussion of both the abilities and the limitations of the newborn infant.

LEACH, PENELOPE. *Your Baby and Child from Birth to Age Five.* New York: Alfred A. Knopf, 1980.

This authoritative, up-to-date book by a developmental psychologist describes in detail the behavior and development of the newborn, as well as that of the older infant and child.

PATTERSON, GERALD R. *Living with Children: New Methods for Parents and Teachers,* rev. ed. Champaign, Illinois: Research Press, 1976.

A distinguished researcher who has studied operant learning processes in children describes how behaviorist learning principles can be applied to children's behavior in everyday life.

STRATTON, PETER (Ed.). *Psychobiology of the Human Newborn.* New York: Wiley, 1982.

Important researchers in newborn behavior and development summarize and discuss findings on a wide range of topics concerning early growth and development.

TOUWEN, BERT. *Neurological Development in Infancy* (Clinics in Developmental Medicine No. 58), Philadelphia: J. B. Lippincott (Spastics International), 1976.

This definitive study of the development of infant behavior provides a detailed portrait of the early development of reflexes, as well as other infant behaviors.

5

FROM
ACTION
TO
THOUGHT:
COGNITION,
PERCEPTION,
AND
LANGUAGE

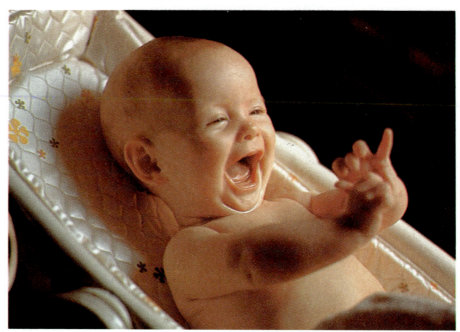

CHAPTER OUTLINE

5

FROM ACTION TO THOUGHT: COGNITION, PERCEPTION, AND LANGUAGE

Imagine yourself in a state of consciousness in which all you know is what you are doing at a particular moment. You are lying in your crib looking at your mobile, when suddenly a face appears above it, apparently materializing from nowhere. You watch the face intently, but then, just as suddenly, it disappears. At this instant, it ceases to exist for you. In its absence, your eyes once again focus on the mobile—but now a bottle appears just above your face, moves around for a few seconds, and disappears. It, too, ceases to exist. You make no connection between these events and the subsequent familiar feeling of a nipple touching your lips; you do not know that you are about to be fed. Instead, when you feel the nipple, you simply open your mouth and start sucking on it. As you do, your whole world is filled with the feeling of sucking and swallowing.

This is the world of the young human infant, a world in which objects and people exist for the infant only when he is looking at them, hearing them, grasping them, or acting on them in some other way. For him, out of sight is not only out of mind; it is out of existence. And whatever is in sight at the moment is not coordinated with his other actions and perceptions. The 3-month-old does not relate one action to another. When he is being diapered, for example, he does not know that the face he sees one second, the voice he hears the next, and the hands that are hoisting him by his ankles all belong to the same person.

This almost unimaginable way that infants have of knowing the world is what developmental scientists call sensorimotor intelligence. It is a "knowledge" of things that is limited to what the infant can do to them, how he can act on things through his senses and his movements. The infant does not understand that objects and people have an existence of their own, independent of the sensorimotor actions he performs on them. That understanding, and its corollary—that the child also has an independent existence, a self—develop at about age 2, when symbolic thought begins.

This chapter describes how sensorimotor intelligence progresses toward representational intelligence—that is, how the infant develops from knowing-through-action to symbolic thought. And with the beginning of symbolic thought comes the blossoming of language.

PHYSICAL DEVELOPMENT

In the first two years of life, doing and knowing are more closely related than at any other time. By seeing, hearing, feeling, and manipulating objects (including their own bodies) in various ways and under various circumstances, infants gradually construct an understanding of what objects are like and how they are affected by people and other agents acting on them. Physical development during these years gives infants increasing control over their bodies. As they

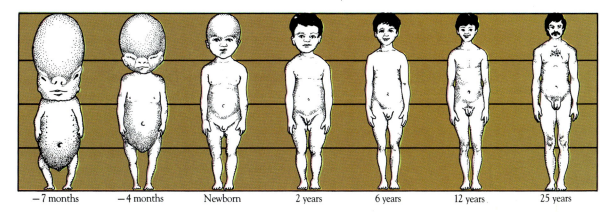

Figure 5-1 Human body proportions from 2 months after conception to adulthood. The head-to-foot direction of physical development is evident: Early in fetal life the head is half the body; at birth it is a quarter that length; and in the adult, one-eighth. Clearly, the head does a great deal of its growing early in life.

become physically able to do more, they are able to learn more about the objects and people around them.

Scientists describe physical development in infancy as having two aspects. One is growth in size and weight (Lampl & Emde, 1983; Tanner 1978), and the other is development of such skills as grasping, sitting, crawling, and walking (Knoblock & Pasamanick 1974). These abilities are usually called **motor abilities** although a more precise term for them is sensorimotor abilities because they all require the simultaneous use of muscles and senses.

In both bodily growth and motor development, the order of development follows two basic patterns: **head-to-foot** (cephalocaudal) and **inner-to-outer** (proximodistal) (Gesell 1954). That is, development proceeds more rapidly in the head and the upper parts of the body than in the lower parts, and more rapidly in the center of the body than in the extremities. For example, infants can suck before they can grasp, and can sit up before they can crawl.

Bodily Growth

Body proportions change markedly between birth and 2 years of age and, following the two patterns of physical development, continue to change in the same general ways until adulthood. Because of the head-to-foot order of growth, the head is much more developed at birth than the rest of the body is; in fact, it is one-fourth the total length of the body. As body growth catches up, the proportion decreases as shown in Figure 5-1, until at adulthood the head is only one-tenth the total body length. Similarly, a baby's legs are very short compared to the trunk, and they become relatively longer with age. Because of the inner-to-outer order of body growth, the trunk of the body develops faster than the arms, which in turn develop faster than the hands.

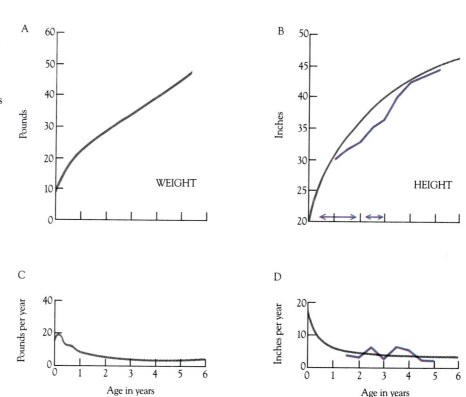

Figure 5-2 The average growth in weight (A) and height (B) from birth to 6 years old. The curves represent both boys and girls because their patterns of growth early in life are very similar. The curves in C and D show the average *rate* of growth for weight and height over these years. You can see that weight and height increase most quickly at the beginning of life. The colored plots on graphs B and D show what can happen when growth has been temporarily retarded. The pattern shown here represents a child who had two periods of starvation early in life (colored arrows). The spurts of growth when the child resumed normal eating can be seen clearly on the graph in D. (Adapted from Tanner 1970; Prader et al. 1963)

The rate of growth during the first 2 years is the most rapid of the child's lifetime (Figure 5-2). At birth, the average baby is about 20 inches long and weighs about 7½ pounds. At 3 months, the baby has gained about 3½ inches in length and about 5 pounds. At age 2, average height is about 34 inches (a 70 percent increase from birth) and average weight about 27½ pounds (almost a 400 percent increase) (Eichorn 1979). It should be emphasized that these figures are averages. Within the normal range, babies' sizes vary widely. Commonly, 2-year-olds weigh as little as 22 pounds or as much as 35 pounds; they may be as short as 31 inches or as tall as 37 inches.

Babies also show wide variations in rates of growth (Lampl & Emde 1983). Some children tend to grow at a relatively steady rate; others, in dramatic spurts. The reasons for these individual differences are often unclear. But extreme growth spurts are known to occur in children whose physical development has been retarded by illness or malnutrition. Many of them have a catch-up spurt in height and weight after they have regained their health (Tanner 1978). It is as if the "production line" for growth, after undergoing a temporary shutdown, increases the speed of growth well above the normal rate to make up for the shutdown.

Motor Abilities

Table 5-1 presents a number of milestones in a baby's motor development. In the table and in the discussion that follows, certain developments are described as occurring at particular times in a baby's life. These ages indicate when about

TABLE 5-1 MILESTONES IN SENSORIMOTOR DEVELOPMENT

AGE	SENSORIMOTOR ACHIEVEMENTS	VOCALIZATION AND LANGUAGE
3 months	Grasps objects, smiles spontaneously, holds head steady when sitting, lifts up head when on stomach, follows object readily with his eyes.	Squeals, coos especially in response to social interaction, laughs.
4½ months	Reaches awkwardly for some objects that he sees, frequently looks at hands, readily brings objects in hand to mouth, holds head steady in most positions, sits with props, bears some weight on legs.	Eyes seem to search for speaker, some consonants are mixed in with cooing sounds, babbling begins.
6 months	Usually reaches for near objects that he sees and looks at objects that he grasps, sits without support leaning forward on his hands, bears his weight on legs but must be balanced by adult, brings feet to mouth when lying on back.	Simple babbling of sounds like "mamama" and "bababa," turns to voice, laughs easily.
9 months	Grasps small objects with thumb and finger-tips, shows first preference for one hand (usually the right), sits upright with good control, stands holding on, crawls, often imitates.	Repetition of sounds in babbling becomes common, some production of intonation patterns of parents' language, some imitation of sounds, understands "no."
1 year	Neat grasp of small objects, stands alone, walks with one hand held by adult, seats self on floor, mouths objects much less, drinks from cup but messily, often imitates simple behaviors, cooperates in dressing.	Produces a few words such as "mama" and "dada," understands a few simple words and commands, produces sentence-like intonation patterns called expressive jargon.
1½ years	Puts cubes in bucket, dumps contents from bottle, walks alone and falls only rarely, uses spoon with little spilling, undresses self, scribbles spontaneously.	Produces between five and fifty single words, produces complex intonation patterns, understands many words and simple sentences.
2 years	Turns single pages in a book, builds tower of blocks, shifts easily between sitting and standing, runs, throws and kicks ball, washes hands, puts on clothing.	Produces more than 50 words, produces a few short "sentences," understands much in concrete situations, shows much interest in language and communication.

NOTE: These behaviors represent a few of the sensorimotor milestones of infancy. The ages shown here are averages for middle-class American children; normal infants show wide variations in the ages at which they develop these behaviors.
SOURCE: Frankenburg & Dodds 1967; Ilg, Ames & Baker 1981; Knoblock & Pasamanick 1974; Lenneberg 1967; Ramsay 1984.

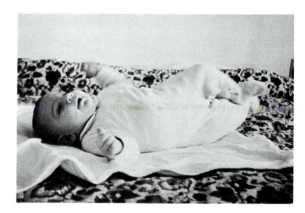

50 percent of American children show a certain ability, but the normal development of many infants departs from this schedule. Some, for example, develop the ability to crawl several months earlier than the average; some, several months later. And some babies never crawl but go directly from sitting to walking.

Generally, parents do not worry much if their child develops more quickly than they expected, but they often agonize over seeming slowness in the development of some motor ability. Such concern is rarely justified, however. Babies differ so much in size and weight, in temperament, in genetic legacy, and in the amount and kind of stimulation they get from their environment that no single developmental timetable could cover all of them (Connolly 1981).

Sitting, Crawling, and Walking   The change in just 12 months from a newborn unable even to hold his own head up to a 1-year-old toddler is as swift and dramatic a developmental sequence as any in human life. A 1½-month-old cannot purposefully change body positions. A 3-month-old, on his belly, can lift his head and chest up and stay propped on his outstretched arms for about 10 seconds. A 4-month-old can sit up if raised to a sitting position and given support, and most 5- or 6-month-olds can sit up for a time without assistance. At this age infants can also roll over.

By 7 months, many babies try to crawl; by about 8 months, most succeed in one way or another. Some babies zip around neatly on their hands and knees; others motor along on their bellies; and some develop unusual styles, such as lying on their backs and scooting forward head-first.

At 8 months, most infants can pull themselves to a standing position by holding on to the furniture, though they usually need help getting back down.

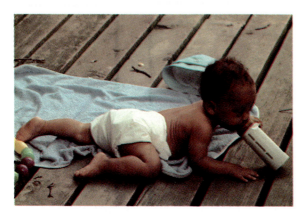

Many 9- or 10-month-olds can cruise, stepping along while holding on to objects in their path. By 1 year, many children walk—and walk and walk. They are so proud of this accomplishment and so determined to keep at it that they may seem outraged when asked to sit in a stroller, or in a highchair just for the time it takes to eat.

At 1 year, children are still awkward in their movements. In the next year, their walking smoothes out, although its grace may be compromised by layers of diapers and rubber pants. Beginning walkers need their arms for balancing, but as their skill increases, toddlers become able to carry a large toy while walking. Before long, they are learning how to run, to climb up stairs, to hop and jump. Skipping takes a while longer.

Reaching and Grasping   At 3 months, the grasping reflex has disappeared, and although the baby's reaching and grasping behaviors are now purposeful, they are not yet skillful. Typically, a 3-month-old will reach toward a desirable toy and swipe at it, but he may be unable to close his hand around it. Frustrated, he may reach for the object with both arms, starting with them far apart and closing in on the toy—finally trapping it between two open hands or, sometimes, two closed fists. By 5 or 6 months, however, the baby can pick up and hold a teething biscuit or cracker and begin to feed himself such things as pieces of banana and pear. The process may be messy, but quite a bit of the food actually ends up in the baby's stomach.

A baby's first two teeth typically arrive during the seventh month, so his mother may start to wean him from breast to bottle at about this time. By this age, the baby is able to hold a cup with handles but cannot really drink from it on his own. By about 1 year, most children can hold and control a cup well enough to drink from it messily. Even when someone holds the cup to his

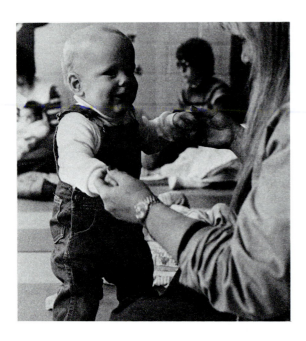

mouth, as much of the drink ends up on his stomach as in it. Between 1 and 2 years, most children learn to handle the cup without spilling much, if any, of its contents.

Sleeping and Waking   One of the most striking indicators of the transformation of newborn into a sensorimotor infant is the establishment of a stable daily cycle of sleeping and waking. By the time they are 3 months old, many babies sleep through the night. After they are fed in the evening, they sleep until 6 or 7 o'clock in the morning, usually to the delight of their parents. At about the same age, the baby may begin to protest the evening bedtime, as if not wanting all the interesting events of the day to come to an end. Many parents are surprised at this new voluntary protest and take it as a signal that the baby is "becoming human." At 6 months, babies still sleep about 15 of every 24 hours— through the night and two naps (Emde et al. 1976).

After they start crawling, at 8 or 9 months, and get involved in exploring, many infants hate to be put down for a nap. By about a year, many babies take just one nap a day, and most will continue to do so until about age 3 or 4.

The Development of the Cerebral Cortex

An essential foundation for most of the developments in behavior during the first 2 years is the physical development of the brain, particularly the cortex. At birth the brain averages about 25 percent of its adult weight, and by 3 months it reaches about 40 percent (see Chapter 4). The brain reaches half its

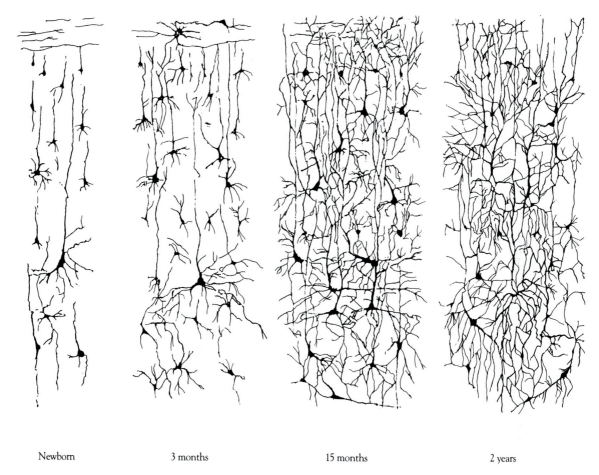

| Newborn | 3 months | 15 months | 2 years |

Figure 5-3 The development of neurons in the cerebral cortex. They grow both in size and in the number of connections between them. The progress of behavior from reflex to action is paralleled—and accounted for in great part—by the progress of cortical development. (Conel 1939–1963).

adult size by 6 months, and almost 75 percent by age 2. This growth is due primarily to an increase in the size of neurons and in the density of connections between them (Figure 5-3), as well as an increase in myelination.

In the cortex, both the areas that control primarily sensory functions and those that control primarily motor functions seem to develop according to the two patterns of physical development (Figure 5-4). Between birth and 3 months, the greatest development in the motor cortex takes place in the areas that control the head, upper trunk, and arms. Between 3 months and 1 year, the areas that control the legs and the hands show substantial development. The same kind of sequence occurs in the sensory cortex, but development there lags

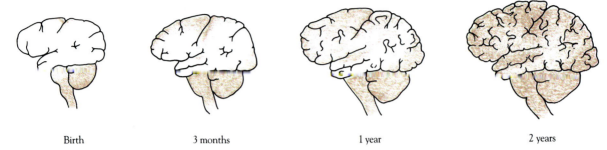

| Birth | 3 months | 1 year | 2 years |

Figure 5-4   Development of the cerebral cortex in the first two years. From between 300 and 350 grams at birth, the brain's weight jumps to more than 500 grams at 3 months, 900 by one year, and more than 1,000 by 2 years. The weight of adult brains ranges from 1300 to 1400 grams. The intensity of color in these drawings shows the comparative degree of maturity of different areas.

somewhat behind that of the motor cortex until about 2 years of age, when it catches up (Tanner 1978). The development of skills shown in Table 5-1 follows the maturation of these brain areas (Woodruff 1978; Lecours 1975).

Besides motor and sensory areas, the cortex also contains so-called association areas. Although little is certain about the specific functions of these areas, it is known that they combine information from the sensory and motor areas and are essential to higher cognitive functions such as anticipation and reasoning. The association areas show major development between 6 months and 2 years, as the infant becomes capable of more and more complex actions.

The correspondence between the development of particular areas of the cortex and particular motor developments is not the only connection between the physical maturation of a child's brain and his increasing abilities. At certain times in infancy, the brain seems to grow overall in spurts, periods of rapid development that appear to correspond closely with the beginnings of new cognitive abilities (Kagan 1982). Recent research findings about these spurts are presented later in the chapter when cognitive development is described.

The dependence of motor development on changes in the nervous system is illustrated by the development of a child's control of bladder and bowels. Babies may be conditioned very early to empty their bladders when they are placed on a potty, but voluntary control appears, on the average, only at 15 to 18 months (Tanner 1970). This order of events reflects the fact that the areas of the cortex necessary for emptying the bladder while on the toilet develop somewhat sooner than those needed to exercise voluntary control. In addition, the sensory neural pathway between the bladder and cortex must be mature enough to transmit the signal that the bladder is full, and the nervous system must be capable of having that signal take precedence over the brain's other ongoing activities, even when the child is deeply involved in some interesting game. Finally, the child must be capable of associating the signal from the bladder with the need to get to the potty. Most children do stay dry during the day by the time they are 18 to 24 months old, but some perfectly normal children do not manage to do so until they are 3 years old.

The Role of the Environment

All motor abilities depend greatly on gene-directed development of the brain and body, but environmental stimulation also plays a central role (Gottlieb 1983). The importance of such stimulation is seen most clearly when it has been lacking. Several studies, particularly of infants in institutions, have shown that a severely restricted environment in infancy can disrupt motor development (Hunt et al. 1976).

In a classic demonstration of this effect, Wayne Dennis (1960) studied infants in several orphanages in Iran. In two of these institutions, infants spent virtually the whole of every day of their first year merely lying in their cribs. The sides of the cribs were covered with cloth (to prevent drafts), so the infants could not see out into the room. The infants were fed by means of bottles propped up in the crib; they never sat on someone's lap, and no one ever held them. In fact, the infants were picked up only when they were bathed—once every other day. They had no toys and almost no social interaction. The few attendants in these understaffed orphanages were kept so busy with the physical care of the infants that they spent no time at all playing with them or interacting with them.

When Dennis tested these infants, he found that their motor development was severely retarded. Whereas almost all normally reared babies can sit alone by 9 months of age, more than half the institutionalized infants between 12 and 21 months of age still could not. And whereas nearly all infants reared normally or in well-run institutions walk on their own long before their second birthday (Clarke & Clarke 1976), fewer than 15 percent of the institutionalized 3-year-olds could walk alone.

Unlike the infants in Dennis's study, normally reared children are picked up, cuddled, and played with, receiving not only emotional and social stimulation but stimulation of their nerves and muscles as well. They learn to adjust their bodies to various ways of being held. Their sense organs and brains process the great variety of information they receive from looking at things from different spatial perspectives and from feeling different skin pressures and muscle tensions. This kind of experience stimulates the development of sensory and motor skills and, presumably, the development of the brain.

For deprived infants, even seemingly small increases in such stimulation can make a great difference. A second classic study by Dennis showed that a mere 15 hours of stimulation during a 1-month period greatly increased the developmental maturity of 1-year-old infants, moving them much closer to the norms for motor development (Dennis & Sayegh 1965).

 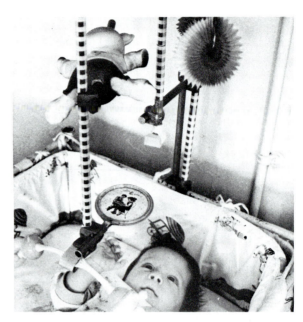

Figure 5-5   Two of the crib environments used by White and Held to test infants' reactions to various amounts of stimulation. (Left) An unadorned crib environment. (Right) The massively decorated environment assembled by White and Held.

Such findings might suggest that for infants' motor development, the more stimulation, the better. Other studies indicate, however, that a moderate amount of stimulation probably has the best effect. One study placed orphanage infants into three environments: the usual sterile institutional crib, with nothing much to look at; a crib enriched with one or two interesting toys; and a crib decorated with a wide array of brightly colored cutouts, mobiles, and toys (White & Held 1966). The babies who had one or two toys within reach in their cribs showed an immediate interest in their environment, attempting to reach out and handle the toys. In terms of looking and reaching, the babies in both the deprived and the greatly enriched environments lagged behind those in the moderately enriched one. In fact, the babies in the greatly enriched crib environment seemed overwhelmed: They ignored the elaborate stimuli and cried a great deal at first. Other studies likewise suggest that large doses of stimulation are not necessary for normal development and may even be irritating and confusing to infants (White 1971). The environments that most babies live in provide enough stimulation for normal motor development.

Figure 5-6 These babies are making important sensorimotor discoveries about the objects in their world—the color and scent of flowers and the soft feel of their petals, the gritty texture of beach sand and the movement of water as it ebbs and flows.

COGNITIVE DEVELOPMENT: THE SENSORIMOTOR PERIOD

When a baby learns to grasp things and bring them toward his eyes and mouth, he experiences all sorts of properties that were not evident before. The infants shown in Figure 5-6, for example, are getting the feel of how fragile a flower is and how hard it is to carry sand. During the first 2 years, each new activity broadens the infant's range of experience tremendously, and each insistent exploration leads to systematic changes in his ways of knowing about the environment. The theoretical perspective that focuses on describing and explaining these changes is cognitive-developmental theory.

THEORY: COGNITIVE DEVELOPMENT

Jean Piaget, who was born in Switzerland in 1896 and died in 1980, was probably the most influential developmental scientist of the last 20 years, even though he never earned a degree in psychology.

Trained as a biologist, Piaget was also interested in philosophy from an early age. In his early twenties, his interest turned to psychology, and he took a job with Theodore Simon, Alfred Binet's collaborator in the construction of the first intelligence test. As he worked with tests of reasoning ability, Piaget became intrigued with children's incorrect answers, which often reflected kinds of mistakes in reasoning that adults almost never make. To understand this qualitative difference between children's thinking and that of adults, Piaget set out to study how cognition, or intelligence, changes with age. (To Piagetians, "cognition" and "intelligence" mean the same thing.) He devised methods of his own for observing children's thinking processes at work, and over the years he and his colleagues at the University of Geneva studied thousands of children. Piaget also chronicled the development of thinking in his own three children (see the essay "Piaget's Observations," in this Chapter) and observed them carefully from birth through infancy and assessed their sensorimotor intelligence by means of simple tests that he constructed (Gruber & Vonèche 1982; Piaget 1983).

Piaget's theory attempts to explain how people develop knowledge and understanding. His biological background led him to see intelligence in terms of an organism's organization and its adaptation to its environment, two characteristics of living things that are not only fundamental but inseparable. For us human beings, organization refers to our biologically inherited constitution—the way our nerves and muscles and sense organs work together. It also applies to the internal workings of our minds. Piaget wrote, "Every intellectual operation is always related to all the others. Every act of intelligence presupposes a system of mutual implications and interconnected meanings" (1963, p. 7).

Adaptation, as discussed in Chapter 2, is vital to every species' survival, and every species is intelligent in the sense that it is adapted to its environment well enough to survive and reproduce. Piaget called this ability practical, or material, intelligence. Adult human beings, however,

are also capable of reflective intelligence; that is, they can think about, or reflect upon, their own experiences and thoughts, and can use reason. Infants are clearly not capable of reason. Yet reason is vital for the ability of human beings to adapt to their complex cultures. Piaget's theory attempts to explain how this development from practical, or sensorimotor, intelligence to reflective intelligence takes place. It describes how the nature of cognitive organization changes as development proceeds.

Although many cognitive-developmental researchers disagree with aspects of Piaget's theory (and with each other), virtually all of them agree on two basic principles. First, people are **active seekers and interpreters** of their experience, not merely reactors to stimulation from the environment, as classical behaviorist learning theory implies. And second, cognitive development produces **qualitative changes** (not merely quantitative ones) in how people think. That is, people don't just know more as they develop; their way of thinking changes.

THE BASIS OF INTELLIGENCE IN ACTION

Piaget and other cognitive-developmental scientists see people as active agents who construct their own understanding of the world. By acting on the world, individuals learn both about it and about their own actions. In this way, they adapt their knowledge to the world. Actions in this sense are voluntary behaviors, including not only bodily movements but also looking, listening, and thinking. In the course of acting upon things, an individual transforms both the things he acts upon and himself. Taking note of these transformations, he **abstracts** from them; that is, he identifies a common element in several transformations and uses it to build a new action that is more mature and more complex (Nelson 1974; Piaget 1983).

When a toy with a small bell in it is hung over the crib of a 7-month-old baby, the baby discovers how to make the bell ring by chance: When he moves his whole body vigorously, the crib shakes, and so the bell rings. But when he makes only small movements or sucks on his bottle or strokes his blanket, the bell does not ring. By comparing the effects of these various actions, the baby constructs the rule that thrashing about produces a tinkling sound.

With this simple rule completed, he can move on to a more complex one. He accidentally hits the toy with his hand and the bell tinkles. In an effort to make it tinkle again, the baby at first goes back to his original action of thrashing about. He has not yet understood that the sound can be brought about in more than one way.

Again by accident, he hits the toy with his hand and the tinkling takes place. This time he learns the rule that hitting the toy with his hand produces a tinkling sound, and now he purposely tries to hit it. At this point he has two actions—thrashing and hitting—that produce the same outcome.

One day the baby's mother unfastens the toy from the crib and puts it into the baby's hand. The baby spontaneously moves his hand about, as babies often do, and the toy tinkles. He quickly learns that moving his hand while holding the toy produces tinkling. Now he has three actions that transform the object from "toy silent" to "toy tinkling."

Over several weeks or months, he repeats these three actions often and eventually abstracts the thing that all three actions share: "Moving the toy makes it tinkle." He has developed a more mature and complex understanding of how to produce the tinkling property of the toy.

In older children the process works the same way, except that they can abstract from their own thinking instead of just from their sensorimotor actions. For example, they acquire an understanding of sex roles—"sex-appropriate" behaviors—through abstracting. They put together what they know about girls and women and about boys and men, and then abstract the attitudes, actions, and styles that differentiate the sexes. Once they have abstracted the principles of behavior of their own sex, they usually try to act in accord with them (Kohlberg 1966; Maccoby 1980).

Schemes

What people abstract as they develop is called a **scheme** (sometimes called *schema*), a structured piece of knowledge about how to do something. For Piaget, a scheme is the cognitive structure that underlies an action or a thought. A scheme may be as simple as how to pick up a chess piece between thumb and forefinger or as complex as the strategy for beating a particular chess opponent. When an infant thrashes about to make the toy tinkle, he is using a simple sensorimotor scheme. When he abstracts the more general rule "Moving the toy makes it tinkle," he has constructed a new, higher-level sensorimotor scheme.

Assimilation and Accommodation

To describe the adaptive nature of knowing, Piaget (1952) uses the concepts of **assimilation** and **accommodation.** Every thought and action employs both processes. When you apply a scheme to an object or event, you try to assimilate the object or event into the scheme. When you adjust that scheme to the particular characteristics of the object or event, you accommodate the scheme to the object or event. For example, when you catch a baseball, you employ assimilation as you strive to reach out and grasp the ball, using a scheme that you devise from your previous experience of catching baseballs. But the ball's speed and direction will vary depending on the wind and the way the bat met the ball. You will therefore employ accommodation, adjusting your actions to account for the characteristics of the ball's movement.

Assimilation and accommodation continually interact. The result is adaptation—schemes become more refined and better able to account for what happens in an individual's world—and this adaptation process produces cognitive development. In Piaget's terms, the process is motivated by the need for **equilibrium.** In trying to make sense of something, the mind seeks equilibrium between assimilation and accommodation.

The infant's grasping provides a useful example of how assimilation and accommodation move a mind toward equilibrium. To a young infant—say, a 2-month-old girl—very few objects are familiar. She must learn about everything from scratch. One way she does this is by using her hands to grasp objects. Perhaps the first thing she learns to grasp is her blanket, sort of pinching it between her fingertips and palm. Once she has a scheme for this action, she uses it regularly. A month later, she discovers the rattle in her crib and tries to grasp it—that is, she tries to assimilate the rattle to her "pinching" scheme for grasping a blanket. When that does not work, she experiences disequilibrium and begins some trial-and-error groping. Eventually, she accommodates her grasping scheme to her experience—she learns to hold the rattle as well as the blanket. When she succeeds in grasping the rattle at will, she has attained a new equilibrium between the application of her grasping scheme to the rattle (assimilation) and the adjustment of her scheme to the properties of the rattle (accommodation).

Of course, this is only the beginning of the infant's grasping experience, for the world is full of things that can be grasped—and of things that cannot be grasped, like floors, and other things that are dangerous to grasp, like flames. With each opportunity for grasping something that she has never grasped before, the infant experiences disequilibrium and must enlarge her grasping scheme to reach still another new equilibrium. Each equilibrium reached produces better adaptation to the world.

Throughout life, a person develops many schemes—at first, only sensorimotor ones, but later on, symbolic ones as well. By means of these schemes, the person tries to "grasp" objects, events, and ideas. When a particular scheme does not work, disequilibrium arises and must be resolved. Its resolution leads to a developmental change in the scheme—an enlarged, better adapted knowledge of the world. In this way, according to Piaget, assimilation and accommodation lead a person through recurring cycles of disequilibrium and equilibrium, and cognitive development moves forward.

This view of intelligence differs sharply from the one embodied in the concept of IQ (DeVries & Kohlberg 1977). In IQ tests, intelligence is treated as a relatively fixed trait that individuals possess in different amounts. A person who scores 120 on an IQ test is said to be more intelligent than someone who scores 90. For Piaget, in contrast, intelligence is an ongoing adaptive process rather than a trait. This process becomes more complex and more abstract with age, so that toddlers can be said to have reached a higher cognitive stage than infants. Piaget and other cognitive developmentalists emphasize the organization of knowledge rather than the amount. (IQ tests and their applications are discussed in Chapter 9.)

QUALITATIVE CHANGE: PIAGET'S FOUR PERIODS

Piaget has identified four periods of cognitive development: sensorimotor, pre-operational, concrete-operational, and formal-operational. Each period is characterized by a different way of knowing, and every child passes through the same periods. The periods represent a type of stage. Historically, *stage* usually has meant a developmental step that meets the following three conditions (Flavell 1971; Wohlwill 1973):

1.   Most important, changes from stage to stage are qualitative; that is, the difference between one stage and the next is one of quality, not simply quantity.

2.   The changes occur abruptly. The new thinking capacities of a 2-year-old emerge rather abruptly, for example (Corrigan 1983).

3.   Several changes appear at the same time. The new thinking capacities of the 2-year-old, for instance, are evident in a number of different areas, such as language, pretend play, and search for hidden objects.

The four periods meet all these conditions, according to Piaget, and they are thus stages. They are called "periods" because they are the most general of all stages, encompassing all intelligence and developing over long age spans (Flavell 1963). The periods are described only briefly here because they are dealt with at length in later chapters.

Until about 2 years of age, the child is in the **sensorimotor period** of cognitive development (Piaget 1952, 1983). As explained earlier, an infant knows things only through his sensorimotor actions on them. Objects and people exist for the baby only when he is actually looking at them, hearing them, or touching, holding, mouthing, or otherwise acting on them. When a 3-month-old loses sight of a rattle, for instance, it stops existing for him; he does not even search for it.

Most 2-year-olds are no longer limited to merely sensorimotor intelligence but have entered the second period of cognitive development, the **preoperational period,** in which they are able to **represent** absent objects—that is, to think symbolically about them. For example, when a toy rolls out of sight under the couch or around a corner, 2-year-olds will search for it with determination, which indicates that they know it still exists (Corrigan 1981). This period, which lasts roughly from age 2 to age 6 or 7 is characterized chiefly by children's ability to symbolically represent to themselves not only absent objects but past and future events. The ability is evident in a large number of new schemes that appear at around age 2, including both searching for objects and pretending. A child can pretend, for instance, that he or one of his dolls is his father going to work. To act out such an event, the child must have in mind some symbolic representation of the event itself (Piaget 1951).

What preoperational children lack, according to Piaget (1951), is the capacity to use their representations logically—to relate different facts to each other consistently, without contradiction, as adults can do. The ability to think in this way first develops in the **concrete-operational period,** from age 6 or 7 until adolescence. At this time, children become able to think logically about familiar concrete things (Inhelder & Piaget 1964).

Figure 5-7 Piaget's four periods of cognitive development. (A) An infant in the sensorimotor stage of development learns about the shape and texture of a ball by looking at it, handling it, and mouthing it, but he does not understand that the ball has an existence outside of his own actions on it. (B) A toddler in the preoperational period has the ability to represent objects, such as a ball, mentally. In fact, he can pretend that the ball is something else—the head on a snowman. (C) A child in the concrete-operational period can think logically and quite systematically about real objects and events in his world. This allows him to learn the complex rules of a game such as baseball or football and to play according to those rules. (D) A person with formal-operational abilities can think beyond the here-and-now. He can plan strategies for ball games and create new plays.

"Grandma always cuts it again so I can have FOUR little sandwiches."

A commonly used test of concrete-operational intelligence is the conservation task, which tests a child's ability to recognize the constancy of a given amount despite changes in its form. In one version of the task, a child is shown two equally large balls of clay and then shown one of the balls being rolled into the shape of a sausage. When asked which has more clay, the ball or the sausage, a child in the preoperational period usually says that the sausage has more because it is longer. This kind of judgment is also evident in the daily lives of preoperational children. For example, they will usually choose a serving of cake that has been cut into several pieces instead of a serving that is the same size but a single piece: To them, more pieces equals more cake. They are also likely to choose a narrow 8-ounce glass of juice over a wide 8-ounce glass: In this instance, taller means more. Concrete-operational children, on the other hand, know that these choices are illogical. "Your glass is taller than mine," they will say, "but I have just as much juice because my glass is fatter."

Although concrete-operational intelligence enables children to think logi-cally about concrete situations, they cannot think logically about hypothetical ideas. Only in the *formal-operational period*, from early adolescence through adulthood, can people deal logically with the possible or hypothetical. Formal-operational abilities are essential for learning and understanding mathematics, science, poetry, and philosophy. In fact, for Piaget, all formal-operational thought is like the thinking used in performing a scientific experiment. Just as the scientist tries systematically to consider all possible outcomes of the experiment and re-late them to the hypothesis being tested, an individual capable of formal-operational thought can approach a problem by systematically trying to consider all the possible causes and solutions. It does not matter whether the problem is a car that will not start, a chemistry experiment that had unexpected results, or a particular moral rule that appears inconsistent with the principle upon which it is based (In-helder & Piaget 1958).

A careful reading of Piaget (1951, 1971) shows that the type of thinking charac-teristic of each cognitive period never simply disappears when a higher period is reached. In each period, a person's ways of thinking not only develop from but include those of the preceding period. That is, the periods form a *hierarchy,* in which each new type of intelligence is built upon and incorporates the type before it (Fig-ure 5-8). An adult may therefore use any of the four types of intelligence, depend-ing on what he happens to be doing at the moment. A chemist conducting an experiment, for example, uses sensori-motor intelligence in pouring liquid from one container to another, concrete-oper-ational intelligence in measuring the liq-uids he pours, and formal-operational in-telligence in devising a particular combination of liquids. Artists and poets

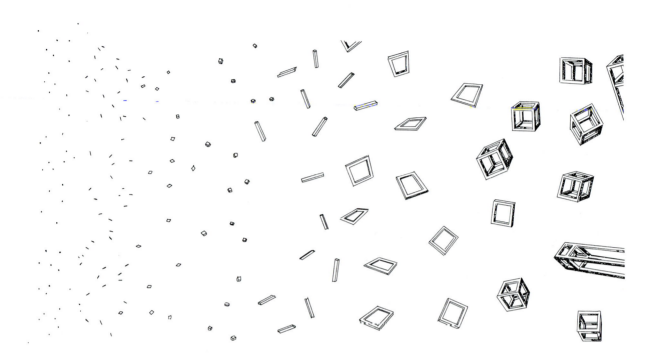

Figure 5-8 A graphic metaphor for the hierarchical nature of intelligence. Each structure in this hierarchy has been developed from the simpler structures to the left of it. In a similar way, as sensorimotor intelligence develops into preoperational intelligence and so on, the earlier levels do not disappear. Instead, they are incorporated into the reorganized structure of intelligence.

may use preoperational intelligence—intuitive thinking—to create images that logic would not produce, then use formal-operational thought to organize these images into a coherent form.

Although most cognitive-developmental researchers agree that the course of development shows some kind of cognitive hierarchy, they disagree about the nature of the stages of development and the processes by which a person moves through them (Flavell 1982; Sternberg 1984). A major focus of these disagreements is the role and importance of the environment.

The Environment and Unevenness in Development

Piaget's analysis of development in terms of four periods implies that the schemes a person is capable of using should show a high degree of consistency. If a child is in, say, the concrete-operational period, then virtually all his capabilities should be concrete-operational. Studies have shown, however, that this kind of consistency is rare (Flavell 1971; Ford 1979). When people are tested on a wide range of tasks, their performance usually indicates thinking characteristic of various stages. The performance of college students, for example, typically reflects at least two stages—formal operations in the students' special interests, such as their major, and concrete operations in other areas (DeLisi & Staudt 1980; Neimark 1975). Piaget (1941) acknowledged the existence of some such unevenness in performance and called it **decalage,** but he tended to minimize both its frequency and its importance (Broughton 1981).

Even children's understanding of conservation, which characteristically begins to develop at the start of the concrete-operational period, shows considerable unevenness. A child may be able to rea-

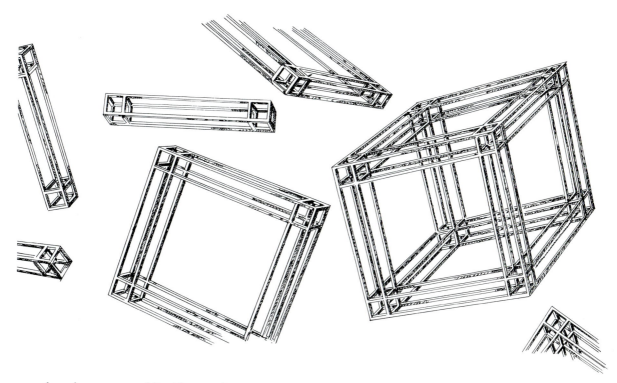

son that the amount of liquid stays the same when juice is poured from a short wide glass into a tall, narrow one. But he or she may be unable to conclude that a ball of clay that is changed to a sausage shape contains no more clay than when it was a ball. Another child may reason correctly about conservation of amount of clay but incorrectly about conservation of amount of liquid. This unevenness in applying what is, after all, the same kind of reasoning to these various physical phenomena probably arises from environmental influences (Pulos & Linn 1981). The first child may have had much experience pouring liquids and little experience with clay or similar substances.

Although Piaget acknowledged that cognitive development can be uneven and agreed that environmental factors contribute to the unevenness, he did not construct his theory to explain how the environment produces it (Piaget 1971).

NEO-PIAGETIAN THEORY

Building upon the work of Piaget and other major cognitive-developmental theorists such as Heinz Werner (1948) and Lev Vygotsky (1962), developmentalists have addressed problems that earlier theorists did not resolve, including how the environment produces unevenness in cognitive development. These researchers and theorists differ somewhat in their approaches to cognitive development and their criticisms of Piaget, but they agree enough on many major points for their ideas to be called a neo-Piagetian theory.

One leader of the neo-Piagetian movement is Jerome Bruner (1973), an American psychologist who emphasizes how children process information about their world, how they construct and control flexible abilities for handling information, and how the environment affects the way they use information. One role of the environment is to provide reinforcement and punishment for specific behaviors, and so neo-Piagetian theory relies on concepts from learning theory as well as those from Piaget.

A basic difference between classic Piagetian theory and neo-Piagetian theory is that whereas Piaget characterizes a *person* as being in a particular stage of development, neo-Piagetian theory characterizes a person's *behavior* as being at a particular level of development. The traditional idea of development by stages suggests that developmental changes occur abruptly, or discontinuously, and that a number of qualitative changes emerge at the same time. The neo-Piagetian idea of development by levels of behavior acknowledges that abilities can appear abruptly, but it does not imply that such changes always occur in a stage-like way, all at once for different abilities.

According to neo-Piagetian theory, each person has many different abilities at various levels, forming a profile of levels, as shown in Figure 5-9 (Biggs & Collis 1982). At a given time, one or two levels are dominant in the profile, and the person can be described as performing, for example, mostly at the concrete-operational level. The profile is likely to become more varied as development proceeds. In infancy, all abilities are sensorimotor. Most abilities of the average 5-year-old are preoperational, but some are still sensorimotor. Adults demonstrate abilities at all levels, although the majority are concrete-operational or formal-operational (Flavell 1970; Piaget 1972).

Another difference between the two approaches is in how general a person's abilities are. Piaget believed that schemes are highly general abilities. Neo-Piagetian theorists, on the other hand, tend to view abilities as specific to the context in which they are learned (Biggs & Collis 1982; Bruner 1973; Cole et al. 1983; Feldman 1980; Fischer 1980; Siegler 1981). That is why, according to their view, unevenness is so common in cognitive development. For an ability to become general, the person must learn how to apply it in a range of different contexts.

Piaget argued, for example, that children develop a scheme for conservation and that this one scheme should apply to all types of conservation tasks. Neo-Piagetian theorists say that, to the contrary, the development of one scheme or ability will not typically bring other, related schemes to the same level at the same time: the child must develop a specific conservation scheme for each type of task. When children practice, say, conservation of amount using a ball of clay, they learn that a sausage made from the ball contains no more clay than the ball does. But they do not automatically generalize that scheme to the conservation of amount of cake or the conservation of liquid (Pinard 1981).

A major criticism of Piaget's theory has been that it does not clearly explain the transitions between periods. It does not state specifically how sensorimotor thought becomes preoperational thought or how preoperational thought becomes operational thought. Neither does it describe precisely how transitions take place within periods, except for the sensorimotor period (Miller 1983). Some neo-Piagetian theorists attempt to explain such transitions more precisely. In particular, several have been able to find and describe distinct developmental levels *within* the Piagetian periods (Biggs & Collis 1982; Case 1980; Fischer 1980; Kagan 1982; Kenny 1983; McCall 1983). These levels and the experimental evidence that supports their existence are presented along with Piaget's theory throughout this book.

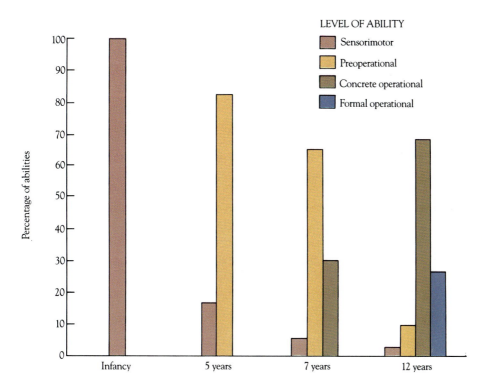

LEVEL OF ABILITY

█ Sensorimotor
█ Preoperational
█ Concrete operational
█ Formal operational

Figure 5-9 These profiles illustrate the patterns of the abilities of one child at four different ages. These are hypothetical percentages, not actual measurements, but they serve to show the variation in periods specified by neo-Piagetian theory. When the child is 7, for example, many of his skills are at the preoperational level, but some are concrete-operational, and a few remain at the sensorimotor level.

The Development of Circular Reactions and Representation: Piaget's View

Piaget made extensive observations of his own children's development (see the essay "Piaget's Observations," in this chapter). He was struck by the insistence with which infants explore their environment during the sensorimotor period. They often repeat a behavior over and over, as if searching to understand the properties of their physical world and the operations of their own bodies. To emphasize the repetitious nature of these behaviors, Piaget (1952) called them **circular reactions.** He noted that they grow increasingly complex during the first 2 years of life, developing from primary to secondary to tertiary circular reactions. He described this development as having six stages.

In the first stage, which encompasses the first few months of life, the baby is capable only of reflexes, such as sucking and grasping (see Chapter 4). These reflexes are the foundation of the circular reactions.

Primary circular reactions, which define the second stage, are repetitions of a single action, apparently for its own sake, and are most common in infants between 1 month and 6 months of age. In one circular reaction, a 3-month-old girl sucks at a pacifier endlessly. If her mother bends over the crib, the infant may stop sucking and begin the circular reaction of looking at her mother's face intently, moving her own head and eyes to keep the face in view as her mother moves around. When the mother leaves, she may start another circular reaction, like repeatedly grasping the edge of her blanket or shirt.

At the third stage, infants perform **secondary circular reactions,** which are most common between the ages of 4 and 12 months. The baby repeats an action in order to affect some object and produce a result she enjoys, such as an interesting sight or sound. In other words, the activity is used as a *means* to repeat or sustain an interesting *end.* A 6-month-old girl, for example, shakes her rattle over and over so that she can listen to the sound. Similarly, she waves her pacifier in front of her eyes repeatedly so that she can watch her arms and hands moving. And she searches for a partially hidden object, as shown in Figure 5-10.

The fourth stage is characterized by the **coordination of secondary circular reactions,** in which the infant uses a familiar action not merely to re-create an interesting sight or sound but to produce a novel end. For instance, at 7 months, Piaget's son Laurent used a familiar means, hitting at things, to achieve the new end of removing an obstacle. He was trying to reach a matchbox, but Piaget positioned a pillow in such a way that Laurent could still see the box but could not reach it. To get to the matchbox, Laurent hit the pillow until it was out of his way (Piaget 1952). Similarly, infants show a major advance in what Piaget (1954) called **object permanence,** the ability to search for hidden objects. Now they can find an object hidden under a screen even when the screen covers it completely (see Figure 5-10). Such behaviors are common between 6 and 14 months of age.

The fifth stage is characterized by **tertiary circular reactions,** performed mostly by children between 11 and 22 months old. The infant not only repeats an action in order to produce an interesting result in an object but also varies the action in order to vary the result. These reactions might be called experiments in action, because the infant seems to be trying out variations in an action to see how they will affect an object. At 11 months of age, for example, Piaget's son began a series of dropping experiments. First, Laurent dropped a piece of bread and watched it fall. He picked it up and dropped it again, this time from up high, and again watched it fall. He repeated dropping the bread

Figure 5-10   The development of the knowledge of object permanence in the sensorimotor period. To a very young infant, her rattle and even her mother do not exist except when she is actually looking at them or touching them. Infants are not born with an understanding of how objects exist in space and time; they must construct the notion of object permanence. The development of object permanence is generally tested in a series of hiding experiments. The infant is shown an object and then watches while the researcher hides it. Piaget described a series of stages in the development of infants' ability to find a hidden object. Gradually over the first two years of life, infants discover that an object continues to exist even when they are not performing a sensorimotor action on it—not seeing, touching, or hearing it. Along with the development of object permanence, babies also come to understand that people too have a permanent existence. Indeed, attainment of the final stage of object and person permanence seems to result in a substantial decrease in distress at separation from the mother: The infant appears to understand that mother is still present somewhere and will soon come back, so there is no reason to be alarmed that she is not visible at the moment.

PRIMARY CIRCULAR REACTIONS: When something disappears from sight, the infant does not even look for it. It is as if the object ceased to exist.

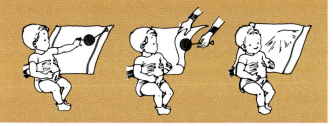

SECONDARY CIRCULAR REACTIONS: If the object is only partly hidden, the infant will search for it. But she will not search for one that is completely hidden, even if she saw it being hidden.

COORDINATION OF SECONDARY CIRCULAR REACTIONS: If the infant sees an object being hidden, she will search for it where she saw it hidden. But if she sees the object moved from the first hiding place to a second one, she will search in the first hiding place.

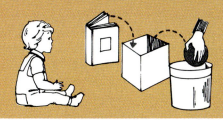

TERTIARY CIRCULAR REACTIONS: The infant will search for a hidden object through any number of displacements that she can see. But if someone secretly hides the toy (for example, pretends to hide it behind a pillow but secretly puts it into his pocket), the infant will not continue to search after finding that the object is not where she last saw it hidden.

BEGINNINGS OF REPRESENTATIONAL THOUGHT: The infant will continue to search for objects even if they have been secretly hidden, showing that she knows the object must exist somewhere.

RESEARCH
PIAGET'S OBSERVATIONS

These excerpts are from Jean Piaget's book *The Origins of Intelligence in Children* (1952). They record Piaget's intensive observations of his three children—Laurent, Lucienne, and Jacqueline—in their infancy. The age of each child is indicated in years, months, and days at the start of each observation; for example, 1;2 (4) indicates that the child was 1 year, 2 months, and 4 days old at the time the observation was made.

Piaget not only observed the infants but created situations to test their capacities, adapting what he did to the particulars of each child and each task. These observations thus demonstrate Piaget's use of the clinical method, which was discussed in Chapter 1 (pages 34–36). Ranging over the first 2 years of life, the records are also a condensed account of the growth of intelligence from action to symbolic thought.

PRIMARY CIRCULAR REACTIONS

Observation 62. At 0;2 (4) Laurent by chance discovers his right index finger and looks at it briefly. At 0;2 (11) he inspects for a moment his open right hand, perceived by chance. At 0;2 (14), on the other hand, he looks three times in succession at his left hand and chiefly at his raised index finger. At 0;2 (17) he follows its spontaneous movement, then examines it several times while it searches for his nose or rubs his eye. . . . At 0;2 (19) he smiles at the same hand after having contemplated it eleven times in succession. . . . At 0;2 (21) he holds his two fists in the air and looks at the left one, after which he slowly brings it towards his face and rubs his nose with it, then his eye. A moment later the left hand again approaches his face; he looks at it and touches his nose. He recommences and laughs five or six times in succession while moving the left hand to his face. He seems to laugh before the hand moves, but looking has no influence on its movement. . . . At 0;2 (24) at last it may be stated that looking acts on the orientation of the hands which tend to remain in the visual field. . . .

Observation 79. Lucienne, at 0;4 (15) looks at a rattle with desire, but without extending her hand. I place the rattle near her right hand. As soon as Lu-

cienne sees rattle and hand together, she moves her hand closer to the rattle and finally grasps it. A moment later she is engaged in looking at her hand. I then put the rattle aside; Lucienne looks at it, then directs her eyes to her hand, then to the rattle again, after which she slowly moves her hand toward the rattle. As soon as she touches it, there is an attempt to grasp it and finally, success. After this I remove the rattle. Lucienne then looks at her hand. I put the rattle aside. She looks alternately at her hand and at the rattle, then moves her hand. The latter happens to leave the visual field. Lucienne then grasps a coverlet which she moves toward her mouth. After this her hand goes away haphazardly. As soon as it reappears in the visual field, Lucienne stares at it and then immediately looks at the rattle which has remained motionless. She then looks alternately at hand and rattle after which her hand approaches and grasps it.

SECONDARY CIRCULAR REACTIONS

Observation 90. At 0;5 (1) Lucienne looks in the direction of her hand which is being held. For example, I clasp her right hand while she looks to the left; she immediately turns in the right direction. Until now such an experiment yielded negative results. A moment later, I place in her left hand (outside the visual field) a bulky object (a gourd), which she immediately tries to grasp but which I retain. She then definitely looks for this hand, even though her arm is outstretched beside her body and thus her hand is hard to see.

At 0;5 (18), Lucienne corroborates these last acquisitions: taking what she sees, bringing the object before her eyes when she has grasped it outside the visual field, and looking in the direction of the hand which is being held.

COORDINATION OF SECONDARY CIRCULAR REACTIONS

Observation 137. At 0;9 (6) Laurent examines a series of new objects which I present to him in sequence: a wooden figure of a man with movable feet, a wooden toucan 7 cm high, a matchbox case, a wooden elephant (10 cm long), and a beaded purse. I observe four quite constant reactions. (1) In the first place a long visual exploration: Laurent looks at the objects which are at first immobile, then looks at them very rapidly (while transferring them from one hand to the other). He seems to study their various surfaces or perspectives. In particular, he folds the purse in two, unfolds and refolds it in order to study the transformations; as soon as he sees the hinge, he turns the object over in order to see it full face, etc. (2) After the visual exploration a tactile exploration begins: He feels the object, especially the toucan's beak, the little man's feet, and gently passes his fingers over the unevenness of the object (the carved wood of the toucan, the beads of the purse, etc.), he scratches certain places (the case of the box, the smooth wood of the elephant, etc.). (3) He slowly moves the object in space: chiefly movements perpendicular to his glance, but already perhaps desired displacements in depth. (4) Only at last does he try the various familiar schemata, using them each in turn with a sort of prudence, as though studying the effect produced. He shakes them, strikes them, swings them, rubs them against the bassinet, draws himself up, shakes his head, sucks them, etc.

TERTIARY CIRCULAR REACTIONS

Observation 148. At 0;10 (16) . . . I place my watch on a big red cushion (of a uniform color and without a fringe) and place the cushion directly in front of the child. Laurent tries to reach the watch directly, and, not succeeding, he grabs the cushion which he draws toward him as before. But then, instead of letting go of the support at once, as he has hitherto done, in order to try again to grasp the objective, he recommences, with obvious interest, to move the cushion while looking at the watch. Everything takes place as though he noticed for the first time the relationship for its own sake and studied it as such. He thus easily succeeds in grasping the watch.

Observation 161. At 1;1 (0) Jacqueline tries to attain a plush cat located on the wood of her bassinet outside her field of prehension. She gives up after a series of fruitless attempts and without thinking of the stick [which she had used earlier in a different situation]. I then put my finger 20 cm above the latter. She perceives the stick, grasps it at once and makes the cat

fall. At 1;1 (28) she is seated on the floor and tries to reach the same cat, this time placed on the floor. She touches it with her stick but without trying to make the cat slide to her, as though the act of touching it sufficed to draw it to her.

Finally, at 1;3 (12) she discovers the possibility of making objects slide on the floor by means of the stick and so drawing them to her; in order to catch a doll lying on the ground out of reach, she begins by striking it with the stick, then, noticing its slight displacement, she pushes it until she is able to attain it with her right hand.

REPRESENTATION

Observation 181. . . . Jacqueline at 1;8 (9) arrives at a closed door—with a blade of grass in each hand. She stretches out her right hand toward the knob but sees that she cannot turn it without letting go of the grass. She puts the grass on the floor, opens the door, picks up the grass again and enters. But when she wants to leave the room things become complicated. She puts the grass on the floor and grasps the doorknob. But then she perceives that in pulling the door toward her she will simultaneously chase away the grass which she placed between the door and the threshold. She therefore picks it up in order to put it outside the door's zone of movement.

This ensemble of operations, which in no way comprises remarkable invention, is nevertheless very characteristic of the intelligent acts founded upon representation or the awareness of relationships.

Observation 183. At 1;6 (8) Jacqueline plays with a fish, a swan and a frog which she puts in a box, takes them out again, puts them back in, etc. At a given moment, she lost the frog. She places the swan and the fish in the box and then obviously looks for the frog. She lifts everything within reach (a big cover, a rug, etc.) and (long after beginning to search) begins to say *inine, inine* (= *grenouille* = frog). It is not the word which set the search in motion, but the opposite. There was therefore evocation of an absent object without any directly perceived stimulus. Sight of the box in which are found only two objects out of three provoked representation of the frog, and whether this representation preceded or accompanied the act is of little importance.

in different ways, over and over. The next day Laurent tried his dropping experiment with a box, a plastic swan, and several other objects (Piaget 1952).

The development of circular reactions reflects increasing cognitive sophistication, but infants' behavior at the end of the sequence shows that they are still in the sensorimotor period. Although they can keep a goal in mind well enough to vary their ways of reaching it, they cannot think about performing actions that they are not physically performing at the moment.

By some time between 16 and 24 months of age, accumulated sensorimotor experience and the increasing maturity of the nervous system have prepared the infant to move from the sensorimotor to the preoperational period. Piaget described the transition as the sixth developmental stage of infancy. It is characterized by *representation,* the ability to perform what Piaget called internal symbolic actions. Representation allows children to think about properties of objects independently of their actions on those objects. Piaget (1952) described how his 16-month-old daughter Lucienne showed her transition from sensorimotor to preoperational intelligence. While Lucienne watched, Piaget put a chain inside a matchbox, leaving the box open about half an inch. Lucienne wanted the chain, and to get it she used a means-end action that she had often used before: She turned the box over. When the chain did not fall out through the small opening, she used another familiar means with more success: She put her finger into the slit, hooked the chain, and pulled it out.

At this point Piaget made the task harder in order to force Lucienne to deal with a problem that she had not yet encountered—opening a box. He put the chain back into the box and left only a very small opening. Lucienne tried to reach through the slit as she had done before, but to no avail. Momentarily stymied, she appeared to study the box. Then, almost perceptibly, she changed from sensorimotor experimentation to representation, symbolically inventing a solution: "She looks at the slit with great attention; then, several times in succession, she opens and shuts her mouth, at first slightly then wider and wider! . . . Soon after this phase of . . . reflection, Lucienne unhesitatingly puts her finger in the slit and, instead of trying as before to reach the chain, she pulls so as to enlarge the opening. She succeeds and grasps the chain" (Observation 180, Piaget 1952).

Opening her mouth wider and wider seemed to be a sensorimotor display of her thoughts about how to solve this problem, using a new scheme based on the idea "make wider." Such sensorimotor signs of mental activity seem to be common only in the transition from the sensorimotor to the preoperational period; they show a connection between the external actions of sensorimotor intelligence and the internal actions of representational intelligence.

Neo-Piagetian Levels of Sensorimotor Development

Neo-Piagetian theory, introduced on page 223, builds on Piaget's work on cognitive development by studying how children process information and how

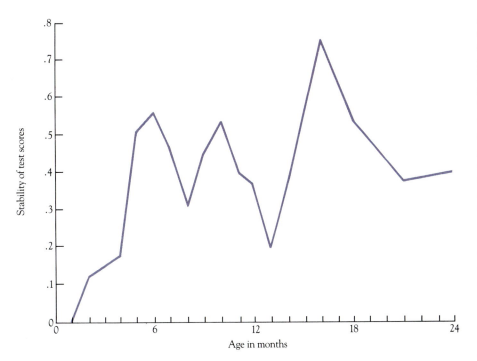

Age in months

Figure 5-11   Changes in the stability of infant test scores. Infants were tested repeatedly on the Bayley Infant Scales during the first two years of life. Their scores on the items that measured cognitive change best for their age group showed four systematic changes that reflected the four levels of infant intelligence. In the first month, infants' scores changed dramatically from one testing to the next, and so the stability of scores— the correlation between them—was 0. Beginning at 2 months, some stability began to appear—the infants began to get consistent scores— as the first cognitive level developed. With the emergence of the second level at about 8 months, stability fell sharply, and it fell again for the third and fourth levels at 13 and 21 months, respectively. The graph is for girls, but boys showed a similar pattern (McCall et al. 1977).

experience affects their behavior. Neo-Piagetian research also focuses on testing such developmental concepts as stage or level. Studies of brain development and performance on standard infant tests suggest that an infant's individual sensorimotor abilities actually do develop through four levels (Kagan 1982; Harris 1983; McCall 1983; Uzgiris 1976).

The infant tests include the assessment of motor abilities such as holding up the head, kicking arms and legs, and grasping small objects. Infants also are tested for more complex responses, such as attention to sights and sounds, ability to grasp and manipulate objects (shaking a rattle or ringing a bell, for example), interactions with the examiner (smiling, cooing, babbling, or imitating), manipulating toys in a meaningful way (putting cubes in a cup or banging spoons together, for example), and looking for a dropped toy or one that the examiner has covered (Bayley 1970). Performance on these tests changes suddenly at roughly 2 months, 8 months, 13 months, and 21 months of age (McCall et al. 1977; McCall 1983). For the first 2 months, infants' performance is erratic, changing even from day to day, but then it begins to be stable as they enter the first developmental level. Later, as infants enter the second, third, and fourth levels, their performance on the tests again changes suddenly. These sudden changes are observed as an abrupt drop in the stability of infants' test scores and then a return to stable performance, as illustrated in Figure 5-11.

Even after scores have stabilized, however, not all the infants' abilities have advanced to the same degree (as stage theory would predict). Some abilities are at the new level, some are not. One hypothesis is that what changes as a child enters each new level is the child's optimal performance—the best the child can do (Biggs & Collis 1982; Fischer & Pipp 1984; Flavell 1982; Siegler 1983). That is, the *capability* for performing at the higher level develops, but which particular behaviors first reveal this new capability depends on the individual infant's interactions with her environment.

Jerome Kagan and Robert Emde suggest that the brain also shows major changes at each level. The electrical patterns of brain waves change systematically as an infant enters each of the four levels of sensorimotor development. The strongest evidence is for the shift to the first level at 2 to 3 months of age, when brain waves during sleep begin to assume the normal pattern for children and adults (Dreyfus-Brisac 1979; Emde et al. 1976). As an infant enters each of the three succeeding levels, brain waves seem to show further rapid changes toward the fully mature form (Kagan 1982).

As Table 5-2 shows, the four levels of sensorimotor development that neo-Piagetians have found coincide roughly with Piaget's stages defined by the three kinds of circular reactions and the beginning of representational thought. The ages given in the table represent the months in which particular levels of ability tend to predominate. The ranges overlap because there is so much variation among individuals and among different abilities in the same individual. They are based on research with middle-class children in Western industrialized nations.

TABLE 5-2 PIAGET'S SENSORIMOTOR STAGES COMPARED WITH NEO-PIAGETIAN SENSORIMOTOR LEVELS

PIAGET'S STAGES	NEO-PIAGETIAN SENSORIMOTOR LEVELS	APPROXIMATE AGES
Reflexes		
Primary circular reactions	Level 1 Single actions	2 to 7 months
Secondary circular reactions	Level 2 Relations of actions	6 to 12 months
Coordination of secondary circular reactions		
Tertiary circular reactions	Level 3 Systems of actions	10 to 20 months
The beginnings of representational thought	Level 4 Single representations	18 to 36 months

Single Actions   A newborn baby has only the reflexes and basic sensory capacities described in Chapter 4. Although she can suck, grasp, look, and listen, these behaviors are not under straightforward voluntary control. The course of cognitive development through the levels of infancy and childhood involves the gradual establishment of voluntary control over increasingly complex actions and thoughts.

By 3 months of age, the baby has gained control over many *single actions,* and these become the basic building blocks of sensorimotor intelligence. A 3-month-old can control only single actions, however, as in Piaget's circular reactions. For instance, she can control her grasping and she can control her looking, but she cannot relate two single actions to each other. That is, she cannot perform one action in order to produce another. She cannot hold her rattle in front of her face in order to see it; nor can she look at a crib toy and use what she sees to help her locate the toy with her hand (Kagan et al. 1978; Kaye 1982; Uzgiris 1976).

Relations of Actions   By about 6 months of age, most babies have begun to coordinate some very simple actions with each other. For example, if a child deliberately holds a rattle in front of her face and looks at it, she has succeeded in combining the two actions (holding and looking) into a single skill. She has constructed a sensorimotor *relation of actions.*

Most of the sensorimotor relations that scientists have investigated connect a means to an end, as in Piaget's secondary circular reactions. In other words, one action is used to bring about or predict a second action. For example, an infant can bang her spoon on her highchair tray to produce a satisfying thumping sound or perhaps to bring her mother running. Many of the baby's means-end relations involve her parents. When she sees her mother's breast, she can predict that sucking will follow shortly. And while she is sucking, she knows that she can look up and see her mother's face. Thus her mother is becoming more predictable and coherent in her mind (Décarie 1965; Sander 1975).

The development of relations of actions requires a major advance in the infant's memory, in that the baby must recall how two actions can be coordinated (Kagan et al. 1978; Zelazo & Leonard 1983). The memory advance is especially evident when the baby uses one action to predict another, as when she produces sounds that she knows will bring a parent to her.

Systems of Actions   Starting at about 10 months, the baby moves beyond relating one particular action to another and can start to coordinate varieties of one action with varieties of another in a *system of actions.* With a system of actions for holding and looking at a rattle, the infant can take the rattle, look at it carefully, grasp it in several different ways, bring it in front of her eyes, examine it from different angles, move it with her hand back to where she picked it up, watch it carefully as it moves, and bring it up in front of her eyes again. All this behavior flows smoothly, because all the parts are integrated in a system that allows the child to remember the connections among the various ways she can hold and look at the toy. By 12 or 13 months, these systems begin to multiply, giving the child a great deal more flexibility and control over her own behavior.

Should she drop the rattle and observe its fall, she may begin to explore other systems of actions by starting a dropping game like the one Piaget's son Laurent played with pieces of bread. In this game, which fascinates many 1-year-olds but often frustrates their parents, the infant drops her toys over the side of the crib and watches as best she can where they fall. Then she fusses and cries until someone picks up the toys and puts them back in the crib. Within a few minutes, she has once again dropped them onto the floor. Rather than being deliberately perverse, an infant who behaves this way seems to be studying the system that connects the dropping of toys with where the toys can be found after they have been dropped.

Infants play many such exploratory games—with people as well as with objects—and they construct sensorimotor systems in the process (McCall 1979; Uzgiris 1976; Zelazo & Leonard 1983). As a child coordinates various actions of her own with characteristics and actions of objects and people, these entities begin to take on some reality of their own. A rattle becomes a combination of certain kinds of looking (shape and color), certain kinds of listening (sound), certain kinds of grasping (shape and weight), certain kinds of touching (texture). The mother's face becomes something that can be looked at, touched, grasped, and even heard. And its physical connection to all the visible, touchable parts of the mother's body can be understood and remembered. It is only when a rattle or person can take on some reality of its own that it can become an object of thought.

Single Representations   The fourth developmental level is characterized by symbolic thoughts, or *representations.* The emergence of this capacity opens a new world of cognitive possibilities for the child (Corrigan 1983; Dasen et al. 1978). One of the most striking new abilities is pretending, as when a 2-year-old acts as if a push toy were a lawnmower or as if a broomstick were a horse. In such make-believe, the child uses one object to symbolize, or represent, another (Figure 5-12).

A Developmental Cycle of Processing Information

Both Piaget (1941, 1950) and Werner (1948) hypothesized that the stages of sensorimotor development in infancy were parallel to those of development in childhood, as if the stages of development for action repeated themselves for representation. In Piaget's (1950, 1983) terms, infants gradually develop the

Figure 5-12 This 2-year-old is pretending that two soda bottles are racing cars. It looks as if the car in his left hand is winning.

ability to *act* logically, but when symbolic thought emerges at the end of infancy, they must start the process over again, slowly developing the ability to *think* logically. Just as over a number of months in infancy, babies construct more and more complex and logical schemes of action, so over a number of years in childhood, children construct more and more complex and logical schemes for symbolic thought as they develop through the preoperational and operational periods.

A number of neo-Piagetian researchers have attempted to specify the nature of this parallel more precisely in terms of mechanisms of information processing—how children use and remember what they do and know (Biggs & Collis 1982; Case 1980; Fischer 1980; Mounoud 1982). They mostly agree that the succession of levels in the development of sensorimotor intelligence reflects a cycle of improvements in memory, and that the cycle recurs in later periods. The cycle is repeated at least once over the course of the preoperational and concrete-operational periods, and again in the formal-operational period, with one cycle leading into the next.

Infants are initially capable of controlling only one action at a time, but during their first 2 years they develop the ability to control relations of actions and then systems of actions. The fourth level of infant development, single representations, is both the high point of sensorimotor intelligence and the first

Figure 5-13 A schematic illustration of the repetitive cycle of cognitive development suggested by neo-Piagetian theory. Note that each cycle begins with control of only single actions or thoughts, develops to relations, then to systems; the next level signals development to a higher organization of intelligence. These developments take place for particular skills, however—not for the child as a whole.

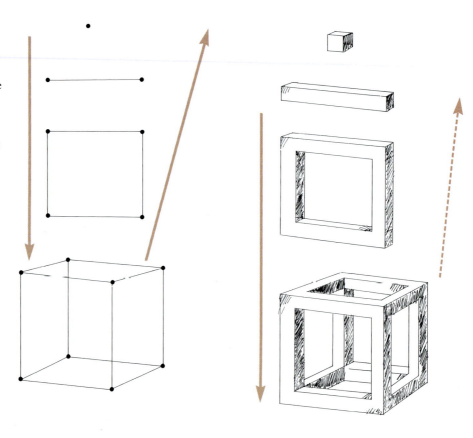

level of representational intelligence (Figure 5-13). The cycle repeats itself as children's abilities develop from single representations, to relations of representations, to systems of representations (see Chapters 7 and 9). This second cycle ends with the emergence of abstractions, or hypothetical schemes, in early adolescence. It may be that this new ability is the beginning of a third cycle extending through adolescence and early adulthood (see Chapter 11).

The improvements in abilities seem to depend upon changes in what is called *working memory,* the number of items that an individual can process at one time (Biggs & Collis 1982; Case 1980). A number of tests of working memory have been devised. For example, infants are shown a series of simple actions, like touching a plate, shoving a spoon, and turning over a cup, and their working memory is assessed by the number of actions they can imitate without reminders. One measure of working memory for older children requires them to read a series of numbers or letters, such as 58139, and then to repeat from memory as many digits as they can. Infants show a systematic increase in their working memory for actions—from one action to a pair of actions (a relation) to two pairs of actions (a system). Then development shifts from actions to representations; over the course of the preoperational and concrete-operational periods, children demonstrate the same kinds of increases in their working memory for representations—from one representation to a pair of representations (a relation) to two pairs of representations (a system). In the formal-operational period, abstractions emerge, and adolescents move through the same sorts of increases in their working memory for abstractions.

Information-processing studies have also shown that during childhood and adolescence, there are significant developments in children's understanding of memory and strategies for using it (Brown et al. 1983). These developments are discussed in Chapters 7, 9, and 11.

PERCEPTUAL DEVELOPMENT

The development of sensorimotor skills during the first 2 years strongly affects a child's entire psychological life. An aspect of life closely related to cognitive development is perceptual development. In fact, many scientists consider perception to be a kind of cognition. As described in Chapter 4, perception is more than mere sensation because it requires an interpretation of sensory information—and interpretation depends on cognition.

Newborns receive visual sensations, but tracings of their eye movements as they look at things indicate that they do not perceive. That is, newborns do not interpret visual stimuli in the way that older children and adults do. They tend to see individual elements that make up a form or pattern but not to perceive the form itself.

Although there is considerable perceptual development in the first few months of life, one experiment illustrates that before 6 months of age, recognition of some forms may remain immature (Bertenthal et al. 1980). When adults see the arrangements of elements in Figure 5-14, they immediately perceive a square in arrangement C. Using habituation procedures, researchers found that 3-month-olds responded to all three of the arrangements as if they were the

Habituation stimulus

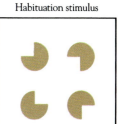

A

Novel stimulus

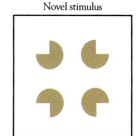

B

Novel stimulus

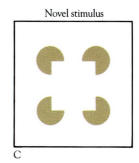

C

Figure 5-14   To the adult eye, a form leaps out of this display only in C; the other patterns are seen as essentially similar to each other. The square in C is a construction by the brain. Does a young infant see it? At 3 months, babies show no more interest in C than in B after they have habituated to A. But at 7 months, they are likely to examine C carefully. Perception has evidently undergone significant development in the interim (Bertenthal et al. 1980).

same. Seven-month-olds, however, paid extra attention to arrangement C, which indicated that they were perceiving a square—or at least some part of that pattern. Five-month-olds showed intermediate behavior, discriminating between the patterns some of the time, but not consistently.

In general, the developmental progression for the perception of patterns shows a similar outline in a number of different perceptual abilities studied by researchers. Newborns show little or no perception of patterns; 3-month-olds perceive only very simple patterns; by 7 or 8 months of age, infants are able to perceive some very complex patterns.

Face Perception

For newborns, faces are simply interesting arrangements of edges between contrasting dark and light areas (Haith 1980). By 3 months of age, however, babies seem to know more about what they are seeing when they look at a face: They tend to concentrate on the eyes (Haith et al. 1977; Maurer & Salapatek 1976). By 5 months of age, they seem to know how the elements of a face should be arranged. In one study, for example, 4-month-olds did not differentiate between a drawing of a face with scrambled features and one with a normal arrangement of features, whereas 5-month-olds did (Caron et al. 1973). By the middle of their first year, babies have had enough experience looking at faces not only to know how the features should be arranged but also to distinguish familiar faces from unfamiliar ones. This ability is demonstrated by a clearcut fear of strangers that develops between 6 and 9 months (Emde et al. 1976).

Little research has been done on facial perception beyond 9 months, but what has been done suggests that development continues into late infancy and on into childhood (Gibson 1969; Carey et al. 1980). Some parents report that their toddler looking through a photo album can point out a picture of Mommy or Daddy that had been taken 10 or more years earlier, when hair, clothing styles, and even the parent's features were noticeably different. And children can often recognize a familiar individual from seeing just a small part of the face. A Halloween mask that leaves the individual's mouth, chin, and head exposed is generally no barrier to recognition.

Depth Perception

Infants can first perceive depth by 2 to 3 months, distinguishing, for example, between a three-dimensional ball and a two-dimensional one (a circle) (Fantz 1966; Pipp & Haith 1977). But the relation of depth to other simple elements of a situation is not fully achieved until 7 to 9 months of age, as shown in an experiment by Joseph Campos testing infants' behavior on an apparatus called the **visual cliff** (Campos et al. 1978, 1982). As shown in Figure 5-15, the visual cliff is a sheet of glass, one side of which rests on a table while the other side extends over a sheer drop of several feet.

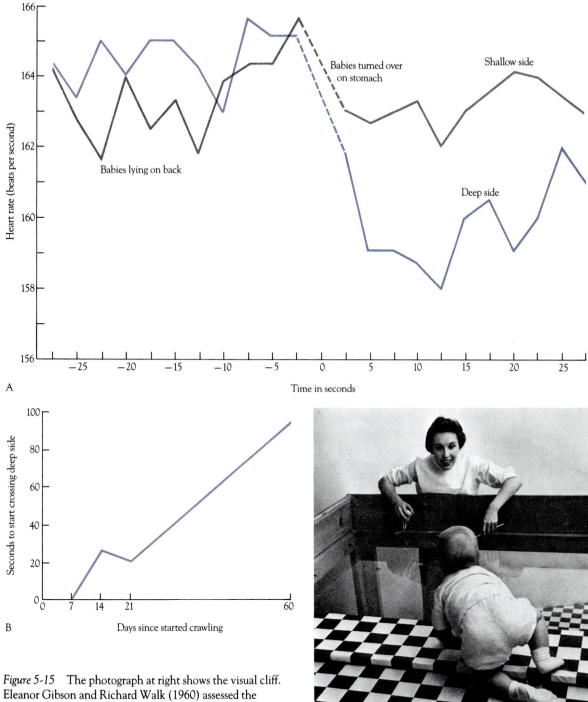

Figure 5-15 The photograph at right shows the visual cliff. Eleanor Gibson and Richard Walk (1960) assessed the perception of the cliff by mobile infants by testing their willingness to crawl across the glass of the "deep" side when their mothers called to them. But it is impossible to use this method for very young infants. (A) Instead, the heart rate of young babies is measured—a lowered heart rate reflects interest but not fear. Joseph Campos and his colleagues (1978, 1982) tested 2-month-olds on the cliff. He first put them on their backs in order to obtain a baseline heart rate. When he turned them over so that they were looking into

the "shallow" side, heartbeat did not change (gray line). By contrast, when he turned them over so that they were looking into the "deep" side, heartbeat decreased (colored line). (B) Campos tested older infants as they were becoming mobile, and discovered that reluctance to cross the "deep" side develops slowly, as a child gains experience in crawling—and, presumably, in falling.

Campos devised a means of testing young babies' reactions to depth on the visual cliff by monitoring the babies' heart rate. A drop in heart rate usually means that a baby is focusing her attention on something, whereas a rise in heart rate means that she is experiencing an emotional reaction such as fear. Infants show no reaction to being placed on the deep side until they are 2 or 3 months old. When they are placed on the deep side at that age, their heart rate decreases, indicating close attention to the depth (Figure 5-15A). They appear to be fascinated by what they see, but they show no fear of falling.

To develop fear of the deep side, a baby must be able to relate the perception of depth to the danger of falling. Consequently, the longer a baby has been crawling, the more likely she is to have had a few falls, and the longer she is likely to hesitate before venturing onto the deep side. In fact, at about 8 months of age, most infants do show fear of the apparent drop on the deep side. Even when urged by their mothers to cross the deep side, they hesitate (Figure 5-15B). Newly mobile infants, then, are generally in greater danger of a serious fall from a high place. A small tumble down a single step or off a low couch might serve as a good learning experience and help keep a baby from launching herself off a porch or down a long staircase.

Self-Recognition: Emergence of the Self

The development of **self-recognition** has been traced in studies that covered all of the first 2 years of a baby's life. These studies—usually observations of babies' behavior in front of a mirror—show the gradual emergence of a definite notion of self, an understanding that one exists as an independent person (Bertenthal & Fischer 1978; Harter 1983; Lewis & Brooks-Gunn 1979).

Before 3 months of age, an infant takes little interest in her own mirror image—or in mirror images of anyone else. She can focus in a sustained way on the image in the mirror, but she looks at her own image in much the same way that she would look at another baby (see Figure 5-16).

Beginning at 4 to 6 months of age, the infant reaches out to touch her own image in the mirror, but without understanding that the image is a reflection. If she sees an interesting toy in the mirror, she will reach into the mirror for it instead of looking toward where the toy really is. But by about 1 year of age, she can use a mirror image to determine where an object is in relation to her own body and reach for it in its actual location, not in the reflection.

At 18 to 24 months, the child's responses to her mirror image show that she is beginning to think of herself as an independent person. In a simple but telling test, an adult surreptitiously applies a spot of rouge to the child's nose before the child goes to look in the mirror. A 1-year-old will not seem to notice anything unusual when she looks into the mirror. But by about 18 months, most children look at their mirror images carefully and then touch or rub their

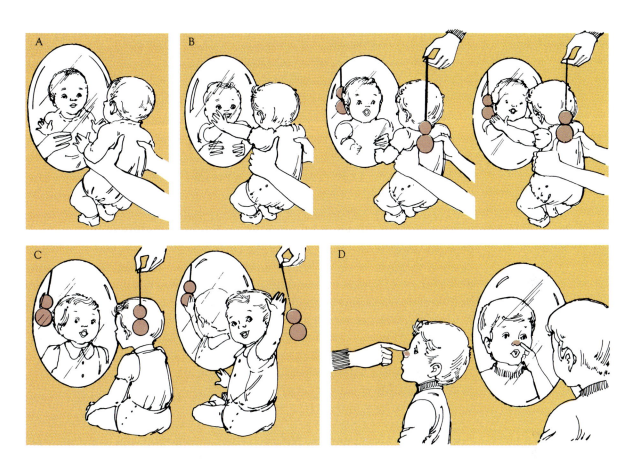

Figure 5-16   The four main steps in the development of self-recognition in a mirror. (A) At about 3 months, the infant merely looks at the mirror image, not even reaching out to touch it. (B) At about 6 months, the infant reaches out to touch his image. If he sees an attractive toy in the mirror, he reaches toward the mirror to grasp the toy. (C) At about 10 months, when the infant sees an attractive toy in the mirror, he uses the information about the toy and how it relates to his own image in the mirror to determine where to reach for the toy itself. (D) At about 18 months, when an adult puts a spot of rouge on the infant's nose and later the baby sees it on the nose of his mirror-image, he will reach up to touch his own nose.

noses or ask "What's that?" These behaviors show that the children recognize their own faces and know what they normally look like in a mirror. A few months later, if someone points at the child's mirror image and asks "Who's that?" the child will say "Me" or give her name.

The ability to represent the self is an important human ability that is absent in most animals, but a few animals do develop notions of self. Although cognitive-developmental researchers are interested mainly in human behavioral development, the concepts of cognitive-developmental theory apply as well to the behavioral development of animals.

SENSORIMOTOR INTELLIGENCE IN ANIMALS

If you have ever had dogs or cats and observed their development from puppyhood or kittenhood, you may have noticed some of the same developmental phenomena that occur in infants. Most animals, at least most mammals, develop through levels of sensorimotor intelligence in ways similar to the development of human infants. But, in most cases, their development seems to be limited to sensorimotor intelligence. Very few ever achieve representation.

Cats have been shown to pass through Piaget's sensorimotor stages (Gruber et al. 1971; Thinus-Blanc et al. 1982). Informally observing the behavior of his kitten Bagel, one of the authors of this book noted many instances of sensorimotor development. Bagel liked to have her belly rubbed, for example, and she learned a relation of actions for producing belly-rubbing: She would simply roll over onto her back in the presence of her owner. If he happened to be sitting near her when she rolled over, her action usually produced the desired end. At first, however, Bagel took no real account of where her owner was relative to her belly: Even if he was sitting across the room, she would roll over expectantly. Gradually, Bagel developed a system of actions for producing a belly rub. She became able to take account of the spatial relation between herself and her owner, rolling over only when he was near enough to reach her.

Dogs, cats, monkeys, and most other animals display intelligence: They learn and they adapt to their environment. But in terms of the scale of human intelligence, they apparently cannot develop beyond sensorimotor skills. Some chimpanzees and gorillas—members of the family of apes, who are more intelligent than monkeys—do demonstrate representational intelligence (Parker & Gibson 1979). For example, Gordon Gallup (1977) has shown that chimpanzees develop self-recognition but rhesus monkeys do not. Gallup put red dye on one ear of chimpanzees and rhesus monkeys while the animals were anesthetized. A control group was also anesthetized but did not have their ears dyed. He then put each of the animals in front of a mirror to see whether it would reach for the strange-colored ear. The chimps with a red ear did; the rhesus monkeys did not. By recognizing themselves in the mirror image, just as 18-month-old children do, the chimps indicated that they were capable of elementary representation.

Gallup recounts a thought-provoking story of a chimp who seemed to think of herself as a human being. The chimp, who was raised by a couple who are researchers, was taught to sort photographs into two stacks, human beings in one stack and animals in another. After she had learned to do this without error, the psychologists slipped the chimp's own photo into the unsorted pile. When she came to her photo, she unhesitatingly put it with the human stack!

The best evidence that apes can achieve representation is the fact that chimpanzees and gorillas can learn to use some language—not spoken language, because apes do not have the anatomical apparatus for producing human speech sounds, but visual language. Chimps and gorillas have been taught to speak with signs—written signs like hieroglyphics or gestural signs of the sort that are used by deaf people (Patterson 1980; Premack 1983; Savage-Rumbaugh & Rumbaugh 1980).

A number of chimps have been taught to use the system of gestural signs called American Sign Language, or ASL. These chimps lived with human families almost as if they were human children. They learned to understand some spoken language as well as ASL, and they were able to put ASL gestures together productively—that is, to use signs in combination with each other and in new contexts. For example, once the chimp Washoe had learned the sign for "more," she used it with other signs she already knew in order to express her wants, saying things such as "More tickle" and "More sweet." Later, she began to put three or more signs together to make sentences: "Hurry gimme tooth-brush" and "You me go in there," for instance. And occasionally she even coined phrases to name things for which she had no sign, such as "water bird" to refer to a swan. By the time she was 5 (roughly the equivalent of 7½ human years), Washoe knew about 150 signs (Gardner & Gardner 1980).

The language ability of another chimp, Lucy, is illustrated by the following story. Lucy was about to have a language-training session with her trainer Roger when he noticed a small pile of excrement on the living room floor. Roger signed "What's that?" to Lucy, who was obviously aware of the offense she had committed. Lucy looked away, as if she had not heard the question. Roger signed again, "You know. What's that?" This time, Lucy answered, "Dirty dirty," the term she uses for excrement. "Whose dirty dirty?" "Sue's" Lucy answered. (Sue was a psychologist working on the project.) Roger replied, "It's not Sue's. Whose is it?" Lucy tried again. "Roger's." "No! It's not Roger's," Roger shot back. "Whose is it?" Lucy finally confessed, "Lucy's dirty dirty," and added, "Sorry Lucy."

Although these chimps obviously are beyond the sensorimotor period of cognitive development, they cannot, according to the evidence gathered so far, progress much beyond early representational intelligence and the primitive use of language. Their capacities seem to be at about the level of 2-year-old children, as explained in the essay "Do Apes Really Use Language?"

RESEARCH

DO APES REALLY USE LANGUAGE?

When the initial reports of the use of sign language by chimpanzees appeared, the scientific community reacted with great excitement. Here was the first instance of a species other than *Homo sapiens* that could communicate through language. Some scholars even wondered if people and chimpanzees might eventually be able to discuss important questions of philosophy and religion.

Reality soon ended such speculation, as it became evident that ape language—and ape intelligence—never reach the heights of human language and intelligence. If apes use language, it is much more primitive than the kind that adult human beings use. Chimps and gorillas do not seem to be able to acquire more than a few hundred words, they do not build complex sentences, and they do not use abstract concepts.

Naturally, the question raised by many researchers now is whether ape language is like human language at all. The answer to this question hinges on the answer to another question: What abilities do apes demonstrate in their signing? For example, do they use single words meaningfully? Do they put words together into grammatical sentences?

Although not all the evidence is in yet, the outline of an answer does seem to be taking shape: Apes can use language meaningfully, but in extremely limited ways. In most respects, their speech is roughly equivalent to a 20- to 24-month-old human child's use of sign language.

One of the most fundamental characteristics of human language is the use of words, and even the most conservative researchers acknowledge that chimpanzees and gorillas use words (Terrace et al. 1980). An estimate of vocabulary size depends on how words are counted. By the most conservative estimates, which count only signs that are used repeatedly over many days or weeks, the signing apes have each learned 100 words or more. The most liberal estimates, which include signs that are used only a few times, exceed 500 words (Weller 1980). As impressive as such vocabularies are, they remain small in comparison to those of human beings. By the time children are 27 months old, most of them know more than 300 words, and their vocabulary continues to increase rapidly for many years (Dale 1972).

Another fundamental characteristic of human language is sentence structure: We use specific rules to combine words into meaningful patterns, and different patterns communicate different meanings. "The mosquito bit John" means something different from "John bit the mosquito," even though both sentences use exactly the same words. As children grow older, they consistently and greatly increase their ability to use such rules, producing an increase in the length of their sentences.

Here lies one of the major limitations of ape language. Chimps and gorillas have been shown to use simple rules, such as placing signs in certain consistent orders in multisign combinations (Gardner & Gardner 1980; Terrace et al. 1980), but they do not seem spontaneously to use more complex rules, such as those applying to subordinate clauses ("I ate the apple that Jim brought"). Indeed, their most common utterances remain short—one or two words—and do not increase steadily with age. Even when they occasionally produce a long utterance, the grammar of the sentence remains simple: "Me eat drink more."

This sort of simple grammar is typical of the early sentences of human children (Brown 1973). In many other features, too, ape communication is similar to the early language of children. First, apes and young children tend to repeat themselves frequently, as when the chimp named Nim said, "Nim eat Nim eat," "Banana me eat banana," and, in one enthusiastic burst, "Give me orange me give eat orange me eat orange give me eat orange give me you" (Terrace et al. 1980). A second feature common to the language of apes and young children is a tendency to directly imitate or copy what an adult has just said, even when the imitation is nonsensical. When a father asks, "What do you want?" for example, a 2-year-old may answer, "What you want?"

In human beings, these features of early language virtually disappear as children grow older, but in apes they seem to remain throughout life. By 3 years of age, children have almost completely stopped repeating and copying (Bloom et al. 1976), but chimpanzees do not ever seem to lessen their use of these behaviors.

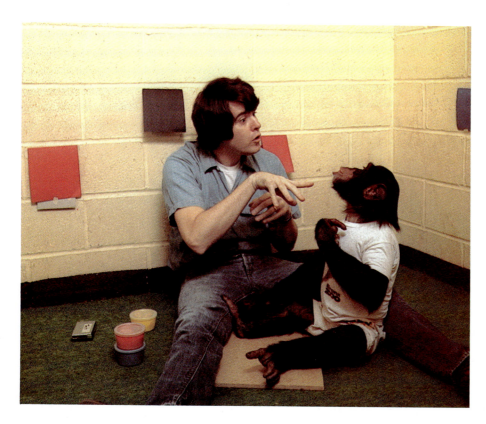

Figure 5-17 Teacher asks "Who?" and Nim answers "Me."

Most of the comparisons of ape and human language suffer from a major problem. All the chimps and gorillas who have been studied used visual signs of some sort, whereas most of the human children studied used spoken language, typically English. American Sign Language (ASL) is at least as different from English as English is from Chinese, and some of the seeming differences between ape language and child language may turn out to be differences really between sign language and English. For instance, word order is one of the most important grammatical features of English, but word order in ASL seems to be much less important (Siple 1978). One reason for this difference is that two words can easily be said simultaneously in ASL—one with each hand. It is impossible to say two words of English simultaneously. Similarly, many grammatical rules in sign language depend on the spatial relationships between the two hands, but there are no spatial relationships between the words in English or any other spoken language.

Nevertheless, the most general conclusions that have already been drawn about ape language are not likely to be changed by the analysis of signing in human children. For example, human adults who speak ASL use many complex sentences that embody sophisticated grammatical rules, so it is unlikely that the absence of complex grammar in ape language results from the use of ASL. Research on ASL is more likely to reveal subtle differences between ape and child, such as the manner in which word order is used or the frequency of repetition and imitation.

The discovery that chimps and gorillas can learn to use simple language is still one of the most exciting scientific accomplishments of the last 20 years, even though ape language has turned out to be much more limited than some scholars at first believed. Chimps and gorillas can speak to us, but what they say is not very profound. It seems clear that "Give me banana" or "Washoe afraid of dog outside" will never give way to "What is the meaning of life?"

EARLY LANGUAGE ACQUISITION

The ability to understand language and to use it, usually through voiced sounds, is part of our genetic inheritance as members of the human species (Chomsky 1965; Dance & Larson 1976). At about 1 year of age, children all over the world begin to talk, communicating with others by means of single words. It is another year or so before they start to use two words in combination, but by the time they are 4 or 5 they are talking a blue streak, using language in a fairly adult fashion. This general process is universal. It does not matter whether a child lives in an American city, a Peruvian village, an Icelandic fishing community, or a Chinese farm commune.

Does this mean that a child who grew up in total isolation would spontaneously begin to speak? No. As explained in Chapter 2, inherited capacities depend on environmental input for their expression. To develop speech, children must hear a language being spoken as part of their social interaction (Slobin 1982). The importance of hearing speech is shown most obviously by the fact that children learn the specific language that is daily spoken to them: Children in China learn Chinese, children in the United States learn English. In addition, although infants who are deaf from birth easily learn a gestural language like American Sign Language if it is used around them, they have a difficult time learning to use spoken language (though with special training some of them do).

The remainder of this chapter concerns children's language during the sensorimotor period, when it consists chiefly of prespeech sounds and single words (see Table 5-1). Chapter 7 describes the acquisition of language after 2 years of age, when children begin to use sentences.

Prespeech Sounds

Each of us is equipped with a vocal apparatus and a brain that permit the articulation of many different kinds of speech sounds, as shown in Figure 5-18 (Lenneberg 1967). Although the word "infant" is derived from the Latin word *infans*, which means without speech, infants can and do vocalize from birth. At about 2 months of age, their vocalizations become more complex as they begin to make cooing sounds that include some of the sounds of spoken language. During the next few months, the number of sounds they make gradually increases, and at 4 or 5 months they begin to string sounds together in what is called **babbling**. Babbling includes a wide range of speech sounds—not only those of the child's native language but others that resemble African tongue clicks, French vowels, and guttural Russian and German sounds (Jakobson 1968).

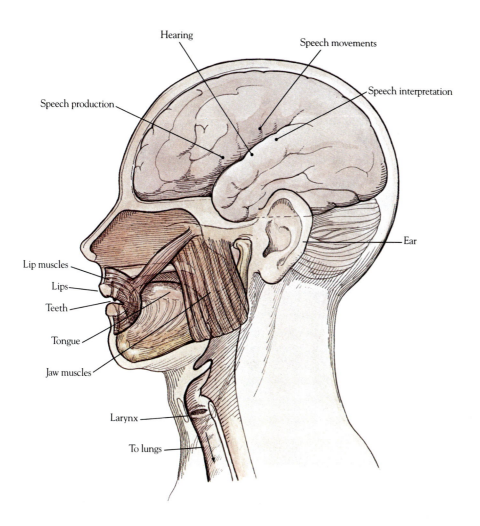

Figure 5-18   The major organs of speech and the areas of the brain believed to be important in speech. The raw material of speech sound is produced by the passage of air from the lungs through the larynx. The air pressure causes fleshy folds projecting from the walls of the larynx (the vocal cords) to vibrate. This sound, resonating in the space formed by the mouth and nose, is shaped, modulated, stopped, and started by rapid and precise movements of the tongue, lips, jaw, and teeth. The movements of these structures are controlled from the motor area along the central fold at the top of the brain. Language competence involves speech reception just as much as speech production, of course. Speech sounds are received by the ear, which transmits the information to the primary hearing area in the temporal lobe of the brain. The function of the two areas of the brain here labelled "speech production" and "speech interpretation" is not certain. It is well established, however, that damage to forward areas is more likely to affect production (the ability to speak) and damage to rear areas more likely to affect reception (the ability to understand speech) (Lenneberg & Lenneberg 1975).

Babies seem to listen to their babbling, connecting their own sound-making to the sounds that they hear. The importance of this process is highlighted by the fact that although children born deaf produce many of the same sounds as hearing children for the first few months of life, the similarity gradually decreases until the age of 6 months or so (Lenneberg 1969). Then, apparently because they cannot hear their own sounds, the babbling of the deaf infants tapers off and eventually ceases.

At about 1 year of age, the beginning of the sensitive period for language acquisition described in Chapter 2, many babies frequently produce long sequences of sounds that have the "shape" of the adult speech they hear but that use no real words (Dore et al. 1976). This imitation of speech intonation is called *expressive jargon.* Although the sounds are meaningless, they give the impression of normal speech if one doesn't listen too closely. One of the authors of this book was once amazed by the apparently sophisticated language ability of Joshua, a 1-year-old son of friends. Through a closed door, he heard Joshua carrying on a long and complex telephone conversation. It turned out, of course, that no one was on the other end of the line and that Joshua was not using words. But his intonation and phrasing were so adult—complete with pauses, as if listening to his telephone partner—that, muffled by the door, the conversation sounded genuine.

The use of expressive jargon shows that children have learned to control their voice and timing well enough to produce the "shape" of adult speech. They will use this ability to imitate not only intonation patterns but the sounds of specific words.

One Word at a Time

Children begin to use language one word at a time. A child's one-word utterances usually refer to concrete things and are short, like "hot" and "mama" (Clark 1983; Dore et al. 1976). Often, they seem to be not so much real words as audible accompaniments to certain sensorimotor actions (Piaget 1951; Corrigan 1977). For example, a child may say "bye-bye" when waving to someone, or "pat-a-cake" (usually said in some shortened form) when clapping, or "light" when flipping a light switch. The child's use of these utterances is very restricted because they are linked to a specific action. At this point, language still requires only sensorimotor intelligence, not representation.

At about 15 to 18 months, on the average, children begin to use words more flexibly. But their language still depends very much on what they are seeing or doing at the moment, as illustrated by Lois Bloom's (1973) study of the beginnings of language in her daughter Allison. Here are two short descriptions of Allison's utterances at 17 months and the contexts in which they occurred. As you can see, virtually all the words Allison used at this time were closely tied to her actions.

LOIS BLOOM	ALLISON
What's Mommy have? (Mother holds cookies.)	
(Allison reaches for cookie.)	*cookie*
Cookie! OK. Here's a cookie for you.	
(Allison takes cookie and reaches with other hand toward others in bag.)	*more*
There's more in here. We'll have it in a little while.	
(Allison picks up bag of cookies.)	*bag*
(Allison tries to get up on chair.)	*up*
(Allison stands on chair, looks over its back at blank wall.)	*away*
Away?	
(Allison turns around.)	*chair*
Chair?	
(Allison sits down.)	*down*

To interpret the meaning of what adults say, children this age often make use of the surrounding context—settings, gestures, facial expressions, tone of voice (Bruner 1982; Greenfield & Smith 1976). That is, much of their understanding derives from their sensorimotor interpretation of the situation rather than from their comprehension of language itself. Allison, for example, probably did not understand the grammar of the question "What's Mommy have?" and so could not understand the question fully. But she could still answer "Cookie," because she saw what her mother was holding up and she heard that her mother's tone of voice indicated a question.

To be able to use language in an adult fashion, the child must move beyond a dependence on immediate context and learn the general meanings of words. In recent years, much has been learned about how this understanding develops.

Processes of Language Development

In learning to use words in many contexts, children seem to rely on a process of abstraction similar to the one they use for cognitive development (MacWhinney 1978; Nelson 1974). Children usually focus their attention on a new word first when it is connected with some sensorimotor action. They compare several situations in which they hear the same word, and then they determine the meaning of the word from what they perceive as similar about those situations. Katherine Nelson (1974) provides an example of how the process of abstraction probably works when a child abstracts the meaning of the word "ball." A mother and her daughter, about 2 years old, are playing with a ball for the first time. The mother uses the word "ball" repeatedly: "Let's play with the ball." "I'm going to throw you the ball." "Now you throw me the ball." "Where's the ball?" "Here's the ball." Such remarks encourage the child to notice and imitate the word "ball" because of its repeated occurrence in the mother's speech. Once she notices the word, she can begin the process of abstraction to determine what it means.

In her first encounter with the ball as she and her mother are playing with it, she notes a number of characteristics that might be relevant:

In living room, on porch

Mother throws, picks up, holds

I throw, pick up, hold

It rolls, bounces

On floor, under couch

This is a lot of information. To hone down the word to its essential characteristics, the child must gather other instances of the word's use and compare this instance with them.

Later, the baby and her mother go to the park, where they play ball with an older girl. On this occasion, the baby notes the following characteristics:

On playground

Girl throws, catches

It rolls, bounces

Over ground, under fence

In comparing the two instances, the baby can begin to see that certain of the characteristics remain constant: The ball rolls, it bounces, and it is thrown. Other aspects, such as where the game takes place and who plays it, vary and so are not essential to the meaning of "ball." From a number of such experiences, the child learns the functions of a ball and what the word "ball" applies to.

A child uses the same process to figure out what balls look like, that is, to identify their key perceptual attributes. Perhaps the child has one ball that is large and round with red and white stripes and another that is white with blue stars, small, and round. A comparison of these sets of characteristics allows her to disregard the irrelevant attributes and abstract the crucial one: roundness.

This process does not always operate as smoothly and efficiently in real life as the ball example suggests. Children make many mistakes while trying to abstract the meaning of a word, and they often shift from one meaning to another. One child used the same word to refer to a dress, a coat, a white hat, and her stroller, and also to request a walk and to report that she had taken one (Leopold 1939–1949). Piaget (1951) described an instance of such misuse, called overgeneralization, by his 14-month-old daughter Jacqueline. While she was standing on a balcony one day watching the scene below, she saw a dog go by and said "bow wow," which she had been using to indicate dogs. Over the next few days, she applied the word to anything she saw passing below the balcony, whether it was a dog, a hen, or a woman pushing a baby carriage.

As these overgeneralizations suggest, determining the meaning of a word is a difficult task. Usually, the adults around the child try to make the task easier by speaking in short, simple sentences that refer to physical activities that are currently going on (Snow & Ferguson 1977). The words that adults direct toward infants have a close connection with the immediate context, and this helps the child to determine their meaning.

Another way adults can help children who are learning to talk is by reinforcing their early efforts to pronounce and use words properly and by providing the child with clear models of what to say. Compare these dialogues recorded by Katherine Nelson (1973):

Mother: Is that a car?

Jane (14 months): Bah.

Mother: Yes, car. Here's another car.

Jane: Gah.

Mother: Car, yes.

Jane: Bah. Daddy.

Mother: Daddy. Daddy's car is all gone.

Paul (17 months, looking at a picture book): Go.

Mother: What? Feel.

Paul: Fe.

Mother: What's that? A dog. What does the dog say? One page at a time. Oh, that one over there. What's that one there?

Paul: Baoh.

Mother: What? You know that.

Paul: Bah.

Mother: What?

Jane's mother supported her attempts to speak by accepting Jane's imperfect pronunciation, expanding her intended meaning, and saying the word correctly so that Jane could try to imitate it. Paul's mother was more critical, giving no reinforcement for any of his attempts and controlling the whole exchange. At 15 months, Jane had a vocabulary of 50 words. Paul did not have a vocabulary that large until he was 20 months old. He also dropped some individual words and stopped using two-word utterances for a while after he had begun to use

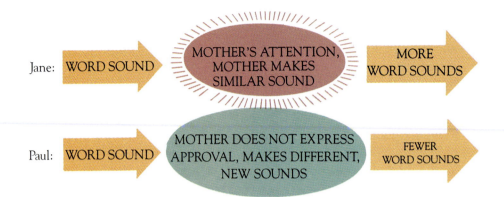

Jane: WORD SOUND → MOTHER'S ATTENTION, MOTHER MAKES SIMILAR SOUND → MORE WORD SOUNDS

Paul: WORD SOUND → MOTHER DOES NOT EXPRESS APPROVAL, MAKES DIFFERENT, NEW SOUNDS → FEWER WORD SOUNDS

Figure 5-19 The interactions of Jane with her mother and Paul with his mother are analyzed here in terms of learning theory. Both children initially emit similar behaviors. Jane receives reinforcement for her behavior in the form of approval from her mother and a sense of being able to communicate. The reinforcement produces an increase in her language behaviors. Paul receives little such reinforcement, and his language behaviors increase much less, or even decrease.

them. It seems likely that his mother's rejection of his primitive efforts was partly responsible (see Figure 5-19).

Jane's mother also aided her by saying the word Jane was trying for, "car," several times. If children are to learn to speak, they must listen to what people around them say and copy it. Parents can help by giving their children models of what the child obviously wants to say. This two-way exchange between parent and child seems to greatly facilitate the child's language development, even when the child does not immediately repeat what the parent has said (Moerck 1980; Wells 1980).

Ten years ago, some psycholinguists thought that imitation was not important in language development, because many children seldom imitate immediately what they have just heard (Bloom et al. 1974; Corrigan 1980). Research on the role of social interaction in language development, however, has shown the important role of imitation and of observational learning in general (Snow 1981). Adults set specific models for what children should say, and children clearly learn from these models. The processes of imitation and observational learning are discussed in the Theory Inset "Social Learning," in Chapter 6.

There are limitations to what children can learn from observation. For instance, they cannot imitate utterances that are far beyond their comprehension. Most 2-year-olds could imitate the phrase "red ball," but none could imitate "The quality of mercy is not strained." Within such limits, however, children do imitate much of what they hear, and thus learn a great deal about how to speak (Clark 1977; MacWhinney 1978).

Individual Differences in Learning to Speak

Children show enormous individual variations in their development of language. They differ not only in the ages at which they begin to speak and the rate at which their speech develops but also in the style of their first communications (Peter 1983). From an early age, some seen to focus on spoken words, whereas others focus more on communicating by gestures and other nonverbal means.

LISA'S 50 WORDS:

Objects						Non-Objects					
Animate			Inanimate			Person-Related				Object-Related	
People	**Animals**		**Personal**		**Impersonal**	**Action**		**Expressive**		**Action**	**Properties**
Daddy	Daisy		Ball	Blanket	Car	See	Sit	Yes	Mine	Woof woof	Cold
Mommy	Puppy		Doll	Shoe	Keys	Outside	Nap	Not now	Hi		Hot
Kenny	Dog		Fork	Sock	Telephone	Go	Up	Want	Please		Where
Me			Water	Pillow	That	Eat	Tickle		Thank you		
			Toast	Pocket		Drink	tickle				
			Juice	Book							

JANE'S 50 WORDS:

Objects							Non-Objects				
Animate			Inanimate				Person-Related		Object-Related		
People		**Animals**	**Personal**			**Impersonal**		**Action**	**Expressive**	**Action**	**Properties**
Daddy	Rhoda	Doggie	Ball	Curler	Noodles	Drawer	Rock	School	Bye	Cuckoo	More
Mommy	Helen	Kitty	Walker	Cracker	Turkey	Key	Porch	Up	Hi	All gone	
Daniel	Lara		Book	Cookie	Pea	Clock	That		Row-row		
Nana	Girl		Glasses	Cake	Ear	Top			No		
Jane	Baby		Watch	Water	Eye	Light					
			Tie	Bottle	Toes						

Figure 5-20 These two 50-word vocabularies of 18-month-old Lisa and 15-month-old Jane are quite different. Virtually all of Jane's vocabulary consists of names of objects—some animate, some inanimate. In contrast, Lisa has many words that she uses for social and expressive purposes—"Hi" and "Thank you," for example—and for actions rather than objects. Lisa might be more sociable and outgoing than Jane, or her mother might emphasize personal and social matters in her own speech, whereas Jane's mother might concentrate on naming things.

One of the best-documented differences in language development is in the type of words that children learn first (Nelson 1981). The initial vocabulary of some children consists primarily of the names of inanimate objects, whereas other children favor words that primarily name or characterize people and offer the opportunity for social exchanges. Figure 5-20 shows the fifty-word vocabularies of two children, one from each group.

Nelson (1981) believes that such individual strategies for learning to talk may reflect a genetically based disposition. A child having an active, assertive temperament, for example, may organize her schemes of the world in terms of actions and seize first on words that characterize those actions, such as "go," "sit," "bump," "hurt," and "boom." A less active but curious baby might concentrate on objects that can be manipulated and first learn words such as "key," "clock," "top," "light," and "drawer." A third infant might be most fascinated by the people around her and first learn the words that ensure social interactions with those people, such as "hi," "nice," "good girl," and "bye bye."

Despite individual differences, every child includes all types of words—names of food and objects, social phrases, and action words—in her first 50-word vocabulary. Many factors undoubtedly contribute to learning that vocabulary, including the parents' styles of speech, the number of siblings and their ages, and the way others react to the child's attempts to speak—whether they reinforce and help shape the child's attempts or reject and belittle them. But despite such differences in learning opportunities and in the amount and kind of encouragement, virtually all 8-month-olds babble, virtually all 18-month-olds speak words, and virtually all 2-year-olds can put two words together to form a primitive sentence.

These achievements, which express the common outlines of language development throughout the human species, are closely tied to the developing cognitive skills of the sensorimotor child. As development in both cognition and language progresses, the quality of the child's social and emotional life also changes. An infant's special attachment to her mother or other principal caretaker can begin only when the baby can distinguish her mother from other people. Separation anxiety—the child's distress when her mother goes out of sight—ends with the understanding that mother exists independently of the child. In a similar way, social development affects cognitive and language development. Children learn language only when people talk to them. And they learn their society's basic social give-and-take first with the earliest "dialogues" of infancy—dialogues that may not even use language.

SUMMARY

PHYSICAL DEVELOPMENT

1. During infancy, as well as throughout childhood, physical development follows two basic patterns: **head-to-foot** (cephalocaudal) and **inner-to-outer** (proximodistal).
    a. These patterns are especially evident in infant bodily growth.
    b. The same patterns apply to the development of **motor abilities** (also called sensorimotor abilities), such as sitting, crawling, walking, grasping, and reaching.

c.   The motor and sensory areas of the cortex of the brain, which develop very rapidly during infancy, mature according to these patterns too.

2.   The *association areas of the brain,* which integrate information from the sensory and motor areas and are essential to higher cognitive functioning, show major development between 6 and 24 months.

3.   Development of motor abilities depends in part on gene-directed physical development, but it is also subject to environmental influences. A moderate amount of environmental stimulation seems to produce the best development of motor abilities.

COGNITIVE DEVELOPMENT: THE SENSORIMOTOR PERIOD

4.   Infants' exploration of their environment leads to systematic changes in their ways of knowing. The theoretical approach that focuses on these changes, *cognitive-developmental theory,* seeks to explain how people develop knowledge or understanding, especially during infancy and childhood. The best-known systematic theory of cognitive development is that of Jean Piaget.

THEORY: *COGNITIVE DEVELOPMENT*

5.   Cognitive-developmental researchers agree on two basic principles:
a.   People are *active seekers and interpreters* of their experience, not merely reactors to stimulation from the environment.
b.   Cognitive development produces *qualitative changes* (not merely quantitative ones) in how people think.

6.   By performing actions and then *abstracting* from the transformations brought about by the actions, a person constructs a general understanding of something. To abstract is to compare several transformations and find an element that they all have in common. The result of a person's abstracting is what Piaget calls a *scheme,* a structured piece of knowledge about how to do something.

7.   The active nature of intelligence is described by Piaget in terms of a continual interaction of *assimilation* and *accommodation.* When people apply a scheme to a situation, they assimilate the situation to the scheme. When they adjust that scheme, they accommodate the scheme to the situation. Schemes thereby become better and better adapted to the person's world. Piaget says that in this process the developing person is seeking *equilibrium* between her schemes and the world of her experience.

8.   According to Piaget, every child develops through four different ways of knowing—four periods of cognitive development.
a.   In the *sensorimotor period,* from birth till about 2 years of age, an infant knows things only through her sensorimotor actions on them. Objects

and people exist for the infant only when she is looking at, hearing, or touching them.

b. During the *preoperational period,* from 2 to 6 or 7 years of age, preschool children can mentally represent objects and people not currently present or events not currently taking place. But they cannot use these representations logically.

c. In the *concrete-operational period,* from 6 or 7 years to early adolescence, children develop the ability to think logically about concrete things they are familiar with.

d. In the *formal-operational period,* from early adolescence through adulthood, the ability to think logically about hypothetical ideas develops.

9.   The cognitive-developmental periods form a **hierarchy,** in which each new type of intelligence is built upon and incorporates the type before it.

10.   Research demonstrates that individuals show unevenness, or **decalage,** in their cognitive development. When tested on a number of tasks, they perform at different cognitive-developmental stages on different tasks. Such unevenness probably arises mostly from environmental factors.

11.   **Neo-Piagetian theory** builds upon Piaget's work and those of other classical cognitive-developmental theorists but addresses problems that the earlier theorists did not resolve, including the role of the environment in cognitive development.

a. Jerome Bruner and others have suggested that cognitive-developmental analyses should emphasize how children process information, how the environment affects that processing, and how transitions occur from one developmental stage or level to the next.

b. Classical Piagetian theory characterizes a person as being at a particular stage of development. Neo-Piagetian theory, on the other hand, characterizes a person's skills as being at particular levels of development. Each person has skills at various levels, although a majority of skills are likely to be concentrated in a few levels.

12.   Piaget described behavior during the first 2 years in terms of six stages characterized by increasingly complex *circular reactions,* actions infants repeat over and over.

a. In the first stage, during the first few months of life, an infant is capable only of reflexes—inborn, automatic behaviors.

b. *Primary circular reactions* (common in 1- to 6-month-olds) are repetitions of a single action.

c. *Secondary circular reactions* (4 to 12 months of age) are repetitions of single actions to produce an interesting end—an effect on some object.

d. In the *coordination of secondary circular reactions* (6 to 14 months of age), the baby uses a familiar means to produce a novel end.

e. **Tertiary circular reactions** (11 to 22 months of age) are variations on a repeated action in order to vary the result in some object.

f. Between 16 and 24 months of age, the infant develops **representation,** the ability to perform internal mental actions and therefore to think about objects independently of her own sensorimotor actions.

13. Neo-Piagetian theory and research builds on Piaget's work but concentrates on how children process information and how experience affects their behavior. Tests of sensorimotor skills and brain development suggest that infants progress through four successive developmental levels in the sensorimotor period.

a. With **single actions,** infants 2 months and older can control one activity at a time.

b. Babies 6 months and older can combine two actions in a **relation of actions**.

c. With **systems of actions,** infants 10 months and older can coordinate variations in one action with variations in a second action.

d. **Single representations,** which begin to appear at about 18 months of age, allow a child to symbolize something.

14. Building upon a hypothesis of Piaget's, neo-Piagetian scholars have suggested that the sequence of sensorimotor levels reflects a **cycle of information processing** that is repeated in later periods of development. For example, just as the infant moves from single actions to relations of actions to systems of actions, the child progresses from single representations to relations of representations to systems of representations. Each step in the cycle seems to involve an improvement in **working memory,** the number of items that the person can process at one time.

PERCEPTUAL DEVELOPMENT

15. Perceptual development during infancy seems to follow the general course of cognitive development. Newborns perceive few patterns if any at all, 3-month-olds can perceive some very simple patterns, and by 7 to 8 months, infants can perceive fairly complex patterns of basic relations between elements.

a. Babies seem to be able to recognize a human face by 3 months and to know how the parts of the face should be arranged by 5 to 8 months.

b. Children can detect depth by 3 months, but they really begin to understand how depth relates to falling only at 7 to 9 months, as experiments with the **visual cliff** have shown.

c. **Self-recognition** shows a reliable sequence of development during infancy, with full self-recognition in the mirror coming at 18 to 24 months.

SENSORIMOTOR INTELLIGENCE IN ANIMALS

16. Many animals seem to develop through levels of sensorimotor intelligence similar to the human ones, but apparently only apes ever reach the level of representation. Chimps and gorillas can develop various kinds of symbolic skills, including sign language roughly equivalent to that of 2-year-old human children.

EARLY LANGUAGE ACQUISITION

17. Although babies vocalize from the time they are born, children learn a language only when they hear people speak it to them.

    a.   At 4 or 5 months, babies produce their first speechlike sounds, called **babbling**—strings of meaningless sounds.

    b.   Before they begin to use words at 1 year, many children master much of the intonation of the language they hear. They produce **expressive jargon,** sequences of sounds that are not real words but have the intonation patterns of real sentences.

    c.   An infant's first words (between 12 and 18 months) are often tied to sensorimotor actions, as when a baby waves her hand and says "bye-bye."

    d.   Only at about 2 years, which is after the emergence of representation, do children readily formulate sentences of two or more words.

18. Children learn the meanings of words through a process of abstraction. They hear a word in several situations, compare the characteristics of each situation, and abstract the relevant characteristics. Adults help toddlers by speaking short, simple sentences to them and talking about concrete objects that are being used at that moment.

19. Reinforcement and observational learning (including imitation) are also important in language learning.

20. Individual children differ widely in how they acquire language—not only in the rate, but also in the way that they learn.

SUGGESTED READINGS

COWAN, PHILIP A. *Piaget: With Feeling.* New York: Holt, Rinehart and Winston, 1978.

The author, an eminent neo-Piagetian scholar, presents Piaget's theory and shows how it can be extended to deal with social and emotional development.

DEVILLIERS, JILL G, and PETER A. DEVILLIERS. *Language Acquisition.* Cambridge, Massachusetts: Harvard University Press, 1978.

An overview of language acquisition, including development in the first two years.

EVANS, RICHARD I. *Jean Piaget: The Man and His Ideas.* New York: Dutton, 1973.

The book contains a brief autobiography of Piaget and an interesting interview in which Piaget discusses his theory.

GRUBER, HOWARD, and JACQUES VONÈCHE. *The Essential Piaget: An Interpretive Reference and Guide.* New York: University of Chicago Press, 1982.

Two of Piaget's colleagues have put together the most definitive and useful single collection of Piaget's works.

ILG, FRANCES, LOUISE BATES AMES, and SIDNEY BAKER. *Child Behavior* (revised edition). New York: Harper & Row, 1981.

From research at the famous Gesell Institute of Human Development, the authors describe the normal sequence of development during the first 10 years. Writing for parents, they deal with most of the problems and issues that normally arise with infants and children, including eating, sleeping, fears, sex, siblings, and school.

LAMB, MICHAEL, and JOSEPH J. CAMPOS. *Development in Infancy: An Introduction.* New York: Random House, 1982.

This textbook includes a thorough review of early perceptual development.

PIAGET, JEAN, and BARBEL INHELDER. *The Psychology of the Child.* New York: Basic Books, 1969.

Piaget and one of his most distinguished collaborators summarize their approach to cognitive development.

6

THE
ORIGINS
OF
PERSONALITY

CHAPTER OUTLINE

In his philosophical speculations about the relation of human beings to the world and about what they can know, Rene Descartes reached this conclusion:

> Even the existence of my own body can be doubted as a possible illusion, a dream. But I who doubt, I who am deceived, at least while I doubt, I must exist, and, as doubting is thinking, it is indubitable that while I think, I am. (*Discourse on Method,* 1637)

6

THE ORIGINS OF PERSONALITY

In other words, "I think, therefore I am." In their cognitive climb from action to thought, infants seem to embody Descartes's words. When the capacity for representation—that is, thinking—has developed, the sense of self emerges: "I am."

Although nearly everyone develops the consciousness of self, the selves that emerge are not alike. Each is unique—each child develops a personality of her own. The scientific definition of personality does not differ much from the way people use the term in ordinary conversation. By ***personality,*** developmentalists mean a person's unique pattern of behaviors—her disposition to perceive things and react to them in her own individual way.

Personality depends on the complex interplay of inborn factors and experience, on the tapestry of heredity and environment discussed in Chapter 2. People in families often point to similarities between their relatives, saying things such as "He's as stubborn as a mule, just like his grandfather" or "She's very adventuresome, like her mother before her." They seem to assume that personality characteristics can be inherited. Scientists are more cautious about making this assumption. They do not know exactly which personality characteristics may be inherited—or indeed whether any are. At birth, infants do differ in temperament, some being placid and easy and others irritable and difficult, but these early dispositions often cannot be seen in the same child at a later age because of the enormous developmental changes that have taken place.

Along with temperament, social learning in the family plays a major role in the development of personality. In the early years, a baby's social environment is dominated by interactions with parents. Parents have personalities of their own, and they also have a battery of expectations about how children should be raised. These expectations generally reflect the parents' social values, which depend in part on the parents' culture and their class background.

Interactions between parents and child seem to go through a sequence of stages as the child develops a self-concept. Toward the end of the first year, a crucial milestone is reached: the establishment of a special relation between parent and child. It is this first social relation that helps the baby gradually become an independent person with a sense of self.

Although developmentalists can be confident that temperament and early social learning in the family lay the foundations for personality, the way these two factors are linked to the adult personality is a matter of much controversy. The final section of this chapter examines the question of continuity in personality: Is it possible to trace adult personality and behavior back to its origins in infant temperament and early experience?

TEMPERAMENT AND CHANGE

A newborn does not yet have a personality, but she does have a temperament. **Temperament** is a characteristic way of responding that seems to depend almost entirely on an infant's physical constitution at birth and perhaps also on prenatal influences, whereas personality is a complex of characteristics that result from an individual's experiences as well as her heredity. In practice, a newborn's temperament is usually defined by measurements of certain behaviors (see Figure 6-1). Once the researchers have identified individual differences among newborns, they measure these behaviors in the same babies at intervals during infancy and sometimes into childhood, in an attempt to answer this question: How does the relatively simple temperament of the young infant develop into the complex personality of the child and adult?

Stella Chess and Alexander Thomas carried out some of the most extensive longitudinal studies, and their findings have been generally supported by other researchers. They followed about 140 children from early infancy to adolescence and also followed hundreds of other children for shorter periods. The children were seen by trained observers and given standard psychological tests, and the parents were interviewed regularly about how their children behaved in specific situations. When the children reached school age, their teachers also were asked to report on specific behaviors (Thomas & Chess 1977, 1980). The researchers found that newborns differed in nine qualities of behaving or responding and that such differences sometimes continued into childhood. Figure 6-1 lists these categories with examples of how they might be expressed by infants and by older children.

The researchers also found that certain of these temperamental qualities tended to occur together. These clusters of characteristics generally fell into three types—the easy baby, the difficult baby, and the baby who was slow to warm up (Figure 6-2). The **easy infant** has regular patterns of eating and sleeping, readily approaches new objects and people, adapts easily to changes in the environment, generally reacts with low or moderate intensity, and typically is in a cheerful mood. The **difficult infant** usually shows irregular patterns of eating and sleeping, withdraws from new objects or people, adapts slowly to changes, reacts with great intensity, and is frequently cranky. The

TEMPERAMENTAL QUALITY	AT 2 MONTHS	AT 10 YEARS
1. ACTIVITY LEVEL (Tendency to be in physical motion)	Moves often in sleep. Wriggles when diaper is changed.	Plays ball and engages in other sports. Cannot sit still long enough to do homework.
	Does not move when being dressed or during sleep.	Likes chess and reading. Eats very slowly.
2. RHYTHMICITY (Regularity of biological functions)	Has been on four-hour feeding schedule since birth. Regular bowel movement.	Eats only at mealtimes. Sleeps the same amount of time each night.
	Awakes at a different time each morning. Size of feedings varies.	Food intake varies. Falls asleep at a different time each night.
3. APPROACH OR WITHDRAWAL (Initial reaction to any new stimulation)	Smiles and licks washcloth. Has always liked bottle.	Went to camp happily. Loved to ski the first time.
	Rejected cereal the first time. Cries when strangers appear.	Severely homesick at camp during first days. Does not like new activities.
4. ADAPTABILITY (Flexibility of behavior following initial reaction)	Was passive during first bath; now enjoys bathing. Smiles at nurse.	Likes camp, although homesick during first days. Learns enthusiastically.
	Still startled by sudden, sharp noise. Resists diapering.	Does not adjust well to new school or new teacher; comes home late for dinner even when punished.
5. INTENSITY OF REACTION (Energy level of responses)	Cries when diapers are wet. Rejects food vigorously when satisfied.	Tears up an entire page of homework if one mistake is made. Slams door of room when teased by younger brother.
	Does not cry when diapers are wet. Whimpers instead of crying when hungry.	When a mistake is made in a model airplane; corrects it quietly. Does not comment when reprimanded.

Figure 6-1 The nine temperamental qualities identified by Thomas and Chess and how they were expressed in the behavior of infants and older children. The lines with the gold background give examples of behavior at high or positive levels of the characteristic. The lines with the brown background give examples of low or negative levels. (Adapted from Thomas, Chess & Birch 1970)

slow-to-warm-up infant typically has a low activity level, tends to withdraw when presented with an unfamiliar object, reacts with a low level of intensity, and adapts slowly to changes in the environment. Fortunately for parents, most healthy infants—40 percent or more—have an easy temperament. Only about 10 percent have a difficult temperament, and about 15 percent are slow to warm up. The remaining 35 percent do not easily fit one of the three types but show some other pattern of the nine categories in Figure 6-1.

How permanent are these temperamental types? Is an infant's temperament set for life? Some children keep a very consistent temperament for several years, at least. Clem, who was in the study just described, was a difficult child. He showed a consistently high intensity of reaction. At 4½ months he screamed every time he was bathed. At 6 months his parents reported that during feeding he screamed "at the sight of the food approaching his mouth." At 9½ months he was generally "either in a very good mood, laughing or chuckling" or else he

TEMPERAMENTAL QUALITY	AT 2 MONTHS	AT 10 YEARS
6. THRESHOLD OF RESPONSIVENESS (Intensity of stimulus required to produce reaction)	Stops sucking on bottle when approached.	Rejects fatty foods. Adjusts shower until water is at exactly the right temperature.
	Is not startled by loud noises. Takes bottle and breast equally well.	Never complains when sick. Eats all foods.
7. QUALITY OF MOOD (Proportion of happy, friendly to unhappy, unfriendly behavior)	Smacks lips when first tasting new food. Smiles at parents.	Enjoys new accomplishments. Laughs when reading a funny passage aloud.
	Fusses after nursing. Cries when carriage is rocked.	Cries when he cannot solve a homework problem. Very "weepy" if he does not get enough sleep.
8. DISTRACTIBILITY (Degree to which extraneous stimulation disrupts ongoing behavior)	Will stop crying for food if rocked. Stops fussing if given pacifier when diaper is being changed.	Needs absolute silence for homework. Has a hard time choosing a shirt in a store because they all appeal to him.
	Will not stop crying when diaper is changed. Fusses after eating, even if rocked.	Can read a book while television set is at high volume. Does chores on schedule.
9. ATTENTION SPAN AND PERSISTENCE (Length of time activities are maintained and tolerance for difficulty)	If soiled, continues to cry until changed. Repeatedly rejects water if he wants milk.	Reads for two hours before sleeping. Does homework carefully.
	Cries when awakened but stops almost immediately. Objects only mildly if cereal precedes bottle.	Gets up frequently from homework for a snack. Never finishes a book.

was screaming. His parents said that "he laughed so hard playing peek-a-boo he got hiccups." At 2 years his parents said, "He screams bloody murder when he's being dressed." When he was 7 years old his parents reported, "When he's frustrated, as for example when he doesn't hit a ball very far, he stomps around, his voice goes up to its higher level, his eyes get red and occasionally fill with tears. Once he went up to his room when this occurred and screamed for half an hour."

Clem was unusual. The kind of continuity that he showed from infancy to childhood is rarely found in developmental studies. In fact, the temperament of the majority of babies changes between the first year of life and the preschool years (Beckwith 1979; Dunn 1979). Circumstances in the child's environment are the most likely agents of this change, and the most important agent in an infant's world is his mother. His mother has a well-developed personality of her own and, for better or worse, these two human beings affect each other.

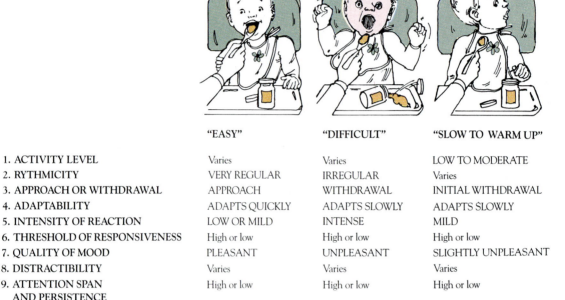

	"EASY"	"DIFFICULT"	"SLOW TO WARM UP"
1. ACTIVITY LEVEL	Varies	Varies	LOW TO MODERATE
2. RYTHMICITY	VERY REGULAR	IRREGULAR	Varies
3. APPROACH OR WITHDRAWAL	APPROACH	WITHDRAWAL	INITIAL WITHDRAWAL
4. ADAPTABILITY	ADAPTS QUICKLY	ADAPTS SLOWLY	ADAPTS SLOWLY
5. INTENSITY OF REACTION	LOW OR MILD	INTENSE	MILD
6. THRESHOLD OF RESPONSIVENESS	High or low	High or low	High or low
7. QUALITY OF MOOD	PLEASANT	UNPLEASANT	SLIGHTLY UNPLEASANT
8. DISTRACTIBILITY	Varies	Varies	Varies
9. ATTENTION SPAN AND PERSISTENCE	High or low	High or low	High or low

Figure 6-2 The clusters of characteristic behaviors that define "easy," "difficult," and "slow-to-warm-up" temperaments. The temperamental qualities measured are listed at left, and the typical ways of responding for each temperament are shown in capital letters. The behaviors printed in lower-case letters do not differentiate between the temperaments. For example, both an easy baby and a difficult baby might have a high attention span.

MOTHER-INFANT INTERACTION

Partly because of her own personality, an individual mother has certain attitudes about what babies should be like and how they should be treated. (The word "mother" here refers to the baby's primary caretaker—usually the infant's biological mother but sometimes a grandmother, nurse, or sitter. Sometimes, but not often, it is the baby's father.) Some mothers have a task-oriented style of dealing with their infants. They consider, for example, that the tasks of child care are not occasions for playing with the baby. They devote their full attention to the tasks (Escalona 1968). These parents carefully diaper, feed, and clean their babies with little talk or play with the child. They set aside other times, when the baby is clean and fed and awake, for playing and talking. Because so much of a mother's time is taken up with the necessary duties of child care, the amount of time these parents spend interacting with their babies is limited.

Other mothers have a high-interaction style, continually talking to and interacting with their babies. They believe that the baby is trying to communicate through her cries and coos, and they attribute all sorts of significance to her sounds. They say that the baby is "scolding" them for being late with a feeding or that she is "asking" for a clean diaper. Because these mothers are always trying to figure out what the baby means or wants, they pay great attention to her sounds, movements, and facial expressions, and so are continually responsive to her.

These are only two possible styles of parenting. There may be as many styles as there are parents. But these two can illustrate the variations in parent-child interaction that result from the coming together of a particular infant's temperament and the parent's personality. Consider, for example, a baby who is slow to warm up, with a low activity level, a low intensity of reaction, and a tendency to respond only to high stimulation. Babies with this temperament do not initiate much interaction themselves. Their low activity level means that they sleep a great deal. When they are awake, they do not make great demands for attention. Even when they are hungry, they are more likely to whimper than to scream loudly. The combination of this temperament and the first type of parenting—the task-oriented style—means that the baby will not receive a great deal of stimulation. This match of baby's temperament and style of parenting is probably less than ideal for the baby.

Bobby was a slow-to-warm-up baby (Thomas, Chess & Birch 1970). As an infant, Bobby rejected new foods—not actively or adamantly; he just let them dribble out of his mouth. When he did that, his parents eliminated the food from his diet and never reintroduced it. When Bobby backed away from other children on a playground, his parents did not encourage him to play with them. They just took him home. When he was 10 years old, Bobby was living on a diet of just hamburgers, applesauce, and boiled eggs. In play, he was a loner. Any activity that required exposure to new people or made new demands on him he reacted to with distaste. Although Bobby was not abnormal—he enjoyed things that he did by himself and at his own pace—it is interesting to speculate what kind of 10-year-old he might have been if his mother and father had had a different style of parenting, one that encouraged him to try new things and to persist until the new experience became a bit more familiar. This type of baby needs a lot of stimulation for his best cognitive and social development, the kind of stimulation he would get from a high-interaction parent.

On the other hand, a difficult baby, whose intensity of reaction and responsiveness are high, might receive so much stimulation from a playful, talkative parent that she would become over-excited, and then tired and irritable. A high-interaction parent may keep stimulating a crying baby whose only need is to be put down and allowed to fall asleep.

In one study, mothers and their infants were videotaped over a period of

Figure 6-3 An infant and mother usually develop a synchronized pattern of relationship. For example, when the baby is ready to wake up (because she is getting used to waking at certain times of day or because she is getting hungry), the mother is likely to be there to pick the baby up, feed and change her, and socialize with her. And the baby increasingly adapts both to the circumstances of her life (developing different patterns of sleep and activity for day and night) and to her mother's handling of her.

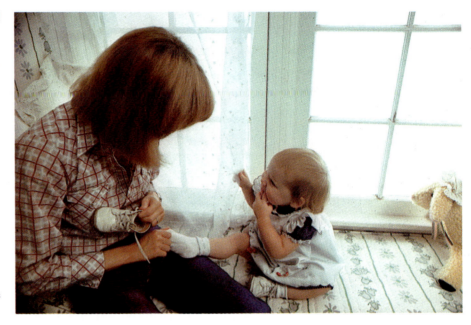

months. The tapes were later analyzed, and individual differences both in babies and in how their mothers interacted with them were recorded (Brazelton et. al. 1974). For example, the researchers noted that the mothers of two similarly tense, overreactive infants responded to their babies very differently. One increased her activity and her stimulation of the baby when the baby looked away from her, which is usually a signal that the baby wants some time out from interacting. The other mother maintained a steady level of activity that, over several months, modulated her baby's overreactivity. Also, she was sensitive to the baby; that is, her responses to the baby's signals were contingent (well-timed), appropriate, and consistent (Lamb & Easterbrooks 1981).

Parents' level of sensitivity to their infants' temperamental characteristics has been shown to have long-term effects on development. One longitudinal study found that children of mothers who responded sensitively to them as very young infants were, at ages 3 to 7, more resourceful and more able to occupy themselves when alone; also, they were assessed as being more satisfied and had better relations with other people (Brody & Axelrod 1978).

The parental characteristics that seem most likely to make a baby more difficult are inconsistency in interaction with the baby, intolerance of the baby's needs, and conflict between parents (Cameron 1977). Major negative changes in the family's social situation, such as divorce, loss of a job, and moving, often seem to produce these parental behaviors and a corresponding

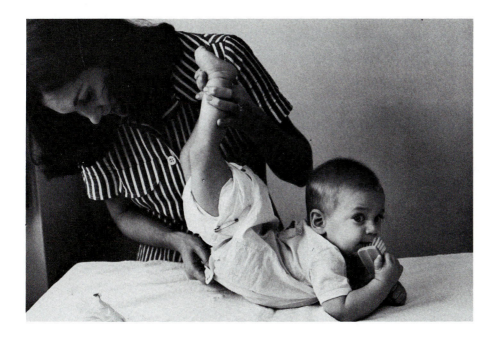

change in the baby's temperament—toward being more difficult. Likewise, improvements in the family's social situation often seem to lead to a much easier temperament (Vaughn et al. 1979).

Major mismatches between parent and infant are rare, and they tend to diminish as each adapts to the other. Both the parenting style of mother or father and the baby's personality are forged from these mutual adaptations.

Getting to Know Each Other

From the time of birth, babies influence their parents as well as being influenced by them. One longitudinal study showed that differences in the behavior of newborns affected mother-infant interaction later, when the babies were 1 year old (Waters et al. 1980). The researchers assessed one hundred babies seven and ten days after birth by measuring motor maturity, physiological regulation, ability to orient to objects and people, and responsiveness to stimuli. When these babies were a year old they were brought back, and they and their mothers were observed to see what kind of attachment relationships existed between them. Attachment is discussed at length later in this chapter; here it is only necessary to note that babies about a year old behave in different ways when their mother leaves them alone or with a stranger for a brief time. Most babies have a secure attachment to their mother: The baby seeks to have mother near and, although he may cry when she leaves, he is easily comforted by her return. The baby is content while his mother is present and will explore his surroundings as long as he knows she is nearby. This behavior shows that he has come to expect his mother to be reliable and sensitive to him, and that he can count on her. A few babies, however, seem unable to be comforted by their mother when she returns from even a short absence. Even though they cry to be picked up, they then struggle to be put down, continue crying, and show signs of anger. These babies are apt to show distress and anxiety even when their mothers are nearby. This behavior indicates that the baby is ambivalent, or uncertain about his mother's ability to meet his needs.

The researchers found that newborns who were more difficult—whose motor immaturity prevented them from adjusting easily to being held, who were more irritable, who often became excited and startled, and who were less responsive to objects and people—were more likely at one year of age to show anxious, ambivalent attachment to their mothers. Mary Ainsworth, who first described these different patterns of attachment (1978), found the mothers of anxious, ambivalent babies to be generally unskilled in holding their babies, interacting with them face-to-face, and feeding them. It is easy to see the ways in which difficult babies could contribute to such problems. They are harder to hold because they cannot adjust their bodies to being held as well as other babies can. Because their internal physiological regulation runs less smoothly, feeding problems are more likely to arise. Their overreactivity would make it more difficult for the mother to learn the baby's signals. And their poorer orientation to sights and sounds could hamper face-to-face interaction.

Clearly then, babies influence the mother-infant interaction. Babies adjust to the way their mothers hold them, feed them, comfort them, talk to them, and change their diapers. Adjustment takes place even in the first week or two after birth. In one study, nine newborns to be put up for adoption were each taken care of 24 hours a day by an experienced nurse for the first 28 days of life (Sander 1975). On the tenth day of this 28-day period, all the nurses exchanged babies. When this switch occurred, infants showed a major increase in crying and in feeding problems. The difficulties occurred no matter which nurse a baby had first and which second. The problems persisted for several days, until the babies and their new caregivers had adapted to each other.

Studies have shown—and it seems obvious—that the more sensitive mothers are to their babies, the more competent and sociable the babies are (Clarke-Stewart et al. 1979, 1980; Waters et al. 1980). But it is much easier to be responsive to a competent, sociable, "easy" baby than to a difficult one. Does maternal responsiveness produce sociable and competent babies, or does infant temperament produce a certain level of maternal responsiveness? Researchers trying to untangle this chicken-and-egg problem have concluded that the influence is reciprocal (Bradley et al. 1979).

The process of interaction between parent and infant is in many ways like the cultivation of a garden (Figure 6-4). The child has certain characteristics

Figure 6-4 These contrasting gardens are an analogy for different possible interactions between parent and infant. Each species of flower or shrub or tree has its own needs; some need a great deal of moisture or sunlight to flourish, some very little. Some are very vulnerable to being choked off by weeds. (Top) If the garden's caretaker allowed the plants to go their own way, unnurtured and unprotected, the result would be a wilderness, where weeds flourish at the expense of more delicate plants. (Middle) If the gardener nurtured and protected the plants but forced them into unnatural shapes and combinations, the plants' natural tendencies would be distorted and much of the garden's beauty would be destroyed. (Bottom) If the caretaker were guided by the nature of his plants, he would plan the garden so that the plants were compatible with each other and each plant grew to be beautiful in its own way.

and grows in certain directions, and her parents can mold her behavior into patterns that build upon those characteristics. Just as gardeners must let themselves be influenced by the characteristics and needs of their plants, so parents must let themselves be influenced by their child if she is to become an effective, healthy person. There must be constant interaction—mutual influence between parent and child (Baumrind 1980; Bell 1979). If this interaction is effective, one of the most important outcomes for the child is that she can rely on those around her when she needs them. That is, she develops a sense of basic trust.

Basic Trust versus Mistrust

Infants must learn the most basic things—how to grasp what they see; how to make vanished objects, including their mother or father, come back; how to get food; how to find comfort when they are upset. They must learn what they can expect of objects, of other people, and of themselves. In other words, they must develop a sense of who or what they can trust and who or what they should mistrust.

Erik Erikson (1963, 1968) suggests that the "cornerstone of a vital personality" is laid in infancy as the baby undergoes this first developmental crisis of Basic Trust versus Mistrust. (Erikson's theory of psychosocial development is described at length in the theory inset "Psychodynamic Approaches," in Chapter 8.) For Erikson, a developmental crisis is a period of encounter between an individual's developing potential and the people and institutions that make up the individual's social environment. These crises occur throughout the life span, from infancy to old age. As a child's physical and cognitive abilities develop, the child is able to deal with the world in new ways, and other people must deal with the child from a new perspective. In the ideal resolution of this first crisis, the infant should develop a sense of **basic trust,** Erikson's term for an essential confidence in the reliability of others as well as a fundamental sense that the self is worthy of confidence. (There should also be a certain amount of mistrust, in the sense that the infant discovers that some objects or people do not behave in consistent or expectable ways.)

The parents, especially the mother, are particularly important in directing the outcome of this first developmental crisis. If the parents are psychologically healthy and comfortable in their caretaking role, they can provide the baby with sensitive care, which gives the baby a sense of being effective (when adults respond to his signals of hunger or discomfort, he knows that those signals are having an effect) and a sense of the world's continuity and reliability.

Erikson also emphasizes that the developing person lives not only in a family but in a larger society. One of the functions of society is to make certain prescriptions about how parents should raise their children.

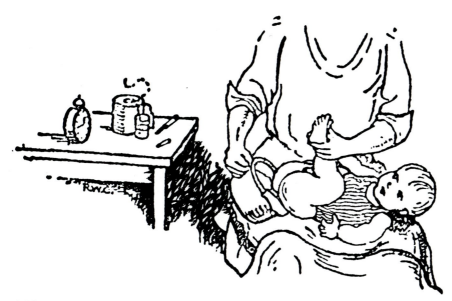

Child-Care Practices

Throughout human history, "experts" have freely given advice to mothers and fathers about child-care practices. Today parents usually obtain this expert advice from pediatricians and books on child care (Clarke-Stewart 1978). Typically, the suggested techniques are presented as the only proper way to raise a child, but in fact they usually reflect the attitudes of the expert's society at least as much as they reflect scientific fact. Within the last 70 years in the United States, there has been a great swing to the opposite in the advice that experts offer, and the change reflects a major change in the attitudes of American society.

During the nineteenth century the dominant view was that the main purpose of child-rearing was to break the child's will, but by the middle of this century the view was that the child should be treated kindly and helped to develop into a strong but sensitive individualist (Gadlin 1978). The advice given in a pamphlet entitled *Infant Care,* published by the United States Children's Bureau, illustrates this change (Wolfenstein 1953). In the first edition, published in 1914, bowel training was to be begun "by the third month or even earlier." Throughout the 1920s and 1930s the same advice continued. Babies were to be firmly toilet trained as early as possible so that by 6 or 8 months of age there would be no more dirty diapers (Figure 6-5).

In the late thirties a new trend began. Mothers of 1938 were told they might begin bowel training as early as 6 months—the time at which mothers of earlier years were supposed to have had their babies fully trained. In 1942, mothers were told not to begin bowel training until 8 or 10 months. By 1951 the recommendation had reached its present-day form: "You can so easily make

Figure 6-5 This drawing appeared in the 1929 edition of *Infant Care,* published by the United States government. The pamphlet gave the following advice to mothers about toilet training. "One method of training the little baby [less than 3 months old] in regular bowel habits is as follows: Hold the baby in your lap or lay him on a table with his head toward your left, in the position for changing his diaper. Lift the feet with the left hand and with the right insert a soap stick or other suppository into the rectum. Still holding the feet up, press a small chamber gently against the buttocks with the right hand and hold it there until the stool is passed. The first time the soap stick is used the stool will come in 5 or 10 minutes. Later the time will be shortened. After the first three or four days or as soon as the baby's bowels will move without a suppository, give up the soap stick." (United States Department of Labor, 1929)

trouble for yourself and the baby if you start training too early. . . . Most babies are not ready to start learning bowel control by the end of the first year. One and a half or two years is a much more common time for them to learn willingly." The same advice is now standard in most books on child care.

Similar changes took place in other advice about child-rearing techniques. In 1914, masturbation was considered a despicable practice that could ruin a child for life, but in 1951 the advice had become similar to that given today: Masturbation in infants and children is normal and should not be a cause for alarm.

The change in attitudes that underlay the changes in child-care recommendations is captured nicely by a simple contrast. In 1928, John B. Watson, the noted behaviorist, recommended the following to parents:

> There is a sensible way of treating children. Treat them as though they were young adults. Dress them, bathe them with care and circumspection. Let your behavior always be objective and kindly firm. Never hug and kiss them, never let them sit in your lap. If you must, kiss them once on the forehead when they say goodnight. Shake hands with them in the morning. Give them a pat on the head if they have made an extraordinarily good job of a difficult task. Try it out. In a week's time you will find how easy it is to be prefectly objective with your child and at the same time kindly.

Today Dr. Benjamin Spock has become the most influential child-care expert, and the advice in his best-selling book, *Baby and Child Care*, is very different from Watson's:

> Don't be afraid to feed her when you think she's really hungry. If you are mistaken, she'll merely refuse to take much. . . . Don't be afraid to love her and enjoy her. Every baby needs to be smiled at, talked to, played with, fondled—gently and lovingly—just as much as she needs vitamins and calories. That's what will make her a person who loves people and enjoys life. The baby who doesn't get any loving will grow up cold and unresponsive. (Spock 1976)

Despite this dramatic reversal in attitudes about training children and in recommended child-care techniques, it is clear that none of these generations of children grew up on the whole as abnormal or unhealthy adults. The particular techniques that parents use in toilet training and other kinds of training seem to be less important than their sensitivity to their baby's particular needs.

The parents' goal in following a recommended set of child-care practices is to make their children effective members of their society—to socialize them. When our society valued the control of sexual expression by adults, children were taught to control that expression in themselves so that they would fit in their society. They were therefore socialized to avoid masturbation and its supposed evil consequences. As the expression of sexuality became more acceptable, masturbation was no longer a behavior that threatened to make the child an "abnormal" adult, so it, too, became more acceptable.

SOCIAL LEARNING AND PERSONALITY DEVELOPMENT

Social interactions between parents and infants begin at birth. From the very beginning, parents and other people try to help babies learn what they will need to function well in their society. What they do to mold the children's behaviors to make them effective members of society is called *socialization,* and the processes by which the children acquire the behaviors are called *social learning.* It is through socialization and social learning that the environment puts its first stamp on personality, and social-learning theory is the main theoretical approach to analyzing these phenomena.

THEORY: SOCIAL LEARNING

Like the traditional behaviorist approach, social-learning theory emphasizes that the environment molds the behavior of child and adult. The traditional theory explains all learning as the result of conditioning. From the earliest days of behaviorism, however, many scholars argued that much human behavior—especially social behavior—was shaped by learning processes more complex than conditioning. In 1941, Neal Miller and John Dollard suggested that, besides conditioning, imitation is also an important part of social learning. Infants and children learn not only by conditioning but by observation and imitation.

From this beginning, other investigators, including John Sears, Eleanor Maccoby, and Harry Levin (1957), expanded social-learning theory further to include the effects of socialization techniques on children's behavior: Do specific child-care practices, such as early toilet training or prevention of masturbation, have particular effects on children's personalities? What are the effects of certain disciplinary and interactional styles, such as authoritarian or permissive approaches to child-rearing? How do the socialization practices of peers, schools, and churches affect children's behavior? In general, how do social practices mold behavior?

Much of the study of socialization aims at understanding how children acquire the general rules and roles of society. Because children cannot understand those rules and roles much before age 2, socialization will not be discussed at length until Chapter 8. The discussion in this chapter is mainly about other social-learning processes that apply to infants and children. Most important are conditioning and imitation.

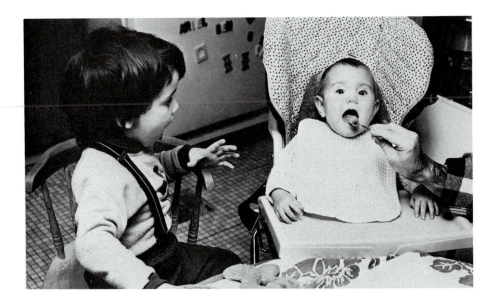

Figure 6-6   Imitation pervades the lives of toddlers.

IMITATION AND OBSERVATIONAL LEARNING

Imitation, the attempt to copy or match the behavior of another person, is certainly an important way of learning from other people. Starting at about 1 year of age, for example, infants imitate simple words that they hear their parents say, and thus they begin to learn to speak. Various scientists have pointed out, however, that imitation is only one form of a much broader social learning process, ***observational learning,*** which is exactly what its name implies: Some new knowledge, information, or behavior is acquired by watching the behavior of others. In this way, the individual can learn without reinforcement or punishment but by observation alone. Rachel, at 13 months of age, has seen that her parents and older sister eat with spoons and forks. She insists on trying to feed herself with her spoon, even though no one has ever encouraged her to do so. In fact, her mother, anticipating the mess, tries to discourage her.

Simple observational learning is a basic process that does not require advanced intelligence. Cats, dogs, and pigeons, for example, can learn through observation (Bullock & Neuringer 1977; John et al. 1968). In a demonstration that has been repeated often, one cat watches another being trained to press a bar for food when a light goes on. When the second cat is put into the experimental situation, it quickly begins to press the bar when the light goes on—much more quickly than the first cat. Through observation, it has learned how to get food. Human beings, of course, are capable of much more sophisticated forms of observational learning.

Albert Bandura (1969), an eminent social-learning theorist, describes in this way how observational learning affects behavior: People observe a behavior and memorize it, or encode it into memory, either as images or as words; later they may imitate the behavior, using their memory to guide their action. But not all behavior learned by observation is later performed. Six-year-old Nicole, for example, sees by watching football on television how the game is played. She also sees that only men play football. She therefore not only learns some rudiments of the game but also learns that girls do not play football. Later, she avoids the neighborhood games that may start up. Social-learning theorists distinguish between learning a behavior by observation and performing it, and they point out that different factors can influence whether a behavior is learned and whether it is performed.

Factors That Affect Observational Learning

One of the goals of learning theory is to specify which factors affect learning and which affect performance. A number of environmental factors have important effects on observational learning.

1. Most obviously, the behavior to be learned must take place in the child's environment, so that she can observe it. A child who never sees people greet each other with handshakes will not be able to learn the greeting by observation.

2. The child should see favorable consequences of a behavior for a *model,* the person that the child is observing. If a child sees that a model is reinforced for performing a behavior, she is more likely to learn the behavior. For example, the applause and attention given to sports heroes and movie stars make boys and girls want to learn these people's behaviors. On the other hand, if a model is punished for a behavior, the child is less likely to learn it.

3. The personal characteristics of the model also have a strong effect on what is learned by observation. Children are more likely to learn from models who are kind and loving than from those who are cold and aloof. They are more likely to learn from models who appear to have power and to control resources. And they are more likely to learn from models who seem similar to them, either physically or psychologically (Bandura 1969; Mischel 1970). These three generalizations suggest why parents are such potent models. For young children especially, parents are the main source of warmth and affection, and the unchallenged holders of power.

Not only the environment but each child's own characteristics and abilities help determine whether the child will learn a behavior that she observes.

4. A child must pay attention to the person performing the behavior. If a child is sleepy, hyperactive, or too young and immature to pay attention to a certain behavior, she will not learn it.

5. The child must be able to remember what she observed. The ability to remember an observed behavior seems to be closely related to the child's cognitive-developmental level (McCall et al. 1977). If a behavior is too complex for the child or if it involves concepts that she does not yet know, she will have difficulty learning it.

Factors That Affect Performance

Social-learning research has shown that children often have learned a behavior from observation even when they do not perform it. For example, two matched groups of children see a model performing the same behavior, but one group sees the model rewarded, while the other group sees the model punished. Many more of the children observing the reward will perform the behavior themselves. Often,

Figure 6-7 Children acquire many of their attitudes and behaviors through observation and imitation. In infancy, parents are the most available and attractive models for social learning. This budding young writer is going to do his best to imitate his mother's literary efforts.

the children who observed the punishment will learn the behavior but will not perform it. If their fear of punishment is removed, however, they may perform the behavior and thus demonstrate that they learned it in the first place (Bandura 1969).

Whether children actually perform a behavior that they have learned depends on several factors.

1. Most important are the reinforcements and punishments that a *learner* receives when trying out the behavior.

2. The reinforcements and punishments that a *model* receives for an action also have a major effect on whether the learner will perform it. As noted earlier, these consequences affect observational learning, but, once a behavior has been learned, they also affect the learner's performance. If a child sees a model being reinforced for doing something, she is much more likely to carry out the behavior than if she sees the model being punished. The reinforcer need not be a tangible object such as food or a toy. For example, if a boy observes his father building a birdhouse with obvious pleasure, the boy is likely to try building something himself.

3. The child's own abilities also determine what behaviors she will perform after observational learning. If the be-

havior is too complex for the child's developmental level or physical skills, she will not usually perform it. A 10-year-old girl may pay close attention to a star basketball player's technique of shooting free throws, and she may remember very well what the player did. But that does not mean that she will be able to do it herself.

SOCIALIZATION PRACTICES

Observational learning is centrally important in development. Parents sometimes do not realize what they are teaching their children through observational learning. When a mother becomes angry and hits her child, for example, she is offering a model of aggression as an appropriate way to express anger—even though her goal may have been to train the child to be *less* aggressive. Consequently, children whose parents use physical punishment are much more likely than other children to get into fights with their peers.

Parents typically employ techniques of conditioning and modeling in more complex, less controlled ways than those that researchers use in the laboratory. They often use complex combinations of operant conditioning, classical conditioning, and modeling to socialize their children, although they may not realize they are using these techniques. To determine the effects of patterns of parental behavior, investigators analyze how particular socialization practices relate to children's behavior. Research of this sort has uncovered several such relations—for one, that when parents use physical punishment, their children are likely to be more aggressive with their peers (Parke & Slaby 1983). Another such finding, mentioned earlier in this chapter, is that inconsistency in the ways parents interact with their babies seems to cause the infants to become more difficult.

COGNITIVE SOCIAL-LEARNING THEORY

In the past, early in the study of child development, the viewpoint of traditional learning theory and that of cognitive theory were so far removed from each other that there seemed to be no way to reconcile the two. Traditional learning theory (see the theory inset "Conditioning and Learning," in Chapter 4) concentrated only on observable behavior (performance) and how *environmental* changes molded it. Because cognitive theory dealt with changes in mental capacities arising at least partly from *biological* maturation, there seemed to be an unbridgeable chasm between the two approaches. Even in its earliest form, social-learning theory reduced the width of that chasm. As social-learning theory has evolved, its separation from cognitive theory has virtually disappeared. Understanding how observational learning takes place, for example, clearly requires knowing about cognitive processes, because a child can observe and remember a behavior without ever carrying it out. A concept of social-learning theory that goes far beyond observational learning and im-

itation is *internalization:* Values, beliefs, and behaviors that a child is taught are taken inside and made a lasting part of the child's personality (Aronfreed 1969).

In recent years, many attempts have been made to integrate the cognitive-developmental approach with analyses of social learning. A new combination called *cognitive social-learning theory* emphasizes both the cognitive processes, such as memory, that underlie learning and the developmental changes that take place in how people learn (Bandura 1980; Parke & Slaby 1983; Zimmerman & Rosenthal 1978).

Early in infancy, babies occasionally show something that appears to be imitation—for example, sticking out their tongue in response to their mother's sticking out her tongue (Maratsos 1982; Meltzoff & Moore 1977). But this simple behavior has proved to be not at all what parents usually mean when they say their babies can imitate. It is unstable, coming and going from minute to minute; and it is crude, in that infants will "imitate" inappropriately, as when they stick their tongue out in response to a moving pencil (Jacobson 1979; Koepke et al. 1983; McKenzie & Over 1983).

By 8 or 9 months of age, there is no longer any question of whether the baby really imitates (Harris 1983; Piaget 1951). Imitation permeates the infant's life. From this age on, much of an infant's learning—and much of his social interaction—involves imitation of some kind.

Later in infancy, at about 1½ years of age, children make a major advance when they become capable of *deferred imitation*—they can imitate a behavior that they had observed some time earlier (McCall et al. 1977). The continuing development of imitation—and observational learning in general—throughout the childhood years will be discussed in later chapters.

Social Learning in Infancy

There are many types of social learning processes besides imitation. One type of observational learning that has recently become a focus of research is **social referencing.** Infants note their parents' emotional reactions, including facial expression and voice, to determine how they should themselves react to some event (Klinnert et al. 1983). When a stranger approaches, babies typically check their mother's face. Even when infants fall down, so long as the fall is not a bad one, they will often not cry unless their mother shows worry or distress.

Parents play yet another important role in their infant's learning. They provide **scaffolding** for the baby's behavior, allowing her to perform a complex behavior that she could not perform alone, and this support helps the infant to develop the more complex form of the behavior (Bullock 1983; Wood 1980). One of the most obvious examples of this is in early walking, when a parent holds the child's hands and balances her so that she can walk. Scaffolding is not always so obvious, however. When a 12-month-old plays ball with her father, they roll a ball back and forth to each other on the floor. In fact, the baby is not very competent at aiming the ball toward her father or at catching it, but her father carefully directs the ball between the baby's legs and reaches out to grab it when the baby tries to return it. When a mother and her 2-year-old are talking, she does a lot of work to support the baby's "dialogue" (Kaye & Charney 1980).

Parents scaffold almost everything the infant does, even the obeying of commands. For a 1- or 2-year-old to obey many simple commands or requests, the parents must carefully create an encouraging situation and direct the child's attention to the act to be done (Schaffer & Crook 1980). If they want the baby to pick up toys and put them in the toy box, for example, they must usually do it first themselves, encouraging the baby to imitate their actions and sometimes making a game of it.

Even in infancy, social learning begins to shape personality. Imitation is both a way of learning and a way of behaving. By imitating her father's behavior with a book, a one-year-old learns that books have interest and value, even though the black marks on a white page are without meaning for her. If a mother's face shows concern every time her baby is allowed to crawl outside the playpen, the baby will, by social referencing, learn something about how dangerous the world is and how to approach new things, and caution may become an important part of the child's personality.

Besides imitation, social referencing, and scaffolding, there may be many other processes of social learning in infants. Researchers have only recently begun to analyze social-learning processes other than imitation, but it already seems clear that parents are central in all of them.

ESTABLISHING THE PARENT-CHILD RELATIONSHIP

Most newborns present a well-defined temperament to their parents. No matter what preconceptions a mother and father may have before their baby's birth, after that event the baby's characteristic way of behaving is the reality they must adapt to. Many parents of a second child are astounded by the difference between the temperaments of the first and second. If the first was a difficult baby and the second an easy one, it may be months before the parents come to believe that this pleasant, undemanding infant is not a quiescent volcano about to erupt at any minute. In the same way, it takes time for a baby to adapt to the parents' tempo and characteristics, partly through social learning.

RESEARCH
AUTISM—A DISORDER
OF COMMUNICATION

An adult asks a child, "Do you want a drink?" The 8-year-old answers, "You want a drink." He probably means that he is thirsty and would like something to drink, but he speaks only by repeating what people say to him. This is a characteristic symptom of a psychological disorder called *autism.* It is rather rare—only about 3 children out of 10,000 display the symptoms. But since the 1940s, when the disorder was first identified (Kanner 1943), autism has been the subject of much research.

Autism appears in infancy, sometimes at the time of birth and virtually always before 3 years of age. There are four major symptoms that clinicians use to identify the disorder (Rutter & Garmezy 1983). First, autistic children do not seek social interaction; in fact, they often actively avoid other people. The lack of responsiveness to people is one of the things that distinguishes autism from other psychoses, such as childhood schizophrenia (Coleman 1980). Most normal babies like to be held and played with from an early age. By 2 or 3 months they smile at other people and seek eye contact, and they arrange their posture in anticipation of being picked up (Emde et al. 1976; Haith et al. 1977). Autistic infants do none of these things. They may respond to social situations or enjoy games that offer them sensory stimulation, such as tickling or being tossed in the air, but they do not initiate interactions or play games that require any direct social interaction between infant and adult, such as peek-a-boo and pat-a-cake.

The second sign of autism is prolonged repetitive behaviors. These children may spend hours performing one or two actions with a single object or with their own bodies. Normal infants and children often repeat behaviors, but the repetition seldom is so prolonged and unvarying; children with other types of severe personality disturbances also rarely show such extreme repetitiveness (Wolff & Barlow 1979). Indeed, autistic babies seem to prefer to be left alone, to spend hours watching their hands move or gazing at a light or rocking in their cribs. Consequently, parents of autistic children have sometimes reported that their infant was an exceptionally "good baby" (Paluszny 1979). As toddlers, these infants do not follow mother around the house. Instead, they prefer to sit in one place for hours, spinning or rolling a toy, usually in a way that has nothing to do with the toy's function. They might hold a toy car upside down, for example, and spin its wheels for hours at a time.

The third symptom is the children's characteristic reaction to interruption of this ritualistic play and to changes in familiar parts of their environment: They often respond with a terrible temper tantrum. Parents report that the slightest change—moving a familiar piece of furniture, for example—may produce a violent tantrum.

The fourth characteristic of autistic children is their severe inability to communicate, in infancy through gestures and later through language. The baby's avoidance of eye contact and difficulty in playing give-and-take games—peek-a-boo, pat-a-cake—are early signs of this deficit. Autistic toddlers may speak a few unconnected words but, in contrast to normal children, they often do so inappropriately, saying "bye-bye" when no one is leaving, for example. Autistic children often scream to indicate that they want or need something, but they make no gesture to help communicate those specific needs. About half the children diagnosed as autistic never achieve useful speech (Rutter 1978). Among those who do eventually use language, many never do it normally. Some speak in a kind of monotone, not using the intonation and pauses of ordinary speech, which normal children begin to use as early as 1 year of age (see Chapter 5). Some autistic children run their words together, as if "youwantadrink" were one word. Some just repeat what people say to them, a behavior called echolalia.

The cause of autism is unknown. Initially, investigators thought that the infants' avoidance of social interactions was a reaction to cold parental treatment (Kanner 1943; Bettelheim 1967). It was suggested that a certain kind of family produced such infants—parents who were intellectual, aloof, efficient, well-off economically, and cold. Subsequent studies have not supported this hypothesis (Achenbach 1984). Families of autistic children fit no particular personality pattern or type of family interaction (Paluszny 1979). The abnormal parent-child interactions that early researchers

Nadia, the girl who created these drawings, was diagnosed as autistic. Yet at age 6 she produced these remarkable drawings. An adult artist could be proud of the skill and spirit these sketches display; orientation, angle, position, and proportion are all correct, and the use of lines is sparing but vivid. Such virtuosity is impossible for all but a few normal 6-year-olds.

may have observed almost certainly were due to the parents' attempts to cope with an extremely disturbed child, who did not respond to them and often actively rejected their loving overtures.

Most researchers now agree that autism is caused by some biological factor, although no one has yet been able to identify it. Autistic children are more likely than normal children to have experienced problems when they were born, such as low birth weight and breathing difficulties (Finegan & Quarrington 1980). In addition, several follow-up studies have found that almost 25 percent of them had epileptic seizures by 18 years of age (Deykin & MacMahon 1980).

Not all autistic children are the same. Some never develop language, but others learn to speak quite well. A few can learn sign language, speaking with their hands, but they cannot learn oral speech (Bonvillian & Nelson 1978). Some show unusual rote memory abilities—memorizing poems, names, or even spatial relationships with little effort. A few have shown remarkable abilities in music, arithmetic, or drawing.

Early studies of autistic children suggested that these children had good cognitive potential and that their low scores on IQ tests resulted from an unwillingness

to perform the tasks rather than an inability (Kanner & Lesser 1958). It is now clear that some autistic children are also mentally retarded. In fact, the main factor determining how well an autistic child progresses seems to be IQ (Rutter 1978). The outlook is very gloomy for autistic children with low intelligence (nonverbal IQ scores below 50): They generally remain grossly handicapped, most never gain communicative language, and almost all must spend their lives in institutions.

Those with more normal intelligence have a fair chance of overcoming many of their childhood deficits in adolescence and early adulthood. Of those who develop reasonably good language skills and show worthwhile educational progress, some are eventually able to live on their own and hold jobs. In one follow-up study of autistic children, half of the normally intelligent ones went on to hold paying jobs as adults (Bartak & Rutter 1976). Even those who are capable of holding a job retain major social deficits, however. If they are fired from their jobs, it is often because their bizarre social behavior offends or annoys fellow workers (Rutter 1976).

In adolescence, some autistic youngsters develop a new awareness of themselves that seems to be similar to what happens to normal adolescents. For the autistic adolescents, however, this awareness means a realization of their own severe social limitations. A program run by Michael Rutter and his colleagues helps these adolescents deal with the emotional distress that this realization brings (Rutter & Bartak 1973). The program also systematically teaches them skills, using role playing and videotapes to show them how to *observe* social and conversational cues. These communication skills, basic to all social interaction, are part of every normal child's behavioral repertoire, beginning with a 3-month-old's smile in response to adult's loving voice, caress, or smile. Autistic adolescents must try to acquire all these skills that normal children learned from the first months of life.

Figure 6-8   The greeting
response.

These elements—newborn temperament, parenting style, and social-learning processes—help explain how parents and their newborn interact when they
are getting to know each other. But these interactions are just the beginning of
a powerful relationship that provides the foundation for all the child's social
development. In the early months of life, its formation is aided by certain
species-specific social behaviors.

Species-specific Social Behaviors

Like other animals, human infants and parents show species-specific behaviors
with each other. An infant is born with many reflexes, such as breathing,
sucking, and swallowing, as described in Chapter 4. But the newborn's behaviors are still very limited. He can cry to get his mother's attention and he can
suck at the breast, but he does not even smile at other people or look them in
the eye.

At the age of 2 or 3 months, his social behavior changes dramatically. When
his mother looks at him, he smiles, looks into his mother's eyes, and "speaks"
with a cooing sound. By 3 months, most infants can sustain a clear-cut social
interaction of this sort in response to their parents' gaze and talk (Hubley &
Trevarthen 1979). An important component of this interaction is the **greeting
response:** The infant opens his eyes wide, opens his mouth in a distinctive
shape, makes a strong cooing sound, and sometimes smiles (Figure 6-8). In fact,
just the sight of a face nearby will evoke the infant's expression, and this
expression almost invariably calls forth a response from the parent—smiling,
talking, touching. In other words, the baby *initiates* the social interaction;

infants and young children actually begin about 50 percent of such interactions, through cries, gestures, or facial expressions such as the greeting response (Bell 1974).

Most parents demonstrate species-specific social behaviors with their infant too, including a greeting response similar to the baby's. They move their head back slightly, raise their eyebrows, open their eyes wide, open their mouth, make a sound, and often smile (Papousek & Papousek 1979). They also speak baby talk, keeping their speech short, repetitive, and simple, and using high pitch with exaggerated changes in pitch (Kaye 1980). Even mothers who have just had their first child use baby talk the first time that they speak to their infant (Fernald & Simon 1984).

Besides performing such stereotyped behaviors, parents tend to mold their other behavior to fit the limited capacities of the infant (Papousek & Papousek 1979). They help the infant to see them, by situating themselves in front of the baby and working to get his attention. They perform simple repetitive acts that are highly predictable and so can be easily grasped and remembered by the baby. And they tend to imitate the baby's actions—opening their mouth when he opens his, cooing when he coos, sticking out their tongue when he sticks out his (Francis et al. 1981). Imitating a 3-month-old's actions is one of the best ways of getting his attention (Field 1977). Later, it becomes one of the best ways of promoting social interaction with an infant or preschooler (McCall et al. 1977; Nadel & Baudonniere 1980). Typically, an 18-month-old will warm up quickly to an adult who imitates her, and children themselves will imitate other children as a means of getting them to play.

These species-specific social behaviors help in forming the parent-child

TABLE 6-1 STAGES IN PARENT-INFANT INTERACTION AND THEIR RELATION TO EMOTIONAL DEVELOPMENT

STAGE	BEHAVIORS THAT INFANT AND PARENT COORDINATE	INFANT'S EMOTIONAL DEVELOPMENT	AGE SPAN
1. Regulation	Sleeping, feeding, quieting, and arousal need to be coordinated into a predictable, comfortable living pattern.	Distress present from birth; emergence of social smile.	0 to 3 months
2. Reciprocal exchange	The first back-and-forth exchanges between parent and infant occur; these exchanges involve feeding, dressing, caretaking, and simple play.	Generally socially responsive: smiles, laughs, becomes excited in response to social interaction and play.	3 to 6 months
3. Infant initiative in exchanges and activities	The first activities are initiated or chosen by the infant, including social exchanges and preferred activities.	Joy at initiating social games and simple nonsocial activities; frustration at failure of intended acts; beginning of specific attachment to parents, as well as separation distress and stranger distress.	5 to 9 months

SOURCE: Sander 1975; Sroufe 1979; Harter 1983. The age span listed for each stage is an average for American children. Infants show wide individual variations in the age at which they pass through these stages.

relationship, but the relationship soon becomes an independent entity that follows its own developmental course. Even in the early months, it keeps changing as the baby develops.

Stages in the Relationship

In the first months of life, the parent-child relationship is based on the child's becoming biologically stable—to ensure his survival. The baby cries when he is hungry or ill or uncomfortable, and the parents respond by providing nourishment and relief of distress. After the baby has developed the capacity for social exchange, the focus of the relationship becomes the baby's attachment to his parents. When the attachment has been securely formed and the baby's cogni-

STAGE	BEHAVIORS THAT INFANT AND PARENT COORDINATE	INFANT'S EMOTIONAL DEVELOPMENT	AGE SPAN
4. Focusing of infant's demands and activities on the parent	Infant attempts to control the availability and responsivity of the parent to the infant's demands and needs; parent is used as secure base from which to explore.	Emergence of strong attachment to parents, including separation distress and stranger distress, sensitivity to parental emotional reactions; social referencing.	8 to 14 months
5. Self-assertion	Infant determines and selects his own goals and intentions apart from the parents.	Elation in mastery; insistence on doing things oneself; rejection of some parental initiatives; moods; caution with new children; control of emotional expressions.	12 to 20 months
6. Independent self-concept	Child establishes a sense of self as independent actor separate from parent; child can communicate about self and intentionally disrupt coordination with parent.	Positive emotional reactions to praise, negative reactions to shame; expression of love, defiance, willfulness.	18 to 36 months

tive abilities have developed sufficiently, the baby begins to establish himself as an independent being, a self. Table 6-1 sets out these stages, as described by Louis Sander, in terms of the behaviors that infant and parent must coordinate and also in terms of the emotional development of the infant.

In the first stage, the **regulation** of basic biological functions, such as eating, sleeping, and relief of distress, is foremost. In most cases, parent and infant establish routines that help the infant to obtain what he needs. The parent establishes certain ways of feeding the baby, changing his diaper, and quieting him and helping him go to sleep, and each of these routines is adapted to fit the baby's temperament, his natural ways of reacting (Fogel 1979). The routines established by each parent-child pair are highly individual, as shown by Sander's study (described on page 270) in which infants had one caregiver for 10 days and then were switched to a different caregiver. After only 10 days had passed, a rhythm had been established between infant and adult, and when a different adult began taking care of the baby, the need to work out a new rhythm led to a large increase in crying and in difficulties with eating.

The second stage sees the beginning of *reciprocal exchange.* From 3 to 6 months, social interactions are established to which both parent and infant contribute (Crawley et al. 1978; Fafouti & Uzgiris 1979). The baby opens his mouth for a spoonful of food, tries to hold the bottle during nursing, adjusts his arms and legs as if to help when he is being dressed, anticipates a touch or a kiss when he sees his mother approaching him. Toward the end of this stage, the infant seems to greatly enjoy ritualized social interactions—laughing loudly when his father blows on his stomach, for example.

The third and fourth stages include two closely related developments. The infant becomes able to initiate social exchanges and play, and at the same time he becomes strongly attached to his mother and other caregivers. The culmination of these developments is a relationship in which the baby often acts as if his mother is a part of him—psychologically attached to him. Most of the research on social development in infancy focuses on this process of attachment (Ainsworth et al. 1978; Campos et al. 1983), and the next section discusses it in detail.

In the third stage, at 5 to 9 months, the infant's *initiative* begins, his desire to start an elementary social interaction or play activity. Thus for the first time, he establishes some personal control over his relationship with his parents. For example, he may click his tongue to start a ritual in which he and his father make clicking sounds back and forth. He holds his arms up so that his mother will hold him. He does many similar things that indicate the beginnings of communication (Bullowa 1979), and he also tries to control his solitary activities. He bounces in his crib to make his mobile move. He grabs his spoon and bangs it against his highchair. During this time, the baby also begins to show some fear of adults that he does not know and some fear at separation from his parents.

The fourth stage brings attachment into full bloom, as the 8- to 14-month-old *focuses* his demands and needs on his parents. The baby blatantly tries to control them, always wanting them near and repeatedly trying to make them carry out particular activities on demand (Green et al. 1980; Hubley and Trevarthen 1979). The infant crawls to his father, grabs his foot, and makes a sound, demanding that his father pick him up. He points at his cup to get his mother to give him a drink. (Pointing is one of the earliest communcative gestures; Fogel 1981.) Babies even like to control their parents in ways that look like teasing. From 9 to 10 months, Seth repeatedly held out his arms as if he wanted to be picked up. When his parents approached, he would then turn away and smile or giggle. It is important for parents to realize that infants who do this sort of thing are not being nasty or malicious. They are simply learning ways to influence their parents and thus differentiating themselves from other people.

At times, the incomplete differentiation of infant from parent is clear. Babies at this age seem to confuse their parents' emotional reactions with their own: If Mommy laughs, baby laughs; if Mommy is upset, baby cries. This emotional contagion is the beginning of social referencing, mentioned earlier, in which infants use their parents' behavior to determine how to evaluate a situation (Campos et al. 1983).

After establishing an attachment relationship, infants move on in the last two stages to make themselves more independent. In the fifth stage, at 12 to 20 months, *self-assertion* develops, the seeds of which could be seen in Seth's teasing. The child begins to assert himself as an individual. He insists on doing things his own way and rejects many parental initiatives. He wants to feed himself, even if most of the food ends up anywhere but in his mouth. He tries to stand and walk, rejecting parental attempts to help him. He often rejects toys or games that his parents suggest, preferring to choose his own activities. If his language were not limited to just a few words, he would say, "Mommy, I want to do it myself."

Starting at about 18 months, the child enters the final stage, in which he not only asserts himself but establishes an *independent self-concept* (Harter 1983; Maccoby 1980). He can talk about himself. He acts proud when praised and ashamed when criticized. He may feel so strongly about having things his way that temper tantrums are frequent, even though his own failure to communicate his wants clearly is often why things do not go his way. This period is often referred to as the "terrible twos."

The major focus in this description of the stages has been the infant's changing personality, because he is developing so fast that he forces major changes in the terms of encounter between himself and his parents. It is important to recognize, however, that these stages are interpersonal, in that development through them requires coordination between parent and child. At each stage, how parents adjust to the child's needs and demands helps determine how the child proceeds to the next stage and, ultimately, the kind of person that he will become. Research on the process of attachment in stages 3 and 4 indicates not only that the parent-infant relationship is important for normal social development but also that individual differences in parent-child relationships seem to affect the child's personality.

Attachment

When most people speak of the attachment between mother and infant, they mean love. But love is not an easy word to use scientifically in any context, so psychologists hesitate to use the word for the emotions of a child less than 2 years old. They prefer to use the term *attachment* for infants' feelings about their mother or father—a tie based on a feeling of affection that is focused on a specific person and is enduring. To measure attachment scientifically, researchers look at a variety of infants' behaviors toward their parent or other caretaker. Among the behaviors they measure are the baby's following the parent with his eyes, the orientation of his body toward her, smiling at her, clinging to and following her, using her as an island of safety from which he can explore the world, and becoming distressed in the presence of strangers.

Attachment changes as infants develop (Ainsworth et al. 1978). Before babies are about 6 months old—that is, before they can readily perceive the difference between faces—attachment to one individual does not exist. These young babies show what might be called indiscriminate attachment, reacting with equal delight to every smiling face. When they begin to be able to single out their mother, they also begin to react to her in specific ways, with sounds and smiles and gestures. During the second 6 months of life, they initiate more and more of these attachment greetings, which are reserved exclusively for parents. Strangers are usually looked over warily. By the time infants are a year old, attachment is strong. At this age, most babies cry with obvious distress when separated from their mothers and often seem to be very uncomfortable with strangers, especially in unfamiliar situations (Zelazo & Leonard 1983). After 1 year of age, the intense attachment to mother begins to wane, and babies show multiple attachments—to brothers and sisters, grandparents, babysitters, and other people important in their everyday lives.

Individual Differences in Attachment   As described by Mary Ainsworth and her colleagues (1978), infants show three different patterns of attachment to their parents. In the healthiest pattern, called *secure attachment* (or Type B), infants unhesitatingly use the mother as a secure base, exploring the environment when they are not afraid and seeking the parent for comfort when they are upset or afraid. When reunited with their mother after a short separation, they seek close contact with her. The large majority of babies fit into this category.

In the other two patterns of attachment, there is some difficulty between parent and child. Babies who show *anxious, ambivalent attachment* (Type C) are more likely to act anxious or distressed even when their mother is present, and they seem to be ambivalent about using their mother as a secure base. When they are upset or when reunited with their mother after a separation, they may seek close contact with her, but the next moment they may resist contact or act angry. In the third pattern, *avoidant attachment* (Type A), infants seem to ignore their mother much of the time instead of using her as a secure base. They rarely show separation distress, and even if the mother has been out of sight for a time, when she returns they may ignore her entirely.

Ainsworth believes that these patterns of attachment result from the ways mothers interact with and respond to their infants. If the mother is responsive in a way that is sensitive to the infant's needs and individual temperament,

Figure 6-9 Mary Ainsworth and her colleagues studied attachment in Ugandan infants as well as in American ones. Here is a photo they took in Uganda of Sulaimann, 35 weeks old, who became extremely distressed whenever his mother had to leave his sight.

then the baby will develop a secure attachment to her. The infant comes to expect that mother is generally accessible and responsive, and consequently develops a sense of security, similar to Erikson's basic trust. If the mother is not sensitively responsive, however, the baby will develop one of the other two attachment patterns. When the mother is slow to respond, less affectionate with the infant, and less skillful in handling him, the baby develops anxious, ambivalent attachment. Avoidant attachment develops, according to Ainsworth, when the mother frequently rejects the baby's overtures for close bodily contact, and it also may be related in some cases to child abuse (George & Main 1979).

So far, there has been little research that has tested these hypotheses about the three types of attachment (Campos et al. 1983; Lamb 1982). The study by Waters et al. (1980) described earlier (page 269) indicated that infants' temperamental characteristics—especially if they had problems with physiological regulation and responded poorly to stimuli—interfered with the establishment of a smooth-running mother-infant interaction in early infancy and, consequently, with the infants' attachment behavior at 1 year of age. Nevertheless, it is not possible to draw any firm conclusions about how much the mother contributes to the pattern of attachment, how much the infant's temperament contributes, or which other factors might play a role (Connell & Goldsmith 1982). Most obviously, researchers have neglected the role of the infant's attachment to his father (or other caregiver), even though many infants are as attached to their fathers as they are to their mothers (Bretherton & Ainsworth 1974; Lamb 1978).

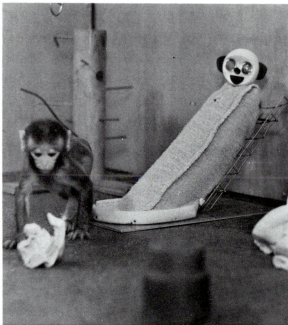

Figure 6-10 (Left) Infant monkey clinging to its surrogate cloth mother. In the background is a wire "mother" of the kind that the infant monkeys ignored. (Right) Infant monkey using the surrogate mother as a secure base from which to investigate a strange object.

Despite these limitations, a large amount of research does indicate that the three patterns of attachment reflect important differences in mother-child relationships and that those differences frequently continue throughout infancy and into the preschool years (Ainsworth 1979; Sroufe 1979).

The Parent as a Secure Base   Most infants have a good relationship with their parents and develop a healthy attachment. These infants use the parent as a *secure base,* an island of safety from which they can explore the world. They come close to their mother, touch or hug her, and then crawl away to explore something. Periodically they come back to check in with her again.

Harry Harlow (1971) carried out a series of experiments with rhesus monkeys, examining the role of the mother-infant relationship in monkeys' development. Some monkeys were raised in isolation, without mother or playmates but with only one or two wire dolls made to look roughly like monkeys. When the doll was covered with terrycloth, the monkey would cling to it as if it were a real monkey mother. Under normal conditions, infant monkeys cling to their mother's fur almost continuously. This contact is an important part of attachment in monkeys. When the "mother" was simply a wire frame supplied with a milk bottle, the monkey would merely drink the milk, never trying to cuddle or cling.

Harlow's research illustrates how important the secure base is. The researchers put some strange and frightening toys into each monkey's room. One was a robotlike toy that had flashing lights for eyes; another was an unusual stuffed animal. The baby monkeys were extremely alarmed, and those with terrycloth

Figure 6-11 An infant monkey who was raised with a comfortless wire mother just huddled on the floor in a terrified heap when confronted by a strange toy.

mothers clung to them with all their might, as shown in Figure 6-10. But soon, from this island of safety, they made quick forays toward the toy to investigate it. Eventually all these monkeys became brave enough to approach the toy, and one of them even tore it limb from limb. The babies raised without either terrycloth mothers or monkey mothers, on the other hand, were overcome with fear in the face of the mechanical toy. They did not run to their wire "mothers"—no comfort or security there. They just threw themselves onto the floor, crying and grimacing like the monkey in Figure 6-11. They never did get up the courage to investigate the new toy.

In a classic study of 10-month-old human infants, the babies showed similar behaviors (Rheingold 1970). Infants were left in a room with their mother, with a stranger, or with some toys. A door was open into an adjoining room that contained a few toys (but no people). Most of the infants who were with their mothers eventually crawled into the adjoining room in order to inspect it (and then crawled back to their mothers). Infants who were left in the first room with a stranger or with toys, on the other hand, simply cried and never did inspect the other room. Infants explored only when they had the security of their mother's presence.

One of the clearest signs that an infant is forming an attachment to mother and using her as a secure base is the appearance of two kinds of distress— stranger distress and separation distress. When an infant sees a stranger, he tends to be wary, especially after the age of 6 or 7 months. If he is touching his mother, he may remain wary or bury his head in his mother's lap and nothing more. But if he is away from his secure base, he will usually cry, showing *stranger distress.* American infants typically start showing stranger distress frequently at 7 to 9 months of age and continue to do so strongly through the rest of the first year, at which time it begins to subside (Emde et al. 1976).

Stranger distress is partly a result of cognitive development but also seems to be intimately tied to the infant's developing attachment to his parents (Campos et al. 1983; Sroufe 1979). He looks at the stranger and recognizes that this person is not his mother or father or anybody else to whom he is attached. Particularly in the absence of an attachment figure to act as a secure base, he is frightened by this stranger. It is interesting that, during the peak period of stranger distress, most infants are afraid only of adults, not of other children. Not until the second year do most of them become wary of unfamiliar infants (Jacobson 1980).

In *separation distress,* the infant is uneasy not because of the presence of a stranger but because of the absence of his mother or caregiver. When he sees his mother walk away or notices that she is gone, he bursts into tears. Like stranger distress, separation distress can begin as early as 4 or 5 months, and it typically becomes intense at 8 or 9 months. It seems to increase in intensity for at least the rest of the first year. After about 15 months it decreases gradually, and by 24 months it is not very common (Emde et al. 1976; Kagan 1979). As described in Chapter 5, as soon as an infant is capable of representation—as soon as he understands that objects and people do not cease to exist when they are out of his sight and hearing—separation distress becomes uncommon. This cognitive development is usually complete by about 2 years of age.

Many psychologists view attachment as the foundation of all subsequent social interaction and love (Harlow 1971; Ainsworth et al. 1978). A number of studies have looked into how infants are affected by the lack of this base of affection.

The Effects of Social Deprivation   In 1915 the death rate of infants brought to foundling homes during their first year of life was astounding. These homes reported death rates ranging from 32 to 75 percent for babies less than 2 years old (Chapin 1915). In the general population at that time, the mortality rate for infants the same age was only about 15 percent. Most experts of the day attributed the high institutional death rate to poor diet and poor sanitation.

In the 1930's, sanitation and diet in such institutions had improved greatly, but the infant death rate remained much higher than normal. After investigating the reasons for this, Rene Spitz (1945, 1965) concluded that institutionalized infants were depressed—physically, mentally, and emotionally—because of a lack of mothering. He called this effect *failure to thrive.*

Spitz studied infants in two institutions. One was a foundling home where babies were kept in cribs in individual cubicles, with one nurse in charge of eight infants. The infants were fed and kept clean but were given very little individual attention and affection—very little mothering. The other institution

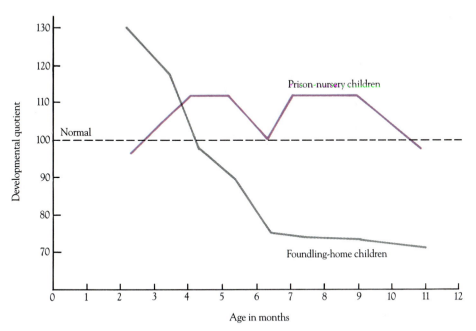

Figure 6-12   The diverging developmental paths of the two groups of institutionalized infants studied by Rene Spitz. The foundling-home children, who received little affection or stimulation from their overworked caretakers, showed a steady decline in their developmental quotient to what Spitz called the "astonishingly low level of 72." (Developmental quotient is a measure of where the infant's sensory-motor abilities and perceptions stand in relation to a norm for his age; normal development is rated at 100.) The prison-nursery babies, who were raised by their mothers, maintained at least a normal level of development throughout the months of study.

was a prison in which delinquent mothers were allowed to care for their own babies in a nursery from birth to the end of the first year.

Both institutions had good medical care and good food, but the social background of the mothers seemed to favor the foundling-home children. Some of their mothers were educated middle- or upper-class young women who could not care for their illegitimate children. On the other hand, all the mothers in the prison had been jailed for prostitution or criminal activity. Yet the babies in the prison thrived, while those in the foundling home did very poorly. The prison babies developed normally and were mostly healthy, but the foundling-home babies showed extreme failure to thrive. They were highly susceptible to disease, and many died. While Spitz was studying the foundling home, an epidemic of measles swept through the home. Of 88 children less than 2½ years old who contracted measles, 23 died. The mortality rate for measles in the community near the foundling home was less than one in 200.

The foundling-home children were also retarded in their psychological development. Their test scores during the first year of age are shown in Figure 6-12, along with those of the prison-nursery children. In the foundling home, of the children between ages 1½ and 2½, only two could walk, say a few words, and eat by themselves. In the prison, on the other hand, many of the 8- to 12-month-olds could do these things.

Spitz attributed the difference between the two sets of babies to mothering—or lack of it. The prison mothers had the time to give their babies more attention than would most mothers, who have homes, jobs, and other children competing for their time. The babies in the foundling home received almost no human attention except feeding and cleaning, and they had little in their cribs to look at, play with, or explore.

When Spitz's results first appeared, some scientists severely criticized them on methodological grounds (Pinneau 1955). The two institutions and the children in them were not exactly the same, and Spitz's conclusion about the need for mothering certainly was far stronger than what the data actually allowed (Thompson & Grusec 1970). But later research has clearly supported Spitz's general conclusion—that infants who are not given attention and affection are likely to fail to thrive and even to die (Rutter 1979).

These results should not be taken to mean that good mothering requires the presence of the baby's biological mother. The person who does the "mothering" can be a father, foster parent, grandparent, or friend. Children adopted into good foster families develop normally, even when they received poor care during early infancy (Tizard 1977). What is important is that the primary caregiver be affectionate and sensitive to the baby's needs and desires (Rutter 1979).

The monkeys in Harlow's experiments who were raised without a terrycloth mother to cling to developed bizarre behaviors much like those of some severely disturbed children. Some rocked back and forth endlessly and paced in their cages for hours. Many of them even bit themselves repeatedly or pulled their own hair out until they were raw.

Partly as a result of Harlow's findings, scientists now view the human infant's attachment to the mother as a species-specific behavior that helps human beings survive the extreme dependency of infancy. John Bowlby (1969, 1973, 1980) and others also have suggested that babies who do not form attachments suffer severe handicaps in their emotional development. Bowlby studied the histories of a number of British children and teenagers who had been brought to him because of delinquency or disturbed behavior. The background factor he found common to many of them was lack of mothering: Either they had spent their early years in institutions or they had been shifted repeatedly from one foster home to another. What seemed to underlie most of their disturbed or antisocial behavior was a severe deficiency in personality. Bowlby described them as "affectionless." They seemed unable to have a genuine emotional relationship with anyone. They were unable to care, unable to love.

The Reversibility of the Effects of Early Experience   Many infants suffer in their development when they are deprived of an affectionate, stimulating relationship with a parent or other caregiver, but the negative effects of environment are not necessarily permanent. One of the most remarkable demonstrations that they can be reversed is a study by Harold Skeels (1942, 1966, and Figure 6-13). Twenty-five infants were being raised in an orphanage where they received adequate health care but very little affection or social

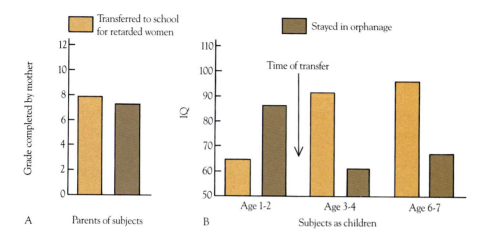

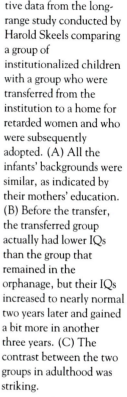

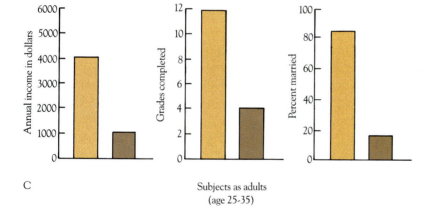

Figure 6-13 Representative data from the long-range study conducted by Harold Skeels comparing a group of institutionalized children with a group who were transferred from the institution to a home for retarded women and who were subsequently adopted. (A) All the infants' backgrounds were similar, as indicated by their mothers' education. (B) Before the transfer, the transferred group actually had lower IQs than the group that remained in the orphanage, but their IQs increased to nearly normal two years later and gained a bit more in another three years. (C) The contrast between the two groups in adulthood was striking.

stimulation. Skeels arranged to have thirteen of these infants transferred from the orphanage to an institute for retarded women. Each baby was "adopted" by one of the women, so that each had a foster mother, and the infants received a great deal of attention and stimulation.

Before the transfer, all these infants were extremely retarded in their development. Their average IQ was around 64. Yet, a year and a half later, the transferred babies' development was nearly normal; they had gained an average of 28 IQ points and were lively and playful. Eleven of the transferred babies were later adopted by families. The twelve infants who had stayed in the orphanage, on the other hand, actually showed declines in IQ.

Twenty-one years later, Skeels did a follow-up study to see whether the effects of the change in early experience had continued into adulthood. Indeed they had. All the adults who had been transferred in infancy, including the two who had not been adopted by families, were self-supporting; half of them had completed high school, and four had attended some college. Eleven of them were married, and nine had children. In contrast, one-third of the subjects who had remained in the orphanage were still institutionalized, and only one of them could be classified as entirely normal.

The improvement in the infants' environment had a striking long-term effect even though the infants were already 19 months old when transferred, and one was already 3 years old. It seems that even at 2 or 3 years—and perhaps even later—intervention in the form of affection and stimulation can bring about a drastic change in the course of development (Tizard 1977).

Harlow and his colleagues have also demonstrated the reversibility of early social deprivation in monkeys. In one experiment, monkeys that had been isolated for 6 months had developed all the bizarre behaviors described on page 296 (Suomi et al. 1974). Some of these monkeys were then placed in cages with monkey "therapists"—3-month-old, normal, healthy females. Young female monkeys frequently initiate social contacts but are seldom aggressive, so it seemed that they would make good therapists. After 6 months of living with the therapists, the behavior of the deprived monkeys had improved substantially and was almost normal. After another 6 months in a large cage with the therapists, the former misfits were completely recovered.

Another experiment with monkeys showed that young monkeys themselves can substitute for many of the functions of mothers. Young monkeys raised together without mothers learned social skills from each other and developed close bonds of affection. Four infant monkeys were raised together in a large cage from the time they were 2 weeks old. During their first 2 months together, they spent most of their time just clinging to each other. As they got older, they began to play with and groom each other. When they were a year old, these monkeys were living happily together. None showed any of the abnormal

Figure 6-14 Infant monkeys raised together without mothers spent much of their first months clinging to each other in this "choo-choo train" configuration.

behaviors shown by motherless monkeys raised in isolation (Harlow & Harlow 1969).

A famous study has shown that peers can substitute for lost human mothers, too (Freud & Dann 1951). The children in the study were six victims of the Nazi regime in Germany—they were concentration camp survivors. Anna Freud (Sigmund Freud's daughter) and Sophie Dann set up a refuge for these survivors at Bulldogs Bank, England in 1945. The children were orphans of Jewish-German origin whose parents had been deported to Poland and killed there in the gas chambers (Table 6-2). As young infants, the orphans had been transferred from one refuge to another before ending up in the Ward for Motherless Children of the Tereszin Concentration Camp. When admitted to the concentration camp, the children were between 6 months and one year old. There they were cared for as well as could be expected, given the limitations. Their caretakers changed often, as Tereszin was a deportation camp, but the children were kept together and spent their infancy together. After the war, the children eventually arrived at Bulldogs Bank, when they were all between 3 and 4 years old.

When they arrived, they were wild, restless, and hostile to the adults. They shouted, screamed, and swore at them—they even spat at and bit them. With each other, however, they were affectionate and extremely caring. They could not bear to be separated. No child would consent to remain upstairs while the others were downstairs. No child would go for a walk unless all the others came along.

Figure 6-15 The orphaned children who survived life in a World War II concentration camp were sent to a refuge set up in England by Anna Freud and Sophie Dann. The somewhat fuzzy photo at left was taken soon after their arrival, in October 1945. The other photo shows them in the summer of 1946.

TABLE 6-2 BACKGROUNDS OF THE CHILDREN AT BULLDOGS BANK

NAME	DATE AND PLACE OF BIRTH	FAMILY HISTORY	AGE OF ARRIVAL IN TERESZIN	AGE AT ARRIVAL IN BULLDOGS BANK
John	December 18, 1941 Vienna	Orthodox Jewish working-class parents. Deported to Poland and killed.	Presumably less than 12 months	3 years, 10 months
Ruth	April 21, 1942 Vienna	Parents, a brother of 7, and a sister of 4 years were deported and killed when Ruth was a few months old. She was cared for in a Jewish nursery in Vienna, then sent to Tereszin with the nursery.	Several months	3 years, 6 months
Leah	April 23, 1942 Berlin	Leah and a brother were illegitimate, hidden from birth. Fate of mother and brother unknown. Brother presumed killed.	Several months	3 years, 5 months. Arrived 6 weeks after the others owing to a ringworm infection.
Paul	May 21, 1942 Berlin	Unknown	12 months	3 years, 5 months
Miriam	August 18, 1942 Berlin	Upper middle-class family. Father died in concentration camp, mother went insane, was cared for first in a mental hospital in Vienna, later in a mental ward in Tereszin, where she died.	6 months	3 years, 2 months
Peter	October 22, 1942	Parents deported and killed when Peter was a few days old. Child was found abandoned in public park, cared for first in a convent; later, when found to be Jewish, was taken to the Jewish hospital in Berlin, then brought to Tereszin.	Under 12 months	3 years

SOURCE: Freud & Dann 1951.

The children's emotional dependence on each other was extraordinarily touching. Each was sensitive to the needs of the others. There was no competition, no rivalry, no jealousy or envy among them. For example, John cried once when there was no cake left for a second helping for him. Ruth and Miriam both gave him what was left of theirs. When Paul lost his gloves during a walk, John took his off and gave them to Paul, never complaining that his own hands were cold.

Eventually, the children began to trust the adults who were caring for them and to form attachments to them. The children were a little retarded cognitively, but that is not surprising. What is surprising is that they were not truly deficient, delinquent, or psychotic, given the circumstances of their early lives. They had attached themselves to each other and thus had learned social interaction by coordinating their giving and getting to each other's needs and temperaments. When they grew up, the children all became effective adults, despite their traumatic childhoods (Hartup 1983).

The Effects of Day Care   Research on attachment, and particularly the work by John Bowlby (1969, 1973, 1980), has been stimulated partly by public concern about *day care* for infants. Articles in popular magazines and books on child care have expressed fears that day care may be detrimental to a child's development. In the 1950s and 1960s, most such articles and books expressed alarm at a mother's going to work before her baby was 3 years old. Although the authors were not specific about the developmental damage that would ensue, they warned that a mother who leaves her infant in order to work will cause "definite injury both to him and to herself" (Miller 1968). At that time the two most widely read publications—Benjamin Spock's *Baby and Child Care* and the United States Children's Bureau's *Infant Care*—both strongly urged mothers to spend full time with their infants in order to avert maladjustments in later life.

In the 1970s, as the women's rights movement became stronger and as more women joined the work force, the tone of these publications changed somewhat. They began to stress the quality of the interaction between mother and child rather than the quantity of time spent together. Dr. Spock's 1976 revision moved the topic of working mothers out of the section called "Special Problems" and stressed the father's role as a caretaker. However, Spock and a number of these popular books continued to doubt that day care in groups was an acceptable substitute for individual care by the mother.

In actual practice, working mothers continue to show a preference for nongroup care (although this may reflect a shortage of suitable group day-care facilities). United States Department of Labor data revealed that 52 percent of preschoolers were cared for in their own homes, either by a parent or other relative (40 percent) or by a sitter (12 percent). Thirty-five percent of the children were cared for singly or in small groups in someone else's home, often

the home of a relative. Only 13 percent went to group day-care centers (Clarke-Stewart 1982).

Researchers have investigated the effects of day care on infants' attachment to their mothers and on their cognitive development, sociability, and competence (Kagan et al. 1978; Rubenstein & Howes 1979). In general, these studies found no ill effects of high-quality day care. When the attachment patterns of children less than 2 years old who had been in day care were compared to those of children raised entirely by their mothers, no differences were found. Even though the children may form attachments to the adults who care for them during the day, they show an overwhelming preference for their mothers, especially when the children are tired or distressed (Kagan et al. 1978; Farran & Ramey 1977). Even infants raised in Israeli collective settlements (kibbutzim), who spend 20 hours a day with a caretaker, are less fearful with their mother and a stranger than with their caretaker and a stranger (Fox 1977).

Cognitive development of children in good day-care centers is just like that of children raised at home. Middle-class children who spend time in day-care centers seem, on the average, to be no different in cognitive functioning from children who remain at home with their mothers (Kagan et al. 1978; Macrae & Herbert-Jackson 1976). There is some evidence that lower-class infants in community-controlled day-care programs may actually benefit intellectually from being there (Andrews et al. 1982).

Social and emotional development also appear to be about the same for children cared for in centers and those reared at home (Rubenstein & Howes 1977). Children who begin day care early are somewhat more likely to interact with peers in the preschool years (MacRae & Herbert-Jackson 1976). They seem to enjoy the simple games that they can engage in with their peers at the center during the day (Belsky & Steinberg 1978; Kilmer 1979). In any case, by 5 or 6 months of age, most infants enjoy being with other children. In the most common form of play, two children manipulate the same objects, taking turns (Table 6-3). By the end of the first year, children actively seek contact with other children, and their play becomes more complex. As they move into the

TABLE 6-3 A SOCIAL INTERCHANGE BETWEEN INFANTS

TIME (SECONDS)	BERNIE (16 MONTHS)	LARRY (18 MONTHS)
0	Puts paper to wall Releases paper Picks paper up from floor Offers paper to Larry	
11		Receives paper from Bernie Puts paper to wall Releases paper Backs away a few steps and looks at Bernie Puts paper to wall Holds paper against wall and looks at Bernie Releases paper Backs away further and looks at Bernie
32	Looks at Larry and picks up paper Puts paper to wall Releases paper Picks up paper from floor Offers paper and vocalizes to Larry	
51		Receives paper from Bernie Puts paper to wall Releases paper Backs away and looks at Bernie
65	Points at paper and looks at Larry	
67		Looks at Bernie and picks up paper Puts paper to wall Releases paper Backs away and looks at Bernie
72	Departs	
81		Looks at Bernie and picks up paper Puts paper to wall Releases paper and departs, following Bernie

SOURCE: Mueller & T. Lucas 1975.

second year, they begin to play coordinated games (Mueller & Vandell 1979).

Most of these studies of effects of day care were carried out in excellent centers with trained staffs, ample facilities, and a low ratio of infants to caretakers—usually 3 or 4 to 1. In centers such as these, children seem to suffer no ill effects of day care. In poorly run or inadequately staffed centers, however, children may be unhappy and may suffer some developmental difficulties (Clarke-Stewart & Fein 1983).

BUILDING THE SELF

Establishing an attachment relation—particularly with the parents—seems to be an important step in the infant's *development of an independent self.* Although little research has been done on this development, several scientists have attempted to describe it.

Separation and Individuation

To establish themselves as independent individuals, children must mentally separate themselves from their mothers. This process is called *separation and individuation* (Harter 1983; Mahler et al. 1975).

The social developments that lead to the emergence of the self begin toward the end of the first year, when an infant is learning to focus his demands on his parents (Stage 4 in Table 6-1). But not all a child's demands can or should be met, so the parents often do things that go against his wishes. His mother takes him in from a walk in the stroller when the baby wants to continue the excursion, or she puts him to bed in the evening even though he wants to stay up with the family. The security the baby feels in his relationship with his mother allows him to explore the limits of what his mother will permit. Such experiences help children begin to understand that they are beings separate from their mothers.

This initial understanding develops gradually into self-assertion, which characterizes the fifth stage of the parent-infant relationship. The baby between 12 and 20 months of age begins to make his own wishes known, even when they clash with his mother's. He might insist on wearing a certain sweater even though his mother wants him to wear one that is not so heavy and hot.

Finally, after the development of representation (discussed in Chapter 5) and the social developments that take place in the parent-child relationship (Table 6-1, Stage 6), the child establishes an independent self-concept. At age 2, he can talk about "I": "I do it." While he is achieving this ability, he is often very negative—disrupting interactions with his parents, saying "no" to everything, becoming angry at interventions by his parents. Although this behavior is often trying for the parents, it seems to be a necessary part of the process of separation and individuation.

Figure 6-16 A well-known transitional object and its owner.

Transitional Objects

Many children help themselves through the difficult time of separation and individuation by focusing some of their attachment on one or two familiar objects that act as a substitute for the secure base of the parent. These are called **transitional objects** because they facilitate the transition from dependent baby to individual self (Winnicott 1971).

Figure 6-16 shows a transitional object familiar to millions—Linus's blanket. The object of attachment is often a blanket, some other piece of soft cloth, or a soft cuddly toy (like the terrycloth mother of Harlow's monkeys). Babies may form the first such attachment as young as 4 or 5 months of age, but most of them form it at the end of their first year or during the second. Some then find it difficult to give up the object until they are 4 or 5 years old. The child usually holds the object when he sucks his thumb or hand, and he takes it to bed with him. Often he wants it with him when he goes from place to place—even from room to room in his own house. After all, you never can tell when you may need it!

No wonder a baby attached to such an object becomes upset when he must be separated from it for a while—for example, when the blanket must be

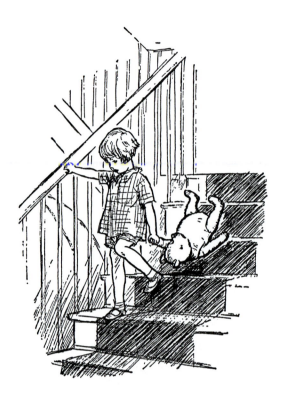

Figure 6-17 Christopher Robin and Winnie the Pooh (who would surely not like to hear himself called a transitional object).

washed. It is very much like giving up a part of yourself as well as giving up a major source of comfort in distressing situations. And the object won't get up and walk out the front door or scold you for tearing up the newspaper.

A. A. Milne (1957) recognized the special relation between a child and his bear in his stories about Christopher Robin and Winnie the Pooh:

> . . . So wherever I am, there's always Pooh,
> There's always Pooh and Me.
> "What would I do?" I said to Pooh,
> "If it wasn't for you," and Pooh said, "True,
> It isn't much fun for One but Two
> Can stick together," says Pooh, says he,
> "That's how it is," says Pooh. . . .

THE CONTINUITY OF PERSONALITY DEVELOPMENT

One of the most basic questions in the study of personality development is whether the personality of the older child and the adult can be predicted from the temperament and the social environment of the infant and young child. An infant's temperament and his social environment today may determine his

TABLE 6-4 THREE RECURRING PERSONALITY TYPES

TYPES OF INFANT TEMPERAMENT	TYPES OF INFANT ATTACHMENT	TYPES OF ADULT PERSONALITY
Slow-to-warm-up	A: Avoidant attachment	Alpha: Steady and cautious
Easy	B: Secure attachment	Beta: Cheerful and spontaneous
Difficult	C: Anxious, ambivalent attachment	Gamma: Moody and irritable

personality and social behavior tomorrow, but do they still do so after many years have passed?

Thus far, researchers have found little evidence for the continuity of personality between infancy and the later years (Beckwith 1979; Dunn 1980). The search for this continuity has proved much more complicated than many scientists expected.

Personality Types

Researchers have devised many different ways of categorizing the personalities of children and adults; interestingly, many find some system of three categories most useful. One example is the three categories of temperament discussed near the beginning of this chapter—easy, slow-to-warm-up, and difficult. The three types of infant attachment described by Ainsworth and her colleagues are similar to these three types of temperament, as shown in Table 6-4 (Goldsmith & Campos 1982; Maccoby 1980). Type A babies tend to avoid contact with their mothers, even in strange situations, and so resemble infants of slow-to-warm-up temperament. Type B babies play and explore easily in the presence of their mother; after separation from their mother or in the presence of a stranger, they quickly and clearly seek contact and affection. This behavior seems virtually the same as that of easy babies. Type C babies behave erratically and are emotionally inconsistent, seeking their mother's attention but at the same time emotionally rejecting her, and so they resemble difficult babies.

Three similar categories appear in research on adult personality and its relation to health, especially the likelihood of having heart attacks. In adulthood, people can be divided into three types: Type Alpha people are steady, cautious, and depend on their own resources—the kind of people that slow-to-warm-up infants might be expected to become. Type Beta people are spontaneous and undemanding, much like easy infants. Type Gamma are irritable, moody, and volatile, like difficult infants.

During adulthood, people of each of these types are consistent for periods of 30 or 40 years, and the type that they belong to can predict certain kinds of physical illness. In one study of physicians in their middle 50s, about one out of four Alphas and Betas had had a serious illness, such as a heart attack, high blood pressure, or cancer. Among Gammas, however, three out of four had had such a major illness, and many of them had already died (Betz & Thomas 1979). Fortunately, much of the risk of illness can be reduced if Gammas work to temper their emotionality and their life style (Friedman 1980).

It might seem reasonable to expect that most adult Gammas had difficult temperaments as infants, but little such continuity has been found. Attempts to predict adolescent and adult personality from infant temperament have thus far met with little success (Thomas & Chess 1977). Only after people have reached adulthood have researchers found personality types to be stable over long periods (Costa & McCrae 1980; Mussen et al. 1980).

Introversion-Extroversion

That no continuity of personality from infancy to adulthood has yet been found does not necessarily mean that none exists. Research on the genetic inheritance of personality suggests that eventually continuity of some kind will be found. It seems likely, for instance, that each person stays fairly consistent throughout life on a scale of introversion to extroversion. An **introvert** tends to avoid stimulation, to be shy, to avoid socializing with new people, and to focus on solitary pursuits. An **extrovert** tends to seek stimulation, to be outgoing, to seek contacts with new people, and to focus on social pursuits. In many behavior-genetic studies of personality in older children and adults, introversion and extroversion appear as characteristics having a large hereditary contribution (Eysenck 1976). Some studies suggest that emotionality and lack of soothability also may be partly inherited (Goldsmith & Gottesman 1981; Plomin & Rowe 1977).

Environmental Influences and the Difficulty of Detecting Continuity

Many sociologists believe that personality is entirely the result of environmental influences—of socialization: "Socialization is the process of social interaction through which people acquire personality and learn the way of life of their society" (Robertson 1981). The sociological explanation traces personality differences in a society to differences in the values of various parts of the society. In this view, each person is socialized to learn the way of life of a particular region, race, religion, socioeconomic class, and family. In fact, many studies (described in later chapters) show that there are consistent personality differences between children of different cultures, socioeconomic classes, and families, because children's values—an important component of their personalities—tend to closely resemble those of their parents and because the parents' values differ according to their culture or class. Continuity of personality, then, would be accounted for by the continuity of the person's environment. A person who grew up and remained in the same neighborhood and social class would be expected to behave in consistent ways throughout life, and also much like others who had been raised under similar conditions.

Developmentalists, too—especially those who take a social-learning approach—recognize the powerful effects of socialization. Studies that have followed individuals from early childhood to maturity have detected little continuity of personality *except* in some traits that are strongly reinforced by socialization, such as dependence in females and aggressiveness in males (Kagan & Moss 1962; Parke & Slaby 1983).

A problem with the sociological view, according to many developmentalists, is that the human being experiences vast developmental changes from birth to maturity even when the environment undergoes no radical change. Because an infant's way of perceiving and knowing the world is so different from a child's, and a child's is so different from an adult's, simply knowing an infant's temperament and environmental history is not enough to determine the kind of person he will become. The two following short biographies illustrate an extreme case, in which similar traumatic childhoods can produce drastically different results. One is the biography of a mass murderer. The other is of a premier actor and movie maker.

C was born in England in 1889. When C's mother and father separated, C was so young that, later, at 5, he did not recognize his father when he saw him. C's mother tried to support C and his older brother but did not succeed. When C was 6, his mother was sent to the workhouse, a public institution that housed able-bodied paupers and made them work. C and his brother were then sent to a school for orphans and destitute children. There, C was separated from his brother, as the school segregated children by age.

Part of the school's program was the punishment period every Friday, attended by all 390 children there. For minor offenses, the punishment was caning, carried out by a 200-pound man with a cane four feet long and as thick as a thumb. For more serious offenses, such as attempting to run away, the punishment was being struck with a birch rod while manacled with wrist straps. Boys who had been birched were sent directly to the doctor for treatment. C was caned at 7. Soon after, his brother elected to leave the school and join the Navy, an option available to 11-year-olds.

Within a year, C's mother had managed to leave the workhouse and find some employment, so C joined her. But the employment did not last long; she went back to the workhouse and C was sent to a different school. Within the year, C received word that his mother had gone insane and had been sent to an asylum. Legally, then, his father was obligated to provide for C and his brother, and they were sent to him.

The father was living in two rooms with a young woman who did not at all welcome the intrusion of two young sons. She drank a great deal, as did the father, who often stayed away for weeks at a time. Occasionally, when the

ESSAY
CHILD ABUSE AT HOME

The most dangerous age for children subject to abuse is between 3 months and 3 years of age. Who hurts or neglects these vulnerable infants? And why do they do it? Most people who read a newspaper article about an abused child think of the parent as a monster, an inhuman creature, but in fact it is our fellow human beings who commit these abhorrent acts. Calling the offenders names or punishing them does not prevent hurt to the victim. Psychologists, sociologists, and physicians study child abuse to learn who does it and why in order to find ways of preventing it. They have found that a complex set of factors interact to produce child abuse. It is not simply the result of a parent's deviant psychological characteristics. The diagram on page 312 shows all the factors that have been found to contribute to child abuse: the society's norms regarding violence, the parent's age, sex, and socioeconomic status, the parents' own experience of growing up, the parent's personality, stress in the family, and particular situations that set off aggression. All these factors can come into play when a child is abused.

SOCIAL NORMS REGARDING VIOLENCE

In American society, the use of force toward children is, on the whole, condoned. We tend to say, with a smile, "Spare the rod and spoil the child." But there are societies in the world that consider corporal punishment of children a barbaric act—the Cheyenne and the Zuni, for example (Prescott 1979). American parents often permit or even encourage schools to use corporal punishment on their children to punish disapproved behavior. Against this background, it should not be too surprising that many, if not most, incidents of child abuse are carried out by psychologically "normal" people who inflict more punishment than they intended because of their anger and temporary loss of self-control (Gil 1979). In a society that condemned physical punishment of children, this fine line between spanking and abuse, so easy to cross, would not exist. Noted psychologist Edward Zigler (1979), in fact, doubts that child abuse will ever be controlled in America because of the society's acceptance of corporal punishment of children.

If spanking is not considered child abuse in our society, how does one define child abuse? In his nationwide study of child abuse in 1970, David Gil adopted the following definition: "Physical abuse of children is intentional, nonaccidental use of physical force, or intentional, nonaccidental acts of omission, on the part of a parent or other caretaker in interaction with a child in his care, aimed at hurting, injuring, or destroying that child." Gil was able to discover a number of facts about abusing adults and the situations that lead to abuse—at least for *reported* cases of abuse.

THE CHARACTERISTICS OF ABUSING PARENTS

Class. Although a sizable number of middle-class parents have been reported as child abusers, far more reported abusers are from the lower socioeconomic classes. In Gil's survey, 60 percent of the families reported as abusers had received public assistance at some time prior to the abuse. One reason that abuse is reported more often among lower-class parents may be that all kinds of violence are more common in these families, and it is therefore easier to slip across the line between punishment and abuse. Another possible reason is that the pressures of poverty create frustration in a parent and the frustration is released in a physical attack on the child. Gil found that nearly half the fathers of abused children were unemployed at some time during the year the abuse occurred, which supports the idea that frustration is a strong causative factor. Even so, it is certainly not a sufficient cause by itself, because most poor people do not abuse their children.

Sex. Both women and men are abusers. In homes with two parents, the father or the stepfather was the abuser in two-thirds of the incidents reported, the mother or stepmother in one-third. However, thirty percent of all the households in which abuse had been reported were homes in which the mother had sole care of the children; there was no father living at home. So it appears that the blame for abuse falls pretty equally on men and women.

Age and Family Size. Although it has been said that extremely young parents are more likely to be abusers, that is not true. Parents of all ages were reported as abusers. It is true, however, that severe injuries to the child are more likely to be inflicted by parents less than 25 years old (Gil 1970).

Among the families in which children were abused, the proportion with four or more children was almost twice as high as the proportion of such families in the population as a whole. Families with many children and little money generally suffer from a lack of living space—too many people in too few rooms, which increases stress and frustration.

Socialization Experience. Abusive parents were often the victims of deprivation and abuse during their own childhoods (Rutter 1979). Although most such adults do not abuse their children, they are more likely to do so than parents who had happier childhoods. The histories of abusing parents often included foster home placement and juvenile court experience. These abused children who grew up to be abusing parents suffered in two ways. They did not learn how to be parents; they had no models but the abusive ones from whom to learn how adults take care of children. Also, because they had suffered emotional deprivation in childhood, they had urgent emotional needs that sometimes focused on their children. They wanted an emotional fulfillment from the child that the child could not possibly satisfy. One researcher stated it this way:

> Basic in the abuser's attitude toward infants is the conviction, largely unconscious, that children exist in order to satisfy parental needs. Infants who do not satisfy these needs should be punished . . . to make them behave properly. . . . It is as though the infant were looked to as a need-satisfying parental object to fill the residual, unsatisfied, infantile needs of the parent. (B.F. Steele, as quoted in Kempe 1971)

THE CHARACTERISTICS OF ABUSED CHILDREN

Although children of all ages are abused, the most dangerous period is from three months to three years, when the child is utterly defenseless. Older children may be able to find ways to run and hide from the abuser; also, they are somewhat less vulnerable to physical damage. It is the infants who are most vulnerable. Many parents who abuse their infants have no idea of the limitations of infants' thinking and control. Case studies show that abusing parents hit the baby because "he wouldn't stop crying" or "wouldn't

obey" or "wouldn't stop wetting the bed" (Gelles 1979). They issued commands to a baby who could not understand those commands or could not control the disapproved behavior.

Some infants, like the difficult babies described by Chess and Thomas (1980), are particular targets of abuse. Babies who are fussy, who cry a lot because they are irritable or have colic, and babies who have some physical or intellectual abnormality are especially vulnerable to abuse (Gil 1970). Prematurely born infants, who are small (usually around five pounds) when dismissed from the hospital and so require frequent small feedings, are more often targets of abuse. Although it hardly seems fair to call being unwanted a characteristic of a child, an unwanted baby—one born to an unmarried woman who gave birth to the baby only because she felt she had no other choice or born to an already overburdened mother—is also more at risk for abuse or neglect. The Massachusetts Society for the Prevention of Cruelty to Children reported that in 50 percent of 115 families studied after an incident of abuse there was unwanted conception (Zalba 1971). Neglect can be as damaging as physical abuse for an infant and is sometimes even more life-threatening. Neglected infants often do not receive enough physical nourishment for normal growth, and many receive so little emotional nourishment that they display the "failure to thrive" syndrome also found in some institutionalized infants (Kempe and Kempe 1978).

SITUATIONAL FACTORS

Adults who use force toward children do not do so all the time. There is usually a situation that "triggers" the abuse, a situation that involves stress and frustration. The frustration may arise from ignorance about child development, about what can be expected from babies in terms of understanding and control. It may arise from the adult's frustration about controlling any part of his life or destiny under conditions of poverty and overcrowding. It may arise from hostility and quarrels between the parents, with frustration released on the child.

One situation that seems common to many families of abused children is social isolation (Garbarino and Stocking 1980). The parents often have absolutely no

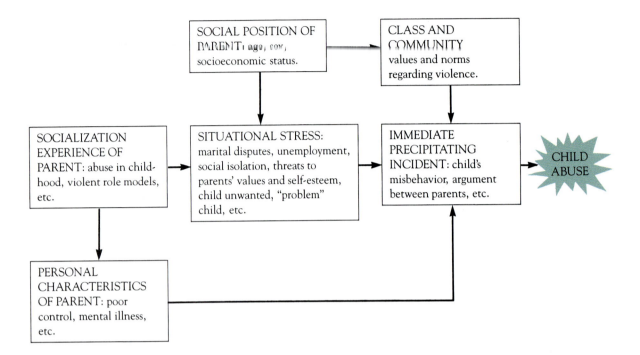

associations outside the home—no contact with friends, neighbors, or relatives, no membership in clubs or associations, no person they can look to for help. They seem unable to believe that others might want to help them in any way. At a point of crisis, whether or not it has to do with a child's perceived bad behavior, these parents have nowhere to turn. Studies have even uncovered the fact that abuse is most likely to occur around dinnertime; one study found that 50 percent of the reported incidents occurred between 6 P.M. and 9 P.M. (Justice and Justice 1976).

PREVENTING ABUSE

All the factors shown in the chart on this page, then, interact in producing abuse. An abusing parent may be psychologically disturbed but is not necessarily so. A normal parent in the midst of a stress-producing situation and presented with a child's persistent crying or misbehavior can lose control and turn discipline into abuse. The abused child may be abnormal in some way—retarded or hyperactive or persistently crying—or the baby may be perfectly normal and generally cheerful. But even normal babies have periods of dis-

tress and crying because of teething or indigestion or earache, and normal 2-year-olds often say "No", not because they are willfully misbehaving but because they are establishing their identity. A situation such as the father's unemployment may be so stressful in one family that it contributes to child abuse, but it may bring the members of another family closer together. Despite the difficulty of writing a scenario that could positively predict abuse, the studies done to date have identified a number of high-risk factors that physicians, psychologists, and social workers can keep in mind in trying to spot the potential for abuse. Most current strategies of intervention are characterized by one sociologist as an "an ambulance service at the bottom of the cliff" (Gelles 1979). That is, treatment of the family—through such groups as Parents Anonymous or by removing the child from the family—takes place only after the child has been battered. Edward Zigler (1979) recommends the following five measures as a start toward preventing abuse.

1. Because many abusive parents have unrealistic ideas about what children are capable of, all high school students should be required to take a course in child care and normal child development. A course in par-

enthood would help not only those adolescents whose experience with their own parents has been deficient but also those who might think it possible, say, to teach their child to read at age 2.

2.   Because premature infants are known to be at risk for abuse, more intensive efforts should be directed toward reducing the incidence of prematurity. Good prenatal care should be promoted for all women, no matter how poor.

3.   Because unwanted children are at risk for abuse, family planning information and advice should be strongly promoted.

4.   Because stress plays such a powerful role in facilitating child abuse, especially in families with four or more children, affordable and attractive day-care facilities should be promoted, so that families can be relieved of the burden of care at least for short periods of time.

5.   Because the social norms in America approve corporal punishment of children, abuse of children is made easier. One possible way of moving toward a change in those norms would be to make it illegal for schools to use corporal punishment.

Ruth S. Kempe and C. Henry Kempe (1978) conducted a study of 350 mothers having their babies at Colorado General Hospital. They interviewed the parents before birth to discover their feelings about the pregnancy, their expectations about the unborn child, facts about the parents' own upbringing, and the social supports the parents had. Then the parents were closely observed during labor and birth and for the first weeks of the children's lives. The observers noted such things as how the mother handled the baby, whether she sought eye contact and held the baby face to face, whether the parents were distant with each other, and whether the mother spoke disparagingly about the baby or made unrealistic complaints about him. On the basis of such measures, the researchers predicted whether each couple would be successful or unsuccessful in parenting. Further research proved that their predictions were correct 77 percent of the time, and that children of parents identified as probably unsuccessful had a significant number of accidents and incidents of abuse, whereas children of parents identified as probably successful had few accidents and no incidents of abuse. The researchers suggest that such assessment programs become widespread in maternity hospitals and that parents who are likely to have difficulty receive regular visits from "health visitors," a sort of visiting nurse who focuses on maternal skills. The health visitor, however, need not have nursing training and, in fact, could be a volunteer rather than a paid professional.

In Sweden, a country with a population of about 8 million, only about ten children per year are hospitalized for maltreatment (Petersson 1976). Sweden has a highly developed system of social welfare. Some of the social services are part of a carefully planned family policy, which includes paid maternity and paternity leaves, a homemaker service for mothers who become ill and for working mothers whose children become ill, day-care centers, preschools, and after-school care centers, and mother-child clinics that keep in close touch with mothers and their children from birth to age 7 (Tietjen 1980). Clearly, such support systems relieve a great deal of stress of the kinds described in this essay, and the efficacy of such programs can be seen in the Swedish child-abuse statistics. Governmental resources—at the national, state, or local level—applied to such programs in the United States would undoubtedly decrease the amount of child abuse here.

young woman was drunk, she would lock the boys out of the house, and they would have to sleep in the streets. Neither the father nor the young woman beat the boys, but no affection was given them. The mother was eventually released from the asylum, and the boys took up residence with her again, in one poor room across from a pickle factory. At the age of 10, C left home to join a troop of traveling entertainers.

P was born in 1929 in Nevada. His mother was a full-blooded Cherokee. She was a trick-rider in rodeos and had married P's father, an Irish cowboy, five years earlier. In the five years after this marriage, they had four children, and the six members of the family traveled around the West, following the rodeo circuit. The family slept in the old truck they traveled in, and although money was scarce, it was quite an exciting life for a young child. His mother and father had formed a show team and rode together until ailments forced them to retire.

When P was 5, the family moved into a house near Reno, Nevada. Troubles between the parents mounted; P's mother started to drink. When P was 6, his mother took the children and moved to San Francisco. She became an alcoholic and had relations with many different men. On several occasions, P tried to run away and return to his father but did not succeed.

His mother then put him into a Catholic orphanage, where he was often struck by the nuns because he wet the bed. After several months the orphanage asked his mother to remove P, and she then put him into a children's shelter run by the Salvation Army. He was still wetting the bed, and a sadistic nurse at the shelter punished him for it by putting him into a tub of ice-cold water and keeping him there. This nurse also called P "nigger" because of his Indian blood. P caught pneumonia because of the cold baths and was sent to a hospital, where he stayed for two months. His father came and got him from the hospital and took him back to the house in Nevada. The two of them lived in the house for a year, and P finished third grade, the last formal schooling he received.

P's father then sold the house, fitted out a kind of primitive trailer, and the two of them took to the road, traveling all over the West. They never stayed in one place very long. They traveled for six years, finally ending up in Alaska. During these years, P's mother died, strangling to death on her own vomit while drunk. His older sister killed herself by jumping out of a fifteenth-story hotel window. His brother, having driven his wife to commit suicide, killed himself the following day.

In his adolescence, P began to argue excessively with his father. At age 16, only a few inches over five feet tall, P ran away and joined the Merchant Marines.

C was Charlie Chaplin, a world-famous comedian and director of movies. P was Perry Smith, hanged for killing four members of the Herbert Clutter family in Kansas. These extremely different outcomes illustrate how hard it is to describe, predict, and explain the origins of personality.

SUMMARY

1. Both inborn factors and experience contribute to the formation of **person-ality,** a person's disposition to perceive things and react to them in a character-istic way.

TEMPERAMENT AND CHANGE

2. Most newborns display individual **temperaments,** certain characteristic ways of responding that depend primarily on physical constitution.
  a. **Easy babies** (about 40 percent of newborns) are regular in their patterns of eating and sleeping, readily approach new objects or people, adapt easily to changes in their environment, react with low or moderate intensity, and are generally cheerful.
  b. **Difficult babies** (10 percent) are usually irregular in their eating and sleeping patterns, withdraw from new objects and people, adapt slowly, react with great intensity, and are generally irritable.
  c. **Slow-to-warm-up babies** (15 percent) have low activity levels, withdraw when first presented with new objects or people, react with a low level of intensity, and adapt slowly to changes in their environment.
  d. Thirty-five percent of newborns behave in ways that do not easily fit into any of these patterns.

MOTHER-INFANT INTERACTION

3. An infant's temperament interacts with his mother's style of caring for him, which is based on her personality and expectations.
  a. Some mothers are task-oriented, not interacting socially with the baby while caring for him physically; others have a high-interaction style, continually talking to and stimulating the child. The interactions of a slow-to-warm-up baby with a task-oriented mother will be very different from those of the same baby with a high-interaction mother, and such interactions help shape the beginnings of personality.
  b. Babies adapt to their caretaker's style of feeding and interacting. A change of caretakers only 10 days after birth causes a baby to become upset—to cry more and have feeding problems.
  c. Babies' temperaments can affect the course of mother-infant interaction. Newborns assessed as being difficult when they were a week old were more likely, at 1 year of age, to show anxious, ambivalent attachment to their mothers.
4. According to Erik Erikson's theory of psychosocial development (described in Chapter 8), early interactions between mother and child determine the

course of the child's first developmental crisis: **Basic Trust versus Mistrust.** If the mother's care allows the baby to develop confidence in the reliability of other people and a sense of himself as a being worthy of care, the baby will develop a sense of basic trust.

5.   Specific child-care practices—early or late toilet training, for example— are less important to personality development than the parents' caring attitude and sensitivity to the baby's needs.

6.   The parents' goal in choosing certain child-care practices is to assure that their children will eventually become effective members of their society.

THEORY: *SOCIAL LEARNING AND PERSONALITY DEVELOPMENT*

7.   **Social-learning theory** focuses both on socialization—what parents and others do to mold children's behaviors to make them effective members of society—and on social learning processes—how children acquire the behaviors that allow them to live comfortably and interact acceptably with other people.

   a.   **Observational learning** is an important process of social learning. Children watch others behave, encode the behavior into memory, and may later perform it.

   b.   Theorists distinguish between **learning** a behavior and **performing** it; each of these aspects of social learning can be influenced by a number of different factors.

   c.   Learning a behavior depends on the child seeing it performed; the consequences of the behavior for the **model,** the person who performs it; the personal characteristics of the model; the amount of attention the child can bring to what she is observing; and the level of the child's cognitive development, including memory.

   d.   Performing a behavior depends on the reinforcement the child receives when she first attempts to perform the behavior; the reinforcement a model receives for performance; and the level of the child's abilities.

   e.   Although traditional learning theory and cognitive theory have differed widely in their approaches to development in the past, the two points of view have now been combined in **cognitive social-learning theory.** This approach emphasizes both the cognitive processes, such as memory, that underlie learning and the developmental changes that take place in how people learn.

   f.   **Internalization** is a concept that combines the ideas of cognitive theory with those of social learning theory: Values, beliefs, and behaviors that a child has been taught are taken inside and made a lasting part of the child's personality. Another important concept of cognitive social-learning theory is **deferred imitation,** when infants become able to imitate a behavior that they have observed some time before.

8. Social learning takes place even early in infancy.
   a. By 8 or 9 months, infants can *imitate* behaviors immediately after they see them. Many infant-parent games involve imitation.
   b. Another type of social learning, which develops around the same age, is *social referencing:* When a novel event occurs, the infant checks the parent's face for an emotional reaction to the event and then reacts the same way.
   c. *Scaffolding* is another means of social learning in infants. Parents support simple parts of a complex behavior until the baby learns them and can perform the entire sequence. For example, parents scaffold the learning of language by supportive dialogue with their 2-year-olds.

ESTABLISHING THE PARENT-CHILD RELATIONSHIP

9. The human species is equipped with a number of species-specific social behaviors that help to establish infant-parent interactions. At 2 or 3 months of age, babies develop a *greeting response*—a particular facial expression and sound—which parents react to socially. Most parents also use a certain facial expression in greeting their infant, as well as baby talk and imitation of the baby's actions.

10. Infant and parent pass through a number of stages in their relationship as the infant develops cognitively and emotionally. In the stage of *regulation* during the first few months, parent and infant establish routines to fulfill the infant's basic biological needs. In the second stage, *reciprocal exchange,* both infant and parent contribute to the first social interactions. The infant begins to exert more control over her social interactions in the third stage, *initiative,* and establishes a strong relationship with the parent in the fourth stage, *focusing.* From the base of this attachment relationship, the infant moves on to establish herself as an independent human being in the fifth stage, *self-assertion,* and the sixth stage, *independent self-concept.*

ATTACHMENT

11. *Attachment* describes the infant's relation to the mother or other principal caretaker between about 6 months of age and about 2 years. Attachment is an enduring tie based on a feeling of affection that is focused on a specific person. Psychologists measure attachment by the baby's following the mother with his eyes, the orientation of his body toward her, smiling at her, clinging to her, and following her when he is able to. Forming an attachment is an important step in the development of the parent-infant relationship.
   a. There appear to be three different types of attachment. *Secure attachment,* the healthiest type; *anxious, ambivalent attachment;* and *avoidant*

attachment. Mary Ainsworth believes that these patterns of attachment reflect the different ways that mothers interact with their babies.

b. Babies also form strong attachments to their fathers.

c. Babies with a healthy attachment use their parents as a *secure base* from which to explore the world. Babies with insecure attachments are less likely to explore.

d. Two signs that an infant is forming an attachment and using the mother as a secure base are *stranger distress* and *separation distress,* which develop in the second half of the first year.

e. The lack of a parent-infant relationship can retard social and cognitive development, as seen when infants raised in certain institutional settings showed *failure to thrive,* that is, were depressed physically, mentally, and emotionally.

f. Such retardation can often be overcome if the environment of deprivation is replaced by one that furnishes affection, support, and stimulation.

g. High-quality *day care* for infants does not appear to damage their attachment to their parents or their social, emotional, or cognitive development.

BUILDING THE SELF

12. Healthy attachment seems to be a necessary step in an infant's *development of a self.* A secure base gives a baby the confidence to explore the world and gain experience.

a. This experience aids in the process of *separation and individuation,* by which the baby learns to think of himself as separate from his mother.

b. During the process of separation and individuation, many infants focus their attachment on an object—a toy or a blanket—in place of the parent. These are called *transitional objects* because they aid in the transition to an independent self.

THE CONTINUITY OF PERSONALITY DEVELOPMENT

13. Psychologists have been unable to find much evidence for continuity of personality from infancy and childhood to adulthood.

a. The three types of infant temperament seem to correspond with three types of adult personality: *Type Alpha,* steady and cautious people who depend on their own resources; *Type Beta,* spontaneous and undemanding people; and *Type Gamma,* irritable, moody, and volatile people. Alpha would seem to correspond with slow to warm up; Beta with easy; Gamma with difficult. However, researchers have not found such a connection in development from infancy to adulthood.

b. One general aspect of personality seems to have continuity over much of the life span—a tendency toward **introversion,** a tendency to avoid stimulation, or **extroversion,** a tendency to seek stimulation.

SUGGESTED READINGS

BRAZELTON, T. BERRY. *Infants and Mothers: Differences in Development* (revised edition). New York: Dell, 1983.

Brazelton, a famous pediatrician, describes the course of development during the first year, highlighting the many variations in the normal behavior of infants.

DUNN, J. *Distress and Comfort.* Cambridge, Massachusetts: Harvard University Press, 1977.

A developmental psychologist discusses what scientists know about what upsets babies, how they can be comforted, and how the parent-child relationship relates to an infant's emotions.

HARTER, SUSAN. "Developmental Perspectives on the Self-System." In E. M. Hetherington (ed.), *Socialization, Personality, and Social Development,* Volume 4 of P. H. Mussen (ed.), *Carmichael's Manual of Child Psychology.* New York: Wiley, 1983.

A definitive but highly readable review of research on the development of the self. It includes an especially good overview of how the interaction between parent and child contributes to the child's personality and sense of self.

KAYE, KENNETH. *The Mental and Social Life of Babies: How Parents Create Persons.* Chicago: University of Chicago Press, 1982.

A well-known researcher on infant development describes how a baby gradually comes to participate in social interaction between parent and child.

NORRIS, GLORIA, and JO ANN MILLER. *The Working Mother's Complete Handbook.* New York: Dutton, 1979.

Two working mothers discuss the increasingly common household in which both mother and father have regular jobs, and they offer some helpful suggestions on how women can manage both parenting and working at the same time.

SPOCK, BENJAMIN. *Baby and Child Care.* New York: Pocket Books, 1976.

This guide to child care has been used by more American parents than any other book. First published in 1945, it still contains a wealth of useful information and advice in a readable, accessible form.

The preschool years dawn with children's recognition that they exist as individuals, separate from their mother and father. As independent beings, then, they are eager to make sense of the world around them. Their rapidly expanding ability to use and understand language lets them tune into that world, listening to mother chatting with the butcher or an older brother gossiping with his friends, and—sometimes with unfortunate results through imitation—father expressing himself to careless drivers in other cars. But the mind that processes all these incoming cognitive and social data is still immature, especially in the early preschool years. For one thing, the child tends to take things literally. If she hears someone say, for example, "I was so mad I hit the ceiling," she might ask, "Did it hurt?" Another difference is that for preschoolers, time seems to have only one dimension—the present. Telling a 3-year-old that she can open her birthday gifts "soon" or "in an hour" conveys very little. The hour might as well be an eternity. The characteristics of pre-schoolers' thought, their remarkable language development, and their physical development from toddler to runner are described in Chapter 7. Chapter 8 examines how a society and its representatives—especially parents—begin training preschoolers to become effective members of the group as well as valued individuals with a sense of self.

UNIT

3

THE

PRESCHOOL

YEARS

7

THE
ABILITY
TO
THINK
AND
TALK

CHAPTER OUTLINE

7

THE
ABILITY
TO
THINK
AND
TALK

The period between the ages of 2 and 6 years spans some of the most impressive developments in a person's life. The physical change from a short-legged, cherubic 2-year-old to a typically slim, athletic 6-year-old is striking. But even more remarkable is the change in competence—in what children can do physically and in the way they understand and deal with the world. Between 2 and 6, children gain control of their bowel and bladder. They learn to undress and then to dress themselves. They learn to get themselves a drink from the faucet and then to pour a glass of milk and make a peanut-butter sandwich. They come to understand what boys and girls are—as well as mothers, fathers, doctors, and firemen—and to comprehend simple social concepts such as "nice," "mean," and (eventually) "polite." They graduate from uttering one and two words at a time to speaking in sentences, chattering away to their mothers, fathers, sisters and brothers, babysitters, even to themselves. They become able to explain why they want something and to ask for explanations of events they don't understand.

Traditionally, scientists have sorted these changes into separate categories—cognitive development, language development, physical development, and social development. Development in each of these areas is not really separate, however. Cognitive development creates the need for more sophisticated speech in order to express the new knowledge. Language development leads children to master new words that embody new ideas. Physical development allows them to do more complicated things than they could earlier, including some things, such as playing games, that bring them into greater social contact with others. Each type of development affects and interacts with every other type.

COGNITIVE DEVELOPMENT: PREOPERATIONAL INTELLIGENCE

Although preschool children have developed beyond the sensorimotor intelligence of infancy, they have their own ways of thinking and understanding that are sometimes puzzling and confusing to their parents and other older people. For example, one 3-year-old asked his father, "Daddy, when you were little, were you a boy or a girl?" Another asked, "Mother, who was born first, you or me?" (Chukovsky, 1968). A 5-year-old, filled with anger and remorse after being spanked for a misdeed, asserted, "Now I'm going to stab myself to death, and you are *not* going to spank me for it." Such statements show not only inexperience and a lack of knowledge. They also show that preoperational intelligence is different in many ways from the thinking of older children and adults.

For one thing, whereas older children and adults are able to think logically, preschool children are not, according to Piaget (1951). Piaget uses the word

"Mommy, when you get old how many grandchildren are you gonna have?"

preoperational to describe thought that occurs before children are capable of
what he calls operations, or "schemes of connected relational reasoning" (Isaacs
1974)—that is, before they can reason logically.

Preoperational intelligence is more than just lack of logic, however. It has
other characteristics, some of them particularly endearing, that are described
later in this section. Among them is egocentrism—the kind of self-centeredness
that leads a 4-year-old to say, "Look, Mommy, the moon follows me wherever
I go." Another characteristic is complexive thinking, a chaining of ideas in
which each is linked to the one preceding or following it but the whole is not
organized into a unified concept. A third characteristic shows up in play; the
newly developed capacity of preschoolers for deferred imitation allows them to
play many pretend games. Deferred imitation demonstrates, too, that preschoolers have acquired considerable powers of memory.

Representation

As described in Chapter 5, pretending is tied to representation, the ability to
think about the properties of things without having to act on them directly. In
fact, the development of representation is the cornerstone of all cognitive
development during the preoperational period.

Recent research suggests that preoperational intelligence develops through
at least two distinct levels, the first roughly between the ages of 2 and 4, the
second between 4 and 6 (Case & Khanna 1981; Gelman 1978; Kenny 1983).

ESSAY:
WHO IS SAINT PATRICK?

The following opinions were gathered by Lin Jakary for the San Diego Reader.

NICOLE SALCIDO
FUTURE ARTIST
AGE 6

Saint Patrick is a man. He sells clothes in a little shop in Mexico. He's about twenty-one years old and he's not very famous yet. Some people know about him because he's really friendly and he helps people and he gives you directions if you're lost. That's why they named a day after him. He likes to wear green and he likes it if you wear green. He's also very nice. You have to be nice to be a saint, but I also think you're supposed to be dead.

MARK ANKER
FUTURE FIREMAN
AGE 5

I saw some programs on Saint Patrick. I also saw a paper clover on the calendar. Saint Patrick grows clovers. Lots of them, like a hundred million trillion. He also grows flowers and trees and fishes. There are little people too small for us to see that live in the clover. They like gold. They close some of the stores and the banks on Saint Patrick's Day so the little people can get some of the gold and celebrate. Or maybe that's just on Christmas and Easter. One thing I know is that they talk Irish. I think they might have trouble with snails munching on the clover. We have some clovers and the snails keep coming and coming.

DEVIN MOTLEY
FUTURE FOOTBALL PLAYER
AGE 5

I know it has something to do with leprechauns. They're little people who live deep in the mountains. They have little houses and they use acorns for doorknobs. They also wear green tights. They wear red shirts. They have yellow hair, white faces, and green hands. They wear silver belts. They have pet dogs. They have good luck because the mountain lions never eat them. Once we were camped about fifty-two miles away from where they lived and one night when everyone was asleep I sneaked out of my tent and I saw one. He was very tiny. I don't know if you know this, but they can jump all the way from North America to South America in one leap. I tried to catch him but he was too fast for me.

KATIE TURNER
FUTURE GYMNAST
AGE 6

Saint Patrick said for all the snakes to get out of Ireland because the snakes were bothering people. He put magic in a shamrock, which is like a rock that's green. When a snake touched the shamrock it died and the other snakes got scared and got out of Ireland. A shamrock is also a green plant with leaves. That's why if you don't wear green on Saint Patrick's Day you get a pinch. . . . I'm half Irish and half fairy. I can see invisible things like shadows and fairies. They give me diamonds but I usually give them away to my friends. I might save one for my mom. Her birthday is on Saint Patrick's Day. My grandfather was one hundred percent Irish, but he died before I was born.

JEREMY HORTON
FUTURE ASTRONAUT
AGE 5½

His name was Mr. Patrick but now they call him Saint 'cause he's such a good fella. He helps people celebrate the planting season, especially if you're planting potatoes and clovers. You can celebrate by having a party and wearing green because clovers are green. I don't have anything all green so I'm going to wear my shirt with green stripes. I've heard that four-leaf clovers are good luck. If you find one, you get rich. If you find two, you get a little less rich. If you find more than two, you lose all your money. It's also a bad idea to put your foot in a patch of clover because you never know what might be hiding in there.

HI AND LOIS

As with the sensorimotor levels of infancy, a child's transition from one of these levels to the next seems to be marked by a spurt in brain development. The growth spurt marking the transition from sensorimotor intelligence to representation occurs at age 2, and the spurt marking the attainment of the second preoperational level occurs at age 4 (Eichorn & Bailey 1962; Fischer & Pipp 1984). Whether there are additional levels between these ages is still controversial (Case 1984). Several neo-Piagetian theories agree, however, that the preschool years mark the beginning of the representational cycle of levels, which eventually leads to operational thought, as explained in Chapter 5. As described in what follows, 2- to 4-year-olds are capable of only single representations, whereas 4- and 5-year-olds develop the ability to coordinate two or more of them.

Single Representations   When a 3-year-old tiptoes into her parents' room and whispers in her mother's ear, "I'm a kitty and I just woked up," she is using a representation. Pretend play, a favorite pastime of preschoolers that becomes possible only when they have become capable of representation, is a good window into the thinking of young children. Observing a child play a pretend game is a way of estimating the sophistication of the child's thought.

Observation of children pretending has shown that when children begin to use representations, at about age 2, they can control only one representation at a time (Corrigan 1983; Dasen et al. 1978; Fenson & Ramsay 1980; Nicolich 1981). At the start, each representation is extremely simple, reflecting just one characteristic of the thing represented. In making a doll act as a person, for example, a child can represent the person doing only one thing at a time—a child walking, a man eating, or a woman washing her hands. As the child builds up her representational ability, she begins to represent the person doing a string of things in sequence, such as a boy walking, then going to the potty, and then eating.

Figure 7-1 The ability to play pretend games marks the development of representation.

Later in development—by age 3 in many children—single representations can include a set of *related* characteristics or actions (Case & Khanna 1981; Inhelder et al. 1972). The child makes a mother doll walk out the door saying that she will be back for supper, get into a car, and drive away. Or the child makes a car go "vroom-vroom," race across the floor and up and down furniture, and crash into all kinds of things.

In these complex single representations, a child combines characteristics not just into sensible scenarios for people or cars but into **social categories,** in which the characteristics hang together in terms of a concrete social concept, such as "mother," "father," "doctor," "nice," or "mean." Instead of making a doctor doll, for example, carry out a string of unrelated or even inappropriate actions, the child can make it do a series of "doctor things"—putting on a white coat, washing its hands, taking a temperature, and giving an injection (Watson 1981). Likewise, she can make her teddy bear act nice—saying that he likes her, sharing his toys with her, and giving her a piece of candy (Hand 1981). Figure 7-2 shows some developments in pretending during the preschool years.

Figure 7-2 These four steps in the development of the ability to pretend reflect a child's cognitive development. (A) In the first pretend games, which mark the transition from sensorimotor to preoperational intelligence, the child simply pretends to be carrying out an action, such as sleeping or drinking from an empty cup: The child behaves *as if* she were going to sleep. (B) Development of representational thinking allows the child to apply this pattern to something outside herself: Bear is behaving as if *she* were going to sleep. (C) Then the complexity of what Bear can do increases to show a social category: Bear is acting as if she were a baby, doing all those things that a baby does—sleeping, eating, playing. (D) As the child advances to the second level of preoperational intelligence, she can relate one social category—the role of mother—to another category—the role of baby. Bear is acting as if she were a baby interacting with another bear, who is acting as her mother.

Typically, children's understanding of the social categories in the family seems to begin with the idea that mothers have long hair, wear dresses, and clean house, whereas fathers have short hair, wear pants, and go to work. Even when their own parents do not fit these stereotypes, children of 3 or 4 years generally learn them anyway (Kuhn et al. 1978). Earlier, they might have imitated Daddy cooking breakfast and washing the dishes, but now their play tends to conform to sex-role stereotypes (Lee 1975):

Morgan: I'll be cooking and you telephone, okay? I'll be the daddy, okay?

Jeff: No, no—mommies cook.

Morgan: Oh . . . I'll cook. I'll be the mommy.

Jeff: Uh?

Morgan: I'll be the mommy.

Jeff: And I'll be the daddy, cause I'm the . . . Good.

Morgan: You'll be ironing.

Jeff: Yes, Daddy'll be ironing.

Morgan: Mommies iron, mommies iron. Not boys . . . not daddies.

Jeff: Oh, and you can cook. (Jeff goes to the ironing board.)

Morgan: No, no, mommies. Daddies don't iron. (Morgan holds the iron to prevent Jeff from ironing.)

Jeff: But . . .

Morgan: When the mommies are gone, daddies iron?

Jeff: Yeah.

Morgan: Oh. (He releases the iron.)

Similarly, their first understanding of other social categories, such as race (black and white) or age (adult and child) tend to be stereotyped (Edwards 1983; Van Parys 1981; Wilson 1978). Parents who would like to see traditional social roles modified are sometimes upset by these attitudes in their children, but there is little they can do. Not until children are several years older can they begin to deal with the complexities of social categories and so disregard traditional stereotypes.

Relations between Representations   Children begin to understand some of the complexities of social behavior when, at about age 4, they start to relate two or more representations to each other (Biggs & Collis 1982; Case & Khanna 1981; Kenny 1983). This ability enables children to master many new categories, because many categories involve relations. The category "man," for example, includes as part of its meaning the relation between man and woman. Only when children can relate man and woman can they understand this part of the meaning of man. Similarly, at this level they can understand other social relationships, such as husband-wife, mother-father, mother-child, and so forth.

Each of these social relationships is learned as a separate combination, however, and so 4- and 5-year-olds tend to confuse combinations that overlap. Mothers as wives and fathers as husbands seem to be particularly perplexing, resulting in remarks such as, "No, Mommy, he's not your husband. He's my Daddy." Nevertheless, the children's cognitive and social advance from earlier understandings is obvious. Previously, they did not even understand that a mother and father have a special relationship to each other as husband and wife. Now they understand that relationship but confuse it with father and mother.

By relating representations, the child can understand **contingencies,** that is, situations in which variations in one factor depend upon variations in a second factor (Piaget et al. 1968). For example, how full the bathtub gets is contingent on how long the water is left running. Children 4 or 5 years old can understand this contingency because they can relate their representation of the amount of water in the tub to their representation of how long the water has been running. Consequently, they can leave the bathroom while the tub is filling and, most times, return before it overflows.

Younger children who are limited to single representations can understand contingencies in a more concrete, sensorimotor way. For example, they must actually watch the tub filling up to know when to turn the water off. Contingencies are such a natural part of adult thought that many parents do not realize the problems their 2- and 3-year-olds have with them. At some time you must have heard the frustrated parent of a young preschooler say something like, "I've told her a dozen times that if she doesn't wear her coat outside when it's freezing, she's going to catch a cold." The easiest way to teach a child at that age is to simplify the task so that it requires only single representations. For example, the parent can make putting on a coat a regular part of going outside: "You always wear your coat when you're playing outside." Then the child needs to understand only that going outside goes together with putting on a coat, not the contingency between not putting on a coat and possibly getting the sniffles.

Some of the cognitive advances made possible by a child's ability to relate representations may not appear to be advances, especially to parents. The first glimmerings of understanding of, say, a social relationship can lead to even more extreme stereotyping than the child showed earlier (Fischer et al. 1984). Because the child can now relate two representations, such as man and woman, she can set them up as opposites, insisting that men should not do woman things and vice versa (Damon 1977; Maccoby 1980). Earlier, the child's stereotypes of man or woman might have had opposing characteristics, but the child did not understand it as an opposition between social roles and therefore did not try to impose it on others. The younger child may say, "Men do these things," but she does not say, "Men do these things, so women shouldn't." The 4- or 5-year-old may begin to neaten up the sex roles in her own mind, insisting that men and women are truly opposites. For instance, 4-year-old Joshua insisted that his mother should wear dresses instead of pants because "Ladies

RESEARCH:
CHILDREN'S VIEWS OF RELIGION

Religion plays an important role in the lives of many children, but there have been few psychological studies of that role. How do children experience religion? Everyday evidence suggests that young children's understanding of religious concepts is different from that of adults: What religious thoughts and feelings go through the minds of those numberless children who fervently sing the hymn about "the cross-eyed bear" (the cross I'd bear)? And what concept of God exists in the mind of the little Connecticut girl who was heard piously reciting The Lord's Prayer as "Our Father who art in New Haven, Harold be they name"?

David Elkind conducted a study of how children acquire a religious identity. He looked at how they came to think of themselves as a Protestant or Catholic or Jew and what they understood those designations to mean. Elkind and his colleagues conducted clinical interviews with about 800 children between 5 and 14 years old, divided almost equally between Catholics, Protestants, and Jews. He found three distinct stages in the development of children's understanding of God and related religious ideas (Elkind 1979).

STAGE I (usually ages 5–7)

At the first stage, children had a global, undifferentiated conception of their religious identity. Here are some questions and typical answers given by these 5- and 6-year-olds:

> Are you Jewish? "Yes." Is your family Jewish? "Yes, well all except my dog, he's a *French* poodle."
>
> Can a dog or a cat be a Catholic? "No." Why not? "They are not a person, they are animals." How are animals different from people? "They walk on four legs."
>
> What is a Catholic? "A person." How is he different from a Protestant? "I don't know."
>
> How do you become Jewish? "God makes you Jewish."

> Can you be a Catholic and an American at the same time? "No." Why not? "I don't know." Are you a Catholic? "Yes." Are you an American? "No."

These youngsters show the same sorts of confusions about religious ideas as about other ideas. They have trouble dealing with more than one class or idea at a time, and although they do associate a denominational term with the concept of God, they seem to think of both God and the denomination as if they were real, concrete objects. It is as if God makes Jews or Protestants just as a baker makes muffins or rolls.

STAGE II (usually ages 7–9)

These school-age children show much more sophistication in their religious thinking:

> Can a dog or a cat be a Catholic? "No." Why not? "Because he can't go to church or receive the sacraments, stuff like that."
>
> How can you tell a person is Catholic? "If you see them go into a Catholic church."
>
> What is a Jew? "A person who goes to Temple and to Hebrew School."
>
> Can you be a Protestant and an American at the same time? "Yes." How is that possible? "Because I live in America and was baptized."

Compared to the religious thinking of the 5- and 6-year-olds, these answers show very little confusion. These children have clear, though entirely concrete, ideas about religious identity. Notice that all their answers relate certain actions—going to church, being baptized—to the religious denomination. Actions seem to be the magic key to understanding religious terms at this stage.

STAGE III (usually ages 10–12)

It is only at the start of adolescence that children's understanding of religious concepts comes close to adults' understanding.

> Can a dog or a cat be Protestant? "No, because they don't have a brain or an intellect."

What is a Jew? "A person who believes in one God and does not believe in the New Testament."

How can you tell a person is a Protestant? "Because they are free to repent and go pray to God in their own way."

How do you become a Protestant? "Well, you are baptized first and worship in the Protestant way and follow Protestant rules."

Can you be a Catholic and an American at the same time? "Yes." How is that possible? "They are two different things—American is a nationality; Catholic is a religion."

Young people on the brink of adolescence no longer define religious ideas in terms of outward behavior. They are capable of thinking about thinking—about beliefs and convictions.

One more study by Elkind concerned children's conceptions of prayer. Not only did he look at how children think about prayer, but he looked at the fantasies and feelings associated with it. Here is one of the interview questions and typical answers by children of various ages (Elkind et al. 1967).

What is a prayer?

Nancy (5 years, 11 months): "A prayer is about God, rabbits, dogs, and fairies and deer, and Santa Claus and turkeys and pheasants, and Jesus and Mary and Mary's little baby."

Jimmy (7 years, 5 months): "That we should have water, food, rain, and snow. It's something you ask God for—water, food, rain, and snow."

Dell (10 years, 6 months): "Prayer is a way to communicate with God. To ask his forgiveness, to ask him if something would go right when it's going wrong."

At first, prayer is simply a word associated with other words—such as the word "God"—that are essentially meaningless for the child. Then it is an action. Finally, it is conceived as a mental activity associated with a system of religious beliefs. At the same time that the children's *understanding* of prayer becomes increasingly

THE FAMILY CIRCUS. **By Bil Keane**

Copyright 1983
The Register and Tribune
Syndicate, Inc.

"I can hardly wait to go to church tomorrow."

"They're havin' a bake sale after!"

differentiated and abstract, the feelings they associate with praying become more individualized and particular. Young children have few feelings connected with praying; praying for them is a scheduled activity—you do it before meals or before bed or at church. In older children, prayer often arises spontaneously in response to particular feelings. Older children tend to pray when they are worried, upset, or lonely—and, less often, when they are exhilarated or grateful.

The role that religion plays, then, in a child's dealings with the world and in his mental and emotional life depends greatly on the child's developmental level.

wear dresses, men wear pants." Similarly, a child may scold a parent who fools around with a toy or sits on a swing and starts to pump: "No. Don't. Only children play. Mommies and Daddies work" (Tucker 1979).

The ability to relate representations brings with it new attempts at social influence. Strategies such as "If you let me play with your truck, I'll let you play with my bucket" become commonplace. Often these first **attempts at social influence** can be pretty bald. Christopher, 4½ years old, knew that his father liked it when he was affectionate, and he knew that he had to have his father's permission to get a snack. The result: "Daddy, I love you. Can I have a peanut-butter-and-jelly sandwich?" Social influence of this type is usually more effective when it is less transparent, but it takes children a while to learn how to be more subtle.

Much of the preschool child's concern is with making sense of the people around her and how they relate to each other (Damon 1977). The ability to represent people and things opens up much of this social world to the child. Social categories like "mother" and "father," social contingencies like "If you're nice to me, I'll be nice to you," and social influence—all these aspects of the child's family and society become accessible to her.

The Social World and Imitation

One of the most important ways in which children learn about the social world is imitation (see the theory inset "Social Learning," in Chapter 6). During the sensorimotor period, before the capacity for representation develops, infants can imitate an action only at the moment they observe it. With their new representational capacities, preschool children can make imitation a major part of their lives because they are capable of what Piaget (1951) calls **deferred imitation:** They can observe an action, represent it to themselves, and then at a later time call up that representation from memory and actively imitate it.

When Benjy, at 2½ years of age, was scolded by his parents, he used his ability for deferred imitation to comfort himself. He sat weeping on the couch, saying "What's a trouble, Benjy? It's all right, Benjy. Don't cry any more—don't cry, Benjy." It had been days or weeks since he had heard his parents comfort him with these words, but he remembered them and used them himself at an appropriate time (Church 1966).

Children's ability to use deferred imitation reflects their developing capacities throughout the preschool period (McCall et al. 1977; Watson 1981). A child capable of single representations can remember an action or a related set of actions and imitate them later. After a visit to the doctor, for instance, the child will play doctor at home by taking her doll's pulse and temperature or by giving it a shot and a comforting pat. A child at the second preoperational level, who is capable of representational relations, can relate a representation

THE FAMILY CIRCUS ®   **By Bil Keane**

Figure 7-3 The young preschooler shows his egocentrism when he assumes that everyone must desire piggy transfers on his shirt.

"Want a piggy on your shirt, Daddy?"

for what a doctor does to a representation for what a patient does and thus understand and remember how the doctor interacted with his patient. Now, after a visit to the doctor, the child may act out not only what the doctor did and said to her but also what she said (or would like to say) to the doctor.

Egocentrism and Perspective Taking

When the child imitates a doctor, she is in a sense taking the doctor's viewpoint. **Perspective taking,** or the ability to take someone else's viewpoint, has been the topic of a large amount of research on preschool children. Piaget (1932) pointed out long ago that preschool children often make serious mistakes in perspective-taking, assuming that another person shares their own view of things.

Everyone who has spent time with preschoolers can describe examples of this **egocentrism,** or the inability to take another's point of view. Three-year-old Tess asked the checker at the supermarket, "Do you like my Aunt Susan?" It did not occur to her that this person did not know her aunt. After Tess had spent an afternoon at the zoo, she said to another stranger (who had not been at the zoo), "Were you afraid of the elephants too?"

Egocentrism in preschool children does not mean that they are selfish or willfully self-centered. It means instead that they center on themselves because they cannot think any other way. They are captives of their own viewpoint.

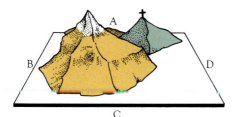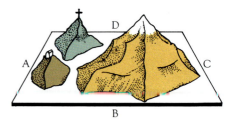

Figure 7-4   The model of
the mountain range used
by Piaget and Inhelder. It
is shown here from all four
sides. The child subjects
in the study also saw all
four sides before they were
seated in front of one of
them. Then the
experimenter moved a
doll around the table and
asked each child how the
scene must look to the
doll. The child was to
respond by picking the
correct view from a set of
ten pictures. Before age 5
or 6, virtually all children
chose the picture showing
their own view of the
model. They were
egocentric—they could
not take another person's
viewpoint.

Zachary, at 2½ years, showed just how extreme egocentrism can be. It was early
evening, and his mother and father were sitting in the living room talking.
Zachary walked up to his mother and asked, "Mommy, can I have a cookie?"
His mother answered, "No, we'll be eating dinner soon." Then Zachary walked
over to his father and asked the same thing, "Daddy, can I have a cookie?" His
father replied, "No, we'll be eating dinner soon." Undaunted, Zachary went
back to his mother: "Mommy, Daddy just said I can have a cookie."

Even when preschool children are shown another person's perspective, they
cannot keep it in mind and coordinate it with their own. The classic laboratory
demonstration of this property of preoperational thought uses a model of a
mountain range like the one shown in Figure 7-4 (Piaget and Inhelder 1967).
The model is quite large, and the child is encouraged to walk around it until
she is familiar with all sides of the landscape. She can see that there are different
objects on the mountains, objects that she can easily identify. After she has
become familiar with the landscape, she is seated on one side of the model,
with one view of the mountain. The experimenter moves a doll so that it has a
different view of the mountain. Then the experimenter shows the child several
drawings or photographs of the landscape and asks her to pick out the one that
shows the doll's view of the mountain range. Preschool children almost invariably choose the picture that shows their own view.

In another task, two children sit on opposite sides of a little wall so that they
cannot see each other. Each child has an identical set of toys or pictures, and
one child is asked to pick a toy and describe it to the other child (Krauss &
Glucksberg 1969; Roberts & Patterson 1983). Young children's efforts in this
task take very little account of the fact that their partner cannot see what is
being described. The following exchange is typical (keep in mind that neither
child can see what the other is doing):

Lynn (pointing): It's this one.
Sheila (picking up a toy): Is this it?
Lynn (pointing again): No, it's this one over here.

The results of such studies have led some psychologists to underestimate the
abilities of preschool children, claiming that all children under 6 years of age

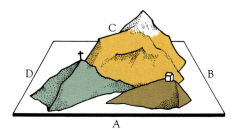
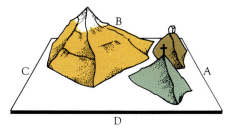

are completely incapable of taking another person's perspective. But research using different situations—for example, ones that require little verbal communication—has shown that preschool children, especially 4- and 5-year-olds, can take another person's perspective (Flavell 1977). In one study, a child sat down in front of a group of toys with her mother and an experimenter. One of the adults closed her eyes while the other adult and the child chose a secret toy that only the two of them would know about. Most 4-year-old children were able to say which adult shared the secret with them and which did not (Marvin et al. 1976). In other words, most children could coordinate their own viewpoint with those of the two adults: They realized that the adult who had helped select the toy—and only that adult—shared their viewpoint, and the secret.

It appears that perspective-taking skills improve as cognition develops through the two preoperational levels. At 2 and 3 years of age, with the capability of single representations, children can take someone else's perspective only in the sense that they can understand a few of that person's characteristics or behaviors. For example, they can understand that a doctor wears a white coat and gives injections. When they pretend that they are a doctor by acting out these behaviors, they are demonstrating a simple type of perspective-taking. Children able to relate representations (at the second level) are capable of perspective-taking in a much stronger sense. They can understand the difference between another person's perspective and their own, as long as they need to keep track of only one or two simple, concrete factors (Whitehurst & Sonnenschein 1978). In the secret-toy task, from the child's viewpoint the choice of toy is not a secret because she helped choose it. She can understand that the adult who also helped choose it shares her viewpoint, and that the adult who was unable to see the choice does not share her viewpoint. Thus, by 4 or 5 years of age, most children have taken a major step away from egocentrism.

Memory

To understand someone else's perspective, and to carry out any other preoperational scheme, the child must be able to remember things—what doctors do, who knows about the secret toy and who does not, what the mountain looks

Figure 7-5 In one of the most common tests of memory, subjects try to repeat a list of numbers or simple words immediately after hearing it. The number of items a subject is able to repeat accurately is one indication of his memory span. This simple test is part of many IQ tests. You can see here that this kind of memory span develops with age to a maximum of about eight items. At about age 4, children have a span of about four unrelated items. (Case 1980; Chi 1978)

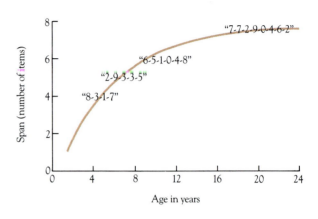

like from the other side. Memory is the ability to encode information, store it, and retrieve it. Generally, memory is described as being of two kinds: short-term and long-term. Information retrieved within a few seconds or minutes of its being encoded is said to be processsed by **short-term memory,** which is also called working memory. Information retrieved days or weeks or years after its being encoded is said to be processed by **long-term memory.** Preschoolers can use both short- and long-term memory. When they have heard a brief list of words or seen a small group of pictures presented by an experimenter, 4- and 5-year-olds can often recall them—immediately after presentation—as well as older children can (Browne & Campione 1972). And their long-term memory is sometimes amazing. Riva, at 4 years of age, went to the supermarket with an adult friend visiting from out of town. Hoping to save time, the friend tentatively asked Riva where the meat counter was. When she easily pointed the way, he asked her about the other items on the shopping list, one by one, and she pointed out the correct location for almost all of them. When 3½-year-old Joshua went to visit some new friends of his mother, they offered him a piece of toast with two kinds of jelly (grape and raspberry). He did not see them again until a year later, but the first thing he said when he walked into the house was, "Can I have a piece of toast with two kinds of jelly?"

No matter how young, all children can remember, but there are developmental changes in memory from infancy through the preschool period and beyond. For example, the ability to repeat back a list of words or numbers soon after hearing them increases as shown in Figure 7-5. However, better memory does not mean only that more items can be remembered. There is also a change in the kinds of things that children can remember and in how they can use their memories. All these changes are related to cognitive developments: the increasing ability to focus attention, the ability to connect ideas with each other in a more logical way, and the ability to devise strategies for remembering.

Infants remember sensorimotor actions, such as how to suck on their pacifiers and how to slap the bathwater so that it makes a good splash. By 2 years of age, most children can recall events that they can understand with schemes at the first preoperational level—single representations. In one experiment, the researcher showed individual 2-year-olds a doll performing an action, such as walking across the table, drinking from a cup, or washing itself (Watson & Fischer 1977). Half an hour later, most of the children were able to recall which action the doll had performed. At home, children this age recall where they left their blanket, who came to visit the day before, or which game their grandmother especially likes to play with them. What they cannot remember are sequences of items or complex social interactions, and they cannot monitor their own memory.

As early as 3 years of age, children begin to understand that they have a memory. Even more important, they can do things to help themselves remember better. In one study, 2- and 3-year-olds were asked to remember which of several cups a toy dog was hidden under, while the experimenter left the room to fetch something. Whereas 2-year-olds seemed unable to devise any strategy for remembering, 3-year-olds used a seemingly obvious one: During the delay, they kept their gaze on the cup that was covering the toy or they touched it (Wellman et al. 1975).

By 4 or 5 years, when they are in the second preoperational level, children can remember sequences of representations that are related to each other. They can remember sequences of objects, such as the order of clothes on a clothesline, the order of pictures in a series, or the order of items on a supermarket shelf (A. Brown et al. 1983). They can also recall sequences of social interactions, such as a story in which one character acts mean and then another acts mean in return (Hand 1981).

In addition, 4- and 5-year-olds can begin to employ strategies for remembering that use relations of representations. For example, when a child knows she will be expected to recall something at a later time, she may ask an adult to remember the item too, as if making a deposit in the adult's memory bank for later withdrawal: "Mommie, I'm putting the mittens in the pocket" (Kreutzer et al. 1975). Another strategy children use is to make a drawing of the item they need to recall. The fact that they use such strategies reveals a growth in sophistication. A child who asks her parent to remember something for her has a good idea—an accurate representation—of what a memory is and how it functions, and she has connected her representation of her own need to remember with her representation of her mother's ability to remember.

Although memory improves throughout childhood, important developmental changes in it take place during the preschool years. Just as with perspective taking, a major advance in memory abilities seems to begin at about 4 or 5 years of age, when children start to be able to recall items of some complexity and when they begin to try to monitor and manipulate their own memories.

Play

Preschool children love to play. They spend hours building and knocking down towers or houses or fences; they play house; they draw and paint pictures; they act out stories with their playmates or dolls. In most cultures and classes, they spend so much of their time in play that developmentalists commonly call the span between ages 2 and 6 the period of play (Rubin et al. 1983; Weisler & McCall 1976). Play is clearly a species-specific characteristic of human children as well as of immature members of some other species (Vandenberg 1978). Play among monkeys and chimpanzees is important for their learning the social patterns of the group and the control of aggression (Harlow 1971).

In infancy, play that the baby initiates is composed mainly of circular reactions—repeated actions, sometimes with variations, such as letting go of toys and dropping them or playing peek-a-boo (see Chapter 5, page 225). In the preschool years, play expands into much of the child's life. Preschoolers love to play games that test and fine-tune their mastery of their bodies—running, climbing, swinging, throwing, and, later, with increased motor control, catching. They like to build things with mud or blocks or cardboard cartons. They like to doodle or draw (see the essay "Learning to Draw"). And they love to pretend—play make-believe games (Fein 1979).

Preschool children love to make believe about all kinds of things—their everyday concerns, new things they have learned, imagined adventure. A boy who has been trying to persuade his mother that he no longer needs an afternoon nap lies down on the grass at 1:30, eyes closed, and at 1:31 proudly informs his mother that he has already had his rest. A girl rising high in the air on a swing makes airplane noises and pretends she is a huge jet taking off into the blue. A boy who is drawing pictures makes them part of a pretend game: He says this drawing is a person, even though he knows it does not look like one, and that drawing is a house, though it is barely recognizable.

During the preschool years, children gradually play less by themselves and more with other children. At 2 years of age, *solitary play* is common. Whether the child makes a tower of blocks, rolls and retrieves a ball, or dresses a doll, she commonly does so by herself. Social play with other children is also frequent, but interaction remains simple, as in the elementary give-and-take in the conversation over toy telephones in Figure 7-6 (Lee 1975).

Parallel play is seen in 2-year-olds and it becomes common by age 3: A child is influenced by the activities of the child next to her, but the two do not actually cooperate in accomplishing a task. For example, both children may play with blocks, but they are unlikely to work together to build the same structure.

AN INTERACTION BETWEEN TWO 2-YEAR-OLDS
HOLDING TOY TELEPHONES:

Jennifer: Hello Mommy.	*Molly:* Hello Douggy.
Molly: Hello Daddy.	*Jennifer:* Hello Do-Do.
Jennifer: Hello Johnny.	*Molly:* Hello Po-Po.

Figure 7-6 Social interaction in the pretend play of 2-year-olds is typically very simple. One common pattern is to carry out variations on a simple theme.

Figure 7-7 Four-year-olds can play pretend games that reflect their new understanding of social categories. Here it appears that "mother" has invited a friend over for coffee and a little small talk.

Children playing in parallel interact much more than was once believed (Mueller & Vandell 1979). Often, they actually seem to be imitating each other. As described in Chapter 5, imitation plays an important social function for young children; it is a way of establishing friendly social relations (Uzgiris 1981). When children playing in parallel imitate each other, they are in fact participating in a close social interaction.

As the complexity of children's representations increases, so does the complexity of their play, both solitary and social. At about 4 years of age, children get better at taking another person's point of view because of the development

RESEARCH:

LEARNING TO DRAW

These ten drawings are from a collection of more than 600 that were made by one child, Randy, between the ages of 3½ and 5½. Randy's father, psychologist Larry Fenson, carefully observed his child's progress from the time the boy first showed an interest in drawing (Fenson 1977, 1978). He had his son explain each picture as he was drawing it and charted the changes in Randy's artwork during the two-year period.

Randy's drawing demonstrates the same basic process that seems to occur in all areas of development, as described by Jerome Bruner (1971, 1973) and others. The child masters individual skills, in this case components of drawing, and then tries out various combinations of them. The combinations then lead to new, more complex skills.

Figure A is one of the first drawings Randy made. As he worked on it, he described in detail the "person" that he was drawing, and the parts of the person are labeled here as Randy described them. The rudiments of the drawing skills that Randy developed in the first few months are already evident in this drawing: curved lines, which quickly developed into circles and ovals (Figure B); long lines with short lines crossing them, like railroad tracks; straight lines with sharp angles, which developed into squares and rectangles (Figure C). Other skills that developed early included filling in figures such as ovals and squares (Figure C) and drawing figures that looked like sunbursts (Figure D). A few months later, Randy developed some new skills, such as enclosure. For example, in Figure E, which he called a flower garden, he drew an enclosure around a variation on tracks. Randy spent several months practicing these simple skills.

Then, about 4 months after he had started drawing, Randy began to combine a number of these simple patterns to form drawings recognizable as a person or object, like the track-circle-sunburst-oval-filled-in person in Figure F. He spent a lot of time practicing these combinations and then one day picked up and copied a man drawn by his brother, who is 3 years older than Randy. In making this copy, Randy began to add hands and feet to his drawings of people, as Figure G shows. Notice that, even in copying, Randy still used the

A

basic patterns that he had developed: For example, the hands are variations on tracks, the head is an enclosure, the eyes and body are rectangles.

For the first 11 months, Randy's drawings all showed increasing mastery and refinement of specific skills and more and more sophisticated combinations of those skills to make figures, especially of people. Then, at the age of 4 years and 5 months, another kind of developmental change took place in the drawings: Randy drew Figure H, a man carrying two suitcases. This was the first time he had drawn a person *doing* something. Starting with this figure, his drawings became more and more storylike, depicting integrated scenes with a number of related objects or people. For example, Figure I shows a mommy and a daddy inside a house. At about the same time that Randy began to represent several related objects or people in his drawings, he also began to show the same kinds of related elements in finger painting, block construction, paper cutouts, and other tasks. Apparently, Randy was beginning to be able to control relations between representations. During the second year of drawing, much of his effort went into mastering and elaborating such relations (see figure J).

Randy's drawings thus illustrate how the developing child "builds" pictures just as he builds all his skills. Elementary components come first: tracks, ovals, sunbursts. Then he combines those components to form representations: drawings of people and objects. And finally he combines the representations to make scenes or stories. The construction of complex skills by combining simpler skills seems to be basic to all behavioral development.

B

C

D

E

F

G

H

I

J

of the second preoperational level of intelligence, and their play becomes much more social. **Cooperative play** begins to predominate (Smith 1978; Weisler & McCall 1976). Now several children will create a city of blocks together (though arguments over who should add which block and when to knock it all down are likely). Or they will play a game of house in which each child takes the role of a family member, and together they act out daily events.

Whether a 4-year-old child is alone or with other children, the content of her play tends to reflect her new level of understanding. For example, social categories such as mother and father become a central focus of play (Lee 1975). Also, the child begins to be able to play games with simple rules, such as crude versions of marbles or hopscotch.

At any age, children's concerns and problems are clearly evident in their pretend play. Suppose that 3-year-old Debby is having some difficulty with toilet training. Like most preschool children, she wants mightily to be called "big" and "child" instead of "little" and "baby": Children wear underpants and use the toilet, whereas babies mess in their pants and have to wear diapers. So whenever Debby has an accident, she is upset with herself. Sometimes, she can be heard in her crib at night, saying to her teddy bear, "Bear has to go potty. Bear has to go wee-wee. . . . Good bear, you're a big bear. You're not a baby." As a solution to many of their concerns and problems, preschool children commonly go beyond merely making Bear go potty—they invent an imaginary playmate. The playmate may take the blame for naughty things the child does or protect her from monsters in the dark or do all the things that she cannot yet do herself (Singer 1973; Pines 1978).

Play, like fantasy in adults, provides a time when children can control things themselves. They can concern themselves more with their own needs, desires, and fears and less with parental demands and reality (Piaget 1951). That is why psychotherapists use play with children to assess what is troubling them and to help them deal with their problems (Harter 1983).

Complexive Thinking and Primary Process

Because play is mostly under the child's control, it shows clearly some of the peculiarities of preoperational thought—its intuitive, prelogical qualities. Preschool children usually have difficulty controlling or coordinating their thoughts. When they can control only single representations, their thinking tends to wander from one thought to another. Even during the second preoperational level, when they are capable of representational relations, they can deal with only the simplest, crudest connections between ideas, so their thoughts still tend to wander.

One result of these difficulties is a kind of thought known as **complexive thinking,** the stringing together of ideas that have no unifying concept or system (Vygotsky 1962). For example, 2-year-old Ruth plays quietly by herself, half-singing, half-saying, "Mind the music and the band and the Band-aid. Ouch!" Although Ruth's ditty seems incoherent, it does have connections. She had begun to sing a line from the song "Yankee Doodle," which goes: "Mind the music and the step and with the girls be handy." But when Ruth says "Mind the music," she thinks of a band, which makes music; the word "band" reminds her of Band-aids, and Band-aids remind her of being hurt. There are connections between some of the ideas, especially those that are next to each other, but no single concept ties them all together.

A poem written by Hilary-Anne Farley, age 5, illustrates a longer sequence of complexive thinking:

Sun Goes Up

I love the juice, but the sun goes up; I see the stars
And the moonstar goes up,
And there always goes today. And the sun
Loves people. But one always dies.
Dogs will die very sooner
Than mummies and daddies and sisters and
Brothers because
They'll not die till a hundred and
Because I love them dearly.

This poem shows other qualities of preoperational thought as well. For example, Hilary-Anne asserts that her family will live long because she loves them dearly. This statement shows a preschooler's egocentrism—she thinks that her own wishes can affect events. When she states that the sun loves people, she expresses a characteristic of preoperational thought called *personification* (or animism), the attribution of human characteristics to objects (Werner 1948). Lialia, 2½ years old, is walking on the beach and sees a ship in the distance. She calls out, "Mommy, Mommy, the ship is taking a bath!" Three-year-old George, asked why he has cut a worm in two, says, "The worm was lonesome. Now there are two of them—it is more cheerful for them that way" (Chukovsky 1968). A 4-year-old sees a cup lying on its side and says, "Poor, tired cup."

These children are not using metaphorical language, as adults do when they say "a proud ship" or "a mean storm" (Winner et al. 1976). Having only recently learned to separate their own actions from those of other people or objects, young children are not yet able to distinguish clearly between properties of objects and characteristics of people. When a ship makes them think of taking a bath or a cup makes them think of lying down to rest, they link these activities directly to the ship or the cup.

All the prelogical qualities of preoperational thought—complexive thinking, egocentrism, personification—can be seen as well in the thinking of older children and adults. When we dream or daydream, for example, we think very much like a preoperational child, according to Piaget (1951), and the thought processes of people with serious psychological disorders resemble those of preschoolers (Holt 1976). This type of adult thought is what Freud (1955) called *primary process* (see the theory inset "Psychodynamic Approaches," in Chapter 8). For instance, people and events in our dreams often shift in the course of a dream. At the beginning, a person might seem to be the dreamer's mother, then somehow the person drifts into someone else, like the dreamer's sister, and then there may be still another change, to the dreamer's best friend. Sometimes we cannot even tell who a person in a dream is, because he or she seems to be a blend of two or three people.

These preoperational qualities of the thought of older children and adults are an example of the general principle (described in the theory inset "Cognitive Development," in Chapter 5) that a person's behavior spans different developmental levels. Even in adulthood, when we like to think of ourselves as basically rational and logical, we sometimes think much as 2- or 3-year-old children do.

During the preschool years, many cognitive-developmental changes take place. Before this period, infants do not distinguish between themselves and their actions on the world. Objects exist only when the baby is acting on them or perceiving them. At about age 2, children become capable of representation, of thinking about the properties of things without having to act on them directly. This capacity marks the first level of the preoperational period. At this level, the child can deal with only one representation—one idea or thought—at a time. At the second level of the preoperational period, beginning at about age 4, children develop the ability to deal mentally with more complex things—representational relations. During the preschool years the child moves through these two levels, building increasingly complex and sophisticated schemes. The egocentric, complexive, magical thinking of infancy gradually gives way to more logical thinking—perspective taking, a better memory, and an ability to separate oneself mentally from one's immediate surroundings.

ACQUIRING LANGUAGE

The preschool years bring an incredible growth in language skills. In late infancy, as explained in Chapter 5, children learn to say a few individual words. By paying attention to context, they can also understand many of their parents' sentences. Six months to a year later, at 2 years of age, their use of language suddenly begins to increase rapidly. The size of their vocabulary increases (see Figure 7-8) and they begin to use many short sentences (Corrigan 1983; Dromi 1984). Some 2-year-olds talk constantly most of the day, even when they are

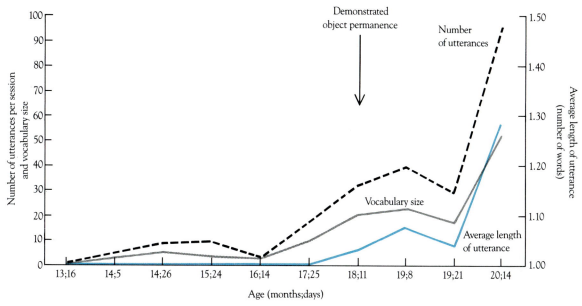

Figure 7-8 These data reflect the progress of just one child, Ashley, but they are typical of how language begins to develop. The experimenter visited Ashley—and a number of other children—for half an hour each week, beginning when the children were about 9 months old. She conducted "interviews" and also tested for object permanence (see Chapter 5). Soon after Ashley demonstrated object permanence—the understanding that objects continued to exist even when she couldn't see or touch them—her use of language increased. She talked more (the number of her utterances went way up) and the size of her vocabulary (the number of different words that she used) increased. She also began to use more two- and three-word utterances (some were "she silly cat" and "close the door"), and so the average length of her utterances rose sharply (Corrigan 1978, 1983).

alone. For the next 3 years and beyond, this language explosion continues as children master their native tongue.

In using language, we represent objects, people, and events in what we say. It should be no surprise that representation in language develops at about the same time as representation in children's imitation, play, and other actions. You will recall from Chapter 5 that uttering words is a sensorimotor ability, just as grasping and looking are (Bates 1976). Uttering individual words does not require representation. One-year-olds, who are not yet capable of representation, can often use a few dozen single words, like "no," "out," "gimme," and "momma" (Bloom 1973; Corrigan 1977). Even cats and dogs may be capable of expressing very simple symbols similar to single words. Pasque, a cat belonging to one of the authors, uses a symbol roughly equivalent to the word "yuk." Whenever she finds something unpleasant or distasteful, whether snow on the ground or a food she does not like, she shakes one of her paws.

Representation does seem to be required for organizing words into simple statements—"Truck red," "Boy hits doll," "Daddy goes bye-bye now" (Bates 1976; Corrigan 1983; Nicolich 1981). Single representations seem to be enough for understanding many simple rules of language, such as the possessive ("Daddy's," "Sam's") and the order of subject before verb ("Boy hits dolly", "I run"). But certain kinds of rules that older children and adults follow cannot be learned by children who can make only single representations. These rules seem to require, at the least, the ability to relate representations to each other (Ingram 1975, Karmiloff-Smith 1979). For example, only at 4 or 5 years do most children begin to use simple polite forms of request, such as "Please give me a little candy" (Bates 1976). To learn this rule for polite discourse, it seems, they must understand the perspective of the person who has the candy. This is not possible before the second level of preoperational intelligence.

Most research on language development has focused on how children acquire the rules that govern our use of language, from its sensorimotor beginnings on. The two types of rules that have been most investigated are rules for communicating in social contexts and grammatical rules for combining words.

Learning Rules for Communicating: Pragmatics

Many of the language rules that children must learn amount to social conventions. When two people talk, for example, they are supposed to take turns: First one person speaks, then the other, and so forth. Even infants in the first year of life seem to follow this rule when someone speaks to them (Kaye 1982). The adult says something; then the infant vocalizes, perhaps in a crude imitation of the adult's sounds; then the adult speaks again, and again the infant vocalizes.

How people use speech in social contexts is called **pragmatics.** Most of the rules are so automatic for adults that we are not even aware that we follow them. In adult speech, for instance, some expressive devices tell the listener not to take what is being said literally. One such device is sarcasm. Another is the use of a question as an indirect request. If you are shivering and say to your roommate, "Is that window still open?" you do not expect him or her merely to answer "Yes." Your words are a request that he or she close the window, and an adult generally realizes that. Young children do not understand such indirect requests, because of their egocentrism and social inexperience. Ask a 3-year-old, "Have you put your tricycle away yet?" and he probably will answer "No" and go on about his business, unaware that the question was intended more as a reminder than as a request for information.

For children, especially very young ones, the simpler pragmatic functions of language are often much more important than the specific meanings of sentences. When preschool children who speak English meet in small groups with preschool children who speak some other language, they may play together for days without seeming to notice that they are speaking different languages. In an exchange observed by one of the authors, an English-speaking 4-year-old walked up with his truck to a French-speaking 3-year-old and spoke in English. The 3-year-old answered in French and they proceeded to play, continuing to speak English and French to each other and acting as if they both understood—

DENNIS the MENACE

"OF COURSE I got a home, Mr. Wilson! You know that!"

Figure 7-9 Dennis displays his lack of pragmatic sophistication.

taking turns, nodding agreement, and so forth. The pragmatic rules in what was being said were similar in English and French, and the meaning of words was generally obvious from the context and from other nonverbal cues such as tone of voice. Only after several days of playing together did the two boys spontaneously note, "Hey, he doesn't speak the same language."

Another conversational convention that is beyond the ability of a young preschool child is the rule that what is being said should be interesting to the listener as well as to the speaker. Because children in the early preoperational period are prisoners of their own viewpoint, they think that what interests them interests everyone. They cannot take account of what might be new or interesting to the listener. For example, they very frequently report their own ongoing actions (Kohlberg et al. 1968; Vygotsky 1962). A child putting a toy into a toy box says "toy in box." Another, sitting at the table and eating some tapioca, says "I eating ioca." A child climbing up on a chair says "up chair." Just imagine an adult indulging in similar self-commentary: "I am sitting down now. I am drinking my coffee."

The egocentrism that leads to endless self-reporting also causes children to assume that other people know what they themselves know. They frequently conduct a conversation as though it were a monologue, changing the subject

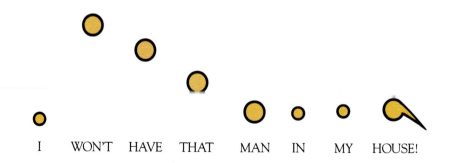

I   WON'T   HAVE   THAT   MAN   IN   MY   HOUSE!

Figure 7-10 Every language has a unique pitch and stress in the way its sentences are spoken. Children learn this aspect of their native language even before they can use words. (See the discussion of expressive jargon in Chapter 5.) Symbols like these, created by linguists, are used to help non-English speakers learn English intonation. The size of a dot indicates how much a syllable is stressed, and the higher the dot, the higher the pitch. The tear-shaped symbols indicate that the pitch changes (falls, in these sentences) while the syllable is uttered (O'Connor & Arnold 1961).

without seeming to be aware of their listener's responses. Starting at about 4 years of age, children begin to handle some of the pragmatic rules that were so difficult when they were younger. When they chatter, they less often just describe what they are doing at the moment. And they are much more inclined to take into account their listener's knowledge and responses.

A well-documented developmental change takes place in pragmatic skill with the rules for polite forms of request. To understand what is polite, one must, of course, consider the viewpoint of another person. In requesting something, older children and adults do not usually say, "Give me some" or even "Give me some?" Instead, to find favor with the possible giver, they use such polite forms as "Would you please . . .?" or "May I have . . .?" or "Could I please have . . .?" These rules are similar in many languages, including English and Italian.

In one study, Italian children ranging in age from 3 to 7 years were told that if they asked the experimenter's puppet, Mrs. Rossi, for candy, she would give them some (Bates 1976). After the children asked for candy the first time, the experimenter had a whispered conversation with the puppet and then said to each child, "Mrs. Rossi wants to give you a piece of candy, but she likes children to ask very, very nicely. Could you ask her once again, even nicer?"

Few 3-year-olds changed their requests at all. Some of the 4- and 5-year olds added "Please" to their original requests, but others only repeated their request in a whisper or asked for less candy: "Give me just a little candy." None of the children used the forms, "Would you give me a candy?" or "I would like to have a candy." In fact, only the children who were about 6 seemed to recognize these forms as nicer ways of making a request.

Not until 6 or 7 years of age do children easily make more subtle requests such as "Gee, it's a long time since I had some candy." They can probably be taught this kind of indirect request earlier, at 4 or 5, because they can begin to understand perspectives then. But only later, when they understand perspectives easily, do these subtle requests seem to come to them naturally.

Thus, children can be only as polite as their cognitive abilities permit them to be. If parents insist that a 3-year-old say "May I please have. . . ." when requesting something, they are likely to be frustrated. The child might be able

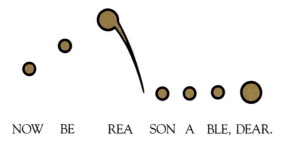

NOW   BE   REA   SON   A   BLE, DEAR.

to learn the sentence by rote, but he or she will not understand its purpose and so will have difficulty using it properly.

Learning Rules for Speaking

Besides rules for communicating in social contexts, preschool children also learn **grammatical rules** for speech—how to form words, phrases, and sentences. As children develop, it becomes increasingly important for them to be able to express such states and relations as possession ("That's my ball"), negation ("No, it's not"), past action ("My mother gave it to me"), and conditional action ("We could play if you brought the ball"). Words must be put together in the proper way if they are to express the meaning that a child intends: "Harry hit Susie" means something different from "Susie hit Harry."

One of the most basic grammatical rules is that language is spoken in sentences. A speaker gives each group of words constituting a sentence a certain pitch and stress, so that listeners can distinguish one sentence from the next. In English, speakers generally drop the pitch at the end of a statement and raise it at the end of certain questions, as shown in Figure 7-10. By age 1, most children recognize these intonation patterns and use them to divide up what they hear into groups of sounds.

Even with speech divided up into such segments, it is an enormous chore for a child to make sense of even one sentence in the flow of spoken language that he hears. According to the linguist Noam Chomsky (1957, 1965), children could not learn language at all if it were not for special adaptations of the human species for acquiring language. Just to learn that the simple past tense in English is formed by adding "ed" to the verb, for instance, a child must do at least three things. First, he must have some understanding of how events happen in time, so that he can distinguish between now and before now. Second, he must be able to divide the stream of sound that he hears into words, which is no easy task. Third, he must listen to how other people express past action and abstract from their examples a general rule for the past tense (Karmiloff-Smith 1984; MacWhinney 1978).

Once he has found a possible rule, he must try it out to see whether other people understand his intended meaning. They do understand when he says "walked" and "dropped" and even "goed," so the child continues to apply this rule for the simple past tense. In effect, he has constructed the rule himself. No one ever says to a 3-year-old, "Add 'ed' to the end of verbs to form the simple past tense." If anyone did, he wouldn't understand. The child cannot state the rule, even approximately, but he knows how to use it.

If all peoples spoke the same language, the process of acquiring language might not seem so complex and mysterious. We might be thought to inherit a tendency to form the past tense with "ed," and so on. But each language has its own rules for forming words, phrases, and sentences. It is clear that children are not born with the ability to learn a particular language, so how do they learn these complicated rules? To answer this question, psycholinguists have studied how children learn to speak in more than 40 different languages, ranging from English to Russian to Samoan to Japanese.

Operating Principles   Some scientists explain the language-learning process by assuming that we all inherit certain species-specific strategies for perceiving speech. Dan Slobin (1973, 1979) calls these strategies *operating principles.* Three of the most important are described below. The idea of operating principles for language is very similar to the idea that newborns have rules for visual scanning, proposed by Marshall Haith and described in Chapter 4. Haith's scanning rules suggest that newborns scan their visual environment in ways that provide the best all-around visual experience. Slobin's operating principles suggest that young children listen to the language they hear in ways that help them discover meaning. These strategies for perceiving speech then make it easier to form rules for producing speech.

OPERATING PRINCIPLE: PAY ATTENTION TO THE ENDS OF WORDS. Many languages express important grammatical meanings by the endings of words. In English, plurals are expressed by adding "s" or "es" to singular nouns, and possession is signaled by a final " 's." Many verbs and adjectives can be changed into nouns by such endings as "ing" ("mean, meaning"), "er" ("listen, listener"), and "ness" ("big, bigness").

OPERATING PRINCIPLE: PAY ATTENTION TO THE ORDER OF WORDS AND WORD SEGMENTS. In English, the standard word order is subject–verb–object, as in "The dog licks the cat." However, some sentences have a different order, as in the passive voice: "The cat is licked by the dog." Young preschool children construct the word-order rule that applies to the vast majority of simple English sentences and ignore the exceptions. When they hear the passive voice, their sticking to standard word order causes them to confuse object and subject. In one study, 3½-year-olds were asked to choose a picture that showed an action expressed in a passive sentence. When the sentence was "The boy is pushed by the girl," virtually all the children chose the picture showing the boy pushing the girl (Fraser et al. 1963).

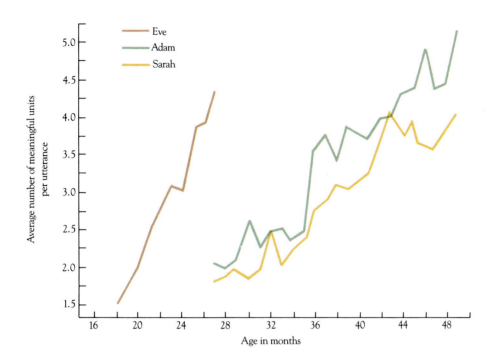

Figure 7-11 The early language development of Adam, Eve, and Sarah was studied intensively by Roger Brown and his colleagues. This chart shows how the three children's utterances grew longer from age 2 to age 4. Each utterance was analyzed into meaningful units (called morphemes by linguists). For example, "Dada going now" contains four meaningful units, because "go" is one unit and "ing" another. Note that Eve acquired language much earlier than Adam and Sarah. Such individual differences are common (R. Brown 1973).

OPERATING PRINCIPLE: AVOID EXCEPTIONS TO LANGUAGE RULES. The misinterpretation of passive sentences illustrates a third operating principle. Children tend to construct a general rule and then use it for everything. Just as they stick to the standard word order when they interpret passive sentences, they use the rule for simple past tense for all verbs: "I goed out without my coat," "I breaked my kite," "I swimmed under water, Mom!"

These operating principles help explain two of the best-known characteristics of children's early speech—telegraphic speech and overregularization.

Telegraphic Speech   Two-year-olds leave out most of the words that an adult would use to express something, saying only the two or three words most important to a sentence's meaning. This early speech has been called **telegraphic** because it resembles the compressed message of a telegram: "Daddy car," a child will say, rather than "Daddy is going to get into the car." The average length of a preschooler's sentences increases steadily with the passage of time, as shown in Figure 7-11.

In English speech, word order is very important, so a young English-speaking child's telegraphic speech almost always follows the rules for word order. If he means "I am playing the drum," he usually says "Play drum," not "Drum play."

In some languages, word order is less important than in English and more variable. Telegraphic speech in these languages is less likely to take account of word order. In Russian, for example, word endings are extremely important and

TABLE 7-1 MEANINGS EXPRESSED IN TELEGRAPHIC SPEECH

MEANING (GRAMMATICAL RELATION)	CHILD'S STATEMENT	SITUATION
NOMINATION (naming; demonstrating existence of)	this necklace	Child is looking at microphone around her neck.
RECURRENCE	more block	Child is taking another block from box.
	'nother wet	Child just wet her pants again.
NEGATION		
Nonexistence	no pocket	Child could not find a pocket in her mother's skirt.
Rejection	no dirty soap	Child pushes away a sliver of soap offered her.
Denial	no dirty	Child is holding up a sock.
AGENT AND ACTION	man cry	A toy man just fell off a toy train.
ACTION AND OBJECT	play it	Child is holding a toy drum.
AGENT AND OBJECT	mommy apple	Mother is giving some apple to the child.
MODIFIER	little mommy	After putting the figure of a mother on a board, the child is putting the figure of a girl there, a little mommy.
POSSESSION	dolly hat	Child points at doll's hat.
LOCATION	cow there	Child points to a cow hanging from a mobile.
LOCATION WITH VERB	throw away	Child is trying to shake a rubber band off her hand.

SOURCE: Adapted from Bloom 1973.

can express many meanings that would be expressed through word order in English. To say "I play the drum" in Russian involves adding an ending to "drum" to show that it is the object of the verb. The word "drum" can thus be placed in different positions in a sentence; because of the ending, its role as the object of the verb doesn't change. Russian 2-year-olds learn the important word endings very early and use those endings in their telegraphic speech, whereas

English-speaking 2-year-olds know hardly any word endings. Russian children are also much more likely to use varying word orders to express the same meaning in their telegraphic speech (Slobin 1973, 1982).

Telegraphic speech in different languages has many variations, but there are also many similarities. In virtually all languages, children using telegraphic speech leave out certain kinds of words: articles ("the," "a," "an"), prepositions ("in," "on," "under," "through"), conjunctions ("and," "but," "because," "when"), and parts of nouns and verbs that mark relatively subtle changes in meaning. They say, for example, "Man cry" when they mean "The man is crying."

Because telegraphic sentences leave out so much, they are generally ambiguous. "Mommy sock" could mean "This is Mommy's sock" or "Mommy has a sock" or "Mommy, put my sock on." If an adult is paying careful attention, however, he or she can usually infer the meaning of the child's telegraphic statements from knowing the child and from the context of conversation. If a girls says "Mommy dock," the adult needs to know first that "dock" is the child's way of saying "sock." If the girl is pointing to one of her mother's stockings, the adult can infer that she probably means "This is Mommy's sock." If she says "Mommy sock" while her mother is dressing her, she probably means "Mommy is putting my sock on" (Bloom 1970, 1973). Examples of the range of meanings conveyed by telegraphic speech are given in Table 7-1.

Overregularization   Among the first things English-speaking children add as their speech becomes less telegraphic are simple endings such as "s" or "es" for plurals and "ed" for the past tense of verbs. Even 2-year-olds use these endings (Brown 1973). At this point, their use of one operating principle becomes especially obvious: Avoid exceptions to language rules. The result is ***overregularization,*** applying a language rule to a word or phrase that does not follow the rule, as in "I goed out and throwed my ball at those gooses." This overregularization is strong evidence that a child knows the rule. Because adults almost never use such forms as "goed" and "gooses," the child could not have learned the words from having heard adults say them (Platt & MacWhinney 1983).

In learning each rule of their language, children seem to go through four phases (Slobin 1979). The age at which they move through each phase depends on the rule being learned, because some rules are learned as early as age 2 and others not until much later. In the first phase of learning the English rule for the simple past tense, for example, children use telegraphic language. At this time, they simply do not employ the rule. A child who has just broken a dish will say "Drop it" or "Break it," even though the action is past. In the second phase the child uses the correct form for some words, perhaps saying "I dropped it." or "I broke it." But rather than having learned the rule, he has just memorized the past forms of some verbs (Berman 1984; MacWhinney 1978).

In the third phase, the child has learned the rule but overgeneralizes it: "I dropped it," "I breaked it." In the previous phase, this same child mechanically used the correct irregular form "broke," but because he now knows the rule and seeks to avoid exceptions, he changes to the incorrect, regular form. Children often resist correction of these forms by adults, as in the following dialogue (Cazden 1968):

Child: My teacher holded the baby rabbits and we patted them.
Mother: Did you say that your teacher held the baby rabbits?
Child: Yes.
Mother: What did you say she did?
Child: She holded the baby rabbits and we patted them.
Mother: Did you say she held them tightly?
Child: No, she holded them loosely.

Eventually, in the final phase, the child uses the correct forms, including both regulars and irregulars: "I dropped it," "I broke it." Still, he may occasionally return to overregularization, especially when it seems needed for clarity:

Dan (age 5):   I found it, Dad!
Father: You what?
Dan: I found it.
Father: What? I didn't hear you.
Dan: I finded it!

Irregular verbs and many other exceptions to language rules are not fully mastered until a child is about 7 or 8 (C. Chomsky 1969; MacWhinney 1978). A few particularly difficult or uncommon rules may take even longer.

Simple Rules Develop First   Children who speak the same language seem to acquire its rules in a similar order: Rules that are simple and used often are acquired first; more complex rules and combinations of rules, later on (Slobin 1982). Samuel, a 2-year-old, uttered the following sentences in the space of 20 or 30 seconds:

Mommy car.
Mommy go?
Go bye-bye?
Jenny come play.
Come play blocks.

Why, instead of "Mommy go" and then "Go bye-bye," didn't Samuel just say "Mommy go bye-bye"? And why not "Jennie come play blocks," instead of "Jennie come play" and "Come play blocks"? The answer is that the single longer sentences require the ability to combine grammatical rules. "Mommy go" uses one rule, for making a subject-verb phrase. "Go bye-bye" uses another, for making a verb-modifier phrase. The child who is just beginning to use these rules cannot yet put them together to form the more complex phrase "Mommy go bye-bye."

Children of 3 or 4 years can combine these simple rules and even add another (the one that says "To form the third-person singular, add "s" or "es" to the verb) to say "Mommy goes bye-bye." But they still have trouble combining more complex rules in a single sentence. For example, there are several ways in English to turn a statement into a question. For a question requiring an answer of yes or no, the speaker reverses the order of the subject and the auxiliary verb. "He will walk" becomes "Will he walk?" For a question beginning with "who," "what," "where," or the like, the question word comes first, followed by the auxiliary verb, the subject, and the main verb: "Where will he walk?" Young children who use questions of the first type—"Will he walk?"—often cannot quite manage questions of the second type. They ask "Where he will walk?" They can apparently add the question word at the beginning of the declarative sentence *or* transpose the subject and auxiliary verb, but they cannot do both in the same utterance (Brown 1968; Slobin 1979). Later, this cognitive limitation disappears.

Because the complexity of a given grammatical form can differ in different languages, the age at which children master the rule for a particular form depends partly on the language they are learning. This phenomenon is especially clear in children who learn two languages simultaneously. In Yugoslavia, for example, many children speak both Hungarian and Serbo-Croatian at home. When speaking Hungarian, these bilingual children are able to correctly express the idea of "into" by 2 years of age. They say, for example, "doll into drawer." But to make the same comment in Serbo-Croatian, they say only "doll drawer," because the rules for expressing "into" in Serbo-Croatian are more complex than in Hungarian (Slobin 1973, 1982).

Similarly, English-speaking children begin to construct compound sentences with relative clauses before their third birthday. All they have to do is tack the relative clause onto the end of the main clause. For instance, "I want the doll" + "that Daddy bought." Turkish children, on the other hand, do not master that grammatical form until they are 5 or so, because to join a relative clause and a main clause they must change both word order and word endings. In essence, a Turk must say, "Daddy's boughten doll I want." To avoid this difficult construction, young Turkish children (and even some adults) usually resort to something like "Daddy bought a doll, huh? I want it." In making such statements, Turkish children show that they understand the relation between the two events—Daddy's prior purchase of a doll, and their present wish to have it—but because of the difficult grammar they cannot combine the related thoughts in a single sentence.

All languages have some such difficult constructions. An example in English

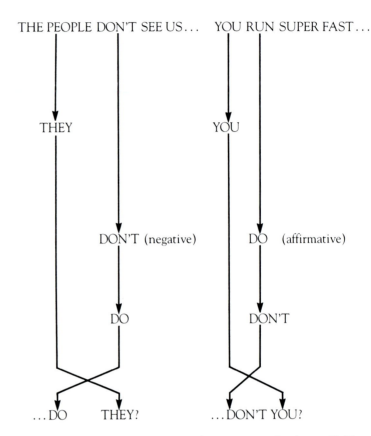

TRANSFORMATION RULES
FOR MAKING A TAG QUESTION: THE PEOPLE DON'T SEE US...   YOU RUN SUPER FAST...

1. If the subject is a noun
or a noun phrase, change it
into a pronoun.

THEY   YOU

2. Locate the auxiliary verb
or supply a missing one.
Determine whether the sentence
is affirmative or negative.

DON'T (negative)   DO   (affirmative)

3. Whichever it is, change
it to the opposite.

DO   DON'T

4. Reverse the order of the
auxiliary verb and pronoun
subject.

...DO   THEY?   ...DON'T YOU?

Figure 7-12   The
formation of tag questions
requires the mastery of the
sophisticated set of
transformational rules
shown here.
Nevertheless, many 4-
and 5-year-olds use tag
questions. The rules are
not conscious, explicit
self-instructions, of
course. No children—and
few adults—could state
them. Yet native English
speakers, even young
ones, follow the rules like
experts.

is the tag question, as in "You want a piece of pecan pie, don't you?" Tag-question forms such as "don't you?" are more complex than they might seem at first (see Figure 7-12), and they develop only at about 4 or 5 years of age. Most preschool children reduce all tag questions to a simple "huh?" (Brown & Hanlon 1970). Many other languages do not have any such complex form but only a polite form similar to "huh?"

Some grammatical forms that are not particularly difficult to understand may enter a child's speech late only because they are difficult to hear. English-speaking children learn relatively early to use the word "is," as in "Here it is," but contractions of the verb, as in "It's here," are learned later. The difference in timing is probably because in most sentences the complete word "is" is stressed and easy to hear, but the "s" sound in "it's" is not as easily perceived.

Because young children can only listen to language, not read it, they often make mistakes due to the way a word or phrase sounds. Even if they are corrected, they may insist that *their* version is right. Typical is the tenacity of a 4-year-old who was overheard firmly correcting the pronunciation of his younger brother: "Moth?" he said incredulously. "What do you mean, moth? It's not moth, Michael, it's mof."

HOW   R   YOU   WAN   YOU   GAD   I   CHANS   SAND   IS

OL   I   LADR.   AD   DOW   GT   ANE   CHRIBLS

Processes of Language Development

Many of the same processes apply both to the learning of single words in infancy and to the learning of grammatical rules: in particular, abstraction, imitation, and reinforcement.

Abstraction   As illustrated in this chapter and Chapter 5, children use abstraction to learn language rules of many kinds (Karmiloff-Smith 1984; MacWhinney 1978). In learning a grammatical rule, for instance, a child abstracts the rule by learning specific words, comparing them, and generalizing them into a rule. First he learns several related words or phrases by rote memory—in the case of the simple past tense, verbs such as "dropped," "walked," "cried". He then compares what is similar and what is different about those words or phrases; from what he perceives as similar (the "ed" sound), he generalizes to produce the rule ("jumped," "hopped," "played").

Apparently, the same process is applied to all rules. To learn how to ask questions such as "What are you doing?" the child compares a number of similar questions, such as "What is he eating," "Where are you going," and "When are we leaving?" From this comparison, he eventually sees that the question word always comes first and the subject and auxiliary verb are transposed, so that "you are doing" becomes "are you doing." Then he generalizes those rules.

Observational Learning and Reinforcement   At one time, many scientists thought that language learning could be fully explained by the behaviorist concepts of conditioning and imitation (Miller & Dollard 1941; Skinner 1957). In their view, children learn language by listening to what adults say, immediately imitating what they hear, and then having their imitation reinforced. Research has since shown, however, that although a few children do seem to learn much of their initial language through frequent, direct imitation of what adults say (Corrigan 1979), most engage in such direct imitation only occasionally. In addition, parents do not often explicitly reinforce their children's utterances for being grammatically correct but focus instead on correct meaning (Brown & Hanlon 1970).

Although imitation and reinforcement alone are not enough to explain the acquisition of language, these processes make important contributions, as social-learning theorists emphasize (Bullock 1983).

Figure 7-13 A few preschoolers start writing before they have had any formal instruction in reading and writing. From adults reading to them and from playing with alphabet blocks and the like, children learn that letters can be matched to sounds. Their own spelling inventions then tell us something about what they hear and about the rules that they create. This message was written by a 4-year-old. It says, "How are you? When you get a chance, send us all a letter. And don't get any troubles." The child's use of "chribls" for "troubles" seems bizarre at first, but if you sound it out, you can see how he came by the spelling. Listen carefully to the "t" in "truck" and compare it to the "t" in "tuck." Then say "troubles" and "chroubles" and compare the sounds. This "mistake" reveals that the child, in learning language, is trying to find out what the rules are by listening, comparing, and abstracting for himself.

FOR BETTER OR FOR WORSE

Preschool children are capable of deferred imitation; they do not need to imitate something immediately in order to learn it. They can remember it and imitate it some time later. As explained in Chapter 6, this learning process, called **observational learning** (Bandura 1969), involves cognition and is not automatic or mechanical. What a child can learn through observation (and then imitate) depends on what he can understand (Clark 1977; DeVilliers & DeVilliers 1978). The possibilities for learning therefore expand with the child's cognitive abilities, although each age still has its limits. The following dialogue between a dejected 3½-year-old and her mother is an example of such limits (Nelson 1973):

> *Child:*   Nobody don't like me.
> *Mother:* No, say "Nobody likes me."
> *Child:*   Nobody don't like me.
> (Eight repetitions of this dialogue)
> *Mother:* No, now listen carefully; say "Nobody likes me."
> *Child:*   Oh! Nobody don't likes me.

Apparently the child's rule for forming a negative sentence with "nobody" as its subject did not permit her to follow her mother's example at this time.

The direct corrections issued by the mother in the preceding dialogue are fairly rare in parent-child interactions. More commonly, adults try to help young speakers by using **expansions,** in which they repeat the child's statement in an expanded or slightly different form (Brown et al. 1969; Snow & Ferguson 1977). Just as in infancy, this imitation of the child by the adult both aids social interaction with the child, as discussed in Chapter 6, and makes an important contribution to the child's developing skills.

In one study, 2½-year-olds interacted with an adult who systematically expanded the child's utterances, as in the following two examples (Nelson 1977). The child and adult were playing together with various toys.

Child: You can't get in.
Adult: No, I can't get in, can I?"

Child: I got it. I reached it.
Adult: You got in under the bed and reached it.

Encounters of these kinds were observed during five one-hour periods spread over two months. In one group of children, the adult concentrated on expanding the children's statements into questions, as in the first example. In another group, the adult concentrated on verbs, as in the second example, in which two verbs were combined in a single sentence. All children showed an improvement in their use of the type of grammatical form that was expanded for their group, and very few showed improvement in the other type. In interactions of this kind, the adult seldom reinforces the child directly by saying "That's good" or "Right" or something similar, and the child does not often directly imitate the adult. But the child seems to learn by the process of observing what the adult says (Furrow et al. 1979).

For children to learn to speak, it is clearly not necessary for their parents to explicitly shape the children's utterances by reinforcement. In fact, parents typically attend to the content of what their children say rather than its grammar (Brown & Hanlon 1970). When a child says "I finded a tiger," the adult's response usually depends on whether the toy the child has found is actually a tiger, not on whether the child has used the correct past tense of "find." Reinforcement is nevertheless important to speech. In one study, for example, 2- and 3-year-olds who were several months behind in their cognitive and language development were reinforced systematically by their parents for saying anything at all and especially for using more advanced speech (Zelazo et al. 1979). The parents would say "That's right" or "Good girl" or would even cheer and applaud the child's speech. As a result of this reinforcement, most of the children showed a major spurt in their language development, in many cases catching up to or surpassing the norms for their age. Parents ordinarily use reinforcement in a similar way as part of their procedures for teaching language (Moerck 1976).

Equally important, children are reinforced by successful communication, and communication with well-formed words and sentences is usually much more successful than communication without words or with poorly formed sentences. For many children, the main reinforcement for their increasingly sophisticated use of language seems to be better communication of their wishes or intentions or love. Although Debbie, 21 months old, may not always receive a cookie when she says "Debbie need cookie," she will receive one often enough to make it worth her while. In any case, someone will usually respond to Debbie's utterance, saying why she can't have a cookie—thereby letting Debbie know that her request was understood—and that is itself reinforcing. When 19-month-old Ruth (precocious in language development) toddles over to her mother and says, "Ruthie wet her diaper. Soaking wet. Change her diaper. Clean diaper," she is clearly communicating her needs (Church 1966). And Ruth quickly gets a clean diaper. And after Ruth has been scolded for some misdeed, she comes over, puts her head in her mother's lap, and says, "Love, Mommie." Love is a word Ruth undoubtedly learned by hearing her mother and father use it with her and with each other, and she knows its reinforcing properties. She has the basic trust that her parents love her, and with words, she can communicate her love for them verbally—reinforcement indeed.

A Special Sensitivity to Language

Preschool children are obsessed with language. They listen to it carefully, and they chatter away to the best of their ability for hours on end. During a few short years, they acquire a large vocabulary and master most of the rules for speaking their native language. By 6 or 7 they speak as well as an adult for most everyday purposes.

This amazing feat of rapid language learning suggests that there is a critical time, or **sensitive period,** for language learning, as described in Chapter 2. Children seem to go through a sensitive period for acquiring language that begins at 1 or 2 years of age, peaks in the later preschool years, and continues to some degree until 13 to 15 years of age (Hecaen 1976; Lenneberg 1969).

The existence of this sensitive period seems to be confirmed by a few cases of so-called wild children, who have grown up in isolation from human society and therefore provide a natural experiment in language deprivation. The term "wild" refers to both their lack of social knowledge and the fact that some of them have actually been discovered living alone in the wild or, seemingly, in the company of wild animals. Of course, the exact nature of the children's deprivation is not always clear. It is usually difficult to determine when they became separated from human society, and why. Some of them may have been abandoned because they were already retarded or abnormal in some other way, and children who have grown up with little human contact have been deprived of more than just language.

Until recently, no wild children had been taught to speak more than a few words after being found (DeVilliers & DeVilliers 1978). In one case, efforts to train the child to speak did have some success. In 1970, a child reared in isolation was discovered in Los Angeles, and good information was obtained on her life history (Curtiss 1977). When Genie was 20 months old, her parents confined her to a small, nearly bare room. Before her confinement, she did hear some speech, but after she was locked away she heard little or none. She was kept locked up in one room for the next 12 years, usually tied down to a potty chair. Her only contact with the world was brief daily visits by her father, who did not speak to her. During her entire confinement, she heard no household conversation, no radio or television—nothing but an occasional noise from the street.

When Genie was found, she was 13½ years old and had already entered puberty. She was very thin because of malnutrition, and she was unable to speak, to stand erect, to use a toilet, or even to chew solid food. It is not surprising that she was emotionally disturbed. Tests showed that Genie understood no language when she was released from her isolation. Her senses were all normal, however, and soon after she was placed in a foster home, Genie began to learn to speak.

In many ways her language development followed the normal course. She learned single words first and then began to combine them into sentences. The kinds of mistakes she made, such as overregularization, were mostly typical of preschool children. And she quickly generalized words such as "dog," which she had learned with a specific object, to classes of objects, just as normal children do.

Some aspects of Genie's language development were abnormal, however. She never learned to use "ed" for the simple past tense. She never asked spontaneous questions. She had some trouble with word order and intonation patterns, which normal infants learn very early. Also, some sounds were hard for her to make. When her case was written about—after 6 years of living with a normal family—Genie could not speak as well as a normal 5-year-old.

Nevertheless, Genie demonstrates the remarkable flexibility of human learning capacities. After more than a decade of total language deprivation, she did learn to speak as well as a 3- or 4-year-old, and her speech may well be continuing to improve. Although her case supports the idea of a sensitive period for acquiring language that ends at about the onset of puberty, it also indicates that much language can be learned after this age, even by a person who has suffered extreme deprivation.

The special human sensitivity for learning language in the preschool years seems to correspond to physical developments during the same period. Certain systematic changes in the brain and the rest of the nervous system at about this time relate closely to speech.

PHYSICAL DEVELOPMENT

During the preschool period, the psychological changes in the child are not the only striking developments. The brain and nervous system grow rapidly and important parts of the brain attain their mature form. The child continues to grow, from a height at age 2 of about 33 inches, on the average, to about 45 inches at age 6. Motor skills also improve substantially. Most 6-year-olds can tie their shoes, catch a ball, and handle fork and spoon with ease. These physical developments correspond closely to changes in cognitive, language, and social behaviors, combining with them to produce normal development.

Language, Cognition, and the Brain

The brain continues to grow rapidly during the preschool period. At age 2 the brain of a child is about 55 percent of its adult size; by age 6, it has grown to more than 90 percent of its adult size (Tanner 1978). This growth is not steady. Most of it takes place before 4 to 4½ years of age. Also, there seems to be a spurt in brain growth at about 2 years of age (described in Chapter 5) and then a large spurt between 3 and 5 years of age, followed by a major decrease in rate of growth from 5 to 6 years (Eichorn & Bayley 1962; Fischer & Pipp 1984). The increase in brain size is due to changes in the organization and size of nerve cells, not to an increase in their number. It is due also to an increase in the number of glial cells that feed and support the nerve cells, and to the increasing myelination of nerve fibers. As described in Chapter 2, myelin is the coating around nerve fibers that serves to channel impulses along the fibers and to reduce the random spread of impulses between adjacent fibers, thus helping the nervous system to function quickly and accurately.

The general developmental changes in language that take place at age 4 presumably correspond to the spurt in overall brain growth. In addition, more specific developmental changes take place in parts of the brain that play important roles in language. The best documented of these changes are called **myelogenetic cycles** (Figure 7-14). Each cycle is a period in which myelin forms in a particular system within the brain (Yakovlev & Lecours 1967). There are three myelogenetic cycles in systems that are important to language (Lecours 1975). The first cycle, in the primitive brain (the brain stem and the limbic system), starts before birth and ends early in infancy. It seems to be associated with the development of babbling. The second cycle takes place in a more advanced part of the brain and takes longer to be completed; it begins around birth and continues until 3½ to 4½ years of age. It seems to accompany the development of speech in infancy and the early preschool years. The third cycle takes place in the association areas of the cortex of the brain, which play a central role in intelligence. Although myelination of these areas begins at birth, it does not near completion until age 15 or later.

Certain sections of the association areas are especially important for speech. Damage to these areas in children or adults produces a loss of the ability to speak; in adolescents and adults, this loss may be complete and permanent. These association areas seem to begin normal, stable functioning at 1 to 2 years of age and approach their adult form in early adolescence (Bay 1975), although

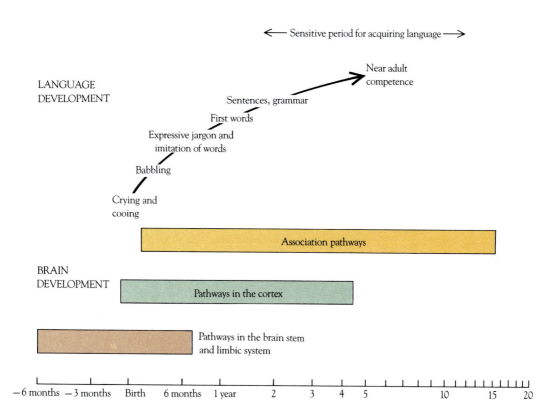

some development probably continues into young adulthood (Yakovlev & Lecours 1967; Tanner 1978). The maturation of these association areas thus seems to correspond closely to the sensitive period for acquiring language.

While the brain is growing phenomenally during the preschool years, especially between ages 3 and 5, the pattern of growth in the rest of the body is very different.

Figure 7-14 Myelo-genetic cycles in the brain and the development of language. The first cycle, in the brain stem and the limbic system, seems to play a part in the development of babbling. The second cycle, in specific areas of the cortex, seems to accompany the early development of speech. The third cycle, in the association areas, begins at birth but proceeds very slowly toward full maturity; it parallels the sensitive period for language development.

Growth in Height and Weight

In their first 2 years after birth, babies quadruple their weight and increase their height by two-thirds. Between 2 and 3 years, children gain only about 4 pounds and grow only about 3½ inches. Between ages 4 and 6, the increase in height slows still further: Children grow about 2½ inches and gain 5 to 7 pounds each year, on the average (Watson & Lowrey 1967).

One consequence of the slower growth rate after age 2 is that most 3- and 4-year-olds seem to their parents to eat less food than they did at 2. Some parents become alarmed at the seeming decrease in their child's appetite, but the change in food intake is normal. Actually, children do not eat less food; they

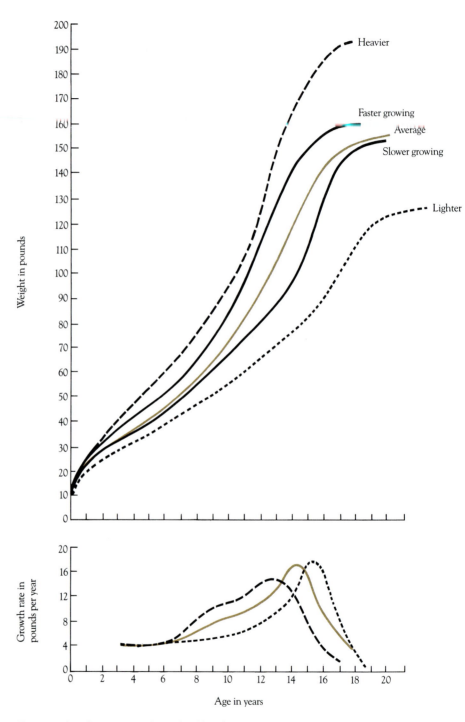

Figure 7-15   The patterns of growth of four boys compared with the average and, below, the rates of growth of two of them compared with the average. You can see that there are wide individual differences.

merely eat fewer calories per pound of body weight. Because they are growing slower, they no longer need as many calories to build their developing muscles, bones, and nerves. Later, when they once again grow faster, they will eat more to keep pace.

Between the ages of 2 and 6, the change in children's body proportions produces a remarkable transformation. Their "baby fat" disappears, their legs lengthen, accounting for a larger proportion of their height, and the relation of head size to body size becomes more adultlike.

Although the general pattern of growth is the same for all normal children, there are wide individual variations. Some children grow slowly compared with the average; some shoot up rapidly. Figure 7-15, which compares the growth patterns of five children from infancy through adolescence, shows how a child whose growth rate is slow may continue to gain in height and weight almost until age 20, while another whose growth rate is fast may be done growing by age 16. If a child's pattern seems unusual—for example, if he or she is very short and growing at a much slower rate than the typical 2 to 3½ inches a year—parents should ask a pediatrician whether the child's growth is within the normal range.

Physical development in the preschool years, like that at all ages, results from the interaction of heredity and environment. When a child has an unusual growth pattern, genetic factors undoubtedly play some role, and sometimes they may be primarily responsible, as for example when both parents are unusually short. But heredity is not always the most important factor. Normal growth requires the collaboration of a healthy environment with genetic processes.

One of the most striking illustrations of this effect is a syndrome called *psychosocial dwarfism,* in which children who suffer prolonged neglect or abuse simply stop growing. In these children, psychological stress produced by their social environment causes the pituitary gland to stop secreting growth hormone. This is known because the condition can be reversed by changing the children's social environment. When they are sent to a hospital or a home where they receive care and affection, they begin to grow again, often at a high rate that partly makes up for their previous slow growth (Tanner 1970).

In one case, 2-year-old Mary G. had been placed in a foster home (Money et al. 1972). Her foster parents did not physically mistreat her, but neither did they offer her affection. When Mary was 4, the foster-placement agency referred her to a hospital because she was not growing normally. She also showed a number of other symptoms, the most notable being a lowered reaction to pain: When she hurt herself, she did not cry or even seem to mind. She was clinically depressed.

In the hospital, Mary was much happier, and after only 3 months there she had grown 1½ inches, an inch more than would normally have been expected in such a short period. She continued to grow well for a while after returning to the foster home, but when she was about 5 her growth slowed again. She also

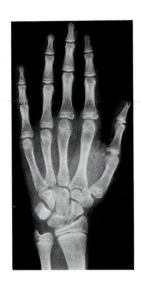

Skeletal age: 14 years

suffered severe insomnia and did not eat well. The foster parents still did not give her any affection, and when she was 6 they asked that she be moved elsewhere. She went back to the hospital for a while and then was placed in another, more satisfactory foster home. In the next year, she grew 3.3 inches.

In body growth, brain growth, and all other aspects of physical and psychological development, genes and environment collaborate to produce normal development. Physical developments, no less than psychological ones, are affected by the environment. A normal, healthy environment is necessary for normal growth of the body and for normal growth of the brain and nervous system.

Skeletal Age: An Index of Maturity

When a child's physical development does not progress normally, physicians need to find out why so that they can determine what, if anything, should be done about it. One tool that can be especially useful for this purpose is the assessment of skeletal age.

As described in Chapter 3, the skeleton begins in prenatal life as cartilage, which is gradually replaced by bone. This replacement process is called **ossification** (*os* is Latin for "bone"). At birth, ossification has really only just begun, and it continues until the end of adolescence. Just how much of a child's cartilage has been replaced by bone can be determined by taking an x ray of the child's hand. By comparing the degree of her ossification with norms for each age, the physician can determine her **skeletal age.** For example, if a short 5-year-old's x ray showed that the ossification of her hand was like that of the average 3-year-old, her skeletal age would be 3. Her physician and parents would then know that she was merely a slow developer and not necessarily fated to become a short adult.

In one actual case, a 10-year-old girl who was very short for her age applied for admission to the Royal Ballet School in England. Most professional dance companies require that female dancers be at least 5 feet 2 inches tall, and the director of the school was unwilling to admit the girl, fearing that her years of intensive training would be for nothing if, as an adult, she were too short to be hired by a ballet company. However, because of the girl's talent the director was persuaded to consult a specialist in children's growth. The specialist took an x ray of the girl's hand and found that her skeletal age was several years below her chronological age. Realizing that the girl was a slow maturer, he predicted that she would be at least 5 feet 3 inches tall at maturity, and the director admitted her to the school. By the end of adolescence, she was 5 feet 4 inches and a professional dancer (Tanner & Taylor 1965).

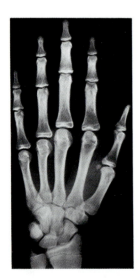

Skeletal age: 16 years

Sex Differences

X-ray standards for skeletal age confirm a difference in developmental maturity between boys and girls. Many people do not notice this difference until early adolescence, when it is most obvious. Anyone who has ever visited a junior high school knows that young teen-aged girls look more mature than boys the same age. In fact, the skeletal age of 13-year-old girls is on the average almost 2 years ahead of that of 13-year-old boys (Tanner 1970). Not only do girls appear to be physically more mature, they *are* more mature.

Even at birth, boys are about 4 weeks behind girls in skeletal age, and the average girl is physically more mature than the average boy throughout childhood. Girls' teeth come in sooner. Girls reach half their adult height at about 1 year and 9 months, whereas boys reach this mark at about 2½ years. Throughout childhood, girls tend to be about the same height as boys the same age even though in adulthood they will be shorter on the average.

During childhood, girls tend to be more advanced than boys in most aspects of behavioral development as well. Many parents of boys think that their son is developing slowly because they mistakenly compare him to his sister or another girl. But girls creep, sit, and walk earlier than boys, on the average. They also talk earlier, gain control of bladder and bowels earlier, and tend to be quicker to master motor tasks that require finely controlled finger movements, such as drawing, tying shoelaces, and writing. Boys have an advantage chiefly in large-muscle coordination: On the whole they are stronger and better at such activities as running, jumping, and throwing a ball.

Despite these differences, boys' and girls' developments are more alike than different. For both sexes, the outline of physical and psychological development in the preschool years is very similar, with girls just slightly ahead of boys.

Motor Development

The union of physical and psychological change is particularly noticeable in the development of motor skills such as running, riding a tricycle, or building a house from toy blocks. The control of movements and the coordination of sensory information with movements clearly require important physical developments. The muscles and bones must be able to make the movements, the sense organs must be able to transmit the sensory information, and the nervous system must monitor and control the entire skill. For example, the nerve fibers necessary for the fine control of movement must be fully sheathed with myelin before they can function efficiently, and myelination of these fibers is not complete until about age 4 or even later (Tanner 1978). The development of these motor skills clearly depends on psychological change as well, in that each skill requires the child to learn some complex new behavior.

A motor skill that is practiced often may develop quickly during the preschool years (Sinclair 1973). For example, Robert and his mother played ball a lot when he was a preschooler. At age 2, Robert's attempts to throw a ball were crude, but he could manage it. He planted his feet, faced his mother, and jerkily pulled his arms out away from his body and then forward with the ball. The ball usually went in the general direction of his mother, but seldom landed

Figure 7-16   A sequence of motor development.

in the same place. He could almost never catch a ball, unless it was thrown gently and carefully so that he could catch it with his arms by clasping it to his chest. By age 3, Robert could already throw the ball much more skillfully, grasping it easily in one hand and aiming it so that it usually came close to his mother. He could catch it much more easily, too, not always having to use the two-armed catch and often catching even a small ball.

At 4 years, Robert had become a fairly graceful thrower and catcher. He threw the ball overhand, shifting his posture like an older child or adult, and aiming with fair accuracy. He also could catch the ball with more grace and less clumsiness, as long as his mother did not throw it in a tricky or unexpected way. From age 5 on, Robert's skills at throwing and catching became more and more graceful, and he could handle unexpected tosses more and more effectively. He began to try new things, like bouncing the ball before he threw it, or kicking it to his mother instead of throwing, or trying to trick her so that she would miss the ball. He started to evaluate his own performance, commenting on what he did well and what he had to improve and asking for help about how he could overcome a problem he had in throwing (Harter 1983).

A 5-year-old who had never before played with a ball would not have Robert's skill. At age 5, his muscles and nerves would probably allow him to reach Robert's skill level in less than the 3 years it took Robert to get there, but he would nevertheless need a lot of practice before he could give Robert a good game of catch.

Mastery of motor skills makes a big difference in a child's everyday life. Not only do children feel competent when they can eat with a fork and spoon, for example, but this skill usually changes their social status. When they are no longer likely to scatter their food all over the table or floor, they are likely to be welcome to join the adults and older children at meals. Joining the family at meals means that they can take part in the conversation and learn the social rules of the dinner table. As preschool children's physical capacities grow and their abilities to think and talk become more sophisticated, their social environment changes: The people around them come to expect more of them as social beings. The next chapter describes the social development of preschool children.

SUMMARY

COGNITIVE DEVELOPMENT: PREOPERATIONAL INTELLIGENCE

1.   The **preoperational period** is the second of Piaget's four cognitive-developmental periods, encompassing the thinking of children from about age 2 to age 6. Preoperational means prelogical.

2.   Research has revealed a qualitative change in a child's thinking within the preoperational period, at about age 4. For this reason, it is useful to consider the period as being divided into two cognitive-developmental levels.

    a.   The ability to construct *single representations* marks the passage from sensorimotor intelligence to preoperational intelligence. Two- and 3-year-olds are capable of representation—they can think about the properties of things without having to act on them, but they can deal with only one representation at a time. At first, a representation includes only one characteristic of an object or person. Gradually, the child expands it to include several characteristics, as in *social categories,* which are clusters of characteristics relating to a concrete social concept, such as "doctor" or "nice."

    b.   At about age 4, children become capable of *relating representations* to each other. For example, children can understand how the category of father relates concretely to the category of mother, and they can understand *contingencies,* in which variations in one factor depend upon variations in a second factor.

3.   The ability to represent makes *deferred imitation* possible. Children can observe an activity and, much later, reproduce it. They do a great deal of this in their pretend play.

4.   Two- and 3-year-olds are not very good at *perspective taking.* They show *egocentrism,* centering on themselves because they are unable to keep another person's perspective in mind as well as their own. By 4 or 5, preschoolers develop some skill in perspective taking.

5.   *Short-term memory,* also called working memory, allows the retrieval of information within a few seconds or minutes of its being encoded, and *long-term memory* allows retrieval after days, weeks, or years. Both types of memory undergo important developments during the preoperational period. The number of things that children can recall and repeat back increases, and there are also qualitative improvements in memory: With every cognitive-developmental advance, children can remember new sorts of things, and they begin to construct strategies for remembering.

6.   Preschoolers play. They love play that lets them exercise their motor skills, such as running and climbing. They also love to play *pretend* games, which exercise their social and cognitive skills. Two-year-olds often play alone, and they also play together but in *parallel play,* without sustained cooperation. At about age 4, *cooperative play* begins to predominate.

7.   One characteristic of preoperational thought is *complexive thinking,* in which ideas are strung together without a unifying concept or system. Another prelogical characteristic is *personification,* the attribution of human characteristics to objects. *Primary process,* a type of thinking that older children and adults show in dreams and in many psychological disorders, shares these characteristics of the prelogical thinking of preschoolers

ACQUIRING LANGUAGE

8. With the development of representation, language begins to blossom. Children strikingly increase their vocabulary and begin to use short sentences.

9. Among the many aspects of language that children must master is *pragmatics,* how people use speech in social contexts. Pragmatics includes fundamental rules for communicating, such as taking turns and not offering your partner information he already has, as well as conversational niceties such as asking for something politely.

10. Children must also learn *grammatical rules* for speech—how to form words, phrases, and sentences that will communicate meaning.

11. Human beings seem to be aided in their learning of language rules by certain strategies for perceiving speech. These *operating principles* are species-specific abilities that help us break up the stream of language we hear into words and word segments and notice their important features. These strategies help a child to form rules for producing speech.

12. Early speech is called *telegraphic* because, like telegrams, it leaves out all words that are not necessary to the message. The meaning of telegraphic sentences—for example, "Mommy sock"—generally cannot be understood outside the context in which they are uttered.

13. At a certain phase in their learning of language rules, children *overregularize.* When they learn the rule that the past tense adds "ed," they say things such as "I goed," even though earlier they had correctly said "went."

14. In any language, children first learn simple rules and those that are frequently used. More complex rules and combinations of rules are learned later.

15. The processes of abstraction, observational learning, and reinforcement all play a part in the acquisition of language.

16. Parents rarely correct the language of their preschool child directly. More commonly, they try to help by using *expansions,* in which they repeat the child's statement in an expanded or slightly different form.

17. The preschool years seem to be the beginning of a *sensitive period* for language learning. Although language is acquired rapidly from age 1 or 2 to age 7 or 8, the sensitive period appears to continue until the onset of puberty. Some language learning seems to be possible even past that time.

PHYSICAL DEVELOPMENT

18. Physical development of the brain and nervous system plays a large part in the cognitive and language developments of the preschool years. Nerve cells grow and form new connections with other cells, and myelin, the nerve coating, forms. There are well-known *myelogenetic cycles,* periods when myelin forms in particular systems within the brain. Research suggests that brain growth takes a spurt at the ages when each preoperational level develops—approximately at 2 and at 3 to 5 years of age.

19. The rate of growth in height and weight slows down at about age 2½ and is fairly slow during the preschool years, but the change in body proportions between ages 2 and 6 is striking. There are wide individual differences in growth during these years, which may arise from either genetic or environmental factors, or both.

20. A good index of a child's physical maturity is *skeletal age,* judged by how much cartilage has been replaced by bone. This replacement process is called *ossification.* On the average, girls show a more advanced skeletal age than boys of the same chronological age.

21. Many motor skills are mastered in the preschool years, from running to dressing oneself to throwing and catching a ball.

SUGGESTED READINGS

CHUKOVSKY, KORNEI. *From Two to Five* (Miriam Morton, translator). Berkeley: University of California Press, 1963.

A famous Russian author of children's tales provides a delightful and informative account of the thought, language, and imagination of preschoolers.

DEVILLIERS, JILL G., and PETER A. DEVILLIERS. *Language Acquisition.* Cambridge, Massachusetts: Harvard University Press, 1978.

A readable and comprehensive textbook outlining the nature of the acquisition of speech in the first 6 years.

FRAIBERG, SELMA. *The Magic Years: Understanding and Handling the Problems of Early Childhood.* New York: Scribner's, 1959.

Not the ordinary manual for parents, this book by a noted developmental psychologist describes the mind of the preschool child and demonstrates that understanding how children think and feel can be enormously helpful to people who live and work with children.

GARDNER, HOWARD. *Artful Scribbles.* New York: Basic Books, 1980.

A fascinating analysis of children's drawings by a famous developmental researcher and author.

GELMAN, ROCHEL. "Cognitive Development," in *Annual Review of Psychology,* 1978, volume 29, pages 297–332.

A competent review of the extensive research demonstrating that preschool children have greater cognitive capacities than predicted by Piaget.

SLOBIN, DAN I. *Psycholinguistics*, 3rd ed. Glenwood, Illinois: Scott, Foresman, 1983.

One of the deans of the study of language development presents his analysis of the field of psycholinguistics, with a special emphasis on the development of language.

TANNER, J.M. *Fetus into Man: Physical Growth from Conception to Maturity*. Cambridge, Massachusetts: Harvard University Press, 1978.

An outline of the nature of physical growth by a major developmental researcher.

8

BECOMING
A
MEMBER
OF
SOCIETY

CHAPTER OUTLINE

8

BECOMING

A

MEMBER

OF

SOCIETY

If you have spent any time with 2- and 3-year-olds, you know that they are always busy, always on the move, running, climbing, and investigating everything in sight. If given free rein, they would happily empty every drawer and cupboard in the house and then pull all the interesting things apart, trying to see how they work. Many are enraged at the notion that they should cease all this activity to take an afternoon nap or go to bed at night. The 2-year-old, with his newly developed sense of self, seems to find pleasure in saying "No"—many times a day.

All this self-centered energy has to be channeled if children are to become social beings, individuals who can deal effectively with other people and function within the set of rules that society prescribes. During the preschool years children begin to be able to see things from the point of view of other people and to understand the rules and categories of their society. As this capacity develops, they make their first efforts to place themselves in their world by recognizing the kind of person they are—boy or girl, black or white, rich or poor—and by deciding who they want to be like—mommy, daddy, grandma, Wonder Woman, Superman.

These changes help broaden the child's world beyond the family. The immediate family is still central, but aunts and uncles, neighbors, television stars, peers, and teachers all begin to assume more importance once infancy is past. These agents help children to channel their activity in socially approved directions and to learn the rules and categories of their society.

SOCIALIZATION

Human beings are social animals. We live in groups—in societies—and in every society children must learn certain attitudes, knowledge, and skills. The process by which we learn how to act in our society is called *socialization.* We learn the behavior and beliefs of our society—we are socialized—both by observational learning and by direct teaching. The teaching may be no more than making sure that a child sees how a certain behavior is done and when it is called for, so that the child will imitate it. At a baseball game, for instance, a father may stand when the national anthem is played, only looking meaningfully at his 4-year-old child, who then also stands and is rewarded with an approving glance. Or the teaching may be direct and verbal: "You must say 'please' when you want more milk," "You must wait your turn," "You must not climb a tree when you're wearing a dress" (Maccoby & Martin 1983).

Norms and Roles

As children are socialized, most of what they learn is the particular social rules and categories specified by their society—that is, its norms and roles (Robertson

1981). Children first become able to understand these social rules and categories after infancy (see Chapter 7), so the preschool years assume a special importance for socialization.

A society's rules or standards of behavior are called **social norms.** Although most norms are never written down, they can govern our behavior, and our expectations of others' behavior, just as effectively as laws. Until recently, for example, a norm related to gender specified that males should open doors for females they are escorting. This norm seems to have changed. Escorted females may now open doors for themselves, but any female who consistently opened doors for her male escort would be considered to be behaving abnormally. An occupational norm governing the relation between employee and boss dictates that the boss may call the employee by his first name but that the employee must call the boss "Mr. Jackson" unless the boss specifically says, "Call me Joe." An age-related norm specifies that children may not interrupt the conversations of adults, whereas adults often feel free to break in on children's "chatter."

A **social role** is a group of norms that defines a specific social category, usually in terms of age, sex, or occupation. In the United States, different norms define the roles of children and adults, men and women, teachers and construction workers. Much of a person's behavior in one of these roles is dictated by the norms that make up role. An individual person, of course, plays a number of roles, and these roles contribute to personality (see Figure 8-1).

"College student," for example, is a social role. You might recall learning that role during your first few months as a freshman. The norms for the role of "high-school student" no longer applied. Your relations with your college instructors probably differed from those that you had with your high-school teachers and required different behaviors and attitudes. Your manner and language with fellow students probably changed too. It's a safe bet that you carefully observed the behavior of other students, at least to find out what *not* to do. Gradually, you became so accustomed to the norms for the role of college student that you could act them out with little or no thought.

People generally consider most of the norms and roles of their own society to be "natural." Children tend to learn them as facts that have the same reality as the wetness of water or the heat of fire. But differences between societies show that norms and roles are social creations, developed and perpetuated because they give a society stability (Benedict 1934; Whiting & Whiting 1975).

Among the Dobus of Melanesia, for example, boys are socialized to be ruthlessly competitive. In the male role, cheating and treachery are regarded as valid, even admirable ways to gain ownership of desirable things. The poorly socialized Dobu male is the man who is friendly and enjoys activities for their own sake rather than for the gain he can expect from them.

Exactly opposite to the Dobus are the Zuñi Indians of New Mexico. Among the Zuñi, boys are socialized to avoid competition, conflict, and the exercise of authority. A boy or man who habitually wins foot races is barred from running because an outstanding runner spoils the games. A well-socialized Zuñi is always

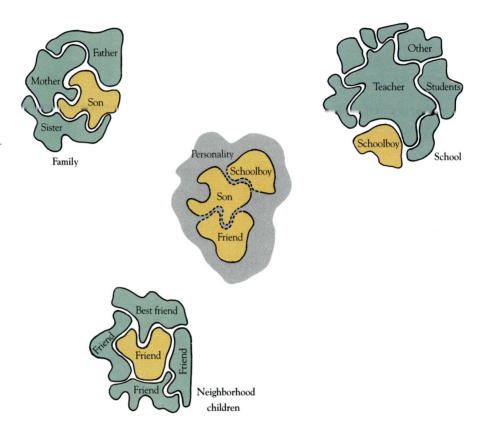

Figure 8-1   Everyone learns a number of social roles, and these roles contribute to the shaping of personality. These are some of the social roles that a child might play. Some of them—schoolboy, for example—will be discarded in later life, when others—accountant or plumber, for example—are added.

cooperative and moderate in emotional behavior. A man who shows turbulent emotion, who competes, and who wants power and authority is considered so abnormal that he is likely to be branded a witch.

A young boy who had learned to behave in accord with Zuñi norms would be cast out by the Dobus—if he survived at all. A boy socialized by the Dobus and sent to live with the Zuñi would be shunned as a witch. But the socialization of the young boy in each society prepares him to be an effective member of that society.

Wild Children

What would a person be like who had not been socialized, who had not been taught what other people expect of him? Some answers to this question may be found in accounts of "wild" children, who from an early age were isolated from human society. Like Genie, described in Chapter 7, some of these children had been kept locked away by their families. Others were found living literally in the wild, abandoned by their parents. The most famous case of this type, the wild boy of Aveyron, was found in 1790 in a forest near Aveyron in France.

Figure 8-2 The wild boy of Aveyron as he appeared in *The Wild Child*, a 1970 film about his emotionally charged life. The film depicts Jean-Marc Itard's attempts to educate the boy.

The boy appeared to be 11 or 12 when he was found and taken in hand by the young physician Jean-Marc Itard. It was Itard's intention to educate the boy, and he kept a journal of his efforts. The quotations in the following account are from that journal (Itard 1932).

When the boy first came under Itard's care, he was "a disgustingly dirty child affected with spasmodic movements and often convulsions, who swayed back and forth ceaselessly like certain animals in the menagerie, who bit and scratched those who opposed him, and who showed no sort of affection for those who attended him; and who was, in short, indifferent to everything and attentive to nothing." Philippe Pinel, a physician famous for his revolutionary treatment of the mentally ill, examined the boy and judged him to be an idiot. Itard disagreed, saying that the boy simply needed to be taught how to live with other people—in other words, that the boy needed to be socialized. He had to learn how to sit on a chair, then to sit at a table and eat with spoon and fork so he could share meals with others. He had to learn acceptable ways of channeling emotions—how to express anger without biting and kicking, how to recognize affection and express it himself in ways that others could understand. He had to be taught to communicate with others and to attend to the words and gestures that they directed to him.

When the wild boy was first found, he uttered only guttural sounds. In the five years that Itard cared for him, he managed to pronounce nothing more than the word "milk" and the expression "Oh, God"—often used by the housekeeper, who offered the boy much affection and care. (Genie, in contrast, learned to speak about as well as a 3-year-old.) The wild boy eventually did learn to read and print some words.

He formed a strong attachment to Madame Guerin, the housekeeper: "Once when he had escaped from her in the streets, he shed many tears on seeing her again. . . . Later, when Madame Guerin reproached him, he interpreted her tone so well that he began to weep." He had learned to feel regret at disappointing people whom he loved and who loved him.

Itard had hoped to socialize the wild boy into a normal adolescent. His hopes were disappointed. Still, the boy did become a clean, affectionate being. Though not able to speak, he understood much of what was said to him. He was greatly changed from the creature who rocked like a caged animal, bit people, and showed no affection. But the complex expectations of a human community were evidently too much for him to meet, having started at the late age of 11 or 12. It is possible, of course, that his difficulties were not entirely due to his late start. He may have had some mental or physical defects that could not be diagnosed in those days. There is no way to know for certain.

Even the simplest, most "natural" human behaviors must be learned, it seems. To eat as human beings do, you must learn their ways. To speak as people do, you must grow up hearing them speak to each other. To love and care for another person, you must receive love and care and see others giving and receiving it. In short, to grow up human, you must live with a human group.

Despite the extreme differences between the Dobu and Zuñi roles for males, men from the two societies would seem very much alike if they were compared with Itard's wild child. Despite all the differences among human societies, socialization fulfills many of the same purposes in all of them.

The Universal Goals of Socialization

The main purpose of socialization in all societies is to teach people to live as members of a group, because it is only in groups that human beings can maintain mastery over their environment. Every society, then, has the same basic goals in socializing its young (Clausen 1966; Robertson 1981). Each individual must learn:

1.   To fulfill physical needs in appropriate ways.
2.   To control aggression.
3.   To master the physical environment.
4.   To master the social environment.

5. To perform essential skills.
6. To behave in accord with the society's moral values.
7. To prepare for the future.
8. To be both an effective individual and an effective member of the group.

Although these goals are universal, the norms and roles that are created to achieve them may differ sharply from society to society. For example, both Dobu and Zuñi men are taught to control aggression, though the "proper" uses of aggression in Dobu and Zuñi societies are very different.

Some types of social roles are also universal. For example, to fulfill the goals of mastering the social environment and behaving in accord with the society's moral rules, all societies have roles that are appropriate for different age groups (Neugarten 1968). Certain behaviors are considered suitable for children but not for adults, or for young unmarried adults but not not for middle-aged couples. All societies likewise have norms that specify appropriate behaviors and attitudes for males and for females. As mentioned in Chapter 2, these sex-role norms are based to some degree on biological differences between men and women—in particular, on the fact that women bear children. However, the world's many cultures define a wide range of behaviors as properly masculine or properly feminine. This shows that socialization is at least as important as biology in shaping masculinity and femininity—and probably more important.

THE ACQUISITION OF SEX ROLES

Sex roles are the set of social norms that prescribe appropriate behavior for males and females. Sex-role definitions provide the basis for stereotypes. In Western societies, for example, men are supposed to be dominant, competitive, logical, and unrevealing of emotion. Women are supposed to be warm, caring, emotionally responsive, and socially adept. When college students in one study were asked to describe their ideal selves, their responses resembled these stereotypes. Male students usually said they would like to be shrewd, critical, rational, practical, dominating, competitive, and ambitious. Female students usually wanted to be loving, sensitive, helpful, sympathetic, and considerate (Block 1973). These college students had obviously learned their society's norms for sex roles, and they seemed to be using these norms to monitor their own behavior and to judge the behavior of others.

The learning of sex roles begins in the preschool years, and by the end of that period, the behavior of boys and girls has become different in many ways. In observing play at nursery schools, researchers have found that boys play much more with objects, such as building blocks and trucks; they do more outside activities, like riding tricycles and playing in the sandbox; and they fight a lot

BEHAVIOR CATEGORY	AGE	NYANSONGO, KENYA	JUXTLAHUACA, MEXICO	TARONG, PHILLIPINES	TAIRA, OKINAWA	KHALAPUR, INDIA	ORCHARD TOWN, USA
DEPENDENCY							
Seeks help	3–6	GIRLS	GIRLS	GIRLS	GIRLS	GIRLS	BOYS
	7–11	BOYS	BOYS	GIRLS	GIRLS	BOYS	GIRLS
Physical contact	3–6	GIRLS	GIRLS	BOYS	GIRLS	GIRLS	GIRLS
	7–11	GIRLS	GIRLS	GIRLS	BOYS	GIRLS	GIRLS
NURTURANCE							
Offers help	3–6	BOYS	GIRLS	GIRLS	GIRLS	GIRLS	BOYS
	7–11	GIRLS	GIRLS	GIRLS	BOYS	GIRLS	GIRLS
Gives support	3–6	BOYS	GIRLS	GIRLS	GIRLS	BOYS	GIRLS
	7–11	GIRLS	GIRLS	GIRLS	GIRLS	GIRLS	GIRLS
AGGRESSION							
Rough-and-tumble play	3–6	GIRLS	BOYS	BOYS	BOYS	BOYS	GIRLS
	7–11	GIRLS	BOYS	BOYS	BOYS	BOYS	BOYS
Insults	3–6	BOYS	BOYS	BOYS	BOYS	BOYS	BOYS
	7–11	BOYS	BOYS	BOYS	BOYS	BOYS	GIRLS

Figure 8-3 Some results of a large-scale cross-cultural study, in which the researchers recorded how often boys and girls in several cultures performed certain kinds of behaviors. This table indicates whether certain behaviors were performed more often by boys or by girls. In most cultures, boys played more roughly than girls, and girls more often sought help from another child or an adult, used physical contact, and tried to resolve problems by suggesting solutions to them. Although the researchers concluded that some behavioral differences between males and females may have a biological base, they also suggested that a number of differences could be attributed to socialization, in particular, the types of work assigned to each sex. At an early age (5 to 7), many girls begin doing housework and caring for younger siblings, which orients them toward helping. Boys are generally sent out to watch animals or to help in the fields, work they do alone (Edwards & Whiting 1980; Whiting & Edwards 1973).

more. Girls spend more time in social interactions, playing in the kitchen, playing with dolls, and listening to stories (Edwards & Whiting 1980; Hutt 1972). Some of the differences between boys' and girls' behavior may be due to biological factors. As Chapter 2 pointed out, boys are more aggressive than girls and this aggressiveness appears to be partly hereditary. But most of the sex-linked differences in children's behavior can be explained by the ways that parents' expectations and behavior with their children differ according to the child's sex. In addition, other adults—teachers, neighbors, grandparents—probably have much the same expectations. Another important possible cause of early behavioral differences between the sexes is each child's own budding understanding of sex roles, a topic that is discussed later in this chapter.

The Expectations and Practices of Parents

When asked how they react to aggression by their sons and daughters, most parents say that they tolerate no more aggression from boys than from girls. What these parents do not realize is that their own sex-role socialization has

caused them to have different **expectations** for sons and daughters. Parents expect boys to be generally more aggressive than girls, so the baseline for unacceptable aggression is actually higher for their sons than for their daughters. Parents might ignore a pushing match among boys that they would be much more likely to stop among girls (Fagot 1978; Huston 1983).

Other expectations that parents have of their children also differ according to the child's sex. In one study most parents of 3-year-old boys said they thought it was important to encourage their sons to do their best, to play competitive games, and to control their feelings. Parents of 3-year-old girls wanted to encourage their daughters to become adept at developing and maintaining relationships with other people, to "wonder and think about life," and to take time "to daydream and loaf" (Block 1973).

Because of their expectations, parents frequently judge a child's behavior as appropriate or inappropriate to the child's sex and reinforce or punish it accordingly. They also shape children's behavior in other important ways. For example, they give their sons and daughters different toys to play with (Fagot 1974; Fein et al. 1975). Although both sexes may receive books, puzzles, blocks, and tricycles, mostly it is girls who are given dolls, dollhouses, and miniature houseware—toys that encourage nurturance—and boys who are given cars and trucks, battle games, and sports equipment—toys that encourage high activity and competition.

The influences that shape sex-typed behavior can be very subtle—almost unnoticeable, in fact. In one study where parents' interactions with their toddlers were observed, the parents reacted negatively to their daughters' running, jumping, and climbing more often than to their sons'. That is, if a son and daughter were making the same amount of noise and bustle, the parents would admonish the daughter but not the son, because they expected the boys to be noisier and more active than the girls. Daughters also received more negative feedback than sons when they picked up and manipulated objects, and sons received more negative feedback than daughters when they asked for help. That is, parents helped their girls when they asked for help but either ignored their boys' requests or told them that they could do whatever it was themselves if they really tried. Yet when the parents were asked about their socialization practices and what they considered appropriate behavior for girls and boys, they said that all of these behaviors were appropriate for both sexes (Fagot 1978). The author of this study suggests that "parents are not fully aware of the methods they use to socialize their young children." It seems that by the time we are old enough to be parents, the norms we have learned about male and female roles are so ingrained that they can influence our judgments and actions without our realizing it.

These conclusions may help explain two differences that researchers have found in the behavior of preschool girls and boys. Girls tend to be more dependent than boys, and boys tend to explore the physical environment more than girls (Goldberg & Lewis 1969; Maccoby & Jacklin 1974). Parents seemingly encourage dependence in girls by responding to their requests for help, just as they discourage it in boys by ignoring their requests or by criticizing them. The reverse is true with regard to explorations of objects and surroundings: Parents encourage this kind of behavior more in boys.

What flexibility there is in these general socialization patterns seems to be applied mostly to girls. Parents tend to tolerate and sometimes even to encourage "tomboy" behavior in girls but often go to great lengths to stamp out "sissy" behavior in boys. Fathers especially are likely to be upset when a son plays "girlish" games or is unaggressive to the point of being unwilling to defend himself (Lansky et al. 1961).

In some areas of social development, parents do not seem to differentiate much in their treatment of girls and boys. Parents react much the same to the sexual curiosity of their preschool sons and daughters; they seem to encourage the same amount of autonomy in both boys and girls (although the baseline for acceptable dependent behavior seems to be different for girls and boys, as pointed out above); and, at least in the early years, they stress achievement equally for boys and girls (Maccoby & Jacklin 1974). So even though parents' direct shaping of sex-typed behavior plays a large part in the acquisition of sex roles, a number of behavioral and personality differences that exist between boys and girls cannot easily be attributed to parents' expectations or teaching practices.

Imitation of parents undoubtedly accounts for some of these differences. Parents are highly effective models—loving, available, nurturant, and powerful (even abusive parents are loving and nurturant some of the time). But it is important to keep in mind the distinction between learning a behavior and

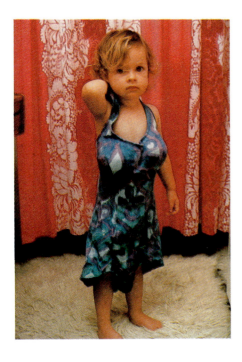

Figure 8-4 An easy way to imitate mother is to put on her clothes. Certain articles of dress, like this bathing suit, are most desirable because they give a girl instant breasts.

performing it. A girl, for example, observes her father's activities as well as her mother's, and so learns a number of "masculine" alternatives to the "feminine" behaviors she sees her mother perform. Yet the girl probably chooses to engage mostly in the feminine behaviors. Why? Part of the answer lies in children's understanding of what it means to be a girl or a boy.

Constructing the Concept of Gender

Young children hear themselves called a boy or girl as soon as they are able to understand language. According to Lawrence Kohlberg, children gradually learn to identify themselves according to this label, and their behavior is increasingly influenced by it (Huston 1983; Kohlberg 1966). In effect, a boy says to himself, "I'm a boy, so I want to do boy things," and a girl says, "I'm a girl, so I want to do girl things."

According to this idea, observational learning and imitation become important ways of learning a sex-role *after* children have placed themselves firmly in the class of girls or boys. Once a child can consistently think "I am a girl," she can begin to organize her behavior around this fact, noting "girl behaviors" in others and trying to imitate them. Generally, a child's understanding of gender labeling does not stabilize until about age 3: many a 2-year-old boy, for example, calls his mother and other females "boys," as he overgeneralizes the category that he belongs to. By 3 or so, however, most children can tell boy from girl, woman from man.

RESEARCH:
CHILDREN'S UNDERSTANDING OF SEX AND BIRTH

Sooner or later, almost all children ask where babies come from. Even if they don't ask, conscientious parents eventually sit the children down and tell them the "facts of life"—always seriously and sometimes in enough detail to confuse a medical student. However accurate and sensible such explanations may be, children take the information and process it at their own cognitive level, usually ending up with a remarkable account of procreation. In interviews with 60 children, all of whom had seen their mothers pregnant and had been given some explanation of their younger siblings' arrival into the family, Anne C. Bernstein discovered that the children's understanding of sex and birth showed distinct levels of cognitive maturity (Bernstein 1976; Bernstein & Cowan 1975).

Preoperational Levels

Geography. The youngest children believed that a baby who exists now has always existed. The only real question is where the baby was before coming to live at the child's house. These children answered the question, "How do people get babies?" as if it were a question about geography.

> You go to the store and buy one.
>
> From tummies.

Here are a few lines from Dr. Bernstein's interview with Antonia, 4 years old.

> *Interviewer:* How did your brother start to be in your mommy's tummy?
>
> *Antonia:* Um, my baby just went in my mommy's tummy.
>
> *Interviewer:* How did he go in?
>
> *Antonia:* He was just in my mommy's tummy.
>
> *Interviewer:* Before, you said that he wasn't there when you were there. Was he?
>
> *Antonia:* Yeah, and then he was in the other place . . . in America.

Manufacturing. Children at this level knew that babies who exist now have not always existed. Therefore, they must be built. Laura, 4 years old, explains:

> When people are already made, they make some other people. They make the bones inside, and blood. They make skin.

Asked how babies start to be in mommies' tummies, Laura replies:

> Maybe from people. They just put them in the envelope and fold them up and the mommy puts them in her 'gina and they just stay in there.

Some children at this level fell into the "digestive fallacy." They had been told something about seeds and tummies and so came up with explanations like this 4-year-old's:

> God makes mommies and daddies with a little seed. He puts it down on the table. Then it grows bigger. The people grow together. He makes them eat the seed and then they grow to be people from skel'tons at God's place. Then they stand up and go someplace else where they could live.

Transitional. Some children who were capable of using concrete-operational thinking in certain areas offered an explanation of birth based on manufacturing but were uncomfortable with that explanation. They seemed conscious that things in their explanation didn't quite add up, but they just could not do any better. Eight-year-old Ursula, for example, describes the father's role in reproduction:

> Well, he puts his penis right in the place where the baby comes out, and somehow it (sperm) comes out of there. It seems like magic sort of, 'cause it just comes out.

Asked why the male contribution is necessary, Ursula says:

> Well, the father puts the shell, I forget what its called, but he puts something in for the egg. . . . I think he gives the shell part, and the shell part, I think, is the skin.

Concrete-Operational Levels

Concrete Physiology. Many 8-year-olds had a pretty good grasp of the physical facts of life. They said that sexual intercourse or the joining of sperm and egg is the cause of procreation. But they still were not really able to understand why genetic material must unite before a new life can begin. One child thought the sperm existed primarily to provide an escort service:

> The sperm reaches the eggs. It looses 'em and brings 'em down to the forming place, I think that's right, and it grows until it's ready to take out.

Preformation. Children at this level, usually 11 or 12 years old, insisted that the baby exists preformed in the ovum or sperm, although they embedded this idea in a complex theory of causation. (Their notions were strikingly similar to the early scientific view that is discussed in Chapter 3.) Although all children at this level mentioned sexual intercourse or fertilization of the egg as necessary for procreation, many seemed embarrassed by being asked to discuss the topic with an adult.

Physical Causality. At about age 12, children began to get the facts straight. They not only understood the physical aspects of conception and birth, including the role of genetic material from both parents; they were also aware of some of the moral and social aspects of reproduction.

Telling Children about the Facts of Life

Many parents of the children interviewed by Dr. Bernstein were surprised at their children's answers. They had explained things thoroughly, they thought, and some had provided books on the subject. But books can be misinterpreted. One 4-year-old boy told a psychologist that some of the mother's eggs never became babies because the daddy eats them up. "It says so in my book," he claimed. And the book did indeed say so—in a discussion of reproduction in fish (Fraiberg, quoted in Bernstein 1976).

When parents explain sex and birth to their children, they should take account of the child's level of understanding and allow the child's own curiosity to be a guide to how much detail to give. Dr. Bernstein suggests that the most accessible explanations will be those that are just one level above the child's current level of understanding. This level can easily be determined by asking the child some simple questions about where babies come from. A 4-year-old who believes that babies have always existed (geographical level), for example, could be given an explanation in terms of manufacturing: "Only people can make other people. To make a baby, you need two grown-up people, a man and a woman, to be the baby's mommy and daddy." A 4- or 5-year-old who takes the manufacturing idea too literally can be told: "Making a real live baby is different from making a doll. A dollmaker takes all the doll parts and puts them together. But mommies and daddies don't do that. They have special things in their bodies they use to make babies. Mommies have tiny eggs and daddies have tiny sperms. When a sperm joins with an egg, they grow into a baby. The baby grows inside the mommy's body."

At all levels, it is important not to inundate a child with facts but to provide enough understandable information to satisfy the child's curiosity. And it is absolutely vital never to make a child feel stupid or foolish because she looks at reproduction in a fanciful way.

This initial grasp of gender labeling seems to be accompanied by a clear preference for the activities and qualities that the child sees as appropriate to his or her own sex. In one study, 3-year-old girls strongly valued stereotyped "girl" things and devalued "boy" things, while 3-year-old boys did the opposite (Kuhn et al. 1978). This stereotyping seems to continue throughout most of the preschool years.

Although most 3-year-olds can apply gender labels accurately, they do not understand how sex roles relate to each other; that is, they do not understand how "boy" is related to "man," or "man" to "woman." The following dialogue between 3-year-old Jimmy and 6-year-old Johnny demonstrates this confusion (Kohlberg 1966):

> *Johnny:* I'm going to be an airplane builder when I grow up.
> *Jimmy:* When I grow, I'll be a Mommy.
> *Johnny:* No, you can't be a Mommy. You have to be a Daddy.
> *Jimmy:* No, I'm going to be a Mommy.
> *Johnny:* No, you're not a girl, you can't be a Mommy.
> *Jimmy:* Yes, I can.

At 4 or 5 years, children are better able to understand social roles. In their play, for example, they can act out the role of mother in relation to child or the role of sheriff in relation to bad guy (Watson 1981; Westerman 1979). Thus for the first time they can really understand how the girl or boy role relates to the woman or man role.

However, 4- and 5-year-olds do not yet understand **gender permanence,** the fact that their gender cannot be changed. They think it is determined by the superficial characteristics of sex roles, such as clothing, hair length, or toy preference. They believe that if these characteristics are changed, the person's sex changes accordingly. As a result, 4- and 5-year-olds are even more inclined than they were at age 3 to treat the boy and the girl roles as opposites and to refuse activities, toys, and clothes that they see as appropriate to the opposite sex (Van Parys 1983). Many parents of 4- and 5-year-old boys have heard them say such things as "I can't wear Penny's sweater. I don't want to be a girl." By the same token, if a girl wants to be a boy, all she has to do, according to children this age, is cut her hair short, wear boys' clothes, and play boys' games, and she will become one (Emmerich et al. 1977; Marcus & Overton 1978).

It seems that until children have a firm understanding that their gender is unchangeable, they find comfort in doing things that are unmistakably labeled as appropriate to their own sex (Ullian 1976). They may even find some cross-sex behaviors threatening. Many 4- and 5-year-olds have nightmares in which their sex is changed or made ambiguous. By 7 years of age or so, children know that nothing they do—not even wearing Penny's sweater—will change their gender. At about the same age, they seem to become much more accepting of variations in behavior relating to sex roles.

Sex roles are only one part of the preschool child's developing sense of who he is and what he wants to be. Other components of the child's personality develop during the preschool years in a similar manner. One of the most important means of personality development in the preschool child is identification.

IDENTIFICATION

Sigmund Freud introduced the term "identification" into psychology, emphasizing how children identify with their parents, especially the parent of the same sex (Freud 1960). The general meaning of *identification* in psychology is virtually the same as it is in everyday language: A child loves or admires another person and so tries to be like him or her. Typically, the child chooses several characteristics or behaviors of the admired person and tries to imitate them.

During the preschool years, children begin to show signs of identifying with their parents, as when 3-year-old Jimmy said he wanted to grow up to be a Mommy. By 5 or 6, identification with parents is usually strong.

As their cognitive and physical capacities change, children need to learn new ways of interacting with others, and identifying with people that they admire provides guidelines for such learning. Throughout childhood, identifications with parents, other family members, older children, teachers, sports or movie stars, even fictional characters, do much to shape a child's personality (Erikson 1968). Identification helps children try on new behaviors, new char-

Figure 8-5 Identification leads children to try out new behaviors, especially the things that mother or father often does.

acteristics, new social roles. It is, in a sense, a process they can use to socialize themselves in response to the society's pressures for socialization.

Because identification is so important for social development in the preschool years and beyond, other psychologists have recognized the significance of Freud's concept and have built upon it. In particular, Erik Erikson's theory of psychosocial development focuses mainly on identification and the construction of an identity.

THEORY: THE PSYCHODYNAMIC APPROACHES OF FREUD AND ERIKSON

FREUD'S PSYCHOANALYTIC THEORY

Sigmund Freud, who was born in Austria in 1856, was one of the founding fathers of psychology. He originated the method of therapy called psychoanalysis and spent 50 years working intensively as a therapist. From the data he gathered in treating patients, Freud formulated a large body of theory to explain how the human mind works. Freud's theory, like the clinical method he developed, is called *psychoanalysis.*

During his career Freud had under his tutelage a number of psychologists who were to become famous themselves, among them Erik Erikson, Alfred Adler, Carl Jung, and Wilhelm Reich. Although many of these students eventually departed from Freudian theory in one way or another, the impact of the psychoanalytic school on the study of psychology has been tremendous.

Freud graduated from the University of Vienna with a medical degree and specialized in neurology. His first psychological work was the attempt to treat hysteria, a disorder whose physical symptoms could not possibly be caused by organic damage or disease. Freud believed that such symptoms had emotional origins and that they would not be affected by conventional medical remedies. At first he tried to treat his patients by hypnotizing them and encouraging them to talk about events and feelings that seemed to be connected with their hysteria. When hypnosis turned out to have drawbacks, Freud tried other means of treatment and soon developed the technique of *free association,* in which patients are urged to express every thought, every memory, every feeling as it comes to them, without censorship or evaluation. Free association is still the basic procedure used in psychoanalytic treatment.

After Freud had treated a number of hysterical patients and collected a body of clinical data, he realized that almost every patient had experienced some sexual difficulty. And he saw again and again that his patients' memories kept leading them back to sexual experiences—real or imagined—in their childhood. In explaining these data, Freud set forth what is probably his greatest contribution to psychological thought, and something that almost all of us today take for granted: the concept of the unconscious.

Libido and the Unconscious

According to Freud (1965), the basic energy fueling all human thought and behavior is libido. **Libido** is a primitive psychic energy that relentlessly seeks pleasure and is closely tied to what becomes sexual behavior in adults. Babies are born with libido much as animals are born with certain drives and instincts. Freud asserted that from the time we are born, we seek to satisfy our libido; this contention caused his dismissal from Victorian scientific circles. In that era it was assumed that sensuality and sexuality did not rear their ugly heads until puberty (and then, perhaps, in males only).

Freud said that as people grow up and learn to become accepted and useful members of their cultures, they channel much of their libidinal energy into nonsexual areas of endeavor. Thus, according to Freud (1960), the energy that produces art, politics, and industry—civilization itself—comes from libido. He called this channeling process **sublimation.** Not all libidinal energy is discharged through this process, however. Much of it remains unsublimated, and primitive desires remain submerged in the mind's unconscious.

The **unconscious,** Freud said, is like the part of an iceberg that lies below the surface of the water. Within it are memories and drives connected with basic processes such as self-preservation and the satisfaction of physical appetites. Under ordinary circumstances, these memories and drives cannot be called up directly into the conscious mind. However, they may surface in disguised or symbolic form—in dreams, slips of the tongue, psychopathological symptoms, and other behaviors (Freud 1963). When thought is dominated by the unconscious in this fashion, it shows what Freud called **primary process** thinking, in which chains of irrational ideas are controlled by impulses from the unconscious. When thought is dominated by the rational, conscious mind instead of by the unconscious, it shows what Freud called **sec-**

ondary process thinking, which is orderly, systematic, and logical.

As a person's secondary-process thinking develops, much of his primary-process thinking begins to seem unacceptable and so causes anxiety when it appears. To reduce this anxiety, the person creates **defense mechanisms.** For example, one may reduce anxiety by employing **repression,** that is, by locking up unacceptable thoughts and feelings in the unconscious so that they are unavailable to consciousness. Repression, in fact, takes place in everyone and is a part of all other defense mechanisms. Sublimation is another defense mechanism, one of the few generally positive ones, according to Freud. Some other common defense mechanisms are shown in Table 8-1.

Id, Ego, and Superego

Besides identifying the dual nature (conscious-unconscious) of the human mind, Freud (1949) depicted personality as consisting of three basic components, the id, the ego, and the superego. He called these components "agencies" of the mind, in an effort to avoid the notion that they are physical things or places in the brain. Instead, each agency has a different role to play in the mind's functioning.

The **id,** which is entirely unconscious, is the reservoir of libido. Its basic moving force is the pursuit of pleasure, its means of pursuit are totally nonrational, and its only operating principle is immediate gratification. According to classical Freudian theory, from birth through early infancy the individual is completely ruled by the id, the only one of the three agencies that exists during this period.

The **ego** is the rational, sensible agency of personality. It begins to develop after the first few months of life in response to the demands of the outer world as chil-

TABLE 8-1 COMMON DEFENSE MECHANISMS

MECHANISM	DEFINITION	EXAMPLE
PROJECTION	Attributing to others one's own unacknowledged or unacceptable feelings.	A middle-aged man who dreads aging says of his wife, "She really hates the idea of getting old."
REACTION FORMATION	Taking an attitude or choosing a behavior that is the exact opposite of what is called for by an impulse that is unacceptable.	A child playing "follow the leader" leads the line of children onto a garage roof even though he has an intense fear of heights.
DISPLACEMENT	Transferring feelings from the person or situation that originally aroused the feelings to another, less threatening person or situation.	A married couple experiencing sexual difficulties find themselves arguing about money or in-laws.
ACTING OUT	Directly expressing an unconscious wish or impulse in order to avoid experiencing the emotion that accompanies it.	A teenager vandalizes his school, breaking windows and furniture and painting obscenities on the walls because in doing so, he avoids dwelling on the shame of failure he has experienced there so often.

dren gradually learn that they cannot always have what they want right away. As the ego develops, children learn to delay gratification of present impulses and wishes in favor of future rewards.

The *superego* starts to develop at about age 6, as children internalize their parents' ideals and standards and make them their own; it later comes to include the values of a person's social class and ethnic group. It is the wellspring for most "shoulds" and "should nots," "musts" and "must nots." But the superego is not a rational agency, as the ego is. It is almost completely unconscious and presses for its goals as blindly as the id does, punishing the ego with feelings of inferiority and guilt if its demands are not satisfied. For example, the superego might push a college student to get all As (in order to be a "good boy") even though the attempt to do so would leave him with no time to make friends or enjoy himself. If the student were to get a B or two because he took time from studying to take part in college social life (a course that the rational ego might endorse), the superego would punish the ego with guilt feelings.

Figure 8-6 An imaginative representation of Freud's notion of the human psyche. The drawing represents two fundamental aspects of Freud's thinking: first, the distinction between the conscious and the unconscious—the unconscious being submerged in a body of water, and second, the division into id, ego, and superego. The id is the great underwater beast, the source of all energy, with the ego (interacting with the outside world) and the superego (submerged) growing out of it.

The ego is the only one of the three agencies that deals directly with the outside world. The id and superego press the ego to deal with the world in a way that will satisfy their wants. The ego has a hard job balancing the requirements of reality with the id's seething needs and the often unrealistic restraints of the superego. The superego and id thus conflict with the ego and with each other. The conscious and the unconscious are likewise constantly in conflict. In Freud's view of human nature, psychological conflict is both central and inevitable.

Stages of Psychosexual Development

Freud (1949, 1960) describes five stages of **psychosexual development.** In each of them a different area of the body is the focus of pleasure. Freud called these areas **erogenous zones.** In his view, the kinds of anxiety and conflict that an adult feels, as well as the relative strengths of id, ego, and superego, depend on what happened to the person during the childhood stages of psychosexual development—on whether the child's search for pleasure was frustrated or overindulged or deflected in some other unsatisfying way.

During the **oral stage,** which lasts into the second year of life, the erogenous zone is the mouth and lips, and pleasure is obtained from sucking. The object of desire is therefore the mother's breast; through the satisfaction of nursing, infants come to love their mother's breasts and, ultimately, their mothers.

During the **anal stage,** the rectum and anus are the erogenous zone. Pleasure is obtained from retaining or eliminating feces. Freud believed that children resist toilet training because they wish to control the timing of this pleasurable function. However, because children love their parents and wish to please them, they eventually learn to eliminate in appropriate places. Establishing this kind of control over bodily functions in response to external demands is a sign that a fully functioning ego has emerged. The anal stage lasts until near the end of the third year.

It is during the **phallic stage** that children first focus on the genitals as a source of pleasure. Children at this stage, between about 3 and 6 years old, are very interested in examining their own sexual organs, and they are curious about those of other people as well. This brief preview of an adult type of sexuality sets the scene for the Oedipus or Electra conflict, involving a child's sexual desire for the parent of the opposite sex (see "The Oedipus Conflict," p. 405). The conflict ends when the child represses this desire and identifies with the same-sex parent. It is this repression and identification that results in the formation of the superego. In identifying with the same-sex parent, said Freud, the child incorporates that parent's values into his or her own personality.

The repression of sexual desire for the opposite-sex parent leads to a general repression of sexuality as the child enters the **latency stage.** At puberty, latency gives way to the **genital stage,** which lasts through adulthood. The focus of pleasure is now the genital area, and the person searches for someone of the opposite sex with whom to share genital pleasure.

According to Freud, a good adjustment at the genital stage is possible only if a person has developed satisfactorily through the earlier stages. Freud thought that many of the symptoms of mental disturbance he saw in his adult patients stemmed from difficulties at one of the earlier psychosexual stages. Frustration of needs at a given stage or excessive indulgence in the pleasures of that stage can lead to **fixation,** in which parts of the person's behavior fail to progress beyond the stage in question. In psychotherapy, one sign of fixation is **regression,** in which a person goes back to using behavior typical of the earlier stage at which he is fixated. For example, a person who commonly has temper tantrums might be suspected of a fixation at the anal stage of the 2-year-old. According to Freud, normal adults, too, may show character traits belonging to earlier stages at which their needs were undersatisfied or oversatisfied. For example, smoking, overeating, or habitual gum-chewing may be adult ways of getting oral satisfactions denied during the oral stage. A strong need to accumulate wealth may be an adult expression of a wish to retain feces, a need frustrated during the anal stage.

Even if a child's needs have not been frustrated or overindulged at early stages, some aspects of each stage of psychosexual development remain in the final organization of adult personality. Oral sex, anal sex, and masturbation are common sexual activities for many adults today. (Freud regarded masturbation as characteristic of the phallic stage.) More generally, most adults enjoy eating beyond the simple satisfaction of hunger, and most enjoy a well-running digestive system, in-

Figure 8-7 Psychoanalytic concepts have been used extensively to interpret literature. Bruno Bettelheim, a renowned child analyst, believes that the enduring attraction of fairy tales lies in their symbolic representation of unconscious drives and conflicts. For example, Bettelheim (1976) sees "Little Red Riding Hood" as representing a premature sexual encounter. The wolf represents the id—violent and selfish—and the hunter represents the ego—social, protective, and realistic. After Little Red Riding Hood ends up in bed with the wolf, the wolf eats her up—that is, she experiences sexual temptation and is then destroyed. But she is cut out of the wolf's belly by the hunter—she is "reborn"—no longer innocent, but wiser and better.

cluding regular bowel movements. The Oedipal urges of the phallic period, too, commonly influence the search for a sexual partner during adulthood. A person may not consciously look for someone like mother or father, but it is not uncommon for a man's wife to have traits that resemble his mother's, or for a woman's husband to resemble her father in some ways.

Freud's theory has strongly influenced not only psychology but also other fields, such as anthropology and literary criticism. Its usefulness for the present-day study of development, however, has been limited because many Freudian concepts are hard to study empirically. The working of the unconscious mind or of defense mechanisms, for example, can only be inferred indirectly—not measured directly. Even so, to ignore these concepts would greatly diminish our understanding of ourselves.

ERIKSON AND FREUD

Erikson began his career in psychology as a student of Freud, but eventually he came to feel that Freud's view of development was too limited, especially in its assumption that personality is determined mostly by relations within the family and is fixed by the end of early childhood. Erikson had seen immense historical upheavals—severe economic depression in Europe and in America, the rise of Hitler and the Nazis, the persecution of Jews, World War II. He came to believe that any theory of psychological development must take into account social, political, and geographical influences on individuals and the prominent effects of individuals on society and history. Freud had not completely neglected those factors, but he did not make them important components of his theory.

Figure 8-8   The eight psychosocial crises described by Erik Erikson.

One of Erikson's major theoretical departures from Freud is his emphasis on the individual's ego and its development. Freud had focused more on the never-ending conflict between id, ego, and superego. For Erikson, the ego is the agency that makes the world coherent for us: It is "where we are most ourselves." When the ego is in control, we are not fantasizing or wishing we could be doing something else (thoughts prompted by the id). Nor are we thinking that we ought to do something or should have done something else in the past (thoughts prompted by the superego). When people are psychologically healthy, their egos are functioning well, screening and organizing most of the impulses, memories, emotions, and perceptions that simultaneously try to enter their thoughts and to demand action. According to Erikson, when the ego is functioning well, the id and superego become its allies. At the right time and in the right place, the ego can let the id have its way—as in sexual abandon—or give the superego its due—as in moral action.

A second major difference between Erikson's and Freud's theory is Erikson's emphasis on the *role of society* in psychological development. "The human being," says Erikson, "at all times, from the first kick *in utero* to the last breath, is organized into groupings of geographic and historical coherence: family, class, community, nation" (1963). Individuals develop within this complex web of social groupings.

Children learn social values and participate in social institutions as an intrinsic part of their development. The developmental course of children growing up in a culture that values ferocity or aggressiveness will be very different from that of children in a culture that values gentleness or noncompetitiveness. The ego develops successfully, Erikson says, when

"at a given stage, [it] is strong enough to integrate the timetable of the organism with the structure of social institutions" (1963). Erikson draws an analogy between prenatal development and psychological development. He says that just as an embryo follows its genetic plan for development, with each organ having its own critical period for forming, a child has a timetable for developing psychological capacities, and each new stage requires a different kind of social interaction if that capacity is to develop normally. The interaction of an individual's developmental timetable with his society's institutions is central to Erikson's theory and is reflected in the name he has given it: the theory of *psychosocial development.*

A third major difference between the views of Erikson and Freud is that Erikson sees development as continuing throughout the *life span.*

ERIKSON'S THEORY OF PSYCHOSOCIAL DEVELOPMENT

Erikson proposes eight stages between birth and old age, each one being defined by a particular kind of encounter between the individual and the social environment. Erikson calls these encounters *developmental crises.* A crisis is not a threat of catastrophe; instead, it is a developmental turning point reached when an individual is mature enough to face important new social requirements or opportunities. Erikson describes each crisis in terms of an opposition between two characteristics, such as trust versus mistrust. Figure 8-8 offers brief descriptions of Erikson's stages. (The stages through adolescence are discussed at length in age-appropriate chapters.) Like Freud's, Erikson's theory is based primarily on his clinical experiences, and it is not easily

BASIC TRUST vs MISTRUST

(birth to 1 year):
Infants learn that they can trust others to respond sensitively to their needs — to care for them. They also come to feel that they are worthy of such care and so trust themselves. Infants who are abused or who are cared for erratically may mistrust their world; they don't know what to expect.

AUTONOMY vs SHAME AND DOUBT

(1 to 3 years):
Toddlers have developed a sense of self and wish to establish themselves as separate individuals, yet they must also begin learning how to comply with social rules. When parents' demands coincide with a toddler's abilities, he develops a sense of autonomy. If his attempts at independent behavior are belittled or if the demands on him are beyond his capacities, he may doubt his abilities to deal with the social world and develop a feeling of shame. Some shame and doubt are necessary to help the child recognize his limits.

INITIATIVE vs GUILT

(3 to 6 years):
Once the preschooler feels himself to be autonomous, he begins to pursue activities on his own, playing games like "house" or "school" with other children and asking to help with chores around the house. His initiative may lead him to overdo things. Because his conscience is beginning to form, parents' over-reactions to transgressions can foster guilt, especially if the parents are extremely rigid or unrealistic. Some guilt is normal, but too much guilt will inhibit initiative.

INDUSTRY vs INFERIORITY

(7 to 11 years):
In all societies, children of this age receive new, adult-like responsibilities. The child must find an area in which his industry wins approval and gives him a sense of mastery. In most Western societies, children apply their industry in schools. If the child sees that his industry is productive — that he is learning valuable things — he will be glad to be industrious. If he finds no area of mastery, he will feel inferior and may shrink from trying new things. Even a child who has mastered something should be aware of areas where his talents are inferior.

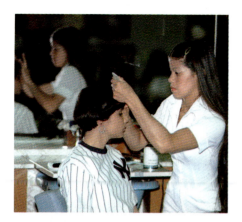

IDENTITY vs ROLE CONFUSION
(12 to 18 years):
The adolescent must integrate all earlier identifications and must recapitulate the psychosocial crises of childhood to formulate an identity, a sense of who she is in relation to her society. The identity comprises a sexual identity, a work identity, and an ethnic identity. Role confusion — uncertainty about one's sexual identity or inability to see oneself in an occupation — is the danger of this stage.

INTIMACY vs ISOLATION
(young adulthood):
A firm sense of identity is the basis for true intimacy. Intimacy is the sharing of oneself with another, in friendship or in work or, most important, in a sexual love relationship. People whose sense of identity is fragile see danger in letting others glimpse their struggle, so they choose isolation, avoiding all contacts that could lead to intimacy.

GENERATIVITY vs STAGNATION
(middle adulthood):
Generativity is primarily the concern for establishing and guiding the next generation — having children and raising and caring for them. It can also include productivity and creativity in work or art. When adults find themselves without children to nurture (or with children but no nurturant feelings) and without some faith in the value of their work, they suffer a sense of stagnation and personal impoverishment.

EGO INTEGRITY vs DESPAIR
(old age):
Ego integrity consists of an acceptance of oneself and one's life cycle as something that had to be, as having order and integrity no matter what psychological or social battles were undergone along the way. Such feelings allow a person to face death without fear. Despair comes if one looks back on one's life and sees it as unsatisfactory yet realizes that the time is too short to start another, better life.

tested by empirical studies. Nevertheless, the theory is a rich and evocative description of the human life cycle.

The idea of ego identity and how it is formed lies at the core of Erikson's theory. **Ego identity** is a person's sense of who he or she is and wants to be—a sense of self that leads to a feeling of inner sameness and continuity in the face of bodily and environmental change. It is also a sense that other people, especially those who matter, perceive and value one in ways that match one's self-perceptions and self-valuations. A mature identity is first formulated in adolescence, but the developmental stages and identifications of infancy and childhood establish the groundwork for it.

Psychosexual and Psychosocial Development

According to Freud, then, a child passes through five stages of psychosexual development, each stage having as its focus of pleasure a certain area of the body: the oral and anal stages in infancy; the phallic stage, which lasts from about age 4 to about age 6; the latency (asexual) stage of middle childhood; and the genital stage, which begins in adolescence and lasts through adulthood. In the phallic stage, the focus of pleasure is the genital area, as it is in adults. This brief preview of adult sexuality sets the stage for the Oedipus conflict, which, in Freud's theory, is the crucial event that leads to identification with the same-sex parent.

The Oedipus Conflict   In Sophocles' tragedy, Oedipus unknowingly murders his father and marries his mother. Freud chose this tragedy as a metaphor partly because his analysis of development in the preschool years focused mainly on boys.

The **Oedipus conflict** takes place because a boy's new phallic orientation makes him feel sexually attracted to his mother (Freud 1949, 1960). Even though he may have only fuzzy notions about what adult sexuality is, he recognizes the emotional relationship between his parents and has some sense of their sexual bond. As a result, he begins to have fantasies about replacing his father as his mother's lover. His sexual impulses may reveal themselves in such typical behaviors as watching his mother dress and undress, touching her body in an exploratory way, making up all kinds of reasons for getting into bed with her, showing delight when his father has to be away on a trip, and saying things like "I'm going to marry you when I grow up, Mommy."

Because the boy wants to replace his father and have his mother all to himself, he has fantasies about harming his father or about his father's going away or dying. But at the same time the child loves and needs his father, so his thoughts begin to scare him: What would he do without his father? In addition, the boy fears his father's power and worries that his father might discover all his hostile fantasies and retaliate. Specifically, Freud says, the boy fears that his father will castrate him.

Dennis The Menace   By Hank Ketcham

"I'll never be in love with anyone but you, Mom . . . . but sometime I might be in LIKE with somebody."

These wishes, fears, and anxieties are eventually resolved. When he is 6 or so, the boy represses his desire for his mother and identifies strongly with his father. After all, if his mother loves his father so much and if his father is such a powerful person, then it must be good to be like his father.

For Freud, this identification means not only that the boy strives to act like his father but that he incorporates what he sees as his father's values. This identification marks the beginning of moral development, as the child begins to use the parental definitions of right and wrong that he has internalized to guide his own behavior. In Freud's terms, these incorporated values are the beginnings of the superego, or conscience.

Freud said that a similar conflict operates in girls at this age: They desire their fathers and have fantasies about getting rid of their mothers. This conflict— sometimes called the **Electra complex,** after a woman in Greek tragedy who led a plot to kill her mother—is resolved much as the Oedipus conflict is. The girl fears her mother's retaliation but recognizes that her father loves her mother, so she represses her desire for her father and identifies with her mother.

For Freud, the successful resolution of the Oedipus or Electra conflict is absolutely necessary for the later development of a proper sexual identity and a conscience, or set of ideals.

Two Psychosocial Stages of the Preschool Years   Erik Erikson's theory of personality development in the preschool years builds on Freud's account of psychosexual development but goes beyond it. Like Freud, Erikson emphasizes the role of the child's emotions and of identification. But just as important in Erikson's view is the role of the child's social environment.

Erikson (1963, 1968) analyzes the preschool years in two stages, which correspond chronologically to Freud's anal and phallic stages but which Erikson describes in terms of psychosocial crises. In each crisis the child must deal with broad issues of who he is and how he relates to his social world.

Erikson calls the first of these two crises *autonomy versus shame and doubt.* This crisis centers on the child's initial attempts at self-control and whether they lead to his being made to feel competent and worthy or incompetent and ashamed. Only in this sense does Erikson's view of this period correspond to Freud's picture of the anal stage and the effects of toilet-training. Erikson points out that "as far as anality proper is concerned, everything depends on whether the cultural environment wants to make something out of it" (1968). In many cultures, toilet-training is simply not an issue. Rigid toilet training can become a battle for autonomy only in cultures that practice it. In other cultures the battle may rage over other issues.

By 2 years of age or so, the child can think of himself as an independent person; through others' responses to him, he begins to form an impression of the kind of person he is. His parents usually recognize his new competence, and they expect him to begin to learn the social rules of their society. The child's task at this time, according to Erikson, is to learn to function both as a separate individual and as a member of his family and society. This helps him to gain a sense of autonomy and to avoid the shame at violating social rules that makes him doubt his own competence.

Bubbly, energetic, and often willful, 2- and 3-year-olds need to learn social restraints. If their parents' demands coincide with their capacities, they can meet the demands and gain confidence in their ability to assert themselves. But some parents set demands so far beyond their children's capacities that they are bound to fail; some exercise such rigid control that their children can make no decisions on their own. In such situations, children become generally ashamed of themselves and doubtful of their abilities to deal with the social world. Intentionally or unintentionally, some parents habitually belittle attempts at autonomous behavior (for example, by laughing at it). Or they make their children feel evil for breaking a rule they do not understand, or dirty for soiling their pants or touching their genitals. The consequence, Erikson says, may be an overwhelming sense of shame.

At the other extreme, some parents change the rules of social behavior from one day to the next or are overly permissive. Consequently, their children have trouble learning what others expect of them. They doubt their ability to deal with other people and feel ashamed of the many social mistakes they make outside the family.

Figure 8-9 (Left.) This young boy seems to radiate autonomy and initiative as he strides purposefully through the streets of his big-city neighborhood. (Right.) On another day, some experience has made the same child withdraw into feelings of shame or guilt.

At this stage, children identify only with their parents or other prime caretakers. Erikson says the child is "deeply and exclusively identified with his parents, who most of the time appear to him to be powerful and beautiful" (1968).

Erikson has tried to emphasize that successful resolution of this crisis requires a balance between autonomy on the one hand and shame and doubt on the other, not the complete elimination of shame and doubt. Children must learn what they should not and cannot do as well as what they should and can do. Shame and doubt thus help direct their behavior. Ultimately they must develop a sense not only of their own autonomy but of its limits.

The second crisis of the preschool years is ***initiative versus guilt.*** Once the child has resolved the first crisis and is firmly convinced that he is autonomous—a person on his own—he begins to pursue activities on his own initiative.

This newly developed ability to understand how things and people relate to each other along with a growing control over their muscles make children eager to become active members of social groups. Many of the games children play at this age recreate social interactions they have seen. They play "house" or "store" or "school." They ask for grown-up chores to do and eagerly take out the trash, carry in the groceries, or set the table. They like to cooperate with other people, and they like to be on the move.

With these new abilities—and an insistence that parents recognize those new abilities—children now move into a new social world. For the first time, they really participate as social beings, people who know how to follow many of the norms and roles of their society. However, their initiative may take them too far. On the one hand, in trying out new things (playing "doctor," perhaps), they may find that they have violated some rule of their newly forming con-

ESSAY:
THE OEDIPUS CONFLICT
ACCORDING TO COGNITIVE THEORY

A cognitive explanation of the Oedipus and Electra conflicts emphasizes how a child's changing understanding influences the child's emotions. At about age 2, the child is in the early preoperational period of development and so has recently gained the ability to think about properties of things independently of his own direct actions on them (Fischer & Watson, 1981). This new representational ability allows the child to think about events that arouse emotion. Sometimes his thoughts scare him, for example, when he thinks about fierce tigers in the backyard or about monsters in the dark.

Also, the toddler at this level cannot take another person's point of view and therefore cannot understand most of the reasons for other people's actions. For example, a certain expression on a child's face or a telltale motion of hands or legs may lead a parent to ask, "Steven, do you have to go to the bathroom?" But the toddler cannot understand that his own behavior is the basis for his parent's question. Instead, he assumes that his mother or father can read his thoughts.

These two aspects of early thought—the child's capacity to be frightened by his own thoughts and his assumption that his parents can read his mind—extend to some degree throughout the preschool years and set the stage for the Oedipus and Electra conflicts. But the actual appearance of these conflicts requires, above all, the ability to understand social roles in the family, such as sex, or gender, roles and age roles. To understand the reciprocal social relationship "husband-wife," a child must be able to understand *both* sex roles and age roles and to relate them to one another. Two- and 3-year-olds cannot even begin to do this. Although they may use the words "boy" and "girl," they do not understand how "boy" is related to "man," and "girl" to "woman." Nor do they understand how either of these pairs is related to "father" and "mother."

By age 4 or 5, children are able to relate mental representations to each other, and they have developed a better understanding of important aspects of family life. They know that a husband is married to a

The toilet monster I never knew about this when I was a child, thank God. There's this thing which lives in the toilet, and *likes* it, and when you go late at night and flush the toilet it *wakes the thing up,* so you better hurry getting out of there. This kid was too slow.

wife and a wife to a husband. They also know that boys grow up to be men, and girls grow up to be women.

One result of this new understanding is that children show their first clear role identifications. They can compare themselves to someone else, often the parent of the same sex, and strive to be similar to that person. However, at 4 or 5, children can mentally control only one reciprocal relationship at a time: wife-husband *or* mother-child. They cannot coordinate two reciprocal relationships simultaneously. Therein lies the cognitive fuse that sets off the Oedipus and Electra conflicts. Children's inability to deal with more than one social dimension at a time leads them to believe that they really can grow up and marry Mommy or Daddy, as the following exchange suggests.

Paul: Mommy, I'm going to marry you.

Mother: But Paul, you can't marry me. You're not old enough.

Paul: Then I'll wait till I grow up, like Daddy.

Mother: But when you're grown up, I'll be as old as grandma.

Paul: Really?

Mother: Yes, you'll be a young man, and I'll be an old woman.

Paul: Well, I'll wait till I'm as old as grandpa. Then I'll marry you.

The characteristics of 4- and 5-year-olds' thinking also explain other aspects of the Oedipus and Electra conflicts. Because the child can relate one representation to another, he can construct the following line of thought. He fantasizes getting rid of his father in order to have his mother all to himself. From that thought, he proceeds to the idea that getting rid of his father means that he would no longer have his father's love and care. This thought frightens him. Being frightened and believing that his parents can read his mind, he then worries that they might punish him for his hostile fantasies.

The confusions and emotional turmoil of the Oedipus and Electra conflicts occur only in cultures and families where children are raised by both mother and father. In cultures with other kinds of family structures, these conflicts do not occur (M. Mead 1963). But according to the cognitive-developmental explanation, preschool children in these other cultures should still show similar confusions about social roles in families.

The confusions of the Oedipus and Electra conflicts disappear when the child reaches the period of concrete operations—usually around age 6. For one thing, the child's egocentrism virtually disappears, and he becomes able to put himself into another person's shoes. For example, he may realize that if his father really should disappear from the face of the earth, his mother would feel very sad. Because his love for his mother is the primary reason for the conflict, his loss of egocentrism allows him to see her point of view and think of her feelings. With the end of egocentrism also comes the understanding that parents cannot really read your thoughts. Most important, the child comes to understand that growing up means more than becoming an adult. Adults grow older, too, so a boy will not "catch up" with his mother. Besides, his mother is already married to his father and therefore cannot also be her son's wife. In this way, when the child can coordinate age and sex roles, the Oedipus and Electra conflicts

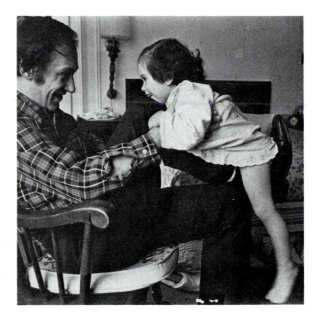

normally become resolved. The entire process is summarized in the table on the facing page.

Cognitive-developmental theory accounts for identification in the same way that it accounts for the Oedipus and Electra conflicts—by tracing the rise of the ability to understand social roles. Although 4-year-olds show an early form of identification, full-blown identification of the type that Freud described requires that a child be able to (1) consider how another person acts in various situations; (2) consider how he himself acts; and (3) compare the other person's actions with his own and adjust his actions to better match the other person's (Kagan 1958). The simultaneous consideration of himself and the other person—the moving back and forth between representations—is possible only when a child has developed the cognitive capacities of the concrete-operational period (Ruble 1983).

COGNITIVE DEVELOPMENT AND THE OEDIPUS CONFLICT

COGNITIVE LEVEL	THE OEDIPUS CONFLICT
PREOPERATIONAL (single representations)	*Setting the stage for the Oedipus conflict* The child cannot understand sex roles or age roles. The child can scare himself with his own thoughts. The child assumes that his parents can read his thoughts.
PREOPERATIONAL (relations between representations)	*Emergence of the Oedipus conflict* The child can understand sex roles or age roles, but when dealing with both sex and age he confuses roles, believing for example that he can take over his father's role as husband. The child can understand concrete aspects of his parents' point of view, but his understanding is so limited that he still assumes they can read many of his thoughts. The child can make simple, crude comparisons between himself and others and therefore shows a rudimentary form of identification. The child can understand single implications of a fantasy. For example, getting rid of father would mean that he would have mother to himself.
CONCRETE OPERATIONAL	*Resolution of the Oedipus conflict* The child can understand the complex relationships between sex roles and age roles. The child can understand his parents' viewpoints in some detail and can therefore recognize that they cannot read his thoughts. The child can compare himself with others on complex and subtle characteristics and can therefore identify with others. The child can understand moral rules and other social norms and thus can form a conscience.

science and so they feel guilty. On the other hand, their new cognitive abilities can lead them to misunderstand, as in an Oedipus or Electra conflict when they imagine themselves as rivals to their parent of the same sex.

Parents need to make the limits of initiative clear: No, Jimmy cannot marry his mother, and Susie cannot spank her baby brother. But if parents overreact, then the child's developing conscience may become overburdened with guilt. Guilt about real social transgressions is necessary, but not guilt about failing to meet the unrealistic expectations of parents or simply about being alive. Too much guilt damages a child's initiative and inhibits normal eagerness to join with others in work and play.

In Freudian theory, identification mainly involves a son's identification with his father or a daughter's with her mother. Erikson's psychosocial theory enlarges Freud's concept. Erikson says that personality development depends on a young person's identification with many people throughout his childhood and adolescence. As a child's cognitive and physical capacities change, he needs to try new ways of interacting with others. He observes how an admired person enacts certain roles, and he tries to emulate, or imitate, that person's actions. In this respect, Erikson's theory serves as a bridge uniting some of Freud's ideas with some of the concepts of social-learning theory.

Identification, Imitation, and Social Learning

Social-learning theory has traditionally emphasized observational learning, especially imitation (see the theory inset "Social Learning," in Chapter 6). Research in this area has shown that young children learn attitudes and behaviors by observing models who are powerful and nurturant and who reward and punish the child (Bandura 1969). For most preschool children, of course, parents are the most powerful and nurturant models.

If the concept of identification is added to social-learning analysis, the child is seen as actually *striving* to be like (identify with) his parents and some other adults. Observational learning may take place for many reasons, but one of the most powerful is the desire to be like someone. When we identify with someone, we observe them closely and try very hard to make ourselves more like them. For the preschool child, most early identifications—and most socialization of all types—take place within the family.

SOCIALIZATION IN THE FAMILY

A child's first efforts to operate as part of a social group take place in the small world of the family. Later, much social behavior will be learned from peers and other **agents of socialization** in the society at large. But the earliest lessons in how to live with others are given by parents.

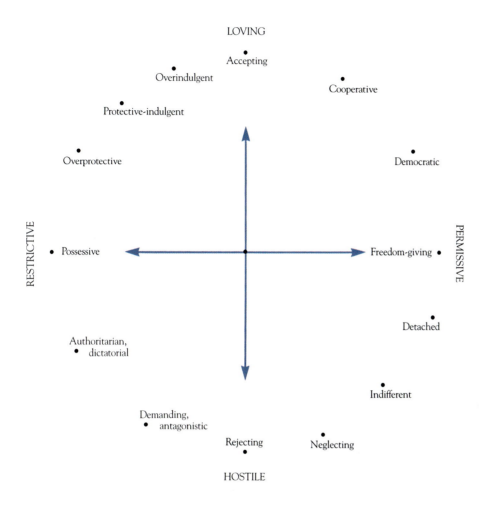

Figure 8-10 Analysis of many different studies of parental style showed that most of parents' behavior toward their children can be described in terms of just two dimensions: how loving the parents are, and how restrictive.

Parents and Parental Styles

Just as there are a variety of styles for mothering young infants, as explained in Chapter 6, so **parental styles** for socializing young children also vary widely. Figure 8-10 summarizes findings from many studies of parental style. It relates various parental characteristics to two major scales of behavior, love–hostility and permissiveness–restrictiveness (Becker 1964; Maccoby & Martin 1983).

Parents nearer the love end of the **love-hostility** scale are accepting and warm. They are sensitive to their children's needs and points of view, and they reward their children's accomplishments, both emotionally and materially. They seek out and enjoy their children's company. Parents near the hostile end of this range are always dissatisfied with their children and continually criticize their personalities as well as their behavior. When these parents are not belittling their children, they are ignoring them.

Parents nearer the permissiveness end of the **permissiveness-restrictiveness** scale do not clearly establish rules of behavior or the consequences for misbehavior. Nor do they consistently enforce any rules that do exist. Parents who are very permissive almost always give in to their children's demands. Very restrictive parents, on the other hand, have strict rules about almost everything and see that the rules are always obeyed. They are unwilling to consider extenuating circumstances when a rule is broken.

Various combinations of the characteristics on these scales correspond to different parental styles. For example, a great deal of love and warmth combined with a high degree of restrictiveness describes parents who are overprotective. Parents who are very permissive with their children and also near the high end of the hostility scale can be described as neglectful.

Is there a systematic relationship between such parental styles and a child's personality characteristics? Numerous studies of this question have brought some consistent correlations to light.

Consequences of Parental Treatment

Most studies that attempt to link children's behavior with treatment by parents look first at the children. What consistent patterns of behavior or personality do many children show that might be traced back to the way their parents treated them? Some of the behaviors in children that researchers have examined are control of aggression, dependence, and competence.

Aggression   In an extensive early study of 5-year-olds, researchers expected to find that children whose parents punished them physically for acts of aggression would show less aggression than other children did (R. Sears et al. 1953). Instead, they found that children—boys, in particular—who had been physically punished for aggression did more pushing and hitting at school than children who had been less harshly punished.

Some subsequent studies have supported this finding: *Aggressive parents tend to have aggressive children* (Parke & Slaby 1983). Parents who punish seem to serve as models for aggressive behavior. In a famous series of studies that examined the effects of the modeling of aggression, groups of preschool children saw an adult insult and hit a large rubber Bobo doll. When children from these groups later played with the Bobo doll, they were much more aggressive with it than were children who had not witnessed the adult's behavior (Bandura et al. 1963) (Figure 8-11).

In a variation on this experiment, groups of children saw either a film in which the aggressive model was generously rewarded for his or her behavior or a film in which the model was severely punished. As expected, children who saw the model rewarded were much more aggressive in their later play than were children who saw the model punished (Bandura 1965). The aggression of

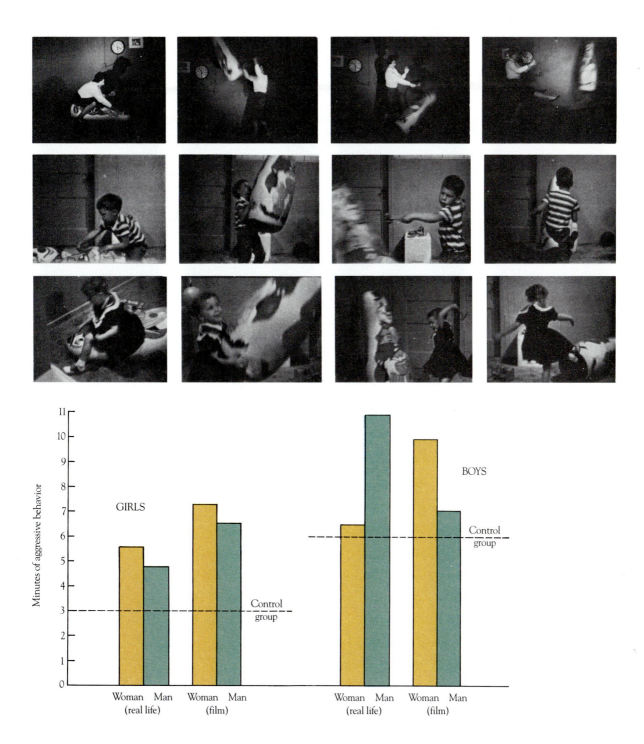

Figure 8-11   The top row of photos shows some of the aggressive behavior modeled by an adult in Albert Bandura's studies. The rest of the photos show children imitating that aggression.

Some of the children were in the same room when the woman attacked the Bobo doll. Other children saw a film of her aggressive behavior. (Some groups of children saw a male rather than a female model.) The control group saw no aggression at all. The chart shows how the children behaved when they were taken to a room containing a Bobo doll and other toys after they had seen the aggressive behavior of the adults. All of the children who had seen aggressive play— whether live or on film—played more aggressively than the controls. Note, however, that the level of aggression for boys in the control group is considerably higher than that for girls.

Figure 8-12 Children almost everywhere use aggression, physical or verbal, once in a while. Sometimes they use it for getting what they want and sometimes to defend themselves. Parents generally try to discourage their children from the first use and to encourage the second.

parents toward their children is usually rewarded, in that the parents get their way.

Almost all parents try to train their children to control aggressive behavior. In fact, control of aggression is one of the universal goals of socialization. Even aggressive parents who unwittingly teach aggression through modeling are trying to teach their children not to hit and kick other children. Many parents make one exception to the no-hitting norm. They tell their children that they should defend themselves when they are the victims of aggression. This defend-yourself norm seems to be a way of teaching independence.

Dependence   Our culture has certain norms about dependence in young children. For example, most parents expect to help a 3-year-old get dressed but think that a 5-year-old should dress himself (except, perhaps, for a little help with shoelaces). Most understand a 2- or 3-year-old's clinging to mother or teacher during the first days of nursery school but disapprove somewhat of a clinging 4- or 5-year-old. Adults in America generally expect to see preschoolers show increasing amounts of independence (autonomy and initiative, in Erikson's terms) as they approach school age.

Despite these age norms, there are wide individual differences in dependent behavior. Some 3-year-olds march off to nursery school with barely a backward glance, whereas some cry for their mother weeks after school has started.

Studies have found several connections between the characteristics of parents and the dependent behavior of their preschool children. The strongest association is between the mother's protectiveness and the child's dependence. Mothers who reward dependence, who become filled with anxiety when their children have a slight illness or are out of their sight, tend to have children who are passive and dependent.

One hypothesis suggests that the overprotective mother and the dependent child reinforce each other's behavior (Martin 1975). It may start with the child's temperamental characteristics. Perhaps the child was the kind of infant that Chess and Thomas (1977) describe as difficult, reacting negatively to unfamiliar things. The mother, alarmed at her infant's violent reactions to new foods, people, and places, decides to keep the child close to her, so that she can intervene at the first sign of distress. The child then may depend more and more on his mother to protect him from distressing events. Or the overprotection and dependence may start because the mother is nervous about her maternal role and duties or unduly fearful about dangers. Through social referencing (see Chapter 6), the child then may take the cue and become fearful about potential dangers. Seeing the child fearful, the mother becomes even more protective. Whatever its origins, once the relationship has begun, both participants keep it going.

Longitudinal studies have found little relation between dependence in the preschool years and dependence in adulthood. Dependent behavior in 6- to 10-year-olds, however, does predict dependence in adulthood—at least for girls. One classic study showed that girls who were dependent in the school years tended to stay that way, but boys who were dependent often became independent adults (Kagan & Moss 1962). This difference in the continuity of boys' and girls' development reveals an interaction between parental style and socialization for sex roles. Norms for the male sex role demand independence. The norm for the female sex role does not demand nearly as much independence, or at least it has not until recently. A boy who notices that he seems less masculine than others because of his dependent behavior may actively search for new models of independent male behavior. In adolescence, male friends often help each other break away from being a "mama's boy." For girls, the social norms permit or even encourage remaining dependent on parents until marriage, and there is less peer pressure to counteract an overprotective parental style.

Aggressiveness and dependence, traits that can create problems for children and their parents, are molded in part by parental style. How does parental style contribute to the formation of more positive traits in children?

Competence and Independence   Diana Baumrind has conducted several studies of the relation between parents' style and the competence and independence of their preschool children (1967, 1971, 1975, 1980). Baumrind assessed the competence of preschoolers in terms of their social responsibility. Children were judged competent if they were friendly, cooperative, and oriented toward constructive achievements. They were judged independent if they showed creativity, assertiveness, and a capacity to be individualistic without being irresponsible.

In assessing parental style, Baumrind looked at the behavior of both mothers and fathers, separately as well as together. In many families, she found one of three parental styles:

1. *Permissive* parents, compared to the others in her study, exercised less control over their children's behavior. They demanded less achievement and accepted behavior that was relatively unsocialized. They also tended to be warm and loving.

2. *Authoritarian-restrictive* parents were cooler, more detached, and highly controlling.

3. *Authoritative* parents, although they firmly enforced rules and demanded high levels of achievement, were warm, rational, and receptive to their children's questions or comments. They seemed to have confidence in themselves as parents.

In general, Baumrind found that children of authoritative parents seem to be the most self-reliant, self-controlled, explorative, and content. The children of permissive parents seem to be the least self-reliant, self-controlled, and explorative. And the children of authoritarian-restrictive parents tend to be more discontented, withdrawn, and distrustful than the others (Baumrind & Black 1967). More specifically, Baumrind proposes that the following characteristics of parental style relate to independence and competence in children:

1. Parents who provide a rich early environment, such as interesting toys and rich social interactions, are more likely to have children with good cognitive skills. Possession of those skills increases a child's self-esteem and leads to competence.

2. Parents who explain why they are delivering punishments or reinforcements are more likely to have competent children. Such explanations improve a child's understanding of social rules. The children of authoritarian-restrictive parents, who do not use reason and explanations, are more likely to be dependent and submissive or passively resistant and less competent. That is, they follow the rules while the parents are around but are inclined to disobey when they think they can get away with it.

3. Authoritative parents, who stress the values of individuality and self-expression, are likely to have independent children.

4. Authoritative parents' firm control of their children's behavior does not restrict the development of independence as long as the parents give the

Figure 8-13 The children of authoritarian-restrictive parents are likely to be dependent and submissive.

children plenty of opportunity to experiment and make their own decisions within the limits defined.

Baumrind's (1980) findings show that the same parental style often affects boys and girls differently. For example, girls whose fathers were punitive tended to be more independent and less conforming than girls whose fathers were warm and accepting. Boys with punitive fathers had trouble forming close friendships and were often unpopular with other children. It seems that for preschool girls, the tension of interacting with a punitive father is more likely to lead to self-assertion than is a paternal attitude of all-enveloping warmth and acceptance. Other studies have found a similar relation for adolescent girls: At least among educationally advantaged girls, a great deal of warmth and support seems to weaken the characteristics that lead to achievement and independence.

Baumrind (1971) also states that the effects of parental practices depend partly on the individual child's personality: "A gentle, sensitive child might well react to high-power directives with passive, dependent responses, whereas an aggressive, vigorous child might react self-assertively or oppositionally, modeling himself after the aggressive parent." Although there is little research

AUTHORITARIAN-RESTRICTIVE PARENTS

GIRLS

BOYS

AUTHORITATIVE PARENTS

GIRLS

BOYS

PERMISSIVE PARENTS

GIRLS

BOYS

that supports the point, sensitive parents probably adapt their socialization methods to each child's personality. In a family with two children, one may be shy and wary of unfamiliar people and events, so the parents might moderate their firmness, finding ways to help this child enjoy the company of others but not insisting on his participating in activities that make him extremely uncomfortable or fearful. The second child might be extroverted—a show-off who seems to demand constant attention. With this child, the parents might have to exert firm and almost constant control, to tone down her obtrusiveness and teach her to forgo the immediate rewards of attention for later rewards that follow achievement.

Siblings

Most families include two or more children, and such factors as birth order and difference in age can have important effects on each child's development. Because family patterns and individual temperaments vary so widely, tracing these effects is an enormously complex task. Nevertheless, a few generalizations can be made.

To begin with, most parents seem to be more closely involved with their first-borns than with their later-borns. They closely monitor the child's development, and they play with and talk to her more, even after the birth of younger children (Dunn & Kendrick 1982; Thomas et al. 1972). In fact, when parents talk to their children as a group, they tend to speak at the level of the oldest child. They also tend to hold higher standards of behavior for the first-born than for later-borns. With a second or third child, parents are apt to be more relaxed and confident. They have learned what to expect and worry less about events that may have made them unnecessarily anxious with their first child.

The intense relationship between parents and first-borns and the parents' high expectations for them seem to produce certain personality characteristics. First-borns tend to be more achievement-oriented than their siblings (Sutton-Smith 1970). More of them appear in *Who's Who*, for example. They tend to

Figure 8-14 Some results of Baumrind's study of how parental style affects preschoolers. The children are represented by behavior profiles constructed from a series of scales arranged in a circle. The scales are dominant to submissive, purposive to aimless, achievement oriented to not achievement oriented, friendly to hostile, cooperative to resistive, and domineering to tractable. The profiles compare the children receiving each of the three parental styles to the "average" boy or girl (center dot in each diagram). The standard that these children were compared with is very different for girls and boys. The average boy is relatively hostile, resistive, and domineering compared with the average girl, who is relatively friendly, submissive, and tractable. Notice that boys and girls can be moved in different directions by the same parental style. Daughters of authoritative parents, for example, are above the average in the aggressive, active, independent dimensions, whereas sons of these parents are much more cooperative, tractable, and achievement oriented than the average boy.

Figure 8-15 A new brother or sister is often hard to take.

be more self-controlled, more conscientious, and less aggressive. On the other hand, they also tend to be more conforming, more anxious, and less socially poised. Largely as a result of their less intense relationship with parents, later-borns tend to be less achievement-oriented than first-borns, and they are more self-confident in social situations and more popular with their peers. Part of their greater social ability with other children probably comes from using older sisters and brothers as models.

Perhaps the most noticeable fact about relations between siblings is that the arrival of a second child is nearly always emotionally upsetting for the first-born, especially if the first-born is less than 3 or 4 years old (Kendrick & Dunn 1980). After all, until the second child arrives, the first-born has no competition for the parents' attention and affection. Even when preschoolers enjoy the new baby, which makes them feel grown up, many decide, sooner or later, that it is time to "send the baby back."

In the ongoing interaction between siblings, the fewer the years that separate children in a family, the greater the influence they seem to have on each other, particularly if they are of the same sex. Siblings far apart in age may be just casual friends, although if an older sibling spends a great deal of time taking care of a younger one, the younger one may identify with him or her almost as strongly as with the parents (Weisner & Gallimore 1977). But children close in age and of the same sex are inclined to compete intensely with each other, especially when they are the first two children in the family.

The competition often takes the form of **deidentification,** or negative identification. In order to carve out a distinct identity, one daughter or son (the younger, usually) watches the other, learns that sibling's behavior, and then tries hard to do the opposite. This process may account for the many families in which two sisters or two brothers appear to have opposite personalities (Loehlin & Nichols 1976; Rowe & Plomin 1981). Parents and others may characterize one child as, say, serious, studious, and conscientious, and the other as light-hearted, unmotivated at school, and careless. Some researchers believe that deidentification is a defense against sibling rivalry (Schachter et al. 1976, 1978). If the siblings claim different turfs, little common ground remains to be used as a battlefield.

Social Class

The nuclear family of parents and siblings is a small social world within the larger one. Therefore, a family's place in the society at large also helps determine how its children are socialized.

One of the most important characteristics of a family's place in society is its **social class.** Sociologists generally classify American families as lower class, middle class, or upper class, depending on family income, the prestige of the head-of-household's occupation, and the education of the parents. These classes are sometimes further divided into three subclasses, giving each class a lower, middle, and upper range. It is thus possible to distinguish, for example, between the chronically unemployed (lower-lower) and skilled factory workers (upper-lower), or between white-collar employees such as sales people or small-business operators (lower-middle) and doctors or corporate executives (upper-middle). How a family raises children can be significantly affected by the class to which the family belongs.

A difference in perspective-taking by parents may be one of the most important differences between lower-class and middle-class styles of rearing children. When helping their children with particular tasks, middle-class mothers typically start from the child's viewpoint and abilities; they base their help on what the child knows and can do. Fewer lower-class mothers take their child's viewpoint and abilities into account (R. Hess 1970; McGlaughlin et al. 1980).

In one series of studies, mothers from classes ranging from upper-middle to lower-lower were observed as they taught their 4-year-olds three simple tasks. Tape recordings of these sessions showed that middle-class mothers were likely to explain to their children how to complete the task, but lower-class mothers tended to use direct commands, simply telling their children what to do and, in some cases, doing it themselves (Hess & Shipman 1965, 1967, 1968).

These excerpts from the tapes illustrate the differences. In this task, the mother was to teach the child how to group or sort a small number of toys.

> *Middle-class mother:* "All right, Susan, this board is the place where we put the little toys; first of all you're supposed to learn how to place them according to color. Can you do that? The things that are all the same color you put in one section; in the second section you put another group of colors, and in the third section you put the last group of colors. Can you do that? Or would you like to see me do it first?"
>
> *Child:* "I want to do it."

This mother gave explicit information about the task and what was expected of the child, she offered support and help of various kinds, and she made it clear that she expected the child to perform.

A second mother's style was less clear and precise. Here is what she said in introducing the same task:

> *Mother:* "Now, I'll take them off the board; you put them all back on the board. What are these?"
>
> *Child:* "A truck."
>
> *Mother:* "All right, just put them right here; put the other one right here; all right, put the other one right there."

This mother relied more on nonverbal communication in her commands. She did not define the task for the child, even in general terms, or tell her what to expect, nor did she provide the child with ideas or information that the child could grasp in attempting to solve the problem.

A third mother was even less explicit. She introduced the task as follows: "I've got some chairs and cars, do you want to play the game?" The child did not respond. The mother continued: "OK, what's this?"

> *Child:* "A wagon?"
>
> *Mother:* "Hmm?"
>
> *Child:* "A wagon?"
>
> *Mother:* "This is not a wagon. What's this?"

Here again, the child did not receive the information he needed to solve or understand the problem. There were marked differences between social classes in the ability of the children to learn from their mothers in these teaching sessions.

The socialization practices of lower-class and middle-class parents differ in other important ways, too. Lower-class parents seem to expect less independent behavior and achievement from their children than middle-class parents do. In preparing a child to start school, for example, lower-class parents stress obedience, respect for authority, and values such as neatness and cleanliness. Middle-class parents tend to emphasize curiosity, eagerness to learn, and self-control (Hess 1970).

When a child misbehaves, lower-class parents are more likely than middle-class parents to use a kind of punishment called "unqualified power assertion" (Hoffman 1960; Maccoby & Martin 1983). That is, they use threats, physical force, or direct commands such as "Be quiet," whereas middle-class parents are more likely to explain why they want the behavior to change: "Be quiet. Daddy's on the phone and I can't hear him when you talk, too."

Figure 8-16   When preschool children were asked to draw a picture of themselves and then to tell a story about the picture, their products revealed class differences. Middle-class children like Rachel (left) generally produced detailed, colorful drawings and stories, showing that they thought well of themselves. The products of lower-class children like David (right) often showed that the children thought poorly of themselves and felt their daily lives to be dull and featureless. (Porter 1971)

Such differences in child-rearing practices between social classes seem to produce some cognitive and social deficits in lower-class children, which may help explain why many enter school without mastery of such basic concepts as color, position, shape, and number, concepts that middle-class parents often stress in talking to their children (Hunt & Kirk 1974). Two agents for erasing these deficits in 2- to 5-year-olds have been explored with some success in the United States—television and preschools. In fact, for preschool children from all social classes, these are probably the most important agents of socialization outside the family.

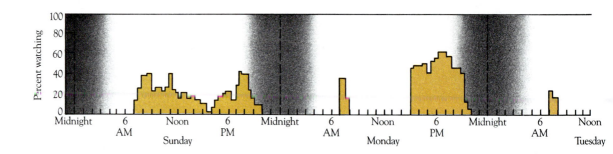

TELEVISION AS AN AGENT OF SOCIALIZATION

Approximately 95 percent of American families own a television set and watch it regularly. Among the most regular viewers are young children.

Children under 6 years old watch television about 2½ hours a day (Leibert et al. 1982). Between ages 8 and 10, viewing time goes up to about 4 hours a day, then begins to diminish in adolescence. So the average child has spent 15,000 hours watching television by the time she graduates from high school. That is much more time than she would have spent on anything other than sleep.

The effects of this convenient "baby-sitter" on the development of young children can only be guessed at, but its power is suggested by some results of the National Survey of Children, sponsored by the Foundation for Child Development (1976). When children were asked to name a famous person they wanted to be like, almost half named someone they had seen on TV—an entertainer or an athlete. These were the children's models.

TV has many positive effects, of course. It widens a child's world beyond the community to include farms and cities, princes and beggars, mountain caves and ocean floors. Every week, a child can discover something new. A girl who has never been inside a concert hall can see a ballet on TV and decide she would like to be a ballerina. A boy who has never been outside a city can see a show about a forest fire and decide to become a naturalist.

Research on the effects of television has focused on three major questions: What do children understand and remember from what they see on TV? What particular negative behaviors, such as aggression, may be induced by TV programs? And can TV be an effective educational medium?

Children's Comprehension of TV Programs

What do preschoolers understand of what they see on TV? In one study, British children watched a *Hercules* cartoon film that was stopped at the height of the drama—when Hercules was in danger from a large rock about to fall on him (Noble 1975). When asked if the story was over, three-quarters of the children

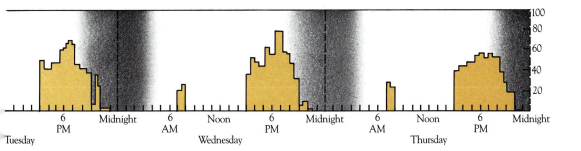

Figure 8-17 The pattern of TV watching by first-grade children in a working-class town near Los Angeles, California. (The data cover just Sunday through Thursday because they were collected in school.) On weekdays, almost a third of the children watch some TV before leaving for school. By 6 o'clock in the evening, about two-thirds of them are watching, and the numbers then drop off gradually until bedtime, which is about 9 o'clock. Although TV watching appears to be a major activity in these children's lives, many of them reported that they were doing other things at the same time they were watching programs—eating or talking or playing with friends and family (Lyle & Hoffman 1972).

5 years old and younger said it was. In other studies, preschool children were shown a simple puppet film and then were asked to arrange twelve photographs from the film according to the story line. Most of the children were unable to put more than two photos into the correct sequence (Noble 1975).

Given the characteristics of preschool children's thinking, these results are not surprising. Because it is hard for a young child to take a point of view other than her own, she cannot put herself in a character's place in order to discern the character's motives or intentions. Nor can she relate the roles of different characters to each other. Consequently, what she perceives are clusters of separate action sequences rather than a story line with a beginning, a middle, and an end. The ability to follow a story line begins at about 4 or 5 years and, by 8 or 9, children can usually follow the details of a simple, concrete story (Collins & Duncan 1984).

Preschoolers may lose the story line and misunderstand motives and intentions, but they find certain characters attractive and are likely to imitate them in later play. Heroes such as Superman and Wonder Woman require no subtle reading of character. They generally announce their intention to "get the bad guys," and their power and strength always win out. Make-believe games involving superheroes may appeal to preschoolers partly because they compensate for a child's lack of power in real life. On the other hand, children have always played such games, even before television. Action and aggression seem to draw the young like magnets.

Aggression and Violence

Before the advent of television, children drew their models for play from stories told or read to them. Many classic children's stories contain aggression and violence. In "Little Red Riding Hood," the wolf eats both Little Red Riding Hood and her grandmother. Eventually, however, they are rescued by a woodsman, who cuts open the wolf's belly with an ax and releases them intact. In "Hansel and Gretel," the children are abandoned by their father and stepmother. The witch captures them in order to eat Hansel, but Gretel foils the witch's plot by pushing her into her own oven and cooking her alive. If you think back on other stories that you heard as a young child, you can probably come up with a long list of grisly tales, full of aggression. Is the violence and aggression presented on TV screens more harmful to children than the aggression in old-fashioned children's literature?

Research suggests that for young children, the answer is yes. First, the vivid, full-color, moving images on the TV screen seem to be much more immediate and affecting than words (Hayes & Birnbaum 1980). Second, the amount of time preschool children spend watching TV is far greater than the amount of time parents have to read to them. Third, the amount of violence and aggression in TV programs is extraordinarily high. Eighty percent of programs portray violence of some kind, and the number of violent acts averages five per program (Signorielli et al. 1982).

Young children who see a great deal of aggression on television seem to be more apt to perform aggressive acts. The Bandura studies described earlier in this chapter (see Figure 8-11) were among the first to document the effect of TV violence. In another study, researchers picked pairs of nursery-school children who showed about the same amount of shoving, hitting, and kicking on the school playground (Steuer et al. 1971). Then one member of each pair was shown a different violence-filled TV program every day for eleven days, while the other was shown a nonviolent program on the same schedule. Afterwards the children were again observed at play. In every pair of children, the child who had watched the violent programs had become more aggressive in his play than the other child. A more recent study also showed more aggression in 3- and 4-year-olds who watched violent TV programs (Singer & Singer 1980).

For older children, the results of studies on the effects of television sometimes contradict each other. For example, one study showed that watching aggression on TV for six weeks produced *less* aggressive behavior in adolescent boys than aggression-free TV did in a control group (Feshbach & Singer 1971). The boys in the control group, however, had had their programs chosen for them by the researchers, and many programs they had been accustomed to watching were kept from them for the six-week period. A replication of this study (Wells 1972) reported that the boys in the control group were frustrated by missing their favorite programs, and this frustration might have caused them to become more aggressive.

The viewing of violence on TV, then, does seem to affect preschool viewers: They show increased aggressive behavior, at least for a short while after the viewing. Whether it has any long-term effects is not known. There seems to be no clear-cut evidence about how older children are affected.

Watching hours of violence on TV each week may confer a kind of emotional immunity to the effects of violence, at least for older children. In one study a group of boys aged 5 to 12 viewed a violent fight in the movie *The Champion* while researchers recorded their heart rates, breathing rates, and perspiration

Figure 8-18   A Sesame Street character imparts information about the letters of the alphabet.

(Cline 1974). The boys in this group, who were known to watch TV more than 25 hours a week, showed significantly less emotional arousal than those who watched less. Continuing heavy doses of TV violence seemed to have lowered the strength of the boys' reactions to it.

Sesame Street

Sesame Street is probably the greatest success story in educational television. Its planners knew that an educational program for children can be successful only if it continuously holds its viewers' interest. Unlike children in classrooms, children watching television can escape a boring lesson with a flip of the switch. So *Sesame Street* has to be entertaining in order to educate. It uses a combination of human characters (both adults and children), unusual puppets, and lively animation to keep its audience engrossed. Each educational segment is no more than a few minutes long, so the children's attention doesn't lag. And humor is an important part of most lessons.

Among the educational goals of *Sesame Street* are to teach the names of letters and numbers, the meaning of relational terms such as "over" and "under," classification skills, the names of simple geometrical forms and some of their functions (as in "circle" and "wheel"), and simple problem-solving skills. Also, through indirect teaching—modeling, that is—the program tries to encourage certain social attitudes and behaviors. It encourages young children to take other people's points of view, to treat others with courtesy and kindness, to respect individual and ethnic differences, and to accept basic rules of justice and fair play.

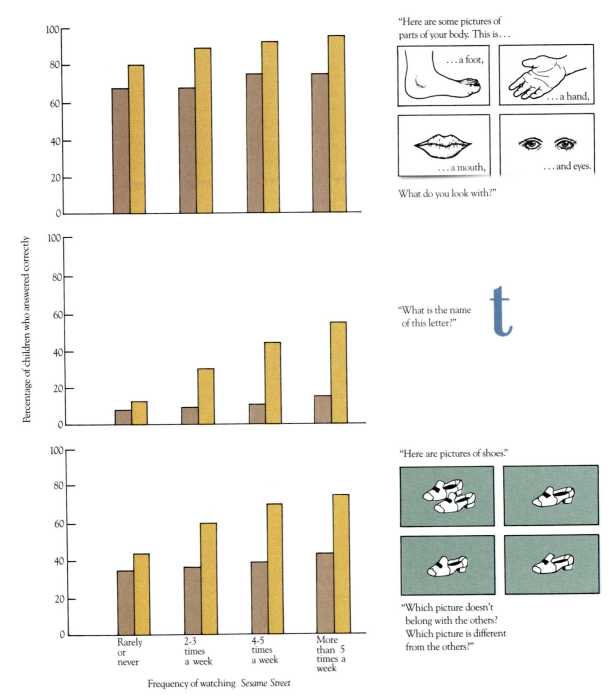

Figure 8-19   A sample of about 1,000 children were tested with questions such as these just before *Sesame Street* went on the air (brown bars) and again at the end of the program's first season (gold bars). These children, between 3 and 5 years old, came from poor inner-city neighbor-hoods, from suburban middle-class neighborhoods, and from rural areas. About half were black, and many were Spanish speaking. The scores of all *Sesame Street* watchers increased as shown, and the more often children watched the program, the more their scores increased.

Although there are other popular educational shows for both preschoolers and older children, only *Sesame Street* has been evaluated thoroughly for its success in meeting its educational purposes. Figure 8-19 shows some results of a large evaluation study run by the Educational Testing Service after *Sesame Street* had been on the air for one year. It showed that both lower-class and middle-class children did learn basic intellectual skills from watching the show and that 3-year-olds profited the most from their year of viewing (Lesser 1974). Perhaps the most striking evidence of the program's success is contained in reports from many schools that first-graders no longer have to be taught the alphabet and numbers.

This evaluation of *Sesame Street* did not test the program's effectiveness as a socializing agent. However, other research has shown that programs such as *Mister Rogers' Neighborhood*, which teach such positive social attitudes as kindness and helpfulness, increase positive behaviors in child viewers, at least in the short run (Stein & Friedrich 1975).

PRESCHOOLS AND DAY CARE

In the second half of this century, preschools have become a major agent of socialization in many societies. In the Soviet Union and other socialist countries, preschools have a carefully constructed curriculum aimed at molding the citizens of tomorrow. Because all citizens in these societies are members of a collective, a basic goal of preschool education is to teach the value of cooperation and group activity. The children learn that their society approves of those who work well as part of a team and disapproves of those who strive for individual recognition. In contrast, American preschools operate according to a variety of principles and curricula, which all generally convey the value of individualism, independence, and competition (Bronfenbrenner 1970; Clarke-Stewart & Fein 1983).

In the United States, the attendance at preschools has increased significantly in the past decade. In 1982, more than 48 percent of the total population of children under 6 years old attended some kind of preschool or day-care center (Clarke-Stewart 1982). Furthermore, kindergarten for 5-year-olds has become an accepted experience, and most kindergartens are part of the public-school system. In 1947, barely half of American 5-year-olds attended any kind of preschool or kindergarten.

Americans have traditionally made a distinction between nursery schools and full-day group care. Nursery schools, which children attend two or three hours a day for social and cognitive "enrichment," have always been considered respectable. But all-day group care for preschoolers has—until recently—been thought of as "a necessary evil to be endured only by children whose mothers had to work. . ." (Robinson et al. 1973). The presumption was that day care provided only physical care, whereas nursery school offered learning experiences.

The idea that mothers work outside the home only because forced to by unfortunate circumstances is the traditional way of thinking about the "ideal"

Figure 8-20 Preschools reflect the values of their society, not only in what they teach but in how they are organized and in what behaviors they encourage and frown upon. Each of the children in this American nursery school (left) is playing on his own or is deciding whether to start a joint building venture. Children in the Soviet preschool (middle) sit in neatly arranged chairs while the group listens to a story. The Chinese preschool (right) has several groups, each engaged in a different activity.

family pattern. That tradition has been breaking down since the 1960s. The growing number of mothers in the work force reflects the change. In 1950, only 12 percent of married women with children less than 6 years old worked outside the home; in 1980 that number had grown to 42 percent. Of single women (divorced or never married) with children less than 6 years old, 56 percent worked, 45 percent full-time (Clarke-Stewart 1982).

In many countries where women are an important part of the work force, the government provides day care. The Scandinavian countries have extensive child-care programs. The Soviet Union and most of the other socialist nations also support extensive preschool services.

During World War II, in response to the need for women in the work force, the United States government paid for children's day care. In the last year of the war, one of every five children between 2 and 5 years old were in day-care centers. When the war ended, government money was withdrawn and most of these centers ceased to exist (Robinson et al. 1973).

In the 1950s, resistance to preschools became more widespread, as many American child-care experts argued that children under 5 would suffer emotionally if they were separated from their mothers for part of every day. This belief was based on research indicating that "maternal deprivation" was harmful to normal development (see Chapter 6).

In the 1960s, however, psychological studies began to suggest that the observed effects of "maternal deprivation" were actually caused by an overall shortage of social and cognitive stimulation. Some researchers came to believe that some children—namely, children from very poor homes—might actually be better off spending part of each day at preschools than spending all of their time at home. The eventual outcome of this change of view was the launching of Project Head Start, financed largely by federal funds.

In the 1970s and early 1980s, as more and more women joined the work force the pressure for day care and for government help in financing it became stronger. But legislators have greatly resisted the idea of government involvement. Partly from preference and partly from necessity, the vast majority of working mothers still make arrangements with relatives or neighbors for care of their children during working hours (see Table 8-2).

TABLE 8-2 CHILD-CARE ARRANGEMENTS
FOR PRESCHOOL CHILDREN OF
WORKING MOTHERS

CARE ARRANGEMENT	CHILDREN USING ARRANGEMENT (%)
In own home	
Father	20
Other relative	20
Nonrelated babysitter	12
Day-care home	
Relative	15
Nonrelative	20
Day-care center	13
Total	100

SOURCE: Clarke-Stewart 1982.

Head Start

Organized as a community-action program, the goal of Head Start was to give poor children the opportunity to overcome any deficiencies in their home education so that they would enter school with skills as well developed as those of middle class children. The hope was that their participation in Head Start for a summer or a year before entering the public schools would substantially improve the performance of these children throughout their schooling. Some of them might then be able to qualify for better jobs in later life, and the cycle of poverty would be broken.

When the project was launched, there were good reasons to be skeptical about its usefulness (Hellmuth 1970). First, no one really knew how to set up an effective preschool. Second, because each community organized its own program, usually in a great hurry, the quality of the programs differed widely. Third, one summer—or even 15 hours a week for a year—may not be time enough to effect major psychological changes.

It was not surprising, then, that the first evaluations of Head Start seemed to show that it was not doing what it was supposed to do (for example, Cicirelli et al. 1969). Although there were some immediate gains in IQ, they seemed to last only a few years at most, disappearing soon after the children started elementary school.

Recent findings have reversed that early evaluation. A large follow-up study done in the late 1970s examined the long-term effects of fourteen different programs similar to Head Start (Lazar & Darlington 1982). The programs used a variety of methods. Some were directed primarily toward the child, some primarily toward the mother, who was shown how to use toys and games to promote her child's development. Some programs were just structured nursery schools; others combined a nursery-school program with periodic home visits by staff who dealt with both parent and child. The success of each of these programs was assessed by studying the progress of a control group of children from the same background who did not participate in the program.

In the follow-up study, researchers collected data on the childrens' school performance and related factors. To almost everyone's surprise, *all* the early-intervention programs had very positive long-term effects.

1.   The children in the intervention programs did better in school than those in the control groups. Fewer of them were assigned to remedial classes and fewer failed a grade. This effect seemed to be greatest when the intervention took place by 4 years of age.

2.   They showed a significant improvement in intellectual functioning, as measured by intelligence tests. Although this increased capacity stayed with them through the first three years of elementary school, it seemed to disappear over the next few years. But it reappeared again in high school.

3. As adolescents, these children felt more competent. Fewer of them dropped out of high school, and more went on to college.

Soon after these findings were made public, Congress voted a large increase in funds for Head Start.

Typical Preschools

Whereas the goals of Head Start and other intervention programs are mainly to teach school-related skills, many preschools focus on social and emotional growth. These programs are generally attended by middle-class children. In fact, in the United States most middle-class parents send their children to such preschools, usually to provide them with playmates in a supportive, stimulating atmosphere. Because there are no national standards for preschools in the United States, these schools differ widely, but most seem to have a common form. Usually, a group has fifteen or twenty 3- to 5-year-olds, with a trained teacher and one or more assistants. Most programs operate 3 or 4 hours a day, 3 to 5 days a week. The equipment usually consists of indoor toys, art supplies, and outdoor playthings such as swings, slides, sandboxes, and tricycles. There are costumes and hats for role-playing games and sometimes a child-size kitchen and tool bench.

Much of the time children play freely with the toys, individually or in small groups. The teacher moves among the children during free play, helping one to see how to solve a puzzle and encouraging another to give someone else a turn at the easel. A good teacher is alert to the "teachable moment" for individual children, the time when a piece of information or a new idea is especially helpful. Sometimes the class does things together—listening to a story told by the teacher, learning to sing songs, or going on an outing to the fire station, the zoo, or some other interesting place.

The developmental effects of middle-class preschools are difficult to pinpoint because evaluation studies have not produced conclusive results. For most middle-class children, preschool seems to be a positive experience but not a necessary one. A child who has not attended preschool but comes from a stimulating home with neighborhood friends and plenty of space to play in will most likely do as well in first grade as a similar child who has gone to a preschool (Robinson et al. 1973).

The goal of all agents of socialization is to increase a child's social competence— to teach children what their society expects of them and to give them the skills needed to meet those expectations. Children are eager to learn those lessons.

They want to know how their world works and how they can be effective members of it. On their own, they discover that identification is one way to learn. Through identification, they socialize themselves. They listen to people they love or admire to find out what those people value, and they watch those people to see how they deal with other people and with the world in general.

Social development in the preschool years is particularly important. During these years, as thinking abilities develop, children learn to play together, to give and take, to wait sometime while others have a turn, and to persist sometimes in a task. By the time they are 6 years old, American children are ready for the social life of a school.

SUMMARY

SOCIALIZATION

1. In the child's preschool years, adults begin the *socialization* of their children, teaching them the attitudes, knowledge, and skills necessary for effective participation in the society. In all societies, there are at least eight basic goals of socialization.

2. Children in all societies begin to learn *social norms,* their society's standards of behavior, and *social roles,* groups of norms that pertain to a specific social category such as age, sex, or occupation.

THE ACQUISITION OF SEX ROLES

3. *Sex roles,* the set of social norms prescribing appropriate behavior for males and for females, exist in some form in all societies. Many of the norms for the two sexes are very different. Sex roles are extremely important components of personality.
  a. Some role prescriptions may be based on biological differences between males and females—in particular, on the fact that females bear children and the fact that males are larger and more aggressive.
  b. One very important determinant of how sex-role differences develop in the behavior of preschool children seems to be *parents' expectations and practices.*

c. Another important factor that determines sex-role differences in the preschool child is the child's developing understanding of what it means to be male or female. According to Kohlberg, the label "boy" or "girl" becomes a major influence on children's behavior as soon as they can identify themselves as one or the other. Three-year-olds already value activities and qualities that belong to their own sex, and, by age 4 or 5, they can understand concretely how male and female roles relate to each other. They still lack an understanding of *gender permanence,* however. Only at about age 7 do children acquire a firm understanding that their gender cannot change.

IDENTIFICATION

4. *Identification,* an important factor in the development of personality, is the imitation of an admired person's attitudes and behaviors. Freud introduced the term in his *psychoanalytic theory* to describe how young children take in their parents' values and thereby acquire a conscience, or superego, and a sex-role identity.

THEORY: *FREUD AND ERIKSON*

5. According to psychoanalytic theory, the basic fuel for all human thought and endeavor is a primitive energy called *libido,* which ruthlessly seeks pleasure. In the course of socialization, much of the libido is channeled, or *sublimated,* into nonsexual areas of endeavor.

6. The *unconscious* is the storehouse of memories and drives connected with basic processes such as self-preservation and the satisfaction of physical appetites. These memories cannot ordinarily be released into the conscious mind, but they can surface in symbolic form—in dreams, for example. Thinking dominated by the unconscious, as in dreams, Freud called *primary process.* Orderly, systematic, logical thinking Freud called *secondary process.*

7. Human beings use *defense mechanisms,* which reduce anxiety by protecting the conscious mind from unacceptable thoughts, to keep such thoughts and impulses locked in the unconscious.

8. Freud also proposed three "agencies" of personality: the id, the ego, and the superego.
a. The *id,* which is entirely unconscious, is the reservoir of libido. Its basic motivation is the pursuit of pleasure, and it is completely nonrational.

b. After the first few months of life, the **ego** begins to develop. The ego is the rational, sensible agency of personality, which seeks to balance the requirements of reality with the id's urgent needs and the unrealistic restraints of the superego.

c. The **superego** is the internalization of the parent's values and ideals. According to Freud, it is formed as a result of a child's identification with the same-sex parent, in resolution of the Oedipus or Electra conflict.

9. Freud described five stages of **psychosexual development,** through which the libido-driven infant gradually becomes a civilized human being. Each stage is characterized by a different **erogenous zone,** an area of the body that is the focus of pleasure: The **oral stage** begins at birth and lasts into the second year. The **anal stage** lasts until near the end of the third year. The **phallic stage,** from about age 3 to age 6, is the first time children focus on the genitals as a source of pleasure. It is during this stage that the **Oedipus** and **Electra conflicts** take place. Children develop sexual attachments for the parent of the opposite sex and wish to usurp the place of the same-sex parent. These feelings cause the children to experience fear of retaliation and, ultimately, anxiety. To relieve the anxiety, they **identify with** the same-sex parent. The repression of sexual desire for the father or mother leads to a general repression of sexuality—the **latency stage,** which lasts until puberty. At puberty, the **genital stage** begins, and it lasts through adulthood.

10. Much mental disturbance in adulthood, Freud thought, arises from difficulties at some stage of psychosexual development. Frustration of needs at a given stage or excessive indulgence in the pleasures of that stage might lead to **fixation** at that stage or **regression** to that stage from a later one.

11. Erik Erikson expanded on Freud's notion of psychosexual development. His theory of **psychosocial development** differs from Freud's theory in three important respects:
    a. It focuses on the **ego** and its development.
    b. It gives full consideration to the **role of society** in psychological development.
    c. It considers development as continuing throughout the **life span.**

12. Erikson divides the life span into eight stages, each of which revolves around a particular **developmental crisis,** an encounter between the person's newly developed capacities and his social environment. The two psychosocial stages in the preschool years are **autonomy versus shame and doubt** and **initiative versus guilt.**

SOCIALIZATION IN THE FAMILY

13. Parents are the most important **agents of socialization** for their young children. Parents differ in their ways of dealing with their children—in their **parental style.** Two general scales that can be used to characterize parental style are **love-hostility** and **permissiveness-restrictiveness.** Various combinations of characteristics along these two scales correspond to different parental styles. **Aggression, dependence,** and **competence** are three types of behavior that have been extensively studied for their relation to parental styles.

14. One series of studies, conducted by Diana Baumrind, identified three types of parental style and found that each style produced different levels of competence and independence in preschoolers.
   a. **Permissive** parents were more warm and loving than others but exercised less control. Their preschool children tended to be the least self-reliant, self-controlled, and exploratory of all those studied.
   b. **Authoritarian-restrictive** parents were cooler, more detached, and exercised a high degree of control. Their preschool children tended to be dependent and submissive, not as competent as others, and more discontented and withdrawn.
   c. **Authoritative** parents firmly enforced rules and demanded high levels of achievement but were warm, rational, and receptive to their children's comments. Their children were likely to be independent, competent, and exploratory.
   d. Parental style always interacts with an individual child's personality, with the result that sensitive parents will try to adapt their socialization methods to each child.

15. **Siblings** can significantly affect each other's development too, although the effects depend on a combination of several complex factors. The most important are birth order, the children's sex, and the number of years that separate them. Siblings may go through a process called **deidentification,** trying to be as different from each other as possible.

16. **Social class** affects parental style. One important difference between classes is that middle-class mothers are more likely than lower-class mothers to base the help they give their children on the child's viewpoint and abilities.

TELEVISION AS AN AGENT OF SOCIALIZATION

17. **Television** is an agent of socialization whose effects are only beginning to be known. Preschoolers tend not to understand the plots of the stories that they watch on TV, but they are affected by the content of what they see. They tend to become more aggressive after watching television violence. TV programs such as *Sesame Street* have been successful in advancing preschool education.

PRESCHOOLS AND DAY CARE

18. **Preschools** are another agent of socialization.

 a. **Head Start** is a large-scale preschool project first funded by the federal government in the 1960s. It was designed to socialize lower-class children for schooling and to give them some basic skills before they entered the first grade. A recent study evaluating long-term effects of such programs showed that they have very positive effects.

 b. Preschools in different societies convey different norms, the norms appropriate to each society. For example, American preschools emphasize independence and self-reliance, whereas Russian and Chinese preschools emphasize group activity and cooperation.

SUGGESTED READINGS

CLARKE-STEWART, ALISON. *Daycare.* Cambridge, Massachusetts: Harvard University Press, 1982.

A working mother who is a developmental psychologist reviews the status of daycare for infants and preschoolers and draws conclusions from research on its effects.

DUNN, JUDITH, and CAROL KENDRICK. *Siblings.* Cambridge, Massachusetts: Harvard University Press, 1982.

An overview of the role of siblings in children's development.

ERIKSON, ERIK H. *Childhood and Society,* 2nd ed. New York: W. W. Norton, 1963.

Erikson presents his theory of psychosocial development and illustrates it with case studies from a number of cultures.

FREUD, SIGMUND. *A General Introduction to Psychoanalysis.* New York: Washington Square Press, 1960.

From 1915 to 1917, Freud gave a series of lectures on psychoanalysis oriented toward a general audience. Even though the theory of psychoanalysis developed further after these lectures, they are still one of the most compelling presentations of the Freudian approach.

————. *New Introductory Lectures on Psychoanalysis.* New York: W. W. Norton, 1965.

Originally published in 1933, this book presents an outline of psychoanalytic theory in its mature form. These "lectures" were never actually delivered but were written as a sequel to the earlier introductory lectures.

LAZAR, IRVING, and RICHARD DARLINGTON, with others. *Lasting Effects of Early Education: A Report from the Consortium for Longitudinal Studies.* Monographs of the Society for Research in Child Development, 1982.

This monograph reports the most definitive study of the long-term effects of preschool programs like *Head Start* on the lives of children from disadvantaged backgrounds.

MACCOBY, ELEANOR, and JOHN A. MARTIN. "Socialization in the Context of the Family: Parent-Child Interaction." In P. H. Mussen (Ed.), *Handbook of Child Psychology.* New York: Wiley, 1983.

An excellent review of how children develop within the family and how parents and children affect each other.

RUBIN, ZICK. *Children's Friendships.* Cambridge, Massachusetts: Harvard University Press, 1980.

A discussion by a noted social psychologist of the nature and development of children's friendships.

WHITING, B. B., and J. W. M. WHITING. *Children of Six Cultures.* Cambridge, Massachusetts: Harvard University Press, 1975.

Two influential developmental anthropologists report the results of the most comprehensive single study of cross-cultural differences in child-rearing.

In 1833 a law regulating child labor was passed in England. It said that children from 9 to 13 years old were not to work more than 48 hours a week in the factories. The mills were closed on Sundays, because work was prohibited on the sabbath. In fact, a religious reformer of the day "was struck with concern at seeing the deplorable profanation of the sabbath" because these youngsters, "released on that day from employment, spend their time in noise and riot, playing at 'chuck'."

Children play. Even these children, after six days of brutalizing work (which earned them the chance to eat enough), took to the streets and played—exuberant games, it appears, games that let them run and shout, exercising muscles and mind that had lain dormant all week. It is not unlikely that children of the 1980s, dropped into the midst of a game of "chuck," would soon catch on and could play right along. Nevertheless, there would probably be important differences between those child-workers of the 1830s and today's schoolchildren. Chapter 9 discusses how schooling affects the way children think; it describes cognitive development and IQ tests, taking up the whole question of what intelligence is and how it relates to physical development and the sharpening of language skills. Chapter 10 examines children's expanding social world—how they learn social and moral behavior.

9

THINKING,
PERCEIVING,
AND
LEARNING
SYSTEMATICALLY

CHAPTER OUTLINE

9

THINKING, PERCEIVING, AND LEARNING SYSTEMATICALLY

At age 6 or 7, most children in the Western world begin their formal schooling. They suddenly begin to spend 5 or 6 hours a day outside the home without parental supervision. Although some children this age are old hands at going to school, having attended nursery school and kindergarten, both children and parents seem to acknowledge that first grade is serious business. Children starting first grade, though often more than a little scared, are usually proud of their new status. And many parents, sometimes mournfully, mark the first day of regular school as the end of their child's babyhood.

The transition to the formal curriculum and instruction of the classroom marks a major change in society's expectations of the child. For some reason, we expect 6- or 7-year-olds to be considerably more competent thinkers than 5-year-olds, and to be more mature in their social relationships as well.

These expectations are not new to the technological age, however; nor are they limited to highly developed societies. Many historical documents indicate that competent thought has long been considered to begin at about this age. English Common Law decreed that a child of 7 is capable of knowing right from wrong and is therefore liable to be tried for a crime. The Catholic Church, too, has long held that children can tell right from wrong at 7 and therefore may begin the act of confession and take their first communion.

In fact, during the Middle Ages, the conception of childhood that we take

Figure 9-1 In many cultures, children at about age 7 are given new, more adult responsibilities. (Left) These children in Quepos, Costa Rica, are taking their first communion in the Catholic Church. (Right) This young herder in the Niger Republic has been assigned the task of hobbling the camels.

for granted did not seem to exist. Philippe Aries argues in his book *Centuries of Childhood* that

> In the Middle Ages, at the beginning of modern times, and for a long time after that in the lower classes, children were mixed with adults as soon as they were considered capable of being without their mothers or nannies, not long after a tardy weaning (in other words, at about the age of 7). They immediately went straight into the great community of men, sharing in the work and play of their companions, old and young alike.

A study of more than fifty rural, preliterate societies showed that in most of them, too, there are major changes in roles and responsibilities between ages 5 and 7 (Rogoff et al. 1976). Children of 6 or 7 are expected to begin to care for younger siblings, to tend and feed animals, or to gather material, such as firewood, that is needed by the group (Weisner & Gallimore 1977).

In Western societies the modern concept of childhood emerged after the Industrial Revolution and has undergone many changes since then, but we still consider the period from age 5 to age 7 as a time of major transformation in children's lives. In fact, a constellation of cognitive and physical changes at ages 6 and 7, called the 5-to-7 shift, seems to account for children's new social roles (Kenny 1983; S. White 1970).

COGNITIVE DEVELOPMENT: CONCRETE-OPERATIONAL INTELLIGENCE

At 6 or 7 years, most children enter the third of the four developmental periods described by Piaget, the period of concrete operations. ***Concrete-operational intelligence*** is the capacity to think logically about concrete things, things that the child experiences directly in everyday life (Inhelder & Piaget 1964). The existence of this capacity is one of the best-established facts about child development, documented by hundreds of studies.

A Logic of the Concrete

In one of the best-known tests of concrete-operational intelligence, a child is shown two identical balls of clay. As the child watches, one of the balls is rolled into a long, thin sausage shape. The child is then asked whether there is more clay in the ball or the sausage or if they are the same. In the preoperational period, a typical answer is "The sausage has more because it's longer." By age 7 or 8, most children will give a concrete-operational answer, explaining that there is the same amount of clay in the ball and the sausage.

According to Piaget, concrete-operational intelligence is composed of ***operations,*** that is, mental actions (or representations) that are reversible (Inhelder and Piaget 1964; Piaget 1983). For example, imagining a clay ball being rolled out to a sausage shape and then rerolled into its original ball is a reversible mental action. Another is knowing that $3 + 5 = 8$ and that $8 - 5 = 3$. By definition, an operation is always part of a mental system that includes both a mental action and its opposite; that is, all operations are reversible. A ***concrete operation*** is a reversible mental action on the real, tangible properties of things. With a concrete-operational understanding of conservation, the child knows that the amount of clay in a ball does not change when its shape changes because she knows that the changes can be reversed or undone. Rerolling the sausage will restore it to the original ball's shape and size. Concrete operations allow the child to ***decenter,*** to move from focusing or centering on one property to coordinating several properties. In the conservation of clay, the preoperational child centers on either the height or the length, but the concrete-operational child decenters, coordinating height with length to form a general concept of total amount of clay.

Neo-Piagetian theory describes this ability to coordinate multiple properties in terms of concrete-operational systems (Biggs & Collis 1982; Case 1980; Fischer 1980; Halford 1982). A concrete-operational system is the capacity to keep in mind several attributes of one object and several attributes of another, and thus to relate (or compare) the two combinations of attributes in a systematic way. A child capable of concrete operations can keep in mind both the length and width of the clay ball and the length and width of the sausage, and

PREOPERATIONAL UNDERSTANDING

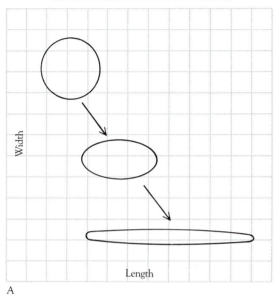

A

CONCRETE-OPERATIONAL UNDERSTANDING

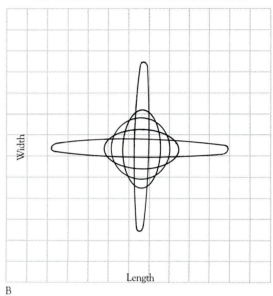

B

Figure 9-2 These two drawings represent the contrast between preoperational thought and concrete-operational thought. (A) When the younger child sees a ball of clay rolled into a sausage shape, he does not see the sausage-shaped clay as *necessarily* identical in amount to the ball it was before, even though he knows that length and width are related. (B) The older child, who has a system for relating widths and lengths, sees that the clay is one object, preserving its identity as a fixed amount no matter how its shape changes.

he can relate these two length-width combinations to each other (Halford 1970; Peill 1975). The capacity to coordinate these combinations in a single concrete-operational system is what allows the child to understand reversibility and to decenter in conservation of clay. He can understand that remolding clay does not change its amount because width and length change jointly and compensate for each other (see Figure 9-2).

You may recall from Chapter 7 that the beginnings of logical thought about concrete things can be seen at 4 or 5 years of age, when children can first relate two representations. When Michael was 4, he could relate the length and the width of one clay ball—saying, for example, that rolling out the ball to make it thinner also makes it longer. But he could not relate the length and width of one ball to the length and width of another. Without the capacity to construct this concrete-operational system, he could not understand that if two balls contain the same amount of clay, then one of the balls and a sausage made from the other ball also contain the same amount of clay.

The attainment of concrete-operational intelligence is a major step in cognitive development. It provides a powerful new tool whose uses extend far beyond understanding the conservation of clay. Children who have concrete-operational intelligence can take another person's point of view, even in fairly complex situations, and relate it to their own, so they can communicate effectively. They can also expand their comprehension of social roles such as mother, father, husband, wife, and lawyer, coming to understand that one person can take on several roles, as when father is also a husband and a lawyer. They can play games with rules, such as hopscotch, baseball, and checkers, which were too complicated for them a year or two earlier. And they can master the tasks they face in school, such as reading and arithmetic.

The development of concrete-operational intelligence allows children to think systematically about their physical and social worlds, and its appearance at the age of 6 or 7 seems to account for the change in what societies expect of children at this age. Yet, like most other major cognitive developments, the development of concrete operations is uneven—both from person to person and within an individual.

Unevenness in Development

Although concrete-operational skills first appear in most children in industrialized countries at age 6 or 7, they can also begin to be formed earlier or later (Feldman 1980). John Stuart Mill, the British philosopher, may have developed the capacity for concrete operations at age 4 or so, because he learned to solve difficult mathematical problems before he was 5. On the other hand, children who develop unusually slowly may not be capable of concrete operations until 10 or 11 years of age.

Whenever concrete-operational thinking does begin to develop, it does not appear all at once, across the board, but at different times in different areas. Specific experiences seem to account for much of this unevenness in cognitive development (Childs & Greenfield 1979; Pulos & Linn 1982). For example, when Michael was almost 6, he could play hopscotch by the rules, which requires a concrete-operational scheme, but he did not understand conservation of clay until he was 7. The fact is that when he was younger Michael had often watched his sister play hopscotch and had wanted desperately to play himself; sometimes he was allowed to join in, even though he did not understand the rules. On the other hand, Michael did not play much with clay until he worked with it in his art lessons in first grade. This difference in experience seems to account for the difference in Michael's cognitive development between these two particular areas. Figure 9-3 shows some other experiences that contribute to the development of concrete-operational abilities.

Some Operational Skills

Although different children concentrate on different areas, all normal children develop many concrete-operational skills during their school years. Most of the

Figure 9-3 Experience with particular objects or substances can help produce concrete-operational understanding about these materials. Playing with water is likely to help a preschooler to understand conservation of liquid when she becomes capable of concrete-operational thought.

topics that Piaget wrote about relate to science, logic, and arithmetic and the use of schemes such as conservation and classification.

Conservation and Necessary Truth   In *conservation tasks,* the experimenter manipulates a substance so that two or more of its attributes vary while some quantity that combines them remains the same. In the clay task, the length and width of one of the clay balls change while the amount of clay stays the same. Several other types of conservation develop during the concrete-operational period, and children may achieve understanding of the various types at very different ages. A child may have a perfect grasp of conservation of clay but not of conservation of liquid, for example (Pinard 1981; Uzgiris 1964).

   In testing for conservation of liquid, an experimenter shows a child two identical jars filled with water and asks whether they are the same. After the child says they are, the water from one of the original jars is poured into a taller, narrower jar while the child watches. Then the child is asked again whether the jars contain the same amount. A 4-year-old usually centers on the height of the liquids and answers that the tall jar has "more." A child who understands

THE FAMILY CIRCUS   **by Bil Keane**

EXPRESS LANE
10 ITEMS OR LESS

3-12
Copyright 1982
The Register and Tribune
Syndicate, Inc.

"Hold it, Mommy! You've got 12 things here!"

conservation of liquid decenters from height and coordinates width with height to form a scheme for total amount of liquid. As a result, he not only says that the amounts of liquid are the same but may insist that they "have to be."

A child's answer that the amounts of liquid "have to be the same" indicates that his mastery of conservation of liquid is so secure that he can think in terms of **necessary truth.** That is, he not only understands that conservation does occur but believes it must (Inhelder & Piaget 1964; Moshman & Timmons 1982). Even if the water in the tall, narrow jar looks like more, the child is able to rely on what he *knows* rather than on what he *perceives.* Other operational skills besides conservation also permit reliance on a source of truth within the self. This new self-reliance allows the 9- or 10-year-old concrete-operational child to become more independent of adults, sometimes in ways that can be a bit trying, especially for the child's parents. For example, one 10-year-old boy assiduously watched his father's speedometer and admonished his father whenever the speedometer went even a mile or two over the speed limit. An 8-year-old girl, accompanying her mother and 1-year-old sister on a trip to the supermarket, protested vehemently when her mother walked to a shelf two steps from the market basket that the 1-year-old was sitting in. The older girl pointed to the sign on the basket and scolded, "Mother! It says right here that you shouldn't leave children unattended in these baskets."

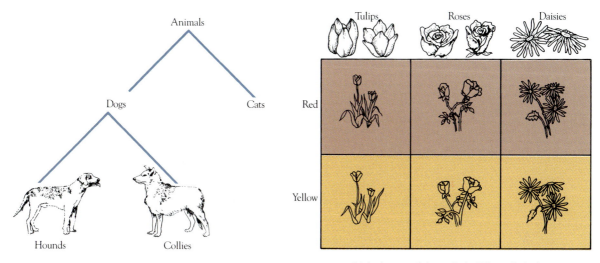

Addition of classes: Collies + Hounds = Dogs

Multiplication of classes: Red x Tulip = Red tulips

Classification and Games   Another type of scheme that has been studied extensively by cognitive-developmental psychologists is **classification.** With concrete operations, children can understand how objects or events fit into categories and how these categories relate to each other. For example, they might recognize "roses," "tulips," and "daisies" as subclasses of the class "flowers." They might also recognize "flowers" as a subclass of the class "plants." The concrete-operational scheme that allows a child to combine several subclasses to form a class and to break a class into subclasses is called **addition of classes.**

The child of age 4 or 5 understands some things about classes. If he is familiar with dogs and cats, for example, he can sort toy dogs and cats into these two classes and even into subclasses, such as spaniels and poodles. But he has trouble relating several classes and subclasses simultaneously. Piaget devised several tasks that demonstrate these limitations (Inhelder & Piaget 1964).

A 4-year-old is given seven toy collies, three toy hounds, and four toy cats (Figure 9-4) and asked to sort them into piles that are all alike. After the child has grouped the toys into collies, hounds, and cats, the experimenter asks some questions. "Which toys are dogs?" The child points to the collies and to the hounds. "Which are cats?" The child points to the cats. "Which are animals?" The child points to all three groups. "Are there more collies or hounds?" The child correctly chooses the collies. "How many collies are there?" The child correctly answers, "Seven." "Are there more dogs or cats?" The child again correctly chooses the dogs.

Then the child is asked a key question: "Are there more dogs or more collies?" The child answers "More collies." "Are there more dogs or more animals?"

Figure 9-4 Addition and multiplication of classes. These two ways of organizing information are basic to many of the ways people deal with their world, and it is only in the school-age years that children become able to use them consistently.

"More dogs," the child says. Another child may answer incorrectly in a different way. He may say that there are the same number of dogs as collies and the same number of animals as dogs.

During the preoperational period, children have this kind of difficulty with classification because they cannot mentally coordinate the classes (dogs and cats) and subclasses (collies and hounds). That is, they cannot simultaneously hold both classes and subclasses in mind and move between them. This inability disappears when the child develops the concrete-operational scheme for addition of classes. By age 7 most American middle-class children can add familiar classes correctly.

In another classification scheme, *multiplication of classes,* two categories are crossed to form joint classes. For example, classes of flowers (tulips, roses, daisies) and classes of colors (red, yellow) can be combined to form joint classes of red tulips, red roses, red daisies, yellow tulips, yellow roses, and yellow daisies. By the time they are 4 or 5 years old, children can sort objects according to a few of these joint classes, but as soon as the objects become at all complicated—with different shades of red, different types of tulips, and the like—the children become confused and can no longer sort correctly (Frith & Frith 1978; Fischer & Roberts 1983). By age 6 or 7, many children understand multiplication of classes, even when the objects vary not only in features central to the classification but also in features irrelevant to it (size, for example, or number of petals).

Addition and multiplication of classes are schemes required for much school-work and in many hobbies and games. A child studying geography must learn the classes of continents, nations, provinces, and cities and see that Europe, France, and Paris are related in one way, and Paris, London, and New York are related in a different way. Organizing a collection of stamps, coins, baseball cards, or bottlecaps also requires classification skills, as does understanding the rules of all but the simplest games. For example, an "out" in baseball can be the result of striking out or being tagged or hitting a fly ball that is caught. "Out" is thus a class that has several subclasses (Figure 9-5). Many other games, from Twenty Questions to Monopoly to poker, also require the addition and multiplication of classes.

Memory

The sophistication of concrete-operational schemes increases greatly between ages 6 and 11. For one thing, as classification abilities improve, memory improves. Information is easier to recall when it is organized, and 11-year-olds, because of their superior classification abilities, are much better at mentally organizing things to be remembered than 6-year-olds are (A. Brown et al. 1983; Moely 1977). Better memory, in turn, makes it possible to use more complex systems—to keep a number of related things in mind while trying to solve a problem or deal with a situation. If asked to memorize lists of words including

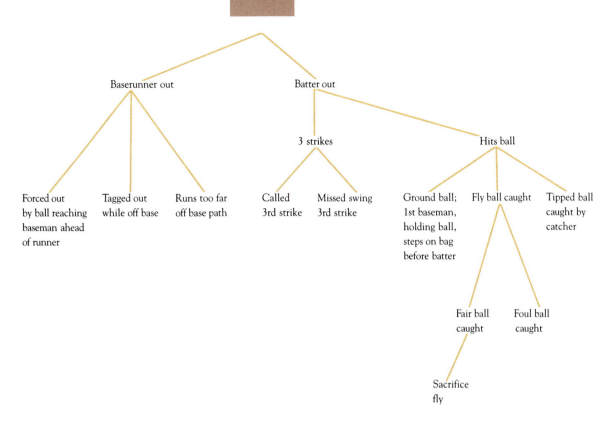

```
                              ┌──────────┐
                              │   OUT    │
                              └──────────┘
                    ┌──────────────┴──────────────┐
              Baserunner out                  Batter out
           ┌──────┼──────┐              ┌──────────┴──────────┐
                                    3 strikes             Hits ball
```

Forced out
by ball reaching
baseman ahead
of runner

Tagged out
while off base

Runs too far
off base path

Called
3rd strike

Missed swing
3rd strike

Ground ball;
1st baseman,
holding ball,
steps on bag
before batter

Fly ball caught

Tipped ball
caught by
catcher

Fair ball
caught

Foul ball
caught

Sacrifice
fly

Figure 9-5 The rules of baseball illustrate how classification skills are applied in everyday situations. Here the addition of classes is used to determine when a play results in an "out."

TABLE 9-1 THE NUMBER OF PLANS FOR REMEMBERING
INCREASES WITH AGE

	NUMBER OF PLANS					
GRADE	0	1	2	3	4	AVERAGE
Kindergarten	8	12	5	0	0	0.85
First	2	18	5	3	1	1.40
Third	0	20	15	8	3	2.45
Fifth	0	20	19	13	6	2.95

SOURCE: Kreutzer et al. 1975.

items that can be organized by class—"apple," "pear," and "banana" as *fruit*, for example—some 8-year-olds organize the items, but many do not. By age 11, most children organize the items they are asked to memorize.

Between the ages of 6 and 11, children also improve in their ability to make inferences in processing information. In one study, 7-, 8-, and 11-year-olds were read eight sentences; some sentences explicitly stated that an instrument was used, and some only implied it. For example, "The boy hit the ball with a bat" and "The workman dug a hole in the ground" (a shovel being implied). Later, when the children were asked to recall the eight sentences, they were given the name of the instrument as a clue in each case. For the 7- and 8-year-olds these clues helped to recall only the sentences that had explicitly contained the word for the instrument. Because of the younger children's inability to infer the instruments in the other sentences, the clues for these sentences rang no bells. The older children, on the other hand, recalled sentences that had only implied the existence of an instrument just as well as those that had actually stated it. These children had inferred that a shovel must have been used to dig the hole (Paris & Lindauer 1976).

During the school years there is also development of what John Flavell (1977) calls **metamemory**—that is, children's awareness of their own memory abilities and of how they can put those abilities to work. Children at 10 and 11 are better at using and monitoring their memories than they were at 6 or 7. They are better at planning, for example, because they can form and keep in mind the goal of remembering something while they try to come up with the means of organizing and storing the information (A. Brown et al. 1983).

This planfulness can be seen in the solutions that children from kindergarten through fifth grade offered for a problem presented in a study of metamemory (Kreutzer et al. 1975). In one problem, the children were asked, "Suppose you were going to go skating with your friend after school tomorrow and you wanted

TABLE 9-2 NUMBER OF CHILDREN CHOOSING OPPOSITES
OR ARBITRARY PAIRS

GRADE	OPPOSITES	ARBITRARY	SAME
Kindergarten	6	10	4
First	10	10	0
Third	18	2	0
Fifth	20	0	0

SOURCE: Kreutzer et al. 1975

to be sure to bring your skates. How could you be really certain that you didn't forget to bring your skates to school in the morning? Can you think of anything else? How many ways can you think of?" The children came up with a variety of plans: thinking about remembering the skates before going to bed; asking their mothers to remind them; putting the skates near their bookbag the night before; leaving a note in plain sight. As Table 9-1 shows, the number of plans the children could suggest increased with their grade level.

Older children are also more aware of the relations between things, and they can use these relations as a memory aid. When shown a list of word pairs, some of which were opposites—for example, black/white—and some arbitrary—Mary/walks—and asked which pairs would be easier to remember, the children responded as shown in Table 9-2. All the fifth-graders knew that it would be easier to remember words that were related to each other.

PERCEPTION

As their concrete-operational abilities improve, children develop not only new ways of thinking but new ways of perceiving. As explained in Chapter 4, **perception** is the relatively automatic interpretation of sensory information to produce an experience of a pattern or meaning. According to Piaget (1969), young children's perceptions of complex stimuli are largely determined by how their sensory systems work—almost "automatically." As children get older, they acquire the ability to override these automatic tendencies and organize the incoming information in a greater number of ways.

In studying developmental changes in perception, psychologists have looked primarily at how children gather perceptual information and how they perceive illusions—mostly visual ones like those in Figure 9-6.

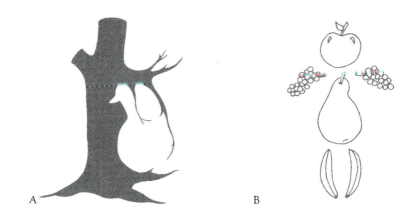

Figure 9-6 Visual illusions used to test perceptual development. (A) This is a figure-ground illusion. Four-year-olds see only the tree—as figure—and all the white as ground. By 7 or 8, many children can see the duck figure as well as the tree, if they are given some help. Only at 10 or 11 do children spontaneously perceive both. (B) This person composed of fruit is a part-whole illusion. Preschool children see such illusions only one way or the other; 5- or 6-year-olds can often see both the whole and the parts but have trouble switching between them (Elkind 1978).

Illusions: Seeing Double

Many of the illusions used for testing are perceptual puzzles in which an object or event can be perceived in two or more ways (Elkind 1978; Vurpillot 1976). Figure 9-6A, for instance, can be seen as either a tree or a duck. At 2 or 3 years old, children often see neither the tree nor the duck. Children of 4 or 5 typically see only the tree. By 7 or 8 years, children can see both, especially if they are given some help. And by 10 or 11 years, most children spontaneously see both. This ability to see two things in one object seems to arise from the reversibility of concrete-operational thinking: Just as children can mentally reverse the transformation of a piece of clay in a conservation task, they can perceptually reverse what they see in an illusion.

Figure 9-6B shows another kind of illusion that can be seen in two ways. Preschool children see such figures only one way, usually whichever way most adults see when they first look at the illusion. That is, they see either the whole—the person—or the parts—the fruit. Children of 5 or 6 years often begin by vacillating ("I see some fruit—no, I see a man"), but when the tester asks the child to name the fruit, the child typically says, "There's no fruit, just a man."

Many items on intelligence tests for children require the ability to see a figure in a number of ways. Figure 9-7 gives two examples of such items, called embedded figures. The easy items in the figure are solved by most 4- and 5-year-olds. By age 6 or 7, most children can solve the more difficult items as well. In these harder items, the figure to be found is disguised somewhat by an overall figure that the child must disregard in order to see the embedded figure.

Mastering these several types of illusions requires the ability to move back and forth perceptually between two or more patterns in the same figure—disregarding an overall pattern to perceive an embedded figure or switching from whole to parts or shifting from one pattern (such as a tree) to another (such as a duck). Such perceptual control is beyond the ability of preoperational children. In a sense, operational schemes allow children to control what they see, which seems to be the key to experiencing these types of illusions.

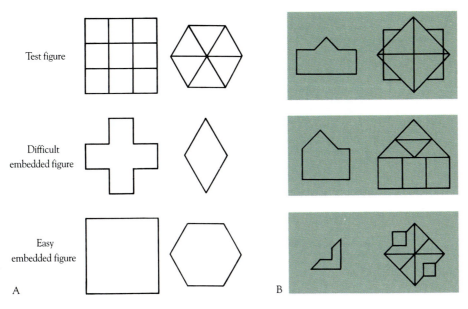

Figure 9-7 (A) These figures were used to test young children's perception of embedded figures. Children of 4 or 5 can trace the outline of the "easy" figures at the bottom in the test figure, but not until age 6 or 7 can they trace out the "difficult" ones (Vurpillot 1976). (B) Some examples of the embedded-figure items used in IQ tests; the task is to find the figure at the left in the one at the right. (From *Embedded Figures Test*, Consulting Psychologists Press, 1971.)

Naturally, these new abilities affect the behavior of children in the everyday world as well as in the laboratory. Among other things, school-age children can find hidden objects—from Easter eggs to friends playing hide-and-seek—much more quickly than younger children can. They can more easily detect objects that naturally blend into the background, like a green bug on a leaf or a frog in a pond or a penny on the ground. By age 10, they can pick out a familiar person's face and voice in a crowd, even when they have met the person only once or twice (Mann et al. 1979).

Searching for Information

Increasing perceptual control is obvious not only in what children can see but in how they search for visual information. By recording children's eye movements, researchers have confirmed that at age 6 or 7 children become able to search for visual information more logically and efficiently. In a task using the complex house figures shown in Figure 9-8, for example, children were asked whether the two houses were identical or different. Most children under age 6 made a cursory and unsystematic visual search. Starting at age 6, most children compared the houses much more systematically, looking back and forth between the corresponding windows to check for differences.

The ability to sustain a visual search improves considerably at about the same age. In one study, children were asked to find all the crosses in a figure that had many. Even 5-year-olds did not manage to find more than a few of the crosses, but by age 6 most children found most of the crosses, and by age 7 they managed to find as many crosses as adults did (Vurpillot 1976).

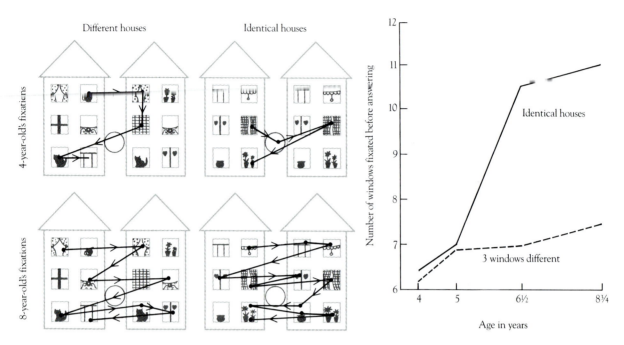

Figure 9-8   Asked whether the two houses are the same, 4- and 5-year-olds make a cursory and unsystematic search, illustrated by the tracings of eye movements shown here. Beginning at age 6, children make a much more controlled and systematic search. The identical houses require many more eye fixations than the different houses to determine whether they are the same, but 4- and 5-year-olds used just about the same number of eye fixations in searching the identical houses and the different ones (Vurpillot 1976).

In perception, as in many areas of behavior, children during the elementary-school years develop abilities similar to those of adults. To bring their abilities to adult level, however, children must not only sharpen their own perceptual skills but develop an accurate sense of what other people perceive.

LANGUAGE AND COMMUNICATION

The ability to take account of other people's perspectives is particularly important when language is used to communicate or to create deliberate effects on others, as in humor. At about age 6 or 7, children get much better at using language for these purposes.

Conversation and Perspective-Taking

In adult conversation it is customary for the speaker to take account of the listener's knowledge of, and interest in, the topic at hand and to tailor his or her remarks accordingly. The speech of young preschoolers, on the other hand, clearly shows an egocentric inability to take another's perspective: They center on their own perspective and converse as though each and every listener shared their knowledge and interests (see Chapter 7). Even at age 4 and 5, most children are capable of taking the viewpoints of other people only in very simple situations (Flavell 1977).

During the grade-school years, there is a striking increase in perspective-taking abilities. In many studies, children of elementary-school age have been asked to take the perspectives of other people: After they hear a story about other people, they are asked to state what each person knows. The ability to take a different person's perspective and keep the details straight is poor at 6 years of age and increases enormously between 6 and 13 years (Edelstein et al. 1984; Feffer & Gourevitch 1960).

Such gains can be seen when children are asked to try to persuade someone to do something for them. A persuasive argument, as all good salespersons know, requires that the speaker take into account the listener's attitudes and needs. Six- and seven-year-olds are not very good at persuasion. When asked in one study to show how they would talk their father into buying them a television set for their room, children this age generally used arguments that took account only of their own wishes: "Oh, Daddy, oh, Daddy, please let me buy a television set. I always wanted one. Oh, please, Daddy, please" (Flavell et al. 1968). Eleven- and twelve-year-olds, on the other hand, used arguments that took account of such things as their father's desire to keep up with the neighbors or his attitude about the importance of education: "Say, Dad, a lot of kids at school are getting televisions for Christmas. Can I have one? Gee, I know a lot of kids that want one. Gee, I could really use it . . . for some of the educational programs that are on TV, and they're real good, and for homework at night some of our teachers want us to watch 'em, and—you know, Johnnie always wants to watch cowboys, and I—I'll never get a chance to watch it down there, so why can't I have it in my room? C'mon, Dad, please."

Humor

School-age children are notorious for their love of bad jokes—those that adults find obvious and rather tiresome. Some children prefer hostile humor. Some prefer puns—jokes that depend on two meanings of one word. And many enjoy jokes about taboo topics—"dirty" jokes about sex or elimination. But despite what adults think of them or their quality and subject matter, the riddles and pranks that so delight children in the early grades show a cognitive maturity that preschoolers do not have (Groch 1974; McCauley et al. 1983).

For example, many of the jokes preferred by school-age children depend on some kind of incongruity—an unexpected situation or outcome, or a play on words (McGhee 1974). Chuck, the 6-year-old nephew of one of the authors, was a tireless practitioner of the ancient trick of sneaking up behind someone, standing to one side, and tapping the person on the opposite shoulder. When

Figure 9-9   Which ending is funnier? Even 4- and 5-year-olds enjoy A more than B. They can see that the incongruity of the upside-down book is resolved by the upside-down boy reading the upside-down book, whereas there is no resolution in B (Pien & Rothbart 1976).

A

B

his victim looked around the wrong way, Chuck went into great fits of giggling, time after time. To enjoy this joke requires perspective-taking: The child must be able to anticipate and savor the victim's reaction. Children of 3 or 4 cannot take the viewpoint of the person whose shoulder is tapped, so they cannot predict the person's surprise at finding no shoulder-tapper where a shoulder-tapper should be. Therefore they cannot understand the joke.

For children—and adults as well—jokes that depend on incongruity are funny when they can be understood but not too easily. If a joke is too easy, it is considered corny. If it is too hard and has to be explained, the humor disappears with the loss of spontaneity. Thus the shoulder-tapping joke is hilarious for a 6-year-old but quite tedious for most adults.

Preschool children can understand and appreciate some jokes (Figure 9-9; Pien & Rothbart 1976), but they tend to be very crude, and favorites are repeated over and over again—to the same listener. For example, 4-year-old Riva was standing outside on a chilly day with an adult friend when she asked, "Are you cold?" To amuse her, the friend responded, "No, I'm John." Riva seemed puzzled for a few seconds and then burst into uproarious laughter. For the next half-hour, she persisted in asking the same question, to which her friend forbearingly gave the same reply. Of course, he also had to ask her if she were cold, so she could reply, "No, I'm Riva."

This very simple kind of pun is about the only kind preschoolers can understand. Before children are able to appreciate plays on words, they need to understand that a word can have more than one meaning, and they must be able to coordinate those meanings. This ability does not appear until the concrete-operational period. One mother's story of how her two sons dealt with "knock-knock" jokes points up the difference between preschoolers and older children on this score. Her older son loved a joke that goes:

Knock, knock.
Who's there?
Irish.
Irish who?
I rish you'd quit talking to me.

Her 3-year-old, not wanting to be left out of the action, also told the joke—often—but his version went like this:

Knock, knock.
Who's there?
Irish.
Irish who?
Irish, will you quit talking to me?

In the elementary-school years children gradually become capable both of appreciating jokes and of using them to entertain others (Fowles & Glanz 1977). As they learn to take account of the listener's perspective, they move beyond the egocentric joy of the mere telling of a joke, and their ability to use jokes to please other people increases greatly. They learn, for instance, that a joke is funniest the first time a listener hears it, rarely funny the tenth time, and hardly ever the twentieth.

Metaphor

In perceptual terms, much humor requires the ability to "disembed" a second meaning of something—to see the fruit as well as the person, so to speak (see Figure 9-6). Another language phenomenon that requires understanding and coordinating two meanings of one word is metaphor. A **metaphor** is a figure of speech that uses a word or phrase in an unusual context in order to suggest an unexpected likeness. For example, the metaphor "amber waves of grain" from the song "America the Beautiful" suggests that a field of wheat or rye blown by the winds looks like golden waves on an ocean.

In pretend play, children as young as 1½ or 2 years may seem to use metaphors or puns of a sort (Gardner 1982; Winner et al. 1979). A 2-year-old, for instance, may twist a car as he moves it up his mother's leg and say "snake." But because preschool children have trouble separating and relating two meanings of the same word, they are unable to use true metaphors. For example, "hard," "sweet," and "bright" can be characteristics of objects or characteristics of people—a bright light, a bright student. In one classic study, preschool children who correctly used such words to describe objects simply denied that the same words could be used to describe people (Asch & Nerlove 1960). By age 7 or 8, many children could correctly use such words for both objects and people, but they had difficulty explaining the relation between the two meanings. Children seem to learn such expressions as "crooked streets" and "crooked politicians" as separate and unrelated vocabulary items. Later, their growing capacity to move mentally back and forth between related ideas allows them to discover the links between such expressions.

By 8 to 10 years of age, most children can guess the meaning of an unfamiliar metaphor such as "The prison guard was a hard rock" well enough to choose the correct meaning on a multiple-choice test: "The guard was mean and did not care about the feelings of the prisoners" (Pollio & Pollio 1979; Winner et al. 1976).

Advances in Grammar

The ability to coordinate two different, related meanings, which is essential to the understanding of jokes and metaphors, also affects many other aspects of children's language, including their understanding of certain grammatical rules.

In complex sentences, children must combine two complete thoughts into a single sentence with a main clause and a subordinate clause: "That's the hat that Daddy bought" combines "That is the hat" and "Daddy bought the hat." "Kathy was angry with Paul because he pulled her hair" combines "Kathy was angry with Paul" and "He pulled her hair." At about age 4, children start to become skilled at using and understanding the simpler complex sentences, such as "That's the hat that Daddy bought." When a complex sentence requires understanding a logical relation between the two clauses, however, children seem to be unable to master the grammatical rule until they have entered the concrete-operational period (Harris 1975).

Sentences containing logical connectives such as "because," "unless," and "although" are difficult for preschoolers. A child less than 6 or 7 years old seems able to understand such clauses only in terms of a concrete situation. In one study, for example, when the experimenter purposely misused "because" to produce an illogical sentence, younger children interpreted the sentence in terms of the concrete situation and failed to see the lack of logic (Corrigan 1975). Children were read sentences such as "Paul pulled Kathy's hair. Kathy was angry with Paul because she kicked him." When asked whether the sentence was true or false, preschoolers said that it was true. They saw no logical problems with the sentence and interpreted the "because" clause as if it meant "and then she kicked him." Yet when asked "What made Kathy angry?" they typically answered, "Paul pulled her hair." Not until age 7 did most children recognize that the sentence misrepresented the cause of Kathy's anger and therefore was false.

The ability to master the logical relations in complex sentences reflects a more general ability that begins to develop with concrete operations—the capacity to deal with the logical relations in language independently of the situation to which it refers (Vygotsky 1962). For instance, grade-school children can be interviewed fairly easily, while children less than 6 or 7 years old have difficulty with most interviews, typically responding to interview questions with incoherent answers or no answers at all (Harter 1982). The older children can make sense of the questions alone, without directly experiencing a real situation to which the questions refer (Olson & Nickerson 1978).

This new capacity plays an important role in how children learn. Schools are set up to promote learning, but most of the techniques used in school depend heavily on learning from language, and they are almost always removed from the concrete subject of the lesson. It is no accident that, in most countries, school begins at 6 or 7 years of age.

SCHOOL: AN ENVIRONMENT
FOR SYSTEMATIC LEARNING

Learning goes on all the time in everyday life. But this informal learning differs in basic ways from the formal learning of the classroom. In everyday life, much learning involves observation and imitation. A child watches an adult or another child do something and tries to do it herself. Or an adult says, "I want you to learn how to do this. Watch me."

In informal observational learning, language often plays a minor part. The general principles or rules that govern an activity to be learned are seldom stated for the child. Instead, the child sees or participates in demonstrations of the activity, and from these accumulated experiences she learns how to do it. A mother painting the bedroom walls with her daughter usually does not begin with a discussion of "how to paint." She demonstrates, saying things like "You have too much paint on the brush" or "Go over that part a few more times."

In contrast, most school learning is conducted mainly through language, and teaching often begins with the verbal presentation of a general rule or with a generalized verbal description. Only later may the rule become connected with the concrete instances from which it has been abstracted (Scribner & Cole 1981). For example, most schoolchildren still learn that "a noun is the name of a person, place, thing, or idea" long before they can point out nouns in sentences (Kenny 1983). They learn that George Washington was "the first president of the United States and the father of his country"—not what he actually did to become president or what he did while in office (Gallatin 1980).

Figure 9-10   The formal education in a school differs in important ways from the informal type of learning through which children learn most games. This school is in the Oasis Dakhla, in the Libyan Desert.

The Effect of Schooling

Formal schooling has a powerful effect on children's cognitive abilities. By studying cultures in which formal schooling is not available to everyone, psychologists and anthropologists have been able to test the cognitive abilities of children who have been to school (perhaps only for a year or two) and children who are entirely unschooled. Their research indicates that even half a year or a year of school can have a strong effect. In a study in Peru, first-graders and children of the same age and social group who were not in school were tested on fifteen different cognitive tasks, ranging from memory to classification to drawing (Stevenson 1982). The schoolchildren performed markedly better on every task than the unschooled children.

School offers children a fairly general cognitive enrichment. But in particular it seems to teach certain approaches to learning and problem-solving. People who have had formal schooling tend to look at a problem as an example of the general class of problems it may belong to. Unschooled people, on the other hand, tend to solve individual problems as if each were new, unrelated to previous ones in their experience. In one study, schooled and unschooled Kpelle children from central Liberia were given a series of sorting problems with cards displaying shapes that differed in color, form, and number (Cole & Scribner 1974; Scribner & Cole 1981). Some problems required the child to pick all the red cards, for example, but to ignore variations in shape (square, triangle, circle) and number (two, three, or four objects). When a child had correctly solved such a problem, the child was given other problems in which color (rather than form or number) was still the basis for solution, but the color was now blue or black. Even though the same principle applied to the original problem and the later ones, unschooled children showed little improvement as they worked through the series. Schooled children, on the other hand, solved later problems much faster than earlier ones. They had constructed a **general rule of solution** for a class of problems.

Because language is the primary means of exchanging information in school, schooled and unschooled people also differ in that schooled people make much greater **use of language** to describe tasks and explain solutions. In a study of Kpelle adults, people were asked first to sort twenty-five familiar objects into groups that "belonged together," then to explain their choices (Scribner 1973). Although many of the unschooled Kpelle adults—particularly those who held paying jobs or those from villages on a road—sorted the objects by category, only those who had gone to school easily explained their sorting choices in terms of a common physical property ("These are all made of wood") or a common function ("These are all used in cooking"). The unschooled adults were unable to explain their groupings except to say "My sense told me these things go together," for example.

Schooling differs from informal learning, then, in giving students **general techniques** for processing information that can be used in many different contexts. The skills of reading, writing, and arithmetic, for example, are general techniques that can be used in all kinds of situations for learning and for solving problems (Ong 1982).

Learning to Read

All normal children learn to speak spontaneously. All that seems to be required is that people speak to them. It is a rare child who learns to read without instruction, however. Coordinating the visual symbols of a written alphabet with the sounds and meanings of a spoken language is a complex task—so complex that how a child learns to read has still not been adequately described.

Information processing is one of the newest and most promising approaches to analyzing reading. This approach assumes that the human mind processes written information in about the same way that a computer does (Siegler 1983). For example, computers that sort bank checks must be programmed ("taught") to read the letters of the alphabet. The program consists of a complete set of step-by-step instructions for **feature extraction,** a method of analyzing the characteristics, or features, that distinguish letters from each other. A simplified program might include the following series of questions about the features of a letter to be identified. The answer to each question is used to extract from the set of all possible letters the ones whose features correspond to what is asked.

A Differentiate graphic symbols   B Decode letters into sounds   C Learn larger units

Figure 9-11   At the very beginning of the process of learning to read, children learn to read aloud because they must match the printed symbols to the speech sounds they are already familiar with. Essentially, they go through the three steps shown here. (A) They learn, by a process of feature extraction, to discriminate letters of the alphabet. (B) Once they can recognize the letters, they decode them into speech sounds. (C) Because many combinations of letters are pronounced differently from the letters by themselves—for example, *oo* in English is different from *o*—they must begin to learn the pronunciation of common groupings of letters. After gaining skill, readers eliminate this step of translation into speech sounds, and they process sounds, words, and meanings simultaneously (Gibson 1965; Doehring 1976).

Question: Is it a closed letter?
Answer: Yes.
Extraction: Then it is *a, b, d, e, g, o, p,* or *q.*
Question: Does it have a straight line in it?
Answer: No.
Extraction: Then it is *a, g,* or *o.*
Question: Does it have a lower loop?
Answer: Yes.
Extraction: Then it is *g.*

Children probably go through a similar process in learning to read the letters of the alphabet, as shown in Figure 9-11 (Gibson & Levin 1975). But human

sure some of that wasn't beginning to sprout too. She closed her eyes happily as she envisioned tall corn blowing in the breeze and herself reaching up on *tiptoes* to pick enough ears for supper. She liked corn so much, golden bantam corn, that as far as she was concerned the family could have it for breakfast, lunch, and dinner. In fact she wouldn't mind having a corn week. Last winter one week had been set aside as potato week when everybody was supposed to eat as many potatoes as possible. The Moffats had had potato pancakes often. It was lucky there was never a squash week, for nobody was very fond

Figure 9-12A   To see how skilled readers use context instead of depending only on the combinations of letters in a word, try to read the obscured word above. Now turn the page and look at the same word in the paragraph in Figure 9-12B. It probably took you no time at all to decipher the word in context.

readers must be able to do more than identify letters. They must relate a letter to a sound and to other letters to form words. They must relate a printed word to its spoken form and to its meaning. They must relate the meaning of a word to the meaning of other words in a sentence. And so on.

One fact confirmed by many studies is that skilled readers do not process printed information letter by letter (Guttentag & Haith 1978). No good reader processes the letters *c-a-t* in sequence to read the word "cat." Good readers process chunks of printed matter. It takes about the same amount of time for a skilled reader to perceive four unconnected letters, one very long word, or four short words that form a sentence. Skilled readers have expectations about letter combinations, word order, and meaning that help them read quickly. These expectations make it possible for them to guess the meaning of an unfamiliar word or the identity of an illegible one from its context (Figure 9-12).

Learning to read, then, proceeds on a number of levels at once rather than on a sequential basis: It involves processing letters, sounds, words, and meaning, all at the same time (Doehring 1976; Knight 1982). Perhaps this multilevel information processing explains why educators have never resolved a question that they have debated for many years: Should children's lessons in learning to read concern letter-sound relations (phonics) or whole-word recognition? Both methods are used, and while phonics seems to be more effective for most children, some seem to learn better with the whole-word method. Once children are familiar with the alphabet and letter-sound correspondences, they use both processes to learn to read. Because this is so, a beginning reading program probably should teach both (Baron 1979).

Figure 9-12B   See Figure 9-12A.

sure some of that wasn't beginning to sprout too. She closed her eyes happily as she envisioned tall corn blowing in the breeze and herself reaching up on tiptoes to pick enough ears for supper. She liked corn so much, golden bantam corn, that as far as she was concerned the family could have it for breakfast, lunch, and dinner. In fact she wouldn't mind having a corn week. Last winter one week had been set aside as potato week when everybody was supposed to eat as many potatoes as possible. The Moffats had had potato pancakes often. It was lucky there was never a squash week, for nobody was very fond

Although some children become adept readers of simple material by the third or fourth grade, many have a hard time learning to read. In fact, some students in the tenth grade do not read as well as some fourth-graders, and some college students do not read as well as some ninth-graders (Educational Testing Service 1974).

Reading is so essential to schoolwork that it affects almost everything a child does in school. Poor readers have difficulty with most of their classes, and this tends to reduce their enthusiasm for school. Children's motivation to do well at school depends greatly on their skill in reading. For the child who has trouble reading, each chapter assignment must seem an Everest of pages, impossible to scale.

Motivation

By the time they enter first grade, most children *can* learn to read, write, add, and subtract. They have the cognitive and physical maturity they need for the tasks required of them in school. But how much they actually learn depends partly on their **motivation,** their need or incentive to learn the skills that the school teaches.

The Social Context   All children are motivated to learn. They all want to understand the world around them. But wanting to learn what schools teach depends on how each child interacts with his or her environment.

The motivation to read, which is probably the key to whether most children learn to read well, can be strongly affected by the attitudes of the parents: their level of interest in their children's performance in school and elsewhere, their hopes for their children's success, and the amount of time they spend actively with their children (Marjoribanks 1978). When children read well enough at first but then fail to improve along with most of their classmates, the change is often due to parental indifference.

The attitudes of peers can also affect a child's motivation to learn to read. In fact, some children are motivated *not* to learn. A study of street "clubs" in one of New York's black ghettos showed that the club members' ability to read was astonishingly low, much lower than that of comparable nonmembers in the neighborhood (Labov & Robins 1969). Not one of the forty-three "Thunderbirds," "Aces," "Cobras," or "Jets" was reading at grade level, and most of these 10- to 16-year-olds were three or more years behind grade level. The researchers of this study, who knew the boys well, concluded that a cultural conflict was responsible for the failure. The boys' values were those of their peer group—of the street culture—which viewed school learning as useless, so there was virtually nothing that a teacher could do to motivate these boys.

Competence Motivation   Even when children are not motivated to learn to read or write, they are motivated to learn many other things. Robert White (1959) believes that all human beings are born with a motive to master their environments. *Competence motivation,* in White's view, helps explain children's curiosity about how things work and their persistence in learning something difficult—such as how to ride a bike or how to read. White's notion of an innate motive for competence is much like Piaget's notion of intelligence as an adaptive mechanism of the human species. We all *need* to deal effectively with our environments (in order to adapt), and therefore we *want* to do so (we are motivated).

Anyone who has watched the efforts of a 1-year-old to stand upright recognizes the strong motivation for competence in that small person. In spite of falls and bumps and bruises, the baby keeps trying until she finally succeeds. When she walks with ease, her pride is obvious. Her motivation to be competent in this necessary human activity is fulfilled.

A child's motivation for competence can grow or diminish over time, depending on the outcome of her efforts. Figure 9-13 shows Susan Harter's (1978, 1983) social-learning analysis of how the process seems to work. Initially, the competence motivation produces independent effort. This effort, in turn, produces either positive or negative feedback, both from the child's own perception of the outcome and from the social environment, usually the important adults in the child's life. When the feedback is positive and the child feels she has succeeded at the task, she then looks forward to new challenges with pleasure, and she puts forth more independent effort. Social approval for her efforts leads her to develop her own internal standards of success and helps her perceive herself as worthy and capable. When the feedback is negative, when the child sees herself as having failed in her efforts and when those efforts are met with social disapproval or indifference, the child's self-esteem suffers. Her competence motivation decreases, and she is likely to avoid challenge, depend on adults more, and therefore fail more often.

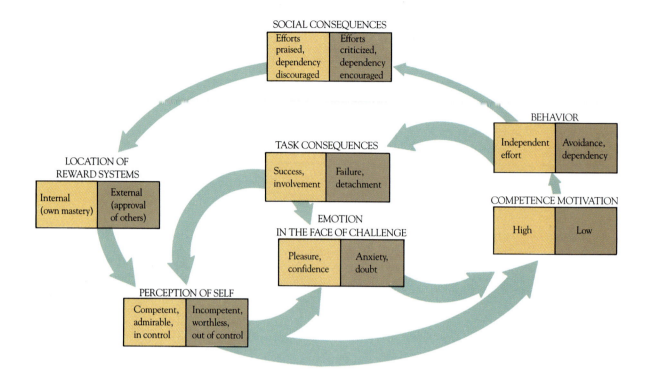

Figure 9-13   A developmental model of competence motivation. The motive to master one's environment—to be competent—can become stronger or weaker depending on the outcome of a child's interactions with her world. The diagram shows the series of factors that operate either positively (gold squares) or negatively (brown squares) to affect motivation. The process feeds back on itself. The drive to mastery produces independent effort, which may produce success at a task and social approval. Such approval encourages the child to develop internal standards of success and to see herself as competent, and success at the task makes her anticipate new challenges with pleasure. Her competence motivation is therefore increased. If a child's efforts are discouraged and her actions disapproved, independence is weakened and self-esteem is lowered. Failure at a task makes her afraid of challenge. She is likely to depend on adults more and thus fail more often. Her competence motivation is decreased (Harter 1978).

The two sketches that follow show how the competence motivation for reading can develop in children who have entered first grade and are beginning to learn to read.

Sarah's mother and father were divorced when she was a year old, and she lives with her mother but spends many weekends with her father. Five days a week, Sarah's mother works from 9 to 3, but she conscientiously spends several hours a day with Sarah—playing with her, reading to her, taking her on visits. During her preschool years, Sarah spent her days with her grandmother and grandfather, who had retired and were at home much of the time. On the weekends that she spends with her father, it is usually just the two of them.

The adults in Sarah's life give her a lot of attention. All of them read to her, and by the time she was 5 she had learned to recognize all the letters of the alphabet and to read some words herself. Every time she points to a new word and reads it, her mother or grandfather or father smiles and tells her what a smart little girl she is.

When Sarah started in first grade, she could answer many of the questions the teacher asked. The teacher often told her how well she read and awarded her many gold stars for her performance. Sarah loves to read, and the teacher gives her extra books to take home.

* * *

Alex is the fourth child in a family of six. He and his parents and brothers and sisters, along with one uncle and a cousin, live in a five-room house. Alex loves sports, and even at 5 years of age he could throw and catch a football better than his 8-year-old brother. No one in the family is much of a reader, so the only books Alex sees are the schoolbooks he or his brothers and sisters sometimes bring home. No one ever read to him.

Alex didn't show much interest in any books because to him the print was just a fuzzy pattern of black and white. He is farsighted. When he started first grade, he knew the names of some letters of the alphabet because he had learned them from watching *Sesame Street.* He could recognize some of these letters on the large posters pinned to the wall around the classroom, but he was unable to connect those patterns with what was printed in his book. When the teacher asked him a question during reading lessons, Alex answered with the first thing that came to his mind. The teacher was displeased and thought that Alex might be retarded. He was restless in class, always hopping up and anxious to do any physical task but never interested in reading. When the teacher sent a note home to Alex's parents about his inattention and restlessness in class, his parents punished him.

After 4 months had gone by, the school nurse discovered Alex's farsightedness, and the teacher sent a note home to his parents saying that he needed glasses. But Alex already felt that he was just no good at reading. After he got the glasses, his classmates started kidding him about them, calling him "Four Eyes," so he tried to avoid wearing them whenever he could.

These sketches illustrate several important ways that events in the child's environment can influence competence motivation for reading. First, observational learning and imitation are important. Seeing other people read, especially people the child loves and respects, increases a child's own motivation. Sarah sees all the adults around her reading books, and so she wants to read them, too. She wants to be an effective and competent reader, like her mother, father, and grandparents.

Second, success and approval reinforce the child's behavior and raise her competence motivation. Approval from other people—especially from the parents and teachers of young children—is usually a strong reinforcer. And success at a given task produces higher self-esteem, which then gives a child the ability to do with less outside approval. The maintenance of high self-esteem becomes reward enough. This cycle of events, which tends to increase competence motivation, is the one that Sarah experienced.

Third, punishment or even indifference from others for attempting to do certain tasks can lower competence motivation in children. A punishing or indifferent environment can produce feelings of inadequacy and, at worst, a feeling that has been called *learned helplessness* (Seligman 1975). That is, when a child's attempts to cope with a certain task bring only pain, whether physical or psychological, the child develops an overall sense of inability. The child not only gives up on that task but is less willing to take on other tasks.

A child's own failures can also produce uncertainty and lowered self-esteem. Alex's experiences with reading confused him and made him feel inadequate. He was also punished by his teacher's and parents' disapproval and his friends' ridicule. One way to avoid future disapproval and ridicule is to avoid the task that produced the psychological pain—in this case, to stop trying to read.

Competence motivation varies from skill to skill. A child may have trouble reading but at the same time take pleasure in successfully learning to play a sport or a musical instrument. Lowered motivation for learning to read probably will not affect motivation for playing softball or practicing the piano.

Particular motives wax and wane as children develop because of changes in the environment and because of developing capacities (Harter 1981). At the beginning of the elementary-school years, for instance, most children show a sharp increase in their ability to understand delayed rewards and work for them, and this ability expands as the child grows older (Mischel 1974; Weisz 1978). Education is full of delayed rewards. Learning to read, write, and do arithmetic leads to better grades in school; and better grades in school lead to approval from parents and teachers and sometimes to tangible rewards; this approval, in turn, often includes hopes for a bright career in the distant future.

Motivation can also be affected by the rate at which perceptual abilities develop during the elementary-school years. Reading is in many ways a series of perceptual puzzles like those discussed earlier in the chapter. To be able to extract letters and words from the pattern on a page, children must have the concrete-operational perceptual abilities that develop in most 6- and 7-year-olds. When children are for some reason delayed in achieving these perceptual abilities—or other abilities that they need to have for school—their motivation is likely to diminish, and they will have problems in learning.

PROBLEMS IN LEARNING

Learning problems are not always the result of poor motivation; they can have many causes. Specific learning disabilities can arise simply because a child is developing certain abilities more slowly than her age mates or because she has perceptual-motor problems arising from physiological or neurological difficulties. General learning problems can result from a child's emotional problems. Or they can come about because of a child's cognitive style, such as her tendency to respond impulsively in learning situations.

Specific Learning Disabilities

Although specific learning disabilities have sometimes been confused with mental retardation, the two are in fact very different. Children who are mentally retarded are generally poor at most tasks, whereas children with a **specific learning disability** have a problem that affects just certain kinds of learning. The causes of such learning disabilities are diverse and not well understood (Vernon 1977).

Some disabilities are simply attributable to **developmental lag,** which exists when children of elementary-school age have not developed certain skills that are typical for their age (Gardner 1975, 1982). For example, mirror writing—writing that moves from right to left with letters formed backward—is a disability in some elementary-school children but is not considered a problem in preschool. In fact, it is quite common there. One of the authors once visited a kindergarten and asked each of the fourteen 4- and 5-year-olds to print her or his name. Seven children wrote their names normally, from left to right; the other seven wrote their names in mirror fashion. Commonly, the same preschool child uses either normal or mirror writing, depending on whether she begins to write at the left or right margin of the paper.

The two-hemisphere organization of the brain seems to account for this phenomenon. Research on animals has shown that when an animal learns a visual shape with one hemisphere of its brain, that shape is often transferred to the other hemisphere as a mirror image (Corballis & Beale 1976). Apparently, many preschool children cannot override this mirror-image effect of the two hemispheres, and so they treat a letter and its mirror image as equivalent.

Normally, a change in brain organization at about age 6 does away with mirror writing (White 1970). Children beyond age 6 somehow suppress the mirror image and stop confusing it with the correct form of the letter. Some children, however, are late in undergoing this change. Consequently, they run into problems in learning to read and write. They cannot consistently discriminate between b and d or p and q, which are mirror images of each other. They have trouble discriminating between the words was and saw, rat and tar. This developmental lag is usually overcome within a year or two.

Another common problem often attributable to developmental lag is inability to pay attention. To cognitive scientists **attention** is the focusing of perception or cognition on an event or object in such a way that most of the details not connected with it are not perceived. Preschool children can keep their attention on a task for a while, but they are more easily distracted than most children of 6 years or older.

Although most 6- and 7-year-olds can concentrate and sustain their attention much better than 4-year-olds, some children begin first grade before they can focus well on what is central to a lesson. Because of this developmental lag, they have learning problems.

Another form of developmental lag linked to attention is *hyperactivity*—an abnormally high activity level together with difficulty in controlling attention and staying quiet in structured situations. Preschool children are normally very active physically. Many cannot sit still for any length of time, and, in most situations, adults do not expect them to. But when a child's activity level is extremely high and uncontrolled, the child may be diagnosed as hyperactive.

In a nursery-school study that included both normal, active children and children diagnosed as hyperactive, two experienced observers could not distinguish between the normal and the hyperactive children when they were playing freely. It was only during structured play, when the children had to remain still for some time and focus their attention on the teacher's directions, that there was a clear difference between the two groups (Schleifer et al. 1975).

Unfortunately, some 6-year-olds are as active in the classroom as preschoolers are in free play. They cannot keep their attention on one task for any length of time but jump from task to task, and they are prone to racing around in the classroom. Many researchers believe hyperactivity has an organic basis, often called "minimal brain dysfunction" (Wender 1971). The exact nature of the disorder is not known, and research suggests that it may not be a single, coherent disorder (Langhorne et al. 1976).

Some children whose behavior disrupts the class's activities are treated by medication. Oddly enough, the medication most often prescribed (amphetamine) acts on adults as a stimulant, or "upper." Such drugs have a so-called "paradoxical" effect on many of these children, calming them down and permitting them to focus their attention better (Barkley 1977). Such medications do not work as well for preschool children diagnosed as hyperactive, and this may indicate some age-related developmental difference.

These drugs' calming effect on hyperactive children of elementary-school age has been taken as evidence of an organic basis for hyperactivity. However, in a study in which bright, normal 10-year-olds were given an amphetamine, the subjects reacted to the drug in much the same way that hyperactive children do (Rapoport et al. 1978). For several hours after a dose of an amphetamine, they were much less active than usual, spoke less, and showed improved attention, faster reaction time, and better memory. This paradoxical result of an experiment with a drug whose effects have been called paradoxical shows that the puzzle of hyperactivity has not yet been solved.

The drugs used to treat hyperactivity can be dangerous, producing addiction and even brain damage. Not every child who is diagnosed as hyperactive should take them, and never without a doctor's supervision. Fortunately, with or without drugs, hyperactivity usually begins to decrease by about 12 years of age and gradually disappears in most adolescents (Weiss 1975).

Models   Copies

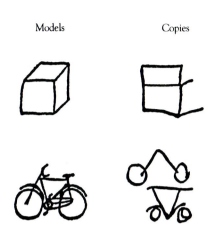

Figure 9-14   Attempts by a dyslexic 9-year-old to reproduce drawings of a cube and a bicycle. Such children are aware, while they are attempting the drawings, that they are having trouble performing the task, and they can see what is wrong with the finished product. Their perception of the forms is fine, but they cannot coordinate the sensory feedback from their muscles and nerves with their perceptions.

In addition to specific learning disabilities connected with developmental lag, *perceptual-motor disabilities,* many of which appear to have some kind of organic cause, also affect learning. For example, a child may have difficulty following oral instructions, apparently because her nervous system is poor either at translating the instructions into actions or at remembering them long enough to act on them. Children may have similar problems with vision or motor abilities. In drawing or writing, a child may be unable to reproduce the patterns she sees, or her perception of them may be faulty. The child may have great difficulty, for instance, in seeing what makes a *T* different from an *F.* Figure 9-14 shows how children with a specific kind of perceptual problem, sometimes called *dyslexia,* attempt to reproduce simple drawings. The poor perceptual-motor coordination that is obvious in these drawings also affects the children's reading ability. Some children with dyslexia are unable to remember the shape of a single letter. Even if they can learn, say, the shape of a capital *F,* they will not recognize a lower-case *f* as the same letter or will not recognize the *F* embedded in a word. Some who can learn to recognize single letters have immense difficulty in combining single sounds into longer units. Dyslexics often are poor at coordinating sight and sound, as well as at coordinating sight and body movements, as Figure 9-14 shows (Klapper 1968).

For reasons not yet understood, the frequency of some learning disabilities differs greatly among groups. Three to ten times as many boys as girls have reading problems, at least in the United States (Maccoby & Jacklin 1974). Also, reading problems seem to be much more common in some countries than in others. English is notorious for its complex spelling, which seems to contribute to a high rate of early reading problems. Written languages that use a symbol for each syllable, like one form of Japanese, seem to be easier to learn to read than languages that use an alphabet. For the mature reader, however, the advantage of an alphabet seems to be that the written symbols that make up the word help to indicate its pronunciation (Gibson & Levin 1975).

Emotional Problems

When children have difficulty learning to read or write or do arithmetic—when they cannot learn a skill that is important for school—they often develop emotional problems. School can become such a negative experience for them that they are upset for much of every school day. But the relation can also go in the other direction: Emotional problems can be the primary cause of learning problems.

A bright child with no perceptual-motor problems may fail to learn because he or she is too emotionally upset to pay attention. Some learning problems of this kind are due to a severe emotional disorder, such as schizophrenia, and are chronic. But in many cases the problems are tied to an upsetting situation. For example, one 8-year-old boy's father was slowly dying of abdominal cancer. The father had had surgery several times to try to prevent the spread of the cancer. The surgeons had removed several organs, including the genitals. The boy had done well in the first two grades, before his father's illness became serious, but in third grade he started doing very poorly, especially in writing. The school did not know about the situation at home, so neither the teacher nor the psychologist could understand why the boy was suddenly failing to learn. In fact, he was simply too filled with sorrow and anxiety to concentrate on his lessons, and his fears focused especially on pencils, because he saw their points as dangerous things that might hurt him. Writing became especially difficult. When the psychologist learned about the home situation, he and the teacher could help the boy deal with his fears and sorrows. The father eventually died, and years later the boy was again doing well in school.

Another boy was sent to a private progressive school at his mother's insistence, even though the father bitterly opposed it. The father dismissed the school as "new-fangled" and predicted that the boy would not learn much there. The mother nagged the boy to succeed, while the father was delighted whenever he failed. Being more anxious for his father's approval and sensing his father's desire that he not learn in the progressive school, the boy so strongly resisted learning that the school could not teach him to read until the true nature of his conflict was finally uncovered (Gates 1941).

Cognitive Style

Besides specific disabilities and emotional problems, a child's cognitive style may be a cause of poor school performance. **Cognitive style** is an individual's disposition to respond to a wide range of cognitive tasks with a similar pattern of behavior (Kogan 1983; Witkin et al. 1962). One of the best known and most important differences in cognitive style is the tendency to respond either immediately, in a rushed, inaccurate manner—that is, with an *impulsive* style—or slowly, deliberately, and accurately—that is, with a *reflective* style.

Figure 9-15 shows a sample from the test devised by Jerome Kagan (1965a)

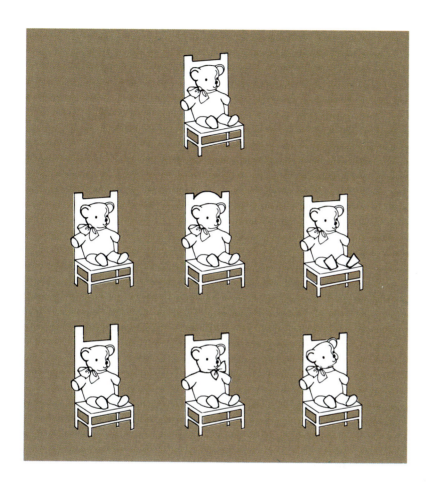

Figure 9-15 A problem like those from Jerome Kagan's Matching Familiar Figures Test. Which of the six figures below is exactly the same as the one above? To answer correctly, it is necessary to make a rather laborious and careful examination of each figure. For this reason, the test discriminates well between children who tend to respond quickly and impulsively (but often correctly on problems where less painstaking care is required) and children who respond slowly and thoughtfully to problems.

to test reflectivity and impulsivity in children of elementary-school age. Some children are highly reflective in performing this test, slowly and carefully checking the bear at the top against all the other bears. Other children impulsively give the array a quick once-over, sometimes looking at only a few items before making their choice, which is usually incorrect. About a third of the children who have taken this test are neither reflective nor impulsive, but such children have not had much attention from researchers (Messer 1976).

Impulsivity or reflectivity seems to be a characteristic disposition of many children, a disposition they display in all sorts of situations. For example, impulsive children immediately answer questions like "What games do you like best to play?" or "What are you poorest at in school?" Reflective children think about their answer for a few moments before they respond (Kagan 1970). According to Kagan, the tendency to respond impulsively decreases somewhat with age and can also be lessened by training. In reading, impulsive children make more errors, perhaps reading "noise" as "nose," or "trunk" as "truck" (Kagan 1965b). They often score lower on IQ tests, not necessarily because they are unable to answer correctly but because they answer carelessly.

INTELLIGENCE TESTS

Learning difficulties in the classroom led to the development of intelligence tests. In 1905, Alfred Binet and Theodore Simon developed the first intelligence test in France. The Minister of Public Instruction wanted some way to identify children who could not profit from instruction in regular classrooms so that they could be transferred to special schools. By trying out many different kinds of tasks and retaining only those that correlated with school performance, Binet and Simon constructed a test that could predict school performance. Within a few years, the tests were being used to predict the scholastic achievement of normal children (Brody & Brody 1976).

The final revision of their test (1911) consisted of five items for each age level from 3 to 15 years, plus five at an "adult" level. These items (which still appear in some form on the most recent American revision of the test, the 1972 Stanford-Binet) included such tasks as remembering a series of numbers, naming common objects, copying a square, putting together the two halves of a bisected rectangular card, finding parts missing from familiar figures, solving complex logical problems, and defining abstract words.

The items were grouped according to difficulty, so that the items in one group were passed by most 3-year-olds, the items in the next group were passed by most 4-year-olds, and so on. The highest group on which a child passed most items determined his **mental age.** For example, if the highest group an 8-year-old passed was the highest one passed by most 8-year-olds, the child was said to have a mental age of 8; if it was the highest one passed by most 4-year-olds, the child's mental age was said to be 4.

Binet originally defined as retarded all children who were at least 2 years behind the average score for their chronological age group. One problem with this definition was that a 16-year-old with a mental age of 14 was considered just as retarded as a 6-year-old with a mental age of 4. To overcome this problem, William Stern (1911) introduced the **intelligence quotient,** or IQ. The intelligence quotient is not a developmental concept, because it is designed to remain constant with age. The IQ is obtained by dividing a child's mental age by his chronological age and then multiplying by 100 to get rid of the decimal. Thus an 8-year-old with a mental age of 6 has an IQ of 75 because $6 \div 8 = .75$, and $.75 \times 100 = 75$. (Many tests now use more advanced statistical methods for calculating scores.) On the average, the IQ that children have at age 8 will be the same IQ that they have when they reach age 12 or 16.

Another widely used intelligence test is the Wechsler. Actually, there are three Wechsler tests—the Wechsler Adult Intelligence Scale (WAIS), the Wechsler Intelligence Scale for Children (WISC), and the Wechsler Preschool and Primary Scale of Intelligence (WPPSI). The Wechsler tests differ from the Binet in that they provide a profile of several intellectual abilities. Each

Wechsler test consists of two general scales, the verbal subscale and the performance subscale, and each subscale consists of several subtests. In the verbal subscale, the subtests assess various skills that require the use of language; in the performance subscale, they assess skills that require spatial manipulation, understanding of pictorial stories, memorization and recognition of symbols, and similar items. The subtests of each general scale are scored separately and then combined to yield, respectively, a Verbal IQ and a Performance IQ. The subtests on the children's test are shown in Table 9-3. The Verbal IQ and Performance IQ can be averaged to give a Full Scale IQ.

These tests are administered individually, but there also are paper-and-pencil intelligence tests administered to groups. Most schoolchildren and military personnel take them, and they are often administered to potential employees.

For children less than 2 years of age, special infant tests have been devised. These tests yield a developmental quotient (DQ) rather than an IQ; they measure an infant's motor abilities and adaptive responses—reactions to visual and auditory stimuli, interactions with another person, and so on. The DQ is calculated in the same way as the IQ, but it is not called IQ because there is virtually no correlation between the scores on infant tests and later IQ scores (Horn 1976). The tests are useful, however, in spotting children with severe mental retardation or specific disabilities, such as hearing or vision problems.

What Do the Tests Measure?

Although it is generally agreed that intelligence tests can predict school performance moderately well, there is no widely accepted definition of what these tests actually measure. Many lay people—and some scholars—believe that IQ is a measure of a global trait called "intelligence." But what is intelligence?

IQ and Intelligence Binet and Simon (1916) defined intelligence as "judgment, otherwise called good sense, practical sense, initiative, the faculty of adapting one's self to circumstances. To judge well, to reason well, these are the essential activities of intelligence." Wechsler (1958) defined intelligence as "the aggregate or global capacity of the individual to act purposefully, to think rationally, and to deal effectively with his environment." These definitions of intelligence are very similar to Piaget's notion of intelligence as an adaptive process, although his tasks for measuring intelligence show differences as well as similarities (DeVries & Kohlberg 1977; Humphreys & Parsons 1979) (see the theory inset "Cognitive Development," in Chapter 5).

Do the tests measure the "faculty of adapting one's self to circumstances" or a person's ability "to deal effectively with his environment?" Is an adult with an IQ of 85 intelligent if he or she is working at a job, raising a family, enjoying

TABLE 9-3 WECHSLER INTELLIGENCE SCALE FOR CHILDREN

SUBTEST	DESCRIPTION	SAMPLE ITEM FOR 6- TO 7-YEAR-OLDS	SAMPLE ITEM FOR 10- TO 12-YEAR-OLDS
VERBAL SCALE			
Information	General knowledge questions.	"Show me your nose."	"Name the days of the week."
Similarities	Find a shared property between two concepts.	"How is a tree like a flower?"	"How is a bus like a bicycle?"
Arithmetic	Mathematical problems to be solved within a time limit.	Child is asked to count a number of objects pictured on a card.	"If you had 4 hats and someone gave you 4 more, how many hats would you have?"
Vocabulary	Definitions.	"What is a bottle?"	"What does 'lazy' mean?"
Comprehension	Practical understanding.	"What should you do if you are lost in a store?"	"Why is it good to have sidewalks?"
Digit span	Ability to remember digits.	"Repeat back '2-9-7.' "	"Repeat back '3-2-7-4-6-1.' "
PERFORMANCE SCALE			
Picture completion	Child is asked to identify parts that are missing from pictures of common objects.	A face without eyes.	A pair of glasses with one arm missing.
Picture arrangement	Cards telling a story are to be arranged in correct order within a time limit.	Three cards showing a man buying an apple.	Four cards showing a boy finding a lost dog.

sports or hobbies, and meeting the demands of daily life? According to the definitions given by Binet and Wechsler, the answer is yes. Yet according to the test scales, a person who scores 85 on a test is not very intelligent. Also some people with high scores on intelligence tests deal poorly with many aspects of their environment. Former President Nixon and his colleagues scored well on intelligence tests, yet a number of them spent time in prisons for a long series of behaviors that were in many ways ineffective or maladaptive.

Intelligence tests do measure some problem-solving skills, in particular those that enable people to do well in school work. And, in fact, IQ scores correlate moderately well with academic success. You will recall from Chapter 1 that correlation coefficients can range from 0.0 to 1.0. In high school, IQ scores and academic grades are correlated at about .60; in college, at about .50 (Lavin 1965; Jencks et al. 1972). The scores also correlate moderately well with career success. A study of people who were part of the Fels longitudinal study showed that childhood IQ scores and adult occupational success were correlated at about .50 (McCall 1977). A correlation of .50 means that 25 percent of the measured variation among adults in educational attainment and career success is accounted for by IQ and 75 percent by factors other than IQ.

SUBTEST	DESCRIPTION	SAMPLE ITEM FOR 6- TO 7-YEAR-OLDS	SAMPLE ITEM FOR 10- TO 12-YEAR-OLDS
PERFORMANCE SCALE (continued)			
Block design	Geometric designs on cards have to be matched by putting together blocks that have variously colored surfaces within a time limit.	Designs are extremely simple.	Designs are more complex.
Object assembly	Cardboard pieces must be put together to form a picture of a common object within a time limit.	Seven pieces to make a person.	Twelve pieces to make a face.
Coding	Child is shown a set of shapes or numbers, each marked with a special mark or symbol. The child must then mark correctly as many as he can of a series of shapes or numbers within a time limit.	Five simple shapes and marks.	Nine numbers and unusual symbols.
Mazes	Child must trace a path out of a maze printed on a piece of paper within a time limit, losing points for entering blind alleys.	Maze plan is very simple with only one blind alley.	Maze plan is more complex, larger, with several blind alleys.

One Intelligence or Many?   Many cognitive scientists believe that intelligence is not a single trait. Statistical analyses of intelligence tests have identified different components, such as the seven "primary abilities" found by L.L. Thurstone (1938): verbal comprehension, word fluency, number (ability to solve arithmetic problems and manipulate numbers), space (visualization of spatial relationships), associative memory, perceptual speed, and general reasoning. The most detailed model of intelligence describes 120 such abilities (Guilford 1977).

One of the most influential formulations of the nature of intelligence says that it is composed of two kinds of general abilities—crystallized intelligence and fluid intelligence (Cattell 1971; Horn 1982). ***Crystallized intelligence*** reflects the kinds of skills that are explicitly taught, particularly in schools: vocabulary, formulas for solving math problems, and information about geography, history, and literature. ***Fluid intelligence,*** according to John Horn (1970), is the factor underlying the central organizing functions in all behavior, especially when the person must use abilities that are not explicitly taught in school or even in society more generally. It includes such basic functions as short-term memory—the ability to hold some bits of information in mind long

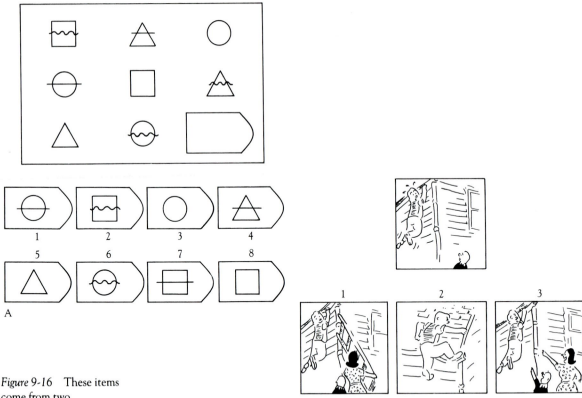

enough to apply them to a task—and reasoning about spatial arrangements or
other nonverbal qualities. The cognitive processes described in Piaget's theory
may also be aspects of fluid intelligence. Fluid intelligence is most clearly seen
in the ability to perform unfamiliar tasks. The Wechsler verbal subtests listed
in Table 9-3 primarily call upon crystallized intelligence, whereas the performance subtests primarily call upon fluid intelligence.

General intelligence is the combination of fluid and crystallized intelligence,
and most problems people have to solve require this combination. Fluid intelligence seems to increase until late adolescence and then to decline somewhat
through adulthood and old age; crystallized intelligence, on the other hand,
rises steadily until age 60 or so (Botwinick 1977; Horn 1982). For this reason,
general intelligence remains fairly steady after childhood.

Heredity and Environment in Intelligence

IQ tests reflect only part of intelligence, which is made up of a number of
distinct components. Nevertheless, they have been the main tool used by
researchers attempting to pin down the relative contributions of heredity and
environment to intelligent behavior.

Some scholars believe that genetic variations among people are by far the
most important determinant of individual differences in intelligence (Jensen
1969; Munsinger 1975). Others are equally convinced that environmental
circumstances are most important (Lewontin 1976; Kamin 1975). Most scholars, however, think that heredity and environment collaborate in complex

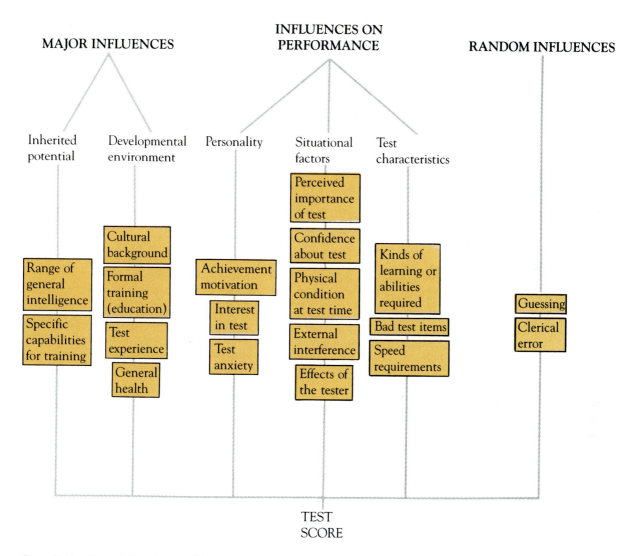

Figure 9-17   Not only hereditary and long-term environmental influences determine scores on an IQ test. Personality characteristics, the character of the test, situational factors (particular conditions when the test is taken), and even some random influences all help to determine the outcome (Goslin 1963; Horn 1976; McCall 1983).

ways from the day of an individual's birth to determine his intelligence. Some sense of the complexity of this interplay is shown by Figure 9-17, which lists some of the possible influences on performance on an intelligence test. Because of its many social and political implications, the question of the role of heredity and environment in the origins of intelligence is much more controversial than most issues in child development. If intelligence is mainly inherited, it may be pointless to try to raise it by changing educational policies, for example. If intelligence is mainly determined by environment, on the other hand, such efforts can be extremely worthwhile.

ESSAY:
THE POLITICS OF IQ TESTING

In 1969, psychologist Arthur R. Jensen published an article titled "How Much Can We Boost IQ and Scholastic Achievement?" This article provoked a controversy among psychologists that is still raging. Jensen's thesis in this and subsequent articles is basically that IQ is very largely an inherited trait and that the inherited IQ of blacks is, on the average, 15 points lower than the inherited IQ of whites. Jensen's findings received a great deal of publicity in the public press also; articles about his ideas appeared in newspapers and popular magazines. A short history of IQ testing in the United States may give some perspective on Jensen's ideas and the reason for their wide publicity. Leon Kamin, in his book *The Science and Politics of IQ,* has traced that history.

IQ TESTS COME TO AMERICA

The originator of the IQ test, Alfred Binet, never believed that his test could "make a distinction between acquired and congenital feeble-mindedness" (1905). In fact, he abhorred the idea that "the intelligence of an individual is a fixed quantity, a quantity which one cannot augment." He said, "We must protest and react against this brutal pessimism" (1913). American pioneers in testing, however, under the influence of Darwin's theories of evolution and popular notions of "survival of the fittest," saw the IQ as a fixed measure of "innate intelligence"—and as an indicator of natural selection for the social order. Famous psychologists such as Lewis Terman, Henry Goddard, and Robert Yerkes equated lower scores on IQ tests with poverty and crime: "Even a superficial investigation shows us that a large percentage of these troubles come from the feeble-minded" (Goddard 1912). Not only was a lower IQ said to be the cause of poverty and crime, it explained social inequality. In a lecture he gave at Princeton University in 1919, Goddard explained that "the different levels of intelligence have different interests and require different treatment to make them happy. . . . The man of intelligence has spent his money wisely, has saved until he has enough to provide for his needs in case of sickness, while the man of low intelligence, no matter how much money he would have earned, would have spent much of it foolishly." The science of IQ testing seemed to be saying that coal miners, whom Goddard later named specifically in this lecture, were obviously persons of low IQ. Their low IQ explained why, when the mines closed for a time, the miners did not have enough money to keep on eating and paying the rent.

TESTING OF IMMIGRANTS

In 1912 Henry Goddard was invited by the United States Public Health Service to administer IQ tests to the immigrants on Ellis Island who were waiting to enter the country. At this time in America's history, most of the immigrants were coming from southern and eastern Europe, whereas earlier waves of immigrants had come from northern European countries. Goddard reported that 83 percent of the Jews, 80 percent of the Hungarians, 79 percent of the Italians, and 87 percent of the Russians were feeble-minded (1913). Such "scientific" data added weight to growing social concerns about the "New Immigration." The newspapers and magazines of the time were filled with articles questioning the ability of these new immigrant groups to be assimilated into the American culture.

America's entry into World War I, in 1917, provided an opportunity for the first mass IQ testing. A written group intelligence test—the Army Alpha—and a supplementary nonverbal test—the Army Beta—were developed and administered to all draftees, some 2,000,000 of them (Kamin 1975). In 1921, an analysis of the scores of some 125,000 draftees was published. One chapter in the analysis was titled "Relation of Intelligence Ratings to Nativity," and the results of the analysis of scores of 12,407 men reporting they had been born outside the United States were shown as in the figure on the next page. The discussion of the results in the report was neutral, saying only, "In general, the Scandinavian and English speaking countries stand high in the list, while the Slavic and Latin countries stand low." Professor Yerkes, senior author of the report, did comment that language handicaps might have depressed the scores of the foreign born. However, the impact of the report was enormous. In fact, it and subsequent books and reports based on the Army data led to passage of the Immigration Act of 1924, which not only specified quotas of annual immigration by national origin, but based those quotas on the census of 1890, before the large immigrations from southern and eastern Europe had begun.

INTERPRETING THE DATA

One of the most influential books based on the Army data was written by Carl Brigham, an assistant professor of psychology at Princeton University and later the first head of the Educational Testing Service. Published in 1923, it was titled *A Study of American Intelligence*. One thing Brigham did was to reanalyze the data on foreign-born draftees in terms of how long they had lived in the United States before taking the test. Brigham discovered the "very remarkable fact" that there was a definite relation between length of residence in the United States and measured intelligence. In fact, immigrants who had lived in this country for at least 20 years before they were tested were every bit as intelligent as native Americans, no matter what their country of origin.

To some, Brigham's data might seem to prove that IQ was greatly affected by exposure to American customs and language. Brigham, however, was certain that IQ tests measure "native or inborn intelligence." His interpretation of the data, then, led him to conclude that the more recent immigrants were simply of poorer stock than the earlier immigrants had been: "We are forced to . . . accept the hypothesis that the curve indicates a gradual deterioration in the class of immigrants examined in the Army, who came to this country in each succeeding five year period since 1902." This "scientific" conclusion raised the specter of a rapid decline in the intelligence of Americans. Americans were faced by further waves of feeble-minded Jews, Slavs, and Italians, who would intermarry with Americans and make the racial stock decline.

It seems that the political temper of the times reinforced—and was reinforced by—the new science of IQ testing. A large proportion of American citizens wanted an end to massive immigration (for economic and other considerations that cannot be discussed here), and the psychologists' findings gave them scientific evidence to

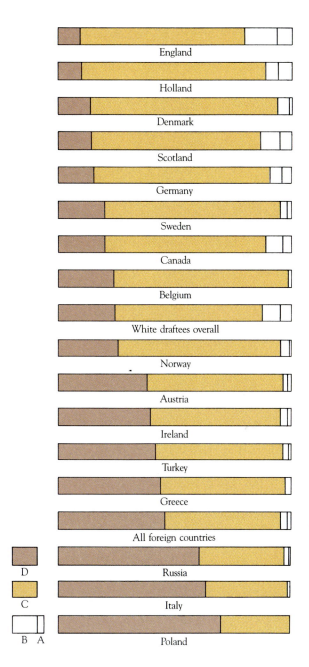

The percentage distribution of letter grades on IQ tests taken by foreign-born men drafted into the United States Army in World War I.

support their arguments. Brigham also warned that "The decline of American intelligence will be more rapid . . . owing to the presence here of the negro" (Kamin, p. 210), which brings us back to Professor Jensen's assertions that blacks are inferior to whites in IQ and that IQ is largely an inherited ability and therefore cannot be significantly altered.

THE TEMPER OF THE TIMES

Jensen's article was published at the end of the 1960s, which had seen the flowering of the civil-rights movement. Until the middle of the twentieth century, access by American blacks to most facets of American life was severely limited. Blacks were barred from many types of jobs—even professional sports. They were barred from participating in many unions. They were refused entrance into many neighborhoods, and most hotels and restaurants. Many attended entirely segregated grade and high schools, which were generally more poorly funded than white schools, and they were denied entrance into many universities. In certain parts of the country, local ordinances kept them from exercising their right to vote.

Many of these bars to participation in society were removed by court decisions and legislation passed in the 1960s. The passage of civil rights legislation aimed at integrating black and white children in schools brought into focus the fact that black children, on the average, scored lower than white children on IQ tests and on academic achievement tests. Educators then came up with preschool programs such as Head Start, meant to offer compensatory education for poor children, primarily black children—to give them the opportunity to overcome deficiencies in their family-based education. As discussed in Chapter 7, Head Start programs varied greatly in organization and curriculum, and most children attended for only a few hours a day. When, after a few years, these children and programs

were evaluated, the initial evaluations showed that little had been gained. The poor and black children were still scoring lower in IQ and schoolwork.

Recall that Dr. Jensen's controversial article was titled "How Much Can We Boost IQ and Scholastic Achievement [by means of compensatory education]?" His answer, essentially, was "Not much." If we examine the temper of that time (which may not be too different from the temper of the current time), we can see that Americans required a satisfactory explanation of why blacks were, on the whole, at the bottom of the socioeconomic ladder. After all, they now had—by law—full civil rights. The answer pointing to the fact that blacks had been the victims of centuries of active discrimination by whites—from the shameful era of slavery to the shameful action of a governor of one of the United States standing in the doorway of a state-supported university and vowing that a black student would never be permitted to enter—was an uncomfortable answer. If the failure of blacks to quickly scale the ladder of success could be laid to some shortcoming in their own makeup—such as genetically determined lower IQ—the discomfort would be much less.

Sixty years after psychologists found immigrants from eastern and southern Europe to be deficient intellectually, it seems almost ludicrous to remember that these people were once thought to be genetically—and therefore irretrievably—retarded. They and their descendants have gone on to achieve great success in intellectual, financial, and artistic endeavors. For reasons having little to do with science, people in that era chose to pay attention to and publicize findings that supported a purely political desire—to end mass immigration. Likewise, the publicity received by Dr. Jensen's findings seems to answer a political need of these times—to rationalize the fact that American blacks are disproportionately represented in the lower socioeconomic stratum of our society. Perhaps sixty years from now, such findings will appear ludicrous to the descendants of this generation.

In their attempts to discover the relative contributions of heredity and environment to intelligence, investigators have mostly studied either twins or adopted children. **Studies with twins** are based on the difference between identical and fraternal twins. In both cases, two children are carried by the same mother and born at the same time, but the different kinds of twins share different proportions of genes. **Identical twins** have exactly the same genes, because they come from a single fertilized egg that splits in two: Their heredity is identical. **Fraternal twins** develop from two separately fertilized eggs, so they share an average of 50 percent of their genes, just as all brothers and sisters do.

If performance on an intelligence test was determined entirely by genes, the correlation between the IQs of identical twins would be very close to perfect— 1.0—even if the twins had been separated early in life and raised in different environments. In fact, it is not that high. If genes nevertheless make a substantial contribution to intelligence, the correlation between the IQs of identical twins—whether the twins are reared apart or together—should be much greater than the correlation between the IQs of fraternal twins, because the fraternal twins share only half as many genes as the identical twins do (Loehlin & Nichols 1976; Shields 1962). In fact, twin studies have revealed such differences, clearly supporting the contribution by genes to intelligence.

Some twin studies also show an effect of environment. The scores of identical twins reared apart tend to differ more than those of identical twins reared together, suggesting that the differing environments of twins reared apart lead to IQ differences (Kamin 1975). In one study, the largest IQ difference in a pair of identical twins was 24 points between Gladys and Helen, who were reared separately. Gladys, who grew up in an isolated region of the Rocky Mountains, had received only 2 years of elementary-school education, whereas Helen had graduated from college (Newman et al. 1937). Indeed, at least 50 percent of the variability in IQ scores seems to result from environmental differences (Plomin & DeFries 1980).

Twin studies have proved to be problematic, however. For one thing, when identical twins are raised together, they tend to be treated very similarly by those around them, so their higher IQ correlation also may be partly the result of their environment. Also, twins who have been separated and raised by different families are rare and hard to find, so data are scarce. Studies of adopted children have proved easier to carry out and have produced abundant and reliable data.

In **studies of adopted children,** the IQs of the children are compared with the IQs of both their biological parents and their adoptive parents. Adopted children share an average of 50 percent of the genes with each of their biological parents. On the other hand, their home and community environment is shared with their adoptive parents, not with their biological parents.

Several of these studies show clearly that both heredity and environment affect intelligence (Skodak & Skeels 1949; Scarr & Weinberg 1976, 1977). In

Figure 9-18 (A) The IQ scores of the adopted children in the study by Skodak and Skeels and of the children's biological mothers (IQ scores were available for only 63 of the 100 mothers). The mean score for the mothers was 85.7, but it was 106 for the children. The environment provided by their adoptive parents allowed the children to gain 20 points in IQ above what would have been expected if they had been raised by their biological parents. (B) Nevertheless, there was a correlation between the scores of the children and the scores of their biological mothers. That is, children of mothers with low IQs tended to have lower scores than children of mothers with high IQs. The correlation is not very high ($r = 0.38$), but it is enough to indicate a hereditary influence on IQ.

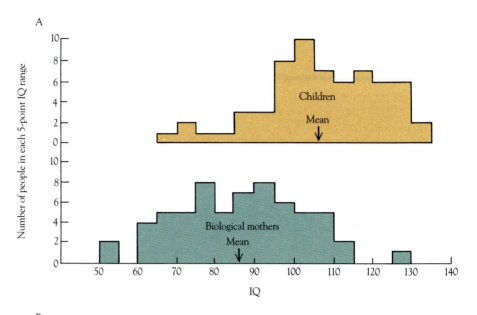

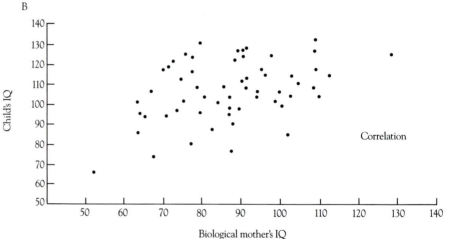

general, the IQ level of the adoptive parents was much higher than that of the biological parents—about 120 for adoptive parents and 90 or so for biological parents—and the environment provided by the adoptive parents was consistent with their own IQ levels, emphasizing learning and education. The IQs of the adoptive children reflected this intellectually stimulating environment. They were around 110, 20 points higher than the biological parents' IQs (Figure 9-18A).

On the other hand, the genetic contributions of the biological parents are also clear. The IQ *rankings* of the adopted children did correspond noticeably to the rankings of their biological parents (Figure 9-18B).

These results illustrate an important genetic concept—***reaction range.*** An individual's genetic make-up sets limits on the general range of his abilities. Given the normal range of environments, his abilities can vary a certain amount within those genetic limits. Some environments support and encourage partic- ular abilities, others suppress them. One estimate of the average reaction range for IQ is about 25 points in normal environments. In the extremely deprived environment of a very bad institution, however, any child will become retarded (Hunt et al. 1976).

Class and Ethnic Background

Lower-class children, on the average, have lower IQs than middle-class chil- dren, and these differences carry over into adulthood. Environmental influ- ences play an even more important role in intelligence in the lower class than in the middle class (Fischbein 1980). This finding makes sense in light of the social-class differences discussed in Chapter 8. Middle-class parents tend to stress intellectual achievement for their children more than lower-class parents do, and they try to foster school-related skills in their children from an early age. They themselves also have had more years of formal education, and their higher incomes make an "enriched" environment easier to achieve.

Some ethnic or racial backgrounds also seem to correlate with lower IQ scores. But a higher than average number of minority-group members belong to the lower class, so the effects of social class and ethnic background are very hard to separate.

A few researchers—most notably Arthur Jensen (1969, 1980)—have sug- gested that the consistently lower average scores of some minority groups are evidence of a hereditary handicap in intelligence. Most researchers, however, find Jensen's conclusion unwarranted and unsound, and believe that ethnic differences in IQ are much more likely to be primarily environmental in origin. Native Americans, blacks, Asian-Americans, and Spanish-speaking groups have formed subcultures in the United States, so their environments—their values and attitudes—differ in some ways from those of the white middle class. Many members of these minority groups (and many researchers) have pointed out that IQ tests reflect the values, attitudes, and knowledge that typify the white middle class. As a result of this cultural bias, members of some subcultures are put at a decided disadvantage when taking these tests.

An example of cultural bias on the Binet test was pointed out by Robert L. Williams (1970), a black psychologist. One question is, "What's the thing for you to do if another child hits you without meaning to do it?" A response is scored correct if the child says something "reasonable," such as "Well, he didn't mean it, so I'd just walk away." The prevalent attitude in some minority communities, however, is that you should strike back at anyone who strikes you, no matter what the circumstances. To do otherwise would represent weakness and might lead others to attack you. A child from such a community who answered "I'd hit him back" would show the intelligence necessary for

1. Who did "Stagger Lee" kill?
   (A) His mother, (B) Frankie, (C) Johnny, (D) His girlfriend, (E) Billy.

2. A "gas head" is a person who has a . . .
   (A) Fast-moving car, (B) Stable of "lace," (C) "Process," (D) Habit of stealing cars, (E) Long jail record for arson.

3. If a man is called a "blood," then he is a . . .
   (A) Fighter, (B) Mexican-American, (C) Negro, (D) Hungry hemophile, (E) Redman or Indian.

4. If you throw the dice and 7 is showing on the top, what is facing down?
   (A) Seven, (B) Snake Eyes, (C) Boxcars, (D) Little Joes, (E) 11.

5. Cheap chitlings (not the kind you purchase at a frozen-food counter) will taste rubbery unless they are cooked long enough. How soon can you quit cooking them to eat and enjoy them?
   (A) 45 minutes, (B) 2 hours, (C) 24 hours, (D) 1 week (on a low flame), (E) 1 hour.

6. "Down home" (the South) today, for the average "soul brother" who is picking cotton (in season) from sunup until sundown, what is the average earning (take home) for one full day?
   (A) $.75, (B) $1.65, (C) $3.50, (D) $5, (E)$12.

7. A "handkerchief head" is . . .
   (A) A cool cat, (B) A porter, (C) An Uncle Tom, (D) A hoddi, (E) A preacher.

8. "Jet" is . . .
   (A) An East Oakland motorcycle club, (B) One of the gangs in "West Side Story," (C) A news and gossip magazine, (D) A way of life for the very rich.

9. "And Jesus said, 'Walk together, children . . .'"
   (A) "Don't get weary. There's a gret camp meeting," (B) "For we shall overcome," (C) "For the family that walks together talks together," (D) "By your patience you will win your souls" (Luke 21:19), (E) "Mind the things that are above, not the things that are on earth" (Col. 3:3).

10. If a pimp is up tight with a woman who gets state aid, what does he mean when he talks about "Mother's Day"?
    (A) Second Sunday in May, (B) Third Sunday in June, (C) First of every month, (D) None of these, (E) First and fifteenth of every month.

11. Jazz pianist Ahmad Jamal took an Arabic name after becoming really famous. Previously he had some fame with what he called his "slave name." What was his previous name?
    (A) Willie Lee Jackson, (B) LeRoi Jones, (C) Wilbur McDougal, (D) Fritz Jones, (E) Andy Johnson.

12. What is Willie Mae's last name?
    (A) Schwartz, (B) Matsuda, (C) Gomez, (D) Turner, (E) O'Flaherty.

13. What are the "Dixie hummingbirds"?
    (A) A part of the KKK, (B) A swamp disease, (C) A modern gospel group, (D) A Mississippi paramilitary group, (E) Deacons.

14. "Bo Diddley" is a . . .
    (A) Game for children, (B) Down home cheap wine, (C) Down home singer, (D) New dance, (E) Mojo call.

15. "Hully Gully" came from . . .
    (A)East Oakland, (B) Fillmore, (C) Watts, (D) Harlem, (E) Motor City.

16. Which word is most out of place here?
    (A)Slib, (B) Blood, (C) Gray, (D) Spook, (E) Black.

The Answers

1. (E) 3. (C) 5. (C) 7. (C) 9. (A) 11. (D) 13. (C) 15. (C) 2. (C) 4. (A) 6. (D) 8. (C) 10. (E) 12. (D) 14. (C) 16. (C)

Figure 9-19 This "intelligence test" was created by Adrian Dove, a black sociologist, to illustrate, with humor, how information and vocabulary common to one culture might be entirely foreign to another.

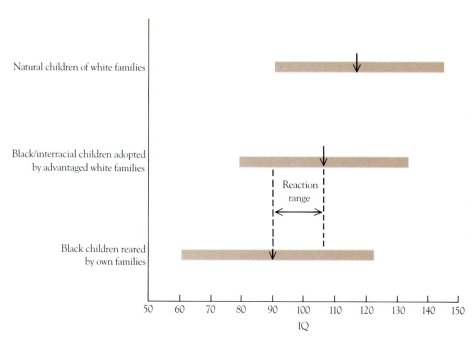

Figure 9-20 The effects of environment on IQ were demonstrated in a study of 130 black and interracial children adopted by white families of high education and income in Minnesota. In that part of the country, black children reared by their own families scored, on the average, about 90 on IQ tests. The adopted black children scored, on the average, 110. The psychologists also tested the natural children of the adoptive parents, who scored, on the average, 120. Thus, the adoptees' scores were closer to those of their step-siblings than to those of their biological parents. The brown bars here represent the range of scores of each group, and the black arrows indicate the group's average. Shown also is the average reaction range, the effect of the environment on genetic potential shown so far in the black children (Scarr & Weinberg 1976).

adapting to his surroundings, but this demonstration would lower his test score.

The vocabulary of IQ tests also seems to show an ethnic bias. Test items frequently use terms that may be commonplace in white middle-class homes but are completely unfamiliar to members of certain subcultures. A test created by a black sociologist might give middle-class whites a feeling for this kind of cultural bias. Try your hand at the intelligence test in Figure 9-19. Then consider the fact that the items that correlate most closely with overall IQ scores on standard intelligence tests are vocabulary questions. Because answers to all the verbal subtests depend on vocabulary, how well would white middle-class people do with a test that used a vocabulary like that in Figure 9-19?

The effects of environment on the IQs of black children are strikingly demonstrated by a study of approximately 100 black children who were adopted in infancy by white middle-class families in Minnesota (Scarr & Weinberg 1976, 1979). On the average, black chldren have been found to attain lower IQ scores than white children—an average IQ of 85 or so instead of 100. The IQ scores of the biological parents in the study were not available, but their educational levels indicated that their IQs were probably average for blacks.

When the children were tested after some years in their adoptive homes, their average IQ was about 110—25 points above the average for blacks and 10 above the average for whites (Figure 9-20). Their achievement in school was above average, too.

Figure 9-21   The relation between birth order, family size, and intelligence. The data on which this chart is based were collected by the military services of the Netherlands. They represent findings on 400,000 individuals, who were tested with the Raven Progressive Matrices Test (see Figure 9-16). These data show that children of larger families and later-born children have lower intelligence than children of smaller families and earlier-born children, although the differences are not large on the average (Belmont & Morolla 1973).

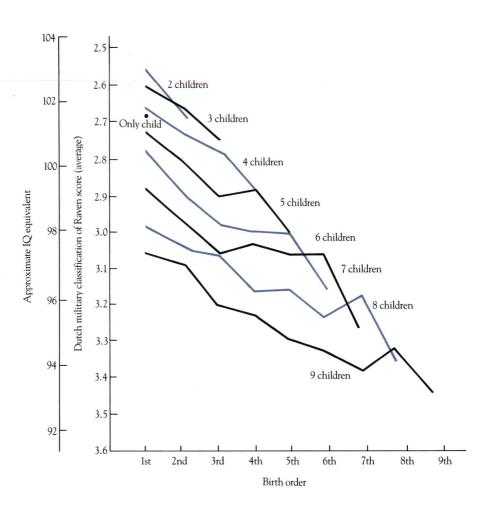

Birth-Order Effects

The IQs of children in the same family differ, slightly but consistently, according to birth order, family size, and the number of years between the births of the children (Zajonc 1983; Zajonc & Markus 1975). The more children in the family, the lower the average IQ of each, as shown in Figure 9-21. This effect is independent of the parents' IQs. Also, later-born children tend to have slightly lower IQs, on the average, than earlier-born children. When the intervals between the children's births are 5 years or more, however, the birth-order effect virtually disappears.

Two factors in the family seem to produce these effects on IQ. First, the level of cognitive development of siblings is important. In families with many closely spaced children, a later-born child interacts frequently with brothers and sisters

who are still at a relatively low level of cognitive development. Later-born children therefore tend to have lower IQs. When the intervals between children are 5 years or more, however, a later child's intellectual development can be stimulated by older brothers and sisters.

Second, having a younger brother or sister to teach stimulates the growth of intelligence. Being born last is therefore a disadvantage. The data show, for example, that the second-born in a family with two children has a slightly lower IQ, on the average, than the second-born in a family with three children. And only children, who are both the first-born and the last-born in their families, have lower IQs, on the average, than first-born children with as many as three younger brothers or sisters.

As these interpretations show, environments can differ even for individuals within the same family. Of course, the effects are not true of all families or of

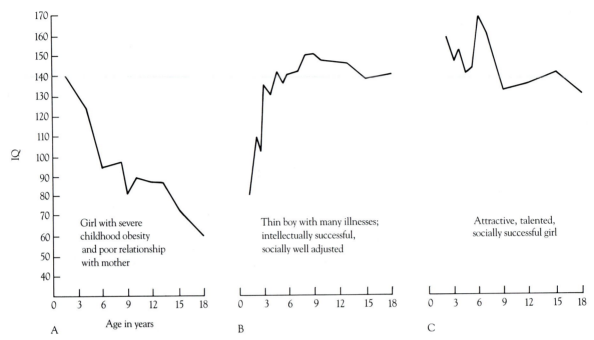

Figure 9-22   An individual's IQ scores may vary over the years. The Berkeley longitudinal study of children from early childhood through adolescence gathered not only IQ scores but also information about the children's family lives and social and emotional development. It was therefore possible to look at a child's personality and circumstances in an effort to explain variations in IQ scores. (A) This girl, whose scores dropped sharply all through childhood, seems to have been crippled emotionally by a neurotic relationship with her mother. The girl was extremely obese, which also made relations with peers difficult. (B) A boy who was handicapped by small stature and ill health seems to have triumphed over those difficulties. He not only had many intellectual accomplishments but was socially well-adjusted as well. (C) The variable scores of this attractive girl reflect intellectual interests in her early school years and then, in high school, her deliberate suppression of intellectual achievement in favor of social activities.

all individuals within a family (Grotevant et al. 1977). But on the average, later-born children in larger families end up with lower IQs than earlier-born children in smaller families.

Change in Individual IQ Scores

Because the environment makes such an important contribution to intelligence, an individual's IQ does not typically remain constant throughout childhood. One of the most detailed reports of changes in individuals' IQs during childhood is based on a longitudinal study—running from early childhood to adolescence—of 153 children in Berkeley, California (Honzik et al. 1948). Although the scores of many children showed little variation, more than half the children showed IQ changes of more than 15 points, and almost 10 percent showed changes of 30 or more points, with some scores going up, some down, and some fluctuating. Figure 9-22 presents the IQ profiles and brief case histories of three children from the study.

Robert McCall and his colleagues (1973) have identified several consistent patterns of IQ change between ages 2 and 17 and have related them to patterns of parental behavior. Children who showed a general increase during childhood had middle-class parents who valued learning and education and consciously attempted to stimulate their children's development. These parents did not think it enough to let their children "develop naturally"; instead, they encouraged them to learn.

Some other children showed a decline in IQ in preschool, but then diverged into two different patterns. Some of them recovered somewhat during grade school and then showed a sharp decline during adolescence. The others continued at a low level during grade school but made a comeback during adolescence. The researchers found that the parents of these two groups differed greatly in the severity of discipline they imposed. The parents whose children scored fairly well in grade school but poorly in adolescence were very lax in their discipline, almost neglectful. In contrast, the parents whose children's IQs remained depressed during grade school but rebounded in adolescence were most severe in their discipline. Both groups of parents tended to belong to the lower class, and neither group attempted to accelerate their children's intellectual development.

Recently, McCall (1983) uncovered still another pattern of systematic change. When a new baby is born, older siblings show a sharp decline in IQ that lasts for several years, but eventually the older siblings' intelligence scores recover. In fact, after some time, their scores rise even higher as a result of having a younger brother or sister (Zajonc & Markus 1975).

The findings of these studies are consistent with the results of other research. Diana Baumrind found that the most competent and independent preschoolers in her sample had parents who were neither authoritarian-restrictive nor permissive (see Chapter 8). Instead, the parents of the most competent preschoolers stimulated their children's intellectual development and set out clear rules of behavior that they enforced firmly but not fiercely.

These patterns of change in IQ may seem to call into question the meaning and usefulness of intelligence tests. But all they actually do is show that IQ is not fixed and that systematic changes in IQ scores during childhood make sense in terms of a child's family environment. Indeed, not only does school performance correspond fairly well to scores on intelligence tests, but systematic patterns of change in IQ tend to be accompanied by the same patterns of change in school performance.

Perhaps the most useful function that intelligence tests can serve is the one Binet originally intended: the identification of children who require special educational help. Also, they can identify children's special strengths and deficiencies, so that schools and parents can build on the strengths and attempt to remedy the deficiencies.

How much of the individual child's difficulty with academic work arises from environmental circumstances and how much from hereditary factors is usually impossible to know because each child's intelligence is the product of an interweaving of both factors from the day of birth. What is important is that during the elementary-school years the tapestry of heredity and environment is still being created, and particular environmental circumstances can affect the design and pattern. Making a child believe, for instance, that he was "born dumb" because he scores poorly on intelligence tests can only damage the pattern. Giving special stimulation and help to a child who has trouble with schoolwork can make the pattern brighter and livelier.

PHYSICAL DEVELOPMENT

Although the IQ scores of some children show large changes, the IQ scores of most children become fairly stable at about 5 or 6 years of age. That is, most children will maintain about the same IQ ranking within their age group as they grow older (Horn 1976). This stabilization of intelligence seems to accompany the development of concrete-operational thought and the beginning of school—it is a psychological change that corresponds to a physical change in the organization of the brain and nervous system.

Between the ages of 5 and 7, most children show a growth spurt, becoming taller and less pudgy and more like an adult. In a sense, this spurt is like a preliminary adolescence, but without sexual maturity (Mead 1963). Other animals typically have just one such growth spurt, ending in a fully adult appearance and including sexual maturity. But we human beings have an exceptionally long childhood, in which our physical development becomes slower and slower (compared to that of other animals) as we mature. The pattern of physical development in the elementary school years illustrates this. After the spurt at ages 5 to 7, children's physical development is slower until adolescence. Children pass through a period of at least 5 or 6 years (ages 6 to 11 or older) in which they are physically and intellectually almost, but not quite, adults. During those 5 or 6 years, they exert a great effort to learn many of the skills they will need in adulthood, an effort not required of other animals.

The Brain and the 5-to-7 Shift

At about age 6, along with the overall spurt in growth, a child's brain undergoes a spurt in growth and function—a spurt that seems to correspond to the development of the new cognitive level of concrete operations. As described in earlier chapters, changes in brain size and function accompany the advance

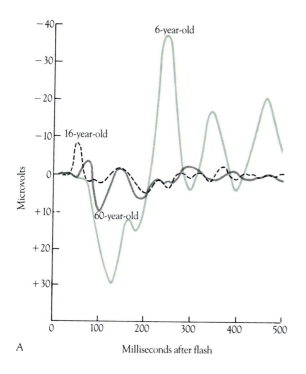

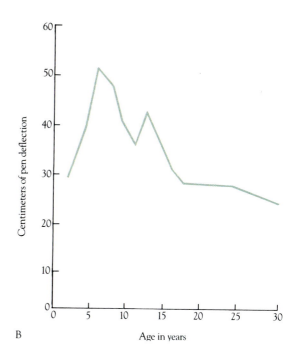

A   Milliseconds after flash   B   Age in years

into every cognitive-developmental level; but the changes that accompany the appearance of concrete operations are the best documented. This cluster of biological and psychological developments signals a major developmental change, the **5-to-7 shift,** so called because of when it takes place (S. White 1970).

In the cerebral cortex, many of the association areas, which play an essential role in intelligence, reach a major milestone at this age: They complete most of their growth of myelin, the material that insulates nerve fibers and permits nerves to transmit impulses faster and more efficiently (Lecours 1975).

At about this time changes also take place in the brain's electrical activity. Brain waves, or electroencephalograms, show a sharp increase to a higher frequency, which is more mature (Epstein 1980). There is also a change in the visually evoked potential, the brain's electrically recorded response to a flash of light (Figure 9-23). Recordings of brain activity show that the magnitude, or amplitude, of this response grows larger through age 6 and then gradually drops off to the adult level, although there is an additional smaller peak in the teens (Milner 1967).

The changes in the brain seem to affect the course of certain brain disorders as well, including PKU and convulsions resulting from fever. You will recall from Chapter 2 that PKU is a hereditary, single-gene disorder that causes mental retardation if it is not treated. To avoid brain damage, children with PKU must be fed a diet low in the protein phenylalanine. But after age 6 or so, the danger of severe mental retardation no longer exists if children are taken off the diet (Brown & Warner 1976; Kagan 1970). Similarly, children who suffer convulsions resulting from fever commonly do so only until about 6 years of age (Carter 1964).

After the spurt in brain growth between ages 5 and 7, there seems to be a

Figure 9-23 The visually evoked potential (VEP) of the brain, roughly speaking, is the response of the visual-information processing area of the cerebral cortex to a sudden flash of light delivered to the eye. (A) The voltage changes in this area of the brain within the first half-second (500 milliseconds) of the flash. Six-year-olds show a much larger fluctuation than older subjects do. (B) The size of this fluctuation is measured by how far a recording pen moves. Why there is a sharp peak at 6 years is not known. A smaller and wider peak in the teens may be related to a shift from concrete-to-formal-operational abilities, just as the peak at 6 years old may be related to the shift from preoperational to operational thinking.

lengthy plateau, a period of little or no growth. In head circumference, for example, children appear to stay virtually the same from ages 8 to 9 (Eichorn & Bayley 1962), and brain waves show no general increase between 8 and 11 years (Epstein 1980).

Bodily Growth

Along with the spurt in brain growth between ages 5 and 7, children show a spurt in height and weight (S. White 1970). In contrast to brain growth, however, height and weight increase steadily during the rest of the elementary-school years. Although growth may be steady from year to year for most children, there are wide individual differences in schoolchildren's heights. The normal range for height at each age is so wide, in fact, that a child of exactly average height at age 7 could fail to grow at all for 2 years and still be within the normal range for height at age 9 (Tanner 1978).

At age 8 in the United States, the difference between the largest and the smallest boy is about 9 inches, and it is nearly the same for girls (Tanner 1978). Across cultures, the range about doubles, so that there may be as much as 18 inches difference in height between the culture with the shortest average 8-year-old and the one with the tallest (Meredith 1971). The shortest children are mostly from Southeast Asia, South America, and islands in the central and south Pacific. The tallest children are mostly from the United States, northern and central Europe, and eastern Australia. Within the American middle class, where virtually all children have healthful food and living conditions, genetic differences are the most important determinant of differences in height. Variations in height between cultures seem to depend more on nutrition and disease, with the tallest children tending to come from countries with abundant food and good medical care.

Motor Skills

Just as steady as a child's physical growth during the elementary-school years is the improvement of his **motor skills**. By age 7, most children can walk and run skillfully, handle their silverware at the table, tie their shoes, manipulate pencils and crayons, and carry out many motor skills nearly as well as adults. From age 7 until adolescence, they continually refine and smooth these skills and gradually extend their capacities over a wide range. Some highly complex motor skills are within grasp during these years. A child who concentrates on mastering the piano, sewing, swimming, or baseball, for example, can become very proficient by 10 or 11 years of age.

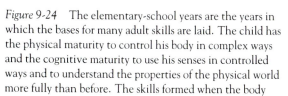

Figure 9-24 The elementary-school years are the years in which the bases for many adult skills are laid. The child has the physical maturity to control his body in complex ways and the cognitive maturity to use his senses in controlled ways and to understand the properties of the physical world more fully than before. The skills formed when the body and brain are ready but still highly malleable are deeply learned and available throughout a person's life. There are few accomplished athletes, musicians, or craftsmen who did not begin to form the skills basic to their area of expertise during their elementary-school years.

These motor skills, together with a new understanding of important social rules and categories, make children ready to become participating junior members of their society. They enter school, join the Scouts or Little League, take music or dancing lessons, and so on—interacting with an ever-widening range of people in an increasing variety of places and activities. The next chapter describes the expanding social environment of the school-age child.

SUMMARY

CONCRETE-OPERATIONAL INTELLIGENCE

1. At about the time children begin their formal schooling, they begin the change from preoperational intelligence to **concrete-operational intelligence,** the third of the four developmental periods described by Piaget. Concrete-operational thought is the ability to think logically about concrete things in the world. An **operation** is a mental action that is reversible. Thus an operation is always part of a system that contains both the operation and its opposite—any operation can always be reversed, or undone, by its opposite.

2. Concrete operations do not emerge simultaneously in all aspects of a child's thinking. Their development is **uneven**—operational systems emerge at different times in different areas of skill, depending partly on a child's experience.

3. Operational thought permits the understanding of **conservation**—that the amount of a substance or the number of objects in a group does not change just because its configuration changes. Children's explanations of conservation demonstrate the change from **centration** in preoperational thought—the centering of attention on one property of an event—to **decentration.** Their explanations also show development of an understanding of **necessary truth**—that certain facts must be true. Because understanding each kind of conservation—clay, liquid, number—is a separate skill, these skills do not usually emerge at the same time.

4. One of the skills developed by almost all children at some time during the period of concrete operations is **classification,** the ability to understand how classes of objects and events are related to each other. The skill that allows a child to combine several classes to form a larger class, or to break down a class into subclasses, is called **addition of classes.** Another classification skill is **multiplication of classes,** in which two sets of classes are intermeshed to form joint classes where they overlap.

5. The scope and sophistication of concrete-operational skills increase between ages 6 and 11 and help make memory better; better memory in turn allows children to use more complex concrete-operational systems. **Metamemory,** children's awareness of their own memory abilities and of how to apply them, also improves during this period.

PERCEPTION

6. The development of concrete-operational skills is accompanied by changes in how children perceive. **Perception** is the interpretation of sensory information to produce an experience of pattern or meaning. Preschool children can rarely perceive more than one pattern in a visual illusion, whereas school-age children can. At age 6 or 7, there is also a major advance in children's ability to search for visual information efficiently.

LANGUAGE AND COMMUNICATION

7. When operational thinking develops, the egocentrism of the preschool child disappears, because children acquire the ability to take *another person's perspective,* coordinating it with their own. Perspective-taking ability greatly improves communication skills because, in conversations, children can take account of what their listener can be expected to know.

8. In the elementary-school years children greatly increase their use and enjoyment of *humor*—puns and jokes—and their understanding of *metaphors.* These changes seem to result partly from their new perspective-taking ability and partly from their concrete-operational capacity to consider simultaneously two meanings or interpretations of one word or event.

9. At the same time, children also begin to be able to deal with the logical relations expressed by the grammar of complex sentences, as in the use of "because" or "unless" to relate two clauses.

SCHOOL

10. Formal schooling leads people to use their intelligence in broad ways that are not tied to specific situations. The skills of reading, writing, and arithmetic are essentially *general techniques for processing information.* Schools teach people how to construct a *general rule of solution* for a class of problems and how to *use language* more effectively.

11. Learning to read proceeds at more than one level at once as shown by *information-processing* analyses of reading. After children learn to recognize features of numbers and letters, they match the letters with sounds, learn words and word orders, and learn meanings all at the same time. Skilled readers process chunks of information on several levels at once; they do not read letter by letter but use their expectations about letter combinations, word order, and meaning to help them read quickly.

12. *Competence motivation,* the desire to be a competent and effective human being who can master his or her environment, is universal. But it is influenced by events in a child's environment: Observational learning from models, success and approval, punishment and failure, and developmental changes in ability all affect competence motivation. In addition, motivation differs in different skills.

PROBLEMS IN LEARNING

13. A child whose cognitive skills are mostly normal but who is poor at certain kinds of learning is said to have a *specific learning disability.*

  a. Some of these disabilities are the result of a *developmental lag;* a child is simply later than his age mates in undergoing a certain developmental change. For example, most children of 6 and 7 develop an increased ability to focus **attention** on a task and ignore irrelevant details, but some are late in developing this ability. **Hyperactivity**—a child's inability to stay quiet and focus his attention—may be the result of a developmental lag, or it may represent an organic disorder whose nature and origin is not yet known.

b.   Some learning problems are caused by **perceptual-motor disabilities,** such as an organically based difficulty coordinating sight with sound.

14.   Learning problems may also arise from children's **emotional problems** or from their **cognitive styles,** their personal disposition to respond to most tasks in a certain consistent way. For example, children who respond very quickly and therefore often inaccurately are called **impulsive,** whereas those who respond slowly and accurately are called **reflective.**

INTELLIGENCE TESTS

15.   The **intelligence quotient,** or **IQ,** is the ratio of a child's mental age (as determined by an IQ test) to his or her chronological age. The most widely used IQ tests for children are the classic Stanford-Binet and the newer Wechsler Intelligence Scale for Children (WISC). The Wechsler test differs from the Stanford-Binet in that it consists of a number of subtests designed to measure specific intellectual abilities. Some are primarily verbal abilities, rendering a Verbal IQ score. Some are nonverbal, rendering a Performance IQ score.

16.   IQ tests correlate moderately well with academic success and with career success, but many other factors also clearly contribute to success.

17.   **General intelligence** appears to have at least two distinct components: **Fluid intelligence** underlies the basic organizing functions in behavior, especially in performing unusual tasks, and **crystallized intelligence** applies to the skills explicitly valued by society, especially those taught in school. Most problems that people have to solve require a combination of the two.

18.   Heredity and environment always collaborate to produce intelligence, and psychologists have attempted to discover how this collaboration functions. **Twin studies** compare the IQs of sets of identical twins, some of whom were reared in different environments, with the IQs of fraternal twins reared together. **Studies of adopted children** examine correlations of the IQs of the children with their biological and adoptive parents; such studies have shown that enriched environments can raise adopted children's IQ; they also show that heredity plays a role because the rankings of the adopted children's IQs correspond with the rankings of the IQs of their biological parents.

19.   It is likely that a person's genetic heritage sets certain limits on intellectual potential in normal environments; these limits are called the **reaction range.** An advantaged environment lets more of that potential be realized.

20. IQ tests may be culturally biased against the lower class and some ethnic and minority groups, because the histories, values, and vocabularies of these groups are different from the values and vocabulary reflected in the tests—those of the white middle class.

21. A child's IQ can be affected by the pattern of births in his family—the number of children in the family, his place in birth order, and number of years between siblings. The more children in a family and the later in the birth order, the lower the average IQ of a child.

22. Many children change little in IQ between early childhood and adolescence, but some fluctuate greatly. Researchers have found certain patterns of change related to social class, parental behavior, and birth of a sibling.

PHYSICAL DEVELOPMENT

23. There is biological evidence that a change in brain functioning takes place between the ages of 5 and 7, in what is called the **5-to-7 shift.** This may account for the development of concrete-operational capacities.

24. Bodily growth during the grade-school years is steady. Both girls' and boys' motor skills—running, jumping, throwing—also show a steady improvement during this period.

SUGGESTED READINGS

BIGGS, JOHN B., and KEVIN F. COLLIS. *Evaluating the Quality of Learning: The SOLO Taxonomy (Structure of the Observed Learning Outcome).* New York: Academic Press, 1982.

The authors apply neo-Piagetian concepts to education and provide concrete examples showing how children show stages or levels in their approaches to problems they are given in school.

FELDMAN, DAVID H. *Beyond Universals in Cognitive Development.* Norwood, New Jersey: Ablex, 1980.

In this eloquent book, a well-known developmental researcher analyzes the development of unusual skills, such as the achievements of prodigies and creative persons.

GARDNER, HOWARD. *Frames of Mind: The Theory of Multiple Intelligences.* New York: Basic Books, 1983.

A famous developmental psychologist outlines the evidence for major individual differences in abilities and suggests that children have a number of distinct intellectual capacities that account for these differences.

10

PARTICI-
PATING
IN
A
SOCIAL
WORLD

CHAPTER OUTLINE

10

PARTICI-

PATING

IN

A

SOCIAL

WORLD

When autobiographers recall their early school days, they rarely write about their studies. Almost always they remember how they made friends or enemies at school and what they learned from a friend or an enemy about fairness or helping or the limits of aggression. Sometimes they recall how a particular teacher encouraged them or made them feel stupid or clumsy and what they learned from teachers about authority, competition and cooperation, or pride of accomplishment. They remember the triumphs and terrors of school social life. The social world of elementary school is a complex one, and it is the first social world most children tackle on their own.

In addition to the family, then, school becomes an important agent of socialization during these years—both through its formal organization and through a child's peers. Of course, children sometimes encounter conflicting norms from these agents. Being a class clown may make you popular with your fellow students—and popularity is an important social value for children—but it is unlikely to gain favor with teachers, who value obedience much more than popularity. Getting all As will bring social approval from your parents and teachers, but it may make you seem like a "grind" or "teacher's pet" to your classmates. Your parents may encourage lively family discussions and encourage you to offer your opinion and to argue in support of it, but your teacher may consider such behavior downright rude. All this social experience—even the conflicts between the various agents of socialization—promotes social development, as children become more able to think systematically about different sets of experiences.

Erik Erikson (1968) characterizes the psychosocial crisis of the school years as one of *industry versus inferiority* (see Figure 8-8). School-age children are not only ready but eager to become productive. In technologically advanced societies such as the United States, much of children's industry is channeled into schoolwork, so that the school experience itself becomes a critical determinant of children's sense of industry and inferiority.

SOCIALIZATION AT SCHOOL

At school, children learn social norms and roles as well as cognitive skills such as reading and writing. In fact, most parents expect the schools to teach norms—to support the parents' own social teachings. But not all parents value the same norms or agree on how schools should operate. Although almost all of them want their children to learn reading and arithmetic, some parents think that schools also should promote obedience to authority and values such as being punctual and courteous; others expect that schools primarily should help their children learn to get along well with others and to express themselves. Sometimes there are major shifts in the general public's attitude toward the role of the schools. In the late 1950s, for example, when the Russians beat the United States in putting a satellite in orbit around the earth, many Americans demanded more and better teaching of basic subjects, especially science and mathematics. In social terms, they were asking for stricter discipline in classrooms so that attention could be focused on learning these demanding subjects. In the late 1960s, when there was strong criticism of technology because of environmental pollution and the uses to which advanced technology was put in the Vietnam war, many people called for more emphasis on such humanistic values as cooperation, openness, and warmth. Because such values cannot easily be transmitted in a tightly controlled social atmosphere, many parents wanted strict discipline replaced by a more democratic classroom structure. Then, in the middle 1970s, when scores on national reading tests were dropping, there was a demand that schools forget about the humanistic values and return to basics—and, of course, more rigid discipline.

In the United States and other pluralistic societies, none of the louder messages ever entirely drowns out the others. Consequently, school systems are asked to pursue different goals, which often seem to be contradictory (Minuchin & Shapiro 1983).

The School Setting

Shifting goals have sweeping effects on the schools, even on the physical organization of the classroom. Most people over 30 recall classrooms in which rows of desks faced the teacher's desk and the blackboard. Many American classrooms still are organized this way. In such **traditional classrooms,** a fixed daily curriculum rigidly follows the clock. The emphasis is on orderly procedure, obeying rules, and learning the three Rs; the teacher leads all the group's activities and does most of the talking.

Many schools now have **open classrooms,** in which small movable tables are arranged and rearranged to fit changing activities. Often, each table contains the materials necessary for one particular learning activity, such as reading, or math, or crafts, or a biology project involving, say, the care of plants or small animals. The children can go from one activity to another, as their interest indicates. The teacher likewise moves around the room, instructing and helping individual children or small groups.

The educational philosophy underlying the open classroom is that children are naturally motivated to learn about their world, and that young children learn best when they work in a concrete way, at their own pace, on something they are currently interested in. Supporters of open classrooms also stress that the free interaction in these learning environments teaches social skills as well as academic ones.

In many large school districts across the country, boards of education have tried to deal with disagreement about educational goals and how to meet them

Figure 10-1 The contrasting physical settings of an open classroom and a traditional one reflect the different educational philosophies underlying them.

by establishing schools of several different forms and allowing parents to choose the form they think best for their children. For example, Jefferson County, Colorado, has three different types of schools: open-classroom schools, fundamental schools (with traditional classrooms, strict regulations, and strong emphasis on the basic skills of reading, writing, and arithmetic), and schools that mix the methods of traditional and open classrooms. Parents who are given the choice can pick the arrangement that seems to support best their own goals of socialization. Those who strongly wish to teach their children values of discipline and order may choose the fundamental schools. Those who believe it is more important for children to be permitted to learn at their own pace and who value good social interactions may choose open classrooms.

Although the arguments for and against traditional and open classrooms are often heated, research has not shown any consistent difference in educational outcome in favor of one or the other of these arrangements. Some children flourish in an open classroom, but others make better progress and feel more comfortable with the direction and discipline of a more traditional organization (Peterson 1977; Ruedi & West 1973).

One study found that children who were compulsive or highly anxious learned to read better when they were taught in a highly structured setting with a step-by-step approach (Grimes & Allensmith 1961). In an open classroom, the compulsive children became upset by what they perceived as disorder or lack of organization, and the anxious children were generally restless and distractible. Children who were neither anxious nor compulsive fared equally well with a structured or unstructured approach. Other research has shown that many children prefer an open classroom and enjoy school more when they are taught in that setting (Horwitz 1979; Minuchin 1976).

In traditional classrooms, the teacher plans all the work for the group. In open classrooms, the teacher guides rather than directs, but children's choices of activities still seem to be strongly influenced by the teacher (Resnick 1971).

Teachers

Almost every adult has grateful memories of a teacher or two who were significant in shaping his life. One such recollection that is especially touching and passionate is Helen Keller's tribute to her teacher and friend, Anne Sullivan: "My teacher is so near to me that I scarcely think of myself apart from her." In her autobiography, Miss Keller recalled the turning point in her young life, a turning point that her teacher made possible.

Helen, who was to become a famous writer and public speaker, had been made blind and deaf by an illness at 18 months of age. When Helen was 7, Miss Sullivan began to teach her the names of things by forming the letters on her hand. At first, Helen imitated the finger movements but did not understand that she was forming a word or even that words existed.

> One day, while I was playing with my new doll, Miss Sullivan put my big rag doll into my lap also, spelled "d-o-l-l" and tried to make me understand that "d-o-l-l" applied to both. Earlier in the day we had had a tussle over the words "m-u-g" and "w-a-t-e-r." Miss Sullivan had tried to impress it upon me that "m-u-g" is mug and that "w-a-t-e-r" is water, but I persisted in confounding the two. In despair she had dropped the subject for the time, only to renew it at the first opportunity. I became impatient with her repeated attempts and, seizing the new doll, I dashed it upon the floor.
>
> [Later] we walked down the path to the well-house, attracted by the

fragrance of the honeysuckle with which it was covered. Someone was drawing water and my teacher placed my hand under the spout. As the cool
stream gushed over one hand she spelled into the other the word water, first
slowly, then rapidly. I stood still, my whole attention fixed upon the motions
of her fingers. Suddenly I felt a misty consciousness as of something forgotten—a thrill of returning thought; and somehow the mystery of language
was revealed to me. I knew then that "w-a-t-e-r" meant the wonderful cool
something that was flowing over my hand. That living word awakened my
soul, gave it light, hope, joy, set it free!

Unfortunately, teachers' effects are not always positive. Dick Gregory, entertainer and black activist, remembers one of his teachers with bitterness: "I
never learned hate at home, or shame. I had to go to school for that. I was
about seven years old when I got my first lesson. I was in love with a little girl
named Helene Tucker. She was always clean and she was smart in school. And
she had a daddy." Gregory's father had left his family, who had to fend for
themselves and were very poor.

> It was on a Thursday, and the teacher was asking each student how much
> his father would give to the Community Chest. I decided I was going to buy
> me a Daddy right then. I had money in my pocket from shining shoes and
> selling papers, and whatever Helene Tucker pledged for her Daddy I was
> going to top it.

The teacher called out all the names except Dick Gregory's. He stood up, raised
his hand, and told the teacher she had forgotten to call his name.

> She turned toward the blackboard, "I don't have time to be playing games
> with you, Richard."
> "My Daddy said he's . . ."
> "Sit down, Richard, you're disturbing the class."
> "My Daddy said he'd give fifteen dollars."
> She turned around and looked mad. "We are collecting this money for
> you and your kind, Richard Gregory. If your Daddy can give fifteen dollars
> you have no business being on relief. And furthermore, we know you don't
> have a Daddy."
> Helene Tucker turned around, her eyes full of tears. She felt sorry for me.
> I walked out of school that day, and for a long time I didn't go back. There
> was shame there.

Although teachers have always affected students' values as well as their
academic skills (Blumenfeld et al. 1979; Le Compte 1978), how a good teacher
inspires students has never been satisfactorily understood. Despite many attempts, no one has been able to make a simple list of methods for becoming the
kind of teacher people remember as having inspired them.

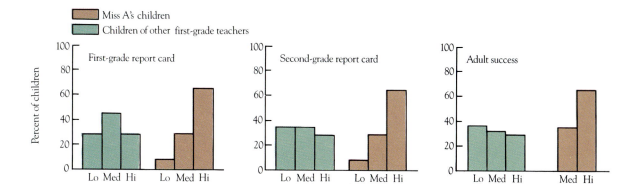

The importance of a good teacher was shown in a study whose original aim was simply to trace the IQ changes that a group of adults had shown during their grade-school years in a poor Montreal neighborhood (Figure 10-2). The researcher noticed that the most successful individuals among the group of 59 he was studying had one thing in common: They all had had Miss A as their first-grade teacher. Miss A taught first grade for 32 years in that neighborhood, and during those years she had used a variety of methods and materials. It appeared that the particular methods or materials she had used did not much matter in the later success of her pupils. What did seem to matter, the researcher concluded, was Miss A's strong conviction that all children were capable of learning what she taught.

The influence of *teachers' expectations* on their pupils' academic progress has been demonstrated in a series of studies by Robert Rosenthal and his colleagues (Rosenthal & Rubin 1978, 1980). These studies showed that a teacher's expectations of a child's intellectual promise can become a *self-fulfilling prophecy*, even when the expectations have no basis in fact. The original expectation itself produces the result that was predicted.

In the first study, the children in all six grades of an elementary school took an IQ test and another test that, the teachers were told, would identify children who were likely to make substantial intellectual gains in the near future (Rosenthal & Jacobsen 1968). The researchers gave each teacher the names of the children who could be expected to "bloom" during the coming school year. Actually, the children's names had been chosen at random. Thus, the only difference between the "bloomers" and the "nonbloomers" was in the minds of the teachers.

Even so, the first- and second-graders who had been called "bloomers" did, in fact, bloom when tested at the end of the school year. They gained an average of 15 IQ points over their scores at the beginning of the year. "Non-bloomers," on the other hand, showed no significant average gain. The IQs of

Figure 10-2 Eigel Pederson, who conducted this study, returned as a teacher to the elementary school he had attended as a child, in a poor section of Montreal. In the school's permanent records, Pederson noticed some significant changes in individual children's IQ scores, which he tried to account for. He discovered that children who had had Miss A as a first-grade teacher were more likely to have gained in IQ, had higher marks in first grade, and were more likely to have kept high grades in second grade, when Miss A was no longer their teacher. Not only that, when the researchers followed up on the adult achievements of 59 former students, they found that Miss A's pupils were much more likely to have well-paying jobs and success in adult life (Pederson 1978).

children in the upper grades did not change in this study, but a later study showed the effect of teachers' expectations on older children as well (Rosenthal et al. 1974).

What the teachers did to turn fictitious promise into actual progress is difficult to say. Among other things, they probably paid more attention to the "bloomers" and gave their efforts more attention and approval. In fact, the teachers rated the children labeled "bloomers" as "happier, more curious, and more interesting" than the other children. These characteristics have less to do with IQ than with the teachers' perception of the children's social skills. Children who receive much encouragement and approval are likely to be happier and more receptive than children who receive less.

Race and social class also can influence teachers' expectations; that is, some teachers expect less in the way of achievement from lower-class children and those belonging to ethnic minorities than from middle-class white children (Minuchin & Shapiro 1983). An upward change in a teacher's expectations, then, possibly could affect such children's performance. In one of Rosenthal's experiments, a group of lower-class Mexican children was included among the children labeled "bloomers," and these children gained even more in IQ than the non-Mexican children did (Rosenthal & Jacobsen 1968). In fact, the "bloomers" whom the teachers had rated as most "Mexican-looking" gained the most in IQ. Perhaps this was because they were the children from whom the teachers, under ordinary circumstances, would have expected the least.

Like the Rosenthal studies, most studies of the effectiveness and influence of teachers examine changes in children's IQ or academic performance, not in the social values that a teacher may have been responsible for. Performance on an IQ test is easy to measure, and the measure is reliable; social and personality characteristics, in contrast, are much more difficult to discover and rate. Nevertheless, there are some indirect ways of discovering what values teachers generally want to impart. For example, a survey of 650 teachers asked which qualities the teachers valued most in their students. The teachers listed both intellectual qualities—being industrious, versatile, receptive to the ideas of others—and social ones—being courteous, energetic, obedient. The quality ranked first by most teachers was a social rather than an intellectual one—being considerate of others. Qualities that teachers ranked surprisingly low included courage and independence in judgment (Torrance 1963). Other studies report similar findings (Minuchin & Shapiro 1983).

An analysis of the educational system by Philip Jackson (1966) helps explain why teachers encourage values such as courtesy and consideration more than independence and courage. Jackson points out that the school, in effect, has two curriculums. One is the *academic curriculum,* and the other is the *social curriculum* of courteous conduct, neatness, and punctuality. Most teachers reward children both for academic achievement and for good conduct but

directly punish children primarily for violating the social curriculum—the norms for classroom behavior.

Jackson describes how important patience, resignation, and conformity are, particularly in the traditional classroom. Children spend much of their time simply waiting—waiting for the rest of the class to finish an assignment, waiting for the teacher to come around and check their work, waiting while attendance is taken or the milk money is collected, and so on. Also, students often experience denial and interruption. They may raise their hands repeatedly without being called on. Or they may be enthusiastically involved in a history lesson, but the history lesson must be interrupted when the clock says it is time to begin the arithmetic lesson.

Partly because of the social demands of the classroom, boys are much more likely to get into trouble in school than girls are, especially in the early grades. Some scholars have suggested that boys have trouble in school because most teachers are females. However, studies comparing male and female teachers show that teachers of both sexes tend to reward traditionally "female" qualities (Brophy & Good 1974; Etaugh & Hughes 1975). That is, the social norms of the classroom, no matter what the sex of the teacher, emphasize courtesy and compliance. Such norms do not mesh well with the social norms for masculine behavior outside the classroom, such as courage and independence in judgment. These are the norms that peers promote.

Figure 10-3 Schools are agents of socialization. They not only teach reading, writing, and arithmetic, they have a social curriculum that includes norms promoting courtesy, compliance, and patience.

Figure 10-4   Friends help socialize each other. They can communicate with each other on the same cognitive and social level, and they can offer each other perspectives different from the ones they have learned from their families.

PEERS AND SOCIALIZATION

Although many children have made some friends during the preschool years, usually children in the neighborhood, school brings together a large group of children of the same age who spend all day together, five days a week. These peer groups add a whole new arena for socialization to a child's life. Play and school activities lead a child to learn about competition and cooperation, about conformity and independence. Children help socialize each other in these behaviors, about which family and schools also have lessons to impart (Hartup 1983). In fact, there can be cross pressures on children, when the adult norms differ from the children's. These pressures are discussed later in this chapter.

The Importance of Peers

The main difference between the influence of peers and that of adults is that children play together as equals. When two children debate each other about what is "fair" or "not fair" in a game, what is "mean" or "nice," the perspective of both children is at about the same cognitive and social level. It is therefore easy for them to understand each other. Also, another child's perspective often offers an alternative to the perspective of parents and other authorities. A 7-year-old girl, for instance, may have learned from her mother and father to be very careful not to fall and get hurt. When she hears her friends call her a "scaredy-cat" because she won't jump over a log in Follow the Leader, she has to think about these conflicting views of her behavior. When a 9-year-old boy's friends praise him for his skill in making a skateboard from a plank and an old roller skate, he can compare this new view of himself with his father's frequent comments that he is clumsy.

A study in Norway illustrates the importance of peer groups for the development of social skills, especially *perspective-taking,* the ability to understand another person's viewpoint (Hollos 1974). The researcher tested children growing up in three Norwegian settings: Flathill, a sparsely settled farm region; Innbygda, a small village; and Elverum, a larger town. All are in the same part of Norway, and the inhabitants do not differ much in income, social class, or size of family (usually three children, about 2 years apart).

Children growing up on the farms in Flathill are isolated from all other children. For one thing, getting about is very difficult for much of the year: in spring and fall the land is too boggy to walk over, and in the winter there is much snow and ice. In addition, the social customs in Flathill frown on casual drop-in visits by neighbors. Even when children start school, which is not until they are 7, they are bused (by the milk-delivery truck) to a nearby town only three days a week. The bus takes them home again immediately after class, because the trip takes more than an hour.

Flathill children spend almost all their time with their mothers, brothers,

Figure 10-5   The importance of peer interactions in social development is strikingly revealed in these data from the Hollos study of Norwegian children. Children from the isolated farms and from the village and town performed about equally well on Piagetian tests of concrete-operational thinking. But on tasks designed to measure social cognition the isolated children were far behind their urban age mates, who played together all the time.

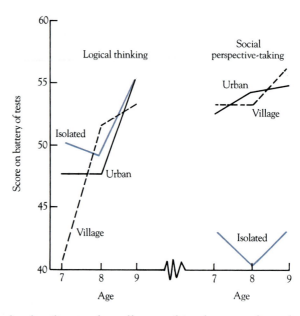

and sisters. In contrast, the families in the village and in the town live close together, and children from different homes play together in groups from the time that they are very young.

Children from these three settings were tested at ages 7, 8, and 9 on two types of tasks: (1) Piagetian tests of such concrete-operational abilities as conservation of quantity and addition and multiplication of classes, and (2) tests of the ability to take another person's perspective. Figure 10-5 shows how the three groups of children performed on the two types of tasks. On classification and conservation tasks, all three groups improved with age and did about equally well by the time they were 9. But on perspective-taking, the isolated farm children—who had not had a chance to spend time with a peer group—scored far below the village and town groups. Their relative lack of social interaction seems to have made them poorer at taking another's point of view.

School-age children, then, help each other learn how to think about social life—that is, to think about events from the point of view of others who may be participating in the events. This ability lies at the heart of satisfying social interactions. But it is only one of the important social skills that peer groups help children acquire. The peer group is also a powerful agent for teaching norms and promoting conformity to them.

Norms and Conformity

In popular use, the word "conformity" tends to convey disapproval. Some people, in fact, use it only to mean a kind of slavish following of other people's taste or behavior. However, as used by social scientists, the word ***conformity*** refers simply to behavior that is in accord with a norm or group of norms. As explained in Chapter 8, social norms are essential to the functioning of society. We all learn what behavior our culture expects of us in various settings, and we generally conform to those expectations. This kind of conformity oils the wheels of social intercourse. People know what to expect of each other and therefore get along together in a wide variety of situations.

There is also a dark side to conformity, however, one that has been of special interest to some psychologists. It is the way in which the pressure to conform to the group can affect a person's expression of opinion or judgment. In a classic experiment, Solomon Asch (1951) had groups of seven or eight adults judge the length of lines. Each judgment involved a pair of cards, one with a single line (the standard) and the other with three lines of noticeably different lengths, one of which was the same as the standard's. The announced goal of the experiment was to test perception. This was to be done by having each member of the group, in turn, choose aloud which of the three lines matched the standard. Actually, all but one of the people in each group were stooges, confederates of the experimenter, and the actual goal of the experiment was to see whether the announced judgment of the real subject was affected by that of the rest of the group. Now and then, the stooges picked the wrong line on purpose, thereby presenting the real subject with a dilemma. The subject could easily see which line was correct, and the experimenter had asked him to "please be as accurate as possible." Yet to pick the correct line would be to go against the group's judgment. So great was the pressure to conform that about a third of Asch's subjects yielded to the group.

A similar experiment was carried out with groups of children from 7 to 13 years old by Ruth Berenda (1950). She found that 93 percent of the children between 7 and 10 conformed to the false majority, but fewer of the children between 11 and 13 conformed. In a similar experiment with kindergarten children, very few 5-year-olds conformed to the group's judgment (Hunt & Synnerdale 1959). Parents who might worry about their school-age children's blind conformity to a pack of friends in matters such as smoking or drinking or skipping school can take heart, however, from other experimental results. When a child had even one other person in the experiment whose judgments were the same as his, he was much better at resisting the judgment of the majority (Allen & Newston 1972). Most groups of children are unlikely to be unanimous about many questions.

As the Berenda study indicates, there is a ***developmental trend in conformity*** to peer influences. Later research has shown that the trend corresponds to the development of a child's social and cognitive abilities (Damon 1977; Piaget & Inhelder 1969). During the preschool years, children gradually come to understand the most obvious social norms and roles as well as very simple characteristics of others' perspectives, as described in Chapters 7 and 8. If a situation is at all complex or subtle, however, the relevant norms, roles, and perspectives are beyond them (Maccoby 1980; Selman 1980). Because in many social situations they cannot understand what other people expect of them, they cannot conform to those expectations. As they gradually become less egocentric, they begin to understand that people can have different thoughts and perceptions about the same social event. With this understanding, they can gather more information on social norms and roles.

During the late preschool and early grade-school years, children often show a desire for rigid conformity to each new norm or role that they come to understand. By age 6 or 7, they have learned most of the common norms of behavior for everyday roles such as boy and girl, parent and child, teacher and pupil. As a result, they may become outraged if a parent or teacher behaves in a way that does not fit those norms. One 7-year-old, for example, asked his mother not to sing out loud around the house when his friends were over, because mothers don't sing. The concrete-operational skills of children in this age range have developed enough for them to understand and deal with numerous social norms, but they tend to treat these norms as if they were fixed and unchangeable.

At about age 11, children become more flexible about social roles and norms. They start to see that norms and roles are somewhat arbitrary: People created them, and people can change them (Adelson 1975; Harter 1983).

Popularity and Leadership

Participation in peer groups not only teaches social norms and social skills such as perspective taking, but it also directly changes what is important to a child: For the first time, such social traits as popularity and leadership become significant. In any group of children, there are a few who are known for their **popularity** (Hartup 1983). Their friendship is actively sought by most of the others in the group. Also, there are usually one or two whom no one seeks out, who remain on the fringe of the group hoping for a few faint signs of acceptance or recognition (Coil & Dodge 1983; Furman 1980).

To study popularity in a group, most researchers begin by constructing a **sociogram** of friendship choices in the group. The members of the group are asked to name a few children they would like to work with, sit near, or walk home from school with, and so on, or they are simply asked to name their best friends in the group. Children named most often by others are assumed to be popular. The two sociograms in Figure 10-6 reflect developmental differences in social relations between age 6 and age 11. After completing the sociograms, researchers assess the children's personality traits, either by tests or through observations and ratings. The measures of popularity and personality are then correlated to see which personality traits are related to acceptance and rejection by peers.

Most studies of this type have produced findings that are not very surprising.

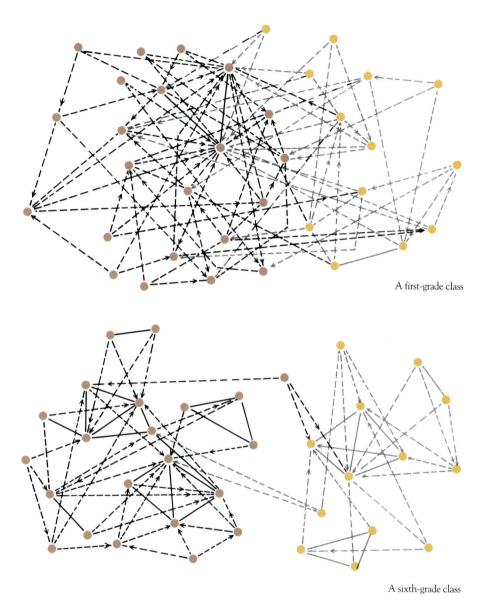

A first-grade class

A sixth-grade class

Figure 10-6 These sociograms were constructed by asking each child in the class to write on a piece of paper his or her first three choices of a person to sit near. A choice is shown by a dotted line with an arrow pointing to the chosen person. A solid line indicates a mutual choice. Brown circles are girls; gold ones are boys. The first-grade sociogram shows that few of the choices are mutual; 6-year-olds are not yet very aware of how other people feel about them. Still, two girls in the class appear to be very popular—many of their classmates chose them. Note that there are many boy-girl choices, unlike the sixth-grade sociogram, where the choices are almost totally segregated by sex. The sixth-grade sociogram also shows the emergence of cliques, recognizable by networks of mutual choices. These children are mature enough to recognize others' feelings toward them and to form friendships based on mutual feelings.

Popular children are friendlier and more outgoing than less popular children. They are generally good-looking, and the boys are good athletes. As a rule, they are well adjusted. Of course, because these characteristics are related to popularity only by correlations, the question arises, are children popular because they are sociable and well adjusted, or does their popularity inspire them to be friendlier and make them better adjusted? The existing data do not permit an answer.

Popular children also seem to be brighter than their peers. Perhaps such children have more advanced social skills. Perhaps they can take their friends' viewpoints in more subtle and complex ways than other children can and therefore are able to respond to them with more empathy. It seems that the ability to take another's perspective is a factor in children's popularity (Goslin 1962).

Many of the personality characteristics that are related to popularity also relate to a child's *leadership* status in a group. Children who are leaders, either elected or unofficial, tend to be friendly, outgoing, good-looking, well adjusted, bright, and good at perspective-taking (Hartup 1970). One further trait that leaders show, especially leaders of boy's groups, is assertiveness or aggressiveness. The aggressiveness is modulated by the child's other positive personality traits and is often used in behalf of the group. Leaders fight back when provoked and they engage in a lot of rough-and-tumble play, but they know the limits of aggression and use it in socially acceptable ways—to subdue a bully, for example, or to enforce fair play.

Aggressiveness by itself is not a characteristic of children who are leaders. In fact, unprovoked, sneaky, or disruptive aggression is characteristic of unpopular children (Lesser 1959; Winder & Rau 1962). For children to be leaders, they must display and handle aggression in ways prescribed by their culture or subculture. The following description of a leader is from a study of boys' groups discussed at length in the next section of this chapter. This boy emerged as leader of a group of lower-class boys:

> Rogelio's words began to count more and more. This erect, self-confident boy had an almost uncanny ability to call plays and make selections which won the game without hurting anyone's feelings. . . . Juan was the best fighter in the group . . . but they knew that Rogelio could hold his own [and] remarked that Rogelio was the best one to have along to keep them out of trouble. In two months' time, Rogelio was the acknowledged leader, though he had never competed or come into conflict with Juan. (Sherif & Sherif 1964, pp. 28–29)

Cultural Differences: Competition and Cooperation

Some of the best documented cultural differences in socialization by peers can be seen in norms for *competition* and *cooperation* (Werner 1979). The dominant cultural norm in the United States—and in most Western industrial nations—is that competition is good and proper behavior. Many individual Americans dislike the emphasis on competition, and there are other norms (such as the Golden Rule) that conflict with the competition norm. Still, whether it is openly stated, as in business and sports, or only implied, as it often is in schools, competition is encouraged.

In American grade schools, individual achievement is clearly a major goal,

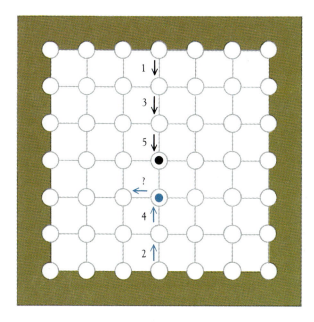

Figure 10-7 The two-player game invented by Kagan and Madsen to measure cooperation and competition. The board shows the situation after 5 moves have been played. The goal is to get your marker into the circle originally occupied by the other player's marker. It is now the second player's turn, and he must choose either to move or to stay and block the first player's path. If he chooses to stay, then the first player must choose whether to move or to block. The game must end by 24 moves for the winner to receive a toy. Children from a Mexican farming community very rarely chose to block, whereas Anglo-American children from a low-income area in Los Angeles blocked so much that sometimes neither won a toy.

Proportion of moves
that blocked opponent

Mexican	Anglo
2%	24%

and competition is the way to achieve that goal. Every child in a classroom competes against all the other children for high marks, just as individual American adults compete against each other for better jobs and higher pay.

Russian society deals with competition in a different way. Competition is discouraged between individuals but encouraged between groups. Grade-school classrooms, for example, are usually divided into several groups, which compete against each other for good marks and approval (Bronfenbrenner 1970; Smith 1976). In Russian society at large, norms generally discourage individual competition. Marxist doctrine states that goods should be distributed "to each according to his needs." That is, individuals should not have to compete with each other for a fair share of the society's products. Groups such as collective farms, however, do compete against each other in trying to get, for example, the best yields per acre, because the central government acknowledges winning groups with public praise and other rewards.

Some studies suggest that American children have been so thoroughly socialized for competition that they often compete even when it would be to their benefit to cooperate. In one study, experimenters set up a two-player game in which markers were to be moved across a board as shown in Figure 10-7 (S. Kagan and Madsen 1972). The goal of the game was for one player to get his marker into the circle originally occupied by the other player's marker. Players were not allowed to move their markers into circles occupied at the time by another player's marker, but they were allowed to use up a turn by not moving at all. When the markers were in each other's way, each player had a choice of blocking the other player or moving to avoid him. The children were told that the first to reach the opposing player's original circle would receive a plastic chip redeemable for a toy—but only if the game ended in less than twenty-four turns. If the game took longer than that, no one received anything. Each pair of children was to play the game eight times, taking turns at making the first move.

If the children had cooperated, moving aside when one was in the other's path, each could have won every other game and received four toys. But of the sixteen pairs of American 7- to 9-year-olds playing the game, only two pairs cooperated and ended up with four toys apiece.

When the same game was played by sixteen pairs of rural Mexican 7- to 9-year-olds, the outcome was very different: Eleven pairs walked off with four toys for each child. While the American children as a group lost twenty-two toys, the Mexican children as a group did not lose even one toy. Most of the Mexican children avoided conflict. Only five of the sixteen pairs used the strategy of blocking at all. As a group, the American children blocked ten times as often as the Mexican children did. The few times that a Mexican child did block, the other child in the pair seldom resisted by counterblocking. Instead, he moved aside to let the first child pass. In these Mexican pairs, the distribution of the eight toys was often unequal. The blocker got all or most of them.

The difference between these two neighboring cultures in socialization for competition is striking. American children sometimes compete even when it is not in their best interest to do so, whereas Mexican children sometimes avoid competing even when it is in their interest to compete.

Although individual and group competition are so sharply ingrained in American behavior, competitive relationships can be turned into cooperative ones under certain circumstances. A classic study in social psychology by Muzafer Sherif and his colleagues (1961) demonstrates how. Twenty-two fifth-grade boys were brought together in a summer camp near an old Jesse James hideout in Oklahoma called the Robbers Cave. The boys, who all came from the same ethnic background and social class, were divided into two matched groups. At first, each group engaged in activities on its own. Friendships were formed within each group, leaders came to the fore, and each group chose a name and a symbol to represent it: the Eagles and the Rattlers.

The experimenters promoted competition between the two groups by pitting them against each other in swimming contests, ball games, tugs-of-war, and the like. The rivalry became fierce. Active hostility developed between the groups and led to aggressive encounters such as fights and raids. One group changed leaders because its members felt the former leader was not a strong enough competitor. Each group became more cohesive in the face of its common enemy, demanding that all members of the group conform to the group's standards and attitudes.

After the groups had begun to show active hostility and conflict, the researchers tried to get them to cooperate. They brought the Eagles and Rattlers together for special occasions—movies, goodwill dinners, and the like. But the groups would not cooperate. The special occasions just led to more fighting.

Finally, the researchers contrived several emergency situations in which the groups had to work together to reach a goal that both groups valued. For example, it was announced that the water tank had broken and that all the boys were needed to find the break and repair it. If the tank was not repaired, the camp would have to close early. After several such experiences in which the boys all worked together to achieve a **shared goal,** the relations between the two groups changed entirely. Competition became cooperation, and friendships formed between individual Rattlers and Eagles.

SOCIALIZATION IN THE FAMILY

Even though peers are important agents of socialization during the school years, a child's parents remain most influential in teaching social norms and in shaping behavior and personality. In many ways, interactions between parents and children remain stable during the school years, although some do change. Some effects of earlier parent-child relations first become evident at this time. Developmental changes in the child also produce some changes in the family, and the family itself may change in a way that affects the child, as when a younger child is born, parents are divorced, or one parent dies (Maccoby & Martin 1983).

Parental Styles

Parents' characteristic ways of treating their children, called **parental styles,** change fairly little from the preschool years through the school years (see Chapter 8). Such consistency can be detected only by detailed longitudinal studies of families. One of the most thorough of such investigations, the Fels study reported by Jerome Kagan and Howard Moss (1962), clearly demonstrated this consistency. For example, mothers who were restrictive with their daughters tended to be consistently so, at least throughout the child's first 10 years. Restrictiveness was measured in terms of how hard a mother tried to impose her own standards on her child. Restrictive mothers paid little attention to the child's abilities and interests. They just rigidly required that the child do what they thought the child ought to do, and they used threats and punishments to deal with transgressions.

The daughters of restrictive mothers tended to be passive and dependent during the school years, as shown by the following case from the Fels study. The first description of Ellen and her mother is when the child was 3, and the last is at age 14.

Home visit, 3 years: The mother told Ellen not to pick the ears off a toy rabbit. Ellen said, "I did pick it off," with some evidence of impudence. Mother said, "What are you doing, defying me or something?" and she struck Ellen two or three light blows with a knitting needle, which brought on a few tears.

Home visit, 5 years: The mother did not think the [Fels] nursery school was good for Ellen. After she had been attending, it took several weeks to cure her of being "fresh."

Nursery-school summary, 5 years, 8 months: Ellen was not a talkative child. She seemed to be silent most of the time. She played with other children, as a follower. She usually cooperated with them and with adults. Ellen gave the impression of being constantly alert for adult interference. She seemed to play most freely when she felt most free from adult scrutiny. She seemed distrustful of any new situation and paused to size it up carefully before entering into it. After her initial shyness, she seemed to enjoy nursery school thoroughly.

Interview notes with the mother, 8 years: The mother seemed to take a sheltering or protective attitude toward the children, not allowing or encouraging them to do things for themselves, such as take their baths, comb their hair, or care for themselves at the table. She didn't allow the children far from home, for she was afraid something would happen to them.

Interview with Ellen, 10 years: Ellen seemed to be very much afraid of adults. She was extremely shy with the interviewer and talked so low that the interviewer could hardly understand her. She was exceedingly inept at verbalization. At the slightest question that had to do with judgment of her position relative to someone else, she just would say that she didn't know. She didn't know whom she liked or disliked and couldn't describe any aspect of her personality.

Day-camp summary, 10 years, 3 months: Ellen seemed to be playing a passive role in relation to her environment. She was nonassertive, nonaggressive, not verbal. She was often dumbly patient and appealing. Her outgoing moments seemed to be mainly responses to objects and materials. She drank in the activity of others and stayed parallel, keeping a safe distance.

Home visit, 14 years, 2 months: The mother ignored Ellen's presence in the room except to tell her to go get something, to stop doing something, or to make some derogatory statement about her appearance. In response to this biting sarcasm, Ellen grinned sheepishly. Ellen was readily submissive to the commands that her mother made. For example, her mother told her in stentorian tones to close the garage doors and bring her the keys. Ellen said meekly that she had already done so. The mother then felt called upon to say imperiously "Well, bring me the keys," and Ellen jumped to do her bidding.

A restrictive mother does not inevitably produce a passive, dependent daughter, however. As another excerpt from this case study suggests, the relationship between parent and child is reciprocal: Each is affected by the other's behavior. In an interview with a Fels staff person, the mother talked not only about Ellen (who was then 11) but also about Ellen's two sisters, one older, one younger.

> The mother said, "I have always tried to suppress them (Ellen and her older sister), but I have let the younger one go." The youngest girl, apparently, has a more spirited personality and gets away with so much that, as the mother said, "It simply drives the others mad; they would like to kill her." This was said with much humor, as if she finds the rivalry between the girls an amusing spectacle. I had the feeling that she enjoys the youngest girl's spunk, and she is now contemptuous of the mild manner of the suppressed older girls.

Most likely, the mother did not simply "let the younger one go." Some aspects of the youngest's temperament or some change in the home environment or both probably allowed her to keep her spirit in spite of her mother's restrictiveness. Even though parental treatment may be consistent and some outcomes of that treatment can be predicted on the average (for example, the parental styles that promote children's self-esteem, discussed later in this chapter), the chemistry between parent and child is so complex that merely knowing the parents' practices does not allow one to predict with certainty how they will affect a particular child.

Although parents' treatment of each child is generally consistent, the child's development necessarily brings some changes. Parents may treat their newborn infants mostly according to the parents' own expectations about what children *should* be like and how they *should* behave. Infants can be seen almost as objects to be acted on, to be molded to fit the parents' expectations. But 9- and 10-year-olds have some well-developed personality traits and "minds of their own," so the relationship between parent and child must change with time (Maccoby & Martin 1983).

For example, another finding of the Fels study was that mothers' criticism of their 1- to 3-year-old daughters correlated positively with the daughters' striving for achievement in adulthood. In contrast, mothers' critical treatment of girls between 3 and 10 years old seemed to have no effect on the girls' adult attitudes toward achievement (Kagan and Moss 1962). Kagan and Moss suggest that the difference grew from the interaction between developmental changes in the children and the parents' goals. The mothers who were critical of their preschool daughters had the overall goal of forming in their daughters a sense of independence; these mothers may or may not have continued to be critical as the girls grew up. The mothers who did not begin to criticize their daughters until after the preschool years were mostly reacting to some specific irritating behavior, such as getting into trouble at school or neglecting household chores. The goal of these mothers in criticizing was not a broad, character-forming one; they were aiming to change specific behaviors.

Figure 10-8 The role of the father in the development of the child has been studied as little among nonhuman primates as it has in human beings, and for similar reasons. The mother does by far the larger share of the rearing in all primate species. But many primate fathers—gibbons, for example—do take some part in child care. In many other species, chimpanzees and gorillas, for example, interactions between child and adult male are infrequent or irregular.

What has just been said about parents' attitudes and behaviors toward their children applies to both parents, but you have probably noticed that all the specific findings discussed so far concerned only mothers. This is because psychologists have typically studied the mother and then acted as if she represented both parents. The father's role in the family has become the subject of research only in the past decade (Lamb 1978; Weinraub 1978).

Fathers

Fathers and mothers traditionally play different roles with their infants. A large part of the mother's role is caretaker. Interaction between fathers and infants is much less frequent and generally more playful. Fathers' play also tends to be more physical, with more jouncing and bouncing and more surprises, than mothers' play. Even though fathers interact with infants much less, many infants have as strong an attachment to their fathers as they have to their mothers (see Chapter 6; Bretherton & Ainsworth 1974; Lamb 1976).

In most families, the mother is primarily responsible for the care of infants and young children. Even when an infant is not breast-fed, the mother usually does most of the bottle-feeding. She also is usually the one to bathe the baby, change the diapers, do the dressing and undressing, toilet-train, and take the child to the doctor's office for check-ups. The mother also does most of the talking to the baby. One study (of only 10 families) reported that during the first 3 months fathers spent an average of only about 37 seconds a day talking to their young infants (Rebelsky & Hanks 1971). One study found that the average American father spent 12 minutes a day with his children (Stone 1972).

In the past decade, with an increasing number of mothers joining the work force, it would seem that fathers' participation in child care should have increased. In a number of families, there has been an increase, especially in families where the mother works full-time and both parents have the attitude that the roles of men and women should be equal. Fathers in such families are more likely to get involved at the very beginning; they attend prenatal classes and are present at their infant's birth (Russell 1978). However, these fathers are still the exception. At best, most fathers contribute two hours a day to the running of the household. One study (Kellerman & Katz 1978) asked parents to say which of 89 child-rearing responsibilities were best done by mothers and which by fathers. Most parents considered half of the tasks to be the mother's exclusive responsibility. (These included the giving of all physical care, training in correct ways to behave, and anything having to do with music, literature, or art.) The parents considered one-third of the 89 tasks to be joint responsibilities. (These were tasks having to do with education and discipline.) Only 8 items on the list (about 10 percent) were considered to be the father's sole responsibility. (These were mainly guidance in assertiveness, mechanical skills, and sports.)

In fact, whether the wife works or not, the best predictor of how much time a man spends on child-rearing and other household tasks is his own working schedule: Men who work 40 hours a week spend about two hours a day doing things around the house; men who work 50 hours a week spend an hour a day (Clarke-Stewart 1982). Some companies have set up flexible working hours to allow employees who are parents to balance their schedules so that their children have at least one parent at home for most of the working day. A study of such working parents found that after a year of flexible scheduling, male and female roles had not changed: Child care was still the mother's primary responsibility; for fathers, work was the top priority (Bohen & Viveros-Long 1981).

In general, fathers seem to be less nurturant and more consistent in enforcing rules with their children than mothers are. In interviews about their relationships with their children, mothers tend to emphasize their wish to keep their children free from anxiety, whereas fathers talk about their responsibility to teach the children moral and personal values. Interviews with children between preschool and high-school age suggest, in turn, that they generally detect this difference between the mother's and father's roles—they see their mother as affectionate and nurturing and their father as strong, competent, and somewhat frightening (Emmerich 1961; Kagan & Lemkin 1960).

A father's style may have particular effects on the attitudes and personalities of his sons and daughters. For example, girls tend to show higher achievement if their fathers participate in child-rearing, especially if the fathers encourage the girls' independence and performance (Hoffman 1973). A study of the family backgrounds of women who supported or opposed the aims of the women's rights movement showed striking differences between the fathers of the two groups (Worrell & Worrell 1971). Women who opposed the movement had fathers who had treated them like fragile flowers, to be loved, appreciated, and protected carefully. Women who supported the movement had fathers who had given them acceptance and affection in more moderate amounts and had allowed their daughters considerable autonomy.

Fathers seem to have an effect on their sons' self-esteem: Boys with high self-esteem report a closer relationship with their fathers than boys with low self-esteem do (Coopersmith 1967). Fathers also have a crucial influence on whether their sons will be delinquent (Glueck & Glueck 1959; Lynn 1974). The fathers of delinquent sons are often punitive, aggressive, and at the same time neglectful. They treat their sons erratically; they frequently pay no attention to them (sometimes because the fathers are drunk), and when they do pay attention, it is often to ridicule or brutalize them. Most delinquents see their fathers as neglectful, as failing to protect them and offering them little or no direction.

Single-Parent Families

The frequency of divorce has risen more than 700 percent in the United States since 1900: One out of three marriages now ends in divorce. It has been estimated that four out of ten children born in the 1970s will spend some time in a one-parent family (Clarke-Stewart 1982). In more than nine out of ten divorces of couples with children, the mother retains custody of the children, although fathers are usually required to help support them. Public attention to the father's equal right to custody has increased, but the courts' traditional position that "children belong with their mother" remains strong for the most part, especially if the children are young.

Generally, fathers are given the right to take the children for weekend or holiday visits, and at first they tend to exercise these visitation rights regularly. But after a few years, many fathers lose contact with their children, either because of the difficulties of "weekend parenting" or because the father takes up a new relationship (Hetherington et al. 1978).

Adjusting to life in a **single-parent family** is not easy. Besides the emotional injuries to parents and children before and during most divorces, there are economic crises. Many mothers must go to work full-time. Child-care or alimony payments by the father, though they may strain his resources to the breaking point, usually are not enough to maintain the standard of living that the family had before the divorce.

The effects of a divorce on children's emotional well-being depends on a number of circumstances—the age of the children, the level of hostility between the parents, how the parents explain the separation, whether the parents use the children as pawns in their own emotional battles, and, probably most important, how the parent who has custody of the children adjusts to life after divorce. No matter how favorable these circumstances may be, most children feel some emotional distress when their parents divorce. Some imagine that they are responsible for the break-up and they suffer from guilt. Some feel rejected by the parent who leaves. Some become depressed or hostile (Wallerstein & Kelly 1980).

A longitudinal study of divorced and intact families (Hetherington et al. 1978, 1982) found that during the first year after a divorce the parents with custody exercised less control over their children than they had before, probably because of all the emotional and material adjustments both they and the children had to make. They made fewer demands on the children and did not communicate with them as well as before the divorce. During the second year, however, the situation improved. The mothers established better and more consistent relations with their children, who likewise began to adjust better.

Divorced families are not the only single-parent families. According to the 1980 census, approximately 3 percent of children lived with mothers who had not ever married. The combination of increased divorce and increased childbirth out of wedlock means that in 1980 a full 20 percent of American children lived with only one parent, almost always the mother (United States Bureau of the Census 1982). What are the effects of growing up in a family with only a mother? Several negative effects have been found, and in general these are more severe for boys than for girls. Children from mother-only families tend to perform less well on standardized intelligence tests and in school (Biller 1974; Shinn 1978). As with all negative effects of living in a single-parent family, this one does not occur if the family functions well and the children have close contact with loving adults other than their parents.

There are negative effects also on social and emotional development. Boys in mother-only families seem to have some difficulty achieving a clear masculine identification, especially if their fathers are absent during the preschool years.

Figure 10-9 Single parents (who most often are single mothers) usually have a busy schedule, juggling the responsibilities of work and housework and the need to care for their children's physical and psychological health.

A preschool boy is likely to show less traditionally masculine behavior, being less assertive and more dependent on other boys and avoiding rough-and-tumble play. These effects usually diminish or disappear as other males—friends, teachers, uncles, his mother's man friends—begin to serve as models. Some data also suggest that boys in mother-only families have trouble controlling their impulses and forgoing immediate gratifications in favor of long-term goals (Biller 1970). It should be noted, however, that several studies have found no differences between boys raised with and without fathers (Barclay & Cusumano 1967; Biller & Bahm 1971).

Girls seem to be generally less affected by living in a mother-only family than boys are, but their social development shows some effects. One study found that the effects differed depending on whether the father had died or was absent because of divorce (Hetherington et al. 1978, 1982). Both daughters of widows and daughters of divorcees reported feeling anxious around males, but their behavior at a dance and their responses to a male interviewer revealed that they coped with their anxiety in different ways. Girls whose fathers had died were shyer and more inhibited around males than girls from intact families were, whereas daughters of divorced parents were bolder and more flirtatious. It may be that the daughters of divorcees viewed their mothers' single lives as unsatisfying—even though the mother's memories of her married life were negative—and had decided that, in order to be happy, it was essential to have a man. The daughters of widows—who tended to sanctify their dead husband—may have decided that few males could live up to their father's image or may have transferred the feeling of awe and deference connected with it to all males.

Problems in relationships with the opposite sex seem to continue into adulthood for many men and women who grew up in single-parent families. They are more likely to get divorced and to feel lonely and less likely to report having a satisfactory sex life (Biller 1976; Shaver & Rubenstein 1980). On the other hand, many of these men and women do have good sexual relationships and successful marriages. Other harmful effects of the father's absence have been claimed for both boys and girls, but most of the studies that produced these claims were done some time ago and have been criticized as methodologically unsound (Herzog & Sudia 1968).

The safest conclusion seems to be that living with just one parent does not automatically have ill effects. In fact, several studies indicate that children are better off in a stable single-parent home than in a two-parent home that is strife-ridden (Ahlstrom & Havighurst 1971; Rutter 1971). The effects of divorce depend in great part on how the parent with custody of the children handles the situation. After the first year, most of the worst effects disappear as parent and children adjust to their new situation (Hetherington et al. 1978). The absence of ill effects in many families attests to the developmental adaptability of both parents and children.

On the whole, the three main socializing agents during the school years—the school, the peer group, and the family—cooperate to teach the child many of the same values. But in some ways, they also compete.

CROSS PRESSURES: ADULTS VERSUS PEERS

Dealing with different social agents can be difficult. Conflicts arise, with one agent encouraging the child in one direction and another agent encouraging him in a different direction. One of the most common difficulties is the conflict between peers and adults (Hartup 1983).

Cultural Differences

The balance between the influence of peers and adults can differ greatly in different cultures. In many countries, a child's friends and classmates are much less important agents of socialization than they are in the United States.

School-age children in Switzerland, for example, depend much more on the advice and consent of adults than American children do. In one study, American and Swiss children were told the following story about a child their own age: "A group of children want to give a surprise party for their scout leader. One boy has accepted the responsibility of decorating the room. He wonders who he should ask for advice, his homeroom teacher or a student who is so artistic that he has won a scholarship to the museum's art classes" (Boehm 1957). The children were asked whose advice they thought the boy in the story should seek. Almost 70 percent of the Swiss children said he should ask the teacher, whereas 92 percent of the American children thought he should depend on his talented young friend.

Another group of studies examined children's reactions to dilemmas involving conflict between adult norms and peer pressure (Bronfenbrenner et al. 1965; Devereux 1970). Children in England, Germany, Russia, and the United States were asked such questions as, "Would you go to a movie recommended by friends but condemned by adults? Would you act as a lookout while some friends put a rubber snake in a teacher's desk?" Those who showed the strongest inclination to go along with their friends were the English children. As the researchers explain, English children spend the least time alone and the most time away from their parents, with groups of peers unsupervised by adults. The American and German children were less influenced by their peers than the English children were but much more than the Russian children.

A further study in this series confirmed a large difference between American and Russian children on this matter (Bronfenbrenner 1967). Groups of Russian and American 12-year-olds were asked to answer questions about conflicting pressures from peers and adults under one of three different conditions. One group of each nationality was told that their answers would be kept strictly confidential—no one but the researchers would see them. Another group was told that their answers would be made available to parents and teachers. The third group was told that their answers would be shown only to the class.

Even in the groups that were assured of confidentiality, the Russian children were less inclined than the Americans to act in ways that adults would disapprove. When the children throught their answers would be posted for adults to see, the responses of Russian and American children were closer to each other and also much more in line with adult social rules. The greatest difference between the two nationality groups emerged when the children thought the rest of the children in the class would see their responses. Under these circumstances, most Russian children showed even greater allegiance to adult rules than they did when they thought they were answering in confidence. In contrast, many more American children promised mischief than they did when they thought their answers would be kept confidential.

Clearly, children in the United States are greatly influenced by their peer groups. American children's confidential answers showed that some would prefer not to pull pranks, but the peer-disclosure condition showed that they would not want their friends to know about their reluctance. If a child like this were really asked by his friends to keep watch while a rubber snake was being put in a teacher's desk, the child would probably participate in the prank, despite his reluctance, in order to avoid his friends' disapproval.

The Russian children's opposite reaction—to keep their friends from knowing anything about their willingness to go against adult rules—stems from Russian practices of socialization. In the Russian educational system, beginning with nursery school, children's groups are used as a means of reinforcing the society's adult values. Children are encouraged to help each other obey the rules, and groups are often given the responsibility of rewarding their members who do well or punishing those who break rules. From their earliest years,

Figure 10-10 These two posters illustrate two laws of the Pioneers, a Communist youth organization for children in their early teens. The one on the left, which reads, "A Pioneer is a friend to children of all the nations of the world," seems to express values like those of Western organizations such as the Boy Scouts. The other, which reads, "A Pioneer tells the truth and treasures the honor of his unit," stresses a code that is not considered particularly good form in the West: One boy is shown reporting on the misbehavior of another (who has carved his name on the desk) to the authorities. In the background is a picture of a child martyr in the Soviet Union, a boy who was killed by villagers for informing on his father, who was collaborating with anti-collectivization forces.

Russian children are taught that it is their duty to report children who break rules (Figure 10-10).

The two societies, then, deal very differently with the relation between peer socialization and adult socialization. In Russia there is almost no conflict between conformity to adult social rules and conformity to peer-group pressures because the peer group is taught to support the adult rules. In the United States, on the other hand, conflict between peer norms and adult norms is expected and, for the most part, is treated leniently by adult authorities.

Some social scientists believe that strong American peer allegiance is a fairly recent result of social changes that have tended to segregate children from adults—larger and more centralized schools, more group child care for preschoolers, and more "permissive" child-rearing techniques than were common a generation or two ago (Bronfenbrenner 1970). The "us against them" attitude of children has a long history in the United States, however. One of the most famous children in American literature, Huckleberry Finn, has been winning admirers for a hundred years as he chafes against adults' rigid notions about what children should be:

> The Widow Douglas she took me for her son, and allowed she would sivilize me; but it was rough living in the house all the time, considering how dismal regular and decent the widow was in all her ways; and so when I couldn't stand it no longer I lit out. I got into my old rags and my sugar hogshead again, and was free and satisfied. (Twain 1971)

How Much Conflict?

Cross pressures between adults and peers are real, but for most children the conflict is not very strong (Hartup 1970). In the United States, most adults think that children should have a group of friends and spend a lot of time playing with other children. Most American parents worry if their school-age children keep to themselves. In other words, the adult norm for children's behavior supports the formation of children's groups and their activities.

Even when the norms of adults and child peers seem to differ, the conflict may be more apparent than real. For example, suppose a girl's mother has said that she should always tell her mother if her friends do something bad. When her best friend writes on a bathroom wall or steals a pack of gum, should she tell her mother? Most American children 8 years of age or older do not tell on their friends. But how many American adults would really approve of a child's "squealing" on his friends whenever adult authority demanded it? Most parents surely would like to know when their children's friends do something criminal or dangerous, but there is an *adult* norm that subtly supports "no squealing." Think of all the gangster movies in which "the squealer" is depicted as a despicable, weasel-like character. What appears to be a conflict between child peer norms and adult norms is not much of a conflict after all.

Conflicts may result from unrealistic norms laid down by the family. In the grade-school years, children try to find and follow socially acceptable rules for how to deal with the world. If the rules they are taught or modeled by their family are unsatisfactory, they will try to learn from their friends. Extremely overprotective parents may set rules that forbid their children to ride bicycles or play games in which there is the slightest chance of injury. If the child's peers condemn his behavior as abnormal—"sissy" or "chicken" or "scaredy-cat"—he will reconsider his parents' rules in light of the fact that all the other kids are allowed to ride a bike or climb on the playground equipment.

Even in England and the United States, where peer groups are the most influential, research findings suggest that children who most consistently support peer decisions come from troubled families (Devereux 1965, 1966). The families of these children tend to be punitive or permissive to the point of neglect, and the children do not feel very strong affection for their parents. It seems that these families do not provide adequate norms. In the very permissive

Figure 10-11 Children in groups do influence each other, but the children's norms are usually not very different from what adults consider acceptable behavior.

families, adult norms simply are not clear; in the punitive families, they are harmful, either to the child's physical well-being or to his self-esteem.

The popular press sometimes blames the behavior of gangs of delinquent youngsters on their adherence to peer norms and their disregard of adult standards. Yet the single most consistent characteristic of delinquents is the character of their family life (Bachman 1970). The parents of children who join delinquent gangs often have police records themselves or are alcoholics. Relationships within the family are often hostile and filled with physical abuse, or the parents simply don't care what their children think or do. These children first learn violence and disregard for social rules at home, then they follow antisocial norms in their peer groups (Ahlstrom & Havighurst 1971).

The conflict between peer norms and adult norms, then, seems to have been greatly exaggerated. Most of the time, peer-group norms are part of a wider framework of what adults consider acceptable behavior for groups of children. When children's peer norms do violate society's standards of proper behavior, the families themselves usually play a major role in supporting the antisocial behavior.

MORAL DEVELOPMENT

In a sense, the system of rules that makes social life possible is embodied in a culture's morality. Besides the moral rules encoded in written laws, each society has unwritten moral rules—specifying, for example, that people should help each other under certain circumstances. If you see a person drowning and you have a good chance to save him, the unwritten moral rules say that you should try. No one will put you in jail if you do not, but many adults would blame themselves for not acting. Their conscience would bother them.

What people call a conscience is a product of moral development. The child is not born with morality, or a conscience, but develops it gradually. The most clearly spelled out theory of the development of moral judgment is Lawrence Kohlberg's.

THEORY: A COGNITIVE-DEVELOPMENTAL APPROACH TO MORAL JUDGMENT

Jean Piaget attempted in some of his early work (1932) to analyze the development of moral judgment in children. Although he discovered many interesting facts, he did not devise a developmental sequence of moral stages. Building upon the work of Piaget and of the American psychologist James Mark Baldwin (1894), Lawrence Kohlberg has formulated a more complete cognitive-developmental theory of how moral reasoning develops.

Kohlberg (1969) has proposed a sequence of six qualitatively different ways of making moral judgments—that is, six stages of reasoning about moral issues. According to him, the course of moral development depends largely on the course of cognitive development. As people progress through the Piagetian periods of cognitive development, their way of understanding the social world changes, and one of the most important aspects of this social understanding is moral judgment.

Like Piaget's periods of cognitive development, Kohlberg's stages form a hierarchy. That is, the understanding at each stage does not simply replace that of the preceding one but rather builds upon it. At each new stage, the person reorganizes the reasoning of the previous stage and incorporates it into a new cognitive structure, or scheme.

Kohlberg's theory has aroused controversy (Damon 1978; Kurtines & Greif 1974), and he himself has revised parts of it (Colby et al. 1983; Kohlberg 1978).

The theory is summarized here in its classic form. The problems with it will be explained in appropriate places in this and later chapters.

THE STAGES OF MORAL DEVELOPMENT

The six moral stages are grouped into three levels of moral judgment: the preconventional level, the conventional level, and the principled level. The two stages at each level are characterized by the same general type of moral judgment, but in two different forms.

The Preconventional Level

The first two stages of moral development, which make up the preconventional level, can begin in the preoperational period of cognitive development (Kitchener 1983; Kuhn 1976). During these stages, a person's moral judgments are based only on direct physical consequences and on the person's own needs. Events that have unpleasant consequences are judged to be bad, and events that have pleasant consequences are judged to be good. Judgments take no account of a person's intention in engaging in an action.

STAGE 1: PUNISHMENT AND OBEDIENCE ORIENTATION. In this stage, moral judgments of an act are based only on its physical consequences and on how it is judged by authorities. An act is bad because Mommy or Daddy says it is bad, because the child is punished for the act, or because it causes damage or injury. An act is good because Mommy or Daddy says it is good, because the child is rewarded for doing it, or because it has pleasant consequences.

For example, suppose a preschool girl is asked to judge who is worse, a boy who was punished for accidentally spilling his milk or one who also accidentally spilled his milk but was not punished. At Stage 1, she would say that the punished one was worse, even though neither boy spilled the milk intentionally. A child at this stage is obedient to people she perceives as having superior strength or prestige because they have the power to bestow rewards and punishments.

STAGE 2: MARKETPLACE ORIENTATION. Physical consequences and the judgment of authorities are still important at this stage, but other people's points of view begin to be taken into account. A child at Stage 2 is willing to do what she perceives as a good deed for someone else if she can be sure that she'll get something she needs in exchange. That is, she will barter good for good in a marketplace. "I'll let you play with my truck if you give me half of your candy bar." This stage is often called the stage of "You scratch my back and I'll scratch yours."

The Conventional Level

At this level, individuals begin to understand conventional morality—what people in the society think is good or bad. Moral judgment becomes a matter of what other people approve of and what pleases them. An act that does not conform to social standards is considered bad. Moral development at this level begins during Piaget's concrete-operational period (Colby et al. 1983; Kuhn 1976).

STAGE 3: GOOD-BOY/GOOD-GIRL ORIENTATION. In this stage, the standards of a person's family and friends are general standards of behavior for that person. A "good girl" or "good boy" is one who conforms to these social standards—or at least tries to.

One major development during this stage is the ability to judge not only an act itself but the intention of the person

Preconventional level
Stage 1: Punishment and obedience

"I'd better do what's good for me!"

Stage 2: Market place

"I have to remember that they're after something, too."

Conventional level
Stage 3: Good-boy/good-girl

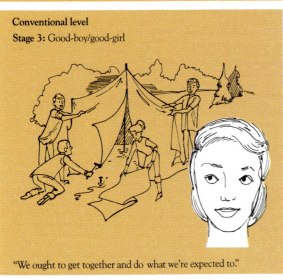

"We ought to get together and do what we're expected to."

Stage 4: Law and order

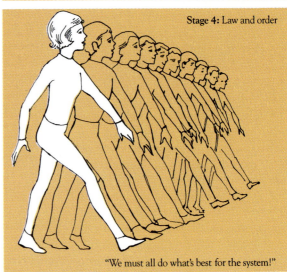

"We must all do what's best for the system!"

Principled level
Stage 5: Contractual-legalistic

"I am going to uphold what we've all agreed is best."

Stage 6: Universal ethical principle

"I must act as a rational person seeking the best for all."

who performs it. At Stage 3, a person would judge it bad for someone to drive above the legal speed limit because people in general judge speeding to be bad. But if the driver did not intend to speed—if the speedometer malfunctioned, for example—the person would say that the speeder was not really being bad.

STAGE 4: LAW-AND-ORDER ORIENTATION. "Following the rules" is still the measure of morality in this stage, but the rules are those of the wider society, not just of family and friends. The person comes to understand for the first time that laws and rules are necessary for a smoothly

Figure 10-12 Kohlberg's six stages of moral development are illustrated here, emphasizing the growth of the ability to take another perspective. This ability grows with social interaction in the same way that a person's grasp of the physical world grows with physical experience. At Stage 1, the individual is not capable of taking any point of view besides her own. Moral rules therefore appear to be arbitrary and completely external. As she begins to be able to take another's perspective, she sees that one's behavior must be regulated according to more than just "what happens to me" (Stage 2). Conventional morality begins with Stage 3, when the person can imagine what "people" think is good or bad; "I" becomes "we." This awareness matures into the understanding of Stage 4, that morality is a matter of the whole society's point of view rather than merely a way of managing relations among individual people. At the principled level, the individual begins to rise above the "we" point of view to take even larger perspectives. At Stage 5, she sees things from the viewpoint of a person who wants to make life workable within an agreed-upon social framework. Finally, Stage 6 is based on the perspective of "all people everywhere." The thinker at this stage recognizes an individual's responsibility to try to make moral judgments that are right for everyone, whether or not the judgments are socially agreed upon.

functioning society. Obeying laws and authorities to maintain the social order is therefore seen as moral.

A person at Stage 4 would disapprove of driving over the speed limit not merely because people in general think it is bad but because it is illegal: governments have enacted laws that forbid speeding in order to protect lives.

The Principled Level

In the final two stages of moral development, individuals move beyond conventional morality; they formulate general moral principles that can apply to societies other than their own and can also be used to judge their own society's laws and change them. Their basis for judging an act, then, is how it accords with their moral principles. According to Kohlberg (1969), a person can enter these two stages early in Piaget's formal-operational period, which begins in adolescence. More recent research, however, suggests that these stages may not begin until early adulthood (Colby et al. 1983).

STAGE 5: CONTRACTUAL-LEGALISTIC ORIENTATION. At this stage, the individual understands that social regulations are flexible and subject to change. Laws and rules of conduct are based on contracts, or agreements among people. People in a society agree to set up regulations that they feel are needed to maintain the social order and at the same time to guarantee as many individual rights as possible while maintaining the social order. Different societies consequently have different rules and laws. Circumstances may require changes in the rules, and, after rationally discussing alternatives, people can agree to change them.

The moral principles of an individual at this stage in general direct her to be fair and rational, to avoid violating others' rights, and to concern herself with the will and welfare of the majority. Acts are judged to be immoral when they violate the rights of others under the terms of the social contract.

STAGE 6: UNIVERSAL ETHICAL-PRINCIPLE ORIENTATION. A person at this final stage of moral development has passed beyond the boundaries of her own society in forming her moral principles. She has formed for herself abstract principles, applicable to all societies, that call above all for justice, equality of human rights, and a respect for the dignity of every human being. The Golden Rule can be seen as one such universal ethical principle: "Do unto others as you would have them do unto you."

A person at Stage 6 strives to act in accordance with her own principles, even though they might be at odds with her society's laws and rules. She is more concerned about self-condemnation than about censure by others. For example, Martin Luther King, Jr., led civil rights marches and sit-ins in the 1960s even though they violated various laws, because he was trying to eliminate the injustices that existed for black people and other minorities.

MORAL DILEMMAS

A person's moral stage can be assessed with Kohlberg's Moral Judgment Interview, in which several moral dilemmas are presented and people are asked to explain their reasoning in arriving at solutions to the dilemmas (Colby et al. 1983). The best-known dilemma is this one:

> In Europe, a woman was near death from cancer. One drug might save her, a form of radium that a druggist in the same town had recently discovered. The druggist was charging $2,000, ten times what the drug cost him to make. The sick woman's husband, Heinz, went to everyone he knew to borrow the money, but he could only get together about half of what it cost. He told the druggist that his wife was dying and asked him to sell it cheaper or let him pay later. But the druggist said "No." The husband got desperate and broke into the man's store to steal the drug for his wife. Should the husband have done that? Why?

What matters for scoring moral stage is not whether a person decides that Heinz was right or wrong but how the person explains the decision. Table 10-1 lists typical responses to the drug-stealing dilemma, both pro and con, in terms of motives for engaging in the act or not. It is the kind of motive rather than being for or against the act that determines how the answer is scored.

PATTERNS OF MORAL JUDGMENT

All people in the world go through the same sequence of moral stages, according to Kohlberg. That is, the stages are **universal.** Moral-dilemma tests have been presented to people in several cultures; in most cases, the same developmental sequence seems to hold (Edwards 1982). Figure 10-13 presents data that support the universality of the stages (Kohlberg 1969).

Although the order of progression through the stages seems to be fixed and universal, many people stop short of Stage 6. In fact, the data collected by Kohlberg and his colleagues indicate that some adults' moral judgments remain at Stage 1 or 2, and most judgments by adults are made at Stage 3 or 4 (Colby et al. 1983; Kohlberg 1969). Also, a person's progress from stage to stage does not occur as a sudden jump. Typically, about 65 percent of a person's judgments are at one stage, while the rest are distributed at lower and higher stages.

Development of moral judgment from

TABLE 10-1 MOTIVES FOR STEALING OR NOT STEALING THE DRUG

	PRO	CON
STAGE 1 Action is motivated by the avoidance of punishment, and "conscience" is irrational fear of punishment.	If you let your wife die, you will get in trouble. You'll be blamed for not spending the money to save her, and there'll be an investigation of you and the druggist for your wife's death.	You shouldn't steal because you'll be caught and sent to jail if you do. If you do get away, your conscience would bother you thinking how the police would catch up with you at any minute.
STAGE 2 Action is motivated by the desire for reward or benefit. Possible guilt reactions are ignored, and punishment is viewed in a pragmatic manner.	If you do happen to get caught you could give the drug back and you wouldn't get much of a sentence. It wouldn't bother you much to serve a little jail term if you have your wife when you get out.	You may not get much of a jail term if you steal the drug, but your wife will probably die before you get out so it won't do you much good. If your wife dies, you shouldn't blame yourself. It wasn't your fault she had cancer.
STAGE 3 Action is motivated by the anticipation of disapproval by others, actual or imagined.	No one will think you're bad if you steal the drug, but your family will think you're an inhuman husband if you don't. If you let your wife die, you'll never be able to look anybody in the face again.	It isn't just the druggist who will think you're a criminal; everyone else will too. After you steal, you'll feel bad because you've dishonored your family. You won't be able to face anyone again.
STAGE 4 Action is motivated by the anticipation of dishonor (that is, blame for failure of duty) and by guilt over concrete harm done to others.	If you have any sense of honor, you won't let your wife die because you're afraid to do the only thing that will save her. You'll always feel guilty that you caused her death if you don't do your duty to her.	You're desperate and you may not know you're doing wrong when you steal the drug. But you'll know you did wrong after you're punished and sent to jail. You'll always feel guilty for your dishonesty and lawbreaking.
STAGE 5 Action is motivated by concern for the respect of equals and of the community (assuming that their respect is based on reason rather than emotions) and concern for one's own self-respect (that is, to avoid judging oneself as irrational, inconsistent, and lacking in purpose).	You'd lose other people's respect, not gain it, if you don't steal. If you let your wife die, it would be out of fear not out of reasoning it out. So you'd just lose self-respect and probably the respect of others too.	You would lose your standing and respect in the community and violate the law. You'd lose respect for yourself if you're carried away by emotion and forget the long-range point of view.
STAGE 6 Action is motivated by concern about self-condemnation for violating one's own principles.	If you don't steal the drug and let your wife die, you'd always condemn yourself for it afterward. You wouldn't have lived up to your own standards of conscience.	If you stole the drug, you wouldn't be blamed by other people, but you'd condemn yourself because you wouldn't have lived up to your own conscience and standards of honesty.

SOURCE: Adapted from Kohlberg 1969.

Figure 10-13   (A) Children and adolescents (ages 7, 10, 13, and 16) were presented with moral dilemmas like Heinz's problem, and their answers were scored for stage of moral development. These profiles of the results show that early-stage answers were more often given by younger children, whereas late-stage answers were more often given by older children. The orderly way these profiles change supports Kohlberg's idea that people invariably progress through the stages in this order. (B) Boys in three different cultures were presented with moral dilemmas; the results shown here support the idea that the stages are universal and are not restricted to our culture. (Kohlberg 1969)

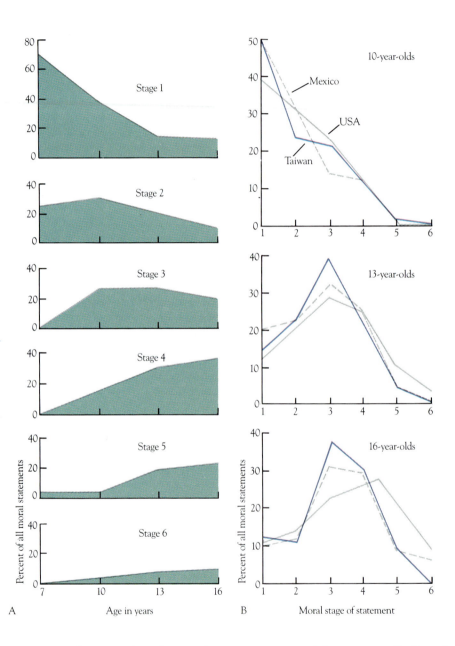

A   Age in years

B   Moral stage of statement

one stage to the next takes place in the same way that it does in other cognitive areas, according to Kohlberg. Presented with a situation that requires a moral judgment, a person uses her existing cognitive schemes to interpret the situation as best she can. Sometimes her existing schemes will not let her make sense of

some aspects of the situation. In Piaget's terms, the person has been presented with information that she is unable to assimilate; therefore, her thought is in disequilibrium. The person must revise some cognitive scheme—accommodate—in order to understand the new material.

It is the disequilibrium induced by failure of a scheme that leads to moral development. For this reason, if a person has not been faced with sufficiently challenging situations, she may not develop to the highest moral stage that she is capable of. Consequently, a person's moral stage will not typically correspond to her Piagetian period. Most people perform at a lower moral stage than would be expected from their Piagetian period. For example, a person who demonstrates formal-operational abilities in Piagetian tasks may perform only at moral Stage 2. If this person experiences situations that induce moral disequilibrium, then her formal-operational abilities may allow her to advance to the higher stages, according to Kohlberg.

Moral Judgment and Moral Action

An early, classic study of cheating that used 10,000 schoolchildren as subjects found no connection between the children's stated moral principles and how much they cheated (Hartshorne & May 1928–30). Children who, in interviews, piously denounced any form of cheating nevertheless did cheat sometimes. The researchers found, in fact, that whether a child cheated did not depend on the child's "honesty" or other traits. Instead it depended on how important a particular test or task was to the child and on how great the risk of detection was.

Some studies have found a few characteristics that seem to be correlated with cheating. For example, children with high IQs seem to cheat less in school than those with low IQs. Of course, brighter children may simply have less need to cheat on academic tests, or less confidence that they can improve their scores by copying someone else's answers. In fact, when bright children are given a nonacademic, game-type task to do, the positive correlation between high IQ and no cheating disappears (Hartshorne & May 1928; Howells 1938).

The relation between moral stage and cheating may seem easy to predict on the basis of Kohlberg's theory, especially for some of the stages. At Stage 2, children presumably do not hesitate to cheat as long as they are not worried about being caught and punished. At Stage 4, on the other hand, children understand their society's moral rules and should normally obey them and not cheat.

The relationship does not seem to be that simple, however. Cognitive and personality factors both seem to influence moral behavior. In one study, a personality factor called "ego strength" helped to determine whether a child cheated (Krebs 1967). Before the study began, school-age children were tested for stage of moral judgment and also for "ego strength," which was assessed by measuring IQ and attention span. Children with high IQs and long attention spans were considered to have high ego strength, and those who scored low on both measures were said to have low ego strength. Of the children at Stage 2, many with high ego strength cheated, but far fewer with low ego strength did. Of the children at Stage 4, few of those with high ego strength cheated, but

RESEARCH:
REASONING ABOUT
FAIRNESS OR JUSTICE

William Damon (1977), using simpler, more concrete moral tasks than Kohlberg, found that children as young as 8 years old used the idea of *justice*, or fairness to others, in making moral judgments and acting on them. Yet if children of that age are presented with Kohlberg's moral dilemmas, they score at Stage 1 or 2—supposedly, they are unable to use the concept of justice or fairness. In one of Damon's tasks, groups consisting of four children—three the same age and one younger—were assigned to make bracelets. At the completion of the task, the experimenter offered the children a reward of ten candy bars to be divided among the group, but before the candy was handed out, the younger child was called from the room. The three remaining children were then asked to decide how the ten candy bars should be distributed.

Here is some dialogue showing the reasoning of three 4-year-olds about the distribution of the candy bars. (Jennifer, the younger child, had already left the room.)

Experimenter:	How do you think we should give them out?
Jonathan:	(Gives 2 to everyone, has 2 left over. Then takes the extra 2 for himself.) I'm going to take these and eat them for supper.
Experimenter:	What do you think, Ben? Do you think they (the extra 2) should go to you and Jonathan?
Ben:	(Nods yes.)
Experimenter:	What do you think, Kerri?
Kerri:	No.
Experimenter:	What way do you think would be best?
Kerri:	I don't know.

Experimenter:	What do you think, though? Put them out again, and let Kerri give them out.
Kerri:	(Gives 2 to Ben, 2 to Jonathan, 2 to herself; sets aside 2 for Jennifer.)
Experimenter:	What about these two?
Jonathan:	These 2 go for me and Ben.
Experimenter:	Is that what you wanted to do?
Kerri:	(Nods no.)
Experimenter:	What do you think, Jonathan? You think two and two, three and three? Do you think that way would be fair?
Jonathan:	Yes.
Experimenter:	Why would it be fair?
Jonathan:	'Cause I hate girls.
Experimenter:	Kerri doesn't think it's fair.
Ben:	I do. I hope Jenny would.

Jonathan:	Yeah, Jenny would, cause she always thinks.
Experimenter:	O.K. So the two boys want to give the boys more, and Kerri wants to give everybody the same? Does anyone think they might change their mind?
All children:	No.

Here are three 10-year-olds debating the distribution problem. (Dennis, the younger member of the group, has left the room.)

Experimenter:	We talked with you all and couldn't decide, so we thought you should decide together. What do you think is the best way to give it out?
Craig:	Would Dennis get some?
Experimenter:	If you think so.
Norman:	He has to be here too.
Experimenter:	Well, you all decide among you.
Bonnie:	I was thinking, we could give it out one a bracelet, because Dennis did one and we all did three. Or give two-and-a half to everybody. That way everybody gets the same thing.
Craig:	Maybe he (Dennis) should get one and we get three.
Norman:	No. It ain't fair
Bonnie:	Also, Dennis is younger and he left earlier.
Experimenter:	So far you've got one for Dennis, three for you, Craig, three for you, Norman, and three for you, Bonnie.
Bonnie:	(Mumbles something.) That's what he (Dennis) should get.

Norman:	No. He's not. That's what I'm getting at. That's what I'm putting in your mind, in your mind, in his mind (stated rather belligerently, pointing to each member of the group).
Bonnie:	Well, let's split these in half. Everybody gets two and a half.
Norman:	Right.
Experimenter:	What do you think? Do you agree, Craig?
Craig:	(Does not reply.)
Norman:	It's the best way. Everybody gets the same amount.
Bonnie:	Craig's is the prettiest, Norman's is the neatest, and I did the most.
Craig:	And Dennis has . . . a lot of pink.
Experimenter:	What do you think, Bonnie?
Bonnie:	I think we should cut this in half.
Experimenter:	What do you think, Norman?
Norman:	We should cut it in half.
Craig:	That's what I thought at first.

In Damon's study, all the groups of 8-year-olds and 10-year-olds reached a consensus that gave each member of their group, including the absent younger child, two and a half candy bars—the fairest possible distribution.

Figure 10-14   The results of Krebs' study of cheating. First each child was tested for moral stage and then for what was designated as ego strength (a combination of IQ and attention span). Then each child was given an opportunity to cheat. The colored part of each circle represents the proportion of children who cheated in each category. Most children with high ego strength at Stage 2 of moral development cheated, whereas few of those with high ego strength at Stage 4 cheated. The bright, attentive "marketplace" thinkers (Stage 2) evidently saw their chance and took it, whereas the bright, attentive "law-and-order" thinkers (Stage 4) had the strength to obey their own moral rule.

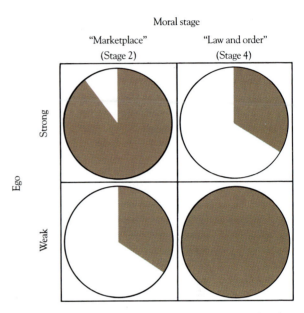

many of those with low ego strength did (see Figure 10-14). Apparently the children at Stage 2 who were bright and attentive found opportunities for cheating that their less intelligent, less watchful peers missed. The bright, attentive children at Stage 4, on the other hand, seemed to have the ego strength to obey the rules, as their morality dictated, whereas few of the children at Stage 4 with low ego strength could resist the temptation.

Other studies have tried to relate behaviors besides cheating to Kohlberg's stages of moral judgment. These behaviors include participation in protests against social injustice (Haan et al. 1968), distribution of valuable goods among individuals in an equitable way (Gunzburger et al. 1977), and decisions about abortion (Gilligan & Murphy 1979). These studies indicate that, for the most part, the higher the stage of moral judgment, the more likely it is that people will also perform actions that are generally considered moral.

It should be possible to make a clearer connection between moral behavior and stage of moral judgment, but research has been hampered by problems of measurement and methodology (Kurtines & Grief 1974; Rest 1983). For example, the stories that Kohlberg uses to assess moral judgment are extremely complex, as the Heinz story certainly is. The complex and abstract nature of Kohlberg's dilemmas apparently can cause people to reason at lower moral stages than they are actually capable of. Simpler stories and methods have revealed higher moral stages in younger children (Damon 1977; Kuhn 1976; Lee 1971). Thus, the relation of stage to moral action can depend on the method of testing. Fortunately, some of these problems seem recently to have been resolved (Colby et al. 1983; Gibbs et al. 1982), and so it may now be possible for more conclusive research to be done.

The Social Learning of Moral Behavior

Primarily because of these methodological problems, some investigators have found fault with Kohlberg's approach. Social-learning researchers, for example, have used modeling to lead children to imitate moral behavior at stages lower than those the children had demonstrated initially (Bandura & McDonald 1963; Hand 1981). This drop in stage indicates that much of what people call moral behavior is controlled by social-learning factors: observational learning, reinforcement, and punishment.

Children are especially likely to imitate a behavior if the person modeling the behavior is powerful or nurturant or receives a reward. For example, in several experiments on moral behavior, one group of children learned a game by watching a model play it and then donate half his winnings to charity (Aronfreed 1968; Bryan & Walbek 1970). A control group simply received instructions about how the game was played. Later, all the children had a chance to play the game, win prizes, and donate some of them to charity. In every experiment, many more of the children who had seen the charitable model were generous in their donations.

Perspective-Taking and Social Experience

By observational learning, children can learn not only specific moral behaviors, such as giving to charity. They can also learn about the model's perspective. The ability to take another person's perspective is one of the most important influences on moral judgment and action (Selman 1980). Consequently, children's social experience with other perspectives necessarily affects their moral development. Consider the following interactions between two mothers and their 7-year-old sons, each of whom has just been caught stealing money from his mother's purse.

> *First mother:* You're nothing but a common thief. You want to end up in jail? I'm going to tell your father when he gets home, and don't be surprised if he pulls out the strap.
>
> *Second mother:* Taking other people's money is stealing, and you must not steal. The money you took, I was going to use it to buy groceries for all of us. You took the money to get yourself some toys and candy, but people can't always have what they want. I want a new dress for Aunt Sally's wedding, but I know that I can't use the grocery money to buy it, no matter how much I want it. Suppose you came home for dinner one night and there was no dinner because there was no money to buy groceries. You'd be hungry and so would I and Dad and your sister. If stealing was OK, then Frank could take your skateboard and Burt could take your mitt. How would you feel about that?

The first child, who was punished without any explanation of why stealing is wrong, probably learned nothing about perspective-taking. The scolding merely reinforced his Stage 1 reasoning about stealing: Avoid stealing to avoid punishment. The second child at least had a chance to hear another's perspective on stealing, as well as on sharing in the family. Perhaps he didn't realize before that even his mother cannot get everything she wants when she wants it. Her explanation thus gave him a model for carefully considering different perspectives in the future.

Social interactions that promote perspective-taking also typically promote moral behavior. Several studies (Figure 10-15) have shown that active training in taking perspectives (through role-playing for example) can greatly decrease problem behavior such as juvenile delinquency (Chandler et al. 1974; Silvern et al. 1979).

Social intercourse of all kinds offers opportunities for perspective-taking, whether it is participation in the family, interaction with fellow students, or playing games. The experience of perspective-taking in all these areas of a child's life promotes moral development.

External and Internal Controls.   Social-learning theorists emphasize that a person may have perspective-taking ability, or any other ability, and still not use it. Whether or not a person does perform a particular behavior and keep on performing it depends partly on the reinforcements and punishments that he receives for it.

Social approval, especially by such important people as a child's parents, is one of the most powerful reinforcers of moral behavior. As children learn that certain kinds of actions bring the approval or disapproval of their parents, they begin to monitor their own behavior in view of the expected consequences. According to Justin Aronfreed (1968), this is what leads to the establishment of conscience.

Aronfreed has outlined a range of moral controls running from external to

Figure 10-15   Michael Chandler used these cartoon sequences to assess the ability to take other people's perspectives. In each of the sequences, something happens to the main character, and then in the middle of the story a new character enters who does not know what happened earlier in the story. In his experiments, Chandler first asked children to tell the entire story. Then he asked them to tell the story as it would be seen by the character who entered in the middle. Children who can explain the difference between what they know and what the new character knows receive a high score for perspective-taking ability. In Chandler's studies, many juvenile delinquents and emotionally disturbed children generally scored lower than normal children did. When these delinquents and disturbed youngsters with poor perspective-taking skills were trained in perspective taking, their problem behaviors decreased in comparison with those of similar children who did not receive the training. (Chandler 1973; Chandler et al. 1974)

internal. Reinforcement and punishment are **external controls,** environmental events that help determine a child's behavior. **Internal controls** are influences within the child that guide behavior. For example, a child might resist the temptation to steal because of external controls, such as fear of being caught and displeasing his parents, or because of the internal controls called conscience, such as the desire to avoid feelings of anxiety and guilt. The development of internal controls is, of course, one of the goals of the socialization of moral behavior.

According to Aronfreed, children are likely to develop strong internal controls when parents *specify* exactly what behavior is being rewarded or punished and *explain* why the behavior is being rewarded or punished. The explanations—as long as they are not far beyond the child's ability to understand—help the child see cause and effect more accurately. Consequently, the child will be better able to control his or her own behavior in a similar situation in the future.

For example, a father is playing Monopoly with his 7-year-old son David and catches him taking money from the bank and putting it into his own pile. If the father quits the game, saying that he won't play with a cheater, he cannot be sure what lesson his son will learn. Does the boy really know what "cheating" is? Maybe he thought he just needed an edge because his father always beats him at this game.

A parent who wants his child to develop internal controls might stop the play and define the behavior that he disapproves of: "You can't just take money from the bank whenever you need it. The rules of the game say that the bank pays you only when you pass Go or get certain Chance or Community Chest cards. Taking money from the bank any other time is really cheating." The father could then punish David by interrupting the game, an activity that David was really enjoying: "I won't finish this game now, because I don't have any fun playing with someone who's cheating. But if you won't cheat again, I'll finish the game after dinner." He could also suggest that David try to imagine what the game would be like if everyone cheated. The fun of games consists of playing to win within the rules. If you cheat, a lot of the fun and challenge goes out of the game. With this kind of explanation, the father is enriching David's perspective-taking skills and helping him to control his own actions.

SELF-ESTEEM AND THE CRISIS OF INDUSTRY VERSUS INFERIORITY

When school-age children act in ways that contradict their newly developing moral values, they may not only feel guilt but undergo a lowering of self-esteem. It is during the school years that children begin to be able to think systematically

about what they themselves are like and to identify things about themselves that deserve esteem or criticism. Self-esteem (or lack of it) thus becomes an important part of the child's personality (Harter 1983).

Figure 10-16 Charlie Brown and Lucy represent two extremes in self-esteem.

Erik Erikson (1968) captures this concern of school-age children in his fourth stage of psychosocial development, the crisis of **industry versus inferiority.** Children of this age are ready and eager to take a greater part in the wider social world around them—in schools, peer groups, and the family. Sooner or later, they become dissatisfied and disgruntled unless they develop a sense of being able to make and do things competently. Children who find no area of family or school life to be competent in will develop a sense of inferiority. But children who find that they can accomplish things—real and potentially practical things—gain a sense of industry, an eagerness to move into the world of adulthood. According to Erikson, resolution of this crisis requires that children also recognize their areas of inferiority, realistically perceiving where their skills are poor. In that way, they can concentrate their industry on areas where they are competent and thus bring about a sense of accomplishment.

Feelings of being a worthwhile and significant person affect all aspects of children's behavior, as discussed in Chapter 8. When children believe they can achieve the goals they set for themselves, their belief can become a self-fulfilling prophecy. High self-esteem tends to bring success, which in turn reinforces self-esteem (Greenwald 1980).

Families and Self-Esteem

During middle childhood, the family has a powerful influence on the development of self-esteem. In a large study of the basis of self-esteem (Figure 10-17), Stanley Coopersmith (1967) studied 85 fifth- and sixth-grade boys. On the basis of special questionnaires, he ascertained which boys had high and which low self-esteem. He found that the parents of boys with high self-esteem consistently showed three interconnected ways of relating to their children:

1. They were extremely accepting of their children.
2. They nevertheless set clearly defined limits on the children's actions.

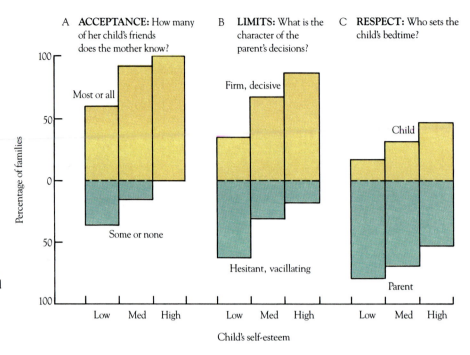

A **ACCEPTANCE:** How many of her child's friends does the mother know?

B **LIMITS:** What is the character of the parent's decisions?

C **RESPECT:** Who sets the child's bedtime?

Most or all

Some or none

Firm, decisive

Hesitant, vacillating

Child

Parent

Percentage of families

Low Med High   Low Med High   Low Med High

Child's self-esteem

Figure 10-17 Coopersmith's study of self-esteem revealed three factors in parent-child relations that had a major influence on a child's self-esteem. A mother who was very *accepting* of her child as a person was almost certain to know her child's friends. Although only a few mothers did not know their child's friends, many more of these mothers had children with low self-esteem. Parents who failed to define and enforce clear *limits* of acceptable behavior were more likely to have children with low self-esteem. Within the framework of the limits that they set, parents who permitted more individual expression were showing that they *respected* their children's judgment. For example, more parents who let their children set their own bedtime had children with high self-esteem.

3. They enforced those limits. Within the framework of the limits they set, these families permitted freer individual expression and more deviation from conventional behavior than families whose children were not as high in self-esteem.

Clear, realistic limits are helpful to children partly because they reduce uncertainty and lessen the chance of unintentional failure to meet parental standards. When standards are ambiguous, children are obviously less likely to know what is called for, and are therefore less able to evaluate their own behavior. Clear standards can contribute to children's sense of competence. Also, with clearly defined standards that are consistently enforced, children do not have to worry that their parents might change their minds unexpectedly. They need not be anxious about what *might* happen to them.

The parental style that Coopersmith found to be associated with high self-esteem closely resembles the style that Diana Baumrind (1967, 1971) calls **authoritative.** As explained in Chapter 8, parents who have an authoritative style tend to have competent and independent preschoolers. Authoritative parents firmly enforce rules and demand high levels of achievement, but they are also warm, rational, and receptive to their children's questions and comments. Also, these mothers and fathers have confidence in themselves as parents.

In Coopersmith's study, too, personal characteristics of the parents appeared to contribute to their children's level of self-esteem. The parents of children with high self-esteem were likely themselves to have high self-esteem. The mother's work history was also important: The higher the boy's self-esteem, the more likely it was that his mother was regularly—and happily—employed. (The

RESEARCH:

CHILDREN SPEAK FOR THEMSELVES

Developmental scientists are always describing what children think or how they feel. Educators, too, often answer broad questions about children's capabilities and progress. Even parents are asked to speak for their children. Finally, someone asked the kids themselves. The National Survey of Children, sponsored by the Foundation for Child Development, gave children a chance to speak for themselves (Foundation for Child Development 1976).

A representative sample of more than 2,200 American children between 7 and 11 years of age were interviewed about themselves and their lives—parents, school, friends, TV, the neighborhood, and much more. Overall, most of the children felt good about themselves; 90 percent said, "I like being the way I am."

About their families. 90 percent were happy about their families, but 80 percent said they worried about their families sometimes. In families that the mother described (in a separate survey) as "not too happy," every single child—100 percent—worried.

About half the children living with two parents said they felt afraid when their parents had arguments, and nearly half of the sample said they felt angry "when no one pays attention to you at home."

About the rules at home. Only about 3 percent of the children said they were allowed to "use curse words or swear words," and only 6 percent were allowed to stay up as late as they wanted. One out of four children said they were allowed to have snacks and eat whatever they wanted. One in six children said their parents seldom or never enforced family rules.

About TV. The power of TV was clear in the children's answers to the question, "Can you tell me the name of a famous person you want to be like?" The greatest percentage naming a particular group named TV entertainers (28 percent). Another 13 percent named sports figures, whom they had undoubtedly seen on TV. Not even 7 percent named a political figure, and fewer than 2 percent named an artist or scientist.

More than half the children reported that they were allowed to watch TV whenever they wanted, and more than a third said they could watch whatever programs they wanted. The survey linked TV to children's fears: Children who were heavy TV watchers (4 or more hours a day) were twice as likely as other children to report that they "get scared often."

About neighborhoods and fear. More than two-thirds of the youngsters said they felt afraid "that somebody bad might get into your house." And a quarter of them were afraid that someone would hurt them when they went outside. When asked "Who is the person you are most afraid of?" the children were much more likely to name a real person than an imaginary figure. About a third mentioned someone specific who had threatened or hurt them in the past—a neighborhood or school bully—and an additional 15 percent named someone in their own family. "My father" led the list of feared family members.

Most of the children's fears were not imaginary. Some children live in neighborhoods and communities where violence and crime abound. And the children's reports of actually having been threatened or hurt while playing outside tally with their fears: 40 percent said they had been bothered by older children while playing outside; and 13 percent said that they had been beaten up.

About school. When asked how they felt about going to school, more than three-quarters of the children said "I love it!" or "I like it." At the same time that they had these general positive feelings about school, the children had misgivings: Two-thirds said they worried about tests at school and felt ashamed when they made mistakes in class. Schoolwork seems to be a source of much anxiety, shame, and frustration for many American children.

One thing that made children unhappy with the school environment was a disorderly atmosphere. Nearly one out of three black children said they would rather go to another school, and the leading reason for wanting to transfer was the fighting and "fooling around" that occurred in their current school.

Figure 10-18 Children in the act of building self-esteem, confidence, and willingness to take risks. This is most easily shown in play, but risks of more subtle kinds—social and intellectual risks—can be just as intense and exciting and call for just as much daring.

working mothers of children with high self-esteem often said that they would continue working even if they did not have to.) The relation between the father's work history and the boy's self-esteem was not as clear. The prestige of the father's occupation did not correlate with self-esteem, nor was there a clear relation between the father's social class and the child's self-esteem, except that boys whose fathers were often unemployed tended to have low self-esteem.

When children develop feelings of inferiority instead of self-esteem, the process commonly begins with parents who treat their children in a rejecting, distant, or autocratic way. Parents who are overly permissive may actually be distant—indifferent except when trouble arises, at which point they may punish the child harshly for breaking rules that the parents never really established. The child, uncertain of how he or she is expected to behave and unable to predict what may happen in the future, feels stupid and powerless. Parents who are autocratic, who demand absolute compliance with their rules without allowing any discussion of limits and reasons for standards, indicate to their children that the children are not worthy of respect. The children come to feel unimportant and become overly passive and compliant.

According to the Coopersmith study, the development of a sense of inferiority or a sense of self-esteem has important effects on other behaviors and attitudes of the child.

Correlates of Self-Esteem

The way children actually perform—in school, with their peers, and in the family—affects their self-esteem and is affected by it. In the Coopersmith study, for example, boys with high self-esteem showed less conformity, more creativity, and better academic achievement.

Coopersmith had his subjects take part in a conformity experiment like those described earlier in the chapter. They judged the lengths of lines after a group of other children had all chosen the same incorrect line. Among the boys with high self-esteem, 63 percent stated their own correct judgment even though it did not conform to the group's judgments, but only 12 percent of those with low self-esteem did so. High self-esteem evidently contributes greatly to the ability to resist conformity.

On various tests of creativity, the children with high self-esteem consistently performed in a more innovative and original way than did children with low self-esteem. Also, they earned better grades in school and performed better on IQ tests.

The relation between self-esteem and these types of performance is by no means perfect, however. Parental style, for example, may affect a child's self-esteem in a way that has nothing to do with her own competence. An independent, creative, intelligent child whose parents make her feel that nothing she says or does is important can draw little self-esteem from her strengths.

Self-esteem lies at the core of the personality. How people feel about their own worth colors all their dealings with the world. Even when people with low self-esteem have success in school or work or personal relationships, they tend to thank their lucky stars instead of applauding their own efforts (Harter 1983; Wylie 1979).

Parents are not the only people in the child's world who can help her experience success and know that she is responsible for it. If her friends admire her for her sense of humor or her skill in drawing, she may begin to feel better about herself. If a teacher compliments her on her singing voice and dramatic talent and gives her a role in the school play, the child can experience a success that she can applaud herself for.

As the child moves into the challenges of adolescence, self-esteem becomes a more complex psychological matter. It is built upon the experiences of earlier years but goes beyond them. Children can experience feelings of self-worth or inferiority, but adolescents gain the power to examine such feelings in themselves. As described in the following chapter, adolescents become able to think about and evaluate their own thoughts and feelings.

SUMMARY

SOCIALIZATION AT SCHOOL

1. Most parents expect schools to teach social norms that support the parents' goals in socialization, but different families have different norms, and even when there seems to be some general public consensus, historical events can cause goals to change.

2. Different social norms are reflected in the organization of classrooms. In *traditional classrooms* chairs are arranged in rows facing the teacher, who leads all class activities in a closely scheduled curriculum. In **open classrooms** groups of children sit at small tables, each group engaged in a different activity, and the teacher moves from group to group. Traditional classrooms support the

norms of discipline and orderliness; open classrooms help foster social skills and support what is assumed to be children's natural desire to learn.

3. A teacher can be extremely important in influencing a child's self-concept and intellectual life. *Teacher's expectations* for an individual student can greatly affect the student's achievement. Expectations for high achievement have been shown to be a *self-fulfilling prophecy:* When experimenters randomly chose some children as "bloomers"—having high potential to learn—and revealed their names to their teachers, the "bloomers" showed a significant increase in IQ scores and academic achievement.

PEERS AND SOCIALIZATION

4. A child's friends—peers—help in the development of social skills, especially *perspective-taking.* Because they are at almost the same cognitive and social level, peers can easily understand each other's point of view and gain experience in social life. Children isolated from peers are slower to develop perspective-taking skills.

5. There is a *developmental trend in conformity* to peer influences, corresponding to a child's cognitive and social abilities. Because preschool children's egocentrism often does not allow them to understand what others expect of them, they rarely conform. By age 6 or 7, children have come to understand many norms; however, they view them in a concrete way, as fixed and unchangeable, so they are likely to conform. By age 11, because they can see that norms of behavior often vary from one situation to another, children become less likely to conform.

6. *Popularity*—being sought as a friend by numbers of children—is often studied through the use of *sociograms,* diagrams of friendship choices in a group. Once the sociogram has pinpointed the popular children, their personality traits are assessed. As one would expect, popular children are friendly, well adjusted, and often good-looking. Because they also seem to be brighter than their peers, it may be that they are able to take their friends' perspectives better than other children.

7. Children who are *leaders* in a group show many of the characteristics of popular children. In addition, they are more assertive, or aggressive, but they control their aggressiveness, using it in socially acceptable ways—to enforce fair play, for example.

8. There are marked cultural differences in socialization for *competition* and *cooperation.* In the United States, norms encourage competition; sometimes the norm is so powerful that children compete even when it is in their best interest to cooperate. In other cultures, such as rural Mexico, cooperation is

stressed, and children from such cultures may cooperate even when it is in their best interest to compete. Competition can best be turned to cooperation if the competing groups or individuals recognize **shared goals,** an important outcome that both sides value.

SOCIALIZATION IN THE FAMILY

9. Parents' characteristic ways of treating their children, called **parental styles,** are fairly consistent from the preschool years through the school years. They may change, of course, in response to the children's cognitive and social development.

10. Fathers' and mothers' roles differ with infants; mother-infant interactions often take place during physical caretaking, whereas father-infant interactions are less frequent but more playful. In later childhood, too, most fathers spend far less time with children than mothers do.

    a.   Fathers generally seem to be less nurturant and more restrictive than mothers.

    b.   Fathers' styles tend to affect their daughters in particular ways. Girls whose fathers participate in child-rearing and encourage independence tend to achieve more academically and in careers than girls whose fathers either had little to do with child-rearing or were overprotective.

    c.   For sons, fathers' behavior is a crucial determinant of delinquency; fathers of delinquents are often alternately punitive and neglectful. Also, a close father-son relationship helps produce high self-esteem in the son.

11. The effects on a child living in a **single-parent family,** which most often has a mother as the single parent, depends in large part on how the parent handles the situation.

    a.   Some studies have indicated that boys in mother-only families have some difficulty in achieving a clear masculine identity.

    b.   Girls' social development appears to be affected by the father's absence; daughters of divorcees are bolder and more flirtatious around men than girls in intact families, and daughters of widows are shyer and more inhibited.

CROSS PRESSURES: ADULTS VERSUS PEERS

12. How children perceive and react to cross pressures from adult and peer norms differs in different cultures. English and American children are much more inclined to go along with peer norms that conflict with adult ones than are children in Russia, where the peer group is socialized to support adult rules.

THEORY: *MORAL DEVELOPMENT*

13. Moral development, according to Lawrence Kohlberg, depends greatly on cognitive development. There are six stages of moral development, at three levels. The stages appear to be *universal,* appearing in the same order in all cultures studied.

   a. At the preconventional level, moral judgment is based solely on direct physical consequences and on the person's own needs. At this level are **Stage 1: *Punishment and obedience orientation*** and **Stage 2: *Marketplace orientation.*** These stages can appear during the preoperational period of cognitive development.

   b. At the conventional level, moral judgment is based on what other people approve and what pleases them. At this level are **Stage 3: *Goodboy/good-girl orientation*** and **Stage 4: *Law-and-order orientation.*** These stages can develop once concrete-operational intelligence has begun to develop.

   c. At the principled level, moral judgment is based on general moral principles that the person has formulated and that can apply to societies other than the person's own. The stages at this level are **Stage 5: *Contractual-legalistic orientation*** and **Stage 6: *Universal ethical-principle orientation.*** These stages can develop after formal-operational intelligence has developed.

14. Children can learn moral behavior through observational learning, through social interactions that promote perspective-taking, and through reinforcement or punishment of moral actions.

15. *Conscience,* or ***internal control*** of moral actions, is more likely to develop in children whose parents specify exactly what behavior is being rewarded or punished and explain why the reward or punishment is being administered. In contrast, ***external controls*** influence behavior through fear of being caught or of displeasing parents.

SELF-ESTEEM AND THE CRISIS OF INDUSTRY VERSUS INFERIORITY

16. School-age children undergo the psychosocial crisis of ***industry versus inferiority,*** according to Erik Erikson. They wish to be industrious—to accomplish practical things—and when they find success in some area, their self-esteem grows.

   a. Parents of children with high self-esteem were found to be extremely accepting of their children, to set clearly defined limits for their behavior, and to enforce those limits.

b. Parents whose children develop a sense of inferiority are likely to be rejecting, autocratic, or distant. Distant parents may actually be overly permissive.

c. Children with high self-esteem are likely to conform to others less than those with low self-esteem. They also tend to be more creative and to achieve better marks in school.

SUGGESTED READINGS

DAMON, WILLIAM. *Social and Personality Development: Infancy through Adolescence*. New York: W. W. Norton, 1983.

A comprehensive, up-to-date book portraying how development arises from both the effects of society on children and the needs of individual children to build their own unique identities.

HARTER, SUSAN. "Developmental Perspectives on the Self-System." In P. H. Mussen (Ed.), *Carmichael's Manual of Child Psychology*. New York: Wiley, 1983.

In this exciting analysis of research on the development of self, a well-known scholar provides a definitive portrait of factors influencing the development of self-esteem.

HARTUP, WILLARD. "Peer Relations." In P. H. Mussen (Ed.), *Carmichael's Manual of Child Psychology*. New York: Wiley, 1983.

A definitive review of how children relate to and influence each other throughout childhood.

KOHLBERG, LAWRENCE. *Essays on Moral Development*. New York: Harper & Row, 1981.

A collection of Kohlberg's most important papers presenting his theory of the development of moral judgment.

LAMB, MICHAEL (Ed.). *The Role of the Father in Child Development*, 2nd ed. New York: Wiley, 1981.

In this collection of articles on a neglected topic, the authors describe what is known about how fathers affect their children's development.

MINUCHIN, P. P., and EDNA K. SHAPIRO. "The School as a Context for Social Development." In P. H. Mussen (Ed.), *Handbook of Child Psychology*. New York: Wiley, 1983.

This article reviews the pervasive influence of the school on social development, including not only its effects on individual children, but also its role in the shaping of broader issues, such as desegregation and sex-role stereotyping.

REST, JAMES. "Morality." In P. H. Mussen (Ed.), *Handbook of Child Psychology.* New York: Wiley. 1983.

A balanced review of the research on cognitive-developmental approaches to moral judgment, especially Kohlberg's approach.

WALLERSTEIN, JUDITH S., and JOAN BERLIN KELLY. *Surviving the Breakup: How Children and Parents Cope with Divorce.*

This report on the California Children of Divorce Project presents the results of this major study in a readable style that makes them useful to lay people who deal with children.

Some societies signal the passage from childhood to adolescence with a ceremony that is dramatic and sometimes painful. Boys may be circumcised as part of the ceremony. Girls may be sent into isolation at their first menstruation and remain away from everyone for months. But when the ceremonies are done—when the boy has come through the painful rite and the girl returns from seclusion—the two are recognized by the community as adults. In these societies, there is no long transition from childhood to adulthood.

In contrast, most technologically advanced societies expect adolescence to intervene between childhood and adulthood. Because such societies are complex and often change rapidly, the period of adolescence allows young people time to prepare for finding a place in the swiftly moving stream of their culture and getting a firm foothold. The goal of this transition period is the formation of a personal identity—adolescents' knowledge of who they are in relation to the society around them. The physical developments that change child to adult begin the process of identity formation; the cognitive changes that accompany the physical changes make it possible (Chapter 11). And the social changes that loom ahead in the form of adult choices and responsibilities make it necessary (Chapter 12).

UNIT

5

ADOLESCENCE

11

BEGINNING

TO

THINK

ABSTRACTLY

CHAPTER OUTLINE

11

BEGINNING
TO
THINK
ABSTRACTLY

Unlike earlier developmental periods, adolescence has neither a clear beginning nor a definite end. The beginning of adolescence is usually said to be marked by *puberty* (the physical changes that result in reproductive maturity), but some young people's bodies don't start to develop sexually until they are well along in their teens. The end of adolescence is even more difficult to define, because no precise physical signs mark the passage to adulthood. In psychological terms, the end of adolescence can be distinguished in any of several ways. It can be said to occur, for example, when young people cease to be dependent on their parents—when they have launched a career or started a family of their own. Or it can be said to occur when young people have developed a clear sense of their own identity—when they can formulate their own answers to the question "Who am I, and what do I value?" In terms of the first definition, a 24-year-old graduate student who is still financially dependent on her parents would have to be called an adolescent. In terms of the second definition, however, the graduate student would probably be called an adult because she has a sense of who she is and what she values—at least she has committed herself to training for a particular career.

The authors of this text have chosen to treat adolescence as beginning at about age 12, because most young people in industrialized nations seem to begin a significant cognitive change at about this age and because many young people start puberty at about 12. The authors have chosen age 18 as the end of adolescence for three reasons. First, most of the physical growth of adolescence is complete by age 18. Second, young people are—for some purposes—legally defined as adults at 18 or 19. Third, and most important, significant social and psychological differences separate high-school students from high-school graduates. Most high-school graduates go directly into the job market and soon become independent of their parents, financially and psychologically, and most of those who go instead to college leave home and begin training for some kind of career.

PHYSICAL DEVELOPMENT

Physical growth during adolescence is more rapid than at any time except the 9 months of prenatal life and the first 2 years after birth. Unlike a 1-year-old, however, adolescents are conscious and often hypersensitive observers of their own physical growth. Girls may look frequently at their profiles in the mirror, checking on the ripening of their breasts. Boys may be equally attentive to the size of their genitals and the growth of body hair. And both worriedly compare their own development with that of their friends and schoolmates. By the time they are 18, boys and girls have just about reached the size and shape they will have as adults, although there are wide individual differences in the timing of the body's changes.

Figure 11-1 Adolescents are conscious and often hypersensitive observers of their own physical growth.

The Onset of Puberty

Puberty begins when a part of the brain called the hypothalamus, following genetic instructions, signals the pituitary gland to send out hormones. These pituitary hormones cause other glands (among them the thyroid, the adrenal gland, and the gonads) to produce hormones that stimulate growth of the body and development of adult sexual characteristics. Puberty ends when males and females are sexually mature, capable of begetting or bearing children. Many physical changes of adolescence, however, continue after puberty has ended (Petersen & Taylor 1980).

As in all human development, the onset of puberty results from the interaction of genetic and environmental factors. The timing of **menarche** (the onset of menstruation), for example, is only partly controlled by genes. Since 1850, the age at which menarche occurs has been declining in Western countries (Figure 11-2), and the reasons probably include better nutrition, particularly in

Figure 11-2 The age at menarche, the first menstruation, has been declining in several northern European countries for about a century. Recently, the decline has slowed down or stopped in some places (Tanner 1978). The size of the overall decline is controversial and may not be as large as the extreme points on the graph suggest. There is general agreement, however, that age at menarche has declined at least 2 years during the period shown in the graph. (Roche 1979)

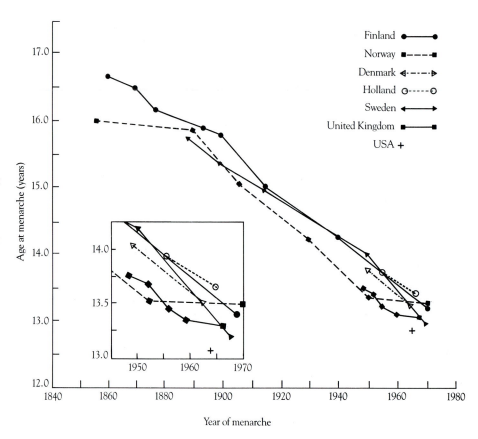

infancy, and fewer diseases because of widely used inoculations and medical care. Inoculations during infancy may themselves be partly responsible not only for the earlier onset of menstruation but for the increase in adult height of men and women during the last century. The physiological stress produced in infants by inoculations may permanently alter their hormone balance in a way that accelerates growth and brings on maturity earlier (Whiting 1965).

Evidence for the role of such environmental factors in the timing of menarche can be seen by comparing girls in technologically advanced societies with girls in other cultures (Tanner 1978). Recently, the average age at menarche seems to have leveled off in Western countries, and it now appears to be steady at 12.5 to 13.2 years. In New Guinea's isolated highlands, the average age at menarche is 18.8, whereas in Megiar, a more urban center on the coast, the average age is 15.6. Among the poorly nourished Bantu in South Africa it is 15.4, but among upper-class girls in Africa it is much lower: 13.4 in Kampala, capital of Uganda.

Genetic factors may also contribute to differences between groups. For example, upper-class Chinese girls in Hong Kong appear to experience menarche earlier than upper-class European girls living in comparable climates, even though both groups presumably get the best possible nourishment and medical care (Tanner 1972). The fact that the trend toward earlier menarche is currently leveling off in well-nourished, medically protected populations suggests that in these populations the environmental factors that have been lowering the age have had about as much impact as they can have on the hereditary possibilities. That is, the upper limit of the genetic reaction range may have been reached (see Chapter 2).

In both sexes, the physical changes of puberty follow a regular pattern, whether they begin at 11 or at 18. Over the course of about 2 years, there is a swift increase in body size, a change in body shape and in the relative amounts of muscle and fat, and rapid maturation of the reproductive system.

Growth of the Body

All adolescents experience a **growth spurt,** a period of a year or more during which they grow about twice as fast as they did throughout childhood. At the peak of this spurt, boys are growing an average of 3.5 inches a year, and girls an average of 3.0, as shown in Figure 11-3 (Tanner 1978). The age at which this growth spurt takes place varies greatly from individual to individual, even within the same community, and variations from what seems "normal" are often upsetting for boys and girls who mature considerably earlier or later than their friends.

Whatever the individual differences, girls have their growth spurt 2 years earlier, on the average, than boys do. For American girls, the average **peak-growth age** is 12; for boys, it is 14. Everyone is familiar with the contrast in appearance of girls and boys in seventh and eighth grades. Most girls by eighth grade have blossomed into young women, whereas most of their male classmates still look like children. Some adolescent girls almost complete their adolescent spurt before some boys the same age even begin theirs.

Changes in height during this period are accompanied by striking changes in body proportions. The parts of the body that reach adult size first are the head, hands, and feet. Increases in head size often go unnoticed, but the rapid growth of hands and feet can be dismaying to some adolescents, who may feel that their bodies are out of control and fear that the rest of their bodies will never catch up with their oversized hands and feet. In addition, the legs grow faster than the trunk, and adolescents stop growing out of their jeans (at least in length) a year before they stop growing out of their jackets.

There is also a spurt in muscle growth and a decline in development of fat. Boys actually lose fat, whereas the rate of fat accumulation in girls decreases but does not result in an absolute loss of fat, so that female adults naturally have a higher proportion of fat to muscle than males do. The increase in strength is especially striking in boys. Before adolescence, boys and girls of similar size and

Figure 11-3 The major
features of adolescent
physical change for girls
and boys. The curves
represent the average
growth in height from age
8 to age 18. The first
appearance of secondary
sexual characteristics is
shown by the average age
of occurrence. These
events may begin several
years earlier or later in an
individual's normal
development, but the
order of their occurrence
is usually as shown here.
The first menstruation, for
example, typically occurs
after a girl's growth has
begun to slow down.
Enlargement of a boy's
testes normally precedes
the growth spurt. (Tanner
& Whitehouse 1976;
Tanner 1978)

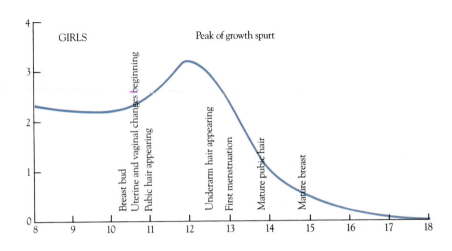

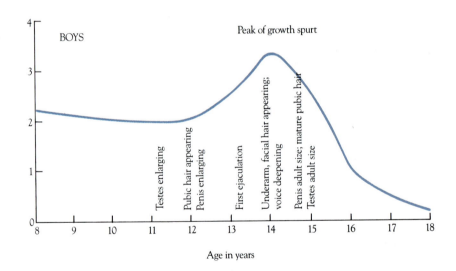

shape are also similar in strength. But at the end of the growth period, boys' muscles are both bigger and stronger than those of girls; that is, they can exert more force per ounce of muscle. Relative to their size, boys also develop larger hearts and lungs, greater capacity for carrying oxygen in the blood, a lower heart rate while at rest, and a greater capacity for neutralizing the chemical products of muscular exercise that produce a feeling of fatigue (Archer 1981).

These physiological differences help explain why males have traditionally been the likelier candidates for hunting, warring, and heavy labor. They also explain why, in a given sport, superior male athletes can usually outperform superior female athletes. However, it should be noted that in their chosen sport, superior female athletes can generally outperform the great majority of

Figure 11-4 (Top) These three girls are all 12 years old, but the rate at which they are maturing is obviously different. (Bottom) The two boys here are both 14 years old, but the boy in the USA tee shirt is a late maturer, whereas his friend is maturing relatively early. Besides the difference in their heights, the taller boy has most likely developed some sexual characteristics that are still to come in the shorter boy.

males. On the average, adult females show greater endurance and sounder health than males. They have a greater average ability to endure long-term stress, their bodies use energy more efficiently, they have greater resistance to disease, and they live much longer (Tavris & Offir 1983).

Before puberty, boys and girls have much the same shape. During adolescence, the differences in shape emerge that attract males and females to each other. As boys gain muscle and lose fat, their broader shoulders contrast with their narrow hips and small buttocks to produce the male form that females admire. Girls' hips grow broader and their breasts develop, resulting in the sexually attractive female form. As these changes in body size and shape are taking place, boys' and girls' reproductive systems and sexual organs are also maturing.

Sexual Maturation

The most rapid development of the reproductive system takes place at about the same time as the growth spurt (Tanner 1978). Figure 11-3 shows the average age of development of sexual characteristics for adolescents in the United States. Although the ages vary widely, the sequence of developmental events in sexual maturation is usually the same for everyone. The sequence in girls usually proceeds as shown in Figure 11-3A. Breast development and the appearance of pubic hair usually precede menarche, which, as noted earlier, occurs at about age 13 in industrialized nations; however, it can occur normally as early as age 10 or as late as 16. Menarche indicates that the uterus is mature. Even so, some girls may not be capable of becoming pregnant for a year or two after they begin to menstruate because their ovaries have not yet started to release eggs.

In boys, the first sign of puberty is most often an acceleration in growth of the testes and scrotum, followed shortly thereafter by the appearance of pubic hair. About a year after the testes start to grow, the penis starts to grow. Although 12.5 years is the average age at which penis growth begins, it starts normally in some boys as early as 10.5 years or as late as 14.5 years. Boys become capable of ejaculation about a year after penis growth starts, but the actual time of first ejaculation is to some extent culturally determined. (It may occur later in cultures where sexual expression is repressed.) Ejaculations in early puberty are unlikely to contain sperm, because active sperm are not usually produced until the testes have reached almost adult size. The changes in a boy's voice are completed fairly late in adolescence.

Psychological Reactions to Physical Change

Almost all adolescents are preoccupied with their physical development. The new cognitive abilities of adolescents, described in the next section of this chapter, help make them both conscious witnesses of changes in their own bodies and calculating comparers of themselves with others. How adolescents react to the changes in their own bodies depends in large part on what they have learned to expect (Petersen & Taylor 1980). For one reason or another, many parents do not discuss sexual maturation with their children before it begins to take place. A boy may be alarmed and perhaps ashamed by nocturnal emissions (ejaculations during sleep) if he has not been prepared for them. To a girl who knows little or nothing about menstruation, it can be a frightening and puzzling event:

> I didn't know about it. She (mother) never told me anything like that. I was scared. I just started washing all my underclothing hoping that my mother won't find out but she came and caught me, she caught me washing it, and she started laughing at me. I mean she told me it wasn't anything to worry about, it's something that happens, you know, but she didn't tell me what it meant and stuff like that. (Konopka 1976, p. 47)

For girls who are fortunate enough to be prepared by their mother or a teacher, the beginning of menstruation can be a prideful event:

> I had my first period at 12, knew about it before and wasn't scared. I thought I was feeling pretty good. Cause then I would know I was growing up to be a lady, you know. And I really had a nice feeling. (Konopka 1976, p. 48)

When an adolescent compares herself with her friends and sees that she is "behind schedule," she is likely to become anxious. Her friends or parents or doctor may reassure her that she will, without doubt, begin developing soon, but the difference between developing *now* and *soon* can be a vital one. If given three wishes, late developers would probably use one of them to get instant maturity.

For late-maturing boys the wait can be especially painful. Being shorter and weaker than their classmates, they may find themselves excluded from many activities and social rewards. For example, they can rarely play on school athletic teams, which are an important source of prestige in most American schools, and they may have difficulty getting dates with the fully developed young women in their classes. Differences in size and physical performance between early- and late-maturing boys are greatest between ages 14 and 16 (Clausen 1975), and early maturers have big advantages during this period as well. Their classmates view them as competent and tend to choose them as leaders, and their parents and teachers treat them more like adults.

This combination of factors may have a decided effect on the personalities of late-maturing boys. In one study, some late maturers showed immature atten-tion-seeking behaviors—the "class clown" phenomenon (Mussen & Jones 1957). Some had lower self-esteem, feeling that others rejected them. And some had defiant feelings toward their parents, who evidently still treated the boys according to their immature physical status.

Many of the boys in this study were retested when they were young adults (average age, 33) to see whether there had been any lasting personality effects of late or early maturing (Jones 1965). Physically, there was no longer much difference between the groups, but some personality differences remained. The men who had matured early in adolescence felt, much more strongly than the late maturers did, that they had leadership qualities and that others turned to them for advice and help. Personality tests showed them to be more responsible and self-controlled. In fact, the characteristics they had displayed as teenagers seemed to have stayed with them and to have matured.

The men who had been late-maturing teenagers appeared to be more adaptable and less compliant than the early maturers. They were more assertive and perceptive, but also touchier. Coping with the problems of being small and weak (even temporarily) in a world that values size and strength seemed to have given the late maturers some insights and flexibility that the early maturers lacked.

One study found differences between social classes in the effects of early and late maturing (Clausen 1975). Being tall and muscular at an early age had stronger social effects in working-class groups than it did in middle-class groups. Perhaps this was because strength is more central to a working-class life style, in which muscle is often needed on the job and aggression tends to be expressed in more overt and physical ways. The difference between classes was most evident in a boy's status within his peer group. Working-class adolescents had a greater admiration for early maturers than middle-class boys did and were much more likely to look to them for leadership. The working-class boys also showed greater disdain for smaller, weaker age mates.

The difference in age of physical maturation seems to have less psychological effect on girls than on boys. Well-developed girls in seventh through ninth grade seem to have a bit more prestige with their female classmates than less mature girls do, but in sixth grade the more mature girls have somewhat *less* prestige (Faust 1960).

How individual adolescents experience the swift changes in their bodies, how they feel about their bodies after comparing themselves with their peers, and how others react to their changing physiques all contribute to the beginnings of a self-definition (Higham 1980). The biological changes and the social responses to those changes give partial answers to the question "Who am I?" With the changes of puberty comes the sense that one is no longer a child and must therefore give up some childish ways of relating to the world. A 15-year-old girl, recalling what she felt right after she began menstruating, said, "I started thinking that I couldn't ride my bike and couldn't do things that made me feel like a baby" (Kagan 1972).

The Development of the Brain

The new thinking abilities that develop during adolescence help young people deal with the physical and social changes of puberty. The exact relation between the timing of these new abilities and the timing of puberty has been unclear (Ljung 1965; Tanner 1970). Several studies suggest, however, that cognitive abilities in adolescents undergo two rapid changes, one at the very start of puberty, at 10 to 12 years, and another at the end of puberty, at 14 to 16 years (Biggs & Collis 1982; Kenny 1983; Tomlinson-Keasey 1982).

Adolescents also seem to show spurts in brain development that correspond with these changes in cognitive abilities. Typically at about 10 to 12 years and 14 to 16 years, their brains develop at an unusually high rate, and their brain waves show dramatic spurts at the same ages (Epstein 1980; Rabinowicz 1978). These findings, like those concerning the beginning of earlier cognitive-developmental levels, show that a brain-growth spurt may correspond with the development of each new level of thinking.

Most studies of cognitive development in adolescence, including those of Piaget, imply that some change in brain organization takes place during this time and that this change makes possible the beginnings of abstract thought (Tanner 1972; Tomlinson-Keasey et al. 1978, 1982). Scientists do not yet understand the nature of the brain change, but the nature of the cognitive changes in adolescence is well documented.

COGNITIVE DEVELOPMENT: FORMAL OPERATIONS

The period of formal operations is the fourth and last cognitive-developmental period studied and described by Piaget. Development from concrete-operational thought to formal-operational thought usually begins at 10 to 12 years of age and continues throughout adolescence (Inhelder & Piaget 1958; Martarano 1977).

Operations, as Chapter 9 explains, are reversible mental actions or representations—that is, reversible thinking processes. Concrete operations are reversible mental actions applied to real properties of things. Using concrete operations, children can think logically about real things in the immediate physical world. **Formal operations** are reversible mental actions applied to hypothetical properties of things. (The term "formal" refers to the ability to think about the form of statements and ideas instead of just about the concrete reality represented by the words.) With formal operations, adolescents can think logically about hypothetical things.

The difference between concrete operations and formal operations is illus-

RESEARCH:
BRAIN SPURTS AND
PIAGETIAN PERIODS

A central question in the study of human development is the relation between cognitive and physical development. Most developmentalists believe that there ought to be some relation between the two, especially between changes in the brain and periods or levels of cognitive development. However, both scientists and journalists have been too quick to move from interesting findings on brain development to unjustified claims about cognitive development.

Research on the relation between spurts in brain development and Piagetian periods illustrates both the potentials and the pitfalls of studying the connection between physical and cognitive development. Herman Epstein, a biologist, proposed a simple hypothesis: Whenever children enter one of Piaget's periods, their brains show unusually rapid growth, much more rapid than when they are within a period. Although direct measures of brain growth are scarce, several longitudinal studies have collected data on growth of the head,

especially its circumference, which is closely related to brain size. Analyses of these data supported Epstein's hypothesis. Children seemed to show spurts in head growth at the approximate ages for the beginnings of the concrete-operational period, the formal-operational period, and the second level of formal operations (Epstein 1974). There were inconsistencies in some of these data and problems with Epstein's interpretations (McQueen 1982), but in general his predictions seemed to hold.

Epstein (1980) also used another measure of brain growth to test the hypothesis. The brain normally emits electrical waves, which are measured by the electroencephalograph (EEG), and these waves are affected by cognitive activities such as thinking and problem solving. Some of the waves also show systematic development with age, and Epstein tested whether the development of these waves demonstrated spurts at the same ages as head-growth spurts. In data from several studies of brain-wave development, spurts did occur at approximately the same ages. Also, the inconsistencies that arose with the head-growth data seemed to be absent from the brain-wave results.

Unfortunately, these findings quickly led Epstein and others to make unwarranted claims about cognitive

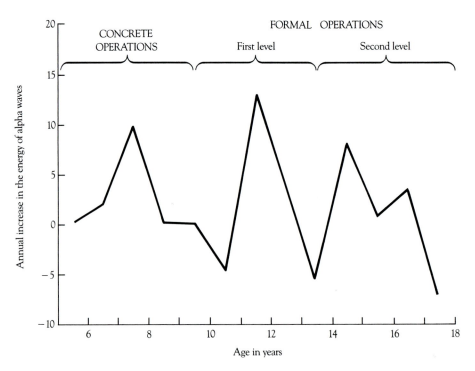

development and education. Based almost entirely on brain-growth curves like that in the graph on the facing page, they began to make prescriptions about how children should be educated. One of the most publicized statements was that children are incapable of learning new skills at the ages of little or no brain growth, such as 12 to 14 years (Epstein 1978; Toepfer 1979). At this time, it was claimed, they can only consolidate skills they have already learned, and so schools should make no effort to teach new skills in seventh and eighth grades. Such prescriptions were not based on studies of children's actual ability to learn new skills at these ages. Instead, they involved enormous assumptions based on the findings about brain growth.

A few investigators have begun to test Epstein's hypothesis more thoroughly. One study searched for a plateau or decline in skill learning between sixth and eighth grade and found instead continued growth in skills (Petersen & Kavrell 1983). Another investigation examined how spurts in head circumference related to spurts in performance on an intelligence test by individual children studied for many years (McCall et al. 1983). Again the hypothesis was not supported: There was no correlation between the cognitive changes

and the spurts in head growth. A third study tested whether individual children actually do grow in spurts and how any such spurts relate to the children's developmental levels (Lampl & Emde 1983). Every child in the study did grow in spurts—not only for head circumference but for other types of physical growth as well, such as height and weight. For the individual children, however, spurts in head circumference showed no clear relation to change in developmental level.

What conclusion can be drawn about the relation between brain growth and Piagetian periods? In investigations of large groups of subjects, some broad characteristics of the brain do change in spurts during the ages when new periods are beginning. Also, individual children do seem to grow in spurts, and some of the spurts coincide with the start of a Piagetian period. Spurts in head growth for individual children, however, do not appear to coincide with spurts in their cognitive development. Clearly, conclusions about how schools should educate children are not warranted from these findings. They suggest that there is only a broad, nonspecific relation between brain development and Piagetian periods. They do not support the argument that children cannot learn new skills during times when their brains are growing slowly.

trated by a task used in studies of logical thinking (Cummins 1978; Osherson & Markman 1975). The experimenter and the subject (either a child or an adolescent) sat at a table on which there were a number of poker chips of various colors. The experimenter explained that she was going to make certain statements about the chips, and the subject was to indicate whether each statement was true, false, or impossible to judge. The experimenter then concealed a colored chip in her hand and said, "Either the chip in my hand is green, *or* it is not green" or "This chip is green, *and* it is not green." Sometimes she held up a chip so the subject could see it, and she made exactly the same statements.

Preadolescent subjects replied only in terms of what they actually saw instead of in terms of the logic of the experimenter's statement. When the chip was visible, the children judged both statements to be true if the chip was green and to be false if the chip was red or blue. When the chip was concealed, they said that they could not tell whether the experimenter's statement was true or false. The children were unable to reason about the logic of the experimenter's statements independently of what they saw.

Adolescents and adults, on the other hand, focused on the statements. They knew that to judge the truth or falsity of the experimenter's statements, no concrete evidence was necessary. They could make their judgments on the basis of purely logical relations among hypothetical statements: That the chip was either green or not green had to be true; that it was both green and not green had to be false.

This study confirms one of the major findings by Piaget and his collaborator Barbel Inhelder about the difference between concrete operations and formal operations. When adolescents have developed formal operations, they can think about the *possible* as well as about the concrete and actual (Inhelder & Piaget 1958). Presented with a problem, children try to solve it with the concrete materials at hand, generally by trial and error. Adolescents can imagine a number of possible realities. That is, adolescents can formulate *hypotheses* about solving a problem and then mentally consider the possible results of their hypotheses. Furthermore, when they test for the truth or falsity of a hypothesis, adolescents are able to consider systematically *all possible combinations* of relevant factors.

The classic experiment used to demonstrate the appearance of this new ability is the *combination-of-liquids problem* (Inhelder & Piaget 1958). A child or adolescent is presented with four beakers of clear, odorless liquid, labeled 1, 2, 3, and 4, and a smaller bottle, also containing a clear and odorless liquid, labeled g. The experimenter first demonstrates that adding a few drops of g to some combination of the other liquids will turn the mixture yellow. The subject is then asked to find the correct combination and also to state what effect each liquid has on the reaction that produces yellow (Figure 11-5).

Many children in the period of concrete operations mix g with each of the four numbered liquids and then give up, saying "I tried them all." Prompted by the experimenter to go on and try combinations of the numbered liquids plus g, they may continue attempting to solve the problem, but their efforts are haphazard. Even if they happen to come upon a combination that does turn yellow, they cannot explain why. That is, they cannot explain the function of the various liquids in the combination.

Adolescents at the period of formal operations attack the problem systematically. They know that they must try all possible combinations, treating each combination as a hypothesis. Consequently, they usually plan before they begin pouring, and many ask the experimenter for pencil and paper in order to map out their approach and keep track of their results.

Usually they start by trying g with each of the four numbered liquids. Then they try all possible combinations of 1 plus one other liquid with g: $1 + 2 + g$, $1 + 3 + g$, $1 + 4 + g$, and so forth. When they have done the systematic testing, they can usually explain the effect of each liquid. Numbers 1 and 3 together with g produce yellow. Number 4 prevents the color from forming because $1 + 3 + g$ turns yellow, whereas $1 + 3 + 4 + g$ does not. Number 2 has no effect because both $1 + 3 + g$ and $1 + 2 + 3 + g$ turn yellow, whereas $1 + 2 + g$ does not.

It is true that without formal operations, children can form and consider some kinds of hypotheses. Even preschool children do so when they wonder "What if a bear got into the house?" School-age children do so when they think, "What if my mother found out what I'm doing now?" Children who have developed conservation abilities can form the hypothesis that the amount of clay does not change when a ball of clay is rolled into a sausage shape. But they can check their hypothesis only by comparing it with concrete reality—that is, by rolling the sausage back into a ball. Even children with concrete operations cannot judge the logic of a hypothesis, nor can they compare several hypotheses to see whether they are logically consistent with each other. According to Piaget, the ability to think logically about hypotheses appears only with the use of formal operations.

Piaget's studies of the development of formal-operational thinking dealt almost entirely with hypothetical thinking about scientific problems. But many neo-Piagetians have argued that the abilities developed during this period are broader than these particular formal operations. Starting at 10 or 11 years, children develop the capacity to **think abstractly** about anything—to understand the intangible concepts that link groups of concrete concepts. And this capacity does not emerge full-blown at 10 to 12 years of age but develops through at least two cognitive levels, one at 10 to 12 years, and another at 14 to 16 years (Arlin 1975; Biggs & Collis 1982; Kenny 1983; Tomlinson-Keasey 1982).

Single Abstractions

The general ability to think abstractly first appears with the development at age 10 to 12 of the first level of formal operations, single abstractions. In building a

Figure 11-5 Attempts by an 11-year-old and a 13-year-old to solve the combination-of-liquids problem. Barbel Inhelder and Jean Piaget (1958) developed this task in order to present subjects with a problem that could be solved only by systematically experimenting with combinations. The 11-year-old here, after trying to produce a yellow color by adding *g* to single liquids, immediately tries putting all the liquids together. He continues experimenting, but unsystematically. Even help from the experimenter does not get him to the right conclusion. The 13-year-old proceeds much more systematically, even trying all the remaining two-liquid combinations after he has found the correct one, just to see if another will work.

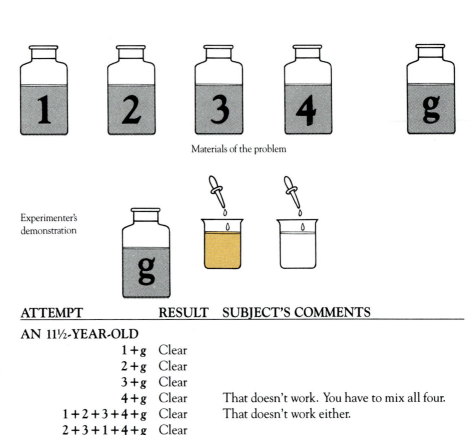

Materials of the problem

Experimenter's demonstration

ATTEMPT	RESULT	SUBJECT'S COMMENTS
AN 11½-YEAR-OLD		
1 + g	Clear	
2 + g	Clear	
3 + g	Clear	
4 + g	Clear	That doesn't work. You have to mix all four.
1 + 2 + 3 + 4 + g	Clear	That doesn't work either.
2 + 3 + 1 + 4 + g	Clear	
4 + 2 + 3 + 1 + g	Clear	
3 + 4 + 1 + 2 + g	Clear	
1 + 4 + g	Clear	
2 + 3 + g	Clear	
3 + 4 + g	Clear	
2 + 1 + g	Clear	I wonder if there isn't water in all of them!
3 + 4 + 1 + g	Clear	
2 + 3 + 4 + g	Clear	
1 + 4 + 2 + g	Clear	
3 + 1 + 2 + g	YELLOW	That's it.

(Experimenter) *What do you have to do for the color?*

Put in **2**.

(Experimenter) *All three are necessary?*

One at a time it doesn't work. It seems to me that with two it doesn't work; a liquid is missing.

(Experimenter) *Are you sure that you have tried everything with two?*

Not sure.

ATTEMPT	RESULT	SUBJECT'S COMMENTS
2 + 1 + g	Clear	
3 + 1 + g	YELLOW	It works! It's **1** and **3**!
		(Experimenter) *Tell me what effect the bottles have.*
		1 is a colorant, **2** prevents the color; no it doesn't prevent it because it worked. **3** takes away the effect of **2**, and **4** doesn't do anything.

A 13-YEAR-OLD

		You have to try with all the bottles. I'll begin with the one at the end.
1 + g	Clear	
2 + g	Clear	
3 + g	Clear	
4 + g	Clear	It doesn't work any more. Maybe you have to mix them.
1 + 2 + g	Clear	
1 + 3 + g	YELLOW	It turned yellow. But are there other solutions? I'll try.
1 + 4 + g	Clear	
2 + 3 + g	Clear	
2 + 4 + g	Clear	
3 + 4 + g	Clear	It doesn't work. It only works with…
1 + 3 + g	YELLOW	
		(Experimenter) *Yes, and what about **2** and **4**?*
		2 and **4** don't make any color together. They are negative. Perhaps you could add **4** in **1 + 3 + g** to see if it would cancel out the color.
1 + 3 + 4 + g	Clear	Liquid **4** cancels it all. You'd have to see if **2** has the same influence.
1 + 3 + 2 + g	YELLOW	No, so **2** and **4** are not alike, for **4** acts on **1 + 3** and **2** does not.
		(Experimenter) *What is there in **2** and **4**?*
		In **4** certainly water. No, the opposite, in **2** certainly water since it doesn't act on the liquids; that makes things clearer.
		(Experimenter) *And if I were to tell you that **4** is water?*
		If this liquid **4** is water, when you put it with **1 + 3** it wouldn't completely prevent the yellow from forming. It isn't water; it's something harmful.

single abstraction, a person grasps an intangible characteristic of a broad category of objects, events, or people—courage, law, justice, or the concept of a variable in algebra, for example. Able to think abstractly, adolescents are no longer bound to particular, concrete objects and their tangible characteristics. They can rise to new intellectual heights using concepts that unite many concrete things by means of a single general idea. Their new ability shows itself in the ways they think about politics, about their relationships with other people, and about themselves.

Schools begin to teach certain simple abstractions in late grade school and junior high. In math classes, for example, students begin to learn the concept of a variable: In an equation, x stands for anything—an unknown number. With concrete operations, children can learn the value of x only in one or a few specific problems, such as $x + 4 = 7$ and $x + 2 = 5$. They treat x as if it means "fill in the blank," but they have no general concept of what x means. To understand that x stands for a variable or an unknown, the adolescent must start by relating two instances of x that have been demonstrated, say $x - 5 = 10$ and $4 + x = 7$. Then she must extend the meaning of x to other demonstrated instances, such as $100/x = 4$ and $5x = 35$. By comparing the use of x in a growing number of instances, she can begin to use it herself to stand for any number in an equation. Unlike the younger child, she can go beyond solving a few concrete problems that contain an x because she has a general concept of a variable or an unknown number.

In developing a single abstraction, a person begins with at least two concrete instances that embody the abstract concept and compares them (Biggs & Collis 1982). From the comparison she begins to extract the concept. This development is shown by the way in which the understanding of particular types of conservation (such as conservation of liquid and conservation of number) leads to the general abstraction of conservation of quantity. For example, a concrete understanding of conservation of liquid requires a child to coordinate the height of the water in a container with the width of the container to form the idea that the total amount of water does not change, as described in Chapter 9. But this concrete scheme by itself does not require a child to understand the general concept of conservation. The child knows merely that the amount of water stays the same in this one type of task.

To form the abstract idea of conservation, the adolescent combines her understandings of two or more specific kinds of conservation, such as conservation of amount of liquid and conservation of substance when a clay ball is flattened and reshaped. Comparing these two specific conservations allows her to abstract a general concept of conservation: Even though two or more attributes of a substance vary, some quantity that combines those attributes is conserved, or remains the same (Figure 11-6). Indeed, a person may even overgeneralize this concept, inferring conservation when there is none (Fischer et al. 1983; Pinard 1981). The volume of gas such as air, for example, does

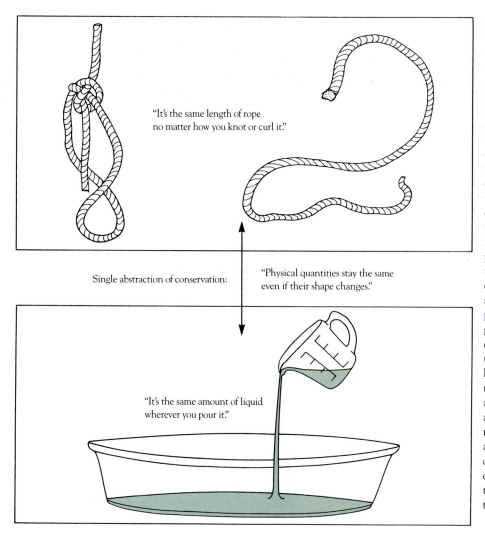

"It's the same length of rope no matter how you knot or curl it."

Single abstraction of conservation:

"Physical quantities stay the same even if their shape changes."

"It's the same amount of liquid wherever you pour it."

Figure 11-6 With concrete-operational intelligence, a child can relate the length and shape of a rope before and after it is knotted and can tell you that knotting affects shape but not length. The same child can relate the height and width of water in one container to its height and width in another and so can tell you that pouring the water does not change its amount. She can probably tell you similar things about conservation of pieces of clay. What she cannot tell you is that physical substances, in general, conserve quantity during such transformations. This knowledge requires making an abstraction about conservation, an ability that develops, as a rule, in adolescence. This ability is no longer tied directly to physical observations; it is built on the connections between the several observations.

not stay the same when the gas is transferred to a new container of a different size.

The ability to combine a number of concrete instances, holding them all in mind at once, is what allows the adolescent to construct abstractions. This process is further illustrated by the way children and adolescents solve verbal analogies like those in Figure 11-7. To solve such analogies, a person must first understand the connection between the pair of items in the first set of terms ("bell" and "bicycle") and then consider the possible connections between the items in the second set of terms (between "wheel," "engine," "toot," "four," or "horn" and "car"). To complete the analogy, the person must compare the connection of "bell" and "bicycle" with the connection of the correct item to

Figure 11-7 Verbal analogies used in a study of the reasoning powers that emerge with adolescence (Lunzer 1965). Problems like these commonly appear on intelligence tests. Almost all adolescents 13 and older could solve the analogies in A ("horn," "kennel," "soldier"), but 9-year-olds couldn't manage any better than guesswork. The 9-year-olds were able to solve analogies like the ones in B because they can go down the list and pick the word that "goes best with" the cue words "hard" or "see." Such a strategy does not work with the analogies in A because only one word, "four," can be rejected as not "going best" with "car"; "wheel," "engine," and "toot" could all do as well.

A.	BELL	is to	BICYCLE	as:	B.	BLACK	is to	WHITE	as:
	WHEEL							STEEL	
	ENGINE							STONE	
	TOOT	is to	CAR.			HARD	is to	SOLID	
	FOUR							SOFT	
	HORN							BLUE	
	LION	is to	LAIR	as:		KNIFE	is to	CUT	as:
			RABBIT					FORK	
	DOG	is to	KENNEL					EYE	is to	SEE.
			FOX					EAR	
			SET					SHARP	
	SHEEP	is to	FLOCK	as:					
	HERD								
	PACK	is to	REGIMENT.						
	SOLDIER								
	SWARM								

Answers: (A) horn; kennel; soldier. (B) soft; eye.

"car." By considering one pair and then the other, adolescents can abstract what it is that both pairs share: The first item in both sets is attached to the second item in order to sound a warning. Thus, coordination of the connection between "bell" and "bicycle" with the connection between "horn" and "car" produces a single abstraction. Most younger children are unable to complete such analogies. They can solve only analogies like those in Figure 11-7B. These problems can be solved simply by picking the item that "goes best" with the given word; there is no need to coordinate the two pairs (Lunzer 1965).

The newly developed abstract thinking abilities of adolescence are applied not only to academic matters such as algebra and verbal analogies. Adolescents spend a lot of time thinking about themselves and their relationships with other people and their society. Their new cognitive abilities allow them to organize these thoughts in dynamic new ways.

Thinking about Politics

Joseph Adelson's findings on the development of political thinking illustrate the difference between the concrete intelligence of children and the abstract abilities of adolescents. Adelson and his colleagues interviewed more than 450 11- to 18-year-olds from several Western nations and from all social classes (Adelson 1975; Gallatin 1980). Their aim was to discover *how* young people think about ideology and political structures, not *what* they think about political parties and specific issues. To avoid the problems that could be caused by asking questions about specific political matters, the interviewers devised a series of questions about a hypothetical new society to be established by a thousand people on an uninhabited island in the Pacific Ocean. The questions were designed to reveal ways of thinking about law, government, and politics. They ranged from very specific ("Should the government require citizens over 45 to have annual medical examinations?") to very general ("What is the purpose of laws?").

Before age 12 or 13, most youngsters showed little grasp of such abstract ideas as authority, individual rights, and democracy, or even of the concept of a society. Compare the typical answers of these four boys to the question, "What is the purpose of laws?" (Adelson et al. 1969).

An 11-year-old: Well, so everybody won't fight and they have certain laws so they won't go around breaking windows and stuff and getting away with it.

A 13-year-old: To keep the people from doing things they're not supposed to like killing people and . . . if you're in the city, like speeding in a car and things like that.

A 15-year-old: To help keep us safe and free.

An 18-year-old: Well, the main purpose would be just to set up a standard of behavior for people, for society living together so they can live peacefully and in harmony with one another.

The two younger children, especially the 11-year-old, answered the question with concrete instances. The 11-year-old cited "laws" that he has probably had experience with—rules that he has heard invoked at home or at school to prevent fighting or to keep windows from being broken. The 13-year-old makes a fuzzy attempt at generality—"to keep people from doing things they're not supposed to"—but mainly mentions specific laws against killing and speeding. The older adolescents did not rely on concrete examples in their answers. Both referred to general concepts abstracted from concrete instances. From the many separate laws that the older adolescents knew about, they distilled an essential purpose that could be stated in abstract terms—in terms of "the law," not one law or a few laws.

The development of an understanding of political and legal processes can also be seen in the answers of children and adolescents to a series of questions about the assassination of civil rights leader Martin Luther King, Jr. Shortly after the assassination, the young people were asked such questions as "When the killer is found, how do you think he should be treated? Why do you think Dr. King was shot? What do you think made the person who shot Dr. King do it?" The answers given by 9- and 10-year-olds were concrete and personalized (Table 11-1). Most children, for example, recommended a specific punishment for the killer (the electric chair, for example), and many attributed a personal motive to the killer: "He hated King," they said, or "The killer had a friend or

TABLE 11-1 REACTIONS TO THE ASSASSINATION OF
MARTIN LUTHER KING, JR.

QUESTION	RESPONSE	AGE 9–12	12–15	15–18
How should the killer be treated?	Punishment	68%	56%	26%
	Fair trial	14	28	63
Why do you think Dr. King was shot?	Personal reason	30	26	5
	Cause, conspiracy	40	31	59
What made the person do it?	Personal motive	32	36	0
	Hate, prejudice	32	18	35

SOURCE: Siegel 1977.

relative killed in race riots." Most 16- and 17-year-olds, on the other hand, suggested that the killer receive a fair trial and viewed the event in terms of political ideology. Typical statements were "He was shot because he was a symbol of his race" or "He was killed because he tried to do something for the Negroes."

The results in Table 11-1 reveal a clear contrast between the concrete thinking of children and the ability of adolescents to use abstractions. As the author of this study states, "A specific punishment or a personal motive are concrete representations of institutions and events, while the idea of justice through a trial or a political ideology are abstractions. Both the development of the understanding of law and the increasing depersonalization of events and motives represent the growth of the child's ability to form abstractions about the political process" (Siegel 1977, p. 285).

The cognitive development evidenced in how adolescents think about politics, compared to how children think, is also seen in how adolescents perceive other people and how they think about themselves.

Understanding Other People

To study how people think about other people—a topic that is sometimes called *person perception*—researchers usually ask individuals to describe someone they know. Such studies have been extensive, and they clearly show that adolescence works a major change in how people view others. As children develop into adolescents, the focus of their descriptions shifts from physical characteristics and concrete psychological qualities to abstract personality characteristics and social relationships. Here are two descriptions by children 7 and 10 years old of people they know (Livesley & Bromley 1973).

7-year-old: She is very nice because she gives my friends and me toffee. She lives by the main road. She has fair hair and she wears glasses. She is 47 years old. She has an anniversary today. She has been married since she was 21 years old. She sometimes gives us flowers. She has a very nice garden and house. We only go in the weekend and have a talk with her.

10-year-old: He smells very much and is very nasty. He has no sense of humor and is very dull. He is always fighting and he is cruel. He does silly things and is very stupid. He has brown hair and cruel eyes. He is sulky and 11 years old and has lots of sisters. I think he is the most horrible boy in the class. He has a croaky voice and always chews his pencil and picks his teeth and I think he is disgusting.

Personal qualities are almost totally absent from the younger child's description. The only personal characteristic noted by the 7-year-old was that the woman was "nice," and her niceness consisted of giving candy to the child. The description also lacks an organizing theme. The 10-year-old used many personal characteristics in her description—"nasty," "silly," "sulky"—and some qualifying words—"very," "always." But the information is still strung together with almost no organization except for the general theme that the child does not like the boy she is describing. Appearance, details of behavior, and mannerisms are all jumbled together and are given equal emphasis. As they do in these two descriptions, children frequently divide people into two simple classes—those they like and those they dislike (Harter 1982).

Descriptions by adolescents 14 or 15 years old show the difference a capacity for abstract thought makes (Livesley & Bromley 1973).

Andy is very modest. He is even shyer than I am when near strangers and yet is very talkative with people he knows and likes. He always seems good-tempered and I have never seen him in a bad temper. He tends to degrade other people's achievements, and yet never praises his own. He does not seem to voice his opinions to anyone. He easily gets nervous.

She is very quiet and only talks when she knows a person very well. She is clever in one sense, and she comes out top of her class. She is very reserved, but once you get to know her, she is exactly the opposite. It is very unusual to see her not attending to the lessons. At some time or other all our minds wander, but hers never seems to do so. One of the things I admire in her is she is very tidy.

The qualities attributed to the people in these descriptions are abstract personality traits, drawn from both the describer's own experience and the described person's behavior in different social circumstances—for example, "He is even shyer than I am when near strangers and yet very talkative with people he knows and likes." When the girl in the second passage is described as "clever in one sense," the implication is that there are other ways to be clever, which this girl lacks. Perhaps she has no sense of humor or is not creative. Behind the statement that Andy "tends to degrade other people's achievements, and yet never praises his own" lies the assumption that most people who degrade other people's achievements are trying to make their own seem more important. Adolescents frequently point out such apparent contradictions in people's behavior; they recognize the complexities in people's personalities (Hand 1981; Harter 1982).

As these examples show, adolescents no longer rely on concrete characteristics and events as their only sources of ideas about people. They can organize and combine information to produce a fairly mature description of another person, including analysis of social relationships and his or her mental life—thoughts, desires, motives, and fears.

Understanding Oneself

Children's thinking about themselves undergoes the same sort of development as their thinking about other people (Harter 1983; Rosenberg 1979). In adolescence, self-descriptions shift dramatically toward abstract personality characteristics and social relationships. This change plays an influential part in the efforts of adolescents to build a sense of their own identity—who they are, what is important to them, and where they are going.

This development in self-definition is apparent in the following autobiographical descriptions. In the study that produced these statements, subjects were asked to write twenty answers to the question "Who am I?" (Montemayor & Eisen 1977).

> *A 9-year-old:* My name is Bruce C. I have brown hair. I have brown eyebrows. I'am nine years old. I love! Sports. I have seven people in my family. I have *great!* eye site. I have lots! of friends. I live on 1923 P. Dr. I'am a boy. I have a uncle that is almost 7 feet tall. My school is P. My teacher is Mrs. V. I play Hockey! I'am almost the smartest boy in the class. I *love!* food. I love fresh air. I *love* school.

> *An 11-year-old:* My name is A. I'm a human being. I'm a girl. I'm a truthful person. I'm (not) pretty. I do so-so in my studies. I'm a very good cellist. I'm a very good pianist. I'm a little bit tall for my age. I like several boys. I like several girls. I'm old-fashioned. I play tennis. I am a *very* good swimmer. I try to be helpful. I'm always ready to be friends with anybody. Mostly I'm good, but I lose my temper. I'm not well-liked by some girls and boys. I love sports and music. I don't know if I'm liked by boys or not.

> *A 17-year-old:* I am a human being. I am a girl. I am an individual. I don't know who I am. I am a Pisces. I am a moody person. I am an indecisive person. I am an ambitious person. I am a very curious person. I am a confused person. I am not an individual. I am a loner. I am an American (God help me). I am a Democrat. I am a liberal person. I am a radical. I am a conservative. I am a pseudo-liberal. I am an atheist. I am not a classifiable person (i.e.—I don't want to be).

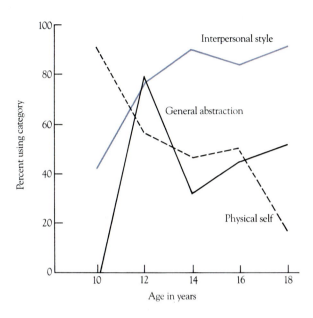

Figure 11-8 Percentage of subjects using certain categories in their answers to the question, "Who am I?" (Montemayor & Eisen 1977)

The 9-year-old described himself in concrete terms—his physical characteristics, family activities, school performances, and particular things he likes. He made no references to abstract personality characteristics or to interpersonal dealings. In contrast, the 11-year-old described herself as truthful, helpful, old-fashioned, and good, and she expressed concern about her social relationships with other girls and boys. Notice also that she placed herself into a broad abstract category—human beings. In this study, very general abstract categories like human being, person, and "speck in the universe" were almost never used by 9- and 10-year-olds but jumped to 80 percent of the answers given by 11- and 12-year-olds. After 12, use of these broad abstract categories dropped off to about 40 percent, as adolescents began to use narrower, more particular abstract categories and to depict interpersonal or psychological styles (shy, calm) or patterns of belief (conservative, pacifist).

The 11-year-old's self-description sounds more like that of the 17-year-old than like that of the 9-year-old, but the older adolescent's self-description more clearly shows the abstract and integrative powers of the adolescent mind. Adolescents can think about their own thoughts in a way not possible for younger children. They can take their own mental constructions as objects to reason about: They can think about thinking (Elkind 1974). The 17-year-old has apparently examined her thoughts about wanting to do well in school and wanting to be recognized as an important person in some line of work, so she has come to the conclusion that she is "ambitious." She has taken account of certain contradictory aspects of her personality and judged herself "confused." She has also examined her thoughts in terms of how well they match the labels

Jessica 9

Edward Hopper

Figure 11-9   This contrast between a 9-year-old's drawing of herself and Edward Hopper's self-portrait, painted at age 17, dramatizes the difference between self-perceptions of children and the self-perceptions of older adolescents and young adults.

"liberal," "radical," and "conservative," and has concluded that these popular descriptions of political beliefs do not fit her very well.

Abstract Relations

Between 14 and 16 years of age, adolescents develop the second level of the formal-operational period, a more sophisticated form of abstract thinking involving *abstract relations*—the ability to coordinate two or more abstractions (Biggs & Collis 1982; Fischer et al. 1983; Jaques et al. 1978; Kenny 1983). They can therefore understand how variations in one abstraction predict or correspond with variations in another. An older adolescent may be able, for example, to understand how to coordinate the abstraction of conformity with the abstraction of individualism.

One of the first areas to which the adolescent is likely to apply these concepts is her own behavior. A girl may see herself as a conformist at school, where she wears the same kinds of clothes as everyone else and generally expresses the same kinds of opinions about her work. But she may see herself as an individualist socially, because she has unconventional friends and wears her own distinctive clothes in their company. By constructing abstract relations, she can coordinate these two abstractions with each other, and one result is that she sees herself as a different kind of person in these two situations—even a contradictory person. This ability is what the 17-year-old girl demonstrated when she purposely described herself in contradictory terms.

The ability to coordinate two abstractions in a relation, which first develops at age 14 to 16 at the earliest, produces an enormous surge in the capacity of adolescents for using abstractions skillfully. When they could handle only a single abstraction, they could not compare even two abstractions, so their new cognitive power tended to be confused and confusing. If they tried to use two abstractions at the same time, such as liberal and individualist, they mixed them up. In the words of one adolescent, it was "like being in a fog." Once they have the ability to relate and compare two abstractions, the fog begins to lift.

Understanding the Social Context of People's Actions

Most personality concepts are abstractions, and so are most social concepts, such as society, politics, and social class. School-age children have great difficulty thinking about society at all (Furth 1980). Young adolescents can think about society in a general way but have difficulty analyzing how it affects human behavior. When they begin to construct abstract relations, older adolescents gain the ability to relate personality concepts to social concepts, and they can then begin to think about people as social creatures whose behavior takes place within a web of social circumstances (Broughton 1978; Kitchener 1983; Rest 1980).

Studies of the understanding of social class vividly demonstrate the emergence of the ability to relate social concepts to personality (Leahy 1983; Naimark & Shaver 1984). When children between 5 and 10 years old were asked to describe rich and poor people and to indicate how they are similar or different, they offered concrete descriptions that were based on appearance and possessions and that recognized few similarities. Fourteen-year-olds placed much less emphasis on appearance but still described the differences between the rich and poor in terms of their possessions, their behavior, and their use of money. (For example, "The poor waste their money, whereas the rich save or invest theirs.") Not until age 17 did adolescents take account of social context in comparing the two economic classes. Their operating definitions of rich and poor reflected their thinking about how social structure affects people (some people are poor because they are old) and how it is affected by people (the rich have political power).

Understanding people's characteristics and actions in this way within the larger social framework becomes possible only in later adolescence, at the second level of formal operations, when the individual can relate abstractions to each other. In his study of the development of political concepts, Joseph Adelson (1972, 1975) asked a question that nicely reveals the development of the ability to relate actions to a social context: "Most people who go to jail and are released seem to end up there again. Why?" Typical answers by grade-school children showed little appreciation for the complexity of the human motives: "Well, they don't know anything, and you have to teach them a lesson" or "Well, it is in his mind to do it and keep doing it over again." The responses of the adolescents 15 and older show a much better appreciation of this complexity. The fact of going to jail itself, they said, "produces a grudge against others," makes people "become bitter or feel mocked," and affects people's definitions of themselves—people in jail "establish themselves as being a criminal."

Another question asked by Adelson in his survey about the hypothetical island society illustrates the point even more strikingly because the question concerned his interviewees personally: "Some people suggested a law which would require children to go to school until they were 16 years old. What would be the purpose of such a law?" (Adelson & O'Neil 1966). Only 10 percent of children less than 15 years old offered society-oriented explanations, whereas most older adolescents could envision long-term effects on the community from lack of education. Many adolescents 15 and older stressed the impact of education on the community's future: "So children will grow up to be leaders" and "To educate people so they can carry on the government."

Adolescents analyze their own motives too, asking themselves things like "Am I helping this person for *her* sake, or just to impress other people? Am I going to college because I chose to or just because my family expected me to go? Did I refuse to join tomorrow's demonstration because I really disagree with that method of protest or because I'm scared I might get into trouble?" Before adolescence, such introspection is not possible, and not until the late teens or early twenties are most people very good at it (Kitchener 1983).

Across a wide range, then, adolescent thinking moves from the personal and concrete toward the general and abstract. One of these advances, the new ability to deal with the social context of individual behavior, brings with it a major change in moral reasoning.

MORAL DEVELOPMENT

The most comprehensive theory of moral development is the one proposed by Lawrence Kohlberg (presented at length in the theory inset "A Cognitive-Developmental Approach to Moral Judgment," in Chapter 10). The theory describes six stages of moral development (Table 11-2). The first three stages seem to accompany the preoperational and concrete-operational cognitive-developmental levels of the preschool and school years, whereas stages 4 through 6 develop in adolescence and adulthood.

In most of his earlier published works, Kohlberg asserted that Stage 4 moral judgment, showing a law-and-order orientation, could develop before adoles-

TABLE 11-2 KOHLBERG'S STAGES OF MORAL DEVELOPMENT

STAGE	ORIENTATION	BASIS OF MORAL JUDGMENT
1	Punishment and Obedience	Physical consequences of an action or what authorities say
2	Marketplace	What satisfies the person's own needs
3	Good-boy/Good-girl	How closely an action conforms to standards held by family and friends
4	Law and Order	Laws and the rules of one's own society
5	Contractual-Legalistic	Agreements, or contracts, among people, which may differ in different societies or change with time
6	Universal Ethical Principle	Abstract principles of justice, formulated by the individual and applicable to all societies, that call for equality of human rights and respect for the dignity of all

cence, during the concrete-operational period of cognitive development. But research since then by Kohlberg and others has forced a change in this position. It now seems clear that because preadolescents are unable to understand such abstract concepts as law and society (Adelson 1972, 1975), they are limited to moral Stage 3. That is, they consider what their family, teachers, and friends think is right and wrong, but they cannot take a broad institutional view of morality (Broughton 1978; Kitchener 1983; Rest 1979).

Kohlberg's own data suggest that Stage 3 reasoning begins in childhood and that Stage 4 reasoning does not develop until early adolescence (Colby et al. 1983; Kohlberg 1969). (In Figure 10-13, note that 10-year-olds show little Stage 4 reasoning while 13-year-olds show much more.) When Kohlberg's complex and troublesome methods of assessment are replaced with simpler ones, it becomes clear that Stage 4 begins to develop right on the heels of the capacity for abstract thinking (Edwards 1982; Lee 1971; Rest 1976). As they grow into adolescence and their Stage 4 moral reasoning emerges, young people can begin to refer to society's moral standards in deciding what is right and wrong. In society's terms, what is right is doing one's duty, showing respect for authority, and maintaining the social order for its own sake. Violation of the law or disruption of the social order is, by definition, evil.

Like all abilities, Stage 4 moral reasoning does not develop overnight. Young adolescents (12-, 13-, and some 14-year-olds), for example, already have an overall **authoritarian bias.** (Authoritarians believe that people should *always* respect and obey those in power.) The bias develops in childhood in relation to parents, teachers, police officers, and the like, and the young adolescent transfers it to her views about government, law, and politics. It drops off sharply in middle and late adolescence. When the answers given to Adelson's (1972) interview questions were judged on a scale of authoritarianism, 85 percent of young adolescents scored high on authoritarianism, but only 17 percent of high-school seniors scored high.

Young adolescents may use Stage 4 judgments to justify authoritarianism, but as they develop more sophisticated abstractions about law, society, and the effects of society on human behavior, they tend to go beyond authoritarianism. Their understanding of the role of law in maintaining social order becomes more flexible. For instance, when they are told that a certain law is not working out as expected, they may suggest changing the law; most young adolescents only propose that the law be enforced more vigorously.

As the moral abstractions of adolescents become more and more complex, their moral judgments may develop past Stage 4 to stages 5 and 6. Judgments at these stages go beyond the perspective of one's own society to a more relativistic type of thinking that takes in a wide range of societies. To reach these higher stages, a person must come to understand that values and institutions, including laws, change according to place and situation. Different countries and even different states or provinces within the same country have different laws. Laws change with the times, and courts may interpret laws differently according to the circumstances. The ability to appreciate the relativity of such cultural "absolutes" as the law rarely develops until after high school (Kitchener & King 1981; Perry 1970).

Whether an individual actually reaches the more sophisticated forms of moral judgment of stages 5 and 6 depends largely on the breadth of the person's experience in social perspective-taking. The cognitive advances of adolescence make it possible to take other people's perspectives on complex moral matters. But if the adolescent encounters only people who have the same point of view as his own—or who are at the same moral stage—his moral judgment is not likely to advance (Turiel 1969). During high school and afterward, the social world of most young people does expand substantially. As they begin to enter the world of adults, they usually meet people from very different backgrounds, and in their schoolwork or reading they come across a diversity of human perspectives. The more experience with perspective-taking that young people have, the more likely it is that their moral thinking will advance (Rest 1981; Selman 1980).

All normal adolescents develop the capacity for abstract thought, which allows them to have new perspectives on morality, society, religion, politics, other people, themselves—anything they put their minds to. Just what they actually do put their minds to is determined in large part by the circumstances of their environment.

Figure 11-10 Uniformity of environment and social relations, whether it is imposed or accidental, reduces an adolescent's opportunity to encounter stimuli that lead to cognitive development. During the "Cultural Revolution" in China, many adolescents were members of the Red Guards, groups whose aim was not only to eliminate active dissent but to punish people whose attitudes were "incorrect." The guard members all held the same beliefs and were united in their zeal, which often led to violence. Interviewed a decade later, when they were adults and the Cultural Revolution was long past, many members regretted the violence and could excuse their behavior only by saying that the group's unanimity kept them from questioning their acts.

COGNITIVE DEVELOPMENT AND THE ENVIRONMENT

At the same time that their abstract thinking abilities are developing, adolescents are acquiring knowledge. In school they learn about literature, political science, history, biology. From television and newspapers they learn about current happenings in government, technology, sports. In their ever-widening social sphere they learn about different attitudes, beliefs, and ways of interacting with others. The quantitative growth of knowledge is particularly significant at this point because it gives adolescents "food for thought," pieces of information that can be used to construct abstract concepts.

Before children have the capacity to organize and apply information systematically, acquiring it cannot have the same effect. Adelson (1972) found, for example, that many children have acquired a good deal of data about politics. They know the names of the major parties and officeholders, and a little about elections. But they cannot give order and meaning to the bits and pieces. Just as children in the early preschool years can count from 1 to 10 without grasping the principle that these numbers represent an ordered series, so young adolescents seem to acquire random pieces of political information without being able to give them coherent meaning.

The kinds of information that adolescents acquire depends on their environ-ment, especially their family environment. Among the young adolescents Adelson surveyed, those who knew the most about politics and were most deeply involved in political talk and thinking came from politically active families. The interest of these adolescents in politics was based not only on the political information they had acquired but also on the emotional currents in the family—a kind of striving for family unity (Adelson 1972; Maccoby & Martin 1983). In the same way, adolescents from families who play musical instruments, go to concerts, and listen to records are likely to know more about music than others and to participate more than others in the making of music (Shuter 1968).

As abstract thinking capacities increase, adolescents can select pieces of information from memory and compare them systematically with each other and with new pieces of information. If a new piece is inconsistent with a piece already learned, this spark can set off reasoning processes that lead to a reorga-nization of ideas, as in the following example:

> *Established proposition:* Parents are omnipotent and omniscient.
>
> *New information:* My parent has just lost a job (misunderstood me, behaved irrationally, or any other such failing).
>
> *New proposition:* If my parents were omniscient, they would not be tainted with failure and vulnerability.

Most adolescents eventually settle this inconsistency by denying the truth of the first proposition (Kagan 1972).

Here is a reorganization of ideas that many adolescents struggle with:

> *Established proposition:* God loves people.
>
> *New information:* The world contains many unhappy people.
>
> *New proposition:* If God loved people, God would not make so many people unhappy.

The first proposition is one that the adolescent probably has held for a long time and that serves as the basis for a whole set of beliefs. He can resolve the contradiction posed by the new information in a number of ways—for example, by supposing that God has some unknown purpose in making people unhappy, or by denying the existence of God, or by asserting the existence of some evil force in the world. The accumulation of knowledge can therefore advance an adolescent's cognitive development by turning up contradictions that can be resolved only by abstract thinking.

Originally, Piaget and many Piagetians assumed that formal-operational abilities developed in a unified way rather than unevenly (Broughton 1981; Piaget 1957). They believed that if adolescents could not demonstrate formal-operational thinking in science class, for example, then they were incapable of

Figure 11-11 Adolescents who devote a great deal of time and effort to the visual arts are likely to develop the ability to use abstract and logical skills in the fine arts, but they probably will not be able to think abstractly about cars and the functioning of internal combustion engines. The opposite holds true for adolescents who devote thought and effort to machines.

any formal-operational thinking. Much evidence indicates that adolescents and young adults show the same unevenness in formal-operational tasks that appears in other abstract tasks. That is, they are able to perform some formal-operational tasks but not others (Kenny 1983; Martarano 1977).

This unevenness appears to be partly the result of environmental factors. For example, an adolescent who is interested in cars and who has learned the functions of all parts of the engine, transmission, and chassis may first display abstract thought in dealing with car troubles. When a car won't start or is running poorly, he may be able to use his abstract and logical abilities to systematically consider all possible sources of the problem and to test out which is the correct one. The same adolescent might or might not be able to demonstrate abstract thought in a chemistry laboratory or an English class. An adolescent who reads a great deal of poetry and poetry criticism and who writes poems will be able to use abstract thought in analyzing poetry but may or may not be able to think abstractly about chemistry or the internal-combustion engine.

Unevenness in the development of abstract schemes continues in adulthood. Adults as well as adolescents apparently develop their abstract abilities to a high degree in some areas but develop them only minimally or not at all in other areas. In his later writings, Piaget (1972) himself has suggested that formal-operational thought is likely to appear first in areas where adolescents and adults have a special interest or aptitude.

Cultural Differences in Abstract Thought

Many cross-cultural studies have seemed to show that people in nontechnological cultures do not develop formal-operational thought—or, in some cases, even concrete-operational thought (Dasen 1977; Inhelder et al. 1974). Unevenness in the development of abstract thought explains the puzzling result.

Figure 11-12 (A) The chart shown here represents the Puluwat navigator's abstract system for navigation. (The Puluwatans themselves do not draw such charts, as they have no written language.) Combining knowledge of star positions relative to the position of his canoe, the knowledge of positions of other islands in the area relative to the position of his own island, and the knowledge of the canoe's speed relative to prevailing wind and wave conditions, the navigator can set and follow a course. (B) Training of future Puluwatan navigators through pebble maps of the stars and surrounding islands. (C) A Puluwatan navigator at work.

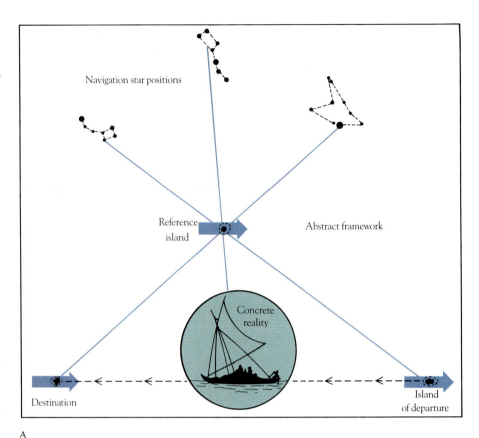

Navigation star positions

Reference island

Abstract framework

Concrete reality

Destination

Island of departure

A

B

C

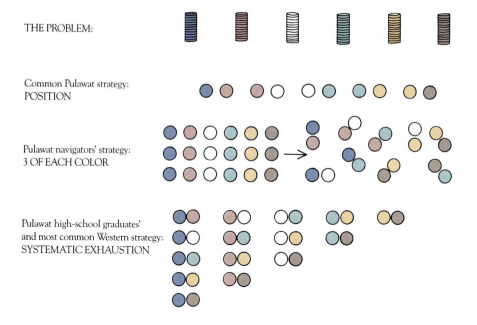

THE PROBLEM:

Common Pulawat strategy:
POSITION

Pulawat navigators' strategy:
3 OF EACH COLOR

Pulawat high-school graduates'
and most common Western strategy:
SYSTEMATIC EXHAUSTION

Figure 11-13 The task is to make as many nonmatching pairs as possible from the six stacks of colored chips. The "best" strategy for solution, shown at the bottom, is to make all possible pairs with one color, then move on to the next color, omitting any pairs that duplicate those from the first sorting, and so on. Most adolescents and adults from the Western world use that strategy, but the only Puluwatans to do so were the two who had completed high school on a nearby island (and who were not navigators). The Puluwatan navigators used a strategy that was more sophisticated than that of other Puluwatans, but it was not adequate to solve this Western type of logical problem.

Because most of the experiments asked non-Western people to do Western-type scientific problems (often using materials that were unfamiliar to them), it is likely that cultural differences, not absolute differences in cognitive level, were responsible for many of the negative results (Cole et al. 1971; Greenfield 1976; Super 1980). People in non-Western societies may, in fact, develop abstract reasoning in areas that are not tested by Western tasks. Some anthropologists' detailed accounts of everyday life in various cultures support this argument. Thomas Gladwin (1970), for example, describes how the people on Puluwat, a small island in the South Pacific, build their boats and navigate them to other islands, sometimes hundreds of miles distant. Gladwin sailed with the men of Puluwat and learned their navigational system, which is based on the movements of the stars, ocean currents, wind direction and velocity, geography, and presence of specific forms of ocean life. Gladwin found that "abstract thinking is . . . a pervasive characteristic of Puluwat navigation."

The navigational system is taught first by formal instruction. The islanders use no written langauge, so masses of factual information must be committed to memory. For instructional purposes, the master navigators use pebbles to construct star maps and maps of island locations. Puluwat navigators who looked at Gladwin's printed star charts quickly recognized their meaning and pointed out and named stars on them (see Figure 11-12).

Although Puluwat navigators undoubtedly use abstract thought, they do not perform well on standard Piagetian tasks designed to test formal operations. In one instance, for example, Gladwin had a number of Puluwatans do the colored-tokens combination task shown in Figure 11-13, in which stacks of chips of six different colors are to be arranged in as many nonmatching color pairs as possible. The "good" strategy used by Westerners was used by only two Puluwat men—the only two from the island who had gone through the Western-type high school on the nearby island of Truk.

THE LIMITATIONS OF ADOLESCENT THOUGHT

Some of the limitations of adolescents' thinking result from limited experience, but more fundamental limitations result from the fact that cognitive development is not completed at the onset of adolescence. Cognitive development continues during adolescence and early adulthood (Biggs & Collis 1982; Case 1980); in fact, people do not seem to reach their highest capacity for abstract reasoning until approximately age 25 (Broughton 1978; Fischer et al. 1983; Kitchener & King 1981). Young adolescents are limited to the first level of formal operations: single abstractions. They cannot relate one abstraction to another. Even when older adolescents develop the next level, abstract relations, they cannot master the complex interrelations of many abstractions.

In his studies of adolescent political thinking, Adelson (1972) noted that even though older adolescents often used sophisticated abstract concepts such as conservatism, law, society, and justice to answer questions about politics, few of them showed any ability to relate many of these concepts to each other. Only one adolescent of the 450 surveyed, an 18-year-old, had developed a scheme for governing society, a fully elaborated political philosophy that prescribed who should hold power, how leaders should be selected and trained, how they should exercise power over the rest of society, and how members of the society should behave and interact. Constructing such a coherent ideology requires the ability to understand a system of abstractions, an ability very few adolescents have (Richards & Commons 1983). For example, few high-school students can comprehend such systems of abstractions as evolutionary theory or the theory of musical composition. These systems can usually be understood only in adulthood.

The inability of adolescents to form relations between multiple abstractions makes it hard for them to distinguish between what they themselves think and what they think other people are thinking. This limitation expresses itself in a kind of **adolescent egocentrism** (Elkind 1978), somewhat like the egocentrism of preschool children, who assume that everyone sees things from the same perspective that they do. These egocentric cognitive distortions of adolescents do, in fact, have much in common with the unsystematic, unrealistic ways in which preschool children use representations—but there is an important difference. Egocentrism pervades all of the preschooler's thinking, whereas it is evident in adolescents mostly when they are trying to think abstractly.

One consequence of adolescents' egocentrism is that they spend a good deal of their time playing to an imaginary audience, in the belief that everyone pays as much notice to them as they pay to themselves. For example, because adolescents focus so much on the physical changes they are experiencing and on their appearance generally, a teenage boy may walk into a roomful of busy strangers and think that everyone is aware that he is wearing dental braces, or has some acne, or is wearing jeans that look "too new." Along the same lines,

FUNKY WINKERBEAN

when young people are feeling critical of themselves, they believe that their audience (which is, after all, their own cognitive construction) is judging them with equal severity. And when they are full of self-admiration, they believe that their audience is likewise impressed.

Egocentrism sometimes shows up in adolescents' thinking about their future roles in society (Harter 1983; Inhelder & Piaget 1958). If the adult role they imagine for themselves seems incompatible with what the society appears to permit, they often think about transforming the society rather than modifying their own imagined role. That is, they have trouble distinguishing their own needs as individuals planning a life program from the complex and varied needs of the society at large.

This same sort of thinking seems to account for at least some **adolescent idealism.** That is, adolescents often think that what they believe to be good and right for themselves is also good and right for society in general. With the overly simple abstractions of early adolescence, they have difficulty separating society from themselves, and so they project themselves onto society (Kitchener 1983; Perry 1970). Their apparent idealism can thus actually stem from an unrealistic egocentric moralism. In Adelson's studies of adolescent political thinking, there was a decline in such idealism as adolescence progressed. It was not that the adolescents became more cynical; instead, they became more realistic and pragmatic.

A large sample of adolescents surveyed in Detroit was asked what might be done if a city council was unresponsive to the concerns of the average person

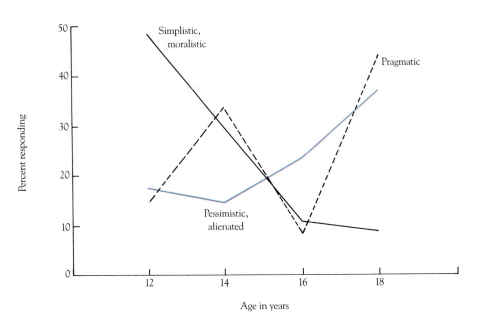

Figure 11-14 Asked what might be done if a city council was unresponsive to the concerns of the average citizen, children and adolescents responded in one of three ways: simplistically, pessimistically, or pragmatically. With age, the proportion of pragmatic and pessimistic answers increased greatly, while the number of simplistic answers decreased. (Gallatin 1972, 1980)

(Gallatin 1972, 1980). The adolescents' answers fell into three groups: simplistic or moralistic ones, pessimistic ones, or pragmatic suggestions. Figure 11-14 shows the major types of response by age. The most simplistic or moralistic answers expressed either indignation or a primitive notion of action: "That's not fair" or "Talk to them real nice." The pessimistic answers expressed despair: "There is nothing you can do." The pragmatic answers suggested mounting a campaign to elect different people to the council or forming a collective-action group to confront the council. Note that the percentage of pragmatic responses increased the most with age, although the number of pessimistic answers also increased. Adelson (1975) suggests that during adolescence young people often develop from a naive moralism toward a more complex and more realistic set of attitudes. He argues that mature idealism may be possible only in late adolescence or adulthood, when cognitive mastery and self-confidence combine to give moral impulses a rational structure.

Two processes contribute to the waning of adolescent egocentrism. One is the growing cognitive sophistication of adolescents, and the other is their widening sphere of social interactions. Discussions between adolescent friends are very important in pricking the bubbles of adolescent egocentrism (Youniss 1982). One adolescent tests his concepts of, say, world betterment on a friend, the friend finds fault with them, and the adolescent goes back to his cognitive drawing board, refashioning his thought in ways that bring it closer to reality. Of course, it is the adolescent's capacity to think abstractly that allows him to restructure his concepts in this way.

Despite the limitations of early abstract thought, abstraction is the beginning of cognitive adulthood. It affects every aspect of adolescent behavior—even language, which to all appearances was mastered years ago.

LANGUAGE DEVELOPMENT

The capacity for abstraction affects language at many different levels. It influences the way language is spoken, the way concepts are used, the understanding of the structure of language, the way language is written, and the purposes for which language is used.

Pragmatics: Speech in Social Contexts

Pragmatics is the study of how speech is used in social contexts. Scientists who study pragmatics are less interested in the formal characteristics of a statement, such as its grammar, than in its social purposes. As explained in Chapter 7, young children must learn how to use speech socially, and how good they are at it depends on the level of their cognitive development. When trying to get someone to give them something, children, as they mature, pass from the declarations and commands of the preschooler ("Give me a cookie") to more polite forms ("May I have a cookie, please") to elaborately camouflaged requests ("Boy, a cookie would sure taste good now") (Bates 1976).

The new cognitive abilities of adolescents allow them to use spoken language for more complex social purposes. They are able to gain the information they want without even asking a direct question (for example, when they pump a mutual friend to find out whether a certain person of the opposite sex finds them attractive). They can use pointed sarcasm and irony. They can use subtle means of persuasion. One of the best-documented cases of this developmental change is the use of a ritualized word game called "sounding" or "playing the dozens" (Labov 1972). This game, which seems to be played exclusively by male ghetto youths, calls for clever, biting insults to be exchanged in front of a group, according to specific rules. The purpose of the game is for each boy to show off his verbal skills and his mental quickness. Everyone recognizes that the insults are not to be taken as true statements about the boys or their families.

To begin, one boy throws out a challenging insult to a second boy, who must reply with an insult of his own. The insults move back and forth between the two boys, with each trying to top the other while the rest of the group listens and evaluates the insults, applauding the clever ones and scorning those that are contrived or weak. When one of the two boys cannot come up with a good enough reply, the other is considered the winner. By custom, the insults contain as many obscene words and ugly images as possible. The topic of the insults is usually the antagonist's mother. One reason for their heavily sexual content is undoubtedly the sexual changes that are occurring as a result of puberty. The same sort of exchange is common in Turkey among adolescent boys (Gumperz & Hymes 1972). There, too, obscenity is required, particularly references to a boy's availability as a passive homosexual partner.

A common traditional form of the game requires that the insults be in rhymed couplets, as in the following sanitized example:

> Iron is iron and steel don't rust,
> But your momma's built like a Greyhound bus.

In recent times in the United States, rhymed insults have given way to a freer form in which the insults are loosely organized around a single topic or follow a particular construction. Here is an exchange of the latter kind, using the construction "Your mother is so . . . that she . . . ." It was recorded at a gathering of a gang called the Cobras (Labov 1972):

> Your mother so old she got spider webs under her arms.
> Your mother so skinny she could split through a needle's eye.
> Your mother so skinny she do the hula hoop in a Applejack.
> Your mother so low she can play Chinese handball on the curb.

This verbal ritual has a well-defined structure, and it requires a good sense of pragmatics, that is, a good sense of what the speaker intends by his remark and of how to use language for social effect. For example, if someone throws out an insult, the first thing the listener must do is decide whether it is intended as a challenge to a sounding match or as a genuine personal insult. If a sounding match develops, he must maintain the general form and content of the initial insult and take account of the perspectives of his opponent and his audience.

Words and Concepts

Adolescents' widening range of pragmatics is only one of the reasons they can perform so cleverly in sounding matches. They also are more sophisticated in their understanding of words and the abstract concepts behind them. Younger children, who lack abstract abilities, are not good at sounding. They can neither understand the rules of the discourse nor invent the required clever word plays. Here is an exchange between two children of elementary-school age:

> Your mother got funky drawers.
> Your father got funky drawers.

Children simply do not have the cognitive abilities that sounding requires.

Figure 11-15 *Mad* magazine has a very strong and enthusiastic following among adolescents but is read by few younger children. The *Mad* features shown here help explain why adolescents enjoy the magazine while their younger brothers and sisters don't. Both features are satires; they use language in an ironic way in order to poke fun at some aspect of modern life. Double-meaning, exaggerations, mimicry, parody are used to point out absurdities and contradictions in people and events. Appreciation of satire requires a sophistication in the use of language that younger children do not have.

This developmental difference has a major effect on the general comprehension of language. For example, it affects the way children and adolescents understand words that they have not heard before. Researchers have studied this effect by giving children and adolescents a series of sentences containing a nonsense word and asking them to discover its meaning (Werner & Kaplan 1952):

All the children will LIDBER at Mary's party.

The police did not allow the people to LIDBER on the street.

The people LIDBERED about the speaker when he finished his talk.

People LIDBER quickly when there is an accident.

The more flowers you LIDBER, the more you will have.

Jimmy LIDBERED stamps for all countries.

In this task, grade-school children used a number of primitive reasoning processes, which resulted in incorrect answers. For example, some children picked a word merely because it sounded like the nonsense word: One child said that "lidber" sounded like "leave," so that must be the word. Children also confused the meaning of the nonsense word with the meaning of the entire sentence. One child responded to the sentence "People talk about the BORDICKS of others and don't like to talk about their own" with "People talk about other people and don't talk about themselves, that's what BORDICK means." This same child interpreted another sentence in the series, "People with BORDICKS are often unhappy," as meaning "People that talk about other people are unhappy because, say, this lady hears someone talking about her and then she'll get mad." Adolescents rarely made these kinds of errors. They were able to compare the use of the word in each sentence and come up with a meaning that suited them all ("gather," in the example given above).

In one study a researcher asked grade-school children, adolescents, and adults whether they knew what nouns, verbs, adjectives, and prepositions were (Anglin 1970). Parts of speech are taught in most schools beginning in second grade, so most of the subjects, including third- and fourth-graders, said they knew and gave correct definitions of several of the categories. But when everyone was asked to sort the twenty words shown in Figure 11-16 according to parts of speech, none of the grade-school children could do it. Many of the adolescents and all the adults could.

Children can learn the definition of a part of speech—"A noun is the name of a person, place, thing, or idea." They may also become fairly good at reproducing the model sentences in grammar workbooks, which makes it appear that they understand parts of speech. But a true understanding of grammar requires the ability to analyze the function of a word in a sentence, and such an ability requires abstract thinking. For example, such words as "fire" or "herd" can function as either nouns or verbs, and such words as "ideal" or "cold" can function as adjectives or nouns.

Understanding the grammatical structure of language is an important component of another new language ability that begins to develop in adolescence: the ability to write effective prose. Along with learning the abstract grammatical rules and categories of their language, adolescents can learn rules for writing well.

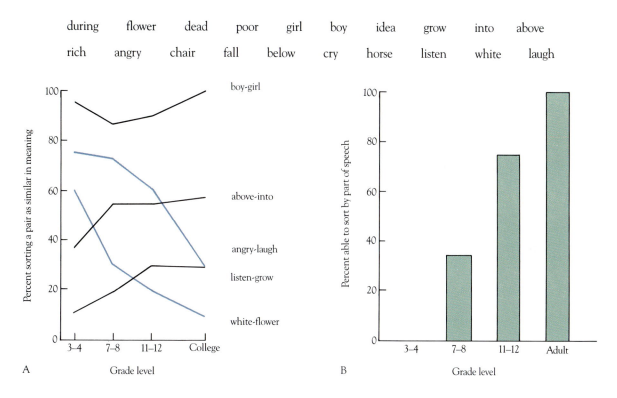

Figure 11-16 Although children for the most part speak with grammatical correctness from early in development, understanding the grammar of a language requires abstract thinking abilities. (A) When children and adolescents were given this group of words and asked which of the 20 "mean the same thing," they sorted the words as shown. Besides opposition of meaning, there was little basis for sorting this group of words except part of speech. Words of the same part of speech (black lines) were paired more frequently by adolescents and adults than by children. Words representing different parts of speech (colored lines) were much less frequently paired by the older subjects. (B) When asked by the experimenter to sort the words by parts of speech, none of the third- and fourth-graders could do so, even though they claimed to know what nouns, verbs, and prepositions were. Many of the adolescents and all the adults succeeded. (Anglin 1970)

Writing Effective Prose

Written language is very different from spoken language. Most of the basic grammatical rules are the same for both, but the pragmatic rules are not (Bereiter & Scardamalia 1982; Olson 1977). When people speak to each other, they are usually face to face, so they can constantly monitor their listener's reactions and adapt what they say to the listener's level of understanding and interest. When someone writes, no reader is present. Many writers therefore develop an abstract conception of their readers, an "ideal audience" to write for. Also, oral communications are usually short—a few sentences at most before the other person replies—so not much organization of content is neces-

Figure 11-17   Two letters to Aunt Mary written by Nicole Connell, one when she was 9 years old, the other when she was 15.

Dear Aunt Mary,

I went to Colorado Springs with Bobby, Mommy, and Grandmom. For Halloween i was a three-headed monster. I got 42¢ for going treak or treating. I got some candy. I'm going to a new school called Jefferson Middle School. I'm having Spanish. I'm also having typing. Thank you for my Birthday gift. How are you? I won two tickets to the Denver Symphony Orchestra. Bobby and me go to art school. I'm making a house with doors, a roof that goes on and off and furnture. I wrote you another letter for thanking you for my Birthday present. HOw are the dogs? The End.

Nicole

Dear Aunt Mary,

Thank you for the card you sent me. I appreciate the fifty dollars which will be put in the bank.

I'm now a sophomore at George Washington High School. The fight to get on the bus has not changed. Freshmen, who go to GW, still have to watch out for juniors and seniors who want to initiate them. Some action has been taken against it. I was one of the lucky freshmen; I wasn't initiated. During the first of this year I will be taking computer lab, physics, college algebra, and the rest of the usual courses.

I am still taking dance at Cherry Creek but not as much as I want. My coin collection is improving. I built a model rocket with a built in camera which I launched twice. The first time I launched it I forgot to put film in the camera, and the second time everything went okay except for some guy who deliberately stepped on it.

P.S. See you soon.

Sincerely yours,

Nichole Connell

---

sary. Written communications are generally longer. Even a letter to a friend may contain eight or ten paragraphs, forty or more sentences.

Because of the complexity of writing, children write poorly (Hunt 1970; Scardamalia et al. 1982). If they write as they speak, much of their prose is almost incomprehensible. Even when they have had some instruction in shaping sentences and constructing paragraphs, their prose does not flow smoothly but is choppy and awkward, as shown in Figure 11-17. Good writing requires a logical organization of ideas. A writer must highlight his most important points, making sure that they are adequately introduced and clearly set out. Children have difficulty identifying the most important ideas in a prose passage that they read so it is not surprising that they cannot organize their own ideas in advance of writing them down (A. Brown & Smiley 1977). Indeed, they even have trouble thinking of things to write about (Siegler 1983).

Adolescents, on the other hand, can begin the long process of learning to write effective prose. They can analyze the relative importance of various ideas and develop effective procedures for conveying them. They can learn how to

ORIGINAL PASSAGE:

Aluminum is a metal. It is abundant. It has many uses. It comes from bauxite. Bauxite is an ore. Bauxite looks like clay. Bauxite contains aluminum. It contains several other substances. Workmen extract these other substances from the bauxite. They grind the bauxite. They put it in tanks. Pressure is in the tanks.

REWRITINGS:

A Fourth-grade child. Aluminim is a metal and is abundant. It has many uses and it comes from bauxite. Bauxite is an ore and bauxite looks like clay. Bauxite contains aluminum and it contains several other substances. Workmen extract these substances from the bauxite. They grind the bauxite and put it in tanks. Pressure is in the tanks.

An eighth-grade adolescent: Aluminum is an abundant metal, has many uses, and comes from bauxite, which is an ore that looks like clay. Bauxite contains several other substances. Workmen extract these from bauxite by grinding it, then putting it in pressure tanks.

A twelfth-grade adolescent: Aluminum is an abundant metal with many uses. It comes from ore called bauxite that looks like clay. It contains aluminum and several other substances which are extracted from the bauxite. They grind the bauxite and put it in pressure tanks.

A skilled adult writer: Aluminum, an abundant metal of many uses, is obtained from bauxite, a clay-like ore. To extract the other substances found in bauxite, the ore is ground and put in pressure tanks.

Figure 11-18 K.W. Hunt gave children, adolescents, and adults a short written passage and asked them to rewrite it. The elementary-school rewritings were awkward and choppy—almost as bad as the original passage. The rewritings of adolescents were often much better, smoother prose. And of course, skilled adult writers composed the best prose of all. Notice how with age not only does the prose become smoother, but the passage actually becomes shorter because of the greater efficiency of the prose.

paragraph and to make well-formed sentences that lead logically from one to another. They can learn how to vary sentence structure to maintain a reader's interest. They can even learn how to structure an entire essay, with an introduction, an argument, and a conclusion.

Abstract Goals

An orator or a writer usually tries to achieve at least one or two abstract goals in each speech or composition. For example, an orator may try to communicate an abstract quality, such as courage, freedom, or power. The pursuit of an abstract goal does much to give a speech or an essay a sense of purpose. Virtually no research has been done on how the use of abstract goals in language develops, but some cases have been described for the universal human nonverbal language—music (Gardner 1983; Shuter-Dyson & Gabriel 1982).

Some children learn to play musical instruments and even to compose music when they are very young. A few of these children are recognized as prodigies.

They have a good sense of melody and rhythm, and they are exceedingly good at the technical aspects of playing an instrument. When prodigies reach adolescence, however, a major change seems to appear in the way they play. The player apparently comes to understand that music can communicate a mood or an emotion or a message to its listeners. He thinks about what emotion or message the composer wanted to convey in a given piece of music and about his own experience of similar emotions. Exceptional musicians somehow manage to communicate that emotional experience to their audiences by their playing. This awareness of communication and its integration with musical technique requires abstract thought.

Even the greatest musical prodigy of all time, Mozart, showed development in his music during adolescence, and especially afterward. Though Mozart wrote many pieces of music while he was a child and a young adolescent, biographers and music critics agree that his compositions before age 13 have a "juvenile quality" (Davenport 1956). At age 13, Mozart visited Italy with his father and studied Italian music. His technical skills became apparent when the young adolescent, after only two hearings, wrote down from memory the musical score for *Allegri's Miserere,* a nine-part choral work played only in the

Figure 11-19 Mozart as an adolescent. He is seated at the clavier (a forerunner of the modern piano), and the music in front of him is thought to be one of his early, incomplete compositions for that instrument.

Sistine Chapel of the Vatican during Holy Week and never shown to anyone but the musicians who played it. At 14, Mozart went on to write an opera (*Mitridate, Re di Ponto*), another when he was 19 (*Il Re Pastore*), and many other compositions, but these are rarely heard today. Compared to his later works, they are not very good. As one biographer says,

> In reviewing the numerous instrumental compositions of Mozart's youth, we are struck with the effort he made to master his ideas. The quartet and symphony productions of this period show many beautiful thoughts not yet turned to due account, but which he resumed and more fully developed in subsequent compositions. (Holmes 1878)

Although Mozart wrote some very good music during late adolescence, he did not create the music that brought him immortality until he was a mature man. Only after he had married and had become independent of his father did he join mature emotion to his technical skill.

Adolescence, then, touches everything a young person does. Besides the obvious bodily changes that come with puberty, the new ability to abstract gives adolescents great new cognitive power. It affects not only their capability for schoolwork, it also affects how they understand other people, how they reason morally, how they use speech, how they write, and—most significantly for themselves—how they understand their own personality and existence. In a sense, as the next chapter shows, the major goal of adolescent development is this new understanding of the self, this new personal identity.

SUMMARY

1. ***Adolescence,*** the long period between childhood and adulthood, is not a universal phenomenon. In this text, adolescence is said to begin at about age 12 and to end at age 18, at the time most adolescents graduate from high school.

PHYSICAL DEVELOPMENT

2. ***Puberty*** is the collection of physical changes that result in reproductive maturity. It begins when the hypothalamus, in the brain, following genetic instructions, signals the pituitary gland to send out hormones. These hormones then stimulate other glands to produce hormones that stimulate growth of the body and development of sexual characteristics.

3. The time of the onset of puberty reflects the interaction of both genetic and environmental factors. ***Menarche,*** for example, the onset of menstruation, generally occurs earlier in well-nourished populations with good medical care. The age of menarche has been decreasing since 1850 in Western countries, and it now seems to have leveled off at 12.5 to 13.2 years.

4. All adolescents experience a ***growth spurt,*** a period of a year or more during which they grow about twice as fast as they did during childhood. The age at which this growth spurt occurs varies greatly from individual to individual, but, on the average, girls experience it two years earlier than boys do. The average ***peak-growth age*** for American girls is 12; for boys, it is 14.

5. Body proportions change drastically during puberty. There is a spurt in muscle growth and a decline in development of fat. Boys' muscles become both bigger and stronger than those of girls; they develop the broad shoulders and narrow hips that make them attractive to females. Girls' hips grow broader and their breasts develop, resulting in the physically attractive female form.

6. Coinciding with the growth spurt is a rapid development of the reproductive system. The sequence of developmental events in sexual maturation is usually the same for everyone. Figure 11-3 shows the sequence for boys and for girls.

7. Although the sequence is the same, the age at which young people go through the sequence varies widely, and individuals who develop much earlier or much later than their peers sometimes suffer psychological discomfort. For boys especially, maturing late can be a problem. Late maturers are shorter and weaker than their peers and so are treated more like children by parents and teachers. Early maturers are treated more like adults, and their classmates look to them for leadership. These differences appear to have both short-term and long-term psychological effects. As adults, early maturers were found to be more responsible and self-controlled and to think of themselves as having leadership qualities; late maturers were more insightful and flexible, but they tended to be touchy.

8. Along with the physical changes of puberty, there appears to be some change in brain organization. The physical nature of that change is not yet known, but the cognitive changes are well documented.

COGNITIVE DEVELOPMENT: FORMAL OPERATIONS

9. At about age 12, children begin to be able to think abstractly. At this time the cognitive **period of formal operations** begins—the fourth and last cognitive-developmental period described by Piaget. Operations are reversible mental actions. Concrete operations are reversible mental actions applied to real properties of the world. In contrast, formal operations are applied to hypothetical properties of things; they constitute, in a sense, thinking about thinking. The term "formal" refers to the ability to think about the form of statements and ideas instead of just about the concrete reality represented by the words.

   a. With formal operations, adolescents develop the ability to think about the **possible,** instead of just the concrete and actual.
   b. Given a problem, adolescents can formulate a number of **hypotheses** about its solution and can predict some possible outcomes of their hypotheses just by thinking about them.
   c. When testing the truth or falsity of a hypothesis, adolescents are able to consider systematically **all possible combinations** of relevant factors.
   d. In sum, formal operations allow adolescents to think logically about hypothetical things.

10. Development of the capacity to think abstractly is not restricted to the logical, scientific type of thinking studied by Piaget. Neo-Piagetians contend that adolescents can **think abstractly** about anything.

   a. Early in adolescence, **single abstractions** develop. This allows adolescents to understand an intangible attribute that characterizes a broad category of objects, events, or people, such as the concepts of courage, law, or justice.
   b. Single abstractions develop from comparing at least two concrete instances that embody the abstract concept. For example, in comparing

conservation of liquid and conservation of substance, an adolescent may be able to formulate an abstract understanding (a general concept) of conservation that he can apply to all concrete instances, namely: Even though some attributes of a thing may vary, the general quantity that combines the attributes stays the same.

11.   The ability to think abstractly can be seen in studying the difference between children's and adolescents' thinking about politics. Children under 13 cannot grasp abstract ideas such as authority, individual rights, democracy, or even the concept of a society. They explain political events in concrete and personal terms, while adolescents explain them in terms of political ideology or abstract concepts such as justice or rights.

12.   Abstract thinking abilities are also revealed in how adolescents think about other people, sometimes called ***person perception,*** and about themselves. Studies in which children's self-descriptions or descriptions of others were compared to those of adolescents show that whereas children focus on concrete physical characteristics, activities, and some simple psychological qualities—for example, "nice" and "kind"—adolescents use a large number of ideological and belief categories, intentions, motives, and general personality traits in their descriptions.

13.   In the middle teenage years (15 or 16), adolescents develop a more sophisticated form of abstract thinking—the ability to coordinate two or more abstractions in what are called ***abstract relations.*** This new ability allows them to understand how variations in one abstraction—conformity, for example—predict or correspond with variations in another—individualism, for example.

14.   With abstract relations, adolescents can understand the context of people's actions; they can relate an individual's actions to his personal history and to the influence of the society he lives in. They can think about how people fit into society and how society's needs affect people's lives. Children cannot do so.

MORAL DEVELOPMENT

15.   The ability to think abstractly makes it possible for adolescents to reach Kohlberg's Stage 4 of moral development, the stage of ***law and the maintenance of the social order,*** because they can now understand concepts such as law and society. Adolescents at Stage 4 tend to take their society's viewpoint in judging what is right and wrong. (Preadolescents judge right and wrong in terms of what their family, teachers, and friends think is right and wrong—Stage 3.) In society's terms, good behavior consists in doing your duty, showing respect for authority, and maintaining the social order for its own sake.

16.   Early in the development of Stage 4 moral reasoning, young adolescents display a pervasive ***authoritarian bias*** in their views about government and law; that is, their judgments show an underlying belief that people in power should always be respected. This strong authoritarianism drops off in middle and late adolescence, as adolescents develop more complex and sophisticated abstractions.

17. Advances through Stage 4 and, later, stages 5 and 6 of moral development depend greatly on the breadth of a young person's experience in social perspective taking. The cognitive advances of adolescence make it possible for adolescents to take other people's points of view on complex moral matters (person to person or through books), but they must be exposed to such points of view if their moral thinking is to advance.

COGNITIVE DEVELOPMENT AND THE ENVIRONMENT

18. Environmental factors affect all of cognitive development during adolescence. For example, adolescents are most likely to apply their abstract reasoning powers to areas of life about which they have acquired a great deal of information. Adolescents from politically active families generally show more sophisticated abstract reasoning about politics than adolescents without such a strong background of political information. Acquisition of information also tends to set up situations in which adolescents learn a set of inconsistent ideas. To resolve such inconsistencies, adolescents must apply abstract reasoning.

19. Environmental factors thus produce unevenness in cognitive development. Some adolescents apply their abstract reasoning capacities to literature; others, to auto mechanics.

20. When peoples of non-Western cultures are tested for abstract reasoning powers—usually with tests designed to elicit formal-operational, logical thought—they often do not perform well. Such results probably reflect unevenness in abstract thinking. That is, these non-Western peoples apply their abstract thinking capacities to areas of life that the tests do not cover.

THE LIMITATIONS OF ADOLESCENT THOUGHT

21. The limitations of adolescent thought arise from young adolescents' inability to form relations between multiple abstractions. Although they can reason abstractly about one area of political thought, for example, they cannot construct a comprehensive political ideology whose concepts can be applied to all political questions.

22. The inability to coordinate abstractions gives rise to **egocentrism** in adolescents, because they are limited in their ability to relate their own thoughts to what other people are thinking. Because adolescents focus so much of their thinking on the physical changes they are undergoing, they often egocentrically assume that others are equally interested in their appearance.

23. The inability to relate abstractions to each other can also explain some aspects of **adolescent idealism.** When an adolescent envisions how he will fit into his society in the future and the imagined fit is not good, then he may think of transforming the society rather than of changing his own imagined role. That is, the adolescent confuses his own point of view with the point of view of the society.

LANGUAGE DEVELOPMENT

24. The capacity for abstraction affects language use.
   a. Adolescents acquire a good sense of **pragmatics:** They are able to use spoken language in complex ways in their social interactions—in sarcasm or irony, for example.
   b. They become more sophisticated in their understanding of the abstract concepts behind words.
   c. They can grasp the grammatical principles underlying the structure of a language.
   d. They can learn to write effective verbal communications, taking account of the needs of a potential reader and organizing the ideas to be presented. They can learn to use the special rules of composition.
   e. They can pursue abstract goals and attempt to communicate abstract qualities such as freedom or power.

SUGGESTED READINGS

BELL, RUTH, and others. *Changing Bodies, Changing Lives: A Book for Teens on Sex and Relationships.* New York: Random House, 1980.

Written by members of the Teen Book Project, this book about the many changes that occur in adolescence describes how different adolescents experience and deal with those changes.

COMMONS, MICHAEL L., FRANCIS A. RICHARDS, and CHERYL ARMON. *Beyond Formal Operations: Late Adolescent and Adult Cognitive Development.* New York: Praeger, 1983.

A collection of articles representing much of the most important research on cognitive development beyond what Piaget called formal operations.

EDWARDS, CAROLYN P. "The Comparative Study of the Development of Moral Judgment and Reasoning." In R. L. Munroe, R. Munroe, and B. B. Whiting (Eds.), *Handbook of Cross-cultural Human Development.* New York: Garland, 1980.

This review of cross-cultural research on the validity of Kohlberg's stages reveals that people in different cultures do indeed seem to show the stages, despite enormous differences between cultures in their specific modes of moral reasoning.

GILLIGAN, CAROLE. *In a Different Voice: Psychological Theory and Women's Development.* Cambridge, Massachusetts: Harvard University Press, 1982.

An eloquent argument that the portrait of women in developmental science has been distorted by the attempt to place women in frameworks that were built to describe the development of men.

GRUBER, HOWARD E. *Darwin on Man: A Psychological Study of Scientific Creativity,* 2nd ed. Chicago: University of Chicago Press, 1981.

In this intellectual biography of the creator of the theory of evolution, a distinguished cognitive-developmental researcher sets forth an exciting developmental analysis of Darwin's construction of the concepts of evolutionary theory.

12

CREATING
A
PERSONAL
IDENTITY

CHAPTER OUTLINE

12

CREATING A PERSONAL IDENTITY

Adolescents in all societies must build a sense of self before they assume the responsibilities of adulthood. In some societies, that task is fairly simple. Social roles and duties are assigned by the tribe or village according to strong and well-defined traditions. A young man assumes the role of hunter or metal-worker, as well as husband and father. A young woman assumes the role of weaver or farmer, as well as wife and mother. There are few choices to be made.

In modern, technologically advanced societies, young people not only must choose what roles and duties they will assume, they must construct a personal ideology—a set of values that helps direct them toward their adult goals (Kagan 1972; Kitchener 1983). In effect, adolescents ask themselves: What kind of person do I want to be? What kind of lover, friend, or parent? What kind of worker or achiever?

Making these choices is not easy, especially for someone whose body is changing from month to month and whose emotions are sometimes so strong that they threaten to get out of control. Adolescents long for independence at the same time that they yearn to remain protected and cared for. They often feel helpless, then angry at family or friends for making them feel helpless—and then guilty about their anger. Most adolescents want a sense of being unique at the same time that they are afraid to reveal any deviation from the ways of their crowd. They are very vulnerable to criticism of themselves at the same time that they may be harshly critical of parents and society.

Although parents remain a major source of values and goals for adolescents, friends take on an increasingly important role in helping each other study choices and discover new perspectives. In middle and late adolescence, when young people become sexual beings, close friends of the opposite sex become as important as friends of the same sex in helping each other build a sense of self. The broad social context of a young person's life also affects the choices to be made: The choices are different in times of war and peace, affluence and depression. The range of choices—the possibilities for achievement—may also be wider or narrower depending on the young person's social class, sex, or ethnic background. These numerous influences and choices all contribute to the young person's struggle to make the transition from child to adult while she is trying to form an identity.

THE GOAL OF ADOLESCENT DEVELOPMENT: A PERSONAL IDENTITY

The formation of an identity—what Erik Erikson calls the *crisis of identity versus role confusion*—is the central stage in his theory of psychosocial development (see the theory inset "Psychodynamic Approaches—Freud and Erikson," in Chapter 8). As the climax of the development of the child and the

"I am *not!*"

"I was at home only in the realm of my imagination. . . . Therefore, I had to become an actor, and create for myself a fantastic personality."

"The hardship to which I was subjected was superficial—only a symptom of the deep disease of color prejudice. I should try, if possible, to root out the disease and suffer hardships in the process."

Figure 12-1 Erikson has written a number of "psychohistories" of historically important people, biographies that probe the processes of their identity formation. These studies examine the growth of personality in light of each individual's social and historical context. These portraits show three of Erikson's subjects both early in life, at a crucial point in their identity development, and later, when they had given full expression to their identity. (Left) Martin Luther, the founder of Protestantism, was a young Catholic monk when he bellowed the words, "I am not," in response to hearing a scripture reading about a "dumb spirit" confronted by Christ. To Erikson, these words express the tremendous conflict Luther felt about accepting the Church's authority as intermediary between the individual and God (and also his own father's authority), and they were a turning point in the formation of Luther's identity as a revolutionary. (Middle) George Bernard Shaw, the renowned English playwright, recognized early in his life that he did not fit comfortably into his society, which viewed him as eccentric. This quotation reveals his self-knowledge and his decision about what to do with himself. (Right) Gandhi as a young man was a successful British-educated lawyer who had embraced Western ways; later, he fought British colonial rule in India. His identity crisis began with an incident in South Africa (another British colony), where Indians were discriminated against as "coloreds." He was thrown off a train for refusing to give up his seat to a white man. This quotation reflects the importance of that incident to his identity formation and lifelong struggle.

foundation for the development of the adult, it is the pivot of psychosocial development. Erikson emphasizes how important establishing a personal identity is when he says, "In the social jungle of human existence there is no feeling of being alive without a sense of identity" (1968, p. 130). An identity gives the self continuity, a sense that the person remains the same no matter what role she is playing. The individual's behavior differs in important ways when she is at work, at home with the family, or traveling, but the sense of self in these situations—the "I"—should not refer to completely different identities, such as I-the-boss, I-the-mother, I-the-guest. The I, the identity, should be solid and continuous and should integrate the different roles that the person plays. Adolescence is the time to start to forge this identity (Bourne 1978).

According to Erikson (1963, 1968), creating an identity during adolescence requires integrating all the identity elements formed during childhood: Trust and mistrust, autonomy and shame, initiative and guilt, industry and inferiority must all be tied together in some shape that society will recognize as worthwhile (Blos 1979).

The adolescent must also review other elements from childhood, particularly her childhood identifications (see Chapter 8). Identifications begin to occur in the preschool and elementary-school years, long before the person is capable of forming a coherent personal identity (Kagan & Phillips 1964; Ruble 1983). In **identification,** the child compares herself to another person and strives to be more like that person in concrete ways, trying to move or talk like that person or to share his or her interests. These childhood identifications may be integrated as parts of an individual's personal identity in adolescence, but they are not the same as a sense of identity. In forming an **identity,** the adolescent weighs and balances ideas about self and society. Thus, creating an identity requires abstract thinking beyond the concrete details of childhood identifications (Barenboim 1981; Erikson 1974).

Forming an Identity

The formation of a personal identity is a difficult process. Not only does it require very active and laborious cognitive and emotional efforts, but it takes place at a time when the body is changing rapidly and when sexual impulses are increasing dramatically. Erikson (1968, 1974) compares the adolescent trying to integrate all these elements to a trapeze artist. She must let go of her safe hold on childhood and reach out for a firm grasp on adulthood. One reason adolescents band together so closely is that they can help each other through this trying time of experimentation with new self-images. Even the "falling in love" of adolescents is often a way to try one's self out, to see a blurry new identity reflected by someone who cares and so to gradually clarify the image.

In attempting to create an identity, the adolescent is subject to several dangers (Marcia 1980). One danger is **identity confusion,** which comes about

Figure 12-2 As Erik Erikson says, adolescents are like trapeze artists; they have to let go of childhood while reaching out for a firm grasp on adulthood.

when other people seem to perceive the adolescent very differently from the way she sees herself. Without support from others, it is hard to establish a stable sense of identity. This may be the root problem of the late-maturing adolescent boys discussed in Chapter 11 (Mussen & Jones 1957). These 15- and 16-year-olds who had not yet gone through puberty were still perceived by their parents and classmates as children, although they felt themselves just as mature psychologically as others their age.

Another danger in this stage of life is ***identity foreclosure:*** A person whose sense of self is still unformed may accept an identity that is imposed from outside, perhaps a stereotype that does not require thoughtful integration with her own special characteristics. For example, a young person who is labeled "delinquent" may seize on that label and say, "OK, that's who I am—then I'll value what delinquents value and do what they do." In cultures that severely restrict a person's identity choices, identity foreclosure is common. A person who is forced into a particular occupation or role because of social class, sex, or race has little choice but identity foreclosure. Black Africans in South Africa, for example, by law cannot take part in many of their society's roles. Their educational, occupational, and interpersonal possibilities are severely limited by their country's restrictive race laws.

Identity in Society

Identity formation depends not only on a young person's specific experiences and circumstances but also on the society, and so it is psychosocial. The adolescent must answer the question, "Who am I in relation to the society in which I live?" Social institutions and economic forces provide the framework within which identity is formed (Elder 1980).

In societies that change little from generation to generation and allow for little social mobility, the social framework of a person's life is likely to remain constant. But sometimes political or social forces reshape the frame, and individuals must then reshape their identities. Their personalities must be flexible enough to adapt to new conditions, yet stable enough to provide a sense of continuity of self.

One of the most drastic social changes in modern times in the United States was brought about by the Great Depression of the 1930s. The generation that went through adolescence in that decade illustrates how social change affects personal identity.

THE SOCIAL CONTEXT OF IDENTITY FORMATION

The decade of the 1920s—the Roaring 20s—was a period of social revolution in the United States. After World War I (and in some ways because of it), there was a dramatic shift from strict Victorian prewar standards of behavior to more relaxed standards in regard to dress, drink, male-female relations, and much more. The 20s were also a very prosperous time. After World War I the economic balloon expanded until 1929, when it burst and the Depression began. The stock market crashed; banks and businesses failed; thousands of men lost their jobs and their life savings. Many families that had been comfortably middle class in the 20s became poor in the 30s.

In 1931, the Berkeley Institute of Human Development began a longitudinal study of adolescent development, called the Oakland (California) Growth Study. The children, 84 boys and 83 girls, were in fifth grade when the study began, and they and their families were studied intensively and continuously from 1931 until 1939. Follow-up surveys of this group were conducted through the 1960s, by which time many of these Depression adolescents had adolescent children of their own.

Glen Elder (1974, 1980), a sociologist, analyzed the data from this study in an effort to determine how the Depression had affected people who had been adolescents during those hard times (Figure 12-3). He was particularly interested in families that had suffered a major loss of income and status. Statistics show that average family income in Oakland declined about 40 percent between 1929 and 1933. Small businessmen lost their businesses, and workmen lost their jobs. Most investments became worthless, and savings disappeared. Parents were unable to feed and clothe their families without charity or government assistance—a Depression innovation that many people found hard to accept. Many men, raised to believe that any man who could not support his family was worthless, suffered a shattering loss of self-esteem.

In many such families, Elder found, there was a shift of power from the father to the mother. As the father's role declined, the mother's role grew more important. Often, the mother both worked at odd jobs to bring income into the household and served as the main decision maker and emotional resource. Because the mother was so busy and the family so poor, the adolescent children were given important adultlike responsibilities. This shift of responsibilities had major effects, which differed greatly for girls and boys.

Adolescent girls were given many housekeeping duties. Because they had not even a slight hope of education beyond high school (who could afford it?) and because jobs were so scarce, they concentrated on a domestic future. Middle-class girls whose families had suffered severe losses tended to marry early. In the Roaring 20s, the feminist movement had flowered. The great prosperity and liberal social norms of that decade had encouraged young women to think of their future in terms of education and career. The Depression greatly constricted these possibilities. Young women were forced by social circumstances to adopt a more traditional female identity as homemaker and mother.

The father's loss of status in the family and the mother's extra burdens had a different effect on boys, serving to liberate them from parental controls at an early age. Teen-age boys took jobs, if they could find them, to help keep the family afloat. In their work or search for work, these young adolescents dealt as one adult to another with many men and women outside the family. The circumstances of the Depression thus accelerated the development of these boys toward adult roles as breadwinners and achievers. In fact, as adults, men whose families had suffered a drastic loss of income when they were boys showed higher motivation to achieve than men whose family incomes had not dropped so much.

The effects of social circumstances on the identities of the men and women in this study continued to be evident in later life. As adults, the women continued to be family-centered, viewing care of their children as their most significant responsibility. The men did not appear to have suffered from delay

Figure 12-3 (A) A good index to the course of the Depression in Oakland, California, is the number of building permits issued each year. Traced here, along with the course of the Depression, is the course of the Oakland Growth Study, whose data Glen Elder used in his study of the effects of the Depression on personality development.

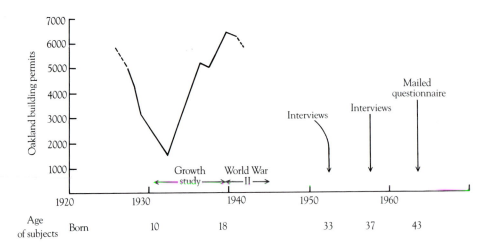

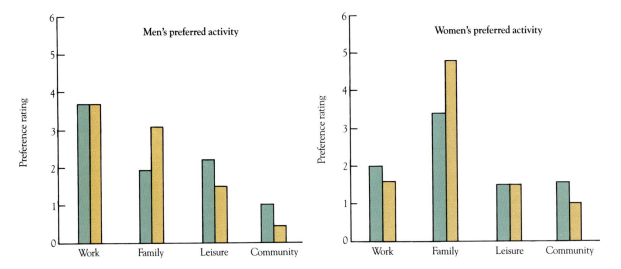

(B) The gold bars here represent children of families who suffered a loss of more than 60 percent of their income; the green bars represent children of families who suffered a loss of only 15 or 20 percent. In interests, the men and women of the hard-hit families showed a much greater concern with family life, as if wishing to make up for the disruptions of those hard times.

or lack of higher education. Their early entrance into the life of work and their need to achieve were enough to make them generally successful in their adult vocations. The men were also more family-oriented as adults than were Depression adolescents whose families had not suffered major financial losses. In the 1920s, when these people were born, their parents did not intend to bring them up in poverty. Most parents did not plan to place the major burdens of housekeeping on their daughters or to send their sons out to earn money for groceries and rent. But when the Depression came, the parents had to adapt their ways of socializing their children to the unexpected hard times.

Elder's work illustrates two points that had previously been difficult to document. First, the historical context of growing up has important effects on the course of human development, including the personal identity formed in adolescence and early adulthood. Second, within the identity they choose, most people have the flexibility to adapt to major social changes during their adult years, to modify rather than to lose their sense of identity.

Any great cultural or social changes—in fact, all broad social influences—are experienced by individuals through what happens in their daily life. Adolescents learn about life's possibilities—and impossibilities—from their relationships with parents and friends and from the adults and books they encounter in high school. These influences all make important contributions to an adolescent's self-image.

ADOLESCENTS AND THEIR PARENTS

Despite the many influences from outside the home during late childhood and adolescence, the family remains the most important influence in the formation of an adolescent's personality and identity.

Shared Values and Goals

For most American adolescents and their parents, the generation gap is a myth. Adolescents tend to follow in their parents' footsteps, taking on values, beliefs, and goals that are very much like those of their parents (Conger 1973; Coopersmith et al. 1975). Most adolescents choose their friends from the same social class that their parents belong to. Their religious beliefs and frequency of church attendance are usually similar to those of their parents. Their educational and career goals tend to match their parents' educational and job levels or to be a bit higher. They are generally Democrats if their parents are Democrats, Republicans if their parents are Republicans, and uninterested in politics if their parents are uninterested.

The similarity of the values held by adolescents and their parents does not come only from the parents' role as socializers of their children. Adolescents, even more than infants and children, have a role in socializing their parents. For example, they often explain and interpret emerging values and life styles for their parents. In special cases, such as families that have resettled in a new country, this assistance from their adolescent children is especially valuable to parents. But adolescents in the average family also play a major role in helping their parents adjust to change.

Even in the warmest, most responsible families, tension between generations occurs from time to time. But in most cases the source of the tension is not conflicting goals or values. Almost all parents want to move their adolescent children toward independence and a place in adult society, and almost all adolescents want to achieve the same goal. The turmoil seems to arise because the adolescent both wants and does not want to make independent decisions and because the parents waver between treating the adolescent as a child and as a responsible adult. Disagreement over the timing of new rights and responsibilities, then, rather than over goals and values, seems to underlie most disputes between adolescents and their parents (Campbell 1969; Hartup 1983). Often the adolescents argue for earlier rights and the parents for earlier responsibilities.

Despite occasional tensions, most adolescents feel that they get along well with their parents. In a Gallup poll, adolescents were asked, "How well would you say you get on with your parents—very well, fairly well, or not at all well?" Almost all said that they got on well: 56 percent said "very well," 41 percent said "fairly well," and only 2 percent said "not at all well" (Gallup 1977).

It may be that value conflicts between generations in the United States and many other Western nations are minimal because rapid change and development are considered normal. Parents, as well as adolescents, expect values and styles to change. In societies that have seen little change for many generations, sudden social change can open a wide gap between parents and children. Such a gap may soon become evident in some Middle Eastern countries, where the sudden increase in national income from oil has produced rapid industrialization and considerable new wealth.

Parental Style and Adolescent Personality

The role adolescents play in socializing their parents depends partly on the parents' child-rearing style. Most parents seem to adopt one of a small number of distinct styles, and each style seems to produce some predictable personality characteristics in adolescents (Maccoby & Martin 1983). In her studies of families of preschool children, Diana Baumrind found that many parents could be classified as having one of three child-rearing styles: authoritative, authoritarian-restrictive, or permissive, as described in Chapter 8 (Baumrind 1971a, 1971b; Baumrind & Black 1967). She also found a small but identifiable group, the harmonious family. In a later review of literature dealing with adolescent

ESSAY:
ADVICE WITHOUT CONSENT

Parents of every generation believe that their experience allows them to see essential truths and values hidden to their adolescent children, and they feel it their duty to reveal those truths and teach those values. They want to warn their children about what they perceive as dangers, and to encourage them to follow virtuous and rewarding paths. But youth has its own necessities—one of which is to acquire experience. Also, times may change from generation to generation, and a parent's advice, based on his experience, may be irrelevant to the forces a young person faces.

Alan Valentine collected a volume of letters written by fathers to their sons. He calls it *Fathers to Sons: Advice Without Consent* (1963). Most of these fathers—or sons—are well-known figures, because it is the letters of important figures that are most likely to be preserved and published. (Letters to adolescent girls are undoubtedly much fewer in number because, in the past, young ladies generally did not leave home until they married.) Some of the letters reproduced here are admonishments about bad behavior; some are advice about specific matters; some are general lessons in living.

GAMBLING

Charles Kingsley (1819–1875), author of *Westward Ho!* and *The Water Babies,* wrote to his son about the evils of gambling:

My Dearest Boy,

There is a matter which gave me great uneasiness when you mentioned it. You said you had put into some lottery for the Derby and had hedged to make it safe. . . . Now all this is bad, bad, nothing but bad. Of all habits gambling is the one I hate most and have avoided most. Of all habits it grows most on eager minds. Success and loss alike make it grow. Of all habits, however much civilized man may give way to it, it is one of the most intrinsically *savage*. Historically it has been the peace excitement of the lowest brutes in human form for ages past. Morally it is unchivalrous and unchris-tian. . . . I hope you have not won. I should not be sorry for you to lose. If you have won I should not congratulate you.

Your Loving,
Pater

MONEY AND CAREER

Leopold Mozart (1719–1787), father of composer Wolfgang Amadeus Mozart (1756–1791), allowed the young man to go off and seek his fortune (though Wolfgang's mother accompanied him). The young man, however, dawdled along the way, enjoying a new-found social life. His father grew impatient, and the last straw came when the young Mozart wrote that he had discovered a lovely young singer and wanted to take the girl with him to Italy and introduce her to the opera world there.

My Dear Son!

. . . Listen to me in patience. You are fully acquainted with my difficulties in Salzburg—you know my wretched income, why I kept my promise to let you go away, and all my various troubles. The purpose of your journey was two-fold—either to get a good permanent appointment or, if this should fail, to go off to some big city where large sums of money could be earned. Both plans were designed to assist your parents and to help on your dear sister, but above all to build up your own name and reputation in the world. The latter was partly accomplished in your childhood and boyhood; and it now depends on you alone to raise yourself gradually to a position of eminence such as no musician has ever attained.

You owe that to the extraordinary talents which you have received from a beneficent God; and now it depends solely on your good sense whether you die as an ordinary musician, utterly forgotten by the world, or as a famous *Kapellmeister*, of whom posterity will read—whether, captured by some woman, you die bedded on straw in an attic full of starving children, or whether, after a Christian life spent in contentment, honours and renown, you leave this world with your family well provided for and your name respected by all. . . . You think all your ill-considered fancies are reasonable and practicable as if they were bound to be accomplished in the normal course of nature. You are thinking of taking her to Italy as a prima donna. Tell me, do you know of any prima donna who, without first having appeared many times in Germany, has walked on to the stage in Italy as a prima donna? . . . What impresario would not laugh, were one to recommend to him a girl of sixteen or seventeen, who has never yet appeared on a stage! . . . How can you allow yourself to be bewitched even for an hour by such a horrible idea, which must have been suggested by someone or other! Your letter reads like a romance.

MZT.

FIGHTING

Richard Harding Davis (1864–1916), war correspondent and novelist, was hazed as a freshman at Lehigh University and evidently didn't take the harrassment without fighting back. He wrote and described the affair to his father, a newspaper editor, who wrote back:

Old Boy:

I'm glad the affair ended so well. I don't want you to fight, but if you have to fight a cuss like that do it with all your might, and don't insist that either party shall too strictly observe the Markis O'Queensbury rules. Hit first and hardest so that thine adversary shall beware of you.

Dad

STUDY HABITS

Dr. Benjamin Rush (1745–1813), a physician and patriot during the American Revolution, wrote to his 16-year-old son at Princeton about study habits:

My Dear Son,

. . . I was much pleased to find that you begin to appreciate time. Recollect, my dear boy, your age and the years you have lost. Improve every moment you can spare from your recitations in reading useful books. Your uncle's library I presume will always be open to you, where you will find history, poetry and probably other books suited to your age. The last King of Prussia but one used to say, "A soldier should have no idle time." The same thing may be said of all schoolboys. Their common plays and amusements I believe instead of relaxing, often enervate their minds and give them a distaste to study. I do not advise you against such exercises as are necessary to health, but simply to avoid sharing in what are commonly called "plays." The celebrated Mr. Madison, when a student at the Jersey College, never took any part in them. His only relaxation from study consisted in walking and conversation. Such was the character he acquired while at college, that Dr. Witherspoon said of him to Mr. Jefferson (from whom I received the anecdote) that during the whole time he was under his tuition he never knew him to do or say an improper thing.

Remember the profession for which you are destined. Without an extensive and correct education you cannot expect to succeed in it.

Heinrich Marx, father of Karl (1818–1883), was a cultivated, prosperous lawyer and judge. At the age of 19, Karl wrote to his father describing his life at the university. Karl worked, he said, day and night. He read Latin and Greek, which were not part of the required curriculum. He wrote poetry. He attempted to evolve a philosophy of law. . . . All this in addition to the lectures and readings for class. Heinrich wrote back, criticizing Karl for *too much* studying and comparing him to his more balanced and comfort-loving fellow students:

Indeed these young men sleep quite peacefully except when they now and then devote the whole or part of a night to pleasure, whereas my clever and gifted son Karl passes wretched sleepless nights, wearying body and mind with cheerless study, forbearing all pleasures with the sole object of applying himself to abstruse studies: but what he builds today he destroys again tomorrow, and in the end he finds he has destroyed what he already had, without having gained anything from other people.

At last the body begins to ail and the mind gets confused, whilst these ordinary folks steal along in easy marches, and attain their goal if not better at least more comfortably than those who condemn youthful pleasures and undermine their health in order to snatch at the ghost of erudition, which they could probably have exorcized more successfully in an hour of speech in the society of competent men—with social enjoyment in the bargain.

POLITICS AND CAUSES

Phillips Brooks (1835–1893), a member of one of Boston's oldest leading families, became an Episcopal bishop. His father, William Gray Brooks, a businessman, wrote in 1864 to warn him about his radical tendencies:

My Dear Son,

. . . We have seen the notices of your Thanksgiving sermon in the "Independent" and the "Anti-Slavery Standard." You seem to be in favor with the radicals of that stamp. Don't go too far. It will require all your best judgment to know just how far to go. . . . Are you not going too fast to advocate the entire freedom and equality of the negro, even to the right of suffrage, as I understand from those notices that you do? I cannot believe that it is best or advisable to introduce another foreign element into our elections; it certainly cannot raise the standards of our right of suffrage or the character of the candidates. Let us keep the ballot box as pure as we can. However you may argue the point of the races being intellectually equal, yet politically to my mind there is no question. I hope I shall never live to see it, and for the sake of my children I hope it will never be done. *Don't go too far.* How many good causes have been injured, nay ruined, by that. Go on in aid of the Freedmen as much as you may please, but such a measure as that is not to their aid in the present state of affairs.

Yours affectionately,
Father

Poet Percy Bysshe Shelley (1792–1822) and his friend Thomas Jefferson Hogg were expelled from Oxford in 1811 for refusing to say they were not the authors of a pamphlet titled *The Necessity of Atheism.* Shelley's father, Sir Timothy Shelley, was outraged at his son's radical actions and attitude.

My Dear Boy:

I am unwilling to receive and act on the information you gave me on Sunday, as the ultimate determination of your mind.

The disgrace which hangs over you is most serious, and though I have felt as a father, and sympathized in the misfortune which your criminal opinions and improper acts have begot: yet you must know that I have a duty to perform to my own character, as well as to your younger brothers and sisters. Above all, my feelings as a Christian require from me a decided and firm conduct towards you.

If you shall require aid or assistance from me—or any protection—you must please yourself to me:

1st   To go immediately to Field Place and to abstain from all communications with Mr. Hogg, for some considerable time.

2nd   That you shall place yourself under the care and society of such gentleman as I shall appoint, and attend his instructions and directions he shall give.

These terms are so necessary to your well-being, and to the value, which I cannot but entertain, that you may abandon your errors and present unjustifiable and wicked opinions, that I am resolved to withdraw myself from you, and leave you to the punishment and misery that belongs to the wicked pursuit of an opinion so diabolical and wicked, as that which you have dared to declare, if you shall not accept the proposals. I shall go home on Thursday. I am your affectionate and most afflicted Father.

Some fathers are more careful about putting their distress down on paper. When Samuel F. B. Morse (1791–1872), future inventor of the telegraph, wrote his father in 1810 from Yale that he wanted a career as an artist, his father did not write a discourse about that radical notion but answered only:

Dear Finley,

I received your letter of the 22nd today by mail.

On the subject of your future pursuits we will converse when I see you and when you get home. It will be best for you to form no plans. Your mama and I have been thinking and planning for you. I shall disclose to you our plan when I see you. Till then suspend your mind.

Your affectionate father,
J. Morse

PHILOSOPHY OF LIFE

Mahatma Gandhi (1869–1948), leader of the Indian struggle against British colonial rule, spent much of his early life in South Africa, where he was imprisoned more than once for promoting racial equality by means of passive resistance. He wrote from prison in 1909 to his 17-year-old son Manilal, who later helped his father's cause in India:

My Dear Son, I have a right to write one letter per month and receive also one letter per month. . . . I chose you because you have been nearest my thoughts in all my reading. . . .

How are you? Although I think you are well able to bear all the burden I have placed on your shoulders and that you are doing it quite cheerfully, I have often felt that you required greater personal guidance than I have been able to give you. I know too that you have sometimes felt that your education was being neglected. Now I have read a great deal in prison. I have been reading Emerson, Ruskin and Mazzini, I have also been reading the *Upanishads*. All confirm the view that education does not mean a knowledge of letters but it means character building. It means a knowledge of duty. Our own (*Gujarati*) word literally means training. If this is the true view, you are receiving the best education-training possible. What can be better than that you should have the opportunity of nursing mother & cheerfully bearing her ill temper, or than looking after Chanchi & anticipating her wants and behaving to her so as not to make her feel the absence of Harilal or again than being guardian to Ramdas and Devadas? If you succeed in doing this well, you have received more than half your education. . . .

Amusement only continues during the age of innocence, i.e., up to twelve years only. As soon as a boy reaches the age of discretion, he is taught to realize his responsibilities. Every boy from such stage onward should practice continence in thought & deed, truth likewise and the not-taking of any life. . . . If you practice the three virtues, if they become part of your life, so far as I am concerned you will have completed your education—your training. . . .

And now I close with love to all and kisses to Ramdas, Devadas and Rami.

from Father

One of the most moving letters written by a father to a son was written by Nicola Sacco (1891–1927), one week before he was executed for murder. Sacco and Bartolomeo Vanzetti, ardent Socialists, were considered by many to be innocent of the crime they purportedly committed. That period—the dawn of the union movement—was one of the times of drastic repression of "Reds" in America, and many people all over the world thought that Sacco and Vanzetti were victims of the temper of the time. Sacco wrote to his 13-year-old son Dante, who had been permitted to visit him in jail before the execution. Sacco had been in prison for seven years.

My dear Son and Companion:

I never thought that our inseparable life could be separated, but the thought of seven dolorous years makes it seem it did come, but then it has not changed really the unrest and the heartbeat of affection. . . .

Well, my dear boy, after your mother had talked to me so much and I had dreamed of you day and night how joyful it was to see you at last. To have talked with you like we used to in the old days—in those days. Much I told you on that visit and more I wanted to say, but I saw that you will remain the same affectionate boy, faithful to your mother who loves you so much, and I did not want to hurt your sensibilities any longer, because I am sure that you will continue to be the same boy and remember what I have told you. I know that and what here I am going to tell you will touch your sensibilities, but don't cry Dante, because many years have been wasted, as your mother's have been wasted for seven years, and never did any good. So, son, instead of crying, be strong, so as to be able to comfort your mother, and when you want to distract your mother from the discouraging sadness, I will tell you what I used to do. To take her for a long walk in the quiet country, gathering wild flowers here and there, resting under the shade of trees, between the harmony of the vivid stream and the gentle tranquility of the mother-nature, and I am sure that she will enjoy this very much, as you surely would be happy for it. But remember always, Dante, in the play of happiness, don't use all for yourself only, but down yourself just one step, at your side and help the weak ones that cry for help, help the persecuted and the victim, because they are your better friends; they are the comrades that fight and fall and your father and Bartolo fought and fell yesterday for the conquest of the joy of freedom for all and the poor workers. In this struggle of life you will find more love and you will be loved. . . .

Dante, I say once more to love and be nearest your mother and the beloved ones in these sad days, and I am sure that with your brave heart and kind goodness they will feel less discomfort. And you will also not forget to love me a little for I do—O Sonny! thinking so much and so often of you.

Best fraternal greetings to the beloved ones, love and kisses to your little Ines and mother. Most hearty affectionate embrace.

Your father and companion

The final letter to be quoted contains no advice. Written by engineer and architect Benjamin Latrobe (1764–1820), while he was planning flood control of the Mississippi, to his son John on the occasion of John's sixteenth birthday (1819), it is a letter that must have warmed the receiver's heart:

My dear Son:

At the table at which I am sitting to write to you, and to congratulate myself on occasion of his birthday that I have a son such as you, I presume that my head is at least four feet below the present level of the water in the Mississippi, while yours is raised two or three hundred feet above the tide. You will be pleased to observe that I am congratulating myself in the first instance, but also most sincerely congratulate you that you are now sixteen and have hitherto given nothing but pleasure and satisfaction to your parents. May God preserve you, my dear boy, what you now are, an honest, upright and generous being, conscious of the errors of his own heart and head, and indulgent to those of his fellow beings, never looking for his own gratifications in the injury done to others, but always making self subordinate to humanity, to friendship and to justice.

Your truly affectionate father and friend,
B. Henry Latrobe

personality and families of adolescents, Baumrind (1975, 1980) described the styles of adolescents' parents in similar terms. She found that certain parental styles seemed to produce, in adolescent children, particular ways of dealing with the world.

Authoritative parents, in Baumrind's terms, hold their children to clear, consistent standards but are flexible and willing to learn from their children. The adolescent children of such parents tend to be **socially active and responsible:** committed, individualistic, and self-reliant. Their parents are interested in their activities, warmly rewarding those they think are desirable and strongly criticizing the undesirable ones. They explain their own actions and attitudes and encourage their children to do the same. In her survey of the literature, Baumrind found that parents of socially responsible adolescents tended to be of high social status; on personality tests, they showed high self-esteem.

Authoritarian-restrictive parents are more controlling and less flexible, restrictive though not harsh or punitive. They tend to have adolescent offspring who are either **traditionalists** or **extreme conformists.** That is, the adolescents tend to act in conventional ways, but some of them actively support social conventions (traditionalists) whereas others conform in a more passive, automatic way (extreme conformists). In Erikson's terms, adolescents with authoritarian parents are quite likely to show identity foreclosure, uncritically adopting the traditional roles espoused by their parents (Marcia 1980).

The parents in what Baumrind calls **harmonious families** try to develop principles for resolving differences with their children instead of setting up rules and standards for their children to obey. They emphasize harmony, equanimity, and rationality rather than obedience, order, or achievement. Adolescents raised in harmonious families tend to be **humanists,** individualistic and socially responsible but with no desire to become rich or famous. The main difference between these adolescents and the children of authoritative parents is that humanists are not highly motivated to achieve in social or economic arenas, even though their parents are often wealthy and successful. Of the small number of adolescents in this category studied by Baumrind (1971c), many wanted to pursue creative vocations, such as art or music.

Adolescents who have serious **emotional or behavior problems** tend to have parents who fail to show love and concern for them and whose styles are permissive or inconsistent (Baumrind 1975; Maccoby & Martin 1983). Permissive parents are undemanding and have unclear expectations for their children. Inconsistent parents have very changeable standards, or else the two parents have very different styles and never resolve their differences. Common emotional problems of adolescents from such families include alienation and a general attitude of hopelessness and withdrawal; common behavior problems include delinquency. Generally, girls are more likely to have emotional problems, and boys are more likely to have behavior problems (Duke 1978).

These serious problems should not be confused with short-term individual

Figure 12-4 This girl's act of shoplifting does not necessarily mean that she is a delinquent. Delinquency implies a pattern of illegal or destructive behavior.

behaviors that might be considered problems by some adults. Many adolescents go through short periods when they withdraw from social or academic activities, and many try out a few minor delinquent acts, such as stealing cigarettes or gum from the neighborhood store (Gold & Petronio 1980). Surveys show that a substantial percentage of American high-school seniors of both sexes have tried marijuana and alcohol and have had sexual intercourse (Jessor & Jessor 1977; Kandel et al. 1978). Most of these adolescents do not have serious problems. The term "delinquency" as used in this chapter refers to a *pattern* of illegal or destructive behavior, not merely a few misbehaviors.

Adolescents who become chronic delinquents, whether from middle-class or lower-class families, often have parents who treat them harshly and arbitrarily, heaping verbal and physical abuse on them (Bandura & Walters 1959; Hetherington et al. 1971). Sometimes one parent is extremely punitive and the other is not, so discipline is inconsistent. The parents do not respect their children, and the children therefore develop low self-esteem (Rosenberg & Rosenberg 1978). Because these adolescents are so exploited by their parents, they learn exploitation as a means of operating in the world. Because their parents' aggression toward them has been successful as a tool of power, they imitate the aggressive behavior. Because the parents' punitiveness is also arbitrary and inconsistent, the adolescents do not learn a standard of behavior (except perhaps that people should do whatever they have the power to get away with).

In general, then, even when adolescents have difficulty adjusting to society, their outlook resembles that of their parents. Aggressive delinquents resemble their aggressive parents. Alienated adolescents resemble their disillusioned parents. Socially responsible adolescents resemble their rational, achievement-oriented parents. Traditional, conforming adolescents resemble their authoritarian, traditional parents.

Temperament and Personality Development

It seems intuitively obvious that everyone has a core of temperament that stays pretty much the same throughout development, a core that shows through despite the influence of parental style. Parents may vow, for example, that their first daughter was stubborn and persistent at birth and at age 18 still is, whereas their younger daughter was intense and explosive at birth and at age 16 still is. Although this intuition may ultimately prove correct, research on temperament does not support it (Thomas & Chess 1977, 1980).

Temperament, discussed in Chapter 6, refers to characteristic ways of behaving that are somehow related to a person's biological constitution and therefore are partly innate. Infants generally demonstrate one of three temperaments: easy, difficult, or slow to warm up (see Figure 6-2). Infants showing these temperaments have been followed into adolescence. Several aspects of their temperaments showed some consistency over the first 5 years of life, particularly activity level, adaptability, and intensity of response. But beyond the preschool years into later childhood and adolescence, only a few people clearly maintained a consistent temperament.

Tracing the long-term influence of temperament is no easy matter, however. The personalities and identities of adolescents and adults are so complex that researchers cannot even be sure where to look for temperamental consistency. When an adolescent is slow to make new friends or hangs back from involvement in unfamiliar activities, for instance, the cause may be a "slow to warm up" temperament, but it may just as well be a general cautiousness learned from parents, a lack of self-esteem, a temporary emotional upset, or a combination of such factors.

Apparently only one firm conclusion about the role of temperament in personality development can be reached at this time: The relations between parents and children seem to be the most important general influence on the course of personality development. Even when people show a consistent temperament, their relations with their parents seem to help explain this consistency. Children tend to remain difficult, for example, when they never establish a secure, supportive relationship with their parents. Such a difficult relationship is just as likely to produce a difficult adolescent personality as an infant's temperament is.

The family, then, is the major socializing influence throughout infancy and childhood and remains so during adolescence (Maccoby & Martin 1983). Parents and their children tend to share the same values and goals. Adolescents tend to have personality characteristics that resemble those of their parents. And developmental changes in temperament from infancy to adolescence seem to be determined primarily by the nature of relations between parents and child.

Although the family is the central influence, adolescence brings with it a great increase in the strength of another influence—peers. Association with other adolescents becomes very important during these years, although this does not usually lessen the importance of the family unless there is trouble within the family itself (Hartup 1983; Jessor & Jessor 1977). Many parents recognize that other adolescents play an essential role in their children's efforts to work out an identity—a role that the parents themselves cannot easily play. Parents usually see the growing interest of adolescents in their peers as desirable, and they encourage their children to become active in adolescent society.

ADOLESCENT SOCIETY

Friends are probably more important in adolescence than at any other time of life. Parents remain important, but parents cannot provide all that is needed for the creation of a personal identity. If your parents tell you that you are handsome or beautiful, it hardly counts because they are prejudiced in your favor. You need friends of both sexes who find you attractive. You also need to know how much of what you think and believe has been "implanted" by your parents. To work this out, you need friends to discuss things with, friends with somewhat different outlooks and viewpoints. Adolescence begins the process of breaking away from family and establishing yourself as an independent person, and adolescents need each other as supports and security while the slow process of disengagement is going on (Blos 1979; Hartup 1983).

Even though adolescence is not as emotionally stormy a period as some scientists and the popular press have made it out to be, strong emotions do come to the fore and need to be talked over (Josselson et al. 1977a, b). Anger at parental restrictions, shame about some real or imagined social mistake, joy at a special date—discussing these things with a friend who is understanding and supportive can help make a good experience better and a bad experience less bad.

Patterns of Friendship

In middle adolescence, the need for a "best friend" or two is exceptionally strong. At this point in development, the young person becomes conscious of himself not only as changing but changeable and so comes to realize that in

Figure 12-5   This adolescent is playing the "staring game" with a friend. Almost everyone remembers playing the game during adolescence. The point is to outstare your opponent, looking directly into her eyes, keeping a straight face, and refraining from blinking. This is a game you play only with someone you like, because it has an element of intimacy. Also, it offers a chance to try out self-control and the ability to affect other people (can you make your friend break down first?) within the safety of friendship.

many ways he can transform himself, determining the kind of person he will be. Besides cosmetic and style transformations—long or short hair, jogging pants or jeans—the 14-, 15-, or 16-year-old believes that he can construct virtually any personality he wants for himself. When trying out potential ways of being, he needs a mirror, and a close friend can provide one (Sullivan 1953).

During different phases of adolescence, friends serve different functions (Douvan & Adelson 1966; Hartup 1983). At the very beginning of adolescence is the **shared-activity phase** of friendship. During this phase friends are not as important for talking things over with as they will be later. At 12 or 13, friends are for doing things together. The focus is on the activity rather than on identity and personality. When young adolescents are asked what qualities they want in their friends, they say friends should be easy to get along with, not selfish or show-offs.

When middle adolescents, in the **shared-identity phase** of friendship, describe what they want in a friend, their answers reflect their increased ability to think more abstractly about human relationships (Youniss 1982). Rather than requiring someone to share concrete activities with, they want a friend who can offer emotional support and understanding, someone who is sensitive to their needs and who is loyal. There are many special secrets to share at this age, especially sexual ones. The adolescent's detailed descriptions of important intimacies—"Then she said . . . then I said . . . then she touched . . . then I . . ."—call not only for attentive listening and supportive analysis but also for careful guarding from ears that might not understand, including, usually, those of parents.

The importance of friends in middle adolescence is also reflected in the formation of cliques or crowds based on shared attitudes and interests (Coleman 1980). In most high schools, the athletes band together and date cheerleaders and other "popular" sociable girls. The intellectuals form another group, which may put out the school's literary magazine or newspaper. The hot-rodders stick together, and the dopers, or "heads," stick together. In certain communities, other cliques form, such as groups of surfers in California coastal schools.

Members from the different groups might get to know each other in class, in the band, or in putting on a play, but choosing a steady date or close friend from a clique very different from your own can cause trouble. For example, if a

girl from the intellectual crowd becomes attracted by the verve and daring of a hot-rodder who also plays a terrific saxophone, she will have trouble bringing him to her crowd's parties. Her crowd probably will not enjoy his company, and he will not enjoy the literary and philosophical talk that the crowd considers a good time.

The need to build an identity causes adolescents to cling to friends whose interests and experiences are somewhat similar to their own. Experiences must be compared and contrasted between friends, but there must be a common starting point that allows sharing and comparison. Adolescent egocentrism, discussed in Chapter 11, probably contributes to the need for friends of similar backgrounds. A friend who serves as a mirror is also, in a sense, an audience, and it would be too confusing to an emerging identity if the audience booed the hero and applauded the villain.

Late adolescence brings a third phase in what young people value in their friends, the *individuality phase.* With it comes a decrease in the importance and stability of cliques. Friends must still be able to share confidences, but the value of the friend as a mirror is largely replaced by an appreciation of the friend's own personality and talents. At 17 or 18, after physical growth and maturation are nearly complete and after some years of experience with adolescent and adultlike roles, the young person has a better sense of personal identity and begins to value friends for their individuality, for what they can contribute to the friendship in the way of interest and stimulation.

Social Isolation and Self-Esteem

Not all adolescents find themselves in crowds or cliques—or even with any good friends at all. Why is it that some young people are left out of adolescent social life or even actively rejected by their peers?

Answers to this question are suggested by a survey of 5000 adolescents that attempted to discover the causes and consequences of high and low self-esteem (Rosenberg 1965, 1979). In many cases, the main reason for social isolation seemed to be low self-esteem. In interviews, fully 65 percent of the adolescents in this study with very low self-esteem said that they were lonely. Their low self-esteem made it difficult for them to seek friendship from other adolescents. Also, their low self-esteem often led to juvenile delinquency (Rosenberg & Rosenberg 1978). In the interviews, adolescents who had very low self-esteem described their relations with other people as awkward and difficult. Because of this feeling of awkwardness, they rarely took the initiative in forming friendships, and they avoided joining in extracurricular school activities. Finding themselves unworthy, these adolescents were certain that other people would not like them or find them appealing. They sought isolation because they felt that they could not fully reveal their unworthy selves to others.

In the interview, one boy said, "When you are small it's much easier making friends because you don't feel you are going to embarrass yourself meeting new people. . . . But when you get older it's not so easy. You begin to think what a fool you can make of yourself in the eyes of a person you don't know. I kind of become shy and withdrawn." Others talked about the facades they had erected around their self-distrust and how they kept others from getting close enough to see beyond the facade. A girl said, "I don't know why, but I have always tried to hide—I've never said anything outright that would give anybody my real feelings—that I was unhappy. Usually I am a relatively gay person. Yet my teachers—if I have been quiet in class or something like that—will ask me after class what happened, because I'm usually such a gay person. And being as I'm not usually happy, I'm deceiving people in that point."

The factor most closely correlated with low self-esteem was the parents' lack of interest in their child—indifference to the child's activities, friends, grades, hobbies. Even adolescents whose parents were punitive showed higher levels of self-esteem than those with indifferent parents.

According to Erikson (1963), the major crises of childhood determine self-esteem, even before children are capable of forming an identity. Without parental enthusiasm and support for their efforts at autonomy, initiative, and industry—their efforts to learn and to do, to become effective agents in the world—children give up on themselves. They may decide that they can have little effect on the world, that they are inferior to other children. The low self-esteem that develops in childhood can then carry over and become a predominant part of an adolescent's newly created identity. A negative identity, unfortunate enough in itself, also keeps the adolescent from forming the close friendships that could lead to a more positive identity.

Low self-esteem and social isolation in adolescence result not only from cold, indifferent parents. Peers also have an important influence. For example, the crowd may follow the dictates of prejudice and reject minority students, such as black students in a mostly white school or white students in a mostly black school. Or they may reject someone whom they perceive as "weird." This type of social rejection by peers also leads to lowered self-esteem (Harter 1983; Rosenberg 1975).

Fortunately, most adolescents do not suffer social rejection or isolation. Many who do have poor self-images still manage to find a close friend or two, and the resulting interactions can help them build a more positive identity.

The Development of Heterosexual Groups

In early adolescence, most children have very few friends of the opposite sex. But by late adolescence and early adulthood, many of a person's friends are typically of the opposite sex. This change usually develops through five phases, in which the make-up of groups and cliques as well as the patterns of individual friendship change (Figure 12-6; Coleman 1980; Dunphy 1963).

In the first phase, the friendship patterns of childhood are still in force. Boys have their groups and girls have theirs, and the two rarely meet. During the

Figure 12-6 Development in adolescent peer groups. A crowd is a group of adolescents of about the same age who live in the same area. The crowd gets invited to the same large parties. Each crowd is made up of several cliques. (Dunphy 1963)

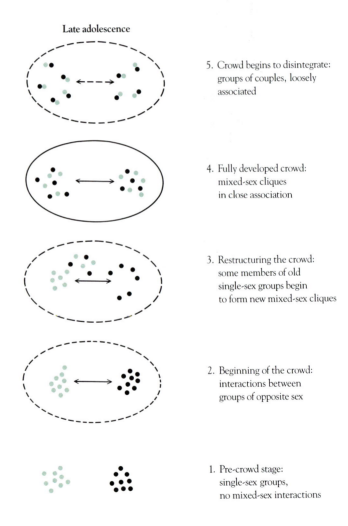

Late adolescence

5. Crowd begins to disintegrate: groups of couples, loosely associated

4. Fully developed crowd: mixed-sex cliques in close association

3. Restructuring the crowd: some members of old single-sex groups begin to form new mixed-sex cliques

2. Beginning of the crowd: interactions between groups of opposite sex

1. Pre-crowd stage: single-sex groups, no mixed-sex interactions

Early adolescence

second phase, boys and girls get together, but only in groups. They might all bike over to the pool together for a swim, yet when the last towel has been snapped and the last Coke drunk, the girls go their way and the boys go theirs. In the third phase, a few girls and boys start seeing each other without the whole crowd, as when three couples go to the movies or bowling. This group becomes a heterosexual "mini-clique," though its members are still part of their original male or female groups.

After this heterosexual breakthrough, the fourth phase begins: Virtually all the boys and girls get together in small groups, and closely related heterosexual cliques form what is called a "crowd." Usually, the cliques join forces for special occasions like dances and big parties. In late adolescence, the fifth phase starts: Young men and women become couples, and some of them consider marriage. These relations with the opposite sex make an important contribution to the adolescent's emerging sense of identity.

SEX AND IDENTITY

During adolescence young people become sexual beings. Their bodies mature sexually, and, as an important component of their personal identity, they build a *sexual identity.* A sexual identity includes both one's experience with sexual behavior or sexuality (physical acts of intimacy) and one's general understanding of one's sex role. Adult sexual behavior is possible only after puberty, but the learning of sex roles—the attitudes and behaviors that a society deems appropriate for females and males—begins at a very early age, as explained in Chapter 8. Starting in adolescence and continuing throughout adulthood, these two aspects of sexual identity interact in complex ways. Adolescents' first experiences with sexuality, for instance, both affect and are affected by their attitudes about themselves as males and females (Miller & Simon 1980).

The relationship between sexuality and the formation of identity in adolescence demonstrates very well how biological and environmental factors interact in the formation of personality. The physical changes of puberty, directed by the genes, give adolescents the physical capacity to have sexual intercourse. But actual sexual practices—whether an adolescent has sexual relations, with whom, how, and how often—are largely the result of learning all through childhood and adolescence, particularly the social learning of sex-role behavior (Beach 1965; Miller & Simon 1980).

Social Learning and Sex

The importance of social learning in sexual matters has been demonstrated even in monkeys. Harry Harlow's group raised rhesus monkeys in isolation, some for 6 months, some for a year, as described in Chapter 6 (Harlow & Novak 1973). The monkeys were raised in cages without any chance to play with or see other monkeys. When a monkey that had been isolated was put in a playroom with other adolescent monkeys, it displayed a number of bizarre behaviors.

One of these was incompetent sexual play. Normally raised monkeys of this age play a lot at chasing and mounting, precursors to the serious business of sex that will develop several years later. The isolated ones simply did not know how to play. Those who had been isolated for 6 months tried to participate, but they would aimlessly grasp monkeys of either sex by the head and throat instead of chasing and mounting like normal monkeys. Those who had been isolated for one year were no good at all at sexual play; as adults, these monkeys were unable to perform sexual intercourse. The anatomical and hormonal development of the isolated monkeys was normal. At puberty, the males achieved erection and the females demonstrated periods of sexual arousal. But because they grew up without being able to learn the ordinary childhood behaviors—the give and take of presexual play that forms the foundation for sexual behaviors—they were sexually incompetent.

Human beings almost never experience the extreme isolation that these monkeys did, but human sexual behavior demonstrates the effects of learning in other ways. Cross-cultural differences in the sexual behavior deemed appropriate during adolescence are a good example (Christensen & Carpenter 1972; Ford & Beach 1951). Some cultures are very permissive about premarital sexual behavior and may even foster it. Young people in such cultures freely engage in sex play as children, and they sometimes have intercourse as soon as it is physically possible. Other cultures forbid even knowledge about sex until after marriage. In these cultures, sexual activity during adolescence is rare. Still other cultures have a double standard, expecting girls to remain chaste until marriage while permitting boys to have sex wherever they can find it. This double standard prevailed in Western culture for a long time and still has considerable power.

If sex were as powerful a biological need as hunger or thirst, these wide variations in sexual activity would not be seen. No culture can set standards saying that the quenching of thirst or the satisfying of hunger must be put off until, say, a marriage ceremony has taken place. No person can choose not to eat or not to drink for a lifetime, but many individuals in various cultures choose to remain celibate throughout life, usually for religious reasons. Social learning clearly plays an important part in sexual activity.

Another social factor that helps set the stage for adolescent sexual behavior is the reaction of adults to the start of puberty. At puberty, adult society begins to acknowledge adolescents as sexual beings. In Western countries, preadolescent boys and girls are often allowed to bathe or sleep together, but adolescent boys and girls are not allowed to. Even if the young adolescents do not have the sexual urges ascribed to them in these situations, they do learn that sleeping

"To tell the truth, I wish I'd been born back before sex."

and bathing together, as well as other activities, have suddenly acquired sexual meaning. Because society assumes sexual motives in the young adolescent, the boy or girl feels impelled to learn more about such motives, and what they learn directs their first diffuse impulses into sexual channels (Petersen & Taylor 1980; Simon & Gagnon 1972).

With the stage now set, adolescent boys and girls start to test out their new sexual capacities. Most adults do not talk to their children about the children's (or the parents') sexual behavior, so these experiments with sexual capacities and identities can be among the first tests of competence and quests for self-acceptance that adolescents conduct entirely on their own.

Biological Bases

The physical changes during adolescence, described in Chapter 11, are drastic and far-reaching. Before puberty, the differences between boys' and girls' bodies are minor, with the exception of the genitals. During puberty, however, many of the hormones released are sex-specific. In boys, secretion of the male hormone testosterone greatly increases; secretion of the female hormone estrogen rises sharply in girls. It may be that such sex-specific hormones produce not only differences in sexual anatomy between female and male adolescents but also differences in sexual physiology and response (Tanner 1970).

Boys and young men tend to be more active sexually than girls and young women, as shown by several large surveys (Kinsey et al. 1948, 1953; Miller &

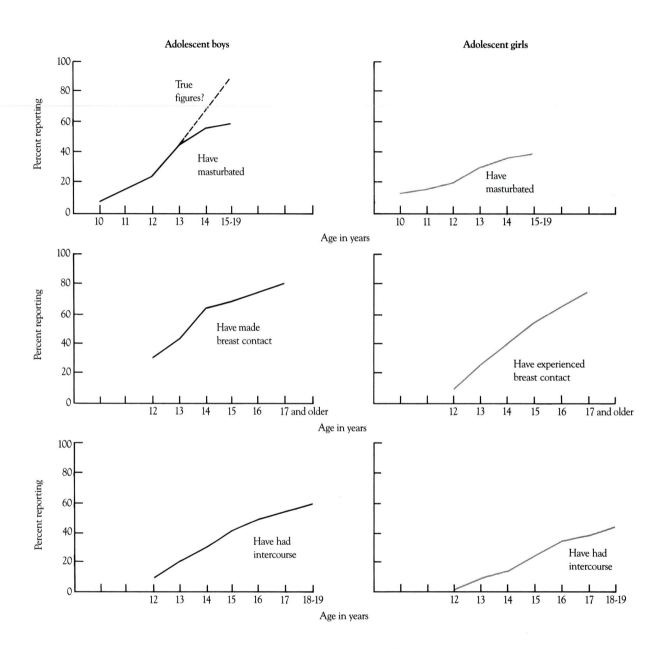

Figure 12-7 Data from the Sorensen survey of adolescent sexuality about three "milestones" of sexual behavior. These data come from the adolescents, who answered questions about their own sexual behavior and attitudes. For this reason, in addition to the line on the graph indicating how many boys reported masturbating, there is a dotted line, based on data from other studies (Gagnon & Simon 1970; Kinsey et al. 1948), which indicates what the actual numbers probably are. It seems that the boys answering the Sorensen questions under-reported their masturbation if they began to masturbate as late as age 14 or 15. (The other results shown here may also be inexact representations of actual behavior, because people are often reluctant to give honest answers about such personal matters.)

Simon 1980; Sorensen 1973; Hunt 1974). Most adolescent boys masturbate, but only about 40 percent of adolescent girls do. Boys more often masturbate to orgasm, and boys require less physical stimulation to arouse them, on the average. The peak of sexual activity, as measured by frequency of orgasms, occurs during adolescence for males but during the late 20s or the 30s for most women. Also, boys are much more likely to be promiscuous, seeking many sexual partners. For every adolescent girl who fits this category of "sexual adventurer," four boys fit the category (Sorensen 1973).

Sex researchers have suggested that the biological differences between adolescent boys and girls set the stage for later learned differences (Gagnon & Simon 1973). Boys' penises are much more prominent and easy to find than girls' genitals, and most boys can reach orgasm much more quickly and easily than most girls. Males have erections frequently even as infants. During childhood, these erections continue, and they are especially likely to accompany emotional reactions, nonsexual as well as sexual, and strenuous physical activities such as climbing trees. Consequently, boys easily discover that their penises are especially sensitive and that touching and rubbing them when they are erect is highly pleasurable.

At puberty, the frequency of erections and the sensitivity of the genitals increases sharply. The "quick trigger" of most adolescent boys means that they will discover orgasms even if they masturbate only rarely. This biological capacity for arousal in young males becomes specifically sexual through learning. As Alfred Kinsey says, "By his late teens the male has been so conditioned that he rarely responds to anything except a direct physical stimulation of genitalia or to psychic situations that are specifically sexual. . . . The picture is that of the psychosexual emerging from a much more generalized and basic physiologic capacity *which becomes sexual as an adult knows it* through experience and conditioning" (1948).

The situation is different for girls. The clitoris is the center of sexual pleasure, and it is small and hidden away in the vulva (Masters & Johnson 1966). Girls are therefore less likely to discover it and the pleasure it can provide, and they are less likely to be reminded of it repeatedly, because their excitement does not produce such an obvious result as an erect penis. Also, most girls seem to take longer to reach orgasm than boys, so they are less likely to discover orgasms even if they do find that touching the clitoris is pleasurable.

Social learning of traditional sex roles interacts with these biologically based differences between males and females, accentuating them in many cases (Maccoby 1980; Rossi 1978). For example, many norms for the masculine role (in the United States and a great number of other societies) emphasize achievement and conquest, so sexual activity becomes linked with competition. Some adolescent male groups have masturbation contests to see who can have orgasm the fastest or who can ejaculate the farthest. Adolescent boys compete with each other, bragging about "making out" with more girls than their peers.

Figure 12-8   Data from the Sorensen survey about adolescents' reactions to their first experience of sexual intercourse. Note the difference between girls' and boys' reactions. For boys (green bars), the event seems to be an establishment of themselves as adventurous, powerful beings. For girls (gold bars), it is more likely to be a learning experience.

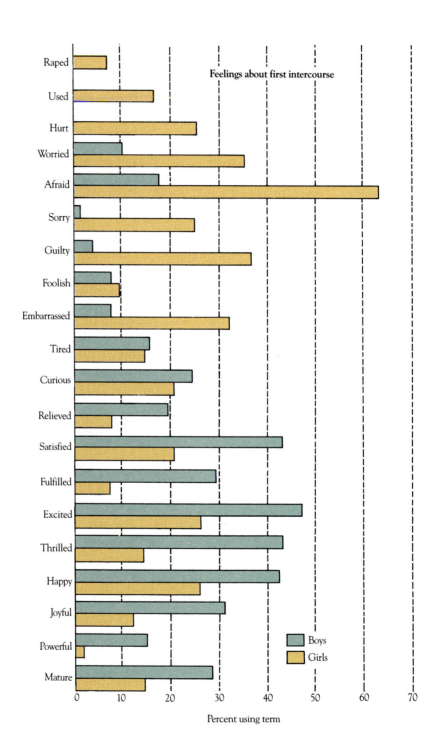

For girls, even the most important signal of sexual maturity—menstruation—is tied to the capacity for motherhood. The norms for the feminine sex role emphasize attractiveness, romance, and nurturance. As Simon and Gagnon (1969) point out, "While boys are learning physical sex, girls are being trained in the language of love and the cosmetic values of sexual presentation. . . . At no point is sexual expression valued in itself, independent of the formation of families."

Consequently, love, romance, and affection are a much more important component of sex for girls than for boys. In one survey, about 24 percent of adolescent boys indicated that they would lie to a girl, telling her that they loved her even when they did not, just so that she would have sexual relations with them (Sorensen 1973). Virtually no girls said they would do so. For most adolescent girls, sexual activity is conducted not just for the sex itself but as part of a romantic relationship with a boy they are dating regularly. The most common type of sexual relation in later adolescence was serial monogamy, which requires breaking up with one lover before forming a new sexual relationship with a different partner. Twice as many girls as boys were serial monogamists.

A mutual relationship may be more important to a girl's attainment of sexual pleasure than to a boy's because a girl's relative lack of experience with masturbation and orgasm and her slower sexual response requires a caring partner who is sensitive to her sexual needs. The fact that most women have the highest frequency of orgasms not in adolescence but in their late 20s or their 30s may reflect women's need to have a caring relationship and knowledgeable partner to develop their full sexual response.

The Sexual and Social Revolution

Male and female roles and sexual behavior are not biologically fixed but are the result of the interaction of biology and social learning. Thus, they can change, and they do. The twentieth-century sexual revolution (or fast-moving evolution, at least) has had many social consequences. Sexual behavior has changed drastically, and sex roles have moved away from many of the traditional prescriptions distinguishing males from females. The revolution has demonstrated, among other things, that many differences between the sexes decrease substantially when society stops prescribing sharp differences in sex roles.

Adolescent Sexual Behavior   In the famous Kinsey reports on sexuality in America, 32 percent of male and 10 percent of female adolescents reported they had had intercourse by age 15 (Kinsey et al. 1948, 1953). These figures were a shock to many people and probably represented a major increase over the percentages at the turn of the century. Since the Kinsey report, the frequency of adolescent sexual activity has continued to increase. In the

Sorensen survey, conducted in the early 1970s, 44 percent of males and 30 percent of females 15 and younger said they had had intercourse. For ages 16 to 19, 72 percent of boys and 57 percent of girls reported having had intercourse.

Although boys are still more active sexually than girls, the increase in activity since Kinsey's time has been greater for girls (Hunt 1974; Zelnick & Kantner 1980). Thus, the male lead in most types of sexual behavior is decreasing dramatically. In the Sorensen survey, fully 80 percent of adolescent boys and 75 percent of adolescent girls had engaged in some kind of sex with another person, ranging from petting to sexual intercourse. In Scandinavian countries, which typically show new patterns of sexual behavior before the United States and other European nations, the proportions of males and females having premarital intercourse are currently about the same, almost 100 percent (Christensen & Gregg 1970). Some studies suggest that the same may soon be true in the United States (Miller & Simon 1980; Jessor & Jessor 1977).

Homosexual contacts also seem to have increased somewhat, especially among boys (Sorensen 1973). Among younger adolescent boys, 5 percent report one or more homosexual experiences; among older ones, 17 percent have had such an experience. About 6 percent of girls have had a homosexual experience, with no difference between younger and older girls. Many adolescents have an accepting attitude toward homosexual sex: 41 percent agree that "it is all right for two people of the same sex to have sex together if both want it."

These findings do not mean that the number of homosexuals is increasing, if the word "homosexual" is taken to mean a person who has sexual contacts exclusively with people of the same sex. The number of people who are exclusively homosexual seems to be stable at about 2 to 4 percent of the adult male population and 0.5 to 1 percent of the adult female population (Katchadourian & Lunde 1974). Especially among adolescents, most homosexual contacts appear to reflect a willingness to try out various sexual behaviors with close friends. Most adolescent sexual experimenters, however, will remain primarily heterosexual throughout their lives.

Many reasons have been suggested for the general increase in sexual behavior during this century. Birth control devices and cures for venereal disease have become easily available. Society has become much more accepting of natural human drives and needs, including sex. Child-rearing practices have become more permissive. Many parents, for example, do not discourage masturbation by their children. Major studies, especially the Kinsey reports and the Masters and Johnson investigations, have demonstrated that many sexual behaviors publicly called immoral are in fact widely practiced. Such disclosures have led more people to feel free to engage in these behaviors. But one of the major factors affecting sexual behavior has often been overlooked—the number of years between sexual maturation and marriage.

The onset of puberty in the Western world has decreased by approximately 3

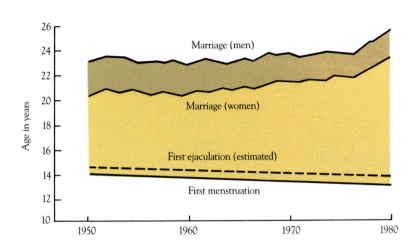

Figure 12-9   The widening gap between onset of puberty and age at marriage.

years during the past century (see Chapter 11). Between the first part of this century and the 1950s, the average age at marriage also decreased (Duvall 1971), although not as much as the decrease in age of puberty. But since the 1960s, the age of marriage has been increasing (Figure 12-9), and adolescent attitudes toward marriage indicate that the age is likely to continue increasing. This gap between puberty and marriage—close to 10 years on the average—generates a kind of biological pressure for change in the norms that govern premarital sex: Is it reasonable to expect adolescents to wait longer and longer after puberty to begin sexual activity?

Unfortunately, the large increase in sexual activity among adolescents has not been accompanied by a similar increase in knowledge about birth control and disease prevention. Most teenagers do not use a birth control device the first time they have intercourse, and many do not use birth control regularly: About 75 percent of those who had intercourse six or more times in the previous month always used birth control (Sorensen 1973). Fortunately, the percentage of teenagers using birth control does seem to have increased in recent years, but a large majority still do not use it regularly (Zelnick & Kantner 1980).

Amazingly, many adolescents, especially those who have intercourse only occasionally, seem to believe that merely wanting not to get pregnant is enough to prevent it. Among girls who had had intercourse recently and had not used birth control, nearly half indicated that if a girl did not want to have a baby, she would not get pregnant, even without birth control (Sorensen 1973). One of the reasons for this misunderstanding is probably that many adolescents, with only simple abstract reasoning skills, still have trouble reasoning in terms of chance or probability. They cannot understand that every time they have intercourse, there is a certain probability of getting pregnant, even if they have not gotten pregnant before (Baizerman 1977).

A large proportion of adolescents say that they do not know where to go to obtain contraceptive information. Among all adolescent girls having intercourse without birth control, 89 percent said that they did not know where to go for contraceptives (Sorensen 1973). Nor are many adolescents aware of how to deal with venereal diseases. About 1 in 10 of all adolescents reports having had syphilis or gonorrhea, and the proportion is higher for young adults. The high proportion of youngsters with one of these serious diseases constitutes an epidemic. Antibiotics cure these diseases easily in most cases, and many cities now have treatment clinics that are inexpensive and that promise confidentiality. But because some adolescents are unaware of the symptoms of venereal disease or are afraid to seek treatment, the epidemic continues to spread.

Along with the increase in sexual behavior and openness about sex, the sexual revolution has brought important changes in attitudes about sexuality to all segments of Western society. In the past, in the United States, there were major differences between social classes and religious groups in sexual attitudes, but these differences are decreasing sharply in younger people. Age is now the most important factor distinguishing permissive attitudes about sex from more conservative ones (Hunt 1974). In the Sorensen survey, 69 percent of adolescents agreed that "Anything two people want to do sexually is moral, as long as they both want to do it and it doesn't hurt either one of them." This liberal attitude toward sex does not mean that adolescents favor promiscuity. Adolescents take their sexual behaviors very seriously and generally restrict their partners to people they really care about.

These increasingly open attitudes toward sex reflect profound alterations in attitudes about sex roles, love, and the institutions of marriage and the family.

Sex Roles   In the United States, boys have traditionally been socialized to be independent, courageous, logical, active, and competitive, and to suppress displays of emotion. Girls have traditionally been socialized to be sensitive to the feelings of others, tactful, gentle, and quiet, and to be able to express emotions (Broverman et al. 1972). These traditional definitions of sex roles seem to be eroding sharply (Block 1976).

Contrasting masculine and feminine sex roles are changing to roles with more shared norms. In sexual behavior and attitudes, too, the trend is toward more similarity rather than toward larger male-female differences (Tavris & Offir 1983; Offer et al. 1977; London 1978). For example, the double standard is rejected by most adolescents, except for many younger girls. Among older adolescents in the Sorensen survey, 69 percent of boys and 71 percent of girls agreed that "so far as sex is concerned, I think that what is morally right for boys is morally right for girls too."

To today's adolescents, a sexual relationship implies close personal bonds, but most adolescents expect to wait a long time before getting married. They do not think that people should have to get married in order to have sexual

Figure 12-10 The change from earlier, contrasting masculine and feminine sex roles to more flexible ones that share more norms is reflected in the similarity of clothing styles for young men and women.

relations, and many of them feel that two people should be able to live together without being married. They see marriage as too important a relationship to be entered without knowing a great deal about your partner and about how the two of you get along together. They emphasize mutuality as the most important aspect of a relationship, whether or not it has the legal sanction of a marriage license. The relationship should not be one of coercion or submission on anyone's part—including society's. They want mutual affection, mutual understanding, and mutual concern for each other's problems. "Love is seen as participation in a self-fulfilling relationship; it embraces both parties, while each maintains his and her own individuality" (Sorensen 1973, p. 365).

Even when the traditional sex roles were strongly in force, many people of both sexes did not behave according to them, and there were many more likenesses between the sexes than the stereotypes indicated (see Chapter 2). Now that sex roles are becoming more flexible and more similar for both sexes, the fact of sexual likeness is becoming more and more obvious: More girls are feeling free to ask boys for dates, to pursue careers, to have premarital sexual relations, and much more. More boys are coming to believe that love is an important component of sex, that household duties should be shared by both members of a couple, that careers are not just for money and status but for personal fulfillment, and much more. Although important differences in sexual anatomy and physiology will always remain, many differences in behavior and attitude are beginning to disappear.

In the past, men were taught it was their responsibility to support the family, whereas women were taught they should be mothers and housewives first and workers second—if at all. These traditional prescriptions have had important effects on the way men and women feel about achievement, on how they perform in school, and on the kinds of jobs they seek. Although such prescriptions still have considerable power, in these issues of career and achievement, as in sexual behavior, the differences between the sexes are beginning to decrease sharply (Rossi 1977).

ACHIEVEMENT MOTIVATION, SCHOOL, AND CAREER IDENTITY

Until adolescence, girls tend to do better than boys in school. Most social scientists believe this difference arises from the fact that girls are more mature than boys, on the average, and more concerned about the approval of teachers and parents. During high school, however, boys overtake girls and begin to get higher grades (Maccoby & Jacklin 1974). This change seems to take place because boys come to realize that the kind of work they do as men will have a very substantial effect on their sense of identity. As a result, their anxiety about their future increases sharply and they start working harder at school (J. Coleman et al. 1977).

Traditionally, adolescent girls have expected to base their sense of identity on family and home activities and on their husbands' careers rather than their own. Partly for this reason, competing for good grades in high school and college has been viewed as too assertive or aggressive for a truly feminine woman, especially if the competition includes males. In response, some capable adolescent girls "leave the field," doing adequate work in school but not their best. Others keep trying, but as Eleanor Maccoby (1963) has written, they confront a difficult situation: "Suppose a girl does succeed in maintaining throughout her childhood years the qualities of dominance, independence, and active striving that appear to be requisites for good analytic thinking. In so doing, she is defying the conventions concerning what is appropriate behavior for her sex. She may do this successfully, in many ways, but I suggest that it is a rare intellectual woman who will not pay a price for it, a price in anxiety."

Males and Achievement Motivation

In high school, as in life after high school, there are many paths to achievement and recognition. Students can excel at different kinds of academic work—history or English or science—but athletics may be the surest path to popularity for boys. Star athletes in most American high schools gain more popularity and recognition than any other group, including top students (Coleman 1980). Student government is another way to achieve status, and many other school activities—including music, drama, art, and cheerleading—also give teenagers a chance to achieve something. Probably most adolescents have both the ability and the desire to do well in some area that interests them. But why do some adolescents work hard to attain a specific goal and gain recognition while others do not?

One major reason for this difference is the relative strength of their **achievement motivation,** which can be defined as the need to reach specific goals in important areas. The most common way psychologists use to measure the

Figure 12-11 Pictures from the Thematic Apperception Test used by McClelland in his original study of achievement motivation (McClelland et al. 1953). The researcher asked subjects to look at each picture for 10 to 15 seconds and then to turn the picture over and write a story about it in 5 minutes or less. They were asked to explain who the characters were, what their relationship was, and what was going on in the scene and why.

strength of a person's achievement motivation is to show him a number of pictures like those in Figure 12-11 and ask him to write a story about each situation. The Thematic Apperception Test, or TAT, consists of a series of such pictures (McClelland et al. 1953). Stories made up by males with high achievement motivation generally refer to high standards of performance, the pursuit of long-range goals, unique accomplishments, and feelings such as pride or shame aroused by success or failure in achieving something.

Research has shown that the strength of achievement motivation correlates with many standard indicators of success, such as grades in school and economic success (Atkinson 1977; Dweck & Elliott 1983). But traditionally, studies of achievement motivation focused primarily on men who were following the traditional male role; the methods were designed to measure achievement in those terms. In fact, until about fifteen years ago, almost all studies of achievement motivation used only male subjects.

A simple theory seems to explain the strength of the achievement motive in males who follow traditional paths to career success. According to the theory, two different and conflicting tendencies make up achievement motivation: the **tendency to approach success** and the **tendency to avoid failure.** In other words, what a person attempts to achieve results from the combination of his need to accomplish something and his fear of failing at it. In people with high achievement motivation, the tendency to approach success is significantly greater than the tendency to avoid failure. They tend to take on jobs that they see as challenging but not impossible. In contrast, people who fear failure more than they need success prefer tasks that are either so easy that success is certain or so difficult that they cannot be blamed for failing.

One of the classic studies that supports this theory used a ring-toss game (J. Atkinson & Litwin 1960). The men who served as subjects were first measured by the TAT. Then they were asked how far from the peg they wished to stand while tossing the rings. Men with high achievement motivation chose to stand at an intermediate distance from the peg, showing a high tendency to approach success with a low tendency to avoid failure. They faced a challenge but still had a reasonable chance of success. Men with low achievement motivation chose to stand either very close to the peg or very far away from it, demonstrating a tendency to avoid failure that was stronger than their tendency to approach success.

In real life, an adolescent whose fear of failure is stronger than his need for success may make similar choices. A person with good abilities may consistently select only the easiest courses offered at his school, or he may say that he has decided not to try out for the football team because no position but quarterback interests him and he knows he has no chance for that.

Family History   The development of high or low achievement motivation in boys depends partly on how parents interact with them. In the most famous study of this phenomenon, parents interacted with their sons while the boys (ages 9 to 11) attempted to complete tasks such as stacking irregularly shaped blocks while blindfolded or making words from a given set of six letters (Rosen & D'Andrade 1959). Parents were allowed to offer aid and comments, short of solving the problem for their son.

Parents of boys with high achievement motivation clearly wanted their sons to do well on each task. They set standards of excellence on tasks for which the experimenter had set no standard, and when the experimenter did set a standard, they expected their boys to do better than average. At the same time, these parents had a high regard for their sons' competence at problem solving. When a boy did well, his parents reacted with warmth and approval; when he performed poorly, the parents—especially the mother—reacted with disapproval.

The study showed that mothers of boys with high achievement motivation behaved somewhat differently from fathers. The mothers became very emotionally involved with their son's activities. (Enthusiastic involvement was rarely seen in mothers of boys with low achievement motivation.) The fathers, on

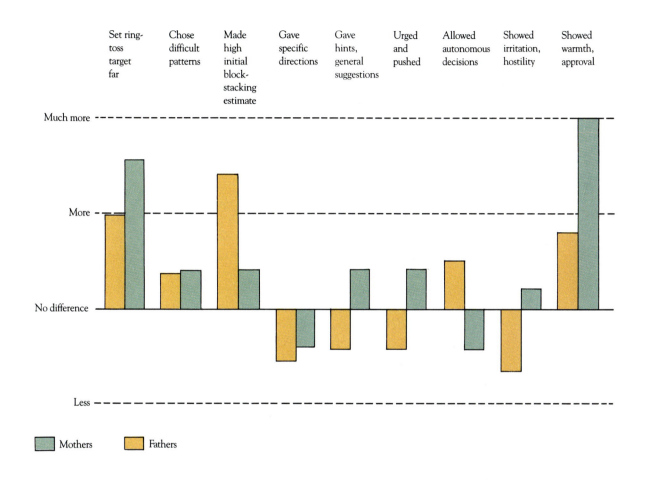

Figure 12-12   How the parents of boys with high achievement motivation compared with the parents of boys with low motivation in the study designed by Rosen and D'Andrade (1959). Mothers' behaviors are indicated by the green bars; fathers' by the gold ones. Note that mothers of boys with high achievement motivation were much more liberal with warmth and praise, and fathers of boys with low achievement motivation were more dominating, giving specific directions and becoming irritated when those directions weren't followed to their liking.

the other hand, were warm and supportive without being strongly involved emotionally. Apparently giving their sons training in independence, they refrained from being pushy or domineering. Fathers of boys with low achievement motivation, in contrast, were more dominating, more likely to criticize, and less warm than the fathers of boys with high achievement motivation (Figure 12-12).

What seems to be most important is that the parents set high but achievable standards and give loving emotional support. The loving relation makes the boy want to live up to his parents' achievement goals for him, and the achievable standards prevent him from being excessively anxious about his performance. This family pattern, which also explains patterns of school performance, resembles the authoritative family style that tends to produce socially active and responsible children, as found by Baumrind (1975).

Middle-class students who are underachievers in school, who earn considerably lower grades than their IQs suggest they should be receiving, often come from families with the opposite pattern. The parents are not warm or supportive, they are restrictive, and they often set impossibly high standards for their children (Morrow & Wilson, 1961). That is, they show a cold authoritarian-restrictive family style like that described by Baumrind.

Social Class   Social class is also important in determining a boy's achievement motivation. In adolescence, as earlier, boys from middle- and upper-class homes tend to show higher achievement motivation than boys from lower-class homes. This difference is reflected in the attitudes and ambitions adolescents have about their future work. In one study of tenth-graders, lower-class adolescents tended to prefer "a job that doesn't bug me"—one with little responsibility and much time off (Bachman 1970). Middle- and upper-class adolescents tended to prefer "a job that pays off"—one with chances for getting ahead. For all classes, family relationships were also important in determining ambition. Adolescents who felt close to their parents and whose parents were not punitive tended to be more ambitious, no matter what their social class.

Although lower-class and middle-class adolescents define success in similar ways, their opinions on how to attain it differ (Katz 1964). Middle-class adolescents usually say that individual effort and personal worthiness make for success. Lower-class adolescents usually say that success depends more on factors over which an individual has no control—on luck or fate. As explained in Chapter 8, these perceptions reflect the realities of middle-class and lower-class life. In general, people with little money, little education, and low-status jobs lack worldly power. They tend to have less control over the circumstances of their lives than members of the middle class do (Leahy 1983).

Although the public schools are supposed to teach everyone the skills needed for upward social mobility in the United States, for many lower-class students the school does not fulfill that promise. On the average, lower-class children enter grade school behind their middle-class peers in language and number skills, and the gap between the two groups becomes larger instead of smaller as they proceed through the grades (Coleman et al. 1966; Bachman 1970). So far, despite considerable effort and experimentation by educators and others, no solution to this serious social problem has been found, except for early intervention in the preschool years (see Chapter 8).

Nonetheless, the model of achievement motivation that has been described (the strength of motivation depends on the relative amounts of need for success and fear of failure) does predict the motivation of boys regardless of social class.

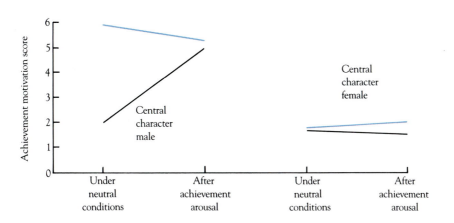

Figure 12-13 The strength of achievement motivation, as measured by stories told about TAT pictures, depended greatly on whether the central character in the picture was a female or a male. Girls' scores are indicated by blue lines, boys by black lines. (McClelland et al. 1953)

The model is less successful in predicting the motivation of girls, partly because it assumes a traditionally masculine orientation toward a career and partly because it ignores the anxiety that accompanies achievement in many women.

Females and Fear of Success

From the very beginning, research on achievement motivation in women produced findings that were different from those for men. For example, one early study was designed to arouse achievement motivation: After creating stories for a few TAT pictures, the subjects were given a problem-solving task (such as anagrams) and told that the task tested a person's intelligence and ability to evaluate and organize material. Then the TAT test resumed. For males, this procedure increased achievement-motivation scores: Their scores after doing the task were higher than their scores before the task. But females showed no such increase (McClelland et al. 1953).

There was an important difference between the tests for males and females, however. Males were most often shown TAT pictures in which the main character was male, and females were shown pictures in which the main character was female. When both male and female high-school students were shown pictures where the central character was female, the sex difference in strength of achievement motivation was markedly reduced, and both boys and girls failed to show increased scores after doing the task designed to arouse achievement motivation (Figure 12-13) (Maccoby & Jacklin 1974).

The TAT scores thus reflected the traditional sex roles for achievement and career. The lower achievement scores for stories with female characters apparently stemmed from cultural stereotypes about male and female activities and goals, stereotypes that were accepted by the women in the study as well as the men. According to tradition, girls and women are not supposed to seek achievement in careers, so the girls and women in the TAT stories did not, either.

Although these results help explain some of the sex differences found in studies on achievement motivation, they leave unanswered many questions about achievement motivation in females. Matina Horner (1970) has argued that besides a tendency to approach success and a tendency to avoid failure, females have a *fear of success,* which leads to a tendency to avoid accomplishment.

Horner hypothesized that females have a cultural conflict about academic and professional success. For example, a girl may want to do well in school, but she may also think it is unladylike and not in her own best interests to get better grades than most of the boys. Some women may experience two strongly conflicting motives: high achievement motivation and high fear of success. To test her hypothesis, Horner devised a study in which male and female college students completed a story after being given the opening line. Women were given such lines as, "After first-term finals, Anne finds herself at the top of her medical school class." Men were given the same lines except that a male name such as John was substituted for Anne. Figure 12-14 presents contrasting stories, two written by women with high fear of success, two by women with low fear.

In the first study of this type, most of the women's stories fell into three categories. All three indicated concern that Anne's achievement in a male domain was not appropriate for a woman. The largest group of responses expressed fear that Anne's achievement would bring her social rejection, especially from males. A second group reflected doubts about Anne's femininity and psychological health. The third group denied the premise of the story: "Anne is a code name for a non-existent person created by a group of med students. They take turns taking exams and writing papers for her." Or "Anne is really happy she's on top, though Tom is higher than she—though that's as it should be. Anne doesn't mind Tom winning." In this study, 66 percent of the women wrote stories that showed fear of success, whereas only 9 percent of the men wrote such stories. In a later study, adolescents of both sexes wrote stories about both sexes—successful boys as well as successful girls (Monahan et al. 1974). Most members of both sexes wrote glowingly about male success and negatively about female success. The boys were even more negative about female success than the girls.

In follow-up interviews of many of the subjects in Horner's original study, conducted nine years after that study, the fear-of-success measures received support from real-life data (Hoffman 1977). Among women who had scored high in fear of success, in contrast to those who had scored low, many became pregnant when their careers were going "too well," promising to catch up with or overtake their husband's or boyfriend's level of success.

For many women, competition with males seems to increase fear of success. Girls in coeducational high schools have shown more fear of success than girls with similar backgrounds in all-girl schools (Winchel et al. 1974). And women who have thoughtfully decided on a traditionally male career have shown more

THEMATIC LEAD: "After first term finals, Anne finds herself at the top of her medical school class."

TYPICAL RESPONSES:

Congrats to her! Anne is quite a lady — not only is she tops academically, but she is liked and admired by her fellow students. Quite a trick in a man-dominated field. She is brilliant — but she is also a lady. A lot of hard work. She is pleased — yet humble and her fellow students (with the exception of a couple of sour pusses) are equally pleased. That's the kind of girl she is — you are always pleased when she is — never envious. She will continue to be at or near the top. She will be as fine practicing her field as she is studying it. And — always a lady.

LOW FEAR OF SUCCESS

Anne has a boyfriend Carl in the same class and they are quite serious. Anne met Carl at college and they started dating around their sophomore years in undergraduate school. Anne is rather upset and so is Carl. She wants him to be higher scholastically than she is. Anne will deliberately lower her academic standing the next term, while she does all she subtly can to help Carl. . . . His grades come up and Anne soon drops out of med school. They marry and he goes on in school while she raises their family.

HIGH FEAR OF SUCCESS

THEMATIC LEAD: "Anne is sitting in a chair with a smile on her face."

TYPICAL RESONSES:

"Her boyfriend has just called her . . . Oh boy. I'm so excited what shall I wear . . . Will he like me? I am so excited. Ann is very happy. Ann will have a marvelous time.

Anne is at her father's funeral. There are over 200 people there. She knows it is unseemly to smile but cannot help it. . . Her brother Ralph pokes her in fury but she is uncontrollable. . . Anne rises dramatically and leaves the room, stopping first to pluck a carnation from the blanket of flowers on the coffin.

Figure 12-14 The two stories at the top were told in response to the cue line, "After first term finals, Anne finds herself at the top of her medical school class." The one on the left was judged to represent a low fear of success, and the one on the right, a high fear of success. In a later study, women known to be high or low in fear of success were asked to tell a story in response to the cue, "Anne is sitting in a chair with a smile on her face." A typical story from women with low fear of success is shown at left; it is highly positive. The story shown here at right, by a woman with high fear of success, is typical of the bizarre, often hostile stories these women told. Evidently, women do not give up wanting to succeed without experiencing a great deal of anger.

fear of success than women who have opted for a more traditionally female role (Orlofsky 1978).

One of the limitations of all the investigations of achievement motivation, including studies of fear of success, is that they tend to focus on achievement in traditionally masculine realms and ignore achievement in traditionally feminine ones (Gilligan 1982). For example, women consider themselves socially more competent than men, and on the average they are probably right. They are also rewarded for social success. But our cultural values teach both women and men to consider social success a "second-rate" achievement relative to success in academic areas, the marketplace, or in a high-status career. Because fewer women than men achieve success in these business and academic areas, women and men devalue women in general. The extent of the devaluation has been shown by numerous studies. In one of them, boys, girls, men, and women were asked to evaluate the same pieces of writing, but half of them were told the work had been done by a man, and the other half were told that the same piece of work had been done by a woman (Mischel 1974). All groups—male and female, young and old—judged the work supposedly done by the woman to be worse.

Socialization practices encourage women to adopt social and family goals rather than career goals and at the same time to downgrade the value of social and family goals. These practices exact a psychological toll. Females have less confidence in their ability to perform many kinds of tasks, even when they can perform well (Feather 1969; Leventhal & Lane 1970). They feel less in control of their own fates than men do, and they are much more likely to be depressed than men (Shaver & Rubenstein 1980). Women, like lower-class adolescents of both sexes, tend to believe that any success they have comes about because of luck or fate (Brannegan & Toler 1971).

Women who do strive for success in culturally valued areas (those dominated by men) face a reality different from that faced by men. Men who wish to marry can often expect the marriage to help their careers by making their domestic lives less burdensome. But women who wish to marry often must try to fit the responsibilities of housekeeper and mother into their career plans and to adjust their career plans to their husband's job situation. No wonder achievement motivation in adolescent girls and women shows conflicts. The conflicts are real.

Some social scientists have found fault with the research showing fear of success in women (Tresemer 1974); deCharms & Muir 1978). In fact, some have suggested that the techniques designed to measure fear of success are actually measuring fear of failure (Shaver 1976). But even if the findings so far do not present a clear picture of achievement motivation in women, they do indicate at least that achievement for women in traditionally male fields can be troubling and stressful.

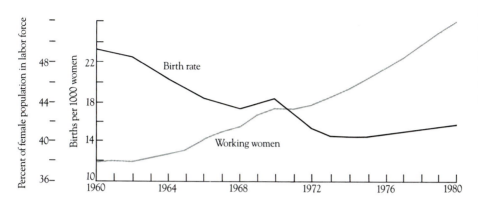

Figure 12-15 These data on the growing number of women in the work force and the falling birth rate over the past two decades reveal how women's roles are changing.

Changing Times

Much of the research on sex differences in achievement motivation was done a decade or more ago, and the last 20 years have seen important changes in cultural values. The near future promises even more changes in the lives of females and males. More young women are going to college, graduate school, and professional school, and ultimately more are going into business, the professions, and politics (Rossi 1977). In the first half of the 1970s, the number of women in college in the United States increased by 30 percent, while the number of men increased by only 12 percent. During the same period, the number of doctorates earned by women increased by 39 percent, while the number earned by men *decreased* by 7 percent (McCarthy & Wolfle 1975). In 1977, women earned more than half of all BAs and more than 40 percent of all MAs. In professional schools, enrollments of women have increased enormously between 1960 and the present (Van Dusen & Sheldon 1976).

Changes in values seem to allow more choices for women and also for men than the traditional sex roles of the past did (Katz 1977; Yankelovich 1978). Women can enter the professions more easily, and men are beginning to place a higher value on getting along well with other people, on family activities, and on such qualities as nurturance and warmth. More young men are willing to share the responsibilities of housekeeping and child rearing with their wives.

Parallel changes seem to be occurring in fear of success. Research indicates that many more men seem to be showing fear of success than did previously, apparently because they are rejecting traditional male roles and values (Hoffman 1974; Orlofsky 1978). And when women show fear of success, as in predicting social rejection for Anne, it does not necessarily mean that they will avoid success in real life. According to some researchers, it is more likely that they have a realistic understanding of the costs they may pay if they reject the

Figure 12-16 One indication of women's changing roles is their increasing participation in sports. Even sports that were once considered exclusively male domains now have female competitors.

traditional female role (Cabellero et al. 1975; Zuckerman & Wheeler 1975).

Despite changes in sex roles and values, the central task for adolescents remains the same—the formation of a personal identity that includes elements for sexual identity and career identity. The formation of this identity does much to determine psychosocial development beyond adolescence. Throughout adulthood, a clear, wholesome, and flexible identity is essential to healthy development. Forming intimate relationships, raising children well, having a successful career, growing old gracefully—all these important tasks of adulthood depend in important ways on the formation of a personal identity.

SUMMARY

1. The climax of social and personality development in adolescence is the formation of an *identity,* the sense of who one is and who one wants to be in the context of one's social environment.

THE GOAL OF ADOLESCENT DEVELOPMENT: A PERSONAL IDENTITY

2. Erik Erikson's theory of psychosocial development describes how earlier developmental stages lead up to the *crisis of identity versus role confusion* in adolescence and how developmental crises continue into adulthood.

    a. Earlier developmental crises sometimes must be relived by adolescents as they struggle to build an identity, because part of an identity is a sense of continuity between what one was and what one will become.

    b. They also somehow must work into their new sense of identity the *identifications* that they formed in childhood.

    c. Some dangers in identity formation are: *identity confusion,* which comes about when other people seem to perceive the adolescent very differently from the way he perceives himself, and *identity foreclosure,* which takes place when an adolescent accepts an identity imposed from outside.

THE SOCIAL CONTEXT OF IDENTITY FORMATION

3. Identity formation depends not only on specific individual circumstances but on broad social forces. People who were adolescents during the Depression of the 1930s and whose family circumstances changed drastically were given adultlike responsibilities earlier than adolescents from families relatively unaffected by the Depression. This affected their identities and their values in adulthood.

ADOLESCENTS AND THEIR PARENTS

4. For the most part, adolescents and their parents share the same values and goals. Parents want to move their adolescent children toward independence and a place in adult society, and adolescents want the same. Conflict seems to arise mainly from the timing of new rights and responsibilities.

5. As in childhood, certain parental styles seem to produce adolescents with particular ways of dealing with the world:

a. Authoritative parents, who hold their children to clear, consistent standards but who are flexible and willing to learn from their children, tend to have adolescents who are *socially active and responsible.*

b. Authoritarian-restrictive parents, who exercise strong control but in an arbitrary way rather than flexibly, tend to have adolescents who are either *traditionalists* or *extreme conformists.*

c. Adolescents from *harmonious families,* who try to set up principles for resolving differences with their children instead of setting up rules and standards for children to obey, tend to be *humanists,* individualistic and socially responsible but not ambitious for wealth or renown.

d. Permissive parents are undemanding and set out no clear expectations for their children, and inconsistent parents have either very changeable standards or unresolved differences in style. Parents with these styles tend to have adolescent children who have *emotional problems,* such as alienation, or *behavior problems,* such as chronic delinquency.

6. Adolescent personality seems to show little or no consistency with infant *temperament,* a characteristic way of behaving that seems to have a biological basis.

ADOLESCENT SOCIETY

7. During different phases of adolescence, friends serve different functions:

a. Early in adolescence, at 12 or 13, adolescent friendships are in the **shared-activity phase.**

b. In middle adolescence comes the **shared-identity phase** of friendship; friends are chosen for their emotional support, sensitivity to the other's needs, and loyalty.

c. Late adolescence brings the **individuality phase** of friendship; friends are chosen for their own personality and talents.

8.   Many adolescents who find themselves socially isolated suffer from low self-esteem, which keeps them from seeking friendships. One factor closely correlated with low self-esteem is parents' lack of interest in their child.

9.   The **development of heterosexual groups** in adolescence appears to go through five phases, from separate groups of boys and girls to heterosexual groups to heterosexual couples.

SEX AND IDENTITY

10.   **Sexual identity** is an important component of the identity formulated in adolescence. Both sexuality and sex roles contribute to sexual identity, and social learning plays a part in both. Different cultures specify very different sex roles and sexual behavior.

11.   The biological changes of puberty produce not only differences in sexual anatomy between males and females but also differences in sexual physiology and response. Adolescent boys tend to be more sexually active than girls, partly because the penis is more prominent and easier to stimulate than female organs.

12.   Biological differences between adolescent boys and girls interact with the social learning of sex roles in ways that often accentuate male-female differences. Norms for the male role in many societies accentuate achievement and conquest, so sexual activity often becomes an area for competition. Norms for the female role emphasize attractiveness, romance, and nurturance, so love and romance become more important components of sex for girls than for boys.

13.   Evidence for the role of social learning in sexual behavior comes from the changes in sexual behavior that have occurred over the past several decades, changes that have coincided with changes in sex-role norms. The frequency of adolescent sexual activity has increased markedly, and the increase has been much greater for females than for males.

14.   Sex roles are changing from contrasting masculine and feminine roles to roles with more shared norms. One important change is that many females now expect to have a career or job instead of expecting to be a wife and mother totally supported by a male.

ACHIEVEMENT MOTIVATION AND CAREER IDENTITY

15. *Achievement motivation,* the need to reach specified goals in important areas, is made up of two conflicting tendencies: *the tendency to approach success* and *the tendency to avoid failure.* In people with high achievement motivation, the first tendency is significantly stronger than the second.

    a. Adolescents with high achievement motivation seem to have parents who set high achievable standards and give loving emotional support.

    b. Adolescents from middle- and upper-class homes tend to show higher achievement motivation than those from lower-class homes.

    c. Females appear to have a third component making up their achievement motivation: *fear of success,* which arises from conflict about the meaning of success in terms of sex-role norms.

SUGGESTED READINGS

ADELSON, JOSEPH (Ed.). *Handbook of Adolescent Psychology.* New York: Wiley, 1980.

A collection of reviews of research on adolescents, written by some of the most important scientists in the field.

DWECK, C., and ELAINE S. ELLIOTT. "Achievement Motivation." In P. H. Mussen (Ed.), *Handbook of Child Psychology.* New York: Wiley, 1983.

A review of achievement motivation and its development, including its relation to intelligence and anxiety.

ERIKSON, ERIK. *Identity: Youth and Crisis.* New York: W. W. Norton, 1968.

The originator of the theory of psychosocial development discusses the concept of identity and how it relates to gender and race.

YOUNISS, JAMES. *Parents and Peers in Social Development: A Sullivan-Piaget Perspective.* Chicago: University of Chicago Press, 1980.

A fascinating analysis of how cognitive development and social development combine in the development of relationships in adolescence.

EPILOGUE

It is hard not to marvel at the process of human development. From a single cell that contains all the genetic information needed to pattern a lifetime of growth, people develop into conscious, intelligent, creative social beings. When researchers study development scientifically, the characteristics that they discover increase their sense of awe, and ours, at this dynamic and complex process.

One of the most fundamental characteristics of development is that it always arises from the collaboration of heredity and environment. Traditionally, child development often was viewed as a kind of unfolding, a simple carrying out of the genetic plan. Modern research makes it clear that what the genes offer is not merely a blueprint for development but also an unfolding array of possibilities. The design that actually develops depends on how the genetic potential interacts with the environmental reality. Part of our human inheritance is great flexibility: Designs can even go back to the drawing board and be reworked in midcourse. For example, an infant's early environment may not allow expression of her full potential for cognitive and emotional growth; but if the environment is changed for the better, she may catch up and realize most or all of that potential.

One of the fundamental characteristics of the human species in all normal environments is that as children grow continuously through the periods of infancy, toddlerhood, childhood, and adolescence, their behavior shows major qualitative changes, reorganizations that permeate all aspects of their lives—how they think and talk, how they feel, how they interact with others, how they view and evaluate themselves and others. Infants' inability to think about things apart from acting on them, for instance, makes them vastly different from the thinking preschooler, and grade-school children's concrete approach to their world makes them vastly different from the adolescent in the throes of both puberty and the emergence of new abstract capacities.

Because children's general capabilities affect so much of their behavior, an adult caregiver can benefit greatly from understanding the abilities of each period of development and how they produce not only specific kinds of skills but also a natural set of concerns, issues, and limitations. Two-year-olds, for instance, are just coming to understand and deal with their separateness from their parents, and so they naturally vacillate between a desire to assert their own competence and a need for love and reassurance. Four- and five-year-olds are gaining a first grasp of social roles and relations, and so they can be expected to caricature those relations in stereotypes that may horrify an unprepared adult. Adolescents are beginning to establish themselves as adults both cognitively and physically, and they show a natural confusion between their passing status as children and their coming status as grown-ups. An understanding of these capacities and limitations can help adults to appreciate children's concerns, to deal with their troubles, and to share in their joys.

Besides describing age-related change and analyzing the nature of the processes underlying it, the scientific study of development has given insight into the environmental conditions that foster healthy development or interfere with it. Just as medical science tells us what food nutrients and environmental conditions are necessary for physical health and growth, the science of development

determines what cognitive, social, and emotional nutrients and conditions young people need for healthy psychological development. Many of these psychological needs of all children have been described in this book. For example, infants need cognitive stimulation and affectionate interchange. When severely deprived of these nutrients, they "fail to thrive," developing at a snail's pace or even dying. Older children need to have someone they value take an interest in their hopes and activities. Without such nourishing interest, they do not learn to value themselves and to believe that what they do can be

worthwhile. In grade school and adolescence, children need to have other children to play with and talk to. Without these peers, they will have difficulty developing a realistic identity and normal adult relationships.

When important people in a child's life are aware of findings like these, they are more likely to provide a nourishing environment that allows the child to realize his or her potential. By the middle of childhood, many children show directly in their feelings how nourishing their environments have been. These two poems about houses—and the people within them—express two very different ways that children may feel about their environments:

By Brian Andrews, age 10

The doors in my house
Are used every day
For closing rooms
And locking children away.

By *Richard Jazen, age 12*

When I walk home from school,
I see many houses
Many houses down many streets.
They are warm, comfortable houses
But other people's houses
I pass without much notice.

Then as I walk farther, farther
I see a house, the house.
It springs up with a jerk
That speeds my pace; I lurch forward.
Longing makes me happy, I bubble inside.
It's my house.

(From *Miracles*, ed. Richard Lewis, New York: Simon & Schuster, 1966)

Although different ways of rearing children clearly have different results, there is no one correct method. Many different ways of raising children can be successful. Indeed, the study of development can be helpful in childrearing mainly *after* one has decided on a set of goals for raising children. Once adults have a set of reasonable goals, they can use knowledge about development to determine the best way to attain those goals, taking account of factors such as the changing capacities and limitations of children from one developmental period to the next and the basic psychological needs of all children.

The young creatures who are the subject of this book change not only from year to year, but almost from day to day. That is one of the fundamental insights of developmental science: Contrary to the medieval belief that children are just small adults, children must go through a long series of developmental changes

to become adults. They are constantly in the process of becoming—infants becoming toddlers, toddlers becoming children, children becoming adolescents, and adolescents becoming adults.

Development does not stop in early adulthood, however. One of the insights of recent research is that development continues throughout adulthood. The changes are not as swift or dramatic, but development—becoming—goes on: becoming a valued member of society through work and then going on to help others to contribute too, establishing a long-term loving relationship, becoming a parent or caregiver and going on to help the young to grow and become competent adults in their own right.

This adult concern for contributing to society and to the next generation is what Erikson calls "generativity." The dependency of the young and the generativity of adults, he points out, are reciprocal: "Mature man needs to be needed, and maturity is guided by the nature of that which must be cared for." This book has striven to give its readers—who are on the path of adult development—insight into the nature and developmental paths of those who must be cared for.

GLOSSARY

abstract In cognitive-development and language development, to identify a characteristic, rule, or action that is common to a number of objects, events, words, or sentences.

abstraction An idea that refers to something that is intangible, not concrete.

accommodation According to Piaget, adjustment of a scheme to an object or event in order to make the scheme better fit the specific characteristics of that object or event. See also **assimilation, equilibrium,** and **scheme.**

achieved social status Social status resulting from some accomplishment by an individual during his or her lifetime; opposed to **ascribed social status.**

achievement motivation A felt need to reach academic or career goals, arising from the relative strengths of two conflicting tendencies: the tendency to approach success and the tendency to avoid failure. A third tendency has been hypothesized, especially for women: fear of success.

adaptation In the theory of evolution, changes in a species that produce behaviors and physiological characteristics that help the species to survive in its particular environment.

addition of classes The cognitive ability to combine several subclasses of objects or events to form a class and to break a class into subclasses.

afterbirth See **placenta.**

agent of socialization A person, group, or institution that teaches social norms and roles, whether directly, as a primary goal, or indirectly.

amniocentesis During pregnancy, withdrawal of amniotic fluid in order to test fetal cells for abnormalities.

anal stage In Freud's theory of psychosexual development, the second stage, in which the erogenous zone is the rectum and anus. This stage lasts until near the end of the third year of life, and it is followed by the **phallic stage.**

anoxia Lack of oxygen during birth.

anxious, ambivalent attachment An attachment pattern signaling some difficulty between parent and child; the infant appears uneasy or distressed even in the parent's presence and is reluctant to use the parent as a secure base.

Apgar scale A measure of a newborn's overall functioning. The infant's heart rate, reflex irritability, muscle tone, color, and breathing are measured on a scale of 0 to 10.

ascribed social status Social status designated at the time of an individual's birth by virtue of some inherited characteristic.

assimilation According to Piaget, application of a scheme to a particular object or event. See also **accommodation, equilibrium,** and **scheme.**

association areas Certain areas in the cerebral cortex that play a central role in intelligence.

attachment The affectional bond that infants show for a person (usually the mother) with whom they have had a stable, long-lasting relationship.

attention The focusing of a person's perceptual and cognitive processes on an event so that the person is unaware of most stimuli not connected with the event.

authoritarian bias A belief that people should always respect and obey those in power.

authoritarian-restrictive parental style According to D. Baumrind, the style of parents who are more detached than others and who exercise a high degree of control over their children without offering explanation or encouraging discussion.

authoritative parental style According to D. Baumrind, the style of parents who are warmer than others, demand high levels of achievement, and firmly enforce rules of behavior but are open to their children's questions and comments and encourage their children to make decisions within the limits defined by the parents.

autonomy versus shame and doubt In Erikson's theory of psychosocial development, the second developmental crisis, which takes place in the early preschool years, when children seek to establish themselves as independent beings.

avoidant attachment An attachment pattern signaling some difficulty between parent and child; the infant seems to ignore the parent much of the time, seldom uses the parent as a secure base, and shows little evidence of separation distress.

basic trust versus mistrust In Erikson's theory of psychosocial development, the first developmental crisis; an infant who masters this crisis develops confidence in the reliability of other people and a sense that the self is worthy of confidence as well as an understanding that he should be wary of some people and situations.

babbling The strings of sounds that infants begin to make at 4 or 5 months of age.

behavioral system A group of related species-specific behaviors that individual members of the species can perform flexibly, in various ways.

behaviorism See **learning theory.**

blind scoring Use of a trained observer who records behaviors without being told about the hypothesis under study or the experimental conditions.

cephalocaudal Pertaining to growth in a head-to-foot or head-to-tail direction.

cerebral cortex The layer of nerve cells that forms the outer covering of the brain and is the primary center for motor functions, sensory discriminations, and intellectual processes.

cesarean section Delivery of a baby through an incision in the mother's abdomen and uterus.

chromosomes In the nucleus of every cell, rod-shaped structures that contain the genes. Human genes are grouped into 46 chromosomes, 23 pairs, including the X and Y chromosomes, which specify an individual's sex: XX female, XY male.

circular reactions In Piaget's theory, repetitious sensorimotor behaviors characteristic of infants.

classical conditioning Also called Pavlovian conditioning. The establishment of a connection between a response (for example, salivation) that normally occurs to a given stimulus (for example, food) and a previously neutral stimulus (for example, a buzzer). See also **conditioned response, conditioned stimulus, unconditioned response** and **unconditioned stimulus**.

clinical method of observation A technique of study in which the observer tries to remain detached but sometimes leads the interaction in order to elicit the behavior that is being studied.

cognition Knowledge, understanding, or the process by which a person acquires knowledge or understanding.

cognitive social-learning theory A synthesis of cognitive-developmental and social-learning theories, focusing on both the influence of the environment on behavior and the cognitive processes that people use in understanding and interpreting those influences.

cognitive style An individual's general disposition to respond to a wide range of cognitive tasks with a similar pattern of behavior.

cohort A group of persons of nearly the same age, who are therefore likely to share some common experiences different from those of younger or older groups.

competence motivation According to R. White, a universal inborn motive to master one's environment.

complexive thinking The tendency to string ideas together into a series in which each idea may be related to the next one but the ideas are not unified by a concept or system.

concrete-operational period The third period of cognitive development, beginning at age 6 or 7 years. It is characterized by the development of logical thinking about concrete events and experiences, but not hypothetical or abstract ones.

conditioned reinforcer In learning theories, a stimulus that increases the frequency of a given response because it has become associated with the primary reinforcer of that response.

conditioned response In classical conditioning, a response to a stimulus that, before learning, did not elicit that response (for example, the salivation of a dog to the sound of a buzzer).

conditioned stimulus In classical conditioning, a stimulus that before learning was neutral but after learning is able to elicit a conditioned response (for example, the conditioned stimulus of a buzzer can cause a dog to salivate).

conservation The ability to understand that some aspects of an object or a substance remain unchanged even though the substance or object is altered in form.

control condition See **control group**.

control group Subjects in a study or experiment who are treated as much as possible like the experimental subjects except that they do not undergo the experimental manipulation.

controlled observation Methods designed to control observer bias; they include written scoring protocols, blind scoring, control groups, and using two or more independent observers.

conventional level of moral development In L. Kohlberg's cognitive-developmental theory of moral development, the second of three levels of moral development. At this level, judgments are based on what other people approve of and what pleases them. It includes Stage 3, (good-boy/good-girl orientation) and Stage 4 (law-and-order orientation).

corpus callosum The bundle of nerve fibers that connects the brain's two hemispheres.

correlation A measure of how well the ranking of individuals on one factor predicts the ranking of the same or related individuals on another factor. A correlation can indicate whether there is any systematic relation between two factors. A **positive correlation** indicates that a high rank on one factor predicts a high rank on another (for example, IQ and school grades). A **negative correlation** indicates that a high rank on one factor predicts a low rank on the other (for example, test anxiety and school grades).

cortex See **cerebral cortex**.

critical period See **sensitive period**.

cross-sectional study A developmental study that simultaneously compares the behavior of groups of people who are similar to one another in all important respects but age.

crystallized intelligence Problem-solving abilities reflecting the kinds of skills that are explicitly taught, particularly in schools. According to Cattell and Horn, crystallized intelligence and fluid intelligence make up general intelligence.

decalage Piaget's term for unevenness in a person's performance on tasks that Piaget created to test cognitive development; that is, evidence that an individual uses thinking characteristic of more than one stage of cognitive development.

defense mechanism A means for reducing anxiety by keeping unacceptable impulses and thoughts in the unconscious from becoming conscious.

deferred imitation The ability to imitate an action that one has observed much earlier.

deidentification   A relationship between siblings in which one (usually the younger) tries to adopt attitudes and behaviors very different from the other's—often in order to avoid direct competition.

dependent variable   In an experiment, the factor that the researcher observes to determine whether it is affected by changes in the independent variable.

developmental crisis   In Erikson's theory of psychosocial development, a developmental turning point or stage in which an individual's maturing capacities are challenged by important new social requirements or opportunities.

developmental quotient (DQ)   A combined measure of an infant's developmental status on several physical and behavioral scales.

difficult temperament   According to Chess and Thomas, the temperament of an infant who shows irregular patterns of eating and sleeping, withdraws from new objects or people, adapts slowly to changes, reacts to stimuli with great intensity, and is often cranky.

discrimination   In learning theories, the process of learning to respond differently to stimuli that differ, even though the difference may be only a slight one.

dishabituation   In learning theories, an increase in response to a stimulus that formerly elicited a low level of responding, or an increase in response to a novel stimulus after habituation to another one. See **habituation.**

DNA   The chemical material that makes up genes.

dominant gene   Some gene pairs are heterozygous, meaning that the genes of a pair carry different chemical instructions. When the instructions of one of the genes completely determine the chemical substance produced by the pair, that gene is said to be dominant; the other gene of the pair is then said to be **recessive.**

Down's syndrome   A set of abnormalities resulting from there being three chromosomes in the twenty-first position instead of the normal two. Severe mental retardation is often an outcome.

dyslexia   A disability of perceptual-motor coordination that makes it hard to perceive differences between the shapes of letters and to reproduce drawings of simple shapes. The main symptoms of the disability are problems in reading.

easy temperament   According to Chess and Thomas, the temperament of an infant who has regular patterns of eating and sleeping, readily approaches new objects and people, adapts easily to changes, reacts with low or moderate intensity to stimulation, and generally displays a cheerful mood.

ego   According to psychodynamic theories, the agency of the mind that is rational and sensible and that deals directly with the outside world. See **id** and **superego.**

egocentrism   In general, the inability to take another person's point of view; in adolescents, the inability to differentiate between one's own attitudes and what one believes others' attitudes to be.

Electra conflict   According to Freud, a universal process in females that takes place during the phallic stage of psychosexual development. The conflict arises from a girl's desire to replace her mother in order to have sole possession of her father; it is resolved by the girl's identification with her mother.

embryonic period   The period of prenatal development from the end of the second week to the end of the second month. Followed by the **fetal period.**

equilibrium   According to Piaget, the state of mind of a person when assimilation and accommodation of a scheme produce agreement between the scheme and the person's experience.

erogenous zone   In Freud's theory of psychosexual development, an area of the body that is the focus of pleasure. The five developmental stages described by Freud are characterized by different erogenous zones.

ethological observation   Also called naturalistic observation. An observation technique by which an observer studies animals or people in their natural environment and attempts to avoid affecting ongoing behavior (by remaining hidden, for example).

expansion   An adult's repetition of a child's utterance but expanded or in a slightly different form.

expressive jargon   The sound sequences many infants make at about a year of age that reproduce the intonation and sounds of the language they hear but contain no real words.

extinction   In learning theories, the reduction in frequency (often to zero) of a behavior by discontinuance of a reinforcement.

extroversion   A relatively enduring quality of personality characterized by outgoingness and the enjoyment of numerous social contacts; opposed to **introversion.**

failure to thrive   A term coined by R. Spitz to describe the depressed state of institutionalized infants.

feature extraction   An information-processing method used by computers to "read" letters or numbers—to distinguish them from each other.

fetal period   The period of prenatal development beginning at the start of the third month after fertilization and ending at birth. Preceded by the embryonic period.

fixation   In Freud's theory of psychosexual development, failure to develop to a further stage because of frustration of needs or excessive indulgence in the pleasures of a given stage.

fixed action pattern   A series of movements or behaviors, performed frequently, that varies little from animal to animal within a species.

fluid intelligence Problem-solving abilities not deriving from school learning. According to Cattell and Horn, fluid intelligence and crystallized intelligence make up general intelligence.

formal-operational period The fourth period of cognitive development, beginning at about 12 years of age. It is characterized by a growing ability to think logically about hypothetical statements and ideas.

free association A basic procedure used in psychoanalytic therapy, in which a patient is encouraged to express every thought as it comes.

gender permanence The understanding that one's gender is permanent, which develops about age 6 or 7. Analogous to object permanence.

gene The basic hereditary unit; a segment of DNA that controls the production of a single bodily substance.

general intelligence The combination of fluid and crystallized intelligence.

generalization In learning theories, a learned ability to respond in a similar way to stimuli that have some property in common.

genital stage In Freud's theory of psychosexual development, the fifth and last stage, in which the focus of pleasure is the genital area. This stage begins with puberty and lasts through adulthood.

genotype The genes carried by a person for any given trait, or a person's total set of genes.

germinal period The first two weeks of prenatal development after fertilization. See also **embryonic period** and **fetal period.**

glial cells Cells that help compose the body's nervous system, especially the brain. Their function is not known with certainty.

grammar In psycholinguistics, the rules actually used by a person (as opposed to written rules) to construct the sentences he or she speaks.

grasping reflex In newborns, closing the hand and grasping in response to a touch on the palm.

greeting response A set of facial gestures and sounds that are made by all human infants in response to other people and that are recognized by them as a greeting. A species-specific human behavior.

habituation In learning theories, a decrease in response to a stimulus that originally had elicited a high level of responding. See also **dishabituation.**

hemispheric specialization For the most part, the right and left halves or hemispheres, of the human cerebral cortex control different sides of the body. They also seem to specialize in different intellectual functions.

heterozygous Pertaining to two genes of a pair that contain different chemical instructions. See **homozygous**.

hierarchy The arrangement of a set of elements in a ranked order. In cognitive-developmental theory, the relationship between the four periods of development, in which each period builds upon and incorporates developments of the preceding period.

homozygous Pertaining to two genes of a pair that contain the same chemical instructions. See **heterozygous.**

hyperactivity A high activity level coupled with difficulty in focusing attention and in remaining quiet in structured situations; a common form of developmental lag.

id According to Freud, the agency of the mind which is the reservoir of libido; it is present from birth onward, and its basic motivation is the pursuit of pleasure. See also **ego** and **superego.**

identification A child's imitating behaviors or adopting attitudes of a person whom the child admires; the process of striving to be similar to another person.

identity, personal The sense of who one is and who one wants to be, given one's social environment.

identity confusion According to Erikson, a problem in identity formation due to other people's perceiving an adolescent in ways very different from the way the adolescent views herself or himself.

identity foreclosure According to Erikson, a problem due to an adolescent's accepting an identity imposed on him or her by others, while his or her own sense of personality is still unformed.

identity versus role confusion In Erikson's theory of psychosocial development, the fifth and central developmental crisis. It takes place during adolescence, when cognitive, social, and personality development can culminate in the formation of an identity.

imitation See **observational learning**.

imprinting A learning mechanism that is active during a short period early in the life of some social species. Its result is the recognition of kindred members of the species and the formation of social bonds with them.

impulsive cognitive style An individual's general tendency to respond to a wide range of cognitive tasks in a rushed, inaccurate manner.

incest taboo The prohibition of the mating of blood relatives, especially between parents and children or between brothers and sisters.

independent variable In an experiment, the factor that the researcher manipulates. See also **dependent variable.**

industry versus inferiority In Erikson's theory of psychosocial development, the fourth developmental crisis. It takes place during the middle years of childhood, when children are eager to accomplish real and practical things and can gain a feeling of self-esteem from those accomplishments.

initiative versus guilt   The third developmental crisis in Erikson's theory of psychosocial development. It takes place during the later preschool years, when children seek to establish themselves as capable of acting on their own.

instrumental conditioning   See **operant conditioning.**

intelligence quotient   See **IQ.**

introversion   A relatively enduring quality of personality characterized by shyness, avoidance of social contacts, and pursuit of solitary activities; opposed to **extroversion.**

IQ   Any standardized measure of intelligence based on a scale in which 100 is defined to be average.

latency stage   In Freud's theory of psychosexual development, the fourth stage, in which there is a general repression of sexuality. This stage extends from about 6 years of age to puberty, and it is followed by the **genital stage.**

learned helplessness   According to Seligman, a profound sense of one's inability to have an effect on things or people; it is produced by an extremely punishing or totally indifferent environment.

learning theory   Also called behaviorism. A theory that focuses on the study of observable behavior and contends that the environment alone, through reinforcement and punishment, is responsible for how children develop.

libido   According to Freud, the primitive psychic energy that fuels all human thought and behavior; it is present from birth onward.

long-term memory   That part of memory that processes information retrieved weeks or years after it is encoded; opposed to **short-term memory.**

longitudinal study   A study in which the same group of subjects is repeatedly tested as they grow older.

low-birth-weight infant   An infant born after a normal gestational period who weighs less than 5½ pounds.

meiosis   The process of cell division that produces sperm cells and egg cells, which have half the normal complement of chromosomes.

menarche   The onset of menstruation.

metamemory   Awareness of one's own memory abilities and of how to apply them to particular memorization tasks.

metaphor   A figure of speech that takes a word or phrase from its ordinary context and uses it in an unusual context in order to suggest a likeness or analogy.

mitosis   The process of cell division that reproduces cells.

model   In observational learning, the person whose behavior is observed.

multiplication of classes   The cognitive ability to combine two classes into a joint class.

myelin   The insulation-like coating that develops around many neurons. It speeds up the transmission of impulses through the neurons and reduces interference between unrelated chemical "messages."

myelination   The growth of myelin to cover nerve cells.

myelogenetic cycle   A period during which myelin forms around nerves within a particular system in the brain.

natural childbirth   A method of childbirth requiring less medication than conventional childbirth in a hospital. The mother is prepared by instruction in the birth process and training in breathing and muscle control aimed at making labor less painful.

naturalistic observation   See **ethological observation.**

natural selection   In the theory of evolution, the higher survival rate of individuals better able to adapt to a particular environment or to environmental changes.

necessary truth   A person's assertion or certainty that a substance "must" have remained unchanged, even though some evidence might indicate otherwise.

negative correlation   See **correlation.**

negative reinforcement   In learning theories, the removal of an aversive event following a behavior with the result that the behavior becomes more frequent.

neuron   The long, thin cells that compose the body's nerves.

nondisjunction   Failure of chromosomes to separate normally during meiosis.

object permanence   The understanding, fully attained at about 2 years of age, that an object continues to exist even when the infant is not looking at, touching, or hearing it.

observational learning   Also called imitation. Acquisition of some new behavior or knowledge through watching the behavior of others.

observer bias   An observer's expectations can unintentionally affect the observer's interpretation of events, causing a biased report of what was seen.

Oedipus conflict   According to Freud, a universal conflict in males that takes place during the phallic stage of psychosexual development. The conflict arises from a boy's desire to replace his father in order to have sole possession of his mother; it is resolved by the boy's identification with his father.

open classroom   A classroom usually having small movable tables and chairs that can be conveniently rearranged to fit different activities. Commonly, it includes special activity centers to which children may move when they like. Teaching is most often done with small groups or individual students rather than with the entire class. See **traditional classroom.**

operant behavior   Any behavior naturally performed, or emitted, by an organism.

operant conditioning   Also called instrumental conditioning. The use of rewards (reinforcement) or punishment to shape or change the frequency of behaviors that an organism naturally performs.

operating principles of language acquisition   According to D. Slobin, a set of strategies for learning language that are inherited as species-specific language abilities of human beings.

operation   In Piaget's cognitive-developmental theory, a mental action, or representation, that is reversible.

oral stage   In Freud's theory of psychosexual development, the first stage, in which the erogenous zone is the mouth and lips. This stage lasts into the second year of life, and it is followed by the **anal stage.**

ossification   The process of replacement of cartilage by bone during development.

overregularization   Application of a language rule to a word or phrase that does not follow that rule, as in "goed."

parallel play   Two or more 2- or 3-year-olds playing side by side but not cooperating.

parental style   A designation of how parents treat their children, based commonly on observations scored according to two broad ranges of behavior, the love-hostility dimension and the permissiveness-restrictiveness dimension.

partial reinforcement   In learning theories, a schedule of reinforcement for a given behavior that delivers reinforcement after some correct performances of that behavior, but not after all of them.

Pavlovian conditioning   See **classical conditioning.**

perception   The organization and interpretation of sensations to give them meaning.

perceptual-motor disability   A group of specific learning disabilities that appear to have some kind of organic cause; dyslexia, for example.

performance   In learning theories, an organism's observable behavior; from changes in performance, it can sometimes be inferred that learning has taken place.

permissive parental style   According to D. Baumrind, the style of parents who, relative to others, are warmer and more loving than others, exercise less control over their children's behavior, demand less in terms of achievement, and accept relatively unsocialized behavior.

personal identity   See **identity, personal.**

personification   The attribution of human characteristics to objects.

perspective taking   Taking another person's point of view.

phallic stage   In Freud's theory of psychosexual development, the third stage, in which children first focus on the genitals as a source of pleasure. This stage extends from about 3 to about 6 years of age, and it is followed by the **latency stage.**

phenotype   An observable trait of an organism, or a set of its traits. A phenotype may or may not accurately reflect a genotype.

phenylketonuria (PKU)   A disorder produced by an abnormality in a single gene pair, causing the body to accumulate destructively high levels of phenylalanine, which is present in many common foods.

placenta   Disc-shaped organ that develops in the uterus to supply oxygen and nutrients to the fetus and carry off its wastes and carbon dioxide. It is expelled from the mother's body after the baby's birth, when it is called the afterbirth.

polygenic   Inheritance depending on the combined effect of a number of genes.

positive correlation.   See **correlation.**

positive reinforcement   In learning theories, a favorable event following a behavior with the result that the behavior becomes more frequent. Also called reward.

pragmatics   The study of how speech is used in social contexts.

preoperational period   The second period of cognitive development, between about ages 2 years and 6 years. It begins with development of the capacity for representational thoughts, and it is characterized by egocentrism and complexive thinking, among other things.

preconventional level of moral development   In L. Kohlberg's cognitive-developmental theory of moral development, the first of three levels of moral development. At this level, judgments are based solely on direct physical consequences and on the person's own needs. It includes Stage 1 (punishment and obedience orientation) and Stage 2 (marketplace orientation).

primary circular reaction   In Piaget's theory, a simple action that is repeated many times, seemingly for its own sake. Most common in infants between 1 and 6 months old.

primary process   According to Freud, thought processes that occur in dreams, daydreams, and some serious psychological disorders. Primary process is characterized by a lack of rationality and logic.

principled level of moral development   In L. Kohlberg's cognitive-developmental theory of moral development, the third of three levels of development. At this level, judgments are based on general moral principles not tied to one's own society's norms. It includes Stage 5 (the contractual-legalistic orientation) and Stage 6 (the universal-ethical-principle orientation).

proximodistal Pertaining to growth in an inner-to-outer direction.

psychoanalysis Psychoanalytic theory and the clinical therapeutic methods that have grown from it.

psychoanalytic theory Freud's theory of psychological and sexual development.

psychodynamic theories Theories based at least in part on Freudian theory.

psycholinguist A person who studies the relationships between language and the behavioral characteristics of those who use it.

psychosocial dwarfism Cessation of a child's growth that is traceable to prolonged periods of abuse or neglect.

puberty The physical changes that result in reproductive maturity.

punishment In learning theories, any event following a behavior with the result that the behavior becomes less frequent.

reaction range The limits set by genetic inheritance on the range of an individual's abilities or traits.

recessive gene See **dominant gene.**

reflective cognitive style An individual's general disposition to respond to a wide range of cognitive tasks in a slow, deliberate, and accurate manner.

reflex An automatic reaction, usually to a specific stimulus. See **grasping reflex, rooting reflex, stepping reflex, sucking reflex,** and **tonic neck reflex.**

regression In psychoanalytic therapy, a return to the use of behavior typical of an earlier stage of psychosexual development. It is a sign of fixation during psychosexual development.

reinforcement schedule See **schedule of reinforcement.**

reinforcer In learning theories, any event following a behavior with the result that the behavior becomes more frequent.

representation In cognitive-developmental theory, the ability to think about the properties of things independently of one's direct actions on them. This ability begins to appear at 1½ to 2 years of age.

reward See **positive reinforcement.**

Rh factor A component of blood. In the great majority of individuals, the component is Rh positive; in the rest it is Rh negative.

rooting reflex In newborns, turning the head in the direction of a touch on the cheek and opening the mouth as if seeking nourishment.

scaffolding A social learning process in infants, in which parents help infants to learn a complex behavior by supporting the learning of simpler components of the behavior.

scanning rules According to M. Haith, inborn neural connections that cause newborns to survey their visual field in ways that promote active visual experience.

schedule of reinforcement In learning theories, the planned distribution of reinforcements for repetition of a given behavior. See also **partial reinforcement.**

scheme According to Piaget, a piece of structured knowledge about how to perform a particular physical or mental action.

scoring protocol In controlled observation, a well-defined list of behaviors to be recorded, with instructions on how to score each of them.

secondary circular reaction In Piaget's theory, an action repeated many times in order to produce an effect that the infant finds interesting or pleasurable. Most common between the ages of 4 and 12 months.

secondary process According to Freud, the orderly, systematic, logical thinking done by the conscious mind.

secure attachment According to Ainsworth, the healthiest attachment pattern of infant to parent, in which the infant is comfortable when in contact with the parent, uses the parent as a secure base, and readily explores the environment but returns to the parent when frightened or upset.

secure base An important aspect of a healthy attachment pattern, in which an infant with a secure attachment feels safe in exploring the environment as long as he or she can have periodic contact with the parent.

self-fulfilling prophecy A person's expectations produce the result that was expected.

sensation The experience that occurs when a sense organ is stimulated; sensory data. See also **perception.**

sensitive period Formerly called critical period. A limited time period during which a development is particularly sensitive to environmental stimulation—either particularly vulnerable (as in the effect of drugs on prenatal development) or particularly able to profit from learning (as in the effect of experience on language development).

sensorimotor period The first of four periods of cognitive development, from about 2 months of age to about 2 years. In this period, an infant's schemes are entirely based in action because the infant is incapable of representation.

sensory capacity Ability to receive and respond to information from the senses—vision, hearing, touch, taste, and smell.

separation and individuation A number of social processes by which infants mentally separate themselves from their parents and establish an independent self-concept.

separation distress Vigorous crying when a parent leaves the infant's presence. It becomes prominent at 8 or 9 months of age and disappears at about 24 months.

sex role A group of social norms that defines appropriate behavior for males or for females.

sexual identity A component of personal identity. A sense of oneself as a practitioner and recipient of sexual behavior; also, a sense of oneself in relation to the norms defining the feminine role or the masculine role.

short-gestation-period infant An infant born after a shorter-than-usual period in the uterus.

short-term memory Also called working memory. That part of the memory that processes information retrieved within a few minutes of its being encoded; opposed to **long-term memory**.

sickle cell An abnormal, sickle-shaped red blood cell. This shape is due to an inherited trait that may be heterozygous, producing few ill effects (and, in fact, offering some protection against malaria), or homozygous, producing sickle-cell anemia, a severe and chronic condition.

sign stimulus A sensory input that regularly elicits a particular fixed action pattern in members of a species.

skeletal age The apparent age of a child's skeleton judged by the extent of its ossification.

slow-to-warm-up temperament According to Chess and Thomas, the temperament of an infant who has a low activity level, tends to withdraw from unfamiliar objects, reacts with a low level of intensity, and adapts slowly to changes in the environment.

social norms A society's standards or rules for appropriate behavior.

social role A group of social norms that defines a specific social category, usually in terms of age, sex, or occupation.

social smile The smile infants display in response to other people, beginning at about 2½ months of age.

social referencing A social learning process in infants, whereby infants watch emotional reactions of others to some new event or object and use that reaction to determine their own.

socialization The process by which children learn the attitudes, knowledge, and skills that enable them to be effective members of their society.

species A group of organisms that share many common characteristics and that can interbreed.

species-specific behavior A behavior that all members of a species perform in much the same way; a behavior characteristic of a species.

specific learning disability In contrast to mental retardation, a physiological or psychological problem that interferes with only a certain kind of learning.

stage A period of development that is qualitatively different in some way from the periods before and after it and that usually incorporates characteristics of preceding periods.

state An infant's degree of arousal, ranging along a continuum from deep sleep to active crying.

stepping reflex In newborns, stepping movements in response to being held upright with the feet touching a surface.

stimulus control In learning theories, the regulation of behavior by a stimulus that is associated with reinforcement.

stranger distress Wariness or crying in the presence of strangers. It begins at about 7 to 9 months and lasts into the second year of life.

sublimation According to Freud, the channeling of the libido's energy into nonsexual areas of endeavor.

sucking reflex In newborns, sucking in response to the feel of something on or in the mouth.

superego According to psychodynamic theory, the agency of the mind that develops as a child absorbs parental and societal rules and standards.

synapse The small space between neurons, across which chemical "messages" travel.

telegraphic speech Early preschoolers' speech, which resembles the language used in telegrams in omitting all but the most essential words of a message.

temperament A characteristic way of behaving or responding, present in early infancy, that seems to depend almost entirely on inborn physical factors.

tertiary circular reaction In Piaget's theory, an action repeated many times in various ways so that the infant seems to be investigating the different results. Most common in infants between 11 and 22 months old.

tonic neck reflex In newborns, when the head is turned to the right side, the right arm is extended straight out while the left arm is bent, in a fencer's posture. The opposite occurs when the head is turned to the left.

traditional classroom A classroom that has a fixed daily curriculum tied to a rigid time schedule and that is usually organized with the teacher at the front of the room and the children at rows of desks in assigned seats. See **open classroom**.

transitional object An object—often a stuffed toy or blanket—that infants become attached to during the process of separation and individuation.

umbilical cord The cord connecting the fetus to the placenta.

unconditioned response In classical conditioning, a response that an organism naturally makes to a stimulus (for example, salivation is the unconditioned response of dogs to food).

unconditioned stimulus In classical conditioning, a stimulus that normally elicits a given response (for example, food normally elicits salivation by dogs).

unconscious   The part of the mind holding memories and drives that are unacceptable in form or content to the conscious mind.

underachiever   A student who earns considerably lower grades than his or her IQ would predict; generally, a person whose achievements are less notable than the level others expect of him or her.

viability   In prenatal development, the point at which a fetus born prematurely is regarded as having some chance of survival. Currently considered to be six months, or 180 days, after fertilization.

visual cliff   An apparatus for testing depth perception in infants; essentially a glass-topped table, one side of which appears to have a sheer drop of several feet.

wild children   Children who grow up in virtual isolation from human society.

working memory   See **short-term memory.**

X-linked trait   A trait that is expressed only in males because the trait is controlled by a gene on the X chromosome for which there is no paired gene on the smaller Y chromosome.

REFERENCES

Achenbach, T. M. *Research in developmental psychology: Concepts, strategies, and methods.* New York: Free Press, 1978.

Achenbach, T. M. "The status of research related to psychopathology." In W. A. Collins (Ed.), *Research on school-age children: A report of the Panel to Review the Status of Basic Research on School-age Children.* Washington, D. C.: National Academy of Sciences Press, 1984.

Adams, M. S., and J. V. Neal. "Children of incest," *Pediatrics,* 1967, 40:55–62

Adelson, J. "The political imagination of the young adolescent." In J. Kagan and R. Coles (Eds.), *12 to 16: Early adolescence.* New York: Norton, 1972.

Adelson, J. "The development of ideology in adolescence." In S. E. Dragastin and G. H. Elder, Jr. (Eds.), *Adolescence in the life cycle.* Washington, D. C.: Hemisphere Publishing Corp., 1975.

Adelson, J., and R. P. O'Neil. "Growth of political ideas in adolescence: The sense of community," *Journal of Personality and Social Psychology,* 1966, 3 (4):295–306.

Adelson, J., B. Green, and R. P. O'Neil. "The growth of the idea of law in adolescence," *Developmental Psychology,* 1969, 1:327–332.

Ahlstrom, W. M., and R. J. Havighurst. *400 Losers.* San Francisco: Jossey-Bass, 1971.

Ainsworth, M. D. S. "Infant-mother attachment," *American Psychologist,* 1979, 34:932-937.

Ainsworth, M. D. S., M. C. Blehar, E. Waters, and S. Wall. *Patterns of attachment.* Hillsdale, N.J.: Erlbaum, 1978.

Alberts, J. R. "Ontogeny of olfaction: Reciprocal roles of sensation and behavior in the development of perception." In R. N. Aslin, J. R. Alberts, and M. R. Petersen (Eds.), *Development of perception* (vol. 1). New York: Academic Press, 1981.

Allen, V. L., and D. Newston. "The development of conformity and independence," *Journal of Personality and Social Psychology,* 1972, 22:18–30.

Allison, A. C. "Protection afforded by sickle cell trait against subtertian malarial infection," *British Medical Journal,* 1954, 1:290–294.

American Academy of Pediatrics, Committee on Nutrition, and the Canadian Pediatric Society, Nutrition Committee. "Breastfeeding: A commentary and celebration of the International Year of the Child," *Pediatrics,* 1978, 62:491–560.

American College of Obstretrics and Gynecology. *Guidelines on pregnancy and work,* National Institute for Occupational Safety and Health publication no. 78-118. Washington, D. C.: U.S. Department of Health Education, and Welfare, 1977.

Amiel-Tison, C. "Neurological signs, aetiology, and implications." In P. Stratton (Ed.), *Psychobiology of the human newborn.* New York: Wiley, 1982.

Andrews, S. R., J. B. Blumenthal, D. L. Johnson, A.J. Kahn, C. J. Ferguson, T. M. Lasater, P. E. Malone, and D. B. Wallace. "The skills of mothering: A study of parent child development centers," *Monographs of the Society for Research in Child Development,* 1982, 47 (no. 6, serial no. 198).

Anglin, J. M. *The growth of word meaning* (Research monograph no. 63). Cambridge, Massachusetts: The MIT Press, 1970.

Antonov, A. N. "Children born during the siege of Leningrad in 1942," *Journal of Pediatrics,* 1947, 30:250–259

Apgar, V., D. A. Holaday, L. S. James, I. M. Weisbrot, and C. Berrien. "Evaluation of the newborn infant—second report," *Current Researches in Anesthesia and Analgesia,* 1953, 32:260–267.

Archer, J. "Sex differences in maturation." In K. J. Connolly and H. F. R. Prechtl (Eds.), *Maturation and development: Biological and psychological perspectives.* London: Heinemann, 1981.

Ariès, P. *Centuries of childhood: A social history of family life.* New York: Vintage, 1962.

Arlin, P. K. "Cognitive development in adulthood: A fifth stage?" *Developmental Psychology,* 1975, 11:602–606.

Aronfreed, J. *Conduct and conscience: The socialization of internalized control over behavior.* New York: Academic Press, 1968.

Aronfreed, J. "The concept of internalization." In

D. A. Goslin (Ed.), *Handbook of socialization theory and research*. Chicago: Rand McNally, 1969.

Asch, S. "Effects of group pressure upon the modification and distortion of judgments." In H. Guetzkow (Ed.), *Groups, leadership, and men*. Pittsburgh: Carnegie Press, 1951.

Asch, S. E., and H. Nerlove. "The development of double function terms in children: An exploratory investigation." In B. Kaplan and S. Wapner (Eds.), *Perspectives in psychological theory: Essays in honor of Heinz Werner*. New York: International Universities Press, 1960.

Ashley, M. J. "Alcohol use during pregnancy: A challenge for the '80s," *Canadian Medical Association Journal*, 1981, *125* (2):141–142.

Atkinson, J. W. "Motivation for achievement." In T. Blass (Ed.), *Personality variables in social behavior*. Hillsdale, N.J.: Erlbaum, 1977.

Atkinson, J., and O. Braddick. "Sensory and perceptual capacities of the neonate." In P. Stratton (Ed.), *Psychobiology of the human newborn*. New York: Wiley, 1982.

Atkinson, J. W., and G. H. Litwin. "Achievement motive and test anxiety," *Journal of Abnormal and Social Psychology*, 1960, 60:52–63.

Bachman, J. G. *Youth in transition* (vol. 2), "The impact of family background and intelligence on tenth-grade boys." Ann Arbor, Michigan: Institute for Social Research, University of Michigan, 1970.

Baizerman, M. "Can the first pregnancy of a young adolescent be prevented? A question which must be answered," *Journal of Youth and Adolescence*, 1977, 6:343–352.

Baldwin, J. M. *Mental development in the child and the race*. New York: MacMillan, 1894.

Baltes, P. B., S. W. Cornelius, and J. R. Nesselroade. "Cohort effects in developmental psychology." In J. R. Nesselroade and P. B. Baltes (Eds.), *Longitudinal research in the behavioral sciences: Design and analysis*. New York: Academic Press, 1979.

Bandura, A. "Influence of model's reinforcement contingencies on the acquisition of imitative responses," *Journal of Personality and Social Psychology*, 1965, 1:589–595.

Bandura, A. "Social-learning theory of identificatory processes." In D. A. Goslin (Ed.), *Handbook of socialization theory and research*. Chicago: Rand McNally, 1969.

Bandura, A. "Self-referent thought: The development of self-efficacy." In J. Flavell and L. Ross (Eds.), *New directions in the study of social-cognitive development*. Cambridge: Cambridge University Press, 1980.

Bandura, A., and F. J. MacDonald. "Influence of social reinforcement and the behavior of models in shaping children's moral judgments," *Journal of Abnormal and Social Psychology*, 1963, 67:274–281.

Bandura, A., and R. H. Walters. *Adolescent aggression: A study of the influences of child-training practices and family interrelations*. New York: Ronald Press, 1959.

Bandura, A., D. Ross, and S. A. Ross. "Imitation of film-mediated aggressive models," *Journal of Abnormal and Social Psychology*, 1963, 66:3–11.

Bang, Vinh. "La methode clinique et la recherche en psychologie de l'enfant." In *Psychologie et epistémologie génétiques: Thèmes Piagétiens*. Paris: Dunod, 1966.

Barclay, A. G., and D. Cusumano. "Father absence, cross-sex identity, and field dependent behavior in male adolescents," *Child Development*, 1967, 38:243–250.

Barenboim, C. "The development of person perception in childhood and adolescence: From behavioral comparisons to psychological constructs to psychological comparisons," *Child Development*, 1981, 52:129–144.

Barkley, R. A., "A review of stimulant drug research with hyperactive children," *Journal of Child Psychology and Psychiatry*, 1977, 18:137–165.

Barlow, G. W. "Ethological units of behavior." In D. Ingle (Ed.), *Central nervous system and fish behavior*. Chicago: University of Chicago Press, 1968.

Baron, J. "Orthographic and word-specific mechanisms in children's reading of words," *Child Development*, 1979, 50:60–72.

Bartak, L., and M. Rutter. "Differences between mentally retarded and normally intelligent autistic children," *Journal of Autism and Childhood Schizophrenia*, 1976, 6:109–120.

Bates, E. *Language and context: Studies in the acquisition of pragmatics.* New York: Academic Press, 1976.

Baumrind, C. "Current patterns of parental authority," *Developmental Psychology Monographs,* 1971, 4(1, pt. 2).

Baumrind, D. "Harmonious parents and their preschool children," *Developmental Psychology,* 1971, 4:99–102.

Baumrind, D. "Early socialization and adolescent competence." In S. E. Dragastin and G. H. Elder (Eds.), *Adolescence in the life cycle.* Washington, D. C.: Hemisphere Publishing Corp., 1975.

Baumrind, D. "New directions in socialization research," *American Psychologist,* 1980, 35:639–652.

Baumrind, D., and A. E. Black. "Socialization practices associated with dimensions of competence in preschool boys and girls," *Child Development,* 1967, 38:291–327.

Bay, E. "Ontogeny of stable speech areas in the human brain." In E. H. Lenneberg and E. Lenneberg (Eds.), *Foundations of language development* (vol. 2). New York: Academic Press, 1975.

Bayley, N. "Development of mental abilities." In P. H. Mussen (Ed.), *Carmichael's manual of child psychology* (vol. 1). New York: Wiley, 1970.

Beach, F. A. (Ed.) *Sex and behavior.* New York: Wiley, 1965.

Beatty, R. A., and S. Glueksohn-Waelsh. *Edinburgh Symposium on the Genetics of Spermatozoa.* Edinburgh and New York: University of Edinburgh and Albert Einstein College of Medicine, 1972.

Becker, W. C. "Consequences of different kinds of parental discipline," *Review of Child Development Research,* 1964, 1:169–208.

Beckwith, L. "Prediction of emotional and social behavior." In J. D. Osofsky (Ed.), *Handbook of infant development.* New York: Wiley, 1979.

Bell, R. Q. "Contribution of human infants to caregiving and social interaction." In M. Lewis and L. A. Rosenblum (Eds.), *Effect of the infant on its caregiver.* New York: Wiley, 1974.

Bell, R. Q. "Parent, child, and reciprocal influences." *American Psychologist,* 1979, 34:821–826.

Belmont, L., and F. A. Morolla. "Birth order, family size, and intelligence," *Science,* 1973, *182:* 1096–1101.

Belsky, J., and L. D. Steinberg. "The effects of day care: A critical review," *Child Development,* 1978, 49:929–949.

Benedict, R. *Patterns of culture.* Boston: Houghton Mifflin, 1934.

Bereiter, C., and M. Scardamalia. "From conversation to composition: The role of instruction in a developmental process." In R. Glaser (Ed.), *Advances in instructional psychology* (vol. 2). Hillsdale, N.J.; Erlbaum, 1982.

Berenda, R. W. *The influence of the group on the judgments of children.* New York: King's Crown Press, 1950.

Berman, R. "From nonanalysis to productivity: Interim schemata in child language." In I. Levin (Ed.), *Stage and structure.* Norwood, N. J.: Ablex, 1984.

Bernstein, A. C. "How children learn about sex at birth," *Psychology Today,* January 1976.

Bernstein, A. C., and P. A. Cowan. "Children's concepts of how people get babies," *Child Development,* 1975, 46:77–91.

Berry, H. K. "Phenylketonuria: Diagnosis, treatment, and long-term management." In G. Farrell (Ed.), *Congenital mental retardation.* Austin, Texas: University of Texas Press, 1969.

Bertenthal, B. I., and K. W. Fischer. "The development of self-recognition in the infant," *Developmental Psychology,* 1978, 14:44–50.

Bertenthal, B. I., J. J. Campos, and M. M. Haith. "Development of visual organization: The perception of subjective contours." *Child Development,* 1980, 51:1072–1080.

Bettelheim, B. *The empty fortress: Infantile autism and the birth of the self.* New York: The Free Press, 1967.

Bettelheim, B. *The uses of enchantment: The meaning and importance of fairy tales.* New York: Knopf, 1976.

Betz, B., and C. B. Thomas. *Johns Hopkins Medical Journal,* 1979.

Biggs, J. B., and K. F. Collis. *Evaluating the quality of learning: The SOLO taxonomy (Structure of the Observed Learning Outcome).* New York: Academic

Press, 1982.

Biller, H. B. "Father absence and the personality development of the male child," *Developmental Psychology*, 1970, 2:181–201.

Biller, H. B. *Paternal deprivation: Family, school, sexuality, and society.* Lexington, Mass.: D. C. Heath, 1974.

Biller, H. B. "The father and personality development: Paternal deprivation and sex-role development." In M. E. Lamb (Ed.), *The role of the father in child development.* New York: Wiley, 1976.

Biller, H. B., and R. M. Bahm. "Father absence, perceived maternal behavior, and masculinity of self-concept among junior high school boys," *Developmental Psychology*, 1971, 4:301–305.

Binet, A., and T. Simon. *The development of intelligence in children* (E. S. Kite, trans.). Baltimore: Williams & Wilkins, 1916.

Block, J. H. "Conceptions of sex role: Some cross-cultural and longitudinal perspectives," *American Psychologist*, 1973, 28:512–526.

Block, J. H. "Issues, problems, and pitfalls in assessing sex differences," *Merrill-Palmer Quarterly*, 1976, 22:283–308.

Bloom, L. *Language development* (Research monograph no. 59). Cambridge, Massachusetts: The MIT Press, 1970.

Bloom, L. *One word at a time.* The Hague, Netherlands: Mouton, 1973.

Bloom, L., and M. Lahey. *Language development and language disorders.* New York: Wiley, 1978.

Bloom, L., L. Hood, and P. Lightbown. "Imitation in language development: If, when, and why," *Cognitive Psychology*, 1974, 6:380–420.

Bloom, L., L. Rocissano, and L. Hood. "Adult-child discourse: Developmental interaction between information processing and linguistic knowledge." *Cognitive Psychology*, 1976, 8:521–552.

Blos, P. *The adolescent passage.* New York: International Universities Press, 1979.

Blumenfeld, P. C., V. L. Hamilton, K. Wessels and D. Falkner. "Teaching responsibility to first graders," *Theory into Practice*, 1979, 18:174–180.

Boehm, L. "The development of independence: A comparative study," *Child Development*, 1957, 28:85–92.

Bohen, H. H., and A. Viveros-Long. *Balancing jobs and family life.* Philadelphia: Temple University Press, 1981.

Bonvillian, J. D., and K. E. Nelson. "Development of sign language in language-handicapped individuals." In P. Siple (Ed.), *Understanding language through sign language research.* New York: Academic Press, 1978.

Botwinick, J. "Intellectual abilities." In J. E. Birren and K. W. Schaie (Eds.), *Handbook of the psychology of aging.* New York: Van Nostrand Reinhold, 1977.

Bourne, E. "The state of research on ego identity: A review and appraisal," *Journal of Youth and Adolescence*, 1978, 7:223–252.

Bowes, W. A., Jr. "Obstetrical medication and infant outcome: A review of the literature." In "The effects of obstetrical medication on fetus and infant." *Monographs of the Society for Research in Child Development*, 1970, 30 (4, serial no. 137).

Bowlby, J. *Attachment and loss*; vol. 1: *Attachment.* New York: Basic Books, 1969.

Bowlby, J. *Attachment and loss*; vol. 2: Separation, anxiety, and anger. New York: Basic Books, 1973.

Bowlby, J. *Attachment and loss*; vol. 3: *Loss, sadness and depression.* New York: Basic Books, 1980.

Brackbill, Y. "Cumulative effects of continuous stimulation on arousal level in infants," *Child Development*, 1971, 42:17–26.

Brackbill, Y. "Obstetrical medication and infant behavior." In J. D. Osofsky (Ed.), *Handbook of infant development.* New York: Wiley, 1979.

Bradley, R. A. *Husband-coached childbirth.* New York: Harper & Row, 1965.

Bradley, R. H., B. M. Caldwell, and R. Elardo. "Home environment and cognitive development in the first 2 years: A cross-lagged panel analysis," *Developmental Psychology*, 1979, 15:246–250.

Brannigan, G. G., and A. Tolor. "Sex differences in adaptive styles," *Journal of Genetic Psychology*, 1971, 119:143–149.

Brazelton, T. B. "Sucking in infancy," *Pediatrics*, 1956, 17:400–404.

Brazelton, T. B., B. Koslowski, and M. Main. "The origins of reciprocity: The early mother-infant interactions." In M. Lewis and J. Rosenblum

(Eds.), *The origins of behavior*. New York: Wiley, 1974.

Bretherton, I., and Ainsworth, M. "Responses of one-year-olds to a stranger in a strange situation." In M. Lewis and J. Rosenblum (Eds.), *The origins of fear*. New York: Wiley, 1974.

Brigham, C. C. *A study of American intelligence*. Princeton, New Jersey: Princeton University Press, 1923.

Brody, E. B., and N. Brody. *Intelligence: Nature, determinants, and consequences*. New York: Academic Press, 1976.

Bronfenbrenner, U. "Response to pressure from peers versus adults among Soviet and American school children," *International Journal of Psychology*, 1967, 2:199–207.

Bronfenbrenner, U. *Two worlds of childhood: US and USSR*. New York: Russell Sage Foundation, 1970.

Bronfenbrenner, U., E. C. Devereux, G. Suci, and R. R. Rogers. "Adults and peers as sources of conformity and autonomy." Paper presented at the Conference for Socialization for Competence, Social Science Research Council, Puerto Rico, 1965.

Bronshtein, A. I., and E. P. Petrova. "The auditory analyzer in young infants." In Y. Brackbill and G. Thompson (Eds.), *Behavior in infancy and early childhood*. New York: Free Press, 1967.

Brophy, J. E., and T. L. Good. *Teacher-student relationships: Causes and consequences*. New York: Holt, Rinehart, & Winston, 1974.

Broughton, J. M. "Development of concepts of self, mind, reality, and knowledge." In *Social cognition* (New directions for child development, no. 1). San Francisco: Jossey-Bass, 1978.

Broughton, J. M. "Piaget's structural developmental psychology, III. Function and the problem of knowledge," *Human Development*, 1981, *24*: 257–285.

Broverman, I. K., S. R. Vogel, D. M. Broverman, F. E. Clarkson and P. S. Rosenkrantz. "Sex-role stereotypes: A current appraisal," *Journal of Social Issues*, 1972, 28(2): 59–78.

Brown, R. "The development of *wh* questions in child speech." *Journal of Verbal Learning and Verbal Behavior*, 1968, 7:279–290.

Brown, R. *A first language: The early stages*. Cambridge, Massachusetts: Harvard University Press, 1973.

Brown, A. L., and J. C. Campione. "Recognition memory for perceptually similar pictures in preschool children," *Journal of Experimental Psychology*, 1972, 95:55–62.

Brown, R. and C. Hanlon. "Derivational complexity and order of acquisition in child speech." In J. R. Hayes (Ed.), *Cognition and the development of language*. New York: Wiley, 1970.

Brown, A. L., and S. S. Smiley. "Rating the importance of structural units of prose passages: A problem of metacognitive development," *Child Development*, 1977, 48:1–8.

Brown, E. S., and R. Warner. "Mental development of phenylketonuric children on or off diet after the age of 6," *Psychological Medicine*, 1976, 6:287–296.

Brown, R., C. Cazden, and U. Bullugi. "The child's grammar from I to III." In J. P. Hill (Ed.), *Minnesota symposium on child psychology* (vol 2). Minneapolis: University of Minnesota Press, 1969.

Brown, A. L., J. D. Bransford, R. A. Ferrara, and J. C. Campione. "Learning, remembering, and understanding." In P. H. Mussen (Ed.), *Handbook of child psychology* (4th ed.); vol. 3: J. H. Flavell and E. M. Markman (Eds.), *Cognitive development*. New York: Wiley, 1983.

Bruner, J. S. "The growth and structure of skill." In K. J. Connolly (Ed.), *Mechanisms of motor skill development*. New York: Academic Press, 1970.

Bruner, J. S. *Beyond the information given: Studies in the psychology of knowing*. New York: Norton, 1973.

Bruner, J. S. "Organization of early skilled action," *Child Development*, 1973, 44:1–11.

Bruner, J. S. "From communication to language: A psychological perspective." In I. Markova (Ed.), *The social context of language*. New York: Wiley, 1978.

Bruner, J. S. "The organization of action and the nature of adult-infant transaction." In M. Cranach and R. Harre (Eds.), *The analysis of action*. New York: Cambridge University Press, 1982.

Bryan, J. H., and N. H. Walbek. "Preaching and practicing generosity: Children's actions and reactions," *Child Development*, 1970, 41:329–353.

Buisseret, P., E. Gary-Bobo, and M. Imbert. "Ocular motility and recovery of orientational properties of visual cortical neurons in dark-reared kittens," *Nature*, 1978, *272*:816–817.

Bullinger, A. "Orientation de la tête du nouveau-né en présence d'un stimulus visuel," *L'Année psychologique*, 1977, *77*:357–364.

Bullinger, A. "Cognitive elaboration of sensorimotor behavior." In G. Butterworth (Ed.), *Infancy and epistemology*. Hassocks, Eng.: Harverster Press, 1981.

Bullock, D. "Seeking relations between cognitive and social-interactive transitions." In *Levels and transitions in children's development* (New directions for child development, no. 21). San Francisco: Jossey-Bass, 1983.

Bullock, D., and A. J. Neuringer. "Social learning by following: An analysis," *Journal of the Experimental Analysis of Behavior*, 1977, *27*:127–135.

Bullowa, M. (Ed.). *Before speech: The beginning of interpersonal communication*. Cambridge: Cambridge University Press, 1979.

Caballero, C. M., P. Giles, and P. Shaver. "Sex role traditionalism and fear of success," *Sex Roles*, 1975, *1*:319–326.

Cairns, R. B. *Social development: The origins and plasticity of interchanges*. San Francisco: W. H. Freeman, 1979.

Caldwell, B. M. "The effects of infant care." In M. L. Hoffman and L. W. Hoffman (Eds.), *Review of Child Development Research*, vol. 1. New York: Russell Sage Foundation, 1964.

Cameron, J. R. "Parental treatment, children's temperament, and the risk of childhood behavior problems, 1: Relationships between parental characteristics and changes in children's temperament over time," *American Journal of Orthopsychiatry*, 1977, *47*:568–576.

Campbell, E. Q. "Adolescent socialization." In D. A. Goslin (Ed.), *Handbook of socialization theory and research*. Chicago: Rand McNally, 1969.

Campos, J. J., S. Hiatt, D. Ramsay, C. Henderson, and M. Svejda. "The emergence of fear on the visual cliff." In M. Lewis and L. Rosenblum (Eds.), *The origins of affect*. New York: Wiley, 1978.

Campos, J. J., B. I. Bertenthal, and K. Caplovitz. "The interrelationship of affect and cognition in the visual cliff situation." In C. Izard, J. Kagan, and R. Zajonc (Eds.), *Emotion and cognition*. New York: Plenum, 1982.

Campos, J. J., K. C. Barrett, M. E. Lamb, H. H. Goldsmith, and C. Stenberg. "Socioemotional development." In P. H. Mussen (Ed.), *Handbook of child psychology* (4th ed.); vol. 2: M. M. Haith and J. J. Campos (Eds.), *Infancy and developmental psychobiology*. New York: Wiley, 1983.

Carey, S., R. Diamond, and B. Woods. "Development of face recognition—a maturational component?" *Developmental Psychology*, 1980, *16*:257–269.

Carlsson, S. G., H. Fagerberg, G. Horneman, C. P. Hwang, K. Larsson, M. Rodholm, J. Schaller, G. Danielsson, and C. Gundewall. "Effects of various amounts of contact between mother and child on the mother's nursing behavior: A follow-up study," *Infant Behavior and Development*, 1979, *2*:209–214.

Carmichael, L. "Onset and early development of behavior." In P. H. Mussen (Ed.), *Carmichael's manual of child psychology* (vol. 1). New York: Wiley, 1970.

Caron, A. J., R. F. Caron, R. C. Caldwell, and S. J. Weiss. "Infant perception of the structural properties of the face," *Developmental Psychology*, 1973, *9*:385–399.

Carter, S. "Diagnosis and treatment: Management of the child who has had a convulsion," *Pediatrics*, 1964, *33*:431–434.

Carter, C. O. "Risk of offspring of incest," *The Lancet*, 1967, *1*:436.

Case, R. "The underlying mechanism of intellectual development." In J. R. Kirby and J. B. Biggs (Eds.), *Cognition, development, and instruction*. New York: Academic Press, 1980.

Case, R. *Intellectual development: A systematic reinterpretation*. New York: Academic Press, in press.

Case, R., and F. Khanna. "The missing links: Stages in children's progression from sensorimotor to logical thought." In *Cognitive development* (New directions for child development, no. 12). San Francisco: Jossey-Bass, 1981.

Cattell, R. B. *Abilities: Their structure, growth, and action.* Boston: Houghton Mifflin, 1971.

Cazden, C. "The acquisition of noun and verb inflections," *Child development,* 1968, 39:433–448.

Chandler, M. J. "Egocentrism and antisocial behavior: The assessment and training of social perspective-taking skills," *Developmental Psychology,* 1973, 9: 326–332.

Chandler, J. V. "Sex differences in the nurturant responses of adolescent children." Doctoral dissertation, University of Denver, July 1977.

Chandler, M. J., S. Greenspan, and C. Barenboim. "Assessment and training of role-taking and referential communication skills in institutionalized emotionally disturbed children," *Developmental psychology,* 1974, 10:546–553.

Chapin, H. D. "Are institutions for infants necessary?" *Journal of the American Medical Association,* January 1915.

Chavez, A., C. Martinez, and T. Yaschine. "The importance of nutrition and stimuli on child mental and social development." In J. Cravioto et al. (Eds.), *Early malnutrition and mental development.* Uppsala, Sweden: Almquist & Wiksell, 1974.

Chi, M. T. H. "Knowledge structures and memory development." In R. S. Siegler (Ed.), *Children's thinking: What develops?* Hillsdale, N.J.: Erlbaum, 1978.

Childs, St. J. R. *Malaria and the colonization of the Carolina low country 1526–1696.* Baltimore, Maryland: Johns Hopkins, 1940.

Childs, C. P., and P. M. Greenfield. "Informal modes of learning and teaching: The case of 'Zinacanteco weaving.'" In N. Warren (Ed.), *Advances in cross-cultural psychology* (vol. 2). New York: Academic Press, 1979.

Chomsky, N. *Syntactic structures.* The Hague: Mouton, 1957.

Chomsky, N. *Aspects of the theory of syntax.* Cambridge, Massachusetts: MIT Press, 1965.

Chomsky, C. *Acquisition of syntax in children from 5 to 10.* Cambridge, Massachusetts: MIT Press, 1969.

Christensen, H. T., and G. Carpenter. "Value-behavior discrepancies regarding premarital coitus in three western cultures," *American Sociological Review,* 1972, 27: 66–74.

Christensen, H. T., and C. F. Gregg. "Changing sex norms in America and Scandinavia," *Journal of Marriage and the Family,* 1970, 32:616–627.

Chukovsky, K. *From two to five* (rev. ed.). Berkeley: University of California Press, 1968.

Church, J. (Ed.). *Three babies: Biographies of cognitive development.* New York: Random House, 1966.

Cicirelli, V. G., et al. *The impact of* Head Start: *An evaluation of the effects of* Head Start *on children's cognitive and affective development* (A report presented to the Office of Economic Opportunity). Ohio State University and Westinghouse Learning Corporation, 1969.

Clark, R. "What's the use of imitation?" *Journal of Child Language,* 1977, 4:341–358.

Clark, E. V. "Meanings and concepts." In P. H. Mussen (Ed.), *Handbook of child psychology* (4th ed.); vol. 3: J. H. Flavell and E. M. Markman (Eds.), *Cognitive development.* New York: Wiley, 1983.

Clarke, C. A. "The prevention of 'rhesus' babies," *Scientific American,* 1968, 119 (November): 46–52.

Clarke, A. M., and A. P. B. Clarke. *Early experience: Myths and evidence.* London: Open Books, 1976.

Clarke-Stewart, K. A. "Popular primers for parents," *American Psychologist,* 1978, 35:359–369.

Clarke-Stewart, A. *Daycare.* Cambridge, Massachusetts: Harvard University Press, 1982.

Clarke-Stewart, K. A., and G. G. Fein. "Early childhood programs." In P. H. Mussen (Ed.), *Handbook of child psychology* (4th ed.); vol. 2: M. M. Haith and J. J. Campos (Eds.), *Infancy and developmental psychobiology.* New York: Wiley, 1983.

Clarke-Stewart, K. A., L. P. VanderStoep, and G. A. Killian. "Analysis and replication of mother-child relations at two years of age," *Child Development,* 1979, 50:777–793.

Clausen, J. A. "Family structure, socialization, and personality." In L. W. Hoffman and M. L. Hoffman (Eds.), *Review of child development research* (vol. 2). New York: Russell Sage Foundation, 1966.

Clausen, J. A. "The social meaning of differential physical and sexual maturation." In S. E. Dragastin and G. H. Elder, Jr. (Eds.), *Adolescence in the life cycle.* Washington, D. C.: Hemisphere Publishing Corp., 1975.

Cline, V. B. *Where do you draw the line? An exploration into media violence, pornography, and censorship.* Provo, Utah: Brigham Young University Press, 1974.

Cohen, Y. "The disappearance of the incest taboo," *Human Nature,* July 1978.

Cohen, L. B., and P. Salapatek. *"Infant perception: From sensation to cognition."* New York: Academic Press, 1975.

Cohen, L. B., J. S. DeLoache, and M. S. Strauss. "Infant visual perception." In J. D. Osofsky (Ed.), *Handbook of infant development.* New York: Wiley, 1979.

Coie, J. D., and K. A. Dodge. "Continuities and changes in children's social status: A five-year longitudinal study," *Merrill-Palmer Quarterly,* 1983, 29:237–260.

Colby, A., L. Kohlberg, J. Gibbs, and M. Lieberman. "A longitudinal study of moral judgment." *Monographs of the Society for Research in Child Development,* 1983, 48 (1, serial no. 200).

Cole, M., and S. Scribner. *Culture and thought: A psychological introduction.* New York: Wiley, 1974.

Cole, M., J. Gay, J. A. Glick, and D. W. Sharp. *The cultural context of learning and thinking.* New York: Basic Books, 1971.

Cole, M., and Laboratory of Comparative Human Cognition. "Culture and cognitive development." In P. H. Mussen (Ed.), *Handbook of child psychology* (4th ed.); vol. 1: W. Kessen (Ed.), *History, theory, and methods.* New York: Wiley, 1983.

Coleman, J. C. *Abnormal psychology and modern life* (5th ed.). Glenview, Illinois: Scott, Foresman, 1980.

Coleman, J. C. "Friendship and the peer group in adolescence." In J. Adelson (Ed.), *Handbook of adolescent psychology.* New York: Wiley, 1980.

Coleman, J. S., E. Q. Campbell, et al. *Equality of educational opportunity.* Washington, D. C.: United States Government Printing Office, 1966.

Coleman, J., H. Herzberg, and M. Morris. "Identity in adolescence: Present and future self-concepts," *Journal of Youth and Adolescence,* 1977, 6:63–76.

Collins, W. A., and S. W. Duncan. "Out-of-school settings in middle childhood." In W. A. Collins (Ed.), *Research on school-age children: Report of the Panel to Review the Status of Basic Research on school-age children.* Washington, D. C.: National Academy of Sciences Press, 1984.

Comenius, J. A. *The school of infancy* (E. M. Eller, trans.). Chapel Hill: University of North Carolina Press, 1956 (originally published, 1633).

Commons, M. L., R. A. Richards, and C. Armon. *Beyond formal operations: Late adolescent and adult cognitive development.* New York: Praeger, 1983.

Conel, J. L. *The postnatal development of the human cerebral cortex* (7 vols.). Cambridge, Massachusetts: Harvard University Press, 1939–1963.

Conger, J. "A world they never knew: The family and social change," *Daedalus,* 1971, 100:1105–1138.

Conger, J. J. *Adolescence and youth: Psychological development in a changing world.* New York: Harper & Row, 1973.

Connell, J. P., and H. H. Goldsmith. "A structural modeling approach to the study of attachment and strange situation behaviors." In R. N. Emde and R. J. Harmon (Eds.), *The development of attachment and affiliative systems.* New York: Plenum, 1982.

Connolly, K. J. "Maturation and the ontogeny of motor skills." In K. J. Connolly and H. F. R. Prechtl (Eds.), *Maturation and development: Biological and psychological perspectives* (Clinics in developmental medicine, no. 77/78). London: Spastics International, 1981.

Coopersmith, S. *The antecedents of self-esteem.* San Francisco: W. H. Freeman and Company, 1967.

Coopersmith, S., M. Regan, and L. Dick. *The myth of the generation gap.* San Francisco: Albion, 1975.

Corah, N. L., E. J. Anthony, P. Painter, J. A. Stern, and D. L. Thurstone. "Effects of perinatal anoxia after seven years," *Psychological Monographs,* 1965, 79:3 (whole no. 596).

Corballis, M. C. "Laterality and myth," *American Psychologist,*" 1980, 35:284–295.

Corballis, M. C., and I. L. Beale. *The psychology of left and right.* Hillsdale, N. J.: Lawrence Erlbaum Associates, 1976.

Corrigan, R. "A scalogram analysis of the development of the use and comprehension of 'because' in children," *Child Development*, 1975, 46:195–201.

Corrigan, R. "Patterns of individual communication and cognitive development." Unpublished doctoral dissertation, University of Denver, 1976. *Dissertation Abstracts*, 1977, 37(10): 53993B.

Corrigan, R. "The use of repetition to facilitate spontaneous language acquisition," *Journal of Psycholinguistic Research*, 1980, 9:231–241.

Corrigan, R. "The effects of task and practice on search for invisibly displaced objects, "*Developmental Review*, 1981, 1:1–17.

Corrigan, R. "The development of representational skills." In *Levels and transitions in children's development* (New directions for child development, no. 21). San Francisco: Jossey-Bass, 1983.

Costa, P. T., Jr., and R. R. McCrae. "Still stable after all these years: Personality as a key to some issues in adulthood and old age." In P. B. Baltes and O. G. Brin, Jr. (Eds.), *Life-span development and behavior*. New York: Academic Press, 1980.

Crawley, S. B., P. P. Rogers, S. Friedman, M. Iacobbo, A. Criticos, L. Richardson, and M. A. Thompson. "Developmental changes in the structure of mother-infant play," *Developmental Psychology*, 1978, 14:30–36.

Crook, C. K. "Taste perception in the newborn infant," *Infant Behavior and Development*, 1978, 1:52–69.

Crook, C. K. "The organization and control of infant sucking." In H. W. Reese and L. P. Lipsitt (Eds.), *Advances in child development and behavior* (vol. 14). New York: Academic Press, 1979.

Cummins, J. "Language and children's ability to evaluate contradictions and tautologies: A critique of Osherson and Markman's findings," *Child Development*, 1978, 49: 895–897.

Curtis, H. *Biology*. New York: Worth, 1983.

Curtiss, S. *Genie: A psycholinguistic study of a modern-day "wild child."* New York: Academic Press, 1977.

Dale, P. S. *Language development: Structure and function*. Hinsdale, Ill.: Dryden, 1972.

Damon, W. *The social world of the child*. San Francisco: Jossey-Bass, 1977.

Damon, W. (Ed.). *Moral development* (New directions for child development, no. 2). San Francisco: Jossey-Bass, 1978.

Dance, F. E. X., and C. E. Larson. *The functions of human communication: A theoretical approach*. New York: Holt, Rinehart, & Winston, 1976.

d'Andrade, R. G. "Sex differences and cultural institutions." In E. E. Maccoby (Ed.), *The development of sex differences*. Stanford, Cal.: Stanford University Press, 1966.

Darwin, C. R. *The origin of species*. New York: Penguin, 1968 (originally published in 1859).

Dasen, P. (Ed.). *Piagetian psychology: Cross-cultural contributions*. New York: Gardner Press, 1977.

Dasen, P., B. Inhelder, M. Lavalée, and J. Retschitzki. *Naissance de l'intelligence chez l'enfant baoulé de Côte d'Ivoire*. Berne: Huber, 1978.

Davenport, M. *Mozart*. New York: Scribner's, 1956.

Davis, A. *Social class influences upon learning*. Cambridge, Massachusetts: Harvard University Press, 1948.

Décarie, T. G. *Intelligence and affectivity in early childhood* (E. P. Brandt and L. W. Brandt, trans.). New York: International Universities Press, 1965.

deCharms, R., and M. S. Muir. "Motivation: Social approaches," *Annual Review of Psychology*, 1978, 29:91–114.

De Lisi, R., and J. Staudt. "Individual differences in college students' performance on formal operations tasks, "*Journal of Applied Developmental Psychology*, 1980, 1:163–174.

Demarest, W. J. "Incest avoidance among human and nonhuman primates." In S. Chevalier-Skolnikoff and F. E. Poirier (Eds.), *Primate biosocial development: Biological, social, and ecological determinants*. New York: Garland, 1977.

Dennis, W. "Causes of retardation among institutional children: Iran," *Journal of Genetic Psychology*, 1960, 96:46–60.

Dennis, W., and M. C. Dennis. "The effect of cradling practices upon the onset of walking in Hopi children," *Journal of Genetic Psychology*, 1940, 56:77–86.

Dennis, W., and Y. Sayegh. "The effect of supplementary experiences upon the behavioral development of infants in institutions," *Child Development*, 1965, 36:81–90.

Descartes, R. *Discourse on method, and other writings.* New York: Penguin, 1968 (originally published in 1637.)

Deutsch, O. E. *Mozart: A documentary biography* (E. Blom and P. Branscombe, trans.). Stanford California: Stanford University Press, 1974.

Devereux, E. C. "Socialization in cross-cultural perspective: A comparative study of England, Germany, and the United States." Unpublished manuscript, Cornell University, 1965.

Devereux, E. C. "Authority, guilt, and conformity to adult standards among German schoolchildren: A pilot experimental study." Unpublished manuscript, Cornell University, 1966.

Devereux, E. C. "The role of peer-group experience in moral development." In J. P. Hill (Ed.), *Minnesota symposium on child psychology* (vol. 4). Minneapolis: University of Minnesota Press, 1970.

deVilliers, J. G., and P. A. deVilliers. *Language acquisition.* Cambridge, Massachusetts: Harvard University Press, 1978.

DeVries, R., and L. Kohlberg. "Relations between Piagetian and psychometric assessments of intelligence." In L. G. Katz (Ed.), *Current topics in early childhood education* (vol. 1). Norwood, New Jersey: Ablex, 1977.

Deykin, E. Y., and B. MacMahon. "The incidence of seizures among children with autistic symptoms." In S. Chess and A. Thomas (Eds.), *Annual Progress in Child Psychiatry and Child Development 1980.* New York: Brunner/Mazel, 1980.

Doehring, D. G. "Acquisition of rapid reading responses," *Monographs of the Society for Research in Child Development*, 1976, 41 (no. 2, serial no. 165).

Dore, J., M. Franklin, R. Miller, and A. Ramer. "Transitional phenomena in early langauge acquisition," *Journal of Child Language*, 1976, 3:13–28.

Douvan, E., and J. Adelson. *The adolescent experience.* New York: Wiley, 1966.

Drachman, D. B., and A. J. Coulombre. "Experimental clubfoot and arthrogryposis multiplex congenita," *Lancet*, 1962, 523–526.

Dreyfus-Brisac, C. "The bioelectric development of the central nervous system during early life." In F. Falkner (Ed.), *Human development.* London: Saunders, 1966.

Dreyfus-Brisac, C. "Ontogenesis of brain bioelectrical activity and sleep organization in neonates and infants." In F. Falkner and J. Tanner (Eds.), *Human growth* (vol. 3). New York: Plenum, 1979.

Drillien, C. M. *The growth and development of the prematurely born infant.* Edinburgh, Scotland: Livingstone, 1964.

Dromi, E. "The one word period as a stage in language development: Quantitative and qualitative accounts." In I. Levin (Ed.), *Stage and structure.* Norwood, N. J.: Ablex, 1984.

Duke, D. L. "Why don't girls misbehave more than boys in school?" *Journal of Youth and Adolescence*, 1978, 7:141–158.

Dunn, J. "The first year of life: Continuities in individual differences." In D. Shaffer and J. Dunn (Eds.), *The first year of life: Psychological and medical implications of early experience.* New York: Wiley, 1979.

Dunn, J. "Individual differences in temperament." In M. Rutter (Ed.), *The scientific foundations of developmental psychiatry.* London: Heinemann, 1980.

Dunn, J., and C. Kendrick. *Siblings: Love, envy, and understanding.* Cambridge, Massachusetts: Harvard University Press, 1982.

Dunphy, P. C. "The social structure of urban adolescent peer groups," *Sociometry*, 1963, 26:230–246.

Duvall, E. M. *Family development* (4th ed.). Philadelphia: Lippincott, 1971.

Dweck, C. S., and E. S. Elliott. "Achievement motivation." In P. H. Mussen (Ed.), *Handbook of child psychology* (4th ed.); vol. 4: E. M. Hetherington (Ed.), *Socialization, personality, and social behavior.* New York: Wiley, 1983.

Dwyer, J. M. *Human reproduction: The female system and the neonate.* Philadelphia: F. A. Davis, 1976.

Edelstein, W., M. Keller, and K. Wahlen. "Structure and content in social cognition: Conceptual and empirical analyses," *Child Development*, 1984.

Educational Testing Service. *Proceedings of the 35th invitational conference on testing problems.* New York: Educational Testing Service, 1974.

Edwards, C. P. "Moral development in comparative cultural perspective." In D. A. Wagner and H. W. Stevenson (Eds.), *Cultural perspectives on child development.* San Francisco: W. H. Freeman and Company, 1982.

Edwards, C. P. "The development of age group labels and categories in preschool children," *Child Development,* 1984.

Edwards, C. P., and B. B. Whiting. "Differential socialization of girls and boys in the light of cross-cultural research." In *Anthropological perspectives on child development* (New directions for child development, no. 8). San Francisco: Jossey-Bass, 1980.

Eibl-Eibesfeldt, I. *Ethology: The biology of behavior.* New York: Holt, Rinehart, & Winston, 1970.

Eichorn, D. "Physiological development." In P. H. Mussen (Ed.), *Carmichael's manual of child psychology* (3rd ed.). New York: Wiley, 1970.

Eichorn, D. H. "Physical development: Current foci of research." In J. D. Osofsky (Ed.), *Handbook of infant development.* New York: Wiley, 1979.

Eichorn, D. H., and N. Bayley. "Growth in head circumference from birth through young adulthood," *Child Development,* 1962, 33:257–271.

Eimas, P. D., and V. C. Tartter. "On the development of speech perception: Mechanisms and analogies." In H. W. Reese and L. P. Lipsitt (Eds.), *Advances in child development and behavior* (vol. 13). New York: Academic Press, 1979.

Ekman, P., and W. Friesen. *Unmasking the face: A guide to recognizing emotions from facial cues.* Englewood Cliffs, N.J.: Prentice-Hall, 1975.

Elder, G. H., Jr. *Children of the Great Depression: Social change in life experience.* Chicago: University of Chicago Press, 1974.

Elder, G. H., Jr. "Adolescence in historical perspective." In J. Adelson (Ed.), *Handbook of adolescent psychology.* New York: Wiley, 1980.

Elkind, D. *Children and adolescents* (2nd ed.). New York: Oxford University Press, 1974.

Elkind, D. *The child's reality: Three developmental themes.* Hillsdale, N.J.: Lawrence Erlbaum Associates, 1978.

Elkins, V. H. *The rights of the pregnant parent.* New York: Two Continents, 1976.

Ellefson, J. O. "Territorial behavior in the common white-handed gibbon, *Hylobates lar.*" In P. C. Jay (Ed.), *Primates: Studies in adaptation and variability.* New York: Holt, Rinehart, & Winston, 1968.

Emde, R., T. Gaensbauer, and R. Harmon. "Emotional expression in infancy: A biobehavioral study," *Psychological Issues* (10, no. 37). New York: International Universities Press, 1976.

Emmerich, W. "Family role concepts of children ages 6 to 10," *Child Development,* 1961, 32:609–624.

Emmerich, W. "Variations in the parent role as a function of the parent's sex and the child's sex and age," *Merrill-Palmer Quarterly,* 1962, 8:3–11.

Emmerich, W., K. S. Goldman, B. Kirsh, and R. Sharabany. "Evidence for a transitional phase in the development of gender constancy," *Child Development,* 1977, 48:930–936.

Engen, T., L. Lipsitt, and M. B. Peck. "Ability of newborn infants to discriminate sapid substances," *Developmental Psychology,* 1974, 10:741–744.

Englund, S. "Birth without violence," *New York Times Magazine,* December 8, 1974.

Epstein, H. T. "Phrenoblysis: Special brain and mind growth periods," *Developmental Psychobiology,* 1974, 7:217–224.

Epstein, H. T. "Growth spurts during brain development: Implications for educational policy and practice." In J. S. Chall and A. F. Mirsky (Eds.), *Education and the brain* (Yearbook of the N.S.S.E.). Chicago: University of Chicago Press, 1978.

Epstein, H. T. "Correlated brain and intelligence development in humans." In M. E. Hahn, C. Jensen, and B. C. Dudek (Eds.), *Development and evolution of brain size: Behavioral implications.* New York: Academic Press, 1979.

Epstein, H. T. "EEG developmental stages," *Developmental Psychobiology,* 1980, 13:629–631.

Erikson, E. H. *Childhood and society.* New York: Norton, 1963.

Erikson, E. H. *Identity: Youth and crisis.* New York: W. W. Norton, 1968.

Erikson, E. H. "Youth: Fidelity and diversity." In A.

E. Winder and D. L. Angus (Eds.), *Adolescence: Contemporary studies*. New York: American Book Company, 1974.

Escalona, S. K. *The roots of individuality*. Chicago: Aldine, 1968.

Etaugh, C., and V. Hughes. "Teachers' evaluation of sex-typed behaviors in children: The role of teacher sex and school setting," *Developmental Psychology*, 1975, 11:394–395.

Eysenck, H. J. "Genetic factors in personality development." In A. R. Kaplan (Ed.), *Human behavior genetics*. Springfield, Illinois: Thomas, 1976.

Fafouti-Milenkovic, M., and I. C. Uzgiris. "The mother-infant communication system." In I. Uzgiris (Ed.), *Social interaction and communication during infancy* (New directions for child development, no. 4). San Francisco: Jossey-Bass, 1979.

Fagot, B. I. "Sex differences in toddlers' behavior and parental reaction," *Developmental Psychology*, 1974, 10:554–558.

Fagot, B.I. "The influence of sex of child on parental reactions to toddler children," *Child Development*, 1978, 49:459–465.

Fanaroff, A. A., and R. J. Martin (Eds.). *Behrman's neonatal-perinatal medicine: Diseases of the fetus and infant* (3rd ed.). St. Louis: Mosby, 1983.

Fantz, R. L. "Pattern discrimination and selective attention as determinants of perceptual development from birth." In A. H. Kidd and J. L. Rivoire (Eds.), *Perceptual development in children*. New York: International Universities Press, 1966.

Farran, D. C., and C. T. Ramey. "Infant day care and attachment behaviors toward mothers and teachers," *Child Development*, 1977, 48:1112–1116.

Faust, M. S. "Developmental maturity as a determinant in prestige of adolescent girls," *Child Development*, 1960, 31:173–184.

Feather, N. T. "Attribution of responsibility and valence of success and failure in relation to initial confidence and task performance," *Journal of Personality and Social Psychology*, 1969, 13:129–144.

Feffer, M. H., and V. Gourevitch. "Cognitive aspects of role-taking in children," *Journal of Personality*, 1960, 28:383–396.

Fein, G. G. "Play and the acquisition of symbols." In L. G. Katz (Ed.), *Current topics in early childhood education* (vol. 2). Norwood, N.J.: Ablex, 1979.

Fein, G. G., D. Johnson, N. Kosson, L. Stork, and L. Wasserman. "Stereotypes and preferences in the toy choices of 20-month-old boys and girls," *Developmental Psychology*, 1975, 11:527–528.

Feldman, D. H. *Beyond universals in cognitive development*. Norwood, N.J.: Ablex, 1980.

Fenson, L. "The structure of one child's art from ages 3 to 4." Paper presented at the meetings of the Society for Research in Child Development, New Orleans, March 1977.

Fenson, L. "The differing roles of drawing skill and conceptual growth in a preschool child's drawings." Unpublished manuscript, San Diego State University, 1978.

Fenson, L., and D. S. Ramsay. "Decentration and integration of the child's play in the second year," *Child Development*, 1980, 51:171–178.

Ferguson, C. A., and D. I. Slobin (Eds.). *Studies of child language development*. New York: Holt, Rinehart, & Winston, 1973.

Fernald, A., and T. Simon. "Expanded intonation contours in mothers' speech to newborns," *Developmental Psychology*, 1984, 20:104–113.

Ferster, C. B., and B. F. Skinner. *Schedules of reinforcement*. New York: Appleton-Century-Crofts, 1957.

Feshbach, S., and R. Singer. *Television and aggression*. San Francisco: Jossey-Bass, 1971.

Field, T. M. "Effects of early separation, interactive deficits, and experimental manipulations on infant-mother face-to-face interaction," *Child Development*, 1977, 48:763–771.

Finegan, J.-A., and B. Quarrington. "Pre-, peri-, and neonatal factors and infantile autism." In S. Chess and A. Thomas (Eds.), *Annual Progress in Child Psychiatry and Child Development 1980*. New York: Brunner/Mazel, 1980.

Fischbein, S. "IQ and social class," *Intelligence*, 1980, 4:51–64.

Fischer, K. W. "A theory of cognitive development:

The control and construction of hierarchies of skills," *Psychological Review,* 1980, 87:477–531.

Fischer, K. W., and S. L. Pipp. "Processes of cognitive development: Optimal level and skill acquisition." In R. J. Sternberg (Ed.), *Mechanisms of cognitive development.* San Francisco: W. H. Freeman and Company, 1984.

Fischer, K. W., and R. J. Roberts, Jr. "A developmental sequence of classification skills and errors in preschool children," manuscript submitted for publication, 1983.

Fischer, K. W., and M. W. Watson. "Explaining the Oedipus conflict." In *Cognitive development* (New directions for child development, no. 12). San Francisco: Jossey-Bass, 1981.

Fischer, K. W., H. H. Hand, and S. Russell. "The development of abstractions in adolescence and adulthood." In M. L. Commons, F. A. Richards, and C. Armon (Eds.), *Beyond formal operations.* New York: Praeger, 1983.

Fischer, K. W., H. H. Hand, M. W. Watson, M. Van Parys, and J. Tucker. "Putting the child into socialization: The development of social categories in the preschool years." In L. Katz (Ed.), *Current topics in early childhood education* (vol. 6). Norwood, N.J.: Ablex, in press.

Flavell, J. H. *The developmental psychology of Jean Piaget.* New York: Van Nostrand, 1963.

Flavell, J. H. "Stage-related properties of cognitive development," *Cognitive Psychology,* 1971, 2: 421–453.

Flavell, J. H. *Cognitive development.* Englewood Cliffs, New Jersey: Prentice-Hall, 1977.

Flavell, J. H. "On cognitive development," *Child Development,* 1982, 53:1–10.

Flavell, J. H., et al. *The development of role-taking and communication skills in children.* New York: Wiley, 1968.

Fleming, A. F., J. Storey, L. Molineaux, E. A. Iroko, and E. D. E. Attai. "Abnormal haemoglobins in the Sudan savanna of Nigeria. I. Prevalence of haemoglobins and relationships between sickle-cell trait, malaria, and survival," *Annals of Tropical Medicine and Parasitology,* 1979, 73(no. 2).

Fogel, A. "Peer vs. mother directed behavior in 1- to 3-month-old infants," *Infant Behavior and Development,* 1979, 2:215–226.

Fogel, A. "Gestural communication during the first six months." In R. E. Stark (Ed.), *Language behavior in infancy and early childhood.* Amsterdam: Elsevier North Holland, 1981.

Ford, M. E. "The construct validity of egocentrism," *Psychological Bulletin,* 1979, 86:1169–1188.

Ford, C. S., and F. A. Beach. *Patterns of sexual behavior.* New York: Harper, 1951.

Foundation for Child Development. *Summary of preliminary results: National Survey of Children.* New York, 1976.

Fowles, B., and M. E. Glanz. "Competence and talent in verbal riddle comprehension," *Journal of Child Language,* 1977, 4:433–452.

Fox, N. "Attachment of kibbutz infants to mother and metapelet," *Child Development,* 1977, 48: 1228–1239.

Fraiberg, S. "Blind infants and their mothers: An examination of the sign system." In M. Lewis and L. A. Rosenblum (Eds.), *The effect of the infant on its caregiver.* New York: Wiley, 1974.

Francis, P. L., P. A. Self, and C. A. Noble. "Maternal imitation of their newborn infants: Momma see, Momma do." Paper presented at the biennial meeting of the Society for Research in Child Development, Boston, April 1981.

Frankenburg, W. K., and J. B. Dodds. "The Denver developmental screening test," *Journal of Pediatrics,* 1967, 71:181–191.

Fraser, C., V. Bellugi, and R. Brown. "Control of grammar in imitation, comprehension, and production." In R. C. Oldfield and J. C. Marshfall (Eds.), *Language.* Baltimore, Maryland: Penguin, 1968.

Freeman, R. D., and L. N. Thebos. "Electrophysiological evidence that abnormal early visual experience can modify the human brain," *Science,* 1973, 180:878.

Freud, S. An outline of psychoanalysis (J. Strachey, trans.). New York: Norton, 1949 (originally published, 1940).

Freud, S. *The interpretation of dreams.* New York: Basic Books, 1955.

Freud, S. *The ego and the id* (J. Riviere and J. Strachey, trans.). New York: Norton, 1960.

Freud, S. *Introductory lectures on psychoanalysis* (J. Riviere and J. Strachey, trans.). London: Hogarth, 1963 (originally published, 1917).

Freud, S. *New introductory lectures on psychoanalysis* (J. Strachey, trans.). New York: Norton, 1965 (originally published, 1933).

Freud, A. *The ego and the mechanisms of defense* (C. Baines, trans.). New York: International Universities Press, 1966.

Freud, A., with S. Dann. "An experiment in group upbringing," *Psychoanalytic Study of the Child*, 1951, 6:127–168.

Friedman, S. "Habituation and recovery of visual response in the alert human newborn," *Journal of Experimental Child Psychology*, 1972, 13:339–349.

Friedman, M. "Type A behavior: A progress report," *The Sciences*, 1980, 20(2):10–11, 28.

von Frisch, K. *The dance language and orientation of bees* (L. E. Chadwick, trans.). Cambridge, Massachusetts: Harvard University Press, 1967.

Frith, C. D., and U. Frith. "Feature selection and classification: A developmental study," *Journal of Experimental Child Psychology*, 1978, 25:413–428.

Fuchs, F. "Genetic amniocentesis," *Scientific American*, 1980, 242 (June):47–53.

Furman, W. "Promoting appropriate social behavior: Developmental implications for treatment." In B. B. Lahey and A. E. Kazdin (Eds.), *Advances in clinical child psychology* (vol. 3). New York: Plenum, 1980.

Furman, W. "Children's friendships." In T. M. Field, A. Huston, H. C. Quay, L. Troll, and G. E. Finley (Eds.), *Review of human development*. New York: Wiley, 1982.

Furrow, D., K. Nelson, and H. Benedict. "Mothers' speech to children and syntactic development: Some simple relationships," *Journal of Child Language*, 1979, 6:423–442.

Furth, H. G. *The world of grown-ups: Children's conceptions of society*. New York: Elsevier, 1980.

Furth, H. G., M. Baur, and J. E. Smith. "Children's conception of social institutions: A Piagetian framework," *Human Development*, 1976, 19:351–374.

Gadlin, H. "Child discipline and the pursuit of self: A historical interpretation." In H. W. Reese and L. P. Lipsitt (Eds.), *Advances in child development and behavior* (vol. 12). New York: Academic Press, 1978.

Gagnon, J. H., and W. Simon. "Prospects for change in American sexual patterns," *Medical Aspects of Human Sexuality*, 1970, 4:100–117.

Gagnon, J. H., and W. Simon (Eds.). *The sexual scene*. Chicago: Aldine, 1970.

Gagnon, J. H., and W. Simon. *Sexual conduct*. Chicago: Aldine, 1973.

Gallatin, J. "The development of political thinking in urban adolescents." Final Report to the Office of Education, 1972.

Gallatin, J. "Political thinking in adolescence." In J. Adelson (Ed.), *Handbook of adolescent psychology*. New York: Wiley, 1980.

Gallup, G. G., Jr. "Self-recognition in primates: A comparative approach to the bidirectional properties of consciousness," *American Psychologist*, 1977, 32:329–338.

Garbarino, J., and S. H. Stocking. *Protecting children from abuse and neglect*. San Francisco: Jossey-Bass, 1980.

Gardner, H. *Art, mind, and brain: A cognitive approach to creativity*. New York: Basic Books, 1982.

Gardner, H. *Frames of mind: The theory of multiple intelligences*. New York: Basic Books, 1983.

Gardner, B. T., and R. A. Gardner. "Evidence for sentence constituents in the early utterances of child and chimpanzee," *Journal of Experimental Psychology: General*, 1975, 104:244–267.

Gardner, B. T., and R. A. Gardner. "Two comparative psychologists look at language acquisition." In K. E. Nelson (Ed.), *Children's language* (vol. 2). New York: Gardner Press, 1980.

Gates, W. H. *The Japanese waltzing mouse: Its origin, heredity, and relation to the genetic characters of other mice*. Washington, D.C.: Carnegie Institution, 1926.

Gates, A. I. "The role of personality maladjustment in reading disability," *Journal of Genetic Psychology*, 1941, 59(1):77–83.

Gazzaniga, M. S. "The split brain in man," *Scientific American*, 1967, 217(August):24–29.

Geber, M., and R. F. P. Dean. "Gesell tests on African children," *Pediatrics*, 1957, 20:1055–1065.

Gelles, R. J. "Child abuse as psychopathology: A sociological critique." In D. G. Gil (Ed.), *Child abuse and violence*. New York: AMS Press, 1979.

Gelman, R. "Cognitive development." *Annual Review of Psychology*, 1978, 29:297–332.

George, C., and M. Main. "Social interactions of young abused children: Approach, avoidance, and aggression." *Child Development*, 1979, 50:306–318.

Geschwind, N. "Language and the brain," *Scientific American*, 1972, 226 (April):76–83.

Gesell, A. "The ontogenesis of infant behavior." In L. Carmichael (Ed.), *Manual of child psychology* (2nd ed.). New York: Wiley, 1954.

Gesell, A., and H. Thompson. "Learning and growth in identical twins: An experimental study of the method of co-twin control," *Genetic Psychology Monographs*, 1929, 6:1–24.

Gesell, A., H. Thompson, and C. S. Amatruda. *The psychology of early growth including norms of infant behavior and a method of genetic analysis*. New York: Macmillan, 1938.

Gibbs, J. C., K. F. Widdman, and A. Colby. "Construction and validation of a simplified group-administrable equivalent of the Moral Judgment Interview," *Child Development*, 1982, 53:895–910.

Gibson, E. J. "Learning to read," *Science*, 1965, 148:1066–1072.

Gibson, E. J. *Principles of perceptual learning and development*. New York: Appleton-Century-Crofts, 1969.

Gibson, E. J., and H. Levin. *The psychology of reading*. Cambridge, Massachusetts: MIT Press, 1975.

Gibson, E. J., and R. D. Walk. "The visual cliff," *Scientific American*, 1960, 202 (April):64–71.

Gil, D. C. *Violence against children: Physical child abuse in the United States*. Cambridge, Massachusetts: Harvard University Press, 1970.

Gilligan, C. *In a different voice*. Cambridge, Massachusetts: Harvard University Press, 1982.

Gilligan, C., and J. M. Murphy. "Development from adolescence to adulthood: The philosopher and the dilemma of the fact." In *Intellectual development beyond childhood* (New directions for child development, no. 5). San Francisco: Jossey-Bass, 1979.

Gladwin, T. *East is a big bird: Navigation and logic on Puluwat Atoll*. Cambridge, Massachusetts: Harvard University Press, 1970.

Glueck, S., and E. Glueck. *Predicting delinquency and crime*. Cambridge, Massachusetts: Harvard University Press, 1959.

Goad, W. B., A. Robinson, and T. T. Puck. "Incidence of aneuploidy in a human population," *American Journal of Human Genetics*, 1976, 28:62–68.

Goddard, H. H. "How shall we educate mental defectives?" *The Training School Bulletin*, 1912, 9:43.

Gold, M., and R. J. Petronio. "Delinquent behavior in adolescence," In J. Adelson (Ed.), *Handbook of adolescent psychology*. New York: Wiley, 1980.

Goldberg, S., and M. Lewis. "Play behavior in the year-old infant: Early sex differences," *Child Development*, 1969, 40:21–31.

Goldman-Rakic, P. S., A. Iseroff, M. L. Schwartz, and N. M. Bugbee. "The neurobiology of cognitive development." In P. H. Mussen (Ed.), *Handbook of child psychology* (4th ed.); vol. 2: M. M. Haith and J. J. Campos (Eds.), *Infancy and developmental psychobiology*. New York: Wiley, 1983.

Goldsmith, H. H., and J. J. Campos. "Toward a theory of infant temperament." In R. N. Emde and R. J. Harmon (Eds.), *The development of attachment and affiliative systems*. New York: Plenum, 1982.

Goldsmith, H. H., and I. I. Gottesman. "Origins of variation in behavioral style: A longitudinal study of temperament in young twins," *Child Development*, 1981, 52:March.

Goslin, P. A. "Accuracy of self-perception and social acceptance," *Sociometry*, 1962, 25:283–296.

Goslin, D. A. *The search for ability*. New York: Russell Sage Foundation, 1963.

Gottlieb, G. "Imprinting in nature," *Science*, 1963, 139:497–498.

Gottlieb, G. "Conceptions of prenatal development: Behavioral embryology," *Psychological Review*, 1976, 83:215–234.

Gottlieb, G. "The psychobiological approach to developmental issues." In P. H. Mussen (Ed.), *Handbook of child psychology* (4th ed.); vol. 2: M. M. Haith and J. J. Campos (Eds.), *Infancy and developmental psychobiology*. New York: Wiley, 1983.

Gould, S. J. *Ever since Darwin*. New York: Norton, 1977a.

Gould, S. J. *Ontogeny and phylogeny*. Cambridge, Massachusetts: Harvard University Press, 1977b.

Green, J. A., G. E. Gustafson, and M. J. West. "Effects of infant development on mother-infant interactions," *Child Development*, 1980, 51:199–207.

Greenfield, P. M., and J. H. Smith. *The structure of communication in early language development*. New York: Academic Press, 1976.

Greenwald, A. G. "The totalitarian ego: Fabrication and revision of personal history," *American Psychologist*, 1930, 35:603–618.

Grimes, J. W., and W. Allensmith. "Compulsivity, anxiety, and school achievement," *Merrill-Palmer Quarterly*, 1961, 7:247–269.

Grobstein, P., and K. L. Chow. "Receptive field development and individual experience," *Science*, 1975, 190:352–358.

Groch, A. S. "Joking and appreciation of humor in nursery school children," *Child Development*, 1974, 45:1098–1102.

Grossman, J. H., W. C. Wallen, and J. L. Sever. "Management of genital herpes simplex virus infection during pregnancy," *Obstetrics and Gynecology*, 1981, 58:1–4.

Gruber, H. E. *Darwin on man* (2nd ed.). Chicago: University of Chicago Press, 1981.

Gruber, H. E., and J. J. Vonèche. *The essential Piaget: An interpretative reference and guide* (2nd ed.). Chicago: University of Chicago Press, 1982.

Gruber, H. E., J. S. Girgus, and A. Banuazzi. "The development of object permanence in the cat," *Developmental Psychology*, 1971, 4:9–15.

Guilford, J. P. *The nature of human intelligence*. New York: McGraw-Hill, 1967.

Guilford, J. P. "Development of intelligence: A multivariate view." In I. C. Uzgiris and F. Weizmann (Eds.), *The structuring of experience*. New York: Plenum, 1977.

Guillemin, J. "Babies by cesarean: Who chooses, who controls?" *The Hastings Center Report*, June 1981, 11(3):15–18.

Gumperz, J. J., and D. Hymes (Eds.). *Directions in sociolinguistics*. New York: Holt, Rinehart, & Winston, 1972.

Gunzberger, D. W., D. M. Wegner, and L. Anooshian. "Moral judgment and distributive justice," *Human Development*, 1977, 20:160–170.

Guttentag, R. E., and M. M. Haith. "Automatic processing as a function of age and reading ability," *Child Development*, 1978, 49:707–716.

Guttmacher, A. F. *Pregnancy, birth, and family planning*. New York: Viking, 1973.

Haan, N., M. B. Smith, and J. H. Block. "The moral reasoning of young adults: Political-social behavior, family background, and personality correlates," *Journal of Personality and Social Behavior*, 1968, 10:183–201.

Hack, M., I. R. Merkatz, and A. A. Fanaroff. "The low-birth-weight infant: Evolution of a changing outlook," *New England Journal of Medicine*, 1979, 301:1162–1165.

Haith, M. M. *Rules newborns look by*. Hillsdale, N.J.: Lawrence Erlbaum Associates, 1980.

Haith, M. M., T. Bergman, and M. J. Moore. "Eye contact and face scanning in early infancy," *Science*, 1977, 198:853–855.

Halford, G. S. "A theory of the acquisition of conservation," *Psychological Review*, 1970, 77:302–316.

Hand, H. H. "The development of concepts of social interaction: Children's understanding of nice and mean." Unpublished doctoral dissertation, University of Denver, 1981.

Hand, H. H. "The relation between developmental level and spontaneous behavior: The importance of sampling contexts." In *Cognitive development* (New directions for child development, no. 12). San Francisco: Jossey-Bass, 1981.

Harlap, S., and P. H. Shiono. "Alcohol, smoking, and incidence of spontaneous abortions in the first and second trimester," *The Lancet*, July 26, 1980, pp. 173–176.

Harlow, H. F. *Learning to love.* San Francisco: Albion, 1971.

Harlow, H. F., and M. K. Harlow. "Effects of various mother-infant relationships on rhesus monkey behaviors." In B. M. Foss (Ed.), *Determinants of infant behavior* (vol. 4). London: Methuen, 1969.

Harlow, H. F., and M. A. Novak. "Psychopathological perspectives," *Perspectives in Biology and Medicine,* 1973, 16:461–78.

Harris, R. J. "Children's comprehension of complex sentences," *Journal of Experimental Child Psychology,* 1975, 19:420–433.

Harris, P. L. "Infant cognition." In P. H. Mussen (Ed.), *Handbook of child psychology* (4th ed.); vol. 2: M. M. Haith and J. J. Campos (Eds.), *Infancy and developmental psychobiology.* New York: Wiley, 1983.

Harter, S. "Effectance motivation reconsidered: Toward a developmental model," *Human Development,* 1978, 21:34–64.

Harter, S. "A model of intrinsic mastery motivation in children: Individual differences and developmental change." In W. A. Collins (Ed.), *Minnesota symposium on child psychology* (vol. 14). Hillsdale, N.J.: Erlbaum, 1981.

Harter, S. "A cognitive-developmental approach to children's use of affect and trait labels." In F. Serafice (Ed.), *Socio-cognitive development in context.* New York: Guilford Press, 1982.

Harter, S. "Cognitive-developmental considerations in the conduct of play therapy." In C. E. Schaefer and K. J. O'Connor (Eds.), *Handbook of play therapy.* New York: Wiley, 1982.

Harter, S. "Competence as a dimension of self-evaluation: Toward a comprehensive model of self-worth." In R. Leahy (Ed.), *The development of the self.* New York: Academic Press, 1983.

Harter, S. "Developmental perspectives on the self-system." In P. H. Mussen (Ed.), *Handbook of child psychology* (4th ed.); vol. 4: E. M. Hetherington (Ed.), *Socialization, personality, and social development.* New York: Wiley, 1983.

Hartshorne, H., and M. A. May. *Studies in service and self-control.* New York: Macmillan, 1928–1930.

Hartup, W. "Peer interaction and social organization." In P. H. Mussen (Ed.), *Carmichael's manual of child psychology* (vol. 2). New York: Wiley, 1970.

Hartup, W. W. "The social worlds of childhood," *American Psychologist,* 1979, 34:944–950.

Hartup, W. W. "Peer relations." In P. H. Mussen (Ed.), *Handbook of child psychology* (4th ed.); vol. 4: E. M. Hetherington (Ed.), *Socialization, personality, and social development.* New York: Wiley, 1983.

Hayes, D. S., and D. W. Birnbaum. "Preschoolers' retention of televised events: Is a picture worth a thousand words?" *Journal of Developmental Psychology,* 1980, 16(5):410–416.

Hebb, D. O. "Heredity and environment in mammalian behavior," *British Journal of Animal Behavior,* 1953, 1:43–47.

Hebb, D. O., and W. R. Thompson. "The social significance of animal studies." In G. Lindzey (Ed.), *Handbook of social psychology.* Cambridge: Addison-Wesley, 1968.

Hecaen, H. "Acquired aphasia in children and the ontogenesis of hemispheric functional specialization," *Brain and Language,* 1976, 3:114–134.

Hecaen, H., and M. L. Albert. *Human neuropsychology.* New York: Wiley, 1978.

Hellmuth, J. *Disadvantaged child* (vol. 3): *Compensatory education: A national debate.* New York: Brunner/Mazel, 1970.

Henderson, N. D. "Human behavior genetics," *Annual Review of Psychology,* 1982, 33:403–440.

Herzog, E., and C. E. Sudia. "Fatherless homes: A review of research," *Children,* 1968, 15:177–182.

Hess, E. H. "Ethology and developmental psychology." In P. H. Mussen (Ed.), *Carmichael's manual of child psychology* (vol. 1). New York: Wiley, 1970.

Hess, R. D. "Social class and ethnic influences on socialization." In P. H. Mussen (Ed.), *Carmichael's manual of child psychology* (vol. 2). New York: Wiley, 1970.

Hess, E. H. *Imprinting.* New York: Van Nostrand Reinhold, 1973.

Hess, R. D., and V. C. Shipman. "Early experience and the socialization of cognitive modes in children," *Child Development,* 1965, 34:869–886.

Hess, R. D., and V. C. Shipman. "Cognitive elements in maternal behavior." In J. P. Hill (Ed.), *Minnesota symposia on child psychology*. Minneapolis: University of Minnesota Press, 1967.

Hess, R. D., and V. C. Shipman. "Maternal attitudes toward the school and the role of the pupil: Some social class comparisons." In A. H. Passow (Ed.), *Developing Programs for the Educationally Disadvantaged*. New York: Teachers College, Columbia University, 1968.

Hetherington, E. M., R. J. Stouwie, and E. H. Redberg. "Patterns of family interaction and child-rearing attitudes related to three dimensions of juvenile delinquency," *Journal of Abnormal Psychology*, 1971, 78:160–176.

Hetherington, E. M., M. Cox, and R. Cox. "The aftermath of divorce." In H. H. Stevens, Jr., and M. Mathews (Eds.), *Mother/child, father/child relationships*. Washington, D.C.: National Association for the Education of Young Children, 1978a.

Hetherington, E. M., M. Cox, and R. Cox. "Effects of divorce on parents and children." In M. Lamb (Ed.), *Nontraditional families*. Hillsdale, N.J.: Erlbaum, 1982.

Higham, E. "Variations in adolescent psychohormonal development." In J. Adelson (Ed.), *Handbook of adolescent psychology*. New York: Wiley, 1980.

Hinde, R. A. *Animal Behavior* (2nd ed.). New York: McGraw-Hill, 1970.

Hinde, R. A. *Towards understanding relationships*. London: Academic Press, 1979.

Hinde, R. A. "The bases of a science of interpersonal relationships." In S. Duck and R. Gilmour (Eds.), *Personal relationships*; vol. 1: *Studying personal relationships*. New York: Academic Press, 1981.

Hinde, R. A. "Ethology and child development." In P. H. Mussen (Ed.), *Handbook of child psychology* (4th ed.); vol. 2: M. M. Haith and J. J. Campos (Eds.), *Infancy and developmental psychobiology*. New York: Wiley, 1983.

Hirsch, H. V. B., and D. N. Spinelli. "Visual experience modifies distribution of horizontally and vertically oriented receptive fields in cats," *Science*, 1970, 168:869–871.

Hoffman, M. L. "Power assertion by the parent and its impact on the child," *Child Development*, 1960, 31:129–143.

Hoffman, L. W. "The professional woman as mother." In *Kundsin, a conference on successful women in the sciences*. New York: Proceedings of the New York Academy of Science, 1973.

Hoffman, L. W. "Fear of success in males and females: 1965 to 1972," *Journal of Consulting and Clinical Psychology*, 1974, 42:353–358.

Hoffman, L. W. "Fear of success in 1965 and 1974: A follow-up study," *Journal of Consulting and Clinical Psychology*, 1977, 45(2):310–321.

Hollos, M. "Logical operations and role-taking abilities in two cultures: Norway and Hungary," *Child Development*, 1975, 46:638–649.

Holmes, E. *The life of Mozart*. London: Novello, Ewer & Co., 1878.

Holt, R. R. "Freud's theory of the primary process," *Psychoanalysis and Contemporary Science*, 1976, 5:61–99.

Honzik, M. P., J. W. MacFarlane, and L. Allen. "The stability of mental test performance between two and eighteen years," *Journal of Experimental Education*, 1948, 4:309–324.

Hooker, D. *The prenatal origin of behavior*. Lawrence: University of Kansas Press, 1950.

Horn, J. L. "Organization of data on life-span development of human abilities." In L. R. Goulet and P. B. Baltes. *Life-span developmental psychology: Research and theory*. New York: Academic Press, 1970.

Horn, J. L. "Human abilities: A review of research and theory in the early 1970s," *Annual Review of Psychology*, 1976, 27:437–486.

Horn, J. L. "The aging of human abilities." In B. B. Wolman (Ed.), *Handbook of developmental psychology*. Englewood Cliffs, N.J.: Prentice-Hall, 1982.

Horn, J. L., and G. Donaldson. "On the myth of intellectual decline in adulthood," *American Psychologist*, 1976, 31:701–719.

Horner, M. "Femininity and successful achievement: A basic inconsistency." In J. M. Bardwick, E. Douvan, M. S. Horner, and D. Guttman (Eds.), *Feminine precedent and conflict*. Belmont, California: Brooks/Cole, 1970.

Horner, M. "Toward an understanding of achievement-related conflicts in women," *Journal of Social Issues*, 1972, 28(2):157–174.

Horner, M. S. "Measurement and behavioral implications of fear of success in women." In J. W. Atkinson and J. O. Raynor (Eds.), *Motivation and achievement*. Washington, D.C.: Winston, 1975.

Horowitz, F. D. (Ed.). "Visual attention, auditory stimulation, and language discrimination in young infants," *Monographs of the Society for Research in Child Development*, 1975, 39 (5–6, serial no. 158).

Horowitz, R. A. "Psychological effects of the 'open classroom,'" *Review of Educational Research*, 1979, 49:71–86.

Howells, T. H. "Factors influencing honesty," *Journal of Social Psychology*, 1938, 9:97–102.

Hubel, D. H., and T. N. Wiesel. "Brain mechanisms of vision," *Scientific American*, 1979, 241 (September):150–162.

Hubley, P., and C. Trevarthen. "Sharing a task in infancy." In *Social interaction and communication during infancy* (New directions for child development, no. 4), San Francisco: Jossey-Bass, 1979.

Humphrey, T. "Palatopharyngeal fusion in a human fetus and its relation to cleft palate formation," *Alabama Journal of Medical Sciences*, 1970, 7:398–426.

Humphreys, L. G., and C. K. Parsons. "Piagetian tasks measure intelligence and intelligence tests assess cognitive development: A reanalysis," *Intelligence*, 1979, 3:369–382.

Hunt, K. W. "Syntactic maturity in schoolchildren and adults," *Monographs of the Society for Research in Child Development*, 1970, 35(1, serial no. 134).

Hunt, M. *Sexual behavior in the 1970s*. Chicago: Playboy Press, 1974.

Hunt, J. McV., and G. E. Kirk. "Criterion-referenced tests of school readiness: A paradigm with illustrations," *Genetic Psychology Monographs*, 1976, 90(1):143–182.

Hunt, R. G., and V. Synnerdale. "Social influences among kindergarten children," *Sociology and Social Research*, 1959, 43:171–174.

Hunt, J. McV., K. Mohandessi, M. Ghodssi, and M. Akiyama. "The psychological development of

orphanage-reared infants: Interventions with outcomes (Tehran)," *Genetic Psychology Monographs*, 1976, 94:177–226.

Huston, A. C. "Sex-typing." In P. H. Mussen (Ed.), *Handbook of child psychology* (4th ed.); vol. 4: E. M. Hetherington (Ed.), *Socialization, personality, and social development*. New York: Wiley, 1983.

Hutt, C. "Sex differences in human development," *Human Development*, 1972, 15:153–70.

Hutt, S. J., et al. "Auditory responsivity in the human neonate," *Nature*, 1968(June 1), 218:888–890.

Ilg, F. L., L. B. Ames, and S. M. Baker. *Child behavior: Specific advice on problems of child behavior* (rev. ed.). New York: Harper & Row, 1981.

Imanishi, K. "Social organization of subhuman primates in their natural habitat," *Current Anthropology*, 1960, 1:393–403.

Imanishi, K. "Social behavior in Japanese monkeys, Macaca fuscata." In C. H. Southwick (Ed.), *Primate social behavior: An enduring problem*. Princeton, N.J.: Van Nostrand, 1963.

Ingram, D. "If and when transformations are acquired by children." In D. P. Data (Ed.), *Georgetown University Round Table on Languages and Linguistics*. Washington, D.C.: Georgetown University Press, 1975.

Inhelder, B., and J. Piaget. *The growth of logical thinking from childhood to adolescence* (A. Parsons and S. Seagrim, trans.). New York: Basic Books, 1958 (originally published, 1955).

Inhelder, B., and J. Piaget. *The early growth of logic in the child* (G. A. Lunzer and D. Papert, trans.). New York: Harper & Row, 1964 (originally published, 1959).

Inhelder, B., I. Lézine, H. Sinclair, and M. Stombak. "Les débuts de la fonction symbolique," *Archives de Psychologie*, 1972, 41:187–243.

Inhelder, B., H. Sinclair, and M. Bovet. *Learning and the development of cognition*. Cambridge, Massachusetts: Harvard University Press, 1974.

Isaacs, N. *A brief introduction to Piaget*. New York: Schocken, 1974.

Itard, J. M. G. *The wild boy of Aveyron* (G. Humphrey and M. Humphrey, trans.). New York: Appleton-Century-Crofts, 1932.

Izard, C. E. *Human emotions*. New York: Plenum, 1977.

Jackson, P. W. "The student's world," *The Elementary School Journal*, 1966, pp. 345–357.

Jacobson, S. W. "Matching behavior in the young infant," *Child Development*, 1979, 50:425–430.

Jacobson, J. L. "Cognitive determinants of wariness toward unfamiliar peers," *Developmental Psychology*, 1980, 16:347–354.

Jakobson, R. *Child language, aphasia, and phonological universals* (A. R. Keiler, trans.). The Hague: Mouton, 1968.

Jaques, E., with R. O. Gibson and D. J. Isaac. *Levels of abstraction in logic and human action*. London: Heinemann, 1978.

Jencks, C., M. Smith, H. Acland, M. J. Bane, D. Cohen, H. Gintis, B. Heyns, and S. Michelson. *Inequality: A reassessment of the effect of family and schooling in America*. New York: Basic Books, 1972.

Jensen, A. R. "How much can we boost IQ and scholastic achievement?" *Harvard Educational Review*, 1969, 39:81.

Jensen, A. R. *Bias in mental testing*. New York: Free Press, 1980.

Jerison, H. J. "Paleoneurology and the evolution of mind," *Scientific American*, 1976, *234* (January): 90–101.

Jessor, R., and S. L. Jessor. *Problem behavior and psychosocial development*. New York: Academic Press, 1977.

John, E. R., et al. "Observational learning in cats," *Science*, 1968, *159*:1489–1491.

Jones, M. C. "The later careers of boys who were early- or late-maturing," *Child Development*, 1957, 28:113–128.

Jones, M. C. "Psychological correlates of somatic development," *Child Development*, 1965, 36:899–911.

Josselson, R., E. Greenberger, and D. McConochie. "Phenomenological aspects of psychosocial maturity in adolescence. Part I: Boys," *Journal of Youth and Adolescence*, 1977, 6:25–56.

Josselson, R., E. Greenberger, and D. McConochie. "Phenomenological aspects of psychosocial maturity in adolescence. Part II: Girls," *Journal of Youth*

and Adolescence, 1977, 6:145–168.

Justice, B., and R. Justice. *The abusing family*. New York: Human Sciences Press, 1976.

Kagan, J. "The concept of identification," *Psychological Review*, 1958, 65:296–305.

Kagan, J. "Impulsive and reflective children: Significance of conceptual tempo." In J. D. Krumholz (Ed.), *Learning and the educational process*. Chicago: Rand McNally, 1965a.

Kagan, J. "Reflectivity-impulsivity and reading ability in primary grade children," *Child Development*, 1965b, 36:609–628.

Kagan, J. "Attention and psychological change in the young child," *Science*, 1970, *170*:826–832.

Kagan, J. "A conception of early adolescence." In J. Kagan and R. Coles (Eds.), *12 to 16: Early adolescence*. New York: Norton, 1972.

Kagan, J. *The second year*. Cambridge, Mass.: Harvard University Press, 1981.

Kagan, J. *Psychological research on the human infant: An evaluative summary*. New York: W. T. Grant Foundation, 1982.

Kagan, J., and J. Lemkin. "The child's differential perception of parental attributes," *Journal of Abnormal and Social Psychology*, 1960, 61:440–447.

Kagan, S., and M. C. Madsen. "Rivalry in Anglo-American and Mexican children of two ages," *Journal of Personality and Social Psychology*, 1972, 24:214–220.

Kagan, J., and H. A. Moss. *Birth to maturity*. New York: Wiley, 1962.

Kagan, J., and W. Phillips. "Measurement of identification: A methodological note," *Journal of Abnormal and Social Psychology*, 1964, 69:442–443.

Kagan, J., R. B. Kearsley, and P. R. Zelazo. *Infancy: Its place in human development*. Cambridge, Massachusetts: Harvard University Press, 1978.

Kail, R. V., Jr. *The development of memory in children*. San Francisco: W. H. Freeman and Company, 1979.

Kamin, L. J. *The science and politics of IQ*. Potomac, Maryland: Lawrence Erlbaum Associates, 1975.

Kandel, D. B., R. C. Kessler, and R. Z. Margulies. "Antecedents of adolescent initiation into stages of drug use: A developmental analysis," *Journal of Youth and Adolescence*, 1978, 7:13–40.

Kanner, L. "Autistic disturbance of affective contact," *Nervous Child*, 1943, 2:217–250.

Kanner, L., and L. I. Lesser. "Early infantile autism," *Pediatric Clinics of North America* (vol. 5). Philadelphia: Saunders, 1958.

Karmiloff-Smith, A. "Language developments after five." In P. Fletcher and M. Garman (Eds.), *Studies in language acquisition*. London: Cambridge University Press, 1979.

Karmiloff-Smith, A. "Structure versus process in comparing linguistic and cognitive development." In I. Levin (Ed.), *Stage and structure*. Norwood, N.J.: Ablex, 1984.

Katchadourian, H. A., and D. T. Lunde. *Fundamentals of human sexuality* (2nd ed.). New York: Holt, Rinehart, & Winston, 1974.

Katz, F. M. "The meaning of success: Some differences in value systems of social classes," *Journal of Social Psychology*, 1964, 62:141–148.

Katz, J. "Evolving relationships between women and men." In *Changing roles of women in industrial societies: A Bellagio conference*, March 1976. New York: The Rockefeller Foundation Working Papers, 1977.

Kaye, K. "Why we don't talk 'baby talk' to babies," *Journal of Child Language*, 1980, 7:489–907.

Kaye, K. *The social and mental life of babies*. Chicago: University of Chicago Press, 1982.

Kaye, K., and R. Charney. "How mothers maintain 'dialogue' with two-year-olds." In D. Olson (Ed.), *The social foundations of language and thought: Essays in honor of Jerome S. Bruner*. New York: Norton, 1980.

Kaye, K., and A. Wells. "Mothers' jiggling and the burst-pause pattern in neonatal sucking," *Infant Behavior and Development*, 1980, 3:29–46.

Keller, H. *The story of my life*. New York: Doubleday, 1954.

Kellerman, J., and E. R. Katz. "Attitudes toward the division of child-rearing responsibilities," *Sex Roles*, 1978, 4(4):505–512.

Kempe, C. H. "Paediatric implications of the battered baby syndrome," *Archives of Disease in Childhood*, 1971 (February), 46:28–37.

Kempe, R. S., and C. H. Kempe. *Child abuse.*

Cambridge, Massachusetts: Harvard University Press, 1978.

Kendrick, C., and J. Dunn. "Caring for a second baby: Effects on interaction between mother and firstborn," *Developmental Psychology*, 1980, 16: 303–311.

Kennell, H.J., et al. "Maternal behaviour one year after early and extended post partum contact," *Developmental Medicine and Child Neurology*, 1974, 16(2):172–179.

Kenny, S. L. "Developmental discontinuities in childhood and adolescence." In *Levels and transitions in children's development* (New directions for child development, no. 21). San Francisco: Jossey-Bass, 1983.

Kessen, W. *The child*. New York: Wiley, 1965.

Kessen, W. "Sucking and looking: Two organized congenital patterns of behavior in the newborn." In H. W. Stevenson, E. H. Hess, and H. L. Rheingold (Eds.), *Early behavior*. New York: Wiley, 1967.

Kessen, W., M. M. Haith, and P. Salapatek. "Human infancy: A bibliography and guide." In P. H. Mussen (Ed.), *Carmichael's manual of child psychology* (3rd ed., vol. 1). New York: Wiley, 1970.

Kimble, D. P. *Psychology as a biological science* (2nd ed.). Pacific Palisades, California: Goodyear Publishing Company, 1978.

Kimmel, D. C. *Adulthood and aging: An interdisciplinary, developmental view*. New York: Wiley, 1974.

King, M. C., and A. C. Wilson. "Evolution at two levels in humans and chimpanzees," *Science*, 1975, 188:107–116.

Kinsbourne, M. *Asymmetrical function of the brain*. New York: Cambridge University Press, 1978.

Kinsbourne, M., and M. Hiscock. "The normal and deviant development of functional lateralization of the brain." In P. H. Mussen (Ed.), *Handbook of child psychology* (4th ed.); vol. 2: M. M. Haith and J. J. Campos (Eds.), *Infancy and developmental psychobiology*. New York: Wiley, 1983.

Kinsey, A. C., et al. *Sexual behavior in the human male*. Philadelphia: Saunders, 1948.

Kinsey, A. C., et al. *Sexual behavior in the human female*. Philadelphia: Saunders, 1953.

Kitchener, K. S. "Human development and the college campus: Sequences and tasks." In *Assessing student development* (New directions for student services). San Francisco: Jossey-Bass, 1983.

Kitchener, K. S., and P. M. King. "Reflective judgment: Concepts of justification and their relation to age and education," *Journal of Applied Developmental Psychology*, 1981, 2:89–116.

Klapper, Z. S. "Psychoeducational aspects of reading disabilities." In G. Nachez (Ed.), *Children with reading problems*. New York: Basic Books, 1968.

Klaus, M. H., and J. H. Kennell. *Maternal-infant bonding*. St. Louis: Mosby, 1976.

Klaus, M. H., and J. H. Kennell. "Parent to infant attachment." In J. H. Stevens, Jr., and M. Mathews (Eds.), *Mother/child, father/child relationships*. Washington, D.C.: National Association for the Education of Young Children, 1978.

Klebanov, D. "Hunger und psychische Erregungen als Ovar und Keimschadigungen," *Geburtshilfe und Frauenheilkunde*, 1948, 8:812–820.

Kline, J., et al. "Drinking during pregnancy and spontaneous abortion," *The Lancet*, 1980 (July 26), pp. 176–180.

Klinnert, M. D., J. J. Campos, J. F. Sorce, R. N. Ende, and M. J. Svejda. "Social referencing." In R. Plutchik and H. Kellerman (Eds.), *Emotions in Early Development*. New York: Academic Press, 1983.

Knight, C. C. "Hierarchical relationships among components of reading abilities of beginning readers." Unpublished doctoral dissertation, Arizona State University, May 1982.

Knoblock, H., and B. Pasamanick (Eds.). *Gesell and Amatruda's developmental diagnosis* (3rd ed.). Hagerstown, Maryland: Harper & Row, 1974.

Koepke, J. E., M. Hamm, M. Legerstee, and M. Russell. "Neonatal imitation: Two failures to replicate," *Infant Behavior and Development*, 1983, 6:97–102.

Kogan, N. "Stylistic variation in childhood and adolescence: Creativity, metaphor, and cognitive style." In P. H. Mussen (Ed.), *Handbook of child psychology*; vol. 3: J. H. Flavell and E. M. Markman (Eds.), *Cognitive development*. New York: Wiley, 1983.

Kohlberg, L. "A cognitive-developmental analysis of children's sex-role concepts and attitudes." In E. E. Maccoby (Ed.), *The development of sex differences*. Stanford, California: Stanford University Press, 1966.

Kohlberg, L. "Stage and sequence: The cognitive-developmental approach to socialization." In D. A. Goslin (Ed.), *Handbook of socialization theory and research*. Chicago: Rand McNally, 1969.

Kohlberg, L. "Revisions in the theory and practice of moral development." In *Moral development* (New directions for child development, no. 2). San Francisco: Jossey-Bass, 1978.

Kohlberg, L. *Essays on moral development*. New York: Harper & Row, 1981.

Kohlberg, L., J. Yaeger, and E. Hjertholm. "The development of private speech: Four studies and a review of theories," *Child Development*, 1968, 39:691–736.

Konner, M. "Evolution of human behavior development and infancy among the Kalahari desert San." In P. H. Leiderman, S. R. Tulkin, and A. Rosenfeld (Eds.), *Culture and infancy*. New York: Academic Press, 1977.

Konopka, G. *Young girls*. Englewood Cliffs, New Jersey: Prentice-Hall, 1976.

Kopp, C. B. "Risk factors in development." In P. H. Mussen (Ed.), *Handbook of child psychology* (4th ed.); vol. 2: M. M. Haith and J. J. Campos (Eds.), *Infancy and developmental psychobiology*. New York: Wiley, 1983.

Kopp, C. B., and A. H. Parmalee. "Prenatal and perinatal influences on infant behavior." In J. D. Osofsky (Ed.), *Handbook of infant development*. New York: Wiley, 1979.

Krauss, R. H., and S. Glucksberg. "The development of communication: Competence as a function of age," *Child Development*, 1969, 42:255–266.

Krebs, R. L. "Some relationships between moral judgment, attention, and resistance to temptation." Unpublished doctoral dissertation, University of Chicago, 1967.

Kreutzer, M. A., S. C. Leonard, and J. H. Flavell. "An interview study of children's knowledge about memory," *Monographs of the Society for Research in Child Development*, 1975, 40(1, serial no. 159).

Kuhn, D. "Short-term longitudinal evidence for the sequentiality of Kohlberg's early stages of moral judgment," *Developmental Psychology*, 1976, 12:162–166.

Kuhn, D., S. C. Nash, and L. Brucken. "Sex role concepts of two- and three-year-olds," *Child Development*, 1978, 49:445–451.

Kurtines, W., and W. Greif. "The development of moral thought: Review and evaluation of Kohlberg's approach," *Psychological Bulletin*, 1974, 81:453–470.

Labov, W. *Language in the inner city*. Philadelphia: University of Pennsylvania Press, 1972.

Labov, W., and C. Robins. "A note on the relation of reading failure to peer-group status in urban ghettos," *The Record—Teachers College*, 1969, 70:395–405

Lamaze, F. *Painless childbirth: Psychoprophylactic method*. Chicago: Henry Regnery, 1970.

Lamb, M. E. (Ed.). *The role of the father in child development*. New York: Wiley, 1976.

Lamb, M. E. "The father's role in the infant's social world." In J. H. Stevens, Jr., and M. Mathews (Eds.), *Mother/child, father/child relationships*. Washington, D.C.: National Association for the Education of Young Children, 1978.

Lamb, M. E. "Parent-infant interaction, attachment, and socioemotional development in infancy." In R. N. Emde and R. J. Harmon (Eds.), *The development of attachment and affiliative systems*. New York: Plenum, 1982.

Lamb, M. E., and M. A. Easterbrooks. "Individual differences in parental sensitivity: Origins, components, and consequences." In M. E. Lamb and L. R. Sherrod (Eds.), *Infant social cognition: Empirical and theoretical considerations*. Hillsdale, N.J.: Erlbaum, 1981.

Lampl, M., and R. N. Emde. "Episodic growth in infancy: A preliminary report on length, head circumference, and behavior." In *Levels and transitions in children's development* (New directions for child development, no. 21). San Francisco: Jossey-Bass, 1983.

Langhorne, J. E., Jr., J. Loney, C. E. Paternite, and H. P. Bechtoldt. "Childhood hyperkinesis: A re-

turn to the source," *Journal of Abnormal Psychology*, 1976, 85: 201–209.

Lansky, L. M., V. J. Crandall, J. Kagan, and C. T. Baker. "Sex differences in aggression and its correlates in middle class adolescents," *Child Development*, 1961, 32: 45–58.

Lassen, N. A., D. H. Ingvar, and E. Skinhoj. "Brain function and blood flow," *Scientific American*, 1978, 239(October): 62–71.

Lavin, D. E. *The prediction of academic performance*. New York: Russell Sage Foundation, 1965.

Law, L. W. "Studies on size inheritance in mice," *Genetics*, 1938, 23:399–422.

van Lawick-Goodall, J. *In the shadow of man*. Boston, Houghton Mifflin, 1971.

Lazar, I., and R. Darlington, with H. Murray, J. Royce, and A. Snipper. "Lasting effects of early education: A report from the consortium for longitudinal studies," *Monographs of the Society for Research in Child Development*, 1982, 47 (nos. 2–3, serial no. 195).

Leahy, R. L. (Ed.). *The child's construction of social inequality*. New York: Academic Press, 1983.

Leboyer, F. *Birth without violence*. New York: Knopf, 1975.

LeCompte, M. D. "Learning to work: The hidden curriculum of the classroom," *Anthropology and Education Quarterly*, 1978, 9: 22–38.

Lecours, A. R. "Myelogenetic correlates of the development of speech and language." In E. H. Lenneberg and E. Lenneberg. *Foundations of language development*. New York: Academic Press, 1975.

Lee, C. L. "The concomitant development of cognitive and moral modes of thought: A test of selected deductions from Piaget's theory," *Genetic Psychology Monographs*, 1971, 83:93–146.

Lee, L. C. "Toward a cognitive theory of interpersonal development: Importance of peers." In M. Lewis and L. A. Rosenblum (Eds.), *Friendship and peer relations*. New York: Wiley, 1975.

Lefkowitz, M. M. "Smoking during pregnancy: Long-term effects on offspring," *Developmental Psychology*, 1981, 17(2): 192–194.

Leibert, R. M., J. N. Sprafkin, and E. S. Davidson. *The early window: Effects of television on chil-*

dren and youth (2nd ed.). New York: Pergamon, 1982.

Leiderman, P. H., S. R. Tulkin, and A. Rosenfeld. *Culture and infancy: Variations in the human experience.* New York: Academic Press, 1977.

Lejeune, J., M. Gautier, and R. Turpin. "Etude des chromosomes somatiques de neuf enfants mongoliens," *Comptes Rendus de l'Academie des Sciences,* Paris, 1959, *248:* 1721–1722.

Lenneberg, E. H. *The biological foundations of language.* New York: Wiley, 1967.

Lenneberg, E. "On explaining language," *Science,* 1969, *164:* 635–643.

Lenneberg, E. H., and E. Lenneberg. *Foundations of language development: A multidisciplinary approach.* New York: Academic Press, 1975.

Leopold, W. F. *Speech development of a bilingual child* (3 vols.). Evanston, Ill.: Northwestern University Press, 1939–1949.

Lesser, G. S. "The relationships between various forms of aggression and popularity among lower-class children," *Journal of Educational Psychology,* 1959, 50:20–25.

Lesser, G. S. *Children and television: Lessons from Sesame Street.* New York: Random House, 1974.

Leventhal, G. S., and D. W. Lane. "Sex, age, and equity behavior," *Journal of Personality and Social Psychology,* 1970, 15:312–316.

LeVine, R. A. "Childrearing as cultural adaptation." In P. H. Leiderman, S. H. Tulkin, and A. Rosenfeld (Eds.), *Culture and infancy.* New York: Academic Press, 1977.

Lévi-Strauss, C. "The family." In H. L. Shapiro (Ed.), *Man, culture, and society.* London: Oxford University Press, 1956.

Lewis, O. "The culture of poverty," *Scientific American,* 1966, *215(October):*19–25.

Lewis, O. *Anthropological essays.* New York: Random House, 1970.

Lewis, M., and J. Brooks-Gunn. *Social cognition and the acquisition of self.* New York: Plenum, 1979.

Lewis, T. L., D. Maurer, and D. Kay. "Newborns' central vision: Whole or hole?" *Journal of Experimental Child Psychology,* 1978, *26:* 193–203.

Lewontin, R.C. "Race and intelligence." In N. J. Block and G. Dworkin (Eds.), *The IQ contro-versy.* New York: Pantheon, 1976.

Lewontin, R.C. "Adaptation," *Scientific American,* 1978, *239 (September):* 213–230.

Lewontin, R. *Human diversity.* New York: W. H. Freeman and Company, 1982.

Lindzey, G. "Some remarks concerning incest, the incest taboo, and psychoanalytic theory," *American Psychologist,* 1967, *22(12):* 1051–1059.

Linton, R. "The natural history of the family." In R. N. Anshen (Ed.), *The family: Its function and destiny.* New York: Harper, 1959.

Livesley, W. J., and O. B. Bromley. *Person perception in childhood and adolescence.* London: Wiley, 1973.

Livingstone, F. B. *Abnormal hemoglobins in human populations.* Chicago: Aldine, 1967.

Livingstone, F. B. "Malaria and human polymorphisms," *Annual Review of Genetics,* 1971, *5:* 33–64.

Ljung, B. O. *The adolescent spurt in mental growth.* Stockholm: Almquist & Wiksell, 1965.

Loehlin, J. C., and R. C. Nichols. *Heredity, environment, and personality: A study of 850 twins.* Austin: University of Texas Press, 1976.

London, P. "The intimacy gap," *Psychology Today,* May 1978, 40–45.

Lorenz, K. Z. *Studies in animal and human behaviors* (Robert Martin, trans.). Cambridge, Mass.: Harvard University Press, 1971.

Lowry, J. T. "Fetal mortality and sex ratio," *Science,* 1979, *206:* 1428.

Lunzer, E. A. "Problems of formal reasoning in test situations." In P.H. Mussen (Ed.), European research in cognitive development, *Monographs of the Society for Research in Child Development,* 1965, *30* (2, serial no. 100).

Lyle, J., and H. Hoffman. "Explorations in patterns of television viewing by preschool-age children." In E. A. Rubinstein, G. A. Comstock, and J. P. Murray (Eds.), *Television and social behavior: IV. Television in day-to-day life: Patterns of Use.* Washington, D.C.: U.S. Government Printing Office, 1972.

Lynn, D. B. *"The father: His role in development."* Monterey, California: Brooks/Cole, 1974.

Lyons-Ruth, K. "Integration of auditory and visual

information during early infancy." Unpublished doctoral dissertation, Harvard University, 1974.

Maccoby, E. E. "Women's intellect." In S. M Farber and R. H. L. Wilson (Eds.)., *The potential of women.* New York: McGraw-Hill, 1963.

Maccoby, E. E. *Social development: Psychological growth and the parent-child relationship.* New York: Harcourt Brace Jovanovich, 1980.

Maccoby, E. E., and C. N. Jacklin. *The psychology of sex differences.* Stanford, California: Stanford University Press, 1974.

Maccoby, E. E., and J. A. Martin. "Socialization in the context of the family: Parent-child interaction." In P. H. Mussen (Ed.), *Handbook of child psychology* (4th ed.); Vol. 4: E. M. Hetherington (Ed.), *Socialization, personality, and social behavior.* New York: Wiley, 1983.

MacFarlane, A. *The psychology of childbirth.* Cambridge, Massachusetts: Harvard University Press, 1977.

Macrae, J. W. and E. Herbert-Jackson. "Are behavioral effects of infant day care programs specific?" *Developmental Psychology,* 1976, *12*:269–270.

MacWhinney, B. "The acquisition of morphophonology," *Monographs of the Society for Research in Child Development,* 1978, *43*(1–2, serial no. 174).

Mahler, M. S., F. Pine, and A. Bergman. *The psychological birth of the human infant: Symbiosis and individuation.* New York: Basic Books, 1975.

Mann, V. A., R. Diamond, and S. Carey. "Development of voice recognition: Parallels with face recognition," *Journal of Experimental Child Psychology,* 1979, *27*: 153–165.

Maratsos, O. "Trends in the development of imitation in early infancy." In T. G. Bever (Ed.), *Regressions in mental development: Basic phenomena and theories.* Hillsdale, N.J.: Erlbaum, 1982.

Marcia, J. E. "Identity in adolescence." In J. Adelson (Ed.), *Handbook of adolescent psychology.* New York: Wiley, 1980.

Marcus, D. E., and W. F. Overton. "The development of cognitive gender constancy and sex role preferences," *Child Development,* 1978, *49*: 434–444.

Marjoribanks, K. "Bloom's model of human development: A regression surface analysis," *International Journal of Behavioral Development,* 1978, *1*:193–206.

Marler, P., and W. J. Hamilton, III. *Mechanisms of animal behavior.* New York: Wiley, 1966.

Marler, P., S. Zoloth, and K. Dooling. "Innate programs for perceptual development: An ethological view." In E. S. Gollin (Ed.), *Developmental plasticity.* New York: Academic Press, 1981.

Martarano, S. C. "A developmental analysis of performance on Piaget's formal operations tasks," *Developmental Psychology,* 1977, *13*:666–672.

Martin, B. "Parent-child relations." In F. D. Horowitz et al. (Eds.), *Review of child development research* (vol. 4). Chicago: University of Chicago Press, 1975.

Marvin, R. S., M. T. Greenberg, and D. G. Mossler. "The early development of conceptual perspective taking: Distinguishing among multiple perspectives," *Child Development,* 1976, *47*:511–514.

Massi, R. K. *Journey.* New York: Knopf, 1975.

Masters, W. H., and V. E. Johnson. *Human sexual response.* Boston: Little, Brown, 1966.

Maurer, D., and P. Salapatek. "Developmental changes in the scanning of faces by young infants," *Child Development,* 1976, *47*:523–527.

McCall, R. B. "Childhood IQs as predictors of adult educational and occupational status," *Science,* 1977, *197*:482–483.

McCall, R. "Qualitative transitions in behavioral development in the first years of life." In M. H. Bornstein and W. Kessen (Eds.), *Psychological development from infancy.* New York: Lawrence Erlbaum Associates, 1979.

McCall, R. B. "Nature-nurture and the two realms of development," *Child Development,* 1981, *52*:1–12.

McCall, R. B. "Exploring developmental transitions in mental performance." In *Levels and transitions in children's development* (New directions for child development, no. 21). San Francisco: Jossey-Bass, 1983.

McCall, R. B., M. I. Appelbaum, and P. S. Hogarty. "Developmental changes in mental performance," *Monographs of the Society for Research in Child De-*

velopment, 1973, 38:(3, serial no. 150).

McCall, R. B., R. D. Parke, and R. D. Kavannaugh. "Imitation of live and televised models in children one to three years of age," *Monographs of the Society for Research in Child Development*, 1977, *42* (5, serial no. 173).

McCall, R. B., D. H. Eichorn, and P. S. Hogarty. "Transitions in early mental development," *Monographs of the Society for Research in Child Development*, 1977, *42*(3, serial no. 171).

McCall, R. B., E. D. Meyers, Jr., J. Hartman, and A. F. Roche. "Developmental changes in head circumference and mental performance growth rates: A test of Epstein's phrenoblysis hypothesis," *Developmental Psychobiology*, 1983, 16:457–468.

McCarthy, J. L. and D. Wofle. "Doctorates granted to women and minority group members," *Science*, 1975, *189*:4206.

McCauley, C., K. Woods, C. Coolidge, and W. Kulick. "More aggressive cartoons are funnier," *Journal of Personality and Social Psychology*, 1983, 44:817–823.

McClearn, G. F., *The early history of the infant welfare movement*. London: Lewis, 1933.

McClearn, G. E., and J. C. DeFries. *Introduction to behavioral genetics*. San Francisco: W. H. Freeman and Company, 1973.

McClelland, D. C. *The achievement motive*. New York: Appleton-Century-Crofts, 1953.

McGhee, P. E. "Cognitive mastery and children's humor," *Psychological Bulletin*, 1974, 81:721–730.

McGlaughlin, A., J. Empson, M. Morrissey, and J. Sever. "Early child development and the home environment: Consistencies at and between four pre-school stages," *International Journal of Behavioral Development*, 1980, 3:299–309.

McKenzie, B., and R. Over. "Young infants fail to imitate facial and manual gestures," *Infant Behavior and Development*, 1983, 6:85–95.

McQueen, R. *Brain growth periodization: Analysis of the Epstein spurt-plateau findings*. Multnomah County Education Service District Education Association, Portland, Oregon, 1982.

Mead, M. *Sex and temperament in three primitive societies*. New York: Morrow, 1963.

Mead, M. "Totem and taboo reconsidered with re-spect," *Menninger Clinic Bulletin*, 1963, *27*:185–199.

Mead, M., and N. Newton. "Cultural patterning of perinatal behavior." In A. Richardson and A.F. Guttmacher (Eds.), *Childbearing: Its social and psychological aspects*. Baltimore, Maryland: Williams & Wilkins, 1967.

Mellin, G. W. "Drugs in the first trimester of pregnancy and the fetal life of *Homo sapiens*," *American Journal of Obstetrics and Gynecology*, 1964, 90: 1169–1180.

Meltzoff, A. N., and M. K. Moore. "Imitation of facial and manual gestures by human neonates," *Science*, 1977, *198*:75–78.

Mendelson, M. J., and M. M. Haith. "The relation between audition and vision in the human newborn," *Monographs of the Society for Research in Child Development*, 1976, *41*(4, serial no. 167).

Meredith, H. V. "Growth in body size: A compendium of findings on contemporary children living in different parts of the world." In H. W. Reese (Ed.), *Advances in Child Development and Behavior* (vol. 6). New York: Academic Press, 1971.

Messer, S. B. "Reflection–impulsivity: A review," *Psychological Bulletin*, 1976, 83(6):1026–1052.

Meyer, M. B., J. A. Tonascia, and C. Buck. "The interrelationship of maternal smoking and increased perinatal mortality with other risk factors. Further analysis of the Ontario Perinatal Mortality Study, 1960–1961," *American Journal of Epidemiology*, 1975, *100*(6):443–452.

Meyer, M. B., B. S. Jonas, and J. A. Tonascia. "Perinatal events associated with maternal smoking during pregnancy," *American Journal of Epidemiology*, 1976, *103*(5):464–476.

Michaels, R. H., and G. W. Mellin. "Prospective experience with maternal rubella and the associated congenital malformations," *Pediatrics*, 1960, 26:200–209.

Miller, M. *Sunday's child*. New York: Holt, Rinehart, & Winston, 1968.

Miller, P. H. *Theories of developmental psychology*. New York: W. H. Freeman and Company, 1983.

Miller, N. E., and J. Dollard. *Social learning and imitation*. New Haven: Yale University Press, 1941.

Miller, P. Y., and W. Simon. "The development of

sexuality in adolescence." In J. Adelson (Ed.), *Handbook of adolescent psychology*. New York: Wiley, 1980.

Milne, A. A. *The world of Pooh*. New York: Dutton, 1957.

Milner, E. *Human neural and behavioral development: A relational inquiry, with implications for personality*. Springfield, Ill.: C. C. Thomas, 1967.

Minkowski, A. "Development of the nervous system in early life." In F. Falkner (Ed.), *Human Development*. London: Saunders, 1966.

Minuchin, P. *Differential use of the open classroom: A study of exploratory and cautious children*. Final Report to the National Institute of Education, 1976.

Minuchin, P. P., and E. K. Shapiro. "The school as a context for social development." In P. H. Mussen (Ed.), *Handbook of child psychology* (4th ed.); vol. 4: E. M. Hetherington (Ed.), *Socialization, personality, and social behavior*. New York: Wiley, 1983.

Mischel, W. "Sex-typing and socialization." In P. H. Mussen (Ed.), *Carmichael's manual of child psychology*. New York: Wiley, 1970.

Mischel, W. "Processes in delay of gratification." In L. Berkowitz (Ed.), *Advances in experimental social psychology* (vol. 7). New York: Academic Press, 1974.

Moely, B. E. "Organizational factors in the development of memory." In R. B. Kail, Jr., and J. W. Hagen (Eds.), *Perspectives on the development of memory and cognition*. New York: Wiley (Lawrence Erlbaum Associates), 1977.

Moerck, E. L. "Processes of language teaching and training in the interactions of mother-child dyads," *Child Development*, 1976, 47:1064–1078.

Moerck, E. L. "Relationships between parental input frequencies and children's language acquisition: A reanalysis of Brown's data," *Journal of Child Language*, 1980, 7:105–118.

Molfese, D. L., R. D. Freeman, Jr., and D. S. Palermo. "The ontogeny of brain lateralization for speech and nonspeech stimuli," *Brain and Language*, 1975, 2:356–368.

Monahan, L., D. Kuhn, and P. Shaver. "Intrapsychic versus cultural explanations of the 'fear of success' motive," *Journal of Personality and Social Psychology*, 1974, 29:60–64.

Money, J., and A. A. Earhardt. *Man and woman, boy and girl*. Baltimore, Maryland: Johns Hopkins University Press, 1972.

Money, J., G. Wolff, and C. Annecillo. "Pain agnosia and self-injury in the syndrome of reversible somatotrophic deficiency (psychosocial dwarfism)," *Journal of Autism and Childhood Schizophrenia*, 1972, 2:127–139.

Montagu, A. "Neonatal and infant immaturity in man," *Journal of the American Medical Association*, 1961, 178:56–57.

Montemayor, R., and M. Eisen. "The development of self-conceptions from childhood to adolescence," *Developmental Psychology*, 1977, 13:314–319.

Morell, P., and W. T. Norton. "Myelin," *Scientific American*, 1980, 242(5):88–119.

Morrow, W. R., and R. C. Wilson. "Family relations of bright high-achieving and low-achieving high school boys," *Child Development*, 1961, 32:501–510.

Moshman, D., and M. Timmons. "The construction of logical necessity," *Human Development*, 1982, 25:309–323.

Mounoud, P. "Revolutionary periods in early development." In T. G. Bever (Ed.), *Regressions in mental development: Basic phenomena and theories*. Hillsdale, N.J.: Erlbaum, 1982.

Movshon, J. A., and R. C. Van Sluyters. "Visual neural development," *Annual Review of Psychology*, 1981, 32:477–522.

Mueller, E., and T. Lucas. "A developmental analysis of peer interaction among toddlers." In M. Lewis and L. A. Rosenblum (Eds.), *Friendship and peer relations*. New York: Wiley, 1975.

Mueller, E. C., and D. Vandell. "Infant-infant interaction." In J. D. Osofsky (Ed.), *Handbook of infant development*. New York: Wiley, 1979.

Muller, E., H. Hollien, and T. Murry. "Perceptual responses to infant crying: Identification of cry types," *Journal of Child Language*, 1974, 1:89–96.

Munsinger, H. "The adopted child's IQ: A critical review," *Psychological Bulletin*, 1975, 82:623–659.

Murphy, D. P. *Congenital malformation* (2nd ed.).

Philadelphia: University of Pennsylvania Press, 1947.

Mussen, P., and M. C. Jones. "Self-conceptions, motivations, and interpersonal attitudes of late- and early-maturing boys," *Child Development*, 1957, 28:243–256.

Mussen, P. H., D. H. Eichorn, M. P. Honzik, S. L. Bieber, and W. H. Meredith. "Continuity and change in women's characteristics over four decades," *International Journal of Behavioral Development*, 1980, 3:333–348.

Nadel, J., and P.-M. Baudonnière. "L'Imitation comme mode d'échange prépondérant entre pairs au cours de la troisième année," *Enfance*, 1980, 77–90.

Nahmias, A., et al. "Herpes simplex virus infection of the fetus and newborn." In A. Gershon and S. Krugman (Eds.), *Infections of the fetus and newborn*. New York: Liss, 1975.

Naimark, H., and P. Shaver. *Social class as viewed by children and adolescents*. Hillsdale, N.J.: Erlbaum, 1984.

Napier, J. *The roots of mankind*. Washington, D.C.: Smithsonian Institution, 1970.

National Institute of Health Consensus Development Summary. "Cesarean childbirth," *Connecticut Medicine*, 1981, *45(3)*:155–162.

National Research Council, Food and Nutrition Board, Committee on Maternal Nutrition. *Maternal nutrition and the course of pregnancy*. Washington, D.C.: National Academy of Sciences, 1981.

National Research Council. *Alternative dietary practices and nutritional abuses in pregnancy: Summary report*. Committee on Nutrition of the Mother and Preschool Child, Food and Nutrition Board, Commission on Life Sciences, 1982.

Needham, J. *A history of embryology* (2nd ed., revised with the assistance of A. Hughes). Cambridge: Cambridge University Press, 1959.

Needleman, H. L. "Lead poisoning in children: Neurologic implications of widespread subclinical intoxication," *Seminars in Psychiatry*, 1973, 5:47–53.

Neimark, E. D. "Longitudinal development of formal operations thought," *Genetic Psychology Monographs*, 1975, 91:171–225.

Nelson, K. "Structure and strategy in learning to talk," *Monographs of the Society for Research in Child Development*, 1973, 38(1 & 2, serial no. 149).

Nelson, K. "Concept, word, and sentence: Interrelations in acquisition and development," *Psychological Review*, 1974, 81:267–285.

Nelson, K. E. "Facilitating children's syntax acquisition," *Developmental Psychology*, 1977, 13:101–107.

Nelson, K. "Individual differences in language development: Implications for development and language," *Psychological Bulletin*, 1981, 17:170–187.

Neugarten, B. L., J. W. Moore, and J. C. Lowe. "Age norms, age constraints, and adult socialization." In B. L. Neugarten (Ed.), *Middle age and aging*. Chicago: University of Chicago Press, 1968.

Newman, H. H., F. N. Freeman, and K. H. Holzinger. *Twins: A study of heredity and environment*. Chicago: University of Chicago Press, 1937.

Newsweek. "The new science of birth." November 15, 1976, pp. 55–60.

Nicholls, E. M. "Pigment spotting in man and the number of genes determining skin and eye color," *Human Heredity*, 1973, 23:1–12.

Nicolich, L. M. "Toward symbolic functioning: Structure of early pretend games and potential parallels with language," *Child Development*, 1981, 52:785–797.

Nilsson, L. *A child is born* (rev. ed.). New York: Delacorte, 1977.

Nishida, T., and K. Kawanaka. "Inter-unit-group relationship among wild chimpanzees of the Mahati Mountains," *Kyoto University African Studies*, 1972, 7:131–169.

Noble, G. *Children in front of the small screen*. Beverly Hills, California: Sage Publications, 1975.

O'Connor, J. O., and G. F. Arnold. *Intonation of colloquial English*. London: Longmans Green, 1961.

Offer, D., E. Ostrov, and K. I. Howard. "The self-image of adolescents: A study of four cultures, *Journal of Youth and Adolescence*, 1977, 6:265–280.

Olson, D. R. "From utterance to text: The bias of language in speech and writing," *Harvard Educational Review*, 1977, 47:257–281.

Olson, D. R., and N. Nickerson. "Language development through the school years: Learning to confine interpretation to the information in the text." In K. E. Nelson (Ed.), *Children's language* (vol. 1). New York: Gardner Press, 1978.

Ong, W. J. *Orality and literacy: The technologizing of the world.* New York: Methuen, 1982.

Orlofsky, J. L. "Identity formation, achievement, and fear of success in college men and women," *Journal of Youth and Adolescence,* 1978, 7:49–62.

Osgood, C. E., G. J. Suci, and P. H. Tannenbaum. *The measurement of meaning.* Urbana, Illinois: University of Illinois Press, 1957.

Osherson, D. N., and E. Markman. "Language and the ability to evaluate contradictions and tautologies," *Cognition,* 1974/75, 3(3):213–226.

Oullette, E. M., H. L. Rosett, N. P. Rosman, and L. Weiner. "Adverse effects on offspring of maternal alcohol use during pregnancy," *New England Journal of Medicine,* 1977, 297:528–530.

Paluszny, M. J. *Autism: A practical guide for parents and professionals.* Syracuse, New York: Syracuse University Press, 1979.

Papoušek, H. "Experimental studies of appetitional behavior in human newborns and infants." In H. W. Stevenson, E. H. Hess, and H. L. Rheingold (Eds.), *Early behavior.* New York: Wiley, 1967.

Papoušek, H., and M. Papoušek. "Early ontogeny of human social interaction: Its biological roots and social dimensions." In M. von Cranach, K. Foppa, W. Lepenies, and D. Ploog (Eds.), *Human ethology.* London: Cambridge University Press, 1979.

Papoušek, H., and M. Papoušek. "The infant's fundamental adaptive response system in social interaction." In E. B. Thoman (Ed.), *Origins of the infant's social responsiveness.* Hillsdale, New Jersey: Lawrence Erlbaum Associates, 1979.

Paris, S. G., and B. K. Lindauer. "The role of inference in children's comprehension and memory for sentences," *Cognitive Psychology,* 1976, 8: 217–227.

Parke, R. D., and R. G. Slaby. "The development of aggression." In P. H. Mussen (Ed.), *Handbook of child psychology* (4th ed.); vol. 4: E. M. Hetherington (Ed.), *Socialization, personality, and social development.* New York: Wiley, 1983.

Parker, S. T., and K. R. Gibson. "A developmental model of the evolution of language and intelligence in early hominids," *The Behavioral and Brain Sciences,* 1979, 2:367–381.

Parkes, A. S. *Patterns of sexuality and reproduction.* Oxford University Press, 1978.

Parmalee, A. H., Jr., and M. D. Sigman. "Perinatal brain development and behavior." In P. H. Mussen (Ed.), *Handbook of child psychology* (4th ed.); vol. 2: M. M. Haith and J. J. Campos (Eds.), *Infancy and developmental psychobiology.* New York: Wiley, 1983.

Passingham, R. E. "Changes in the size and organization of the brain in man and his ancestors," *Brain, Behavior, and Evolution,* 1975, 11:73–90.

Patterson, F. G. "Innovative uses of language by a gorilla: A case study." In K. E. Nelson (Ed.), *Children's language* (vol. 2). New York: Gardner Press, 1980.

Peacock, J. E., and F. A. Sarubbi. "Disseminated herpes simplex virus infection during pregnancy," *Obstetrics and Gynecology,* 1983, 61 (3, suppl.): 13S–18S.

Pederson, E., and T. A. Faucher, with W. W. Eaton. "A new perspective on the effects of first-grade teachers on children's subsequent adult status," *Harvard Educational Review,* 1978, 48(1):1–31.

Peill, E. J. *Invention and discovery of reality.* New York: Wiley, 1975.

Peiper, A. *Cerebral function in infancy and childhood.* New York: Consultants Bureau, 1963.

Perry, W. G., Jr. *Forms of intellectual and ethical development in the college years.* New York: Holt, Rinehart, & Winston, 1970.

Peters, A. M. *The units of language acquisition.* New York: Cambridge University Press, 1983.

Petersen, A. C., and S. M. Cavrell. "Cognition during early adolescence," *Child Development,* 1984.

Petersen, A. C., and B. Taylor. "The biological approach to adolescence." In J. Adelson (Ed.), *Handbook of adolescent psychology.* New York: Wiley, 1980.

Peterson, P. L. "Interactive effects of student anxiety, achievement orientation, and teacher behavior on student achievement and attitude," *Journal of*

Educational Psychology, 1977, 69:779–792.

Peterson, P. L.   "Direction instruction reconsidered." In P. L. Peterson and H. J. Walberg (Eds.), *Research on teaching.* Berkeley, Calif.: McCutchan, 1979.

Petersson, P. O.   *Child health services in Sweden* (Brochure no. 124). New York: Swedish Information Service, 1976.

Piaget, J.   *The moral judgment of the child.* New York: Harcourt Brace, 1932.

Piaget, J.   "Le mécanisme du développement mental et les lois du groupement des opérations," *Archives de Psychologie,* Genève, 1941, 28:215–285.

Piaget, J.   *The psychology of intelligence* (M. Piercy and D. E. Berlyne, trans.). New York: Harcourt Brace, 1950 (originally published, 1947).

Piaget, J.   *Play, dreams, and imitation in childhood* (C. Gattegno and F. M. Hodgson, trans.). New York: Norton, 1951 (originally published, 1946).

Piaget, J.   *The origins of intelligence in children* (M. Cook, trans.). New York: International Universities Press, 1952 (originally published, 1936).

Piaget, J.   *The construction of reality in the child* (M. Cook, trans.). New York: Basic Books, 1954 (originally published, 1937).

Piaget, J.   "Logique et équilibre dans les comportements du sujet." *Études d'Épistémologie Génétique,* 1957, 2:27–118.

Piaget, J.   *The origins of intelligence in children* (M. C. Cook, trans.). New York: Norton, 1963.

Piaget, J.   "The theory of stages in cognitive development." In D. R. Green, M. P. Ford, and G. B. Flamer (Eds.), *Measurement and Piaget.* New York: McGraw-Hill, 1971.

Piaget, J.   "Intellectual evolution from adolescence to adulthood," *Human Development,* 1972, 15:1–12.

Piaget, J.   "Piaget's theory." In P. H. Mussen (Ed.), *Handbook of child psychology* (4th ed.); vol. 1: W. Kessen (Ed.), *History, theory, and methods.* New York: Wiley, 1983.

Piaget, J., and B. Inhelder.   *The child's conception of space* (F. J. Langdon and J. L. Lunzer, trans.). New York: Norton, 1967 (originally published, 1948).

Piaget, J., and B. Inhelder.   *The child's conception of space* (F. J. Langdon and J. L. Lunzer, transl.).

New York: Basic Books, 1969 (originally published, 1966).

Piaget, J., and B. Inhelder.   *The psychology of the child* (H. Weaver, trans.). New York: Basic Books, 1969 (originally published, 1966).

Piaget, J., J. B. Grize, A. Szeminska, and Vinh Bang.   "Épistémologie et psychologie de la fonction," *Études d'Épistémologie Génétique,* 1968, *23.*

Pien, D., and M. K. Rothbart.   "Incongruity and resolution in children's humor: A reexamination," *Child Development,* 1976, 47:966–971.

Pilbeam, D.   "Toward a concept of man," *Natural History,* 1979, 88(2):100–109.

Pilbeam, D., and S. J. Gould.   "Size and scaling in human evolution," *Science,* 1974, 186:892–901.

Pinard, A.   *The concept of conservation.* Chicago: University of Chicago Press, 1981.

Pines, M.   "Invisible playmates," *Psychology Today,* 1978 September, pp. 38, 41, 42, 106.

Pinneau, S.   "The infantile disorders of hospitalism and anaclitic depression," *Psychological Bulletin,* 1955, 52:429–452.

Pipp, S. L., and M. M. Haith.   "Infant visual scanning of two- and three-dimensional forms," *Child Development,* 1977, 48:1640–1644.

Platt, C. B., and B. MacWhinney.   "Error assimilation as a mechanism in language learning," *Journal of Child Language,* 1983, 10:401–414.

Plomin, R., and J. C. DeFries.   "Genetics and intelligence: Recent data," *Intelligence,* 1980, 4:15–24.

Plomin, R., and T. T. Foch.   "Sex differences and individual differences," *Child Development,* 1981, 52:383–385.

Plomin, R., and D. C. Rowe.   "A twin study of temperament in young children," *Journal of Psychology,* 1977, 971:107–113.

Plutarch.   *The Education or Bringinge up of Children* (reprint of 1535 edition). Norwood, New Jersey: Walter J. Johnson, 1969.

Pollio, M. R., and H. R. Pollio.   "A test of metaphoric comprehension and some preliminary developmental data," *Journal of Child Language,* 1979, 6:111–120.

Porter, J. O. R.   *Black child, white child.* Cambridge, Massachusetts: Harvard University Press, 1971.

Potter, M. C. "On perceptual recognition." In J. S. Bruner, R. R. Oliver, and P. M. Greenfield (Eds.), *Studies in cognitive growth*. New York: Wiley, 1966.

Prader, A., J. M. Tanner, and G. A. Von Harnack. "Catch-up growth following illness or starvation," *Journal of Pediatrics*, 1963, *62*:646–659.

Prechtl, H. F. R., and M. J. O'Brien. "Behavioral states of the full-term newborn: The emergence of a concept." In P. Stratton (Ed.), *Psychobiology of the human newborn*. New York: Wiley, 1982.

Premack, D. "Animal cognition," *Annual Review of Psychology*, 1983, *34*:351–362.

Prescott, J. W. "Deprivation of physical affection as a primary process in the development of physical violence: A comparative and cross-cultural perspective." In D. G. Gil (Ed.), *Child abuse and violence*. New York: AMS Press, 1979.

Pulos, S., and M. C. Linn. "Generality of the controlling variables scheme in early adolescence." *Journal of Early Adolescence*, 1981, *1*:26–37.

Rabinowicz, T. "The differentiate maturation of the human cerebral cortex." In F. Falkner and J. M. Tanner (Eds.), *Human growth 3: Neurobiology and nutrition*. New York: Plenum, 1978.

Ramsay, D. S. "Onset of duplicated syllable babbling and unimanual handedness in infancy: Evidence for developmental change in hemispheric specialization," *Developmental Psychology*, 1984.

Rapoport, J. L., M. S. Buchsbaum, T. P. Zahn, H. Weingartner, C. Ludlow, and E. J. Mikkelsen. "Dextroamphetamine: Cognitive and behavioral effects in normal prepubertal boys," *Science*, 1978, *199* (3 February).

Rebelsky, F. , and C. Hanks. "Fathers' verbal interaction with infants in the first three months of life," *Child Development*, 1971, *42*:63–68.

Resnick, L. B. *Teacher behavior in an informal British infant school*. Pittsburgh: University of Pittsburgh Learning Research and Development Center, 1970.

Rest, J. R. "New approaches in the assessment of moral judgment." In T. Lickona (Ed.), *Moral development and behavior*. New York: Holt, Rinehart, & Winston, 1976.

Rest, J. R. *Development in judging moral issues.*
Minneapolis: University of Minnesota Press, 1979.

Rest, J. R. "The impact of higher education on moral judgment development." Paper presented at the Convention of the American Educational Research Association, Los Angeles, April 1981.

Rest, J. R. "Morality." In P. H. Mussen (Ed.), *Handbook of child psychology* (4th ed.); vol. 3: J. H. Flavell and E. M. Markman (Eds.), *Cognitive development*. New York: Wiley, 1983.

Rheingold, H. L., and C. O. Eckerman. "The infant separates himself from his mother," *Science*, 1970, *168*:78–83.

Ricciutti, H. N. "Interaction of adverse social and biological influence on early development: Research and remediation." Paper presented at a symposium of the American Association for the Advancement of Science, Boston, February 1976.

Richards, F. A., and M. L. Commons. "Systematic and metasystematic reasoning: A case for stages of reasoning beyond formal operations." In M. L. Commons, F. A. Richards, and C. Armon (Eds.), *Beyond formal operations: Late adolescent and adult cognitive development*. New York: Praeger, 1983.

Roberts, R. J., Jr. "Errors and the assessment of cognitive development." In *Cognitive development* (New directions for child development, no. 12). San Francisco: Jossey-Bass, 1981.

Roberts, R. J., Jr., and C. Patterson. "Perspective taking and referential communication: The question of correspondence reconsidered," *Child Development*, 1983, *54*:1005–1014.

Robertson, I. *Sociology*. New York: Worth, 1981.

Robinson, H. B., et al. *Early child care in the United States of America*. London: Gordon and Breach, 1973.

Robson, K. S. "The role of eye-to-eye contact in maternal-infant attachment," *Journal of Child Psychology and Psychiatry*, 1967, *8(1)*:13–25.

Roche, A. F. (Ed.). "Secular trends in human growth, maturation, and development," *Monographs of the Society for Research in Child Development*, 1979, *44* (3–4, serial no. 179).

Rogoff, B., M. J. Sellers, S. Pirotta, N. Fox, and S. H. White. "Age of assignment of roles and responsibilities to children: A cross-cultural survey."

In A. Skolnik (Ed.), *Rethinking childhood: Perspectives on development and society.* Boston: Little, Brown, 1976.

Rose, S. *The conscious brain.* New York: Knopf, 1975.

Rosen, B. C., and R. d'Andrade. "The psychological origins of achievement motivation," *Sociometry,* 1959, *22*:185–218.

Rosenberg, M. *Society and the adolescent self-image.* Princeton, New Jersey: Princeton University Press, 1965.

Rosenberg, M. "The dissonant context and the adolescent self-concept." In S. E. Dragastin and G. H. Elder (Eds.), *Adolescence in the life cycle.* Washington, D.C.: Hemisphere Publishing Corp., 1975.

Rosenberg, M. *Conceiving the self.* New York: Basic Books, 1979.

Rosenberg, F. R., and M. Rosenberg. "Self-esteem and delinquency," *Journey of Youth and Adolescence,* 1978, *7*:279–294.

Rosenthal, R., and L. Jacobsen. "Teacher expectations for the disadvantaged," *Scientific American,* 1968, *218*(4):19–23.

Rosenthal, R., and D. B. Rubin. "Interpersonal expectancy effects: The first 345 studies," *Behavioral and Brain Sciences,* 1978, *1*:377–415.

Rosenthal, R., and D. B. Rubin. "Further issues in summarizing 345 studies of interpersonal expectancy effects," *Behavioral and Brain Sciences,* 1980, *3*:475–476.

Rosenthal, R., S. S. Baratz, and C. M. Hall. "Teacher behavior, teacher expectations, and gains in pupils' rated creativity," *Journal of Genetic Psychology,* 1974, *124*:115–121.

Rosow, I. "What is a cohort and why?" *Human Development,* 1978, *21*:65–75.

Rossi, A. S. "Social trends and women's lives: 1965–1985. In *Changing roles of women in industrial societies: A Bellagio conference, March, 1976.* New York: The Rockefeller Foundation Working Papers, 1977.

Rossi, A. S. "The biosocial side of parenthood," *Human Nature,* 1978, *1*(6):72–79.

Rousseau, J.-J. *Emile* (B. Foxley, trans.). London: Dent, 1911 (originally published, 1762).

Rovee, C. K. "Olfactory cross-adaption and facilitation in human neonates," *Journal of Experimental Child Psychology,* 1972, *13*:368–381.

Rovee-Collier, C. K., and L. P. Lipsitt. "Learning, adaptation, and memory in the newborn." In P. Stratton (Ed.), *Psychobiology of the human newborn.* New York: Wiley, 1982.

Rowe, D. C., and R. Plomin. "The importance of nonshared (El) environmental influences in behavioral development," *Developmental Psychology,* 1981, *17*:517–531.

Rubenstein, J. L., and C. Howes. "Caregiving and infant behavior in day care and in homes," *Developmental Psychology,* 1979, *15*:1–24.

Rubin, K. H., G. G. Fein, and B. Vandenberg. "Play." In P. H. Mussen (Ed.), *Handbook of child psychology* (4th ed.); vol. 4: E. M. Hetherington (Ed.), *Socialization, personality, and social development.* New York: Wiley, 1983.

Ruble, D. N. "The development of social comparison processes and their role in achievement-related self-socialization." In E. T. Higgins, D. N. Ruble, and W. W. Hartup (Eds.), *Social cognition and social development: A socio-cultural perspective.* New York: Cambridge University Press, 1983.

Ruedi, J., and C. K. West. "Pupil self-concept in an 'open' school and in a 'traditional' school," *Psychology in the Schools,* 1973, *10*:48–53.

Ruhräh, J. *Pediatrics of the past.* New York: Hoeber, 1925.

Russell, G. "The father role and its relation to masculinity, femininity, and androgyny," *Child Development,* 1978, *49*:1174–1181.

Rutter, M. "Parent-child separation: Psychological effects on the children," *Journal of Child Psychology and Psychiatry,* 1971, *12*:233–260.

Rutter, M. "Institute of Psychiatry: Child psychiatry," *Psychological Medicine,* 1976, *6*(3):505–516.

Rutter, M. "Diagnosis and definition." In M. Rutter and E. Schopler (Eds.), *Autism: A reappraisal of concepts and treatment.* New York: Plenum, 1978.

Rutter, M. "Maternal deprivation, 1972–1978: New findings, new concepts, new approaches," *Child Development,* 1979, *50*:283–305.

Rutter, M., and L. Bartak. "Special educational treatment of autistic children: A comparative study. II. Follow-up findings and implications for services," *Journal of Child Psychology and Psychiatry*, 1973, *14*:241–270.

Rutter, M., and N. Garmezy. "Developmental psychopathology." In P. H. Mussen (Ed.), *Handbook of child psychology* (4th ed.); vol. 4: E. M. Hetherington (Ed.), *Socialization, personality, and social development*. New York: Wiley, 1983.

Sade, D.E., "Inhibition of son-mother mating among free-ranging rhesus monkeys," *Science and Psychoanalysis*, 1968, *12*:18–38.

Salapatek, P. H., and W. Kessen. "Visual scanning of triangles by the human newborn," *Journal of Experimental Child Psychology*, 1966, *3*:155–167.

Salapatek, P. H., and W. Kessen. "Prolonged investigation of a plane geometric triangle by the human newborn," *Journal of Experimental Child Psychology*, 1973, *15*:22–29.

Sameroff, A. J. "The components of sucking in the human newborn," *Journal of Experimental Child Psychology*, 1968, *6*:607–623.

Sameroff, A. J., and P. J. Cavanaugh. "Learning in infancy: A developmental perspective." In J. D. Osofsky (Ed.), *Handbook of infant development*. New York: Wiley, 1979.

Sameroff, A. J., and M. Chandler. "Reproductive risk and the continuum of caretaking casualty." In F. D. Horowitz (Ed.), *Review of Child Development Research* (vol. 4). Chicago: University of Chicago Press, 1975.

Sameroff, A. J., R. Seifer, and M. Zax. "Early development of children at risk for emotional disorder," *Monographs of the Society for Research in Child Development*, 1982, *47*(no. 7, serial no. 199).

Sander, L. W. "Infant and caretaking environment: Investigation and conceptualization of adaptive behavior in a system of increasing complexity." In E. J. Anthony (Ed.), *Explorations in child psychiatry*. New York: Plenum Press, 1975.

Savage-Rumbaugh, E. S., and D. M. Rumbaugh. "Language analogue project, phase II: Theory and tactics." In K. E. Nelson (Ed.), *Children's language* (vol. 2). New York: Gardner Press, 1980.

Savin-Williams, R. C., and D. G. Freedman. "Biosocial approach to human development. In S. Chevalier-Skolnikoff and F. E. Poirier (Eds.), *Primate bio-social development*. New York: Garland, 1977.

Scanlon, J., and J. J. Chisolm Jr. "Fetal effects of lead exposure," *Pediatrics*, 1972, *49*:145–146.

Scardamalia, M., C. Bereiter, and H. Goelman. "The role of production factors in writing ability." In M. Nystrand (Ed.), *What writers know: The language, process, and structure of written discourse*. New York: Academic Press, 1982.

Scarr, S., and R. A. Weinberg. "IQ test performance of black children adopted by white families," *American Psychologist*, 1976, *31*:726–739.

Scarr, S., and R. A. Weinberg. "Intellectual similarities within families of both adopted and biological children," *Intelligence*, 1977, *1*:170–191.

Scarr, S., and R. A. Weinberg. "Nature and nurture strike (out) again," *Intelligence*, 1979, *3*:31–39.

Schachter, F. F., G. Shore, S. Feldman-Rotman, R. E. Marquis, and S. Campbell. "Sibling deidentification," *Developmental Psychology*, 1976, *12*:418–427.

Schaffer, H. R., and C. K. Crook. "Child compliance and maternal control techniques," *Developmental Psychology*, 1980, *16*:54–61.

Schaie, K. W. "Methodological problems in descriptive developmental research on adulthood and aging." In J. R. Nesselroade and H. W. Reese (Eds.), *Life-span developmental psychology: Methodological issues*. New York: Academic Press, 1973.

Schleifer, M., G. Weiss, N. Cohen, M. Elman, H. Cvejic, and E. Kruger. "Hyperactivity in preschoolers and the effect of methylphenidate," *American Journal of Orthopsychiatry*, 45:38–50.

Schreiber, F. "Mental deficiency from paranatal asphyxia," *Proceedings of the American Association of Mental Deficiency*, 1939, *63*:95–106.

Schwartz, B. *Psychology of learning and behavior* (2nd ed.). New York: Norton, 1983.

Scott, J. P. "Critical periods for the development of social behavior in dogs." In S. Kazda and J. H. Denenberg (Eds.), *The postnatal development of phenotype*. London: Butterworths, 1970.

Scribner, S. "Organization and memory among traditional West Africans." Unpublished report, Rockefeller University, 1973.

Scribner, S., and M. Cole. *The consequences of literacy*. Cambridge, Mass.: Harvard University Press, 1981.

Sears, R. R., J. W. M. Whiting, V. Nowlis, and P. S. Sears. "Some child-rearing antecedents of aggression and dependency in young children," *Genetic Psychology Monographs*, 1953, *47*:135–234.

Sears, R. R., E. E. Maccoby, and H. Levin. *Patterns of child rearing*. New York: Harper & Row, 1957.

Seashore, M. J., et al. "The effects of denial of early mother-infant interaction on maternal self-confidence," *Journal of Personality and Social Psychology*, 1973, *26(3)*:369–378.

Seemanova, E. "A study of children of incestuous matings," *Human Heredity*, 1971, *21*:108–128.

Self, P. A., and F. D. Horowitz. "The behavioral assessment of the neonate: An overview." In J. D. Osofsky (Ed.), *Handbook of infant development*. New York: Wiley, 1979.

Seligman, M. E. P. *Helplessness: On depression, development, and death*. San Francisco: W. H. Freeman and Company, 1975.

Selman, R. *The growth of interpersonal understanding*. New York: Academic Press, 1980.

Sharma, S. "Manifest anxiety and school achievement of adolescents," *Journal of Consulting and Clinical Psychology*, 1970, *34*:403–407.

Shaver, P. "Questions concerning fear of success and its conceptual relatives," *Sex Roles*, 1976, *2*:305–320.

Shaver, P., and C. Rubenstein. "Childhood attachment experience and adult loneliness," *The Review of Personality and Social Psychology*, 1980, *1*:42–73.

Shaw, E. "The egg as classroom," *Natural History*, 1976, *85(2)*:72–77.

Sherif, M., and C. Sherif. *Reference groups*. New York: Harper & Row, 1964.

Sherif, M., et al. *Intergroup conflict and cooperation: The Robbers Cave experiment*. Norman, Oklahoma: Institute of Group Relations, 1961.

Shields, J. *Monozygotic twins brought up apart and brought up together*. London: Oxford University Press, 1962.

Shinn, M. "Father absence and children's cognitive development," *Psychological Bulletin*, 1978, *85*:295–324.

Shucard, D. W., J. L. Shucard, and K. R. Cummins. "Auditory evoked potentials and sex related differences in brain development." Paper presented at the Convention of the Society for Research in Child Development, San Francisco, March 1979.

Shuter-Dyson, R., and C. Gabriel. *The psychology of musical ability* (2nd ed.). New York: Methuen, 1982.

Siegel, L. S. "Children's and adolescents' reactions to the assassination of Martin Luther King: A study of political socialization," *Developmental Psychology*, 1977, *13(3)*:284–285.

Siegler, R. S. "Developmental sequences within and between concepts," *Monographs of the Society for Research in Child Development*, 1981, *46(2*, serial no. 189).

Siegler, R. S. "Five generalizations about cognitive development," *American Psychologist*, 1983, *38*:263–277.

Siegler, R. S. "Information processing approaches to development." In P. H. Mussen (Ed.), *Handbook of child psychology* (4th ed.); vol. 1: W. Kessen (Ed.), *History, theory, and methods*. New York: Wiley, 1983.

Signorielli, N., L. Gross, and M. Morgan. "Violence in television programs: Ten years later." In *Television and behavior: Ten years of scientific progress and implications for the 80s*. Washington, D.C.: U.S. Government Printing Office, 1982.

Silverman, D. T. "Maternal smoking and birth weight," *American Journal of Epidemiology*, 1977, *105(6)*:513–521.

Silvern, L .E., J. M. Waterman, W. Sobesky, and V. L. Ryan. "Effects of a developmental model of perspective-taking training," *Child Development*, 1979, *50*:243–246.

Simon, W., and J. H. Gagnon. "On psychosexual development." In D. Goslin (Ed.), *Handbook of socialization theory and research*. New York: Rand McNally, 1969.

Sinclair, C. B. *Movement of the young child: ages two to six*. Columbus, Ohio: Merrill, 1973.

Singer, J. L. *The child's world of make-believe*. New York: Academic Press, 1975.

Singer, W. "Central core control of visual cortex functions," *Fourth Intensive Study Program*, Massachusetts: MIT Press, 1979a.

Singer, W. "Neuronal mechanisms in experience dependent modification of visual cortex function." In M. Cuenod, F. Bloom, and G. Kreutzberg (Eds.), *Progress in Brain Research*. Amsterdam: Elsevier Sequoia, 1979b.

Singer, D. G., and J. L. Singer. "Television viewing and aggressive behavior in preschool children: A field study," *Forensic Psychology and Psychiatry*, 1980, *347*:289–303.

Siple, P. *Understanding language through sign language research*. New York: Academic Press, 1978.

Skeels, H. M. "A study of the effects of differential stimulation on mentally retarded children: A follow-up report," *American Journal of Mental Deficiency*, 1942, *46*:340–350.

Skeels, H. M. "Adult status of children with contrasting early life experiences: A follow-up study," *Monographs of the Society for Research in Child Development*, 1966, *31*(3, serial no. 105).

Skinner, B. F. *The behavior of organisms*. New York: Appleton-Century-Crofts, 1938.

Skinner, B. F. *Verbal behavior*. New York: Appleton-Century-Crofts, 1957.

Skodak, M., and H. M. Skeels. "A final follow-up of one hundred adopted children," *Journal of Genetic Psychology*, 1949, *75*:85–125.

Slobin, D. I. "Cognitive prerequisites for the acquisition of grammar." In C. A. Ferguson and D. I. Slobin (Eds.), *Studies of child language development*. New York: Holt, Rinehart, & Winston, 1973.

Slobin, D. I. *Psycholinguistics* (2nd ed.). Glenview, Ill.: Scott, Foresman, 1979.

Slobin, D. I. (Ed.). *The cross-cultural study of language acquisition*. Hillsdale, N.J.: Lawrence Erlbaum, 1982.

Slobin, D. I., and T. G. Bever. "Children use canonical sentence schemas: A crosslinguistic study of word order and inflections," *Cognition*, 1982, *12*:229–266.

Smith, H. *The Russians*. New York: Times Books, 1976.

Smith, P. K. "A longitudinal study of social participation in preschool children: Solitary and parallel play reexamined," *Developmental Psychology*, 1978, *14*:517–523.

Snow, C. E. "The uses of imitation," *Journal of Child Language*, 1981, *8*:205–212.

Snow, C. E., and C. Ferguson. *Talking to children*. New York: Cambridge University Press, 1977.

Snow, C. E., and M. Hoefnagel-Höhle. "The critical period for language acquisition: Evidence from second language learning," *Child Development*, 1978, *49*:1114–1128.

Sokol, R. J. "Alcohol and abnormal outcome of pregnancy," *Canadian Medical Association Journal*, 1981, *125*(2):143–148.

Sontag, L. W. "The significance of fetal environmental differences," *American Journal of Obstetrics and Gynecology*, 1941, *42*:996–1003.

Sorensen, R. C. *Adolescent sexuality in contemporary America (The Sorensen Report)*. New York: World Publishing, 1973.

Sperry, R. W. "The great cerebral commissure," *Scientific American*, 1964, *210*(January):42–62.

Spitz, R. A. "Hospitalism: An inquiry into the genesis of psychiatric conditions in early childhood," *Psychoanalytic Study of the Child*, 1945, *1*:53–74.

Spitz, R. A. *The first year of life*. New York: International Universities Press, 1965.

Spitz, R. A., and K. M. Wolfe. "The smiling response: a contribution to the optogenesis of social relations," *Genetic Psychology Monographs*, 1946, *34*:57–125.

Spock, B. *Baby and child care*. New York: Pocket Books, 1976.

Sroufe, L. A. "The coherence of individual development: Early care, attachment, and subsequent developmental issues," *American Psychologist*, 1979, *34*:834–841.

Sroufe, L. A. "Socioemotional development." In J. D. Osofsky (Ed.), *Handbook of infant development*. New York: Wiley, 1979.

Stanley, S. M. *The new evolutionary timetable: Fossils, genes, and the origin of species*. New York: Basic Books, 1981.

Stein, A. H., and L. K. Friedrich. "The effects of television content on young children." In A. D. Pick (Ed.), *Minnesota Symposia on Child Psychology* (vol. 9). Minneapolis: University of Minnesota Press, 1975.

Stein, Z., M. Susser, G. Saenger, and F. Marolla. "Nutrition and mental performance," *Science*, 1972, *173*:708–12.

Stein, Z., M. Susser, G. Saenger, and F. Marolla. *Famine and human development: The Dutch hunger winter of 1944–1945*. New York: Oxford University Press, 1975.

Stern, W. *The psychological methods of testing intelligence* (G. M. Whipple, trans.). Baltimore, Md.: Warwick & York, 1914 (originally published in German, 1911).

Sternberg, R. J. (Ed.). *Mechanisms of cognitive development*. New York: W. H. Freeman and Company, 1984.

Sternberg, R. J., and J. S. Powell. "The development of intelligence." In P. H. Mussen (Ed.), *Handbook of child psychology* (4th ed.); vol. 3: J. H. Flavell & E. M. Markman (Eds.), *Cognitive development*. New York: Wiley, 1983.

Steuer, F. B., J. M. Applefield, and R. Smith. "Televised aggression and the interpersonal aggression of preschool children," *Journal of Experimental Child Psychology*, 1971, *11*:442–447.

Stevenson, H. W. "Influences of schooling on cognitive development." In D. A. Wagner and H. W. Stevenson (Eds.), *Cultural perspectives on child development*. San Francisco: W. H. Freeman and Company, 1982.

Stewart, A. L., and E. O. R. Reynolds. "Improved prognosis for infants of very low birthweight," *Pediatrics*, 1974, *54*(6).

Stone, P. J. "Child care in twelve countries." In A. Szalai (Ed.), *The use of time*. The Hague, Netherlands: Mouton, 1972.

Stott, D. H. "The child's hazards in utero." In J. G. Howells (Ed.), *Modern perspectives in international child psychiatry*. Edinburgh: Oliver and Boyd, 1969.

Sullivan, H. S. *Interpersonal theory of psychiatry*. New York: Norton, 1953.

Suomi, S. J., H. F. Harlow, and M. A. Novak. "Reversal of social deficits produced by isolation rearing in monkeys," *Journal of Human Evolution*, 1974, *3*:527–534.

Super, C. M. "Environmental effects on motor development: The case of 'African infant precocity,'" *Developmental Medicine and Child Neurology*, 1976, *18*:561–567.

Super, C. M. "Cognitive development: Looking across at growing up." In *Anthropological perspectives on child development* (New directions for child development, no. 8). San Francisco: Jossey-Bass, 1980.

Super, C. M., and S. Harkness (Ed.). *Anthropological perspectives on child development* (New directions for child development, no. 8). Jossey-Bass, 1980.

Sutton-Smith, B., and B. G. Rosenberg. *The Sibling*. New York: Holt, Rinehart, & Winston, 1970.

Svejda, M. J., J. J. Campos, and R. N. Emde. "Mother-infant 'bonding': Failure to generalize," *Child Development*, 1980, *51*:775–779.

Svejda, M. J., B. J. Pannabecker, and R. N. Emde. "Parent-to-infant attachment: A critique of the early 'bonding' model." In R. N. Emde and R. J. Harmon (Eds.), *The development of attachment and affiliative systems*. New York: Plenum, 1982.

Tanner, J. M. "Physical growth." In P. H. Mussen (Ed.), *Carmichael's manual of child psychology*. New York: Wiley, 1970.

Tanner, J. M. "Sequence, tempo, and individual variation in growth and development of boys and girls aged twelve to sixteen." In J. Kagan and R. Cole (Eds.), *12 to 16: Early adolescence*. New York: W. W. Norton, 1972.

Tanner, J. M. "Trend towards earlier menarche in London, Oslo, Copenhagen, the Netherlands, and Hungary," *Nature*, 1973, *243*:95–96.

Tanner, J. M. *Fetus into man: Physical growth from conception to maturity*. Cambridge, Mass.: Harvard University Press, 1978.

Tanner, J. M., and N. Cameron. "Investigation of mid-growth spurt in height, weight, and limb circumference in single-year velocity data from the London 1966–67 growth survey," *Annals of Human Biology*, 1980, *7*:565–577.

Tanner, J. M., and G. P. Taylor. *Growth*. Alexandria, Virginia: Time/Life Books, 1965.

Tanner, J. M., and R. H. Whitehouse. "Clinical longitudinal standards for height, weight, height velocity, weight velocity, and the stages of puberty," *Archives of Disease in Childhood*. 1976, *51*:170–179.

Tanzer, D., and J. L. Block. *Why natural childbirth?* Garden City, New York: Doubleday, 1972.

Taussig, H. B. "A study of the german outbreak of phocomelia. The thalidomide syndrome," *Journal of the American Medical Association*, 1962, *180*: 1106–1114.

Tavris, C., and C. Offir. *The longest war: Sex differences in perspective* (2nd ed.). New York: Harcourt Brace Jovanovich, 1983.

Temerlin, M. K. *Lucy: Growing up human. A chimpanzee daughter in a psychotherapist's family.* Palo Alto, California: Science and Behavior Books, 1975.

Terrace, H. S., L. A. Petitto, R. J. Sanders, and T. G. Bever. "On the grammatical capacity of apes." In K. E. Nelson (Ed.), *Children's language* (vol. 2). New York: Gardner Press, 1980.

Thelen, E. Rhythmical behavior in infancy: An ethological perspective. *Developmental Psychology.* 1981, *17*:237–257.

Thelen, E., and D. M. Fisher. "Newborn stepping: An explanation for a 'disappearing' reflex," *Developmental Psychology*, 1982, *18*:760–775.

Thinus-Blanc, C., B. Poucet, and N. Chapuis. "Object permanency in cats," *Behavioral Processes*, 1982.

Thoman, E. B., P. H. Liederman, and J. P. Olson. "Neonate-mother interaction during breast feeding," *Developmental Psychology*, 1972, 6: 110–118.

Thomas, A., and S. Chess. *Temperament and development.* New York: Brunner/Mazel, 1977.

Thomas, A., and S. Chess. *The dynamics of psychological development.* New York: Brunner/Mazel, 1980.

Thomas, A., S. Chess, and H. G. Birch. "The origin of personality," *Scientific American*, 1970, *223(August)*:102–109.

Thompson, W. R., and J. Grusec. "Studies of early experience." In P. H. Mussen (Ed.), *Carmichael's manual of child psychology* (3rd ed.). New York: Wiley, 1970.

Thurstone, L. L. *Primary mental abilities.* Chicago: University of Chicago Press, 1938.

Tietjen, A. M. "Integrating formal and informal support systems: The Swedish experience." In J. Garbarino and S. H. Stocking (Eds.), *Protecting children from abuse and neglect.* San Francisco: Jossey-Bass, 1980.

Tinbergen, N. *The study of instinct.* Oxford: Clarendon Press, 1951.

Tizard, B. *Adoption: A second chance.* London: Open Books, 1977.

Toepfer, C. F., Jr. "Brain growth periodization: A new dogma for education," *Middle School Journal*, 1979, *10(3)*:20.

Tomlinson-Keasey, C. "Structures, functions, and stages: A trio of unresolved issues in formal operations." In S. Modgil and C. Modgil (Eds.), *Jean Piaget: Consensus and controversy.* New York: Holt, Rinehart, & Winston, 1982.

Tomlinson-Keasey, C., R. R. Kelly, and J. K. Burton. "Hemispheric changes in information processing during development," *Developmental Psychology*, 1978, *14*:214–223.

Torrance, E. P. "The creative personality and the ideal pupil," *Teachers College Record*, 1963, *65*:220–226.

Touwen, B. C. L. *Neurological development in infancy* (Clinics in developmental medicine, no. 58). London: Spastics International, 1976.

Tresemer, D. "Fear of success: Popular but unproven," *Psychology Today*, 1974, *7*:82–85.

Tresemer, D. "The cumulative record of research on 'fear of success.' *Sex Roles*, 1976, *2*:217–236.

Trivers, R. L. "Parental investment and sexual selection." In B. Campbell (Ed.), *Sexual selection and the descent of man. 1871–1971.* Chicago: Aldine, 1972.

Tucker, J. "The concepts of and the attitudes toward work and play in children." Unpublished doctoral dissertation, University of Denver, 1979. *Dissertation Abstracts International*, in press.

Tulkin, S. R. "Social class differences in maternal and infant behavior." In P. H. Leiderman, S. R. Tulkin, and A. Rosenfeld (Eds.), *Culture and infancy.* New York: Academic Press, 1977.

Tulkin, S. R. and J. Kagan "Mother-child interaction in the first year of life," *Child Development*, 1972, *43*:31–41.

Turiel, E. "Developmental processes in the child's moral thinking." In P. Mussen, J. Langer, and M. Covington (Eds.), *New directions in develop-*

mental psychology. New York: Holt, Rinehart, & Winston, 1969.

Turkewitz, G., H. G. Birch, T. Moreau, L. Levy, and A. C. Cornwell. "Effect of intensity of auditory stimulation on directional eye movements in the human neonate," *Animal Behavior*, 1966, *14*:93–101.

Twain, M. *The Adventures of Huckleberry Finn.* New York: New American Library, 1971.

Ullian, D. Z. "The development of masculinity and femininity." In B. Lloyd and J. Ascher (Eds.), *Exploring sex differences.* London: Academic Press, 1976.

United States Bureau of the Census. *Characteristics of American children and youth: 1980.* Current population reports, P-23, no. 114. Washington, D.C.: U.S. Government Printing Office, 1982.

United States Department of Commerce, Bureau of the Census. *Statistics of school enrollment: Social and economic characteristics of students enrolled in college.* Washington, D.C.: United States Government Printing Office, 1981.

United States Department of Health, Education, and Welfare. *Smoking and health: A report of the Surgeon General.* DHEW publication no. (PHS)79–50066. Washington, D.C.: U.S. Government Printing Office, 1979.

United States Department of Labor, Children's Bureau. *Infant care.* Bureau publication no. 8. Washington, D.C.: U.S. Government Printing Office, 1929.

Uzgiris, I. "Situational generality in conversation," *Child Development*, 1964, *35*:831–842.

Uzgiris, I. C. "Organization of sensorimotor intelligence." In M. Lewis (Ed.), *Origins of intelligence: Infancy and early childhood.* New York: Plenum, 1976.

Uzgiris, I. C. "Two functions of imitation in infancy." *International Journal of Behavioral Development*, 1981, *4*:1–12.

Valentine, A. (Ed.). *Fathers to sons: Advice without consent.* Norman, Oklahoma: University of Oklahoma Press, 1963.

Vandenberg, B. "Play and development from an etho-logical perspective," *American Psychologist*, 1978, *33*:724–738.

Van Dusen, R. A., and E. B. Sheldon. "The changing status of American women: A life cycle perspective," *American Psychologist*, February, 1976.

Van Parys, M. M. "Preschoolers in society: Use of the social roles of sex, age, and race for self and others by black and white children." Paper presented at the biennial meeting of the International Society for the Study of Behavioral Development, Toronto, Canada, August 1981.

Van Parys, M. M. "The relation of use and understanding of sex and age categories in preschool children." Unpublished doctoral dissertation, University of Denver, November 1983. *Dissertation Abstracts International*, in press.

Vaughn, B., B. Egeland, L. A. Sroufe, and E. Waters. "Individual differences in infant-mother attachment at 12 and 18 months: Stability and change in families under stress," *Child Development*, 1979, *50*:971–975.

Vernon, M. D. "Varieties of deficiency in the reading process," *Harvard Educational Review*. 1977, *47*:396–410.

Vore, D., and D. R. Ottinger. "Maternal food restriction: Effects on offspring, development, learning, and a program of therapy," *Developmental Psychology*, 1970, *3*:337–334.

Vurpillot, E. *The visual world of the child* (W. E. C. Gillham, trans.). New York: International Universities Press, 1976 (originally published, 1972).

Vygotsky, L. S. *Thought and language* (E. Hanfmann and G. Vakar, trans.). Cambridge, Mass.: MIT Press, 1962.

Wallace, R. A. *Biology: The world of life* (2nd ed.). Pacific Palisades, California: Goodyear, 1978.

Wallerstein, J. S., and J. B. Kelly. *Surviving the breakup: How children and parents cope with divorce.* New York: Basic Books, 1980.

Warner, J. S., and B. R. Wooten. "Human infant color vision and color perception," *Infant Behavior and Development*, 1979, *2*:241–274.

Warren, N. "African infant precocity," *Psychological Bulletin*, 1972, *78*:353–367.

Washburn, S. L. "The evolution of man," *Scientific American*, 1978, *239(September)*:194–208.

Waters, E., B. E. Vaugh, and B. R. Egeland. "Individual differences in infant-mother attachment relationships at age one: Antecedents in neonatal behavior in an urban economically disadvantaged sample," *Child Development*, 1980, *51*: 208–216.

Watson, J. B. *Psychological care of infant and child.* London: Allen & Unwin, 1928.

Watson, M. W. "The development of social roles: A sequence of social-cognitive development." In *Cognitive development* (New directions for child development no. 12). San Francisco: Jossey-Bass, 1981.

Watson, M. W., and K. W. Fischer. "A developmental sequence of agent use in late infancy," *Child Development*, 1977, *48*:828–835.

Watson, E. H., and G. H. Lowrey. *Growth and development of children* (5th ed.). Chicago: Year Book Medical Publishers, 1967.

Wechsler, D. *The measurement and appraisal of adult intelligence* (4th ed.). Baltimore, Maryland: Williams & Williams, 1958.

Weinberger, D. In *Newsweek*, February 7, 1983, p. 43.

Weinraub, M. "Fatherhood: The myth of the second-class parent." In J. H. Stevens, Jr., and M. Mathews (Eds.), *Mother/child, father/child relationships.* Washington, D.C.: National Association for the Education of Young Children, 1978.

Weir, R. H. *Language in the crib.* The Hague, Netherlands: Mouton, 1962.

Weisler, A., and R. B. McCall. "Exploration and play: Resume and redirection," *American Psychologist*, 1976, *31*:492–508.

Weisner, T. S., and R. Gallimore. "My brother's keeper: Child and sibling caretaking," *Current Anthropology*, 1977, *18*:169–190.

Weiss, G. "The natural history of hyperactivity in childhood and treatment with stimulant medication at different ages: A summary of research findings." In R. Gittelman-Klein (Ed.), *Present advances in child psychopharmacology.* New York: Human Sciences Press, 1975.

Weisz, J. R. "Choosing problem-solving rewards and Halloween prizes: Delay of gratification and preference for symbolic reward as a function of development, motivation, and personal investment," *Developmental Psychology*, 1978, *14*:66–78.

Weller, B. "Growth of the gorillas' vocabularies," *Gorilla*, 1980, *3(1)*.

Wellman, H. M., K. Ritter, and J. H. Flavell. "Deliberate memory behavior in the delayed reactions of very young children," *Developmental Psychology*, 1975, *11*:780–787.

Wells, G. "Apprenticeship in meaning." In K. E. Nelson (Ed.), *Children's language* (vol. 2). New York: Gardner Press, 1980.

Wells, W. D. *Television and aggression: Replication of an experimental field study.* Unpublished manuscript, University of Chicago, 1972.

Wender, P. H. *Minimal brain dysfunction in children.* New York: Wiley-Interscience, 1971.

Werner, H. *Comparative psychology of mental development.* New York: Science Editions, 1948.

Werner, E. *Cross-cultural child development.* Monterey, Cal.: Brooks/Cole, 1979.

Werner, H., and E. Kaplan. "The acquisition of word meanings: A developmental study." *Monographs of the Society for Research on Child Development*, 1952, *15* (1, serial no. 51).

Werner, E. E., J. M. Bierman, and F. E. French. *The children of Kauai.* Honolulu: University of Hawaii Press, 1971.

Westerman, M. A. "Differences in the organization of mother-child interaction in compliance problem and healthy dyads." Doctoral dissertation, University of Southern California, 1979. *Dissertation Abstracts International*, 1980, *40(10B)*:5031.

White, R. W. "Motivation reconsidered: The concept of competence," *Psychological Review*, 1959, *66*:297–333.

White, S. H. "Some general outlines of the matrix of developmental changes between five and seven years," *Bulletin of the Orton Society*, 1970, *20*: 41–57.

White, B. L. *Human infants: Experience and psychological development.* Englewood Cliffs, New Jersey: Prentice-Hall, 1971.

White, B. L., and R. Held. "Plasticity of sensory motor development." In J. F. Rosenblith and W. Allinsmith (Eds.), *Readings in child development and educational psychology* (2nd ed.). Boston: Allyn and Bacon, 1966.

White, C. T., C. L. White, W. Fawcett, and J. Socks. "Color evoked potentials in adults and infants." Paper presented at the meeting of the Society for Research in Child Development, New Orleans, March 1977.

Whitehurst, G., and S. Sonnenschein. "The development of communication: Attribute variation leads to contrast failure," *Journal of Experimental Child Psychology*, 1978, 25:454–490.

Whiten, A. "Postnatal separation and mother-infant interaction." Paper presented at the Conference of the International Society for the Study of Behavioural Development, University of Surrey, England, 1975.

Whiting, J. W. M. "Menarcheal age and infant stress in humans." In F. A. Beach (Ed.), *Sex and behavior*. New York: Wiley, 1965.

Whiting, B. B., and C. P. Edwards. "A cross-cultural analysis of sex differences in the behavior of children aged three through eleven," *Journal of Social Psychology*, 1973, 91:171–188.

Whiting, B.B., and J. W. M. Whiting. *Children of six cultures: A psycho-cultural analysis*. Cambridge, Massachusetts: Harvard University Press, 1975.

Williams, R. L. "Black pride, academic relevance, and individual achievement," *Counseling Psychologist*, 1970, 2(1):18–22.

Wilson, J. G. "Present status of drugs as teratogens in man," *Teratology*, 1973, 7:3–16.

Wilson, A. N. *The developmental psychology of the black child*. New York: Africana Research Publications, 1978.

Winchel, R., D. Fenner, and P. Shaver. "Impact of coeducation on 'fear of success' imagery expressed by male and female high school students," *Journal of Educational Psychology*, 1974, 66(5):726–730.

Winder, C. L., and L. Rav. "Parental attitudes associated with social deviance in preadolescent boys," *Journal of Abnormal Social Psychology*, 1962, 64:418–424.

Winick, M. (Ed.). *Nutrition and fetal development*. New York: Wiley, 1974.

Winick, M. *Malnutrition and brain development*. New York: Oxford University Press, 1976.

Winick, M. "Food and the fetus," *Natural History*, January 1981, 90(1):76–81.

Winner, E., A. K. Rosenstiel, and H. Gardner. "The development of metaphoric understanding," *Developmental Psychology*, 1976, 17:289–297.

Winner, E., M. McCarthy, S. Kleinman, and H. Gardner. "First metaphors." In *Early symbolization* (New directions for child development, no. 3). San Francisco: Jossey-Bass, 1979.

Winnicott, D. W. *Playing and reality*. New York: Basic Books, 1971.

Witkin, H. A., R. B. Dyk, H. F. Patterson, D. R. Goodenough, and S. A. Karp. *Psychological differentiation*. New York: Wiley, 1962.

Wittig, M. A., and A. C. Petersen (Eds.). *Sex-related differences in cognitive functioning*. New York: Academic Press, 1979.

Wohlwill, J. F. *The study of behavioral development*. New York: Academic Press, 1973.

Wolfe, J. B. "Effectiveness of token-rewards for chimpanzees," *Comparative Psychology Monographs*, 1936, 12:whole no. 5.

Wolfenstein, M. "Trends in infant care," *American Journal of Orthopsychiatry*, 1953, 33:120–130.

Wolff, P. H. "The causes, controls, and organization of behavior in the neonate," *Psychological Issues*, 1966, 5(17).

Wolff, P. H. "The natural history of crying and other vocalizations in early infancy." In B. M. Foss, (Ed.), *Determinants of Infant Behavior* (vol. 4). London: Methuen, 1969.

Wolff, S., and A. Barlow. "Schizoid personality in childhood: A comparative study of schizoid, autistic, and normal children," *Journal of Child Psychology and Child Psychiatry*, 1979, 20:29–46.

Wolman, B. B. (Ed.). *Manual of child psychopathology*. New York: McGraw-Hill, 1972.

Wood, D. J. "Teaching the young child: Some relationships between social interaction, language, and thought." In D. R. Olson (Ed.), *The social foundations of language and thought*. New York: Norton, 1980.

Woodruff, D. S. "Brain electrical activity and behavior relationships over the life span." In P. B. Baltes (Ed.), *Life-span development and behavior* (vol. 1). New York: Academic Press, 1978.

Wooton, A. J. "Talk in the homes of young children," *Sociology*, 1974, 8:277–295.

Worrell, J. P., and L. Worrell. "Supporters and opposers of women's liberation: Some personality correlates." Paper presented at a meeting of the American Psychological Association, Washington, D.C., September 1971.

Wursig, B. N., and M. Wursig. "Day and night of the dolphin," *Natural History*, March 1979.

Wylie, R.C. *The self concept* (rev. ed.); vol. 2: *Theory and research on selected topics*. Lincoln, Nebraska: University of Nebraska, 1979.

Yakovlev, P. I., and A. R. Lecours. "The myelogenetic cycles of regional maturation of the brain." In A. Minkowski (Ed.), *Regional development of the brain in early life*. Oxford: Blackwell, 1967.

Yankelovich, D. "The new psychological contracts at work," *Psychology Today*, May 1978, 46–50.

Yarrow, L. J., F. A. Pedersen, and J. Rubenstein. "Mother-infant interaction and development in infancy." In P. H. Leiderman, S. R. Tulkin, and A. Rosenfeld (Eds.), *Culture and infancy*. New York: Academic Press, 1977.

Yerushalmy, J. "Infants with low birth weight born before their mothers started to smoke cigarettes," *American Journal of Obstetrics and Gynecology*, 1972, 112:277–284.

Young, J. Z. *An introduction to the study of man*. New York: Oxford University Press, 1971.

Youniss, J. *Parents and peers in social development: A Sullivan-Piaget perspective*. Chicago: University of Chicago Press, 1982.

Zajonc, R. B. "Feeling and thinking: Preferences need no inferences," *American Psychologist*, 1980, 35:151-175.

Zajonc, R. B. "Validating the confluence model," *Psychological Bulletin*, 1983, 93:457–480.

Zajonc, R. B., and G. B. Markus. "Birth order and intellectual development," *Psychological Review*, 1975, 82:74–88.

Zalba, S. "Battered children," *Transaction*, July–August 1971, 8:68–71.

Zaporozhets, A. V. "The development of perception in preschool children." In P. H. Mussen (Ed.), "European research in cognitive development: Report of the International Conference on Cognitive Development," *Monographs of the Society for Research in Child Development*, 1965, 30(no. 2, serial no. 100).

Zelazo, P. R. "From reflexive to instrumental behavior." In L. Lipsitt (Ed.), *Developmental psychobiology: The significance of infancy*. Hillsdale, New Jersey: Lawrence Erlbaum Associates, 1976.

Zelazo, P. R., and E. L. Leonard. "The dawn of active thought." In *Levels and transitions in children's development* (New directions for child development, no. 21). San Francisco: Jossey-Bass, 1983.

Zelazo, P. R., N. A. Zelazo, and S. Kolb. "'Walking' in the newborn," *Science*, April 21, 1972, 176: 314–315.

Zelazo, P. R., R. B. Kearsley, and J. Ungerer. *Learning to speak: A manual to aid the acquisition of productive language*. Boston: Center for Behavioral Pediatrics and Infant Development, 1979.

Zelnick, M., and J. F. Kantner. *Family planning perspectives*, 1980, 12:230–236.

Zigler, E. "Controlling child abuse in America: An effort doomed to failure." In D. G. Gil (Ed.), *Child abuse and violence*. New York: AMS Press, 1979.

Zimmerman, B., and T. Rosenthal. *Social learning and cognition*. New York: Wiley, 1978.

Zuckerman, M., and L. Wheeler. "To dispel fantasies about the fantasy-based measure of fear of success," *Psychological Bulletin*, 1975, 82:932–946.

ILLUSTRATION ACKNOWLEDGMENTS

Chapter 1

title page   Bob Peterson/Life Picture Service
1-1   The Bettmann Archive
1-2   *A, B, C*   Carnegie Laboratories, Davis, California;
D   John Blaustein/Woodfin Camp & Associates.
1-3   Sovfoto
1-4   Erika Stone
1-5   Herb Levart/Photo Researchers
1-6   *top left*   Burt Glinn/Magnum; *top right*   Arthur
Tress/Magnum; *bottom left*   J. Kraay/Bruce Coleman;
bottom middle   Larry Mulvehill/Photo Researchers;
bottom right   Ann Chwatsky/Art Resource.
page 15   *middle left*   Group III canon/Bruce Coleman;
bottom left   Ken Heyman; *bottom middle*   Gail
Rubin/Photo Researchers.
1-7   From *Two Worlds of Childhood: U.S. & U.S.S.R.*, by
Urie Bronfenbrenner. Copyright © 1970 Russell
Sage Foundation. Reprinted by permission of
the publisher.
1-8   *top left*   J.Ph. Charbonnier/Photo Researchers;
bottom left   Karen Collidge/Taurus Photos; *right*
Chris Perkins/Magnum.
1-9   Courtesy Sam
1-10   Alice Kandell/Photo Researchers
1-11   Yves de Braines/Black Star
1-13   Ken Heyman
1-16   *photos*   Courtesy Mary C. Potter "On Perceptual Recognition", in J. S. Bruner, R. R. Olver, &
P. M. Greenfields (Eds.), *Studies in Cognitive Growth.*
Wiley 1966, pp. 103-134.

UNIT 1   Vasily Kandinsky, *Study for Composition II*,
The Solomon Guggenheim Museum, New York

Chapter 2

title page   Nina Leen, Life/Time Inc.
2-3   Baron Hugo Van Lawick/National Geographic
Society
2-4   Harry Hartman/Bruce Coleman
page 63   Copyright © 1976 by Sidney Harris—
American Scientist Magazine

2-8   BioPhoto/Photo Researchers
2-10   *left*   Erika Stone; *right*   Pam Hasegawa/
Taurus Photos.
2-11   Thomas McAvy, Life/Time Inc.
2-13   *left*   Erica Stone; *right*   Zoological Society of
San Diego.
2-14   Ken Karp
2-18   Leonard Lessin/Photo Researchers
page 89   Courtesy of Philips Electronic Instruments,
Inc.
page 90   Bruno Barbey/Magnum
2-21   Bruce Roberts, Rapho/Photo Researchers
2-22   Clausen, J. C., et al. *Experimental Studies on the
Nature of Species*, vol. 1. Carnegie Institution.

Chapter 3

title page   Claude Edelman/Black Star
3-1   *left*   National Library of Medicine; *right*   Bettmann Archive.
3-2   Dr. Don Fawcett/Photo Researchers
page 129   *(except bottom mid)*   Claude Edelman/Black
Star; *bottom middle*   BioPhoto/Photo Researchers.
page 133   Ray Ellis/Photo Researchers
3-8   Erika/Photo Researchers
3-9   Abigail Heyman/Archive Pictures Inc.
3-10   David Hurn/Magnum
3-13   D. P. Hershkowitz/Bruce Coleman

UNIT 2   Unknown American artist, Abby Aldrich
Rockefeller Folk Art Center, Williamsburg, Virginia

Chapter 4

title page   Burt Glinn/Magnum
4-1   Hanus Papoušek
4-2   *page 166*   Ed Lettau/Photo Researchers; *page
167 left*   Ray Ellis, Rapho/Photo Researchers; *page
167 right*   J. Fiorentino, *Reflex Testing Methods
for Evaluating C.N.S. Development.*   Courtesy of
Charles C. Thomas, Publisher, Springfield, Illinois.
page 168   The Bettmann Archive
page 169   Bill Stanton/Magnum

4-3 *left* Fritz Menle/Photo Researchers; *right* D. P. Herschkowitz/Bruce Coleman.

page 178 Charles Harbutt/Archive Pictures Inc.

4-9 Suzanne Szasz/Photo Researchers

4-10 Ron James

4-13 Shirley Zeiberg/Taurus Photos

4-16 *all photos* Yakovlev Collection, Armed Forces Institute of Pathology, Washington, D.C.

4-17 Erika Stone/Peter Arnold

Chapter 5

title page William W. Cates/Art Resource

page 208 *top left* Momatiuk-Eastcoot/Woodfin Camp & Associates; *top right* Barry Chase/Black Star.

page 209 *top left* Frostie/Woodfin Camp & Associates; *top right* Frederick Ayer/Photo Researchers.

page 210 *top left* Shirley Zeiberg/Taurus Photos; *top right* D. P. Hershkowitz/Bruce Coleman.

5-5 *left* Joanne Leonard/Woodfin Camp & Associates; *right* Leonard McCombe, Life/Time Inc.

5-6 *left* Momatiuk/Eastcott/Woodfin Camp & Associates; *right* Frederick Ayer/Photo Researchers.

page 221 Bil Keane, courtesy of Tribune and Register Syndicate

5-12 Paul Faris/Black Star

5-15 William Vandivert/Scientific American

5-16 B Champlong-Arep/The Image Bank

5-17 Columbia University/Photo Researchers

Chapter 6

title page W. Beust/The Image Bank

6-3 *page 268* Elyse Lewin/The Image Bank; *page 269* Suzanne Szasz/Photo Researchers.

6-6 Peter G. Aitken/Photo Researchers

6-7 Richard Kalvar/Magnum

page 281 © Joel Gordon 1979

6-8 Sandra Pipp

page 283 From *Nadia: A Case of Extraordinary Drawing Ability in an Autistic Child*, by Lorna Selfe. Academic Press, New York, New York, 1977.

page 285 Suzanne Szasz/Photo Researchers

6-9 Mary Ainsworth

6-10 *all* Harry F. Harlow, University of Wisconsin Primate Laboratory

6-11 Harry F. Harlow, University of Wisconsin Primate Laboratory

6-14 Harry F. Harlow, University of Wisconsin Primate Laboratory

6-15 Sophie Dann

page 302 Group III Nich/Bruce Coleman

6-16 Charles Shulz, Courtesy of United Feature Syndicate Inc.

6-17 E. H. Shepard from *Winnie-the-Pooh* by A. A. Milne, A Dell/Yearling Book

UNIT 3 Mary Cassatt, *Mother and Child*, The Metropolitan Museum of Art, George A. Hearn Fund, 1909

Chapter 7

title page Shirley Zeiberg/Taurus Photos

page 325 Bil Keane, courtesy of Tribune and Register Syndicate

page 327 Dik Browne, courtesy of King Features Syndicate Inc.

7-1 *top left* Frank Siteman/Taurus Photos; *top right* Hanus Papoušek; *middle* Hanus Papoušek.

page 333 Bil Keane, courtesy of Tribune and Register Syndicate

7-3 Bil Keane, courtesy of Tribune and Register Syndicate

7-6 Rothwell/FPG

7-7 Alice Kendell/Photo Researchers

pages 342–343 Larry Fenson

7-9 Hank Ketcham, courtesy of Field Enterprises

page 360 Copyright 1981, Universal Press Syndicate. Reprinted with permission. All rights reserved.

page 368 Reprinted from *Radiographic Atlas of Skeletal Development of the Hand and Wrist*, 2nd edition, by William Walter Greulich and S. Idell Pyle, with the permission of the publishers, Stanford University Press. Copyright © 1950 and 1959 by the Board of Trustees of the Leland Stanford Junior University.

7-16 *top left* Harry Hartman/Bruce Coleman; *top right* M. W. Peterson/The Image Bank; *bottom* Harry Hartman/Bruce Coleman.

Chapter 8

title page W. Steinmetz/The Image Bank

8-2 Movie Still Archives, from the United Artists release *L'Enfant Sauvage* (The Wild Child). Copyright © 1969 Les Films Ducarosse.

8-3 *left* Sovfoto; *right* Constantine Manos/Magnum

8-4 Hanus Papoušek

page 388 Rhoda Pollack/Black Star

8-5 Hella Hammid/Photo Researchers

8-8 *page 399, top to bottom* Carol Simowitz/The Image Bank; James Joern/Bruce Coleman; Barbara Rios/Photo Researchers; Richard L. Hong/FPG.

page 400 *top to bottom* Susan Kuklin/Photo Researchers; Nancy M. Hamilton/Photo Researchers; Shirley Zeiberg/Taurus Photos; Ken Heyman.

page 402 Hank Ketcham, courtesy of Field Enterprises

8-9 *left and right* Ken Heyman

page 405 Gahan Wilson, from *And Then We'll Get Him*, Richard Marek, 1978.

page 406 Alice Kandell, Rapho/Photo Researchers

8-11 Bandura, A., D. Ross, and S. A. Ross. "Imitation of film-mediated aggressive models." *Journal of Abnormal and Social Psychology*, 1963, 66:8.

8-12 Ellan Younk/Photo Researchers

8-13 Suzanne Szasz/Photo Researchers

8-15 James H. Barker

8-16 Porter, Judith D. R., Black Child, White Child, Harvard University Press, 1971

8-18 © 1983 Children's Television Workshop. Used by permission.

8-20 A Ira Berger/Black Star; B I. Budnevich (APN); C Hu Yueh-China Photo Service/ Astfoto.

UNIT 4 Winslow Homer, *Snap the Whip*, The Metropolitan Museum of Art, Gift of Christian A. Zabriskie, 1950.

Chapter 9

title page Burt Glinn/Magnum

9-1 A Eric Kroll/Taurus Photos; B Victor Englebert/Photo Researchers.

9-3 *left* Laimute Druskis/Taurus Photos; *right* Susan Lapides 1980/Design Conceptions.

page 448 Bil Keane, courtesy of Tribune and Register Syndicate

9-5 Gene Tashoff/Photo Researchers

9-10 *left* Kurt Scholz/Shostal Associates; *right* Richard Kalvar/Magnum.

9-11 Ken Karp

9-19 "Chitlin Test," copyright © *New York Times*, July 2, 1968.

page 491 Gilles Peress/Magnum

9-24 *top left* B. Mitchell/The Image Bank; *top middle* Richard Kalvar/Magnum; *top right* Erika Stone; *bottom left* Ethan Hoffman/Archive Pictures Inc.; *bottom right* Andy Levin/Black Star.

Chapter 10

title page Ken Sherman/Bruce Coleman

10-1 *top* Charles Harbutt/Archive Pictures Inc.; *bottom* Burt Glinn/Magnum.

10-3 *left* John Clarke/Shostal Associates; *right* Ted Spiegel/Black Star.

10-4 Bob Adelman/Magnum

page 513 *left* Jack Fields/Photo Researchers; *right* George Holton/Photo Researchers.

10-8 *top left* Zoological Society of San Diego; *top right* Peter Frey/The Image Bank; *bottom* G. Mangold/The Image Bank.

10-9 Erika Stone

10-10 From *Two Worlds of Childhood: U.S. and U.S.S.R.*, by Urie Bronfenbrenner. Copyright © 1970 Russell Sage Foundation. Reprinted by permission of the publisher.

10-11 *top* © Joel Gordon 1978; *bottom* John F. Phillips.

page 542 Gwyneth Hamel

10-15 Michael Chandler

10-16 Charles Shulz, United Feature Syndicate Inc.

NAME INDEX

SUBJECT INDEX